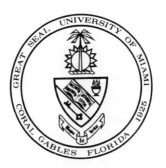

# Correspondence of James K. Polk

VOLUME IX, JANUARY – JUNE 1845

JAMES K. POLK

*Oil on canvas by George Peter Alexander Healy, 1846;
in the Collection of the Corcoran Gallery of Art,
Museum Purchase, Gallery Fund*

# Correspondence of
# JAMES K. POLK

*Volume IX*
*January–June 1845*

## WAYNE CUTLER
Editor

## ROBERT G. HALL II
Associate Editor

1996
The University of Tennessee Press
Knoxville

LIBRARY OF CONGRESS CATALOGING IN PUBLICATION DATA (Revised)
Polk, James Knox, Pres. U.S., 1795–1849.
    Correspondence of James K. Polk.
    Vol. 9 edited by W. Cutler
    CONTENTS: v. 1. 1817–1832.—v. 2. 1833–1834.—v. 3. 1835–1836.
v. 4. 1837–1838.—v. 5. 1839–1841.—v. 6. 1842–1843.—v. 7. 1844.
v. 8. 1844.—v. 9. 1845
    1. Polk, James Knox, Pres. U.S., 1795–1849.    2. Tennessee—Politics
and government—To 1865—Sources.    3. United States—Politics and
government—1845–1849—Sources.    4. Presidents—United States—
Correspondence.    5. Tennessee—Governors—Correspondence.    I. Weaver,
Herbert, ed.    II. Cutler, Wayne, 1938–
    III. Title
E417.A4        1969        973.6'1'0924        75–84005
ISBN 0-87049-947-5

*Sponsored by*

The University of Tennessee, Knoxville

The National Historical Publications and
Records Commission

The National Endowment for the Humanities

The Tennessee Historical Commission

*To*

*Earl J. Smith, Carese M. Parker, James P. Cooper, Jr.*
*Jayne C. DeFiore, and Robert G. Hall II*

# PREFACE

All of the political considerations that made possible the nomination and election of James K. Polk visited the Union's new leader in the formation of his cabinet and the distribution of his patronage. Among the numerous factions within the Democracy, Polk commanded at best the second-hand loyalty of his party's discordant leadership. The distrust of national political and economic consolidation that once had bonded state party alliances and displaced sectional conflicts no longer operated with such force as to maintain anything more than a nominal adhesion to the new administration. Indeed, the friends of both Martin Van Buren and John C. Calhoun declined any close association with Polk and justified their distance on grounds that the new president had been made the tool of a rival leader. To be certain, personal disappointments in the 1844 nomination process and hopeful expectations for the 1848 presidential race fanned the fires of factional division; but those same piques and ambitions might have burned far less wildly had there been no shifting of policy positions on protection and expansion.

Long years of market distress following the panic of 1837 had heightened demands for tariff protection and immigrant disabilities in the manufacturing centers of the North. In the presidential election of 1844 worried Van Buren factions in both Pennsylvania and New York had hoped that their leader's opposition to the immediate annexation of Texas would provide sufficient cover to offset the pressing encroachment of native American influences in Philadelphia and New York City. Nativist appeals, largely to the underemployed masters and journeymen of the cities, had linked the continuance of hard times to cheap foreign manufactures and cheap immigrant labor. Imposition of more stringent terms for naturalization would limit the number of Roman Catholic immigrant voters, who for the most part supported the more religiously inclusive Democracy and its opposition to the spread of business monopolies and the exploitation of waged labor.

Nativists combined economic fears with religious bigotry to convince large segments of the urban electorate to assist in returning America to its Protestant ways, convinced as they were that Jehovah would not shower an idolatrous people with wealth and power. Religious fanaticism rendered it increasingly difficult for the Democracy to hold together its yeoman-mechanic coalitions under the secular banners of hard money, cheap land, low tariffs, and immigrant rights. To further complicate matters, southern calls for westward expansion put the Democracy at even greater risk in those more heavily populated states in which prospective values of land and labor could no longer be calculated apart from the growth of large-scale manufacturing and marketing.

At the state and local levels business development required greater consolidations of corporate capital, larger economies of scale in manufacturing, and closer networks of internal trade. More plainly stated, bigger business needed government financed monopolies, sweated wage labor, and high land prices, none of which supposed advances toward greater national wealth and power were thought to be available without protective tariffs and selective expansion. Of course, the general government could not prohibit its citizens from migrating westward, but how far its protective reach might extend, say to Texas or Oregon or California, rendered the question of protective tariffs all the more unmanageable. During the Polk administration the Van Buren wing of the Democracy would swap the issue of free soil for that of free trade.

Like the more radical wing of the Northern Democracy, leading elements of the South's New Democracy pursued policy directions suited to building their political base at both the state and regional levels. John C. Calhoun and two of his close political associates declined the prestigious diplomatic mission to Great Britain and in so doing distanced themselves from the new administration. Their polite declinations probably reflected their perceptions of Polk's rather dark prospects for settling the seemingly intractable disputes with Great Britain and Mexico. Having built no grass roots constituency of his own and having committed himself to a single term presidency, Polk likely would follow more often than lead; thus the new administration surely would prove a shallow vessel into which to pour vital southern interests.

From Calhoun's point of view the fact that Polk could not retain him as his secretary of state demonstrated the measure of Van Buren's influence in forming the new administration. Nor did the South's chief spokesman for the New Democracy expect to retain his place in the general government; as for an appointment as minister to London he would go only if given a blank instruction to settle questions of expansion and trade on his own. He would have Texas and Oregon without war, for the key to British compromise and in its turn, the door to peace, would be supplied when and only when Congress had reversed the tariff hikes of 1842 and committed the Union to a lower set of tariff numbers. As secretary of state, Calhoun had chosen to read British designs on Texas as an attempt to abolish slavery in that republic and then in the southern states of the Union; and thus he had made expansion into a defensive mechanism for protecting the South's economic and social structures.

In his instructions of August 12, 1844, to William Rufus King, minister to France, Calhoun had accused the British government of using the abolitionist agenda as a pretext for destroying the tropical productions (cotton, rice, sugar, coffee) of the United States, Cuba, and Brazil and substituting like productions from British controlled sources in the West Indies, Egypt, and India. For example, abolition of slave labor in Texas and the American South would bring the cost of cotton production up to Egyptian and Indian levels, which were noncompetitive because of the higher costs of free labor. The British market for cheap cottons could then be moved to tariff-free partners in Egypt and India, cancelling as it were competition from textile manufacturing in the American North. Annexation of Texas would block, of course, British meddling with the South's slave labor system; but protection of American manufactures would bring the young republic into even greater economic conflict and possibly a maritime war with Great Britain. At great expense to their own economy the South had supported one war for the protection of northern trading interests only to find itself later excluded from the benefits of Henry Clay's American system of internal development and capital formation. In recent years radical Democrats in the North had made warfare on free-trade conservatives, and nowhere had the factional struggle proven more violent than in New York.

In 1842 Calhoun had watched with dismay as Silas Wright, Jr., and other Democrats in the New York congressional delegation voted for higher tariffs. Two years later he had lost his Texas annexation treaty in the Senate to a combination of Whigs and Van Buren loyalists. Forcing their sitting governor, William C. Bouck, to step aside in favor of Wright, the radicals had marshaled sufficient numbers of nativist Democrats back into the party line to retain the governorship and carry the 1844 presidential vote. But had not the expediency of those attacks indicated the ruthless tenor and dangerous direction of party politics in the

Union's most populous state. Supposedly the champions of party regularity, many of Van Buren's friends in Congress had returned to Washington City after the presidential victory and defiantly continued their opposition to Texas annexation; that they had done so without the slightest fear of retaliation in the patronage scramble demonstrated how much the new president owed to the northern radicals. Against the weight of that debt the southern wing of the party must remain free to apply its own countervailing stratagems. Calhoun's political friends could see no advantage to close ties with the new administration.

Prior to his inaugural Polk received an avalanche of advice as to the formation of his cabinet and the distribution of his patronage. No one laid out Polk's situation more clearly than Van Buren, whose letter of February 15, 1845, would apply as prophetically to himself as to Polk. The active partisan may combine ostensibly to promote the common cause but generally has a separate interest in view. During the election campaign party men mask their differences; yet when the contest ends and the victory is won, "each is thrown back upon his individual concern & as the objects of all cannot be gratified rivalry & contention take the place of harmony, & we witness such scenes as you are now in the midst of. If the battle is lost all private aspirations are concealed, & harmony reigns in the losing Party." Van Buren urged Polk not to reproach himself, for such conflicts resided naturally in the process of public affairs and could be managed only if there were "steadiness & good intentions at the Helm." With little more than two weeks remaining before the new president's oath taking, Van Buren's lecture on political economy bespoke the same air of diffidence that had characterized his earlier recommendations for filling New York's place in the new cabinet.

A month earlier, on January 18th, Van Buren had responded to Polk's solicitations for cabinet suggestions by reviewing a long line of contingencies: Wright must decline Polk's proffer of the treasury department and remain in the New York governorship; Benjamin F. Butler would make an excellent choice for the state department, but probably would not leave his law practice at this time; under no circumstances would Butler take any lesser place in the cabinet; should state go to someone other than Butler, either Azariah C. Flagg or Churchill C. Cambreleng would serve well at treasury; Robert Armstrong, Jackson's close friend from Tennessee, might fill the western slot; and George Bancroft would top any other candidate for New England's place. Van Buren closed his epistle with the condescending remark "that there is a sort of running opinion amongst us that no man suddenly & unexpectedly raised to the head of the State can succeed." Naturally, he added in a nasty-nice show of civility, "no such deficiencies are to be apprehended" in Polk's case.

On January 30th Polk sent Van Buren a brief note saying that he planned to visit Jackson before leaving on his inaugural trip and that he probably would take one of Van Buren's recommendations, "but which one of them, I think it prudent to leave open until I reach Washington." He invited Van Buren to make any additional suggestions that might come to mind and write to him at Washington City. On February 10th Van Buren wrote back with a brief notice of Butler's pro-annexation views and a longer treatise on the significance of foreign affairs in the coming four years. Polk should appoint a northern man to the state department, "if you can." Van Buren made no additional suggestions.

Naturally Polk took private counsel at the Hermitage with his mentor; and by the time of the president-elect's February 1st departure for Washington City he and Jackson had prepared a tentative slate of cabinet appointments with the following alignment: James Buchanan of Pennsylvania at state, Flagg of New York at the treasury, Andrew Stevenson of Virginia at war, Bancroft of Massachusetts at navy, Cave Johnson of Tennessee at post office, and Robert J. Walker of Mississippi as attorney general. His preliminary selections would include three from the North and three from the South. Buchanan and Walker balanced the key factional split in Pennsylvania; through his marriage Walker had established close family ties to George M. Dallas, whose strong support for Van Buren had effectively blocked Buchanan's presidential bid and had won him a place on Polk's ticket. Final cabinet selections would be made only after appropriate consultations had been held with the leaders of the party in Congress.

Arriving in the capital on February 14th, Polk heard rumors of every description concerning his cabinet preferences and not a little speculation about the impact they might have upon the succession in 1848. Prior to his departure Polk had drafted a form letter with which to request the services of each prospective cabinet officer and to lay out in plain language that any member who chose to run for president or engage in president-making would be expected to resign his post. Also each cabinet member would take personal direction of his department and would not absent himself from his office for any extended period of time. The president-elect's first offer went to Buchanan, who accepted the state department with the singular reservation that he not be expected to suffer "self ostracism," which his friends would never permit him to do! He could not prevent his friends from using his name in connection with the next presidential nomination, but he would agree not to make "any personal exertions for that purpose" without Polk's consent. Having pledged himself to a single term, the president-elect had no intention of consenting to anyone's exertions for the succession.

Flagg's personal involvement in the heated and particularly divisive struggle over the election of U.S. senators in New York brought his selection into serious doubt. In point of fact, Flagg's association with the radicals did not suggest any strong support on his part for Texas annexation. Besides, friends of Bouck had expressed great alarm at the prospect of a Flagg appointment. Not wishing to favor either the Flagg barnburners or the Bouck hunkers, Polk decided to rearrange his cabinet lineup. He would give the treasury post to New England, the war department to New York, and the navy to Virginia. Bancroft, who had served Van Buren most ably as collector of customs at Boston and who had given valuable assistance in putting Polk's name forward at the Baltimore convention, would move from navy to treasury. Benjamin F. Butler or William L. Marcy (in that order of preference) would go into the war department in place of Stevenson. And John Y. Mason, Polk's college classmate and current navy secretary, would remain at his post.

On February 22th Polk advised Van Buren that he had settled on Bancroft for the treasury and explained that southern and northwestern voices had united on a gentleman from the South (Walker) for the second place in the cabinet. Unwilling to accede to their wishes, he thought that Bancroft's appointment would satisfy both North and South; he left unsaid the obvious consideration that the party's southern and western leaders would not agree to Flagg. Van Buren received Polk's letter on February 26th and replied the next day with no little petulance that New York deserved better than the third seat in the cabinet; he took upon himself the liberty of accepting the war department for Butler. Van Buren sent a cover letter explaining that his son Smith Van Buren would hand carry his reply; leaving on February 28th for New York City and a conference with Butler, Smith Van Buren communicated his father's wishes in the matter. By February 25th Polk had invited Butler to take the war department, and two days later Butler had declined on grounds that his pecuniary situation would not permit him to accept; he did mention, however, that he would not have turned down either state or treasury had the one or the other been offered.

Strange to say, pressure from Albany did not change Butler's mind, and on March 1st he renewed his declination and expressed his "anxieties as to the selection you shall make of a Cabinet Minister from New York." In his February 22nd letter to Van Buren, Polk had named Butler or Marcy for the war appointment; Butler's "anxieties" clearly indicated his objection to Marcy. Smith Van Buren picked up Butler's second declination and reached Washington City on March 2nd, one day after Polk had offered the war department to Marcy, whose public persona matched that of any other New York Democrat save perhaps Van Buren and Wright's. For all their later complaints of neglect and humiliation, the New York radicals had given studied attention to foisting off on Polk candidates who either would not accept or who could not be asked. Had Van Buren wanted one of his closest confidants in the cabinet, he would not have excluded Butler from the treasury in favor of Flagg or Cambreleng, neither of whose selection would have acknowledged Polk's headship of the Democracy. In the case of the Calhoun wing of the party, Polk had neither asked nor received its certification, for the Old Democracy of the South had gladly accepted Jackson's annointment of Polk as Van Buren's successor.

Assured that Marcy would accept his assignment, Polk asked John Y. Mason to stay at the navy department. At their meeting on the evening of March 2nd, Mason gave his verbal acceptance, but the next day he wrote Polk that he had changed his mind. As though for emphasis, he sent the president-elect a separate note stating that he had resigned as secretary of the navy. Thus on the day before his inauguration the president-elect faced the difficulty of substituting another Virginian for Mason at the navy department or shuffling his cabinet around to place his friend in a more compatible appointment. What exact course Polk followed in the next forty-eight hours cannot be reconstructed with certainty for want of full and reliable documentation. Several of the key appointment and acceptance letters do not survive, and several carry dates that have been overwritten so as to place the offers and acceptances prior to March 5th, on which day Polk submitted his cabinet nominations to the senate for confirmation. Letters with overwritten dates will appear below as of their overwriting with the original dating noted by the editors. Particular atttention should be given to textual criticism attending the three letters of Mason to Polk on March 3rd and the letter of Bancroft to Polk on March 4th. Polk retained no appointment letters to or from Walker.

The most probable reconstruction of events indicates that Polk sent his official offers to Bancroft, Mason, Johnson, and Walker on the afternoon of March 3rd; receiving Mason's declination later that day, Polk resumed deliberations and decided that evening to switch assignments, giving Walker the treasury, Bancroft the navy, and Mason the attorney-generalship. Probably he discussed the realignment on the day of his inaugural and sent Bancroft, Mason, and Walker new appointment letters. Mason wrote his acceptance of the attorney-generalship on March 5th (date changed to read "March 3rd"). Bancroft's acceptance letter of March 4th referred to Polk's offer of the previous day but did not name the office in question; Polk's written offer to Bancroft of the navy bore the date of March 4th (date changed to read "March 3rd"); and Ban-

croft's retained draft of his acceptance letter, no office named, carried
the date of March 5th. Apart from the mystery of who changed the dates,
and when, the cabinet invitations and acceptances suggest that Polk had
at least one necessary reason for moving Walker to treasury quite apart
from a last-minute appeal from Jacob Thompson of the Mississippi congressional delegation.

Even a cursory examination of Polk's lesser appointments suggests
that the new president tried to accommodate the numerous, often ran-
corous factions at the state and local levels. Candidates with a proven
record of loyalty to the party prior to 1841 received more favor than
any other class. Yet he did not remove or proscribe John Tyler's appointees en masse; nor did he reject Calhoun nullifiers solely for their
ideological preferences. In Tennessee politics Polk had tried to keep
the door of the party open, and such would be his rule for sustaining
the Old Democracy and its sectional coalitions. In the South the most
difficult patronage fight broke out in New Orleans, where Polk named
Denis Prieur to the customs collectorship in place of Thomas Barrett,
chose Alceé La Branche to succeed Martin Duralde, Jr., as naval officer,
and retained Tyler's postmaster, Alexander G. Penn. Polk replaced U.S.
district attorneys in Maryland, Louisiana, Missouri, and West Florida;
selected new U.S. marshals in South Mississippi, Louisiana, Arkansas,
and South Alabama; and replaced three customs collectors in Florida
and three in North Carolina. Removals and resignations brought numerous new faces to the land offices in Mississippi, Missouri, Louisiana,
Alabama, and Arkansas. Perhaps the largest petition drive in the post-
election period urged the appointment of Charles P. Sengstack of Washington City to the post of commissioner of public buildings in the capital;
hundreds of journeymen in Baltimore and Washington City wanted one
of their own appointed in recognition of their party loyalty and civic status. Polk declined to make the necessary removal, although later he did
find a place for Sengstack as warden of the local penitentiary.

In the North two key patronage fights focused factional attention on
the collectorships in New York City and Philadelphia. Six major candidates vied for the lucrative collectorship at New York: Churchill C.
Cambreleng, Jonathan I. Coddington, Azariah C. Flagg, Cornelius W.
Lawrence, Ely Moore, and incumbent Cornelius P. Van Ness. Unable
to satisfy contending factions, Polk chose Lawrence, who had served in
Congress with Polk and for three years as mayor of New York; objections from many quarters registered the protest that Lawrence had too
many close ties to the city's banking interests. Van Burenites Robert H.
Morris, Elijah F. Purdy, and Michael Hoffman garnered the three other
most hotly contested plumbs in New York. Polk gave the collectorship

of Philadelphia to a senior operative in the Family party and Van Buren stalwart, Henry Horn; although nominated twice, Horn failed to receive senate confirmation. James Page subsequently won the appointment to the disappointment of Calvin Blythe, George F. Lehman, Richard Rush, and Henry Welsh. The Buchanan connection did place Lehman in the postmastership and Welsh in the post of naval officer.

Sensitive to the risk of being charged with nepotism, Polk turned away numerous importunities to find places for his family. He did ask that his brother, William, be appointed minister to Naples. William W. "Stingy Bill" Polk, reputedly the richest planter in Arkansas and Polk's some-time creditor, solicited an appointment for his son, Thomas, to be receiver of public monies at Springfield, Mo.; but the president ignored the family tree and made a political appointment instead. William S. Pickett, business partner of Polk's nephew, Samuel P. Walker, wanted the consularship at Marseilles, France, but failed to gain the post because Polk for political considerations could not remove the incumbent. More successful, though more distantly connected members of the family included Josiah F. Polk and James Polk, both of Maryland. Andrew Jackson sought places for two members of his connection, James B. Taggart and Thomas J. Donelson; Polk's particular consideration of Andrew Jackson Donelson must be attributed more to his reward for delivering Texas than to any accommodation of Jackson family interests.

Polk's decision to remove William B. Lewis as second auditor of the treasury and his forced buy out of Francis P. Blair's Washington *Globe* might well have brought down Jackson's wrath for humiliating two of the general's oldest and dearest friends; but the dying hero of New Orleans understood the necessity of launching the new administration in good order and building up the public's confidence in its new leader. Forming a strong cabinet of harmonious members and dispelling the growing distrust between the northern and southern branches of the Democracy required great patience and considerable resiliency. To his credit Polk took the most promising candidates he could recruit to overcome the weakness of his "dark horse" presidency.

## This Volume

Always concerned that the reader's primary focus fall on the text of the document, the editors have limited their annotations to textual criticism and identifications. Persons, subjects, and oblique references have been noted on the occasion of their first mention in this volume; for the full name of persons mentioned subsequently in the text only by surname, the reader will want to consult the index. The editors have transcribed the text faithfully with a strict regard for original spellings, punctuation, and text placement, except for the following rules of normalization:

1. initial words of sentences have been capitalized and ending punctuation marks have been supplied when the syntax is clear (uncertain constructions are noted and rendered without normalization);

2. conventional spellings have been followed except when misspellings have been clearly written;

3. conventional upper and lower case usage has been followed when the writer employed multiple and/or irregular forms of the same character, thus indicating no discernible meaning behind the writer's use of capitals;

4. interlineations, cancellations, and unintentional word repetitions have been ignored unless something more than writing errors may have been indicated;

5. short dashes on the base of the line have been transcribed as commas or periods as the syntax may suggest;

6. redundant punctuation and random flourishes or ink marks have been ignored;

7. superscripts have been brought down to the line, and markings beneath or beside superscripts have been transcribed as single periods;

8. punctuation marks following the abbreviations *st, nd, rd,* and *th* have been deleted;

9. regardless of their position in the original manuscript, the salutation, place of composition, and date have been set on the line or lines immediately below the document's heading;

10. place of composition and full date, if omitted but known to the editors through content analysis, have been supplied in brackets and noted, and misstatements of place and date have been corrected and supplied in brackets with the misinformation noted;

11. the complimentary closing has been omitted, and the omission of same has been indicated by an ellipsis if the closing was written as part of the ending paragraph;

12. the author's signature has been rendered in capitals and small capitals at the end of the text (or supplied within brackets if unwritten or clipped);

13. the inside address has been omitted, but the information has been stated in the head note, along with the document's classification and repository location;

14. textual interventions (ie., words supplied within brackets) have

been made only to complete probable meanings (garbled texts have been transcribed without intervention and so noted); and

15. bracketed ellipses have been added to indicate that a portion of the text has been obliterated by ink blots, sealing wax, or some other kind of damage, and the nature and extent of same has been noted.

The editors' identification and explanatory annotations often have been assembled from standard reference and monographic sources that are so well known and reliable as to obviate the need for citation. These considerations, coupled with a desire to ensure that the endnotes do not overwhelm the presentation of the textual material, have persuaded the editors to forego the naming of sources in their endnotes.

## *Acknowledgments*

Each of the volumes in the Correspondence Series brings additional evidence to bear that the Project's associate editors have contributed so much more to the undertaking than has been accounted for on the title pages. For their scholarship, patience, and friendship the editor gratefully dedicates this volume to Earl J. Smith, Carese M. Parker, James P. Cooper, Jr., Jayne C. DeFiore, and Robert G. Hall II. Thank you for the last five volumes.

For helpful assistance in researching and annotating this volume the editors express their special regard for and appreciation to Brian E. Crowson and James L. Rogers II. We likewise acknowledge the exceptional contributions of Cynthia J. Rogers, who doubled as copy editor and compositor. As with all of the volumes in the Series the editors owe a standing debt to the many scholars who have assisted us in our labors at the University of Tennessee Library, the Tennessee State Library and Archives, the Tennessee State Museum, the National Archives, the Library of Congress, and the New York Public Library. For their continued grant support and encouragement we are particularly indebted to the members of the National Historical Publications and Records Commission, the National Endowment for the Humanities, and the Tennessee Historical Commission and to the staff personnel of the above-mentioned agencies. For their continued backing we renew our prior expressions of appreciation to Jennifer M. Siler and her staff at the University of Tennessee Press.

Knoxville, Tennessee
*December 1995*

WAYNE CUTLER

# CONTENTS

# SYMBOLS

*Document Classification*

| | |
|---|---|
| AC | Autograph Circular |
| ACI | Autograph Circular Initialed |
| ACS | Autograph Circular Signed |
| AD | Autograph Document |
| ADI | Autograph Document Initialed |
| ADS | Autograph Document Signed |
| AE | Autograph Endorsement |
| AEI | Autograph Endorsement Initialed |
| AES | Autograph Endorsement Signed |
| AL | Autograph Letter |
| AL, draft | Autograph Letter, drafted by writer |
| AL, fragment | Autograph Letter, fragment |
| ALI | Autograph Letter Initialed |
| ALI, draft | Autograph Letter Initialed, drafted by writer |
| ALS | Autograph Letter Signed |
| ALS, copy | Autograph Letter Signed, copied by writer |
| ALS, draft | Autograph Letter Signed, drafted by writer |
| ALsS | Autograph Letters Signed |
| AN | Autograph Note |
| ANI | Autograph Note Initialed |
| ANS | Autograph Note Signed |
| C | Circular, authorship attributed |
| CI | Circular Initialed |
| CS | Circular Signed |
| D | Document, authorship attributed |

*xxxi*

| | |
|---|---|
| DI | Document Initialed |
| DS | Document Signed |
| E | Endorsement, authorship attributed |
| EI | Endorsement Initialed |
| ES | Endorsement Signed |
| L | Letter, authorship attributed |
| L, fragment | Letter, fragment |
| LI | Letter Initialed |
| LS | Letter Signed |
| N | Note, authorship attributed |
| NI | Note Initialed |
| NS | Note Signed |
| NsS | Notes Signed |
| PC | Published Circular, authorship attributed |
| PD | Published Document, authorship attributed |
| PL | Published Letter, authorship attributed |
| PL, broadside | Published Letter, broadside |
| PN | Published Note, authorship attributed |

*Repository Designations*

| | |
|---|---|
| CtY | Yale University, New Haven |
| DLC–AJ | Library of Congress, Andrew Jackson Papers |
| DLC–AJD | Library of Congress, Andrew Jackson Donelson Papers |
| DLC–AK | Library of Congress, Amos Kendall Papers |
| DLC–B/R | Library of Congress, Blair and Rives Papers |
| DLC–FP | Library of Congress, Franklin Pierce Papers |
| DLC–JKP | Library of Congress, James K. Polk Papers |
| DLC–LW | Library of Congress, Levi Woodbury Papers |
| DLC–MVB | Library of Congress, Martin Van Buren Papers |
| DLC–WLM | Library of Congress, William L. Marcy Papers |
| DLC–WM | Library of Congress, William Medill Papers |
| DNA–RG 26 | National Archives, Records of the Coast Guard |
| DNA–RG 42 | National Archives, Records of the Office of Public Buildings and Grounds |
| DNA–RG 45 | National Archives, Naval Records Collection of the Office of Naval Records and Library |
| DNA–RG 56 | National Archives, General Records of the Department of the Treasury |
| DNA–RG 59 | National Archives, General Records of the Department of State |

| | |
|---|---|
| DNA–RG 76 | National Archives, Records of the Boundary and Claims Arbitrations |
| DNA–RG 92 | National Archives, Records of the Office of the Quartermaster General |
| DNA–RG 156 | National Archives, Records of the Office of the Chief of Ordnance |
| Ia–HA | Iowa State Department of History and Archives, Des Moines |
| KyLoF | Filson Club, Louisville |
| MB | Boston Public Library, Boston |
| MHi | Massachusetts Historical Society, Boston |
| MdHi | Maryland Historical Society, Baltimore |
| MoHi | Missouri State Historical Society, Columbia |
| NHi | New-York Historical Society, New York |
| NN | New York Public Library, New York |
| NN–Ford | New York Public Library, Ford Collection, New York |
| NNC | Columbia University, New York |
| NNPM | Pierpont Morgan Library, New York |
| NjMoHP–LWS | Morristown National Historical Park, L. W. Smith Collection, Morristown |
| NjP | Princeton University, Princeton |
| PHi | Historical Society of Pennsylvania, Philadelphia |
| PP | Free Library of Philadelphia, Philadelphia |
| ScCleU–JCC | Clemson University, John C. Calhoun Papers, Clemson |
| ScU-SCL | University of South Carolina, South Caroliniana Library, Columbia |
| T–JKP | Tennessee State Library, James K. Polk Papers |
| TxGR | Rosenberg Library, Galveston |

*Published Sources*

| | |
|---|---|
| NCHR | *North Carolina Historical Review* |
| THM | *Tennessee Historical Magazine* |
| THQ | *Tennessee Historical Quarterly* |
| TQ | *Tyler's Quarterly Historical and Genealogical Magazine* |

# CHRONOLOGY

| | | |
|---|---|---|
| 1795 | Nov. 2 | Born in Mecklenburg County, N.C. |
| 1806 | Fall | Moved to Maury County, Tenn. |
| 1812 | Fall | Underwent major surgery by Dr. Ephraim Mc-Dowell in Danville, Ky. |
| 1813 | July | Began study under Robert Henderson at Zion Church Academy |
| 1816 | Jan. | Entered University of North Carolina as sophomore |
| 1818 | June | Graduated from University of North Carolina |
| | Fall | Began reading law in office of Felix Grundy of Nashville |
| 1819 | Sept. | Elected clerk of the Tennessee Senate |
| 1820 | June | Admitted to the bar |
| 1823 | Aug. | Elected to the Tennessee House |
| 1824 | Jan. 1 | Married Sarah Childress of Murfreesboro |
| 1825 | Aug. | Elected to the U.S. House |
| 1827 | Aug. | Reelected to the U.S. House |
| | Nov. 5 | Death of his father, Samuel Polk |
| 1829 | Aug. | Reelected to the U.S. House |
| 1831 | Jan. 21 | Death of his brother Franklin, aged 28 |
| | April 12 | Death of his brother Marshall, aged 26 |
| | Aug. | Reelected to the U.S. House |
| | Sept. 28 | Death of his brother John, aged 24 |
| 1833 | Aug. | Reelected to the U.S. House |
| | Dec. | Chosen to chair the U.S. House Committee on Ways and Means |

| | | |
|---|---|---|
| 1834 | June | Defeated by John Bell for Speaker of the U.S. House |
| 1835 | Aug. | Reelected to the U.S. House |
| | Dec. 7 | Elected Speaker of the U.S. House |
| 1836 | Aug. 6 | Death of his sister Naomi, wife of Adlai O. Harris |
| 1837 | Aug. | Reelected to the U.S. House |
| | Sept. 4 | Reelected Speaker of the U.S. House |
| 1839 | Aug. | Elected Governor of Tennessee over Newton Cannon |
| 1840 | May | Withdrew candidacy for the Democratic vice-presidential nomination |
| 1841 | Aug. | Defeated in gubernatorial election by James C. Jones |
| 1843 | Aug. | Defeated in gubernatorial election by James C. Jones |
| | Nov. | Recommended by the Tennessee Democratic State Convention to be the party's 1844 vice-presidential nominee |
| 1844 | May | Nominated for the presidency by the Democratic National Convention |
| | Nov. | Elected President of the United States over Henry Clay |
| 1845 | Mar. 4 | Inaugurated President of the United States |
| 1849 | Mar. 4 | Yielded office to his successor, Zachary Taylor |
| | June 15 | Died in Nashville of cholera |

# Correspondence of James K. Polk

VOLUME IX, JANUARY – JUNE 1845

# JANUARY 1845

## FROM GEORGE BANCROFT[1]

My dear Sir,                                    Boston. January 1. [1845][2]

Since the election, my heart has often risen to the ends of my fingers, prompting me to send you my congratulations on the glorious result. The events and course of this canvass single it out as the most momentous that has occurred in my day; the whig party brought out all their strength, leaving no reserve force, but pressing every thing into the field; and they were honorably beaten back by a gallant resistance. What was done at the North was done openly by reliance on our principles and trust in one another. In this state, which the tariff and other considerations made the citadel of the whig strength, a larger number of men gave their votes for you, than had ever in Massachusetts given a vote for a democratic president. You would need to know the bitter intolerance and relentless pride of our opponents in this region, to realize how important to me personally was our success; but the temper of your Tennessee whigs will give you some idea of it. The contest, from the early spring, when the Democratic force seemed broken and scattered and exposed to defeat, to the time of the Baltimore convention, the rally of the people in the several states, and the final victory in November, was a succession of the most brilliant scenes, which ever attended an electioneering campaign; and the result is hailed by the party with unmingled satisfaction and joy. The next fifty years may not see another such contest.

After the result was declared, my position in this state induced several gentlemen to solicit me to address you on the subject of the formation of your cabinet. This I declined altogether, because I was unwilling to intrude unsolicited opinions; and because I have the most entire confidence in your own judgment, & independence of that best sort, which springs from the union of Prudence and Courage. Nor should I now have written, had I not learned that my name has been proposed for a place in the cabinet, under circumstances, which might, perhaps, leave on your mind the impression that the suggestion was authorized by me.[3] I count, therefore, so largely on your regard, as to believe you will esteem me as not exceeding the bounds of a just and proper frankness, if I express to you directly, *without consulting any one*, that a place in the cabinet has not seemed to me at this time the place most favorable to my efficiency. Many years of close attention, and continued investigation on my part, have made the public wish somewhat general, that I should as speedily as possible conclude the History which I have undertaken of the United States; and the foreign service in *England*, in *France*, or in *Germany*, is the only position which would favor that end. When I was a very young man, I passed three years and more in France & Germany; and during that period I resided a winter in Berlin; so that the German language as well as the French, is almost as familiar to me as the English. If, in working up your arrangements for the foreign corps, the missions to London & to Paris should be otherwise settled, & the mission to Berlin were offered me, I should certainly accept it. If it were to fall within your views to open such a career to me, I would rather, that the decision should be your own choice, than a result of the representations of my friends; nor should I have troubled you with this communication, had I not feared that some wrong impression might be given to you.

Having thus opened my mind, I recur to the subject which must at first occupy your attention: the composition of your cabinet, and the doctrines of your inaugural. I doubt not your opening address, which will come as a voice from the very heart of the democracy to the nation and to the world, and which will read not in our country only, but from Lisbon to St Petersburgh, will take its place by the side of Jefferson's for fidelity to principle and calm conciliation.[4] I cannot easily express to you how deeply I have at heart the success of you[r adminis]tration[5]; indeed the deepest feeling of interest pervades all the democracy.

GEORGE BANCROFT

ALS. DLC–JKP. Addressed to Columbia. Extract published in M. A. DeWolfe Howe, ed., *The Life and Letters of George Bancroft* (2 vols.; New York: Charles Scribner's Sons, 1908), I, p. 262.

1. Historian and diplomat, Bancroft attended universities in Germany from 1818 to 1822. An ardent Jacksonian, he took an energetic part in securing Northern delegate support for Polk's presidential nomination at the 1844 Baltimore convention. Polk appointed him secretary of the navy in 1845 and eighteen months later named him minister to Great Britain. Acquainted with many English and French scholars, Bancroft pursued additional research on his ten-volume *History of the United States* (1834–74) before returning to the United States in 1849.

2. Erroneously dated "1844."

3. See Robert P. Dunlap to Polk, December 30, 1844.

4. Bancroft probably refers to those portions of Thomas Jefferson's First Inaugural Address devoted to reconciling bitter partisan divisions occasioned by the presidential contest of 1800: "But every difference of opinion is not a difference of principle. We have called by different names brethren of the same principle. We are all Republicans, we are all Federalists. If there be any among us who would wish to dissolve this Union or to change its republican form, let them stand undisturbed as monuments of the safety with which error of opinion may be tolerated where reason is left free to combat it." James D. Richardson, ed., *A Compilation of the Messages and Papers of the Presidents, 1789–1902* (10 vols.; Washington, D.C.: Bureau of National Literature and Art, 1903), I, p. 322.

5. Portions of preceding two words obliterated by sealing wax oil.

## FROM AARON V. BROWN[1]

Dear Sir                                          Washington Jany 1st [1845][2]

My hopes are far from being desponding about Texas at this Session. Benton[3] says he will obey cheerfully & if so the *hesitating* New Yorkers will come in. Our caucus is to night. The proposition of Douglass[4] was prepared at my room & is the one I prefer & a majority of our party, but we will take any other that will reconcile friends.

I have seen Ritchie's response.[5] He will not go into our views—reasons to shew that he is under *suspicion* with the Van Buren men & Benton &Co would war as soon against him as any one—dwells too on his Virginia associates &c &c. But is full of zeal for your administration. If Benton goes right on Texas & Calhoun is not in the Cabinet there would be no insuperable difficulty with the Globe, but you would find it hard to keep in order—give your views further on this point.

There are persons here who talk much of Woodberry[6] for the State Department, going on the supposition that Presidential aspirants are to be excluded. If Buchannon[7] were to go on the Bench, How would it do to give Woodberry the first & Walker[8] the treasury department. Remember the departure of Calhoun might give some dissatisfaction to the South which the appointment of Walker would allay. Woodberry is a no-

ble Democrat, has the unbroken confidence of our party & with all equal
to any of them in general ability. Wickliffe has written to you (he tells
me) tending his resignation[9] whene'r *you* shall chose to accept it. I feel
anxious for him only on account of the shout of joy which the Clayites
would raise over him on his return. What could be done for him to prevent that?

If the two judgeships should lie open in Pennsylvania & N York[10] they
would help you very much in casting your cabinet & I try to do a little in
that line.

Did you mean that I should afflict you so much & so often? Well, if you
did not, remember never to commit yourself by such a request again &
I must especially beg of you to remember that If I sometimes seem to be
arranging & dictating a little *too freely*, that I am a little spoiled by the
incessant court now paying day & night *to the President ad-interim*. Mr.
Tyler & Mrs. Madison & Mr Blair[11] were all receiving the company to
day & really I had a notion *to open shop* myself & could have made quite a
shew among the office seekers! Now let me tell you *a secret*, not to be told
to our most *intimate friend*.[12] I looked carefully at "Mrs. President,"[13]
young & beautiful as she is, & I tell you positively, "*we can beat that*" just
this time twelve months to come, but mind just keep that to yourself.

A. V. BROWN

ALS. DLC–JKP. Addressed to Columbia.

1. Polk's former law partner and longtime friend from Pulaski, Brown served
in the Tennessee Senate and House, 1821–33, in the U.S. House, 1839–45, and in
the Tennessee governorship, 1845–47. From 1857 until his death in 1859, Brown
held the post of postmaster general in the administration of James Buchanan.

2. Erroneously dated "1843."

3. A strong supporter of Jackson and hard money, Thomas H. Benton represented Missouri in the U.S. Senate for thirty years. In November 1844 the
Missouri legislature passed joint resolutions favoring the reannexation of Texas
and instructing its Congressional delegation along those lines.

4. An Illinois teacher and lawyer, Stephen A. Douglas served as a member of
the Illinois House, 1836–37; as Illinois secretary of state, 1840–41; and as a judge
on the state's highest appellate court. He went to the U.S. House as a Democrat
for two terms, 1843–47, before winning election in 1847 to the first of three terms
in the U.S. Senate; Northern Democrats nominated him for the presidency in
1860. On December 23, 1844, Douglas introduced a joint resolution providing
for the annexation of the Republic of Texas.

5. On December 28, 1844, Thomas Ritchie wrote his confidential friend,
Thomas H. Bayly, that he did not wish to accept the proposal, proffered through
Bayly's recent letter, to conduct the new administration's Washington newspaper. Editor of the *Richmond Enquirer* since 1804, Ritchie served unofficially
as political manager of the Virginia Democracy; his strong support of Polk had

placed him at some distance from the Martin Van Buren loyalists. Encouraged at length by lucrative financial inducements, Ritchie formed a partnership with John P. Heiss of Nashville and purchased the Washington *Globe* from Francis P. Blair and John C. Rives on April 12, 1845. Ritchie changed the newspaper's name to that of the Washington *Union* and issued his first number on April 14th. For the text of Ritchie's letter to Bayly, see Charles Henry Ambler, *Thomas Ritchie: A Study in Virginia Politics* (Richmond: The Bell Book & Stationary Co., Inc., 1913), pp. 247–49.

6. Levi Woodbury headed the U.S. Department of the Treasury from 1834 until 1841. Earlier he had served as governor of New Hampshire, Democratic senator from that state, and secretary of the navy. In 1841 Woodbury returned to the U.S. Senate and served until his appointment to the U.S. Supreme Court in 1845.

7. James Buchanan. Brown refers to speculation that Buchanan might be appointed to the U.S. Supreme Court.

8. Pennsylvania born, Robert J. Walker moved to Natchez, Miss., in 1826 and practiced law. He served in the U.S. Senate from 1835 until 1845, when he became Polk's secretary of the Treasury. Subsequently, he served as governor of the Kansas Territory and as U.S. financial agent in Europe during the Civil War.

9. Charles A. Wickliffe served several terms in the Kentucky legislature before winning election to the U.S. House, where he served five terms beginning in 1823; he won the lieutenant governorship in 1836 and succeeded James Clark as governor upon the latter's death in 1839. Henry Clay's chief rival for leadership of the Kentucky Whigs, Wickliffe held the post of postmaster general in the Tyler administration. He offered his resignation to Polk on December 6, 1844. ALS. DLC–JKP.

10. Brown refers to the two vacant associate justiceships on the U.S. Supreme Court.

11. John Tyler, Dolly Payne Madison, and Francis P. Blair. Leader of Washington society from 1801 until 1817, Dolly Madison left Washington at the close of her husband James' administration and remained in retirement until after his death in 1836, when she returned to Washington and enjoyed an active social life until her death in 1849. Founder and editor of the Washington *Globe* from 1830 until 1845, Blair was one of the leading spokesmen of the Jacksonian Democracy; his grudging support of the presidential ticket in 1844 led to his loss of political influence with the new administration and thus to his sale of the *Globe*.

12. Sarah Childress Polk.

13. Julia Gardiner married John Tyler on June 26, 1844.

## FROM MEMUCAN HUNT[1]

Galveston, Texas. January 1, 1845

After congratulating Polk on his election as president, Hunt turns to Polk's cabinet appointments and discusses the views of "the leading public men of

Texas" on this question. Manifesting "great solicitude" on behalf of John C. Calhoun, they hope that Polk will retain him as secretary of state. Because the citizens of Texas revere Andrew Jackson, they also hope that Polk will appoint Andrew J. Donelson[2] as secretary of war.

ALS. DLC–JKP. Probably addressed to Columbia.

1. A native of North Carolina, Memucan Hunt engaged in large-scale cotton planting in Madison County, Miss., before joining the Texas struggle for independence. He served as major general in the Texas army in 1836; as Texas minister to the U.S., 1837–38; as secretary of the Texas navy, 1838; and as commissioner to establish the boundary between the Republic of Texas and the United States.

2. Nephew of Rachel Jackson and private secretary to her husband, Andrew, during his presidency, Donelson became chargé d'affaires to Texas in the fall of 1844 and guided negotiations leading to its annexation in 1845; he later served as U.S. minister to Prussia during the Polk administration.

## FROM CAVE JOHNSON[1]

Dear Sir,                        Washington 2nd Jany 1845

I had the pleasure of receiving yours a day or two since but not time enough to have any hand in the procurement of your Rooms.[2] I should never have yielded to $140 per week. The U.S. Hotel, it is said offered Mr Clay rooms without pay, on account of the increased patronage which would probably arise, & so I suppose if you get off with paying double now, you should not complain.

I enclose you the Copy of a letter, at the request of Messrs. Cobb & Lumpkin; the original will be handed you at the proper time.[3] There is much feeling among the democrats of Geo. to have something done for Stiles who is a good lawyer, an amiable gentleman & who has been by whig management thrown into Lumpkins district & excluded from the next Congress.[4]

I have but little news. T. Ritchie writes to Baily[5] that he will under no circumstances come to Washington, which I regret exceedingly. There has been some conversation about Burke.[6] I doubt whether he will satisfy all tho. a good writer. He was thought to be identified a year ago with Mr. Cn[7] but not so much now as then.

The public talk is stale as to the retention of Mr. Cn. The Southern men speak of it as certain, if he chooses to stay, which is to depend upon the settlement of the Texas question and I suppose the impression is made from the feelings expressed by some of my collegues. There is evidently great apprehension at the North & the South as to the influence that is to give direction to the patronage of the Government. Cliques are formed in all the great cities to try & give it direction to suit their own interests & you will have much trouble to shake them off. Buckhanon[8] is now more talked of, than at the Commencement because, he is not strong enough as a candidate to excite much jealousy. Cass[9] seems but little less exceptionable to northern democrats than Calhoun. Robt. J. Walker is occasionally spoken of also. I fear the Dallas influence in Pen.[10] is not destined to promote the harmony of your admn. & will probably be used if possible to the detriment of Buckhanon.

The Treasury seems generally conceded to N.Y. Wright, Flagg, Marcy & Cambreling[11] seem to be the favorites in the order in which their names are mentioned. Jno P King[12] of Ga. is spoken of, by some southern men, with high commendation.

The P.O. department excites some feeling on account of its patronage. Genl. Saunders, Gov. Hubbard & Madeire[13] are all spoken of here.

For the War, W O Butler, Fairfield,[14] & occasionally Genl Cass, tho. it seems generally thought he will accept only the first.

For the Navy, Jno. Y. Mason,[15] occasionally Fairfield is mentioned in connexion with it. It is generally believed that he has the best chance to be retained & also Elmore or Picken.[16]

R. J. Walker is most talked of for attorney Genl.

In my opinion Genl McKay[17] will be the best that can be selected for either the War, Navy or P.O. tho. not spoken of. It strikes us with some surprise, that no outfits are asked for any European mission. They will probably be asked by the Com. of W & Means, certainly moved in the House.

The Pres had a great crowd. Wm.[18] is the lion of the city & the Admiration of the ladies. The Pres. will give him the Charge to Naples. Bolevar[19] has asked to return the 1st of April. The president will expedite his return so as to appoint Wm. before the 4th March. I expect he will hand you a long list of special favorites to be retained and among them bitter Whigs—for example, Reuben Whitney, Recorder & secretly the Editor of the Madison[20] & his brother in law Miller[21] 2nd asst. P.M. Genl., both to superintend his interests as the candidate of 1848. This is rumor. There is I might say a universal feeling among the Demos for a general turn out of Whigs, much more so than I ever before knew.

I did not intend to trouble you at this time with these things hoping soon to learn more & from better sources. I have not as yet called on Buckhanon. He spent the holy days at home.

I have messages to you every day from friends such as "tell P. to play old hickory on them," "to shake off their cliques, be himself the Pres" &c &c. There is an apprehension among some of your friends that you may listen too favorably to *older politicians with whom you were formerly intimate*, & who may have selfish purposes to attain.

C. JOHNSON

ALS. DLC–JKP. Addressed to Columbia.

1. One of Polk's closest friends and political allies, Cave Johnson practiced law in Clarksville and served seven terms in the U.S. House as a Democrat, 1829–37 and 1839–45. Polk appointed him postmaster general in 1845.

2. Reference probably is to Polk's letter to Cave Johnson, December 21, 1844. Polk relied on Johnson, Aaron V. Brown, and John Catron to secure rooms at the National Hotel in Washington City prior to the inauguration. See Aaron V. Brown to Polk, December 30, 1844, and John Catron to Polk, December 31, 1844.

3. Neither the enclosed copy nor the original letter from Howell Cobb and John H. Lumpkin has been found. Cobb, an Athens lawyer, served as solicitor general of the Western District of Georgia, 1837–41; sat as a Democrat in the U.S. House, 1843–51; and served as Speaker during his final term. He won election to one term as governor of Georgia, 1851–53; returned for one term in the U.S. House, 1855–57; and served as secretary of the Treasury during James Buchanan's administration. A lawyer from Rome, Ga., Lumpkin served one term in the state legislature; won election to three terms in the U.S. House, 1843–49; served as judge of the Georgia Superior Court, 1850–53; returned to the U.S. House, 1855–57; and lost his bid for the Georgia governorship in 1857.

4. A lawyer from Savannah, Ga., William Henry Stiles served as solicitor general for the Eastern District of Georgia, 1833–36; as a Democrat in the U.S. House, 1843–45; and as chargé d'affaires to Austria, 1845–49.

5. Thomas Ritchie and Thomas H. Bayly. A lawyer and judge from Accomack County, Va., Bayly served several terms in the Virginia House of Delegates, 1835–45. Winning election to the U.S. House as a States' Rights Democrat in 1844, he served in that body until 1856. For Bayly's part in recruiting Ritchie to edit the Washington *Globe*, see Aaron V. Brown to Polk, January 1, 1845.

6. Edmund Burke practiced law until 1833, when he became editor of the *New Hampshire Argus*. When the *Argus* united with the Newport *Spectator* in 1834, Burke continued as editor. He served as a Democrat in the U.S. House, 1839–44, and as commissioner of patents, 1846–50.

7. John C. Calhoun.

8. James Buchanan.

9. Lewis Cass, presidential nominee of the Democracy in 1848, served as governor of the Michigan Territory, 1813–31; U.S. secretary of war, 1831–36; U.S. minister to France,1836–42; U.S. senator from Michigan, 1845–48 and 1851–57; and U.S. secretary of state, 1857–60.

10. Johnson's reference is to the rivalry in Pennsylvania between supporters of James Buchanan and the "Family party" of George M. Dallas, Robert J. Walker, and William Wilkins. Identified for many years as a staunch Van Burenite, Dallas helped remove Buchanan's name from the list of potential presidential nominees with his revival of the "Old Hickory Club" in 1843. Polk's friends in the Pennsylvania Democracy warned that Dallas and his associates would op-

pose a Buchanan appointment to the cabinet, use their influence to secure the patronage of the administration, and work to further Dallas' political career.

11. Silas Wright, Jr., Azariah C. Flagg, William L. Marcy, and Churchill C. Cambreleng. U.S. senator from New York since 1833, Wright backed Martin Van Buren for the 1844 presidential nomination; declined second place on Polk's ticket; won election to the governorship of New York in 1844, and served in that post until 1846. A New York legislator and leader of the Albany Regency, Flagg served as secretary of state for New York and as state comptroller for nine years during the 1830's and the 1840's. A strong opponent of the Bank of the United States, he joined the Barnburners and eventually headed that faction of the New York Democracy. A lawyer and New York politician, Marcy served as state comptroller, 1823–29; associate justice of the New York Supreme Court, 1829–31; U.S. senator, 1831–32; Democratic governor of New York for three terms, 1833–39; secretary of war in the Polk administration, 1845–49; and secretary of state, 1853–57. A party stalwart and member of Martin Van Buren's inner circle, Cambreleng engaged in mercantile business in New York and served nine terms as a Democrat in the U.S. House, 1821–39. Van Buren appointed him minister to Russia, 1840–41.

12. John P. King served as a Democrat in the U.S. Senate, 1833–37, and as president of the Georgia Railroad & Banking Co., 1841–78.

13. Romulus M. Saunders, Henry Hubbard, and Samuel Medary. A lawyer active in North Carolina politics since 1815, Saunders lost his bid for the governorship in 1840; having previously served three terms in the U.S. House, 1821–27, he returned to that body and served two more terms, 1841–45. A New Hampshire lawyer, Hubbard sat in the state legislature for several terms before serving first in the U.S. House, 1829–35, and then in the U.S. Senate, 1835–41. He also saw government service as governor of New Hampshire, 1841–43, and as U.S. subtreasurer at Boston, 1846–49. A native of Pennsylvania and printer by trade, Medary edited the Columbus *Ohio Statesman* and in that position exercised great influence among the Ohio Democracy; he subsequently served first as governor of Minnesota Territory, 1857–58, and then of Kansas, 1859–60.

14. William O. Butler and John Fairfield. Butler fought in the Battle of New Orleans; served as an aide to Andrew Jackson; and sat in the Kentucky House, 1817–18. He won election as a Democrat to two terms in the U.S. House, 1839–43; but lost his gubernatorial bid in 1844 to William Owsley, nominee of the Kentucky Whigs. Butler ran unsuccessfully for the U.S. vice-presidency on the Democratic ticket of 1848. A Maine lawyer, John Fairfield sat as a Democrat in the U.S. House and served from 1835 until 1838, when he resigned to become governor of Maine, 1839–43. Fairfield resigned the governorship to fill the seat of Reuel Williams in the U.S. Senate and served from 1843 until his death in 1847.

15. John Y. Mason served as a member of the U.S. House, 1831–37; U.S. district judge for the Eastern District of Virginia, 1837–44; secretary of the navy, 1844–45 and 1846–49; and U.S. attorney general, 1845–46.

16. Franklin H. Elmore and Francis W. Pickens. A South Carolina lawyer and Calhoun supporter, Elmore sat in the U.S. House, 1836–39; presided over the Bank of the State of South Carolina, 1839–50; and served briefly in the U.S.

Senate in 1850. Pickens, a South Carolina lawyer and planter, first won election to Congress as a nullifier and sat from 1834 until 1843; a member of the Nashville Convention of 1850, he served as governor of South Carolina from 1860 until 1863.

17. James I. McKay, a lawyer and Democrat from North Carolina, served in the U.S. House from 1831 to 1849; earlier he had won election to several terms in the state senate and had served as U.S. attorney for the District of North Carolina.

18. Polk's only surviving brother, William H. Polk, practiced law in Columbia and served three terms in the Tennessee House, 1841–45 and 1857–59, and one term in the U.S. House, 1851–53. In December 1844 he traveled to Washington to secure a diplomatic post. President Tyler offered him the position of chargé d'affaires to the Kingdom of the Two Sicilies, but the Senate failed to act on the nomination. Renominated by the new president, William won confirmation on March 13, 1845, and served as U.S. minister to Naples until 1847.

19. William Boulware, a native of Virginia, served as chargé d'affaires to the Kingdom of the Two Sicilies from 1841 to 1845.

20. A Philadelphia businessman and former director of the Bank of the United States, Reuben M. Whitney served as a trusted adviser to Andrew Jackson and to the Treasury Department. During 1833 he assisted Polk in an investigation of the Bank. John Tyler nominated Whitney as recorder of the General Land Office in December 1844, but the Senate rejected the appointment. His relationship to the Washington *Madisonian* is not identified further. See Whitney to Polk, March 17, 1845.

21. A physician and journalist, N. M. Miller became the proprietor of the Columbus *Old School Republican and Ohio State Gazette* in 1841. In 1844 he became second assistant postmaster general, a post he held for about a year. Polk demoted him to third assistant in 1845 and eventually removed him from office.


## FROM THEOPHILUS FISK[1]


Sir,                                           Portsmouth, Va. Jan. 3 1845

I take the earliest opportunity which has been afforded me since my return from Europe to express my warmest congratulations upon the result of the late election. I look upon it, with a heart overflowing with joy, as one of the most signal interpositions of Divine Providence, which has been manifested since the foundation of our government. As a prominent friend in the city of New York remarked to me a few days ago, on my arrival, "the election has Americanized every thing." I felt the force of the remark more fully than I otherwise should have done, from the fact, that I have not met with a single British Tory while passing through England, or in travelling upon the continent, who was not a fiery partisan on Mr. Clay. To this there has not been *one* exception. *All—all*—sympathised warmly, heartily, zealously, with the American whigs in support of their candidate; they manifested the same want of courtesy, to me whenever I expressed my earnest convictions of your success, that their admirers on this side of the water have done under similar circumstances. That the blow has been felt as keenly by them, as by the miscalled whigs of this country, is manifest by the tone of their leading journals since the result was made known. Under all these circumstances, ought not every bosom to swell with profound thankfulness to the Great Giver of all good, that He has been pleased to overrule the machinations of our political enemies?

There has been, since my return, but one draw-back upon my (otherwise) perfect joy. I have seen with the deepest sorrow and regret, an attempt making by those who at first openly opposed your nomination (but who who afterwards assumed a position of "armed neutrality") to monopolize all the credit of the victory, as well as the high places of honour and profit; and in order to succeed, they are sparing no efforts to supplant the very men who laboured the most zealously and sincerely to promote your success. I refer more particularly to the course the friends of Mr. Benton, and some of the friends of Mr. Wright in the State of New York, are pursuing in relation to Mr. Calhoun and his friends. It is their avowed determination *to drive* him from the cabinet.

It is a fact known to a few only, that Mr. Benton and Mr. Wright, when the nomination was first made, determined to do all in their power to defeat your election. Mr. Wright afterwards changed his mind; but not so his leading friends in the State of New York, as is apparent by the difference between his vote for Governor and that cast for Presidential electors.[2] The friends of Mr. Calhoun, who are numerous in New York, worked night and day; and it is to their unflagging zeal that the result in that State has been so glorious.

I have not the slightest suspicion that all the efforts of the disappointed leaders among the friends of Mr. Van Buren, will influence your course in the slightest possible degree. I am too well acquainted with the unwavering firmness of your character, to fear for a moment that all there designs will produce the least possible effect upon your future determination; nevertheless as one of your most devoted admirers, I have felt it a duty to apprize you of the facts as they exist.

Wishing you the most perfect health to enable you to discharge the important duties of the exalted station you have been called to fill ....

THEOPHILUS FISK

ALS. DLC–JKP. Addressed to Columbia.
1. Theophilus Fisk published the Portsmouth *Chronicle and Old Dominion* from 1839 until 1845. In 1844 he travelled to Europe as a courier for the State Department.

2. In the 1844 elections Silas Wright, Jr., polled 241,087 votes in his bid for the New York governorship; the Democratic presidential ticket received 3,499 fewer votes.

## FROM SAMUEL P. WALKER[1]

Dear Sir.                                          Memphis Jany. 3d 1845

I received your letter of the 14th Dec.[2] just as I was *getting off* to Miss. I had written to Knox,[3] before closing the letter. I requested him to say to you that I had a distinct recollection of the settlement between William & yourself[4] but that I did not know what had become of his receipts, vouchers &c.

I staid all night at your plantation with Col. Campbell[5] on the night of the 27th Dec. Your people are all well. Dismukes[6] has shipped 101 Bales cotton & thinks he will make in all 130 to 140 Bales. I presume James Brown[7] has written you that he has employed Mairs[8] for you for the next year. He reached the plantation on the day I left there. Brown recommends him very highly. I staid with Col. Fly[9] as I came up. He knows him well & agrees with Brown in the opinion, that there is no better planter in Miss, that he is honest *very economical* & industrious. It was very well that Brown had made the engagement as Campbell would have dismissed Dismukes any how. He has to much company about him.

I advanced Col. Campbell $150 to pay some accounts in the neighborhood which will be charged to your account at New Orleans.

Maj Bobbitt[10] informed me that he was an applicant for the office of Marshall for North Mississippi. There will be several other applicants— among the number Col. Thos. B. Carroll[11] of Panola County. They both say they will be well recommended. Either of them would, I expect make a good officer. Carroll is said to be an active, energetic & prompt business man. He expects to get all the Miss. influence he can and in addition to get letters from Genl. Jackson Genl Armstrong[12] & others about Nashville.

They talk of uniting and if either of them should be successful of dividing the duties of the office, as it will require the attention of two or three persons any how. I dont know [how] strongly others may be recommended, but I would be very glad to see Carroll get the appointment, particularly, if Bobbitt should withdraw & recommend him.

                                                    SAML. P. WALKER

[P.S.] I recd. a letter from Father a short time since in which he said you would send me your note to close a business arrangement made with Uncle Billy Polk.[13] The money is here in *Gold*. When I get your note I will send you a check on Nashville or Columbia, with whatever premium, I can get for the Gold. S.P.W.

ALS. DLC–JKP. Addressed to Columbia. Extract published in John Spencer Bassett, *The Southern Plantation Overseer* (Northampton, Mass., 1925), p. 174.

1. A Memphis lawyer and businessman, Samuel P. Walker was Polk's nephew and eldest son of James and Jane Maria Polk Walker.

2. Polk's letter has not been found.

3. Joseph Knox Walker, younger brother of Samuel, served as a private secretary to Polk during his presidency. He subsequently practiced law in Memphis and represented Shelby and Fayette counties as a Democrat in the Tennessee Senate from 1857 until 1859.

4. Walker's reference is to William S. Pickett's disposition of Polk's cotton crop. Pickett and Walker operated a cotton brokerage firm in New Orleans and Memphis; Pickett married Walker's sister, Mary Eliza, in 1842.

5. Robert Campbell, Jr., served as Polk's business agent in Columbia. The son of John and Matilda Golden Polk Campbell, Robert used the affix, "Junior," to distinguish himself from his uncle of like name.

6. Isaac H. Dismukes managed Polk's Mississippi estate from 1841 until 1845.

7. James Brown represented Polk's land interests in Mississippi in the 1840's.

8. John A. Mairs became overseer of Polk's Mississippi estate in 1845.

9. Possibly Joshua Fly of Yalobusha County, Miss.

10. William Bobbitt was Polk's business agent in Coffeeville, Miss.

11. Carroll was not appointed to the office.

12. Andrew Jackson and Robert Armstrong. Armstrong served as Nashville's postmaster from 1829 until March 1845, when he was appointed U.S. consul at Liverpool. One of Polk's closest political friends, he managed Polk's three gubernatorial campaigns and coordinated his presidential bid in Tennessee.

13. Reference is to a loan of $9,000 that Polk borrowed from his uncle (Walker's great-uncle), William Wilson Polk of Arkansas. Known in family lore as "Stingy Bill," William Wilson received a captain's commission in the Maury County militia in 1808; he subsequently moved to Middleburg in Hardeman County. By 1840 he had removed to Phillips County, Ark., where he owned one of the South's largest and most profitable plantations.

## FROM ALFRED BALCH[1]

Dear Sir,                                         Nashville 4th January 1845

Individuals who are anxiously and even *indelicately* seeking seats in your Cabinet will complain at their disappointment but, I have observed that the mass of a party have no sympathy in the defeated office seekers. The great matter is to employ those who are so worthy that they cannot be fairly excepted to. If this is done, you will be secure in your position no matter how hot and incessant the fire of the enemy may be. Your perfect protection lies in the choice of men of *real talents* of *energy, virtue, fidelity* and of *immaculate moral characters*.

After you embark from this place you will not have a single moment to devote to any serious important *composition*. You will therefore find it necessary now to shut your doors about you and give your whole mind to your inaugural which will be looked for with great interest here and throughout France and England. It may be well to glance your eye over the inaugurals of your predecessors particularly those of Madison which are written in a perfectly chaste style and are calm dignified and elevated without the least appearance of effort or exaggeration or straining.

The re-annunciation concisely of the principles contained in the Va resolutions of 98 and 99[2] will be acceptable to the Democratic party. Both the great parties into which we are divided, will read with intense interest whatever you may deem it judicious to say upon that absorbing topic the Tariff Act of the 30th of August 42. This act is incurably vicious in itself because it establishes the shocking principle that the labor of one half of the nation shall be *protected* to the injury of the labor of the other half. Observation and experience have satisfied me *perfectly*, that no statesman can long be successful in this country who advocates any system of legislation which is unjust in itself and by consequence oppressive. Mr Clay is a glowing evidence of the truth of this proposition. The planting states in agreeing that the expences of our Goverment shall be met by a duty of 20 per cent ad valorem on imports, with the addition of the cost of insurance freight commissions &c equal to 13 per cent more have done every thing demanded by justice and patriotism for the encouragment of the northern manufacturers. No sensible man can object to *judicious discriminations*. They have heretofore been made and are found even in the compromise act of 32[3] which gave us peace instead of grumbling and discontent.

In the selection of your Cabinet you will look of course for high toned educated *enlightened* men. But, with all the care which you can employ you will have to trust something to luck. You will of course regard it as of the greatest consequence that they should be for James K. Polk *and* the President of the United States. When I was a boy I remember to have heard a great man Wm B. Giles[4] when conversing with a friend about politics remark "one of the great means Sir by which Mr Jefferson is getting forward so successfully is that Madsion Gallatin Dearborne Smith and Breckenridge[5] are his devoted personal and political friends and all have good talents. They all work Sir for the good of the common cause." These observations struck me with great force although I could hardly comprehend them being then only 15 years of age.

Those men who are seeking to become members of your political *fam-*

*ily* by circuitous means are giving in my judgment prima facie evidence at least that they are unworthy of the high positions which they desire to reach. They certainly must want delicacy honor and pride of character. No position can be in my view more palpably true than this that a President of the U States should be left perfectly free to please himself in the selection of his confidential advisers. I have written Ritchie to throw out some strong and striking articles upon this subject to reconcile the public mind to any course you may think proper to pursue on this delicate matter and to repress the angry ebullitions of the disappointed and ambitious aspirants (of whom no doubt there will be a large number) through the deep toned energy of the public opinion.

I fear that you will be annoyed greatly on your journey by a crowd some of whom may not be up exactly to what they ought to be. But, this is one of the inconveniences to which great men are exposed. My Sister Mrs Macombe[6] says she is greatly rejoiced at your election *because Mrs Polk is a first rate Presbyterian*.

ALFRED BALCH

ALS. DLC–JKP. Addressed to Columbia.

1. A Nashville lawyer and influential political strategist, Balch accepted an appointment to a four-year term as judge of the U.S. Middle District of Florida in 1840; he resigned his judgeship before the end of his term and declined all subsequent overtures to run for public office.

2. Balch's reference is to the Virginia Resolutions of 1798, authored by James Madison, and Kentucky Resolutions of 1798–99, written by Thomas Jefferson. Occasioned by Congress' passage of the Alien and Sedition Acts, the resolves held that the general government had assumed legislative powers not delegated by the Constitution and that the states had retained a right to nullify such acts as might be considered unconstitutional.

3. Reference probably is to the compromise tariff of 1833, which effectively ended the nullification crisis.

4. A native of Virginia, William B. Giles won election as an Anti-Federalist to the First Congress and served until 1798. He served as a Democrat in the Virginia House of Delegates, 1798–1800, 1816–17, 1826–27; in the U.S. Senate, 1804–15; and in the governorship of Virginia, 1827–30.

5. James Madison, Albert Gallatin, Robert Smith, Henry Dearborn, and John Breckinridge. Gallatin, a major figure in the early Jeffersonian party, served as a member of the U.S. House, 1795–1801; as secretary of the Treasury, 1802–14; and as minister first to France, 1816–23, and then to Great Britain, 1826–27. Active in Maryland politics, Smith served as secretary of the navy, 1801–09, and as secretary of state, 1809–11. Dearborn served as secretary of war, 1801–09; as collector of customs in Boston, 1812–29; as a U.S. congressman, 1831–33; and as adjutant general of Massachusetts, 1834–43. Breckinridge, a native of Virginia, removed in 1792 to Kentucky where he practiced law and sat in the state legislature, 1797–1801. He served in the U.S. Senate from 1801 until 1805,

when he resigned to become U.S. attorney general, a post he held until his death in 1806.

6. Not identified further.

## FROM J. GEORGE HARRIS[1]

My Dear Sir—                                          Nashville Jan. 4. 1845

I have prepared the matter concerning the late visit of the Louisiana Committee,[2] embodying your reply received on the 2d. Mr. Nicholson[3] says he could not get it into the Union of this morning, but will have it inserted on Tuesday morning next. I performed the duty to Gen Jackson which he entirely approved returning high compliments with his letter for publication.[4]

I yesterday received another letter from *John Jones*.[5] You know I replied to his offer by saying that I would be at Washington early in Feb., and that I would then either accept one of the three propositions made to myself or (as he requested) refer him to some friend of the new administration competent to conduct his paper. It was a reply intended to prevent the possession of his press by either of the annoying *cliques*, and it will have that effect, while it leaves me perfectly free to direct his disposition of it in the most acceptable manner.

I send you his letter, which contains some sensible remarks and some that are not so sensible. With those concerning *himself* I have nothing to do either directly or indirectly. The "P.S.," however gives me a new idea which leads to reasonable conclusions.[6] My belief is that nearly all the officers appointed by Mr Tyler have *deceived* him, and he would be glad to see them removed. Indeed, it is doubtful, in my judgment whether he does not expressly request that no respect be paid to any of his appointments with exception perhaps of a few relatives or particular personal friends.

In a word, I send the letter *merely* as a straw indicative of the *official current* at this moment.

                                                        J. GEO. HARRIS

ALS. DLC–JKP. Addressed to Columbia.

1. A staunch New England Democrat, J. George Harris had been associated with the New London *Political Observer* (Conn.), the *New Bedford Gazette* (Mass.), the Boston *Bay State Democrat*, and the Boston *Morning Post* before assuming the editorship of the *Nashville Union* on February 1, 1839. In March 1843 Harris received a commission from Secretary of State Daniel Webster to serve as special commercial agent of the United States for American tobacco sales in Europe.

2. A committee of Democrats, including Felix Bosworth, Jeremiah Y. Dashiell,

J. S. Crockett, James S. McFarlane, J. M. P. Richardson, and A. D. Green, from New Orleans, La., arrived in Nashville on December 22, 1844, to deliver an invitation to Polk and Andrew Jackson to attend the January 8th anniversary celebration of the Battle of New Orleans to be held in that city. For Polk's response see Polk to Felix Bosworth et al., December 31, 1844.

3. A Democratic member of the Tennessee House from Maury County, 1833–37, and of the Tennessee Senate, 1843–45, A. O. P. Nicholson served an interim appointment in the U.S. Senate from December 1840 until February 1842. He moved to Nashville in 1844 and edited the *Nashville Union* before becoming president of the Bank of Tennessee in 1846.

4. Declinations from both Polk and Andrew Jackson were published in the *Clarksville Jeffersonian* on January 11, 1845, and in the *Memphis Appeal* on January 24, 1845. Harris' reference to publication in the *Nashville Union* has not been found.

5. Harris' reference probably is to John B. Jones' letter of December 23, 1844, in which Jones suggests to Harris the advantages of the new administration's establishing a newspaper that would be independent of the several factions in the Democratic party and devoted fully to Polk's interests. ALS. DLC–JKP. Jones succeeded Thomas Allen as editor of the Washington *Madisonian*. A popular author in the 1840's and 1850's, Jones later published a memoir of his service in the Confederate government, published under the title of *A Rebel War Clerk's Diary* (1866).

6. In his postscript Jones recommends that Polk's administration should remove a "large proportion" of John Tyler's appointees.

## TO MARTIN VAN BUREN

My Dear Sir:                                        Columbia Tenn. Jany 4th 1845
In the spring of 1842, when I had the pleasure to see you last,[1] I confidently anticipated, that you would now occupy the position, in which I have been placed, and certainly no one of your friends more ardently and sincerely desired it than myself. It is scarcely necessary for me to say, that my nomination at Baltimore was unsought and unexpected. Until the moment it was made, it was very far from my thoughts, that any state of circumstances could arise, which could lead to such a result. After it *was* made, there is no one to whom the Democracy of the whole country, are more indebted for their success, than to yourself. The disinterested and magnanimous ground which you so promptly assumed[2] had the immediate effect, to reconcile the party to a nomination, which they had not anticipated, and to produce harmony and union in their action not only in New York, but throughout the Union. My personal thanks are due to you, for the cordial manner in which you gave your powerful support to my nomination, and thereby contributed so largely to secure my election. And now My Dear Sir: in view of the personal and

political relations which have so long existed between us, I feel desirous to have the benefit of your advice, in the discharge of some of the delicate and responsible duties, which must shortly devolve upon me. The first and most important duty, which I will have to perform, will be the selection of my Cabinet. I have reflected much about the *men*, whom it may be proper to call to my aid. There was but one individual about whom my mind was definitively made up, without consultation with any one, as soon as I ascertained the result of the election, and that individual was *Silas Wright* of New York. I accordingly addressed him a letter early in December inviting him to take charge of the Treasury Department. To day I received his answer declining to accept it.[3] In my letter to him I named the Treasury Department, because in my judgment it has become the most important of the Departments, and because of his eminent qualifications to discharge the duties of that station. I most sincerely regret, that for reasons which he assigns, he feels himself constrained to decline accepting *any* situation in the cabinet. I feel inclined to look to New York, for one member of my cabinet. I can have but little hope from the tenour of Mr Wright's letter, that he will reconsider his determination, and I beg of you therefore, that you will suggest to me some other person in New York, whom in your judgment I should select. Your knowledge of the *men* in New York, and their fitness for such a situation is better than mine can be, and I request that you will give me your opinion freely and without reserve. I will be pleased to know your opinion, who would be a proper person to fill the office of Secretary of the *Treasury* or Secretary of *State*, as I think it probable that I will desire to take some one from New York to fill one of these important places. I will be pleased further to have your opinion or any suggestions which you may think proper to make in reference to the *whole* cabinet. Any opinion you may give will be regarded and treated by me as *strictly and sacredly confidential*. When I assure you that I have made no selections, and am under no pledges or commitments express or implied to any one, or to the friends of any one, I hope you will feel no delicacy or hesitation in giving me your opinions and views. I expect to leave home about the 1st and will probably reach Washington about the 20th of February. I hope to receive your answer before I set out on the journey. This letter is intended for *yourself alone*.

JAMES K. POLK

ALS. DLC–MVB. Addressed to Lindenwald, N.Y., and marked "*Strictly Confidential*." ALS, draft. DLC–JKP.

1. Reference is to Martin Van Buren's visit to Columbia in May 1842.

2. Polk's reference probably is to the meeting of a large number of Democrats in New York City on the afternoon of June 4, 1844, convened to respond to the

nominations made at Baltimore. Invited to preside over the gathering, Martin Van Buren declined that honor but expressed his satisfaction at the nominations in a letter read to the crowd. See Martin Van Buren to Gansevoort Melville et al., June 3, 1844. L, copy in the hand of Martin Van Buren, Jr. DLC–MVB.

3. See Polk to Silas Wright, Jr., December 7, 1844, and Silas Wright, Jr., to Polk, December 20, 1844.

## TO SILAS WRIGHT, JR.

My Dear Sir:                Columbia Ten. Jany. 4th 1845

I have received your letter of the 20th ultimo, and exceedingly regret, that you feel yourself constrained by the circumstances which surround you, to decline accepting a place in the Cabinet. In my letter to you I named the Treasury Department for the reasons assigned that in my judgment, it had become the most important of the Departments, and because of your eminent qualifications to discharge its responsible duties. I have awaited your answer in the hope that you would accept & have up to this moment, made no pledges or commitments to any one or to the friends of any one in reference to any of the places in the cabinet. I had hoped to have the benefit of your advice, in considering of the *men*, proper to be selected, for the other places, other than that tendered to yourself. I feel inclined to look to New York, for one member of my cabinet and without consulting with anyone had selected you in preference to all others. As you state that you must decline I avail myself of your remark in the close of your letter that "if any thing in the course of your inquiries and examinations should induce you to suppose, that any information in my possession, or within my reach will be of service to you, I beg you to feel perfectly free to call upon me in the unreserved *confidence* of this correspondence and you shall command my thoughts"; I beg that you will suggest to me the *person* in New York, whom in your judgment I should select. I will be pleased to know your opinion, who would be a proper *man* to fill the place of Secretary of the *Treasury* or Secretary of *State*, as I think it probable that I will take some one from New York to fill one of these important Departments. I hope you will feel no delicacy or hesitation in giving your opinion, of the fitness and qualifications of *men* freely, as I assure you, that what you may say, will be regarded and treated by me as *strictly and sacredly confidential*. Your knowledge of the *men* in New York and of their fitness for such a situation, is better than mine can be, & therefore I desire to have the benefit of your opinion & advice before I make a selection.

I expect to leave home about the 1st and to be at Washington about the 20th February. I hope to receive your answer before I set out on the journey.

JAMES K. POLK

ALS, draft. DLC–JKP. Addressed to Albany, N.Y., and marked "*Copy*" and "*Strictly Confidential*." Extract published in Lyon Gardiner Tyler, ed., *The Letters and Times of the Tylers* (3 vols.; Richmond and Williamsburg, Va., 1884–96), III, p. 156.

## FROM AARON V. BROWN

Dear Sir                                    Washington City January 5. 1845

Let me write this letter about *my own affairs* & presently I will send you one long one about *yours*. I have just closed a long letter to Jonas E. Thomas[1] about offering again for Congress & about my nomination for Governor &c. I do not know exactly whether I have written right or not. Look at it & see. I wrote it under a notion that I shall go raving distracted if I do not soon assemble my children around me somewhere so as to redeem a most solemn pledge to see after them in their raising & education.[2] How this could be done in case of success in the Governors election I can readily see, but in case of defeat I should be thrown out of politics altogether, if not out of the State, so I am rather inclined to look to another disposition of myself. I see something in the papers & hear something in the circles here in reference to some position at home or abroad under your administration. Now as I write freely about every body else, so I will say in reference to myself I do not expect or desire any thing of the sort & if even a cabinet position were offerd. I should regard it solely as the suggestion of friendship & should promply decline it from a conviction that others more able could be selected & whose geographical position would make it more proper than it should be differently conferd. But no matter about that. The Ritchie arrangement has fallen through as I wrote you & I have asked your further advice on the subject. I have some reasons to believe that if Blair would sell out his interest on reasonable terms a gentleman[3] would buy him out becomeing a dormant partner of Brown & Rives[4]—I having the exclusive controul over the interest so purchased & the sole Editor of the concern, drawing *one fourth of the profits* of the whole for my Editorship. This would secure sufficient profits (as I made no advancement & incured no liability in the purchase) to enable me to set up here with my children going to school every day from my own house &c & so attain the great desideratum of which I am in persuit. Well such the plan. Would I have the capacity & tact for such position? I know I would not *on many* occasion & on many *subjects* but I could command (out of my share of profits) someone else of your & my selection, who could remedy that. It takes at least two writers for such an establishment. Kendall[5] you know (as he says he will often do anyhow) could help us sometimes & others, but I should count on having one able & skilful writer *allways* in place & under pay for the service. Thus the establishment would be exclusively & distinctly devoted to your administration—taking sides with no aspirant, opposing none, but vindicating all as far as practicable. In other words my partialities to your administration, my devotion [to] no particular line of succession &c might safely be relied on to keep the paper in such position as would ensure general harmony in the Democratic party. But how would present cliques look upon it. All (except Benton) would be pleased. Cass knows me & has corresponded with me & would approve it. Wright knows my feelings toward him & would not be averse. All parties of the South would be pleased. As to Benton I suppose he alone would not like it, but he would soon see in its course that no injustice would on any occasion be done to him. But after all what would *you* think about it? Every thing will depend on that? It is a mere notion which I will abandon in a moment & without regret if you can think of a better arrangement.

But would Blair sell out—this is not known, but I think it likely he might be induced to do so, especially if a chargé to Naples after Bill[6] was tired & a sufficent time had elapsed to avoid animadversion & the Senate in a bitter fire for confirmation, were thrown in his way. But now you may ask *if all this shall fall through* & come to naught, what about the nomination for governor. Why if it must be so, I will submit, but I declare to you I had rather be the Solicitor of the Treasury or the Comr of the Genl Land office, or to rent a brickyard in this or some other Town than to go through the vituperation & abuse of another campaign in Tennessee. If you well bethink you, I have been a long time on the battlefield, before you were, before Cave Johnson by several years, & indeed I might say *many* years before he ever broke a sweat upon him in the *Jackson* cause. My contest with old Andrew Erwin in *1823* through old Lincoln has never been exceeded since in bitterness & violence.[7] I advert to these things currente callamo,[8] to shew that it is natural at this time of life, to begin to long a little for repose.

I close this however, in order to write you on other subjects relating less to myself....

A. V. BROWN

ALS. DLC–JKP. Addressed to Columbia and marked *"Confidential."* Polk's AE on the cover states that he received this letter on January 13, 1845.
1. A successful lawyer and farmer, Jonas E. Thomas represented Maury Coun-

ty in the Tennessee House, 1835–41, and sat for Maury and Giles counties in the Tennessee Senate, 1845–47.

2. Upon the death of his wife, Sarah Burruss Brown, in May of the previous year, Brown was left with five youngsters to rear: Aaron, Charles J., Laura Louise, Myra M., and Walter.

3. Brown's reference probably is to a group of potential investors for the administration newspaper; this group included Simon Cameron, William M. Gwin, James Walker, and John P. Heiss. They approached Polk's friends with offers of financial support for the purchase of either the Washington *Madisonian* or *Globe*, or for the creation of a new administration organ. See Aaron V. Brown to Polk, January 6, 1845.

4. A shrewd businessman, John C. Rives shared the ownership of the Washington *Globe* with Francis P. Blair from 1833 until 1845. Rives reported congressional debates in the *Congressional Globe* for the period 1833 to 1864.

5. A newspaperman and member of Andrew Jackson's "Kitchen Cabinet," Amos Kendall served as postmaster general from 1835 until 1840. In 1842 he edited a Washington biweekly, *Kendall's Expositor*. The following year, he issued a prospectus for a biography of Jackson, but never finished it. In 1844 Polk engaged Kendall to draft his inaugural address.

6. William H. Polk.

7. Andrew Erwin, a native of Virginia, speculated in early land sales in middle Tennessee; he settled first in Davidson County and then moved to Bedford County, which he represented for one term in the Tennessee House, 1821–23. A principal figure in Tennessee's anti-Jackson faction, Erwin ran unsuccessfully for the Tennessee Senate against Brown in 1823 and again unsuccessfully for the U.S. House against Polk in 1825.

8. Latin expression meaning "with a running or rapid pen."

## FROM AARON V. BROWN

Dear Sir                                        Washington City Jany 5th 1845

Dr. Gwin[1] last night held a long conversation with me in relation to the vews & wishes of Mr. Calhoun, & I doubt not that it was with the view of its being communicated to you. He says that Mr. C.[2] has no expectation of looking forward to the presidency, & that he expects soon to take an occasion so publickly to declare in order that his enemies may have no excuse for assailing him & his friends cease to hold him up in that light. That on your arrival he expects to converse freely with you on all the great measures of your administration & if he finds (as he doubts not he shall) that there is sufficient harmony of opinion, he will be willing to remain in his present position. But if from any cause you should prefer another he will retire without the slightest possible dissatisfaction. He further says that he is prepared to cooperate with you on all subjects, even the Tariff yielding every thing that might be considerd ultra on that subject. Now this presents the question, whether such a declaration of *renunciation* (as Mr Ingersoll[3] would say) will make any difference in the determination you might form in relation to his continuance in his present position. He seems disinclined to the trip to England under the notion that any termination of his Oregon labors might be defeated here by his enemies in the Senate & so place him, at the moment of his final retirement from public life rather under the cloud of public disapprobation. If however he could get *secret* instructions before hand from the Senate perhaps it might alter his determination. If Mr. Calhoun were to be retained I have no doubt it would be highly useful to him and to you for him to renounce all views under any circumstances for the succession as it would tranquilize the different factions very much. Still I do not think it would satisfy them altogether. Going on the supposition that Mr C *might* be retained by you he suggested[4] that Mr Van Buren might be offerd. the mission to *England* & he expressd the opinion that he would accept of it. Then he proposed Butler[5] for the Judgeship if it remained open as is now expected & Flagg for the Post office. This he thought would do for N York. As to Pennsylvania he put Buchanan on the Bench & made Reed of Philadelphia[6] Atto Gen*l*. Having also the Vice Presidency, he thought this would do for Pennsylvania. He left Mason in the Navy & gave Woodberry[7] the War office. This was his programme except as I omitted to say he put Walker in the Treasury. Thus it would stand

| | | |
|---|---|---|
| Calhoun | Sec | State |
| Walker | | Treasury |
| Woodbery | | War |
| Reed | | Att Genl |
| Flagg | | Post office |
| Mason | | Navy |
| Mr Van Buren | | Min. England |

This leaves nothing for Genl Cass or his friends in the N.W. Indeed there is no body but himself there to receive any cabinet office. It is now thought by many that he will come to the Senate, though some of his friends think otherwise.

On the whole this would give a very good Cabinet & produce as much satisfaction probably as any other. I dont know much about Reeds lawyership. N York (if Mr. VB[8]) accepted would be sufficiently provided for as they would count largely on the *patronage* of the post office. It is very powerful & efficient in elections. If you could do no better for Woodbery I have no doubt he would take the post office but I do think he deserves a better position. This leaves Tennessee no place & none for the N. West, which could be supplied by inferior places. Remember however all this is his programme not mine, although it combines several names that I would certainly have. I talked with Mason the other day & told him I had not the slightest notion of what you would do, but I apprehended you would find it difficult to retain *all* & if not all, any of the present cabinet, but that I did not doubt your disposition to except him or if that could not be done, to find some situation that would be satisfactory &c &c all of which you know was entirely general & non committal.

I sometimes fear that I shall weary you with all these suggestions, but submit them without the intrusion of my advice in the matter.

We have Texas on the way hopefully. You will see that the debate turns on Douglass's first resolution.[9] Write a letter to Johnson spuring him up to a settlement of this question. He, Dromgoole & McCay[10] are a little suspected of indifference as to whether it be done this session or not. *They are old Hunkers* you know & lean to the regency some say a little too strong.[11]

A. V. BROWN

ALS. DLC–JKP. Addressed to Columbia. Polk's AE on the cover states that he received this letter on January 13, 1845.

1. William S. Gwin, a native Tennessean, physician, and staunch supporter of Andrew Jackson, served as U.S. marshal for Mississippi, 1833–41, and sat one term in the U.S. House, 1841–43. During his congressional service he became an admirer of John C. Calhoun and supported his candidacy for the presidential nomination in 1844. In 1849 Gwin moved from Mississippi to California and represented that state for portions of two terms in the U.S. Senate, 1850–55 and 1857–61.

2. John C. Calhoun.

3. Charles J. Ingersoll, a Pennsylvania lawyer and Democrat, served as a member of the U.S. House, 1813–15 and 1841–49; as U.S. district attorney for Pennsylvania, 1815–29; and as a state assemblyman, in 1830. He went to Prussia in 1837 as secretary of legation and became U.S. district judge for Connecticut in 1853.

4. Brown's antecedent is "Gwin," not "Calhoun."

5. A former law partner and close confidant of Martin Van Buren, Benjamin F. Butler served as U.S. attorney general, 1833–38, and twice as U.S. attorney for the Southern District of New York, 1838–41 and 1845–48. Brown's reference is to an associate justiceship of the U.S. Supreme Court.

6. John M. Read, a lawyer from Philadelphia, served in the Pennsylvania House for one term, 1823–24; he was appointed U.S. attorney for the Eastern District of Pennsylvania and served from 1837 until 1841. John Tyler nominated Read to be associate justice of the U.S. Supreme Court, but the U.S. Senate refused confirmation. He pursued a private law practice until 1858, when he was elected to the Pennsylvania Supreme Court.

7. Levi Woodbury.

8. Martin Van Buren.

9. Brown's reference is to Stephen A. Douglas' introduction of a joint resolution providing for the annexation of Texas.

10. Cave Johnson, George C. Dromgoole, and James I. McKay. Dromgoole, a Virginia lawyer, served five terms in the U.S. House, 1835–41 and 1843–47.

11. Brown's reference to the "old" Hunkers is not identified further; his allusion to "the regency" refers to the friends of Martin Van Buren who in his absence managed from Albany the affairs of the New York Democracy.

## FROM CAVE JOHNSON

My dear Sir,                              Washington 5th January 1845

I fear I stated too strongly in a former letter that S.W. Jr.[1] would not accept a seat in the cabinet if tendered & lest it may have some influence on your mind, I write now to say, that I had a conversation with J. Buckhanon[2] to day and I find that he is under the belief, from a variety of facts which he stated, that Mr. W. would go into the Treasury with great pleasure as he would get rid of dispensing the patronage in N.Y. I find no one, with whom I converse, who is not anxious that he should do so. That opinion was expressed upon the idea that a new cabinet was formed. It is probable that recent events have excited his friends so much, that he would think, that he could not get on harmoniously with Mr. C.[3] The feeling is now much greater agt. Mr. C. than I have known it for years with the Nothern democracy & a great deal of feeling in the southern agt. Mr. W. because it is believed that most of his friends will vote agt. the treaty of annexation and probably agt. annexation at the present session. Many of them who are for annexation wish it done under your auspices when they hope it will be based upon something better than slavery. It has been frequently said within a few days, if Mr. W. takes the treasury, that Mr. C & his friends would be probably satisfied with Elmore or Pickens in the War or Navy & Mr. C. go to England to negotiate about Oregon &c & beside that the principles upon which you would Administer the Gov. would rally the South around you, whilst S.W. Jr. would do more to add strength to the Admn. in the north than any other man, and that the Treasury is not considered the steping stone to the Presidency.

In connexion with this disposition of S.W. Jr. who should go into the State department? I learn to day that Genl C.[4] consents to come to the Senate from Michigan & will be regarded out of the way I presume. Then Buckhanon and Stephenson & Walker.[5] The first is spoken of as being personally and politicaly very friendly with S.W. Jr. They correspond I understand constantly & he is not so much of an aspirant as to hurt him, & that he is well located in Pennsylvania. They would probably harmonize on all subjects. I hear of none for Mr. S. out of Va. The latter[6] is more generally spoken of as Atto. Genl. & would be probably satisfied & glad to receive it. He is considered of late rather attached to the friends of Mr. C.

These are the principal places talked of in the last few days. I had an opportunity of asking Mr. B.[7] today, if there was any ground for the ill feeling said to have been gotten up between his friends and those of Mr Dallas or between Mr D & himself. He knew of none between them personally, but among their friends some unpleasant feelings had been excited in this way. One of the cliques of Philadelphia (Old hunkers) immagined that Mr. D. would have the distribution of the offices in that city and got up *Dallas Clubs, Dallas Associations* &c and talk of him for the succession in 1848. This they hope will give a proper direction to the patronage there, whilst some few of the friends of Mr. B. regard it as a movement intended to prejudice Mr. B's claims, & this is the only foundation he knows of for the talk of a split between them. Personally the best relations exist between them. These things are suggested from several conversations to day & I give you the impressions made on my mind. I think from the little I could gather to day that Mr. B. would be gratified greatly with such an offer.

I thought it probable that if you should think of placing S.W. Jr. in that position you might like to know *certainly*, before hand, what his course would be. In that event *a hint* to me would take me to Albany. Mr. B. expressed the hope today, that your cabinet would be formed & that you would announce it immediately after your arrival & before the inauguration, so as to keep down the excitement that would be got up in behalf of particular individuals, if it was supposed any doubt existed in your mind. I think it probable that Wm.[8] will be nominated next week. We shall know on monday.

C. JOHNSON

N.B. I shall avail myself of some occasion in compliance with your requests to give you my own opinions after I shall have formed them.

ALS. DLC–JKP. Addressed to Columbia. Polk's AE on the cover states that he received this letter on January 13, 1845.

1. Silas Wright, Jr. See Cave Johnson to Polk, December 14, 1844.
2. James Buchanan.
3. John C. Calhoun.
4. Lewis Cass.
5. James Buchanan, Andrew Stevenson, and Robert J. Walker. Stevenson, a lawyer, served several terms in the Virginia House of Delegates before winning

election to the U.S. House, where he served from 1821 to 1834. He presided as Speaker of that body during his last four terms and went to Great Britain as U.S. minister from 1836 until 1841.

6. Robert J. Walker.

7. James Buchanan.

8. William H. Polk.

## FROM AARON V. BROWN

*at Table* H. Rep

Dear Sir                                  [Washington City] Jany 6th 1845

Last night after I had written you Rives (Jno. C.) came to my room & from *the current* of his conversation about Blairs probable views, I should hardly think he could be bought out. I say I doubt it much. I suggested to him to buy him out *himself* & procure a new Editor (on consultation with the administration) & so carry it on on his own book. This did not seem to take as well as I expected. But he had *no idea* of my views as expressed to you.

A. V. BROWN

ALS. DLC–JKP. Addressed to Columbia. Polk's AE on the cover states that he received this letter on January 14, 1845.

## FROM AARON V. BROWN

Dear Sir                                  Washington City Jany 6th [18]45

I wish to make one additional suggestion to former ones about a public press as your Organ.

In many respects it is desirable to retain the Globe our organ. If a new one is started, the Globe will still go ahead the peculiar organ of the northern democracy, & having been superseded, it will now & then join with the Intelligency[1] in giving side blows at least at the administration & full thrusts at its organ. This would be a galling position to the new establishment & toward the close of your administration if not sooner it would be allmost forced to the support the side or sides opposed to the Northern division of the Democracy. It would be much to be desired if any thing like this can be avoided & I think it can by sinking Blair & Rives into mere *proprietors* & selecting a new Editor. Blair going abroad for his own or his daughters health, or not going as you thought proper. Blair I have no doubt if sent far by you after your arrival would in *conversation* give assurances about his course that prima facie would do, but when his election is over & all the government patronage (or nearly all) was secured to him,[2] what assurance would you have that he would not *catch the bit in his teeth* & go his own way. I have seen some evidences of this in the last few years. If he once gets hold on the printing it will [be] out of your power to control him & remember the printer for the Senate is to be elected as early as March.

You will get a long letter from Thompson of Mississippi[3] on this subject. I have not seen it nor is there any affinity between his views & mine & he is writing about a different purchaser from the one in my eye. If a new establishment had to be started perhaps Cameron[4] might do & if things were to take that direction I might still fall *into that* as contemplated in this other arrangement, *on some satisfactory terms.*[5] It is important to have some firm & steady friend interested in the establishment who would hold it up to your administration *all the time* & keep it from finally espousing one of the aspirants to the neglect of the fame & character of the encumbent. Cameron I understand to be a Buchannon[6] man & if he went on the Bench perhaps he might choose to abandon the idea of a paper. I think Thompson might have at least apprised me of his doings as I was in the same house with him & have consulted me on the subject.

A. V. BROWN

[P.S.] Johnson told me to day that *he* would go for Texas in any shape *fair or foul* (so you need not write him) but that he feared Dromgoole & McCay[7] would not. I think we can do without them. It is nothing but the workings of the Old Baltimore leven.[8] They want no good to come out of the rejection of Van Buren. *A.V.B.*

ALS. DLC–JKP. Addressed to Columbia. Polk's AE on the cover states that he received this letter on January 15, 1845.

1. Washington *National Intelligencer.*

2. Francis P. Blair and John C. Rives held the congressional printing contracts until the Senate voted to replace them with Thomas Ritchie and John P. Heiss of the Washington *Union* on December 17, 1845.

3. Brown's reference probably is to Jacob Thompson. A Mississippi lawyer, Thompson served six terms as a Democrat in the U.S. House, 1839–51. He subsequently served as secretary of the interior during the administration of James Buchanan, 1857–61.

4. A Pennsylvania banker and businessman, Simon Cameron won election as a Democrat to fill the U.S. Senate seat of James Buchanan, who resigned to become Polk's secretary of state. Cameron, who served from 1845 until 1849, subsequently won election as a Republican to the U.S. Senate, 1857–61 and 1867–77. Brown's references are to Cameron's possible role in financing a new administration newspaper.

5. See Aaron V. Brown to Polk, January 5, 1845.

6. James Buchanan.

7. George C. Dromgoole and James I. McKay.

8. Reference is to factional conflicts at the Democratic National Convention held at Baltimore, Md., in May 1844.

## FROM ROBERT ARMSTRONG

D Sir                                           Nashville Jany 9th 1845

I sent out the trunk from Purdy[1] by the Stage last night, enveloped the Keys and wrote a note to Langtry[2] to take charge of the trunk.

Capt Fouler of the Felix Grundy[3] says he will be ready by 20 or 25 and will write me again on 15 Int. If he is ready You had better take his boat. Should he fail we will have a boat, suited to the Stage of water, ready with good and truemen in charge.

As I said to you the sooner You can leave the better. It[4] you leave *here* on Tuesday 28th Int. it would give more time and make your March Safe by 15th Feby. You will find delays unavoidable. We will be ready here with a boat any day you name.

R. ARMSTRONG

[P.S.] I am fearfull Donelson will quit his post. If he does not his wife[5] will quit here and go to New Orleans.

ALS. DLC–JKP. Addressed to Columbia. Polk's AE on the cover states that he answered this letter on January 11, 1845; Polk's response has not been found.

1. Not identified further.

2. A Columbia merchant and director of the Bank of Tennessee's branch at Columbia, Hillary Langtry assumed the postmastership of Columbia on January 9, 1844, and served in that post until June 1845.

3. Not identified further. Polk left Nashville on February 1, 1845, aboard the steamboat *China*.

4. Probably a miswriting of the word *If*.

5. Reference is to Donelson's second wife, Elizabeth Martin Randolph, whom he married in 1841.

## FROM AARON V. BROWN

Dear Sir                                     Washington city Jany 9th 1845

A member (Wright) from Indiana[1] called to day to enter a very serious protest against the appointment of Sec of *Treasury* from *N. York*. He says that all the *North West* expects is some of the minor appointments at Washington & in the country—that if a *N York* Sec of Treasury is selected every land agent & other officer in that region will be a Wright man to the great injury (of course) to Genl Cass—so you see how the jealousy runs. He said his colleagues he believd generally desired R. J Walker for that place. I replied that Indiana had done nobly and as it was not likely she could have a Cabinet position offerd her (now that Howard[2] was dead) that her wishes as to others would doubly receive just consideration. Dont you think that was Diplomatic enough?

Annexation is *getting along* more hopefully than when I last wrote you. See Owens speech.[3] Dromgoole has come out with his proposition[4] & coming as it does from the Van Buren clique it is thought to be more reasonable than was expected. If we loose some 6 or 8 Democrats on that, it is said we will gain that number of Whigs. On the whole I think we can carry a general proposition something like that. Our friends are making incipant exertion, to harmonize on the question. On the subject of an administration press evry thing is on the stand still here for your express direction before your arrival or your decision & action on your arrival. It is the first & greatest difficulty in starting your administration.

It is certain that Clingman & Yancey[5] have gone to Baltimore—a Duel no doubt in contemplation—but I do not expect much blood to be shed where there is such a good city police. Yancey's reply to Clingman was exceedingly severe & Clingman's the most wretched tissue of party slang I ever heard. In haste.

A. V. BROWN

[P.S.] I think it likely that your Brother[6] will succeed in his wishes & be off in a few days for home.

If you had any children yourself you would have seen mine at Murfreesboro.[7]

ALS. DLC–JKP. Addressed to Columbia. Polk's AE states that he received this letter on January 17, 1845.

1. Joseph A. Wright served as a Democrat in the U.S. House, 1843–45; as governor of Indiana, 1849–57; and as U.S. senator, 1862–63.

2. Born in South Carolina, Tilghman A. Howard practiced law in Tennessee and won a single term in the Tennessee Senate, 1827–29. In 1830 he moved to Indiana and served as U.S. district attorney from 1833 to 1837. He went to the U.S. House in 1839, but lost his gubernatorial race in 1840. Howard held the post of chargé d'affaires to the Republic of Texas for a brief period prior to his death in 1844.

3. Son of Robert Owen the British industrialist and social reformer, Robert Dale Owen assisted in the founding of the New Harmony community in Indiana in 1826; he served three terms as a Democrat in the state legislature, 1836–38, and two terms in the U.S. House, 1843–47. In a speech to the U.S. House on January 8, 1845, Owen gave his full support to Texas annexation.

4. On January 8, 1845, George Dromgoole introduced a bill in the U.S. House consenting to the admission of a new state, to be named Texas and to be formed

from a portion of the Republic of Texas' territory, the limits of which were to be determined by deputies of a constitutional convention to be elected by its citizens. The new state's republican constitution would leave to the government of the United States the determination of the Republic of Texas' remaining territory; and the new state's constitution and government would be formed prior to July 4, 1845.

5. Thomas L. Clingman and William Lowndes Yancey. Clingman, a lawyer from Asheville, N.C., won election as a Whig to one term in the U.S. House, 1843–45, and subsequently as a Democrat to five terms in that body, 1847–58; he served two partial terms in the U.S. Senate, 1858–61. Yancey, an Alabama Democrat and lawyer, served single terms in both houses of the state legislature, 1841–43, prior to his election to the U.S. House in 1844. Responding to a highly partisan attack on the Democratic party by Clingman, Yancey took the floor on January 7th and in a scathing speech denounced Clingman and demanded the immediate annexation of Texas. The two dueled on January 13th, but neither suffered injury.

6. Reference is to William H. Polk and his application to be named U.S. minister to the Kingdom of the Two Sicilies.

7. See Aaron V. Brown to Polk, December 23, 1844.

## FROM SAMUEL P. WALKER

Dear Sir.                                                    Memphis Jany 9th 1845

By last night's mail I received your letter of the 4th [1] and a letter from Bills & McNeal, [2] enclosing your note to William Polk for Nine thousand Dollars, signed by them. I judge from their letter that they signed the note very cheerfully.

I have delivered your note to W. Howard [3] and herewith enclose you H. C. Walker's [4] check on the Union Bank at Nashville for $9.000.

I expected from Father's letter to have received the money *in Gold*, and had made an arrangement by which I could have sent you a check at a premium of at least 2 pr. ct. In writing to Howard Col. Polk directed him to pay to me, on the receipt of your note, Nine thousand Dollars. He said nothing about the Gold, and Howard sold it, and is unwilling to pay any thing but currency without *special instructions*. He says he will write to Col. Polk what he has done and if he directs him to do so he will pay me the premium. I regret that I cannot send you the funds, as I contemplated, at a premium, but I could do nothing else than receive the amount in Bank notes. I cannot take the liberty of altering your note, *after it is signed*, or I would strike out the obligation to pay it, in specie. There is an understanding between Howard and myself that you are not to be required to pay the note in anything better than currency (by which we mean, specie paying Bank notes) unless Col. W Polk directs him to pay me the premium he rec'd for the Gold.

SAML. P. WALKER

[P.S.] Please say to Mother, Sally is here, safe and well.[5]

ALS. DLC–JKP. Addressed to Columbia. Polk's AE on the cover states that he answered this letter on January 15, 1845; Polk's response has not been found.
1. Letter not found.
2. A merchant and the postmaster at Bolivar, John H. Bills married Ezekiel P. McNeal's sister, Prudence Tate McNeal, on September 9, 1823. A first cousin to Polk and a Bolivar merchant and land agent, McNeal handled Polk's business affairs in Hardeman County.
3. Wardlow Howard married Mary Wilson Polk, daughter of William Wilson and Elizabeth Dodd Polk, in Hardeman County, on December 27, 1834.
4. Not identified further.
5. Jane Maria Polk Walker and probably Sarah Naomi Walker. Polk's sister and mother to Samuel P. Walker, Jane Maria Polk married James Walker on February 24, 1813. Sarah Naomi Walker was Samuel P. Walker's sister.

## FROM GEORGE M. DALLAS

My Dear Sir,                                    10. Jany. 1845
My last[1] laid before you some reflections, to weigh only what you think they are worth, in respect to the formation of your cabinet. I have since reconsidered the subject, and am fortified in my convictions on the points stated. Perhaps I should have been fuller in reference to my reasons for indicating the person who seemed to me fittest to occupy the place of Secretary of State. Indulge me, therefore, with a few more words as to that.

Mr. Walker is, of all men mentioned, the one who will, as a negotiator, be most acceptable to the people of Texas. You know how great a favorite his past course has made him there. He might accomplish the annexation upon terms better than could be procured by others; and his very presence in the department would induce the Texans to hold on to the project of annexation until the next Congress was tried. He is besides a linguist of no common character, and may recommend his views to the inhabitants of those regions either in the French, the Spanish, or the German language as might be found expedient. I advert to these matters an additional to the more important points briefly sketched before.

It is possible that you may have noticed the singular movement in our electoral college which elicited a letter addressed to you, signed by all the electors but one, recommendatory of Mr. Buchanon.[2] I have been visitted by several of these electors, and have had from them a narrative of the curious and improper means adopted to consummate this proceeding. They are not worth detailing. They convinced me, however, that the persons who joined in the letter had not the slightest desire to see it successful, that some of them were excessively averse, and that the whole was a species of imposition devised by an individual who wishes to be appointed Collector of this Port and who conceived that he could thus give force to the recommendation of Mr. Buchanan in his favor. I am unwilling to say a word injurious to Mr. Buchanan; but I should want frankness if I forebore to express, the opinion that his appointment by you would be followed by the worst contigency in this State, & would be immediately made the basis of a division in the democratic ranks. It is a mistake to imagine him possessed of the popularity ascribed by his friends, here in Pennsylvania; beyond our limits, he is held in the high respect to which he is entitled, but he encounters hosts of organized adversaries.

Next to the State Department ranks, in general estimation, the Treasury. As your officer for this I have heard mentioned the following gentlemen. Mr. Woodbury, Gov. Hubbard, Mr. Bancroft, Mr. Benj. F. Butler, Mr. Cambreling, Gov. Marcy, Genl. Dix, Judge Savage, Mr. Richard Rush, Mr. John K. Kane,[3] and perhaps one or two more not imposing enough to be remembered. Of this list, the ostensible names are, from various considerations, the New York ones; and of these, Cambreling and Marcy are foremost.

A Virginian, it is thought, may be invited to take charge of the Navy, and Mr. Stevenson is frequently spoken of as, for that department, unexceptionable. Sometimes, the present Speaker of the House is preferred, and again Mr. Hunter.[4]

For the War Office, there are some admirable nominations: Col. Butler of Kentucky, Genl. Armstrong, your friend and neighbor, Major Donelson, and Mr. Allen of Ohio.[5] I have nothing to justify a preference among these gentlemen, feel quite sure that either would content the Country.

The Post Department has been assigned to many. It may be that you can draw the one from Pennsylvania whom you wish in your cabinet, for this place. If you should ultimately find that to be expedient, I shall be prepared to express, with entire frankness and with a full sense of the responsibility involved, my judgment as to the person to be preferred.

A Sentence as to the Attorney-Generalship, and I have gone the round. There are many named, but very few really fit. It is an undervalued post; but I have always considered it of immense importance to the comfort and confidence of the Executive. One gentleman, not generally mentioned, has occurred to me, while looking over the range of the bar, and there are points about him which your own reflections will bring up as of importance. He has always been democratic, always ardent and popular, always active and eminent as a practitioner; he is an *eastern democrat* of the soundest order; he was forward at the Baltimore Convention, &c. &c. &c. I mean Ralph Ingersoll, of Connecticut.[6]

Thus, a cabinet concocted upon these general views and materials would stand geographically thus: Mississippi, N. York, Virginia, Kentucky or Ohio, Pennsylvania, Connecticut; manifesting a decent respect for the opinions of mankind on the score of locality.

Will you do me the particular favor to say to Mrs. Polk that Commodore Kearney, of the Navy,[7] has confided to my care the pattern of a Chinese satin dress (about 10 yards) with directions that I should present it to her in his name. It is carefully boxed up, and my commission shall be executed with great pleasure on the first opportunity. Mrs. Dallas,[8] to whom the Commodore made a similar present, desires me to describe it as a rich, white or cream-coloured, figured silk of very great beauty and rarity.

Gov. Wright, in a message of most unpardonable length, has not found a single place for the word *"Texas"*![9] Rely upon it, Gov. Shunk[10] will not be so abstemious.

G. M. DALLAS

ALS. DLC–JKP. Addressed to Columbia. Polk's AE on the cover states that he received this letter on January 20, 1845, and answered it on January 21, 1845; Polk's reply has not been found.

1. See George M. Dallas to Polk, December 15, 1844.

2. Having cast their votes for Polk and Dallas, Wilson McCandless and his fellow Pennsylvania electors wrote Polk on December 5, 1844, and urged him to appoint James Buchanan secretary of state. LS. DLC–JKP.

3. Levi Woodbury, Henry Hubbard, George Bancroft, Benjamin F. Butler, Churchill C. Cambreleng, William L. Marcy, John A. Dix, John Savage, Richard Rush, and John K. Kane. Soldier, lawyer, and railroad president, Dix served two years as adjutant general of New York, 1831–33, and one term as a member of the New York House in 1842. Elected as a Democrat to the U.S. Senate seat vacated by Silas Wright, Jr., in 1845, Dix ran unsuccessfully in 1848 as the gubernatorial candidate of the Free Soil party, served in the Union army as a general officer during the Civil War, and won election to the governorship on the Republican ticket in 1873. A New York lawyer, Savage held various state offices prior to his election to the U.S. House, 1815–19; he presided over the state supreme court from 1823 until 1836; and in 1844 he served as a presidential elector for Polk and Dallas. A lawyer, diplomat, and writer, Rush served as U.S. attorney general, 1814–17; as acting secretary of state, 1817; as minister to Great Britain, 1817–25; as secretary of the Treasury, 1825–29; and as minister to France, 1847–49. An unsuccessful vice-presidential candidate on John Q. Adams' ticket in 1828, Rush moved into the Democratic ranks during the

fight over rechartering the Second Bank of the United States. A Philadelphia lawyer and an ardent Jackson Democrat, Kane served from 1832 until 1836 as one of the spoliation claims commissioners appointed under the authority of the 1831 convention with France. He opposed the rechartering of the Bank of the United States, an unpopular position to take in Philadelphia. In 1845 Polk appointed Kane U.S. attorney for Pennsylvania and the following year named him U.S. judge for the Eastern District of Pennsylvania, a post that he held for twelve years.

4. Andrew Stevenson, John W. Jones, and Robert M. T. Hunter. Jones, a Virginia lawyer, served five consecutive terms in the U.S. House, 1835–45, and won election to one term as Speaker in 1843. A lawyer from Lloyds, Va., Hunter served in both branches of the Virginia legislature prior to his election to the U.S. House as a Democrat in 1837; a veteran of four terms, 1837–43 and 1845–47, he won election as Speaker in 1839. Hunter went to the U.S. Senate in 1847 and served until 1861.

5. William O. Butler, Robert Armstrong, Andrew J. Donelson, and William Allen. A lawyer, farmer, and stockman from Chillicothe, Ohio, Allen won election as a Democrat to one term in the U.S. House in 1833 and sat in the U.S. Senate from 1837 until 1849.

6. A lawyer from New Haven, Conn., Ralph I. Ingersoll won election to two terms in the state legislature, 1820–25, and to four terms in the U.S. House, 1825–33; he served as U.S. minister to Russia from 1846 until 1848.

7. Captain Lawrence Kearney, appointed commander of the East India squadron of the navy in 1840, played an important role in formulating the United States' "Open Door" policy with China, which was affirmed in 1844 by the United States' first treaty with China.

8. Sophia Chew Nicklin Dallas.

9. Silas Wright, Jr., delivered his first executive message to the New York legislature on January 7, 1845.

10. A lawyer from Pittsburgh, Francis R. Shunk had served as clerk of the Pennsylvania House and as secretary of the commonwealth, 1839–42. Elected governor in 1844 and reelected in 1847, he served from 1845 until 1848, when ill health forced him to resign.

## FROM ANDREW JACKSON

My Dear Col,                                                    Hermitage Janry, 10th 1845

Your confidential letter has been recd., read with attention and burned, as is my disposition of all such.

I anticipated the reply of Mr. W.[1] as his being asked to take the Treasury left matters to be inferred that Mr Calhoun would remain in the state Dept., and I apprehended that Mr W. would not like to be in the cabinet with Mr Calhoun. It is perhaps better that W. has declined. I took the liberty to write *confidentially* to two of my friends in Washington to

find out, *casually*, who the real democracy thought would make a good
& safe cabinet for the president, and meet the confidence of the democracy. I have just recd. an answer, as well on the question of keeping all,
or any of the Tyler Cabinett in office, as who would be a safe cabinett
to the president. The letters are strictly confidential for my own eye,
I therefore retain them & make only extracts from them.[2] First as to
retaining all or any of Mr Tylers cabinet, it is stated by the writers "altho
we have the kindest feelings for, and intimate assosciation with all, still
we both agree with you that Col Polk should have an entire new cabinett.
To retain them would involve the president elect in the greatest immag-
inable dificulties at the very threshold of his administration—a furious
& exterminating war would instantly be made upon its most prominent
members by a portion of the democratic party. No party considerations
could prevent this. *This we know*, and in such a warfare, it cannot be
expected, that the president could escape *unscathed*, and on this head
closes by saying no member of the Tyler Cabinett ought to be retained."
The foregoing views appear to me well founded & conclusive, and as you
know meets my views as expressed, and is laid before you for your calm
consideration.

They then go on to give their opinion of whom would fill the Depts,
"with signal ability, viz, Stephenson of va. State, Flagg of New York,
comptroler of the Treasury of N. York, Treasury Dept., and I believe he
is one of the best financiers in N York, and John K. Kane. Kane I know
he is an excellent man, of the old Jefferson school, brotherin law to the
Leapers,[3] a perfect Gentleman, and it is added, if the president elect is
disposed to take one of his cabinett from Tennessee A. J. Donelson might
be added if Col Polk wishes to take a cabinett minister from Tennessee,
and Mr Guthree of Louisville Ky,[4] who they think would make one of the
best postmasters in the U. States." So much for the confidential views of
my friends, and I lay it before you merely for your own calm deleberation.
As to Major Donelson, your views expressed to me, I think will meet fully
his, and altho I think highly of Mr Guthree, I cannot but bring to your
view, that Genl McCafee,[5] at the head of the central democratic committee of Ky, has recommended Genl McConly.[6] I would just add, deliberate
well upon these sugestions, but come to no final conclusion untill you
reach Washington. Surely you will do well to select an entire cabinett
fresh from the people as your own, & leave Mr Tylers out to be provided
for, if thought worthy otherwise. Mason & Judge Wilkens are worthy
men.[7] You will find my friends have said nothing as to an attorney Genl.
They leave that to be for wiser Legal heads than they. When I have the
pleasure of seeing you, if I should live to have that pleasure, which is
doubtful & occasions this letter, we will talk the whole matter over.

A good harmonious cabinett is all you want, to have the most success-full administration that has occurred since the days of Washington. We all salute you & yours.

ANDREW JACKSON

ALS. DLC–JKP. Addressed to Columbia and marked *"Confidential."* Published in John Spencer Bassett, ed., *Correspondence of Andrew Jackson* (7 vols.; Washington, D.C.: Carnegie Institution, 1926–35), VI, pp. 360–62.
1. Silas Wright, Jr.
2. Reference is to Jackson's correspondence with William B. Lewis and Francis P. Blair. Jackson's "extracts" follow closely the text of William B. Lewis to Andrew Jackson, January 1, 1845, and Francis P. Blair to Andrew Jackson, January 3, 1845. ALsS. DLC–AJ.
3. John K. Kane married Jane Duval Leiper, daughter of Thomas and Elizabeth Coultas Gray Leiper and sister of William J. Leiper and George Gray Leiper. William J. Leiper of Delaware County, Penn., is not identified further; George G. Leiper, a graduate of the University of Pennsylvania, served one term in the U.S. House, 1829–31.
4. A lawyer in Louisville, James Guthrie sat in the Kentucky House, 1827–29, and Senate, 1831–40; from 1853 until 1857 he served as secretary of the Treasury in the cabinet of Franklin Pierce; in 1865 he won election to the U.S. Senate and served until 1868.
5. A soldier and lawyer from Mercer County, Ky., Robert B. McAfee sat as a member of the state legislature and as lieutenant governor of Kentucky, 1824–28. From 1833 until 1837 he served as chargé d'affaires to Colombia.
6. Jackson probably meant to write McCalla. In his letter to Jackson of November 23, 1844, McAfee recommended John M. McCalla for Polk's cabinet. ALS. DLC–JKP. McCalla served as U.S. marshal for Kentucky during the Jackson and Van Buren administrations; in 1844 he was an electoral candidate on the Democratic ticket in Kentucky; and in 1845 Polk appointed him second auditor of the U.S. Treasury.
7. Originally from Carlisle, Penn., William Wilkins sat in the Pennsylvania House in 1820 and in the Pennsylvania Senate, 1855–57. He served as presiding judge of the Fifth Judicial District of Pennsylvania, 1821–24, and judge of the U.S. District Court for Western Pennsylvania, 1824–31. Elected as a Democrat and Anti-Mason to the U.S. Senate in 1830, he resigned on June 30, 1834, to assume his duties as minister to Russia. He won election to the U.S. House in 1843 and served until February 14, 1844, when he resigned to become John Tyler's secretary of war. He served in that post until March 6, 1845.

## FROM ISAAC McCOY[1]

Dear Sir                                                            Louisville, Ky. Jany. 10. 1845
I write, *not* to ask a favor either for myself or a friend, but, first to congratulate you on the favor bestowed upon you by *Him* who controls

the affairs of men, and to whom we are indebted for prosperity, though our fellow men may be made the agents in its promotion; and secondly, to entreat you to give efficiency to measures for the improvement of the condition of the Indians, for whose welfare, you are aware, I have labored for upwards of twenty six years.

The plan of Indian reform adopted in Genl. Jackson's administration succeeds well, notwithstanding that, for a few years, it has not received the attention and aid from government which I think such a great enterprise merits. In view of this great work, I can truly say, I rejoice in your elevation to the helm which guides Indian affairs, knowing, as I think I do, your regard for that wretched race, and your sentiments in relation to securing them in a permanent residence, under the influence of civil, and religious institutions.

A copy of the proceedings of the late anniversary of the American Indian Mission Association, the Board of Managers of which is located in this City, is forwarded to you.[2]

ISAAC MCCOY

ALS. DLC–JKP. Addressed to Columbia.

1. Born in Pennsylvania and reared in Kentucky, McCoy received ordination as a Baptist pastor in Clark County, Ind., in 1809; he remained in that post for eight years prior to his appointment in 1817 as a missionary to the Indians in the Wabash Valley. In 1828 he assisted in the removal of the Ottawa and the Miami tribes westward and supported subsequent efforts to form an Indian state west of the Mississippi River; he aided the Indians in the surveying and locating of reservation lands provided for by the Indian Removal Act of 1830. In 1842 he became secretary of the American Indian Mission (Louisville), a cooperative venture of Baptist congregations in Kentucky.

2. Enclosure not found.

## FROM CAVE JOHNSON

Dear Sir,                            Washington January 11th 1845

I have not written this week before because nothing had occurred that I thought would interest you until yesterday. Prior to that time, all parties seemed satisfied, that no person here knew any thing about your intentions. Somehow, it was circulated yesterday, that a letter had been recd here that you had determined to retain Mr C.[1] I heard the Editor of the Constitution[2] state the fact publicly with the utmost confidence. Then followed the nomination of Wm[3] as chargé to Naples. These seem to have induced many nothern men to believe that you intended to side with the South agt. the north. Many asked me to day. I could say nothing further than expressing the opinion that you would not decide upon that matter until you reached the City & the north had nothing to fear from you. You can hardly conceive the feeling on each side here upon that subject. I regret the application of so many of our friends to Mr. T.[4] for office, evidently under the belief, that he will grant any thing which he thinks will be agreeable to you under a hope a similar favor will be extended to his friends whom you may find in office, a list of them will be probably left for you with an earnest recomendation. The friends of Mr C. now seem to regard his continuance as certain. The friends of Genl. Cass, will probably press Mr. Walker for the Secretary of the Treasury. The Genl[5] is supposed to be friendly with Dallas, Wilkins & the Porter[6] influence in Pen. & more friendly to the Southern than the nothern democracy & they fear if it is given to N.Y. that the patronage, *in the west* will be used in behalf of S.W. Jr.[7] Mr. Walker you know is connected with that family in Pa.[8]

Mr. Mason does not expect the cabinet to be retained. I think [he] has strong wishes for himself but will not be dissatisfied unless one should be taken from Va. He would be hurt, if one is selected from that State in his place because it would have the appearance, of others being more acceptable to the democracy of Va than himself.

Genl McKay expressed the opinion in my presence the other day, in a way that induced me to think he expected that I would repeat, as to the two highest offices in your cabinet. For State Department he preferred Mr. Buckhanon[9] of Pa & assigned many reasons which will readily occur to you for the preference over Mr. C. or Genl C. or S.W. Jr. He also prefers Mr. Flagg to any other from N.Y. & he supposed the Secy. T. should come from that State. Mr Hannegan[10] desired me to say to you that he thought R.J.W.[11] was the man for the Treasury probably for the reasons above assigned. Nine out of ten think there should be a new cabinet. Kettlewell of Baltimore[12] has just been with me—the man who first started your name in the Baltimore convention. He is very enthusiastic & had much to say about the offices in Baltimore & begs you to retain Genl Marriot[13] in the Custom House in Baltimore. His *only offence* to the democracy as he says, was taking office under Tyler. There is a *general feeling* for a *clean sweep.*

Wm went to Philadelphia on the 8th—has not yet returned. As far as I can learn he has been very cautious in seeming not to know (which I suppose true) anything of your thoughts or wishes or intentions.

C. JOHNSON

ALS. DLC–JKP. Addressed to Columbia. Polk's AE on the cover indicates that he received and answered this letter on January 20, 1845; Polk's reply has not been found.

1. John C. Calhoun.

2. A lawyer and editor from Luray, Va., William A. Harris won election to one term as a Democrat in the U.S. House, 1841–43. He edited the Calhounite Washington *Spectator* and its successor, the Baltimore *Constitution*, which began in October of 1844.

3. William H. Polk.

4. John Tyler.

5. Lewis Cass.

6. David R. Porter. An iron manufacturer and state legislator from Huntingdon County, Penn., Porter won election to two terms as a Democrat to the governorship of Pennsylvania, 1839–45.

7. Silas Wright, Jr.

8. In 1825 Robert J. Walker married Mary Blechynden Bache, a niece of George M. Dallas and great-granddaughter of Benjamin Franklin. In 1818 William Wilkins married Mathilda Dallas, sister of George M. Dallas.

9. James Buchanan.

10. An Indiana lawyer, Edward A. Hannegan served in the state legislature; in the U.S. House, 1833–37; and in the U.S. Senate, 1843–49. From March 1849 until January 1850, he was U.S. minister to Prussia.

11. Robert J. Walker.

12. A Baltimore grocer, John Kettlewell was a delegate to the Democratic Convention of 1844, and appointed naval officer of Baltimore in 1853.

13. A Baltimore attorney and militia general, William H. Marriott was appointed collector of the port of Baltimore in 1844.

## FROM CAVE JOHNSON

Dear Sir,                                           Washington Jany 13th 1845

I heard a fact stated to day in the course of conversation with Genl McK.[1] & a few others, which possibly you may feel some interest in knowing.

Judge King of Philadelpha has been nominated to supply the place of Baldwin & will be rejected.[2] It is confidently said that the place will be offered to Mr. Buckhanon[3] & strenuous exertions are said to have been used to get the nomination for him by the Whigs & to induce him to accept. If he is taken out of politics, they consider Pena safe to them as they believe, that Mr. B would certainly accept, if it came from any other quarter than from Tyler.

I write you this because it may be of some importance in forming your Cabinet, if you wish him in it. You will take the means to secure it, if there is any difficulty between him & others, that you may see he is well provided for. Wm.[4] leaves here tomorrow. His nomination creates some feeling among the democracy, lest it should be construed into a sort of bargain to retain Tyler scamps or pay back by similar kindness.

Clingman & Yancey fought a duel this evening—the result not heard yet. If the news comes in before the mail goes out I will enclose it.

Foster & Milton Brown offered propositions of annexation today.[5] It is probable that we shall carry it through both Houses.

C. JOHNSON

ALS. DLC–JKP. Addressed to Columbia. Polk's AE on the cover states that he received and answered this letter on January 21, 1845; Polk's reply has not been found.

1. James I. McKay.
2. Edward King and Henry Baldwin. A lawyer from Philadelphia, King entered politics as a Federalist but switched to the Democratic party in the 1820's; he served on the bench of the Pennsylvania Court of Common Pleas from 1825 until 1852. John Tyler nominated King to be associate justice of the U.S. Supreme Court on June 5, 1844, but withdrew the nomination on February 7, 1845. Baldwin, a Pennsylvania lawyer and congressman, accepted appointment as an associate justice of the U.S. Supreme Court in 1830; he served on the Court until April 21, 1844, when he died in Philadelphia of a stroke.
3. James Buchanan.
4. William H. Polk.
5. Introduced in the U.S. House on January 13, 1845, Milton Brown's resolutions for Texas annexation called for admission to statehood, creation of four additional states from the annexed territory, and preservation of the Missouri Compromise line. On January 25th the House adopted Brown's resolutions. Also on January 13th, Ephraim Foster offered a similar joint resolution in the U.S. Senate. Foster, a Nashville lawyer and one of the founders of the Whig party in Tennessee, served three terms in the Tennessee House, 1827–31 and 1835–37. Appointed to the U.S. Senate following the resignation of Felix Grundy in 1838, Foster won election to a full six-year term beginning March 4, 1839, but resigned in November of that year, having pledged to leave office should a Democratic majority be elected to the next legislature. He later served an interim term in the Senate from October of 1843 until March 3, 1845. Born in Ohio, Brown moved to Tennessee and lived in Nashville and Paris before settling permanently in Jackson. A member of the Madison County bar, he served as chancellor of West Tennessee, 1837–39, and sat in the U.S. House for three terms, 1841–47.

## FROM SAMUEL H. LAUGHLIN[1]

My dear Sir,                                        Nashville, Tenn. Jany. 13, 1845

Since I saw you last, I have been requested by a very old and very sincere friend of yours, to communicate to you in confidence a wish which he entertains in regard to office, and which, possibly, he has communicated to you directly or through some other friend before this time. The gentleman I refer to is Doctor Alfred Moore, formerly of Murfreesborough, but for many years past a citizen of Limestone County, Alabama. He has some planting interest in south Alabama, where he has one or two sons who are promising young men, and his wish is to obtain the Collectorship or Surveyorship of the Port of Mobile.[2]  He expresses a dislike to every thing like pressing importunity for office, and desires that his application may stand upon his merits and qualifications and the recommendations of his friends who know him well and have known him long. As an old friend, I know him to be a man of worth and integrity, and have no doubt of your possessing the same knowledge of him yourself. It is therefore only in compliance with his wishes, and my duty to him, that it is necessary or proper that I should trouble you with a word on the subject, especially at a time when you must be constantly occupied with more import concerns.

The sudden death of Mr. Thos. H. Fletcher[3] has thrown a gloom over every thing here this morning. You will see the manner of his death by apoplexy stated in the newspapers which are being circulated to-day. He will be buried it is understood with suitable honors on tomorrow.

In reference to our approaching 4th of March Convention,[4] I have written beseechingly to Mr. C. Johnson and Mr. A. V. Brown, to come to an understanding with each other, and to let some of their friends be advised of their positions. I am very clear that Mr. Brown ought to be the man as things stand. I know too, that it would be a point of great importance to you to have one or both of them in the next Congress. If, however, only one of them can remain there, and become Speaker or *leader*, it will probably be as much as can be accomplished. I consider it of vast importance to us in Tennessee during the incoming adminstration, that we should retain our majority in the Delegation, and that Johnson or Brown should be at the head of it. We may carry Ashe's district, and we may loose Blackwell's.[5]  If Blackwell does not run, and Rowles or Torbitt[6] should rule him off, we will, I verily believe, loose the district.

Sam Turney, I fear, will cause us to loose his district in the State Senate, by running for Congress.[7]  He has nearly consummated the same coalition with the Whigs to defeat Cullom which Cullom adopted in '43 to defeat or drive me off,[8] the evils of which I averted by voluntarily giving place with the approbation of my own sense of justice to our party, and the approval of the judgment of yourself, and other friends whose approbation I esteemed more than I did a seat in Congress obtained through the infliction of injury on the Common cause. Neither Cullom nor Turney I fear will view things in the light I did, and that therefore we will suffer detriment in the Governor's and State Senator's election in that district. I hope however for the best. Monroe Savage (who can be elected, but not as easily as Floyd) will be run in DeKalb.[9]  I have interfered as far as I well can to get Floyd for our candidate, but the local democracy at Smithville are for Savage, and Floyd wishes to avoid running unless it is forced on him. I know you feel the solicitude I do, that we should take right steps to secure the legislature, therefore I give you these facts. Minniss[10] at Sparta is in training for the floating seat from White, Fentress etc. It is most probable R. A. Campbell[11] will be in the House from Warren, and W. S. Waterson or L. D. Mercer[12] in the Senate. Trott[13] will represent Cannon. The compliment in Cannon to E. A. Keeble,[14] in naming him for Governor, is to strengthen his hands for anything which may come up in *future*. It is one of Trott's movements.

I have relinquished entirely all claim or wish for any pecuniary means from our friends here, who have sacrificed freely and some of them largely in the late contest. I have sold and am selling such property, nearly the last I have, as will leave me free of all immediate pressure, Kezer and Dr. Smartt[15] having joined their efforts to mine. What I have not to pay with, I will try to earn. A considerable stock of my law library, which cost me greatly over what I can get for it, with other things I am selling, and having sold two negros, will leave me a free man; and being so free, I cannot, and will not, under the circumstances, expect or accept any thing here. Therefore, I pray you, do not do what you proposed in regard to some subscription of W. H. Polk's.[16] He perhaps, can as inconveniently bear taxation as myself; and as I will not receive any thing from others, I cannot consent to receive any thing from him.

I shall feel myself much honored in going to Washington among the friends who will accompany you, and since you suggested that it would be agreeable for me to do so, I will be in readiness to go with you from here. As to other matters after your inauguration, and organization of your Cabinet, I will wait with patience, determined to annoy neither yourself nor any of my friends with importunity. I have a proud desire to see and note the events of the Inauguration and your progress to the city, as it will be the only journey, and public ceremony of the kind I shall ever witness, or have an opportunity of witnessing in my life.

If you lay your hands on two letters, one from L. L. Loving, and one from Hampton Williams,[17] which I handed you at the Inn to read at your leisure, wishing you to see from them the conduct of W. C. Rives in Virginia,[18] and the rascally intentions of the Whigs at the City, I will thank you to enclose them under an invelope to me at McMinnville. Put yourself to no trouble, however, if they have been misplaced.

S. H. Laughlin

ALS. DLC–JKP. Addressed to Columbia, and marked "Private."
1. A McMinnville lawyer and founding editor of the *Nashville Union*, Laughlin served three terms as a Democrat in the Tennessee Senate, 1839–45. Polk

appointed him to the post of recorder in the General Land Office, and the Senate gave its approval on March 16, 1845.

2. Alfred Moore is not identified further. Laughlin's reference to Moore's son or sons possibly refers to Sydenham Moore. Born in Rutherford County, Tenn., in 1817, he practiced law in Greensboro, Ala., served several terms on the Greene County Court, and won two terms as a Democrat in the U.S. House, 1857–61.

3. Thomas H. Fletcher, a Nashville lawyer, represented Franklin County in the Tennessee House, 1825–27, and served as secretary of state from 1830 until 1832.

4. Laughlin's reference is to the Democratic State Convention.

5. John B. Ashe and Julius W. Blackwell. A lawyer from Brownsville, Ashe served two terms in the Tennessee Senate, 1839–43 and one term as a Whig in the U.S. House, 1843–45, for Tennessee's Tenth Congressional District. A Democrat from Athens, Blackwell won election to two terms to the U.S. House, first from the Fourth District in 1839 and then from the Third District in 1843.

6. George W. Rowles and Granville C. Torbett. A Bradley County lawyer, Rowles won election as a Democrat to two terms in the Tennessee House, 1841–43 and 1857–59. Torbett, a Monroe County lawyer, served one term in the Tennessee House, 1841–43, and two terms in the Tennessee Senate, 1843–47.

7. A White County lawyer, Samuel Turney served as a Democrat in the Tennessee House, 1829–35; in the Tennessee Senate as a Democrat, 1839–47, and as a Native American, 1855–57; and in the Tennessee Confederate Senate, 1861–63.

8. A lawyer and Democrat from Overton County, Alvin Cullom served one term in the Tennessee House, 1835–37, and two terms in the U.S. House, 1843–47; he sat on Tennessee's Fourth Judicial Circuit Court from 1850 until 1852. Laughlin's reference is to his decision to withdraw from the 1843 congressional contest in favor of Cullom.

9. Abram Monroe Savage and William Floyd. A Smithville lawyer, Savage won election as a Democrat to one term in the Tennessee House in 1857. Floyd, an Alexandria merchant, served as a colonel in the DeKalb County militia.

10. A Democrat and lawyer, John A. Minnis served two terms in the Tennessee Senate, 1847–49 and 1859–61.

11. Robert A. Campbell, a McMinnville lawyer, is not identified further.

12. William S. Watterson and L. D. Mercer. A Coffee County planter, railroad promoter, and landholder, Watterson served one term in the Tennessee House, 1823–25. A McMinnville merchant, Mercer took an active part in Democratic party affairs in Warren County.

13. A farmer and merchant in Woodbury, Henry Trott served as first clerk and master of the Chancery Court in Cannon County, 1836–42, and represented that county as a Democrat for two terms in the Tennessee House, 1843–47.

14. A lawyer and editor of the Murfreesboro *Monitor*, Edwin A. Keeble served as mayor of Murfreesboro in 1828 and 1855, campaigned successfully as a Democratic presidential elector in 1856, and represented Tennessee in the Confederate Congress in 1864 and 1865.

15. Timothy Kezer and Thomas Calhoun Smartt. Kezer, a Nashville merchant and hatmaker, and Smartt, a McMinnville physician, were Laughlin's sons-in-law.

16. Reference to William H. Polk is unknown.

17. On November 20, 1844, L. L. Loving wrote to Laughlin about election results in Nelson County, Va. ALS. DLC–JKP. Hampton C. Williams, a clerk in the Navy Department's Bureau of Construction and a Democratic party operative, wrote to Laughlin on November 15, 1844, concerning election results in Washington City. ALS. DLC–JKP.

18. A Virginia lawyer and planter, William C. Rives served several terms in the U.S. House and Senate, first as Democrat and then as a Whig. He twice served as U.S. minister to France, 1829–32 and 1849–53.


## FROM AMOS NOURSE[1]

Dear Sir,            Hallowell Me. Jany 16th 1845

Perhaps I ought to believe that no suggestions of a private individual like myself, comparatively obscure & little known, will be considered by the President Elect as entitled to respect or regard. But there are certain considerations which weigh so heavily upon my mind, that I must give them utterance. That they will be received with indulgence, & favor too if they deserve it, an attentive observation of your public course will not permit me to doubt.

Previous to the Baltimore Convention, a wide breach existed in the democracy of this State, growing out of conflicting views on the subject of the Presidency, & other causes, urged with a zeal of pertinacity approaching to recklessness. By your nomination the asperity of feeling previously existing was allayed, & an entire cooperation, for the time, effected; *but there is thus far no cordial union.* Whether there is to be, depends upon developments yet to be made. If the President shall so construct his Cabinet, & so shape his course in other respects, as not to give even a plausible pretext to either section of the party for claiming a victory over the other, division & distraction will soon come to an end. But should the contrary be made to appear by the retention of Mr Calhoun, the calling in of Mr Van Buren, or any other measure similarly significant, no event in prospect can be more certain, than the complete prostration of the democratic party. I am not well advised of the condition of parties in other States, but, if appearances are to be trusted, essentially the same state of things exists in many.

Now, Sir, I beg you to understand, that I do not present this as any *new* view. It is its *importance*, not its *novelty*, that constrains me to urge it, and if, in doing so, I have overstepped the bounds of delicacy you will be good enough to ascribe it to a want of familiar acquaintance with the rules of etiquette that should govern in such cases.

A. Nourse

ALS. DLC–JKP. Addressed to Maury.

1. Postmaster at Hallowell from 1822 until 1841, Amos Nourse moved to Bath, Me., where he practiced medicine and served briefly as collector of customs, 1845–46.

## FROM AARON V. BROWN

Dear Sir                                    Washington City Jany 17th 1845

I have just seen Extra Billy Smith[1] from Richmond who says that there is quite a sensation there at a report that Stephenson[2] is to be your Sec. of State. He says S. is far from being popular & the working democracy would not like such a thing at all. He says that Mr Stephenson himsef freely declares that if such were your intention he has no knowledge of it. I give only the facts without comment. He says also that Ritchie has understood that on the Tariff you intended in your inaugural to assume 30 per cent as a maximum & so upset the compromise etc.[3] On which point I told him to write to R. to be at ease; there was no foundation for such a rumor & moreover my opinion was that no man living except perhaps Genl Jackson knew who would be your Cabinet.

I have recieved no letter lately from you, but suppose when you do break loose you will give me a torrent.

A. V. Brown

ALS. DLC–JKP. Addressed to Columbia. Polk's AE states that he received this letter on January 15, 1845.

1. Governor of Virginia from 1846 until 1849, William "Extra Billy" Smith served in the U.S. House, 1841–43 and 1853–61. In 1844 he served as a presidential elector on the Democratic ticket.

2. Andrew Stevenson.

3. Reference probably is to the 1833 compromise tariff, which provided for the gradual reduction of rates to a maximum twenty percent by 1842.

## FROM JOHN M. NILES[1]

Dear Sir                                    Washington Jany 17. 1845

I have been requested by S. H. Huntington Esqr to forward to you the accompaning letter, & to introduce him to your acquaintance.[2] I know nothing of the contents or object of the letter, but from my confidence in the writer, do not hesitate to comply with his request. Mr H. is a very respectable & intelligent man; has been Judge of our Common Pleas etc, and is a sound democrat. He resides in Hartford Ct.

There is nothing going on here of much interest. The Texas question is the prominent one; & yet, I am sorry to say, it is beset with so many difficulties, or there is such diversity of opinions in relation to the form of action upon it, that the prospect of accomplishing the object, is not very favourable, although there is little doubt, that there are a majority in both houses, in favour of the measure if they could unite on any one of the numerous plans which have been presented for consideration.

JOHN M. NILES

ALS. DLC–JKP. Addressed to Columbia.

1. Prior to his lengthy political career, John M. Niles established and edited the *Hartford Times*. A Democrat, he twice represented Connecticut in the U.S. Senate, 1835–39 and 1843–49; he also served as postmaster general in Martin Van Buren's cabinet from 1840 until 1841.

2. Reference probably is to Samuel H. Huntington to Polk, January 13, 1845. In his letter to Polk, Huntington pledged the continued support of the Connecticut Democracy. A Hartford attorney, Huntington served as clerk of the Connecticut Senate during the 1830's.

## FROM CORNELIUS P. VAN NESS[1]

Dear Sir                                                    New York January 17/45

Although I have not the honor of a personal acquaintance with you, I have concluded to make to you the following communication. At the same time I do not ask or expect any further answer from you than merely an acknowledgement of its receipt, that I may be sure of that fact.

At the close of the last session of Congress President Tyler offered to appoint me Collector of this port, and, after a consultation with some of my friends, I agreed to accept the appointment. I was not, nor have I ever been, what was properly termed *a Tyler Man*, but I was, and am, the *friend* of Mr Tyler. I was wholly opposed, however, to his seperate Convention,[2] and to all the schemes of his partizans who were in favour of a seperate, or third party, organization. I had not then, nor have I ever, attended a Tyler meeting. At the time of my appointment there were a number of Mr Tyler's *pretended* friends who were determined upon a third party organization, and the greatest efforts were made to press me into the measure, with the influence of the Custom House under my charge. I knew the *secret* object was to aid the election of Mr Clay, and I was determined to defeat their schemes. The accompanying copies of a correspondence which, *in reality*, more than any thing else, produced the withdrawal of Mr Tyler,[3] will show you the part I acted. At the moment that I was pressed to the wall by the men in question, I myself set on foot this correspondence, in order at once to put a stop to their action. Nos 1 & 4, that is the originals, were written by my own Assistant Collector (Chief Clerk)[4] and are in my possession in his hand writing, that is, all but the signatures. Pending this negotiation I had to contend with a bitter opposion to a union, on the one side from the men already referred to, and, on the other side, from the friends of Mr Van Buren, who felt mortified at your nomination instead of his. But it was carried through, and perhaps others will tell you the exertions I made. Mr Tyler felt much happier after it was over; was fully satisfied with my course; and continues, as I believe, to place in me the utmost confidence. He is an honest man, and has acted sincerely in your favour; but this, I am sure, it is not necessary for you to learn from me.

As to myself, I have been 40 years in the political field, and have ever used my best efforts to sustain the republican cause. My father[5] was a worker in the same cause, and was one of the electors, in this state, who voted for Jefferson in 1800. In 1840 I stood by Mr Van Buren like a brother, as my printed speeches will show; but from the moment of his fall I was persuaded he could never be reelected, and that it would be the destruction of our party to run him again. I went upon a principle regardless of his merits or demerits. I was fully persuaded that no man, after having been elevated to that high pinnacle, the Presidency of this great country, and having fallen from it, could ever again reach the same elevation. The fall is too great, and he who suffers it becomes too much shattered to recover strength enough to get up to the same spot again. It never has been, nor never will be. But while I was in favour of a new candidate, I did not commit myself to any particular man. I have attended no political meeting since 1840, until during the struggle in your favour. I took charge of the Custom House here on the 8th of July last. In April last our party ran a popular man for Mayor (Mr Coddington)[6] and was beaten by more than 4000 majority. In November we gave you 2000 majority. There are others who can tell you whether I entered with my *whole heart* into the contest, and also how much money was contributed by me, & by those under me, through my influence.

Now, Sir, it is evident that a portion of Mr Van Buren's friends are determined to make the attempt to punish, through you, all those who were not in favour of his being again nominated. They are already declaring who will stay in, and who shall go out. But your character is of so high and honorable a grade, that all just and disinterested men are convinced that the attempt will wholly fail, and that right and justice will prevail under your administration.

I have said that I was attached to no particular candidate previous to your nomination; and I now declare that I am attached to none for 1848. My object is to give your Administration a firm and unwavering support, and faithfully to stand by you while you remain President, be it for *one* or *two* terms. It is a favourite object with certain men in this city to get possession of my office, and for the reason that it can not be used under me to favour certain *cliques*, as distinguished from the party in general. In my hands it will be administered solely with reference to the public interest, and to the honor & fame of your administration; and your friends & your wishes will always be duly regarded & satisfied. It is wanted by the others to be used for *special* & *ulterior* objects, regardless of your wishes, or the interest of your administration. The war upon me has commenced, and, doubtless, will be kept up until March. I have been, and shall continue to be, very liberal to the friends of Mr Van Buren; and indeed to all the sections of the party. But this will not answer the purpose of certain men, as they want all power to be lodged exclusively in their own hands.

I beg of you, Sir, to pardon the freedom with which I have told my story. I have done it in great haste, and under a great pressure of public business. And, in conclusion, I repeat, I expect no answer, except a bare acknowledgement that this has been safely received.

C. P. VAN NESS

ALS. DLC–JKP. Letter marked *"Private & Confidential."*

1. Born in Kinderhook, N.Y., Van Ness moved to Vermont where he served in the state legislature, 1818–20; presided as chief justice of the state supreme court, 1821–22; and served three terms as governor, 1823–26. He went to Spain in 1830 as U.S. minister during Andrew Jackson's administration.

2. John Tyler's convention met at Baltimore on May 25, 1844, and nominated him for president and Richard M. Johnson for vice-president.

3. Enclosures not found. Van Ness probably refers to resolutions adopted by a meeting of Democrats at Charlton House, New York City, on August 6, 1844, requesting that Tyler withdraw from the presidential contest. The first resolution thanked Tyler for his efforts as president, and the fourth resolution appointed a committee to present the resolutions to him in Washington City. In an August 22, 1844, letter to these men, Tyler acknowledged the influence of their resolutions upon his decision to withdraw from the presidential contest, announced on August 21, 1844. For details on the Charlton House resolutions, see Alexander O. Anderson to Polk, August 22, 1844.

4. Cornelius S. Bogardus.

5. Born in Ghent, N.Y., John Peter Van Ness settled in Washington City; won election as a Democratic presidential elector in 1800; and served in the U.S. House from 1801 until 1803.

6. A New York City merchant, Jonathan I. Coddington had been postmaster

of that city since 1836. He lost the mayoral election in 1844 to James Harper, the Native American candidate. Silas Wright, Jr., and Martin Van Buren supported Coddington as Van Ness' replacement; however, the appointment went to Cornelius W. Lawrence, formerly a member of the U.S. House, 1833–34, and mayor of New York City, 1834–37.

## FROM CAVE JOHNSON

Dear Sir,                                        Washington Jany 18th 1845

I write you a line simply to say that I hope you will interpose to prevent William[1] from accepting the appointment of Chargé & I do so because it is rumored about here that such will be the case. There is a good deal of talk about it & of the obligation it will impose on you to retain all the Knaves that Mr. T.[2] may recomend. I have told those who talked to me, that it would be time enough for them to complain when you were called on to act & acted. He will be confirmed without any serious opposition as Foster, Colquit[3] & Hannegan told me to day.

We have been much troubled with our Clerk,[4] who is probably a defaulter for 40 or 50.000. We dismissed him to day *unanimously* & appointed French.[5] Speculations as to your cabinet have subsided for the last week. All concur in the belief that no one knows any thing about it & this is a source of great gratification to your friends. The spirit of proscription runs too high among our friends, simply because so many are wanting offices & so few can be gratified. You will find some difficulty in controlling your temper, after you get here.

Webster, Reverdy Johnson, Jno M Clayton[6] are elected to the Senate & Clay will be here & Calhoun if he be not retained. Cass will come from Michigan. Your Admn will not therefore be a quiet one. It is thought Dickinson and Dicks will be here from N.Y.,[7] probably Reeves from Va. as the Whigs have taken a snap judgment on our friends & fixed the 22nd to go into the election.[8]

C. JOHNSON

ALS. DLC–JKP. Addressed to Columbia.

1. William H. Polk.

2. John Tyler.

3. A Georgia lawyer, Walter T. Colquitt won election as a Whig to the U.S. House in 1839; refusing to support Harrison for president in 1840, he resigned and in 1841 won back his seat as a Van Buren Democrat. He served in the first session of the Twenty-seventh Congress and then went to the U.S. Senate for one term, 1843–48.

4. A resident of Ohio, Caleb J. McNulty defeated Matthew St. Claire Clarke for the office of House clerk on December 6, 1843, and served until removed from

office on January 18, 1845. The House dismissed McNulty for the defalcation of nearly $45,000 in congressional funds.

5. A Democrat from New Hampshire, Benjamin B. French served as clerk of the U.S. House for several years prior to becoming treasurer of the National Democratic Committee in 1848.

6. Daniel Webster, Reverdy Johnson, and John M. Clayton. A Maryland attorney and member of the Maryland Senate, 1821–29, Johnson won election to the U.S. Senate as a Whig in 1845, and served until 1849, when he accepted appointment as U.S. attorney general in the Taylor administration. John M. Clayton won election to a seat in the Delaware House in 1824; served as Delaware's secretary of state, 1826–28; sat in the U.S. Senate as a National Republican, 1829–36, and as a Whig, 1845–49 and 1853–56; presided as chief justice of the Delaware Supreme Court, 1837–39; and negotiated the Clayton-Bulwer Treaty with Great Britain during his tenure as U.S. secretary of state, 1849–50.

7. Daniel S. Dickinson and John A. Dix. Soldier, lawyer, and railroad president, Dix served as adjutant general of New York, 1831–33, and one term as a member of the New York House in 1842. Elected as a Democrat to the U.S. Senate seat vacated by Silas Wright, Jr., in 1845, Dix ran unsuccessfully in 1848 as the gubernatorial candidate of the Free Soil party; served in the Union army as a general officer during the Civil War; and won election to the governorship on the Republican ticket in 1873.

8. Reference is to Virginia's U.S. senatorial contest and the Whig campaign to assure the reelection of William C. Rives. The Virginia legislature postponed the contest until the following session, during which the Democratic majority secured the election of Isaac S. Pennybacker.

## TO JOHN SCHNIERLE[1]

Sir:                                                      Columbia Ten. Jany 18th 1845

I have had the honor to recieve your letter of the 28th ultimo, transmitting to me the Pre-amble and Resolutions "adopted *unanimously* by a large meeting" of my fellow citizens of Charleston, and also the Resolutions of the City Council, conveying to me their "cordial congratulations" upon the result of the late Presidential Election, and inviting me to visit your City on my way to Washington.

It would afford me sincere pleasure I assure your Sir: to acept the invitation, and to exchange personal salutations with my Fellow-Citizens of Charleston and its vacinity, if I could do so, with any convenience.

I regret that necessary engagements will detain me at home until first of the next month, at which time I have made my arrangements to proceed by the usual and most direct route from this part of Tennessee to Washington.

In declining the invitation which you have conveyed to me, I beg you to assure those whom you represent, that I duly appreciate the honor which they have done me, and hope at some future period to have it in my power to visit your ancient City, and make their personal acquaintance.

I have to request that you will tender to the President of the South Carolina Rail Road Company[2] my thanks for "the accommodation of their road" which they offer from Augusta and Hamburg to Charleston.

JAMES K. POLK

ALS, draft. DLC–JKP. Addressed to Charleston. Polk's AE on the cover of John Schnierle's letter of December 28, 1844, states that he replied on January 20, 1845.

1. Mayor of Charleston, S.C., John Schnierle lost his reelection bid in September 1846.

2. Reference is to Charleston businessman, James Gadsden. Gadsden fought in both the War of 1812 and the Seminole War; served as a commissioner for the removal of the Seminole Indians in 1821; won a seat on Florida Territory's first Legislative Council; and presided over the Louisville, Cincinnati, and Charleston Railroad Company in 1830 and its successor corporation, the South Carolina Railroad Company. Appointed U.S. minister to Mexico in 1853, Gadsden arranged the purchase of a small strip of border lands south of the Gila River; the "Gadsden Purchase" would facilitate a more direct southern route to California, should such be the course chosen by Congress for a proposed transcontinental railroad.

## FROM MARTIN VAN BUREN

My dear Sir                                        Lindenwald Jany 18h 1845

I recd. your friendly letter of the 4h only last Eveg. I am therefore compelled to answer it by return mail to secure its reception before you leave home, as you desire. The frank & manly spirit in which you refer to the subject leave it scarcely necessary to say that nothing that transpired at Baltimore had the effect of weakening the strength of my previous personal regard for yourself, or of relaxing in the slightest degree the exertion of my friends and myself to secure your election. If either of the gentlemen for whose benefit the preliminary proceeding of that meeting were gotten up,[1] & who were supposed to have favored them had been nominated, all hope of carrying the ticket in this State would of necessity have been abandoned. Your nomination was therefore recd. with much satisfaction by the honest men of the Party here, & the manner in which it has been sustained is known to all, though it may not be admitted by all. Be then assured that there is not one among your friends who is more sincerely solicitous for the success of your administration, or who will go farther as long as it is carried on upon principles he approves to sustain it than myself. I look forward with a confident hope to see the three administrations of Genl. Jackson, yourself & my own regarded by the Democracy of the land as periods, in which, more than others, sound Democratic principles have advanced, struggled for, & finally established, and constituting, as a whole a bright era in the history of the Republic.

You did as I would have done myself in offering to Mr Wright the Treasury instead of the State Deptmt. He is fit for any thing, but the former, independent of the consideration of the relative importance of the two places to which you refer, is the very one to which his great talents are peculiarly adapted & for which he is, I sincerely believe, better calculated than any other person in existence. But whatever may have been his desire to aid you it was out of his power to do so. His hands were tied by the circumstances of his election. It being apparent that his nomination was essential to our success a very strong desire was evinced that Gov Bouck[2] should clear the way by declining, but this he refused to do to the last moment & the convention were obliged to lay him aside by a direct vote. Even after this he refused to appear satisfied—preserved unbroken silence in regard to the nomination, & shewed indication of a disposition to make himself troublesome after the election, & has since remained at Albany and enterd into a hot canvass in regard to the election of Senators to Congress & State officers, of a cast anything but friendly to Mr Wrights administration. A most anxious desire to carry the State led our friends in the Counties to confer nomination for the legislature upon the adherents of the portion of the Party which chose to call themselves his especial friends, to induce them to give the ticket in general a zealous support, to an extent which together with the loss of our Assembly Ticket in the City of N York,[3] has given them a force in the Legislature requiring the greatest discretion to deal with. One more state election will set all this right, & place the Administration of Mr Wright in smooth water, but in the mean time it is indispensable to the stability of our politics & the welfare of the State that Mr Wright should remain here. He paid me a visit since his election & upon a view of his condition it appeared plain to us that he could not leave his post without injustice to those who had elected him. I have been thus particular upon the point for fear that Mr Wrights native & unfailing resolve in all that relates to himself may have prevented him from stating the reasons of his declination as strongly as they really are. The choice of Senators (of which I am this moment informed) has resulted very well. In Genl Dix you will find a first rate man, firm, intelligent brave, honest talented & a true Democrat. His Colleague,[4] though some what mixed up with the feuds in relation to Gov Bouck, is yet I believe entirely honest, of very respectable talents & with such a man as Genl Dix will I am persuaded answer perfectly well. He removed all apprehension in respect to his feelings towards Mr Wright by an emphatic letter during the Canvass.[5]

For Secy of State you want, above all others consideration, a man of bland manners, good temper, great quickness of perception, industry and high personal character. No one who has not had experience in the matter can form an adequate idea of the encreased facility with which the administration gets along with the Foreign Ministers, (who are themselves made up of all sorts of characters) with such a Secy. They have matters between them to carp at if not quarrel about every day, if there be not a plastic yet safe hand to smooth them away. I know of no man in the Country who would answer these purposes besides being a safe & discreet Counsellor in all things better than Mr Butler if he would take the place. Thinking it probable, that what appears to be the undivided sense of the Country in respect to the inexpediency of taking into the Cabinet men who were or would be suspected of being aspirants for the sucession, might also be yours, I have often reflected upon what it would be best for you to do in the selection of a Secry of State. The objection here refd to would, by the bye, have been one also agt. the selection of Mr Wright, who is placed in that category nolens volens.[6] It would also be important (you being from the South) to have that Secy from the North if, as is I think probable, the action of Congress should result in throwing upon your hands a great portion of the business of the annexation of Texas. Mr Butler introduced the Resolution upon that subject into the B. Convention,[7] agrees with you in favouring the object & if you should happen to take different views as to details, he would after giving and enforcing his opinion, as it would be his duty to do, assist in carrying yours into effect, or in an extreme case, not likely to occur, resign his place. No one in any part of the Union could do more to remove objections & promote conciliation. Knowing, from experience & which no one can know before he tries his hand at Cabinet making, how extremely difficult it is to suit ones self perfectly in such matters, my mind has frequently been turned to this point & I think I cannot be mistaken in believing that he is the man if he can be obtained. Upon this last I cannot speak with any degree of certainty but will tell you all I Know. It being settled that Mr Wright must stay here and knowing Mr Butlers desire to remain in his profession, which is lucrative & the avails of which are more important from the losses he has sustained by responsibilities for his brother[8] (now happily settled) and fearing that he might commit himself beyond the power of retracting I asked him to call on me on his return from Albany at the meeting of the Electors, which he did. I then broached the matter to him as a thing that might happen & begged him to keep his feelings, as well as his declarations upon the subject as uncommitted as possible. He informed me that he had already expressed himself very decidedly against going into the Cabinet if it should be offered to him & that our friends at Albany had made the same appeal to him that I did. We talked the matter over very fully & he promised me not to act hastily in the matter if the contingency occurred but to advise with his friends, evidently, however, anxious that the thing might pass by without imposing upon him the necessity of making a decision in the matter. So the affair now stands although by no means certain I yet hope that a strong letter from Genl Jackson, backed by Mr Wright & myself might induce him to accept. For the Treasury Dept Sir democrats have not adopted him, he would certainly not take it & nor could we advise him to do so. If therefore you for any reason decide to go elsewhere for a Secy of State he will be out of the question & I am sure very happy to be so.

If you decide to fill the Treasury Department from this State I would recommend Mr. Flagg or Mr Cambreling & in the order in which I have placed them. In the great points of integrity, honor, sincerity & every good and great quality which helps to make a good man I know no difference between them & in my personal regards there certainly is none. They are both abundantly fit for the place but If I were obliged to make the selection between them I would take the first named under a belief that he is more practical, has more recent experience & would be more likely to be successful. Still it might turn out otherwise. Mr Flaggs reputation in this State stands higher I think as financier than that of any man who has gone before him ever stood, although they have been very able men at times. He is always cheerful composed & undismayed, like Butler & in the latter respect also like Cambreling who nothing can frighten. You will see Mr Cambrelings own views of the matter by the enclosed letter from him [9] which I send you in the same confidence that I do this & which I wish you would destroy at once, as I have no authority for sending it although I am satisfied he would not blame me. Whether Mr Flagg would accept or not I cannot say as I have it not in my power to consult him & as his name has never been mentioned in our consideration although he was with Mr Wright at my house. I think however Mr Wright would consent to part with him & that he & I could induce him to take the place. Perhaps there is not man living who is more indifferent about promotion or who discharges the duties of any place that is offerd to him with more fidelity. In redeeming the finances of the State he has unavoidably brought himself in contact with the contractors on the public works & they may unite with the late Gov & his friends to oppose Mr Flaggs re-appointment (which is to take place some time in Feby) although I think they will not dare to brave the known sentiments of the state by such an attempt. Yet to prevent further excitement at Albany it would be well if his selection should be decided upon by yourself to make it known at as early a day as is convenient. I have no reason to doubt Mr Cambrelings acceptance. If I can be of any service upon either points, a hint in advance will be improved to the best advantage.

In respect to the Southern & S. Western portions of the Union I have a great reluctance for reasons which it is not necessary to state, to say any thing. I will therefore only remark that if you should think that you ought to take a member from your own State, the selection of Genl Armstrong (if a business man of which I am not fully apprised) would suit best in this region for two reasons 1st on account of his more complete identification with our venerable friend Genl. Jackson & 2nd because he was not a party to the preliminary proceedings at Baltimore. However much our friends were relieved by the final result & however much our Delegates were applauded at home for giving the affair that direction, those proceedings & the object designed to be accomplished by them with the uses there made of the Texas question, have sunk deep into the feelings of the best portions of the Democracy of the North which will every once and a while shew itself maugre all that the most sincere & able friends of conciliation amongst us can do to keep them down. It is therefore wise to avoid as few as that can consistently be done, all measures or steps which must have a tendency to revive recollections which it is for the good of the cause and the Country should pass as rapidly as possible to the receptacle of things lost on earth. In respect to the West generally I concur very fully as to what is said in the enclosed. I do not know whether in view of the late results you will be able to go into that State, but she is great & will always be powerful, is now Democratic in Congress & will soon be so at home & I know the gentleman refd to to be perfectly honest & trust he would be a connecting link of great value with the sincere, & unadulterated Democracy of the West. You will probably take one member from New Engld. I know that the name of Gov Fairfield has been presented to you for I have been asked to aid it by the present Gov & Chief Justice Shepley[10] but declined because I did not intend to interfere in such matters. Although I am not assured of the fact, I yet think it probable that N. Hampshire will also present a name. My own Secy[11] will probably not desire it himself but I can well conceive that besides the desire of aiding you he will have no very strenuous objections to get some rival for the Senator place (about to become vacant) in his own State out of the way. Maine will ask it because She is the largest & has never had a Cabinet Minister & N. Hampshire because she is & always has been *granite*, a well founded pretension & of no mean value. If I were to decide it I should give it to Maine, but I should do so without the slightest disparagement to any of the names which I can imagine will be brought forward from N.H. The Convention you know gave a large vote for Fairfield for Vice President & between him & Gov Hubbard (an excellent fellow) I should think the Democracy of N. England taken together would prefer Fairfield. In point of talents I do not think the difference is very great. Bancroft greatly over tops both in that respect. If he lived in either State I would not hesitate to give him the preference. I have tried him & know him to be fit for any thing, & if you prefer not to decide between your friends in the named States you never would regret having taken him. No administration need fear to meet the public eye & mind that has such names & persons as Butler & Bancroft in it.

You see my dear Sir that I have complied with your request by giving you my views without reserve in respect to most of the subjects you have submitted. The reasons for my reserve in respect to part will I am sure be duly appreciated. I write in the confidence suggested by your letter & after the matters are all disposed of it may be well to dispose of this also. My sincere desire is to be mixed up as little as possible with contests or conflicting interests among friends. Although I have named only three of our political friends in this State there are possibly many others who think their names might well have been included in the list & as I should not have dreamt of interfering unasked in the matter it may not be amiss to guard agt. injury to their feelings when we are no more.

You are quite right in attaching the importance you do the selection of your Cabinet. I have often been struck with the justice & sagacity of a remark of our great & good friend[12] in the earlier stages of his first term. Riding together & talking of the assaults to which we were exposed & those that were anticipated he remarked that according to his understanding of the matter those attacks were much more to be dreaded in the infancy of an administration than after it had been able to get a foothold of its own & that therefore we should devote ourselves unremittingly to make character after which we would have nothing to fear. It is so in respect to all things. When a public man in so elevated a station makes his Debut, every one watches all his acts closely because they have an opinion to form of him & thousands believe that suspicion, though detestable [in private] life, is in respect to public servants a great virtue. After a while they make up their minds for good or for evil. If it be for the former they are slow to listen to fault finders, will take much upon trust & can with ordinary care & honsty be dealt with easily by a man in power—if for the latter there is scarcely any thing he can do that finds favor in their eyes. I know I can trust to your good sense in saying that this difficulty is greater in your case than it has been in several others, when a man has ben long before the public for such a place, passing to it through regular gradations, that majority of the people who elect him have become accustomed to believe implicitly in his capacity & fitness in all things before he enters upon the duties of his office & they are therefore prepared to trust him in advance & it requires the commission of great faults before they can be brought to doubt their long cherished opinions. With the man who is suddenly and unexpectedly raised to the place in question this valuable element of strength is in a great degree wanting & he has to earn that confidence with his first entrance into office by good acts which is spontaneously yielded in the other case. He has to remove the apprehension which will in such cases always arise, though concealed in the minds, of many of his best friends. We have on two occasions been so unsuccessful in this respect in regard to our Chief Magistrates, that there is a sort of running opinion amongst us that no man suddenly & unexpectedly raised to the head of the State can succeed. But in forming that notion sufficient attention has not been paid to the circumstance that in those cases our experience fully proved that those were radical defects of adaptation to the place which no previous training or other circumstances could have obviated & It is our happiness to know from undoubted evidence that on your part no such deficiencies are to be apprehended, & although we cannot hope to see your administration exempt from perils & difficulties we yet have an abiding confidence that all will go well, & we have, what is better a timely & firm disposition to do all in your power to promote & secure that result.

Hoping that you may be able to decipher this scrawl and desiring to be very kindly remembered to Mrs. Polk, & the Genl & wishing you all manner of success ....

M. V. Buren

P.S. You may read this in confidence to the Genl. but to *no one else.*

ALS. DLC–JKP. Probably addressed to Columbia.

1. Reference is to the Baltimore convention's adoption of a two-thirds rule for selection of the party's presidential nominee. Van Buren's reference probably is to Lewis Cass and James Buchanan who supported the two-thirds rule and had aspirations for the nomination.

2. A farmer from Schoharie County, N.Y., William C. Bouck served as a canal commissioner for nineteen years. Defeated in his 1840 bid for the governorship, Bouck, a leader of the Hunker faction of the Democratic party, won election as governor in 1842 and served a single term.

3. Van Buren's reference is to the defeat of New York City's Democratic candidates for the state assembly. Candidates of the Native American party secured all of New York City's thirteen seats.

4. Daniel S. Dickinson.

5. Not identified further.

6. Latin expression meaning "whether or not one wishes to."

7. Reference is to the Democratic party's resolution calling for the reoccupation of Oregon and the reannexation of Texas. Benjamin F. Butler served the Baltimore convention as chairman of the resolutions committee.

8. Reference is to Charles Butler, a New York attorney, philanthropist, and one of the founders of Union Theological Seminary.

9. Enclosure not found.

10. Hugh J. Anderson and Ether Shepley. A lawyer from Belfast, Me., Anderson won election as a Democrat to two terms in the U.S. House, 1837–41; subsequently, he served as governor of his state, 1844–47, and as commissioner of customs in the U.S. Treasury Department, 1853–58. A native of Massachusetts, Ether Shepley represented Maine in the U.S. Senate from 1833 until 1836. He served as an associate justice of the Maine Supreme Court from 1836, and as chief justice, 1848–55.

11. Reference probably is to Levi Woodbury.

12. Andrew Jackson.

## FROM ALEXANDER DUNCAN[1]

Dear Sir                                        [Washington City] Jan 20th 1845

When I parted with you in Tenesee[2] your *hope* was that we would triumph. My response was that we *would*. My confidence appeared to me to be that of inspiration. I think our triumph has been the most glorisous. The democrecy have even gained since the commencement of the government. All the policy questions and measures which ware involved in the contest between Jefferson and the elder Adams[3] ware involved in this and the decision increased in importance in proportion to the number to be effected by its result. This contest decided some importent questions not involved in that (viz) the anxation of Texas and the possession and occupation of Oregon. Our victory is the more glorious because of the fact that all the highhanded measures of the federal party have received a signal rebuke all having been fairly and openly presented for the confirmation or condemnation of the people. No man ever entered upon the executive duties with as clear lights before him as you will on the fourth of March next.

The people have settled every important measure on which it will be your duty [to] act for the first four years of your administration. So far as great and leading measures are concerned you will have little to do but execute the peoples will plainly and distinctly expressed through the Ballet-Box. So far your task will be easy and agreble. You will have a cabinet to make. That will be an unplesent task, and however correct and pure your choice may be you cannot expect to avoid sensure disapointment and dissatisfaction. If I ware capeble of giving you advice, it would be to bring men around you selected from the body the pure and well tried democricy, men who are as well distinguished for their stability of political principles and national economy as for their capasety for the several stations which they are to fill. And above all if you wish to avoid a bed of thorns for yourself and division and destraction to the democratic party to avoid the appoint[ment] of any men to high and influential places who are either aspirents for the Presdincy or who are the avowed friends of aspirents. Alredy is advantage being taken of your promise not to be a candiate for reelection.[4] How far you may have commited yourself on that point I am not advised nor do I care. If your administration is that vigilent bold and independent administration I and many other of your friends have promised it would be (in the event of your election) the American Democricy will pay but little attention to your committee. They will demand that you be a candidate for re-election and the greater the number of aspirents the more importent will it be that you should be a candedate. Since your election candidates have sprung up like Prudence Dee's men[5] and each man is organising his friends and will direct his whole energies political and personal to advance his own interists and secure his own pretentions. All this you will learn when you come into the center of their operations. But though these things may fore-boad disorganization to a superfeciel observer yet I fear nothing, knowing as I do the operations are confined to but a few compared with the great body of the democricy who are capeble of appreciating the value of a correct administration and who too are capeble of appreciating the motives which govern political aspirents and office hunters.

The people have been to recently gulled by great promeses incouraging high hopes to be easily deceived. The entire failure to secure any one of the many advantages which the whigs promised by the overthrow of the democricy will for many years to come secure each correct administration from overthrow by such on simelar means. You have been beset at home I have no doubt. You will be beset on your way here by office hunters enough to exhast your patronage and when you come here you will be beset by ten for every office within your gift (some worthy and some unworthy) many of whom reside in this City or have remained here since the overthrow of the Democricy in 1840 awaiting a change of administration in the hopes of being restored. This class of applicants will be clamerous. *Their* merrets you will be able to appreciate. But all the offices will be filled on your arival by the creatures of Jno Tyler nearly all of whom will profess to be and to have been democrats of the *"true blue"*[6] but most of whom were the friends of Tyler while he was a candidate and would have thrown up their caps for the successful cadidate be he whom he might. This class also you know how to appreciate. Mr. Tyler however expects them to be retained. I know this from several circumstances all of which would be too prolix for me to detail. A few days since I was in conversation with an officer of the Treasury Dept. (a democrat of the right stamp) on the subject of the cabinet officers of the new adminis- tration. I remarked, in order to secure to Col. Polk the unimbarassed choice of a cabinet, every cabinet officer of the present administration would resign; delicacy honour and dignity would dictate and demand such a course. My friend answered that they might *posebly* resign by if they did every man of them expected to be replaced and continued. Mr Tyler has put and retained in office some whigs. Since he has at- tach[ed] himself to the democratic party and claimed its support efforts have been made in various instances to displace those whigs. Mr. Tyler's response has been in most cases, *"These* are my personal friends and I cannot remove them in my time but I will not insist on Col. Polk to *retain them."* I could give many more proofs that Mr. Tyler will expect you to feel yourself eased of the responseble duty of making appointments, and so desireous is he of relieving you from all such responsebelity in this particular that he has permited the Senate to do little else this winter but confirm the nominations of his *particular friends* all of whom he will expect you to retain. But let me assure you the democrecy will expect a *very* different result. Your proclamation declairing all appointments vacent on the 4th of March would much better meet their approbation. You have no conception of the contempt in which the creatures of Jno Tyler are held here and in most parts of the country by both whigs and democrats.

I have named these things to you that you might not be taken by sur- prise and to give you some idea of what the true democrecy expect as well for the peace and dignity of your administration as for the union and strength of the democratic party.

The general course of policy of your adminestration is well understood but we are entertained with numerous speculations in regard to your Cabenet and appointments. It is amusing to witness the rise and fall of Cabenent stocks among the aspirents and those who act with them and expect to partisipate in the gifts of executive patronage. With the democrecy who are uninfluenced by such motives there is but little spec- ulation. They believe all will be as it should be. There is a very good feeling toward Mr. Cave Johnson. It is much desired by many of your true friends that he should have that situation in your cabinet which most requires the union of talents and vigilence and economy. I think his appointment would give encreased strength to your administration.

You know how to estimate his worth. I wish to God you had a Cave Johnson for every importent place you have to fill. Nothing could shake confidence in your administration.

But sir I have forgoten myself. This epistle is too long. I feel a delicacy in intruding upon you at all fearing as I do that you are flooded with letters and communications and if an appology be necessary it will be found in the anxiety that one feels who has devoted his best energies to secure your election and the support of the democratic party and one whose ardour for your success can only be excelled by his ardour in the support of your administration and to make it dignified and honourable will leave nothing undone within his ability. In the strongest confidence that your administration may be all that the true democrecy expect it to be and that like your *most* noble predecesor (Jackson) in great and momentous events (if necessary) you will not hesitate to *"take the responsebility"* on your[self].

A. DUNCAN

ALS. DLC–JKP.
1. A Cincinnati physician, Duncan served several terms in the Ohio House and Senate, 1828–34, and three terms in the U.S. House, 1837–41 and 1843–45.
2. Duncan campaigned for Polk in Middle Tennessee in late October, 1844.
3. Duncan's reference is to the presidential election of 1800.
4. For Polk's single term pledge, see Polk to Henry Hubbard et al., June 12, 1844.
5. Reference not identified further.
6. Quotation from Samuel Butler, *Hudibras*, part I, canto I, line 189.

## FROM DUFF GREEN[1]

Dear sir                                    Washington (Texas) Jany. 20th 1845
A Mr. Leflore of Mississippi said in New Orleans that Colonel Pillar,[2] a neighbour and friend of yours told him that he was[3] in your confidence, and that your chief difficulty was how to get rid of Mr Calhoun. When I first heard this I considered it one of the many rumors put into circulation by the Benton faction to excite a jealousy in the mind of Mr Calhoun's friends. Upon Enquiry I learn that Colonel Pillar is your intimate and confidential friend.

Laflore's statement therefore assumes a more serious character and the more so as I believe that Wright & Benton have formed a coalition with leading Whigs to organize a new party & present you the alternative of a surrender of the government to them or a bitter & unprincipled opposition. Colonel Pillar's declaration to Laflore is a proof that they have approached you through one confidential friend at least & as most men however eminent for wisdom or experience are disposed to yield to the suggestions of personal friends I confess that as Mr Calhoun's self respect will prevent his doing any thing to counteract their machinations, I am not without my apprehensions that this conspiracy may sow the seed of dissention between you, and that in your desire to conciliate Benton and Wright you may array the south against you. I therefore feel it to be, not only my privilege but my duty to say to you that by continuing Mr Calhoun in the Cabinet you do not necessarily array yourself against Benton & Wright. That he was appointed Secretary of State by the unanimous consent of the Senate for the purpose of taking charge of the negociations in relation to Texas and Oregon and that having taken original and decided measures in relation thereto involving the destiny of the south any arrangement of your Cabinet making it necessary for him to leave the state Department would be to take the side of Benton & Wright and to array all your influence against him and the measures to support which you were elected. If you suppose that by doing so you will promote the public interest or advance your own fame you will in my opinion greatly err.[4] It will be charged that regardless of the obligations arising out of the generous confidence and support of Mr Calhoun and his friends without the excuse of personal feeling you have used the power placed in your hands by him & his friends to gratify the malevolence and promote the personal ends of other men.

Do not my dear sir permit your self leave to take offence. I am no court sycophant. I make no pretense of friendship for you. I have no special claims on your personal confidence, but as one who has devoted many years of an eventful life to the cause of the south, as a citizen of Texas wishing annexation and as one deeply responsible for your election, believing that such a concession to northern prejudice will be fatal to the success of your administration and knowing how difficult it is for honest and truthful opinions to reach one in your exalted station, I have ventured, at the risk of giving offence to do you this service.

If you recieve it in the spirit in which it is dictated you will see that it is an act of friendship. If you have made up your mind to conciliate Benton & his faction at the Expense of Mr Calhoun and his friends it can do no injury.

Duff Green

ALS. DLC–JKP. Addressed to Washington City. Extract published in Tyler, ed., *The Letters and Times of the Tylers*, III, 157. AL, draft, in DLC–AJD.

1. A journalist, politician, and industrial promoter, Green edited the Washington *United States Telegraph* from 1825 until 1836. He followed Calhoun in his break with Andrew Jackson in 1831 and supported Henry Clay for the presidency in 1832. From 1842 until 1844, Green served as an unofficial representa-

tive of the United States in Great Britain and France. Returning to the United States in January 1844, he accepted appointment as U.S. consul at Galveston, Texas. Green subsequently founded the New York *Republic* and in its columns advocated radical free-trade policies and reform of the civil and postal services.

2. Greenwood Leflore and Gideon Pillow. A successful cotton planter and entrepreneur in Mississippi, Leflore was chief of the northwest district of the Choctaw Nation; he served in both the Mississippi House, 1835, and Senate, 1840–44. A Columbia lawyer and general in the Tennessee militia, Pillow played a key role at the 1844 Democratic National Convention. He later served as a general officer in the Mexican War and commanded a Confederate brigade during the Civil War. In his draft of this letter Green mentioned that his source for this information was James Hamilton, Jr. A lawyer and planter, Hamilton served as a member of the U.S. House, 1822–29, and as governor of South Carolina, 1830–32. Initially a supporter of Andrew Jackson, he became an outspoken advocate of free trade and a leader of the states' rights party in South Carolina. Hamilton moved to Russell County, Ala., after the nullification crisis of 1833. Enthusiastic in his support for Texas, he served as one of its European commercial agents and later advocated its annexation to the United States.

3. At this point in his draft Green cancelled the phrase "to be a member of your cabinet."

4. At this place in his draft Green cancelled the phrase "You will be charged that you are acting as the agent of Genl Jackson."

TO THOMAS SHERLOCK ET AL.[1]

Gentlemen:                                        Columbia Tenn. Jany 20th 1845

General Armstrong of Nashville has forwarded to me, your letter of the 13th Instant, addressed to him, enclosing a copy of one to myself.[2] In preparing for my journey to Washington, I have made no arrangements, as to the mode or means of conveyance, except, to request my friends at Nashville to have a Boat at that place on the 1st of February, on which day I propose to set out. If any engagement of a Boat from Louisville (of which you speak in your letter to Genl. Armstrong) has been made, it has been done by my friends. I had desired not to trouble my friends, but to travel in the usual mode in which other citizens do, and presumed that I would find no difficulty at this season of the year in finding Boats ascending the Ohio on which I could take passage. I shall deeply regret it, if any arrangements have been made for my accommodation, by different portions of my friends on the route, which may conflict with each other. It would certainly give me great pleasure to accept the services of the Boat which you kindly tender and take passage on her from Louisville, but this I must leave entirely to yourselves and other friends when I reach Louisville. It may be that the Boat on which I leave Nashville may perform the whole trip, but of this I am not informed.

I thank you gentlemen: for the congratulations which you convey to me upon the result of the late political contest, and for the invitation which you give me, "in the name of the Queen City and of Hamilton County" to "become their guest," for as long a period as I can remain at Cincinnati, on my way to the seat of Government. It gives me sincere pleasure to accept your invitation, as it will to exchange personal salutations, with my fellow-citizens of Cincinnati, and Hamilton County, for a short time as I pass on my journey. In answer to your inquiry in which you desire me to inform you at what time I will leave Louisville, I can only say that I will set out from Nashville on the 1st and will probably reach that City on the 4th or 5th of February, and after a short delay, will proceed on my journey.

JAMES K. POLK

ALS, draft 2. DLC–JKP. Addressed to Cincinnati, Ohio, and marked "Copy." Polk also retained an earlier draft of this letter. ALS, draft 1. DLC–JKP.

1. Sherlock and his partner, Patrick Rogers, served as commission agents for a number of steamboats operating out of Cincinnati.

2. On December 13, 1844, Sherlock and two other Cincinnati Democrats, Gideon M. Ayers and A. W. Anderson, invited Polk to be a guest of the city and offered him the use of the new steamboat *Cincinnati* for his passage on the Ohio River. LS. DLC–JKP.

## FROM SILAS WRIGHT, JR.

My Dear Sir,                                        Albany 21 January 1845

Your letter of the 4th Inst. came to me two days since, and that I might have the test of my own opinion by that of our mutual friend Mr. Van Buren, I have delayed an answer to make an inquiry of him as to the two men in the State to whom he would give the places of Secretary of State and Secretary of the Treasury, in case he was to select both from this State. His answer is, this moment received and is precisely what mine would have been to the same inquiry.

Benjamin F. Butler, whom you very well know, would be my selection for Secretary of State, of all the men I know in New York, and were I the President I should select him for that place from all my acquaintances in the Union. I do not say this, however, because I think you should be governed by the same rule which would govern me. Your location is not mine, and other views, arising from that circumstance, may be controlling with you.

Of Mr. Butler I need say little to you, because you must know him about as well as I do, and General Jackson can tell you all about him, as a cabinet counsellor and confidential adviser and friend. I am sure I can say of him, that, if ever I knew a man "who could wear a window in his breast"[1] he is the man. His experience will add to his value, and his learning and pursuits emminently qualify him for any place, and for that particular place.

If I mistake not, you have had some fear that your failure to offer me that place had given an inclination to my reply to your former letter. That is not so. I do not consider myself qualified for the State Department, as I have never given my attention to our foreign relations to any extent, and have never been connected with diplomatic transactions of any character. If you had offered me that place I should have declined it for that cause, and that you did not was evidence to me of the perfect sincerity of the offer you did make, and in which you judged rightly of my capacity and qualifications, so far as I have those which would fit me for any cabinet position. At the same time, your letter was such as to give that offer all the character of an offer of the first place, and it was more than satisfactory, so far as any personal feeling on my part was concerned. I gave you the true ground of my declination, and every day would satisfy you, if you could be with me, that the course was compulsory upon me.

I am sorry to be compelled to say it to you, but we have a contest, within our own party in this state, in reference to Bank and Internal improvement legislation, which forced me into the position I hold and which, it is already apparent, is to be fought over my head, and it would be ruin to our sound policy and the sound portion of our party for me to flee from it.[2] There has been a strenuous effort to carry our troubles to Washington and to surround you with them, and my predecessor[3] took the advantage of our vacancies in the Senate to send there a man you must recollect, Mr. Foster, who was in the H. of R. in 1837, turned conservative, helped to beat you in the election of printer, and to defeat the passage of the Independent Treasury bill.[4] We have just closed a most heated canvass in the legislature, and have succeeded in recalling him and sending there a man, who, if not so used, I might name to you for either of the places you name and give you one of the best of men, except the want of extensive experience. I mean Genl. John A. Dix. You will find him all you want in the Senate, and we trust his colleague[5] will act with him, though he is not the man we should have selected, if we could have avoided it.

For a Secretary of the Treasury I shall name to you Azariah C. Flagg, at present the comptroller of this State. He is a man as honest and pure as Mr. Butler, and quite as clear sighted and firm, but has not Mr. Butler's education. He was brought up a printer, and edited and printed a news-paper[6] for some dozen years. In 1823 he was first elected to our legis-lature, and in the terrible contest of 1824, which you may recollect was most disasterous to us, he exhibited talent, fidelity, and firmness, which at once marked him for public use. In 1826 he was elected Secretary of State, of this State, which place he continued to hold until 1833, when he succeeded me in the office he now holds. In 1839 the whigs turned him out, but our restoration restored him in 1842.

He has more financial reputation than any man who has succeeded him in that place, and as strong a hold upon the honest democracy of the State as any man in it. His mind is as clear as light and his sagacity and firmness are unsurpassed by any of our public men. He and Dix counselled the removal of the deposites by Genl. Jackson, in 1833, when Mr. V. B. and myself faultered, as the Genl. can tell you.[7] He is amiable as an associate, yielding where principle does not forbid, and always cool and self-possessed. He is invaluable to us here, and I fear I cannot get on without him, and yet justice to him and to you demand that I should not withhold his name from you. I do not doubt he would accept such an offer from you, but I have not intimated to him that I am giving you his name.

His integrity and firm adherence to a sound financial policy make him odious to our gambling politicians, and his re-election to his present of-fice may be resisted by them, and possibly with success. It comes on early in February, and the result must transpire before you can get this letter and reply to it. If he should be defeated, that result should make no difference with your action, as it will be certain to place him higher in the affections of our true democracy. It turns out that our present legislature has not been well selected, because too much was yielded to these disaffected spirits for fear of danger to the great result, and you must not be surprised if you see me compelled to make an issue with it for our people, before the session closes. For our future soundness that may be the best thing, though I hope to avoid it. If Mr. Flagg shall not be re-elected, that result must certainly come.

I have not time to say more and not loose a mail. I might give you var-ious other names, but these two are so far prefered by me that I forbear to name others.

I fear this letter may not reach you at home, though I shall address it to you there. I shall, however, send a brief abridgement of it to your address at Washington, under cover to our friend Johnson, so that if it should miss you, you may, upon reaching there, have the names before you.

The extract you make from my former letter[8] was seriously intended as it was written, and I beg you to believe that nothing will afford me more sincere pleasure, whatever cares and troubles I may find in my new position, than to be able, in any degree, to aid you in meeting those you cannot fail to encounter. In much Haste,

SILAS WRIGHT

N.B. This letter is written in the confidence of this correspondence and I have no time to copy.

ALS. DLC–JKP. Probably addressed to Columbia and marked "*Strictly Private.*"

1. Quotation not identified further.
2. Wright's reference is to the growing division within the New York Democracy between the Hunker and Barnburner factions. The Barnburners, identified with Wright, Martin Van Buren, Azariah Flagg, and John A. Dix, supported the "stop and tax" policy for funding state internal improvements. The Hunkers, associated with William Bouck and Daniel Dickinson, favored a resumption of deficit spending to support New York's internal improvement projects. Drafted as the Democracy's gubernatorial candidate in 1844, Wright strengthened the Democratic presidential ticket in the state; and in recognition of that contribution to his victory in New York Polk offered Wright the post of Treasury secretary in the new administration. Wright declined the cabinet offer and served one term as governor of his state.
3. Reference is to William C. Bouck.
4. Henry A. Foster won election as a Democrat to one term in the U.S. House, 1837–39; however, he broke with the party over the Independent Treasury Bill and supported efforts to depose Francis Blair and John C. Rives as printers of the House. He served as U.S. senator from November 30, 1844, until January 27, 1845, when John A. Dix, a Van Burenite, replaced him.
5. Reference is to Daniel S. Dickinson.
6. *Plattsburgh Republican.*
7. Reference is to Jackson's attack on the Second Bank of the United States in which his administration removed federal deposits and transferred them to state banks. Although Wright and Van Buren initially favored delaying removal, pressure from Jackson and opponents of the bank convinced them to support the president's decision.
8. See Polk to Silas Wright, Jr., January 4, 1845.

## FROM CAVE JOHNSON

Dear Sir                                    Washington 22 Jany 1845

I recd yours of the 13th last evening.[1] This morning I met Mr Buckhanon.[2] He informs me that the President has already issued notice to the Senators for a call session of the Senators after the 4th of March.[3] The law makes it his duty.

The son of Col. Barker former collector of Philadelphia, a lad of 17, shot himself last evening—cause unknown.[4]

The Senate laid on the table today the nomination of Judge King of Pa. & rumor says it will be offered to Mr. Buckhanon.

The debate on Texas will be closed the 25th. We think we can pass it as *a State*, letting her have her lands & pay her debts & admit three other states when the population justifies it—making 36.30 the line between the free & slave states—possibly leaving the divisional line out, for settlement when the three others claim admission. The appointment of Wm.[5] continues to excite much talk.

C. JOHNSON

ALS. DLS–JKP. Probably addressed to Columbia.

1. Polk's letter has not been found.
2. James Buchanan.
3. Reference is to a special session of the Senate called to meet on March 4, 1845, to consider executive appointments. Tyler issued the order for the special session on January 8, 1845.
4. James N. Barker, a native of Philadelphia, Penn., served in the War of 1812, and during the 1820's won election to several terms as alderman and mayor of Philadelphia. In 1829 he accepted appointment as collector of customs in Philadelphia and served in that post until 1838 when he became comptroller of the U.S. Treasury. He occupied that position until his death in 1858. Reference to Barker's son is not identified further.
5. William H. Polk.

## FROM AARON V. BROWN

Dear Sir                                    Washington city Jany [25] 1845[1]

Our annexation resolutions passd this evening by a majority of twenty two. The Tennessee Whigs voted with us, but we had to take it on Milton Brown's resolution.[2] *The distinct friends* of Mr. Wright stood out to the last—you never saw greater excitement. The general impression is that it will pass the Senate. Nothing but Texas has engrossd all minds since I last wrote you.

A. V. BROWN

[P.S.] No action yet on the Major's case.[3]

ALS. DLC–JKP. Addressed to Louisville, Ky., in the care of Thomas J. Read. Extract published in Tyler, ed., *The Letters and Times of the Tylers*, III, 157–58.

1. Brown misdated his letter January 24; corrected date has been identified through content analysis.
2. See Cave Johnson to Polk, January 13, 1845.

3. Reference probably is to William H. Polk's nomination as chargé d'affaires to the Kingdom of the Two Sicilies.

## FROM JACOB L. MARTIN[1]

My dear Sir                                                    Paris 25th January 1845

I am sure that I need not congratulate you to convince you of the gratification which I felt at your election to the elevated place which you are shortly to fill. When I left the U.S. all was dark. Everything portended the defeat of the democratic party. Your nomination was the first ray which brightened the prospect because it indicated the possibility of uniting those elements whose discord threatened the party with destruction. Still we dared not count here upon a favorable result, as nearly all the American travellers whom we saw, being Whigs, expressed the greatest confidence in the election of Mr. Clay. Judge then, how great must have been our delight, when the glad tidings reached us of the triumph of the democratic cause in your person. I, who have enjoyed your friendship, had also personal cause of satisfaction, to which the recollection of your amiable and estimable lady contributed greatly. I will not indulge in phrases, for I am sure you believe, that there is not an American to whom your elevation afforded greater pleasure than it did & does to myself. I took the liberty of sending to you by the last packet a number of the Paris National, which contains a little notice of your history and character, furnished by myself.[2] So little justice was done you, there was so much misrepresentation, or affected ignorance of your merits & claims, that I thought it a duty to furnish my humble testimony in the matter.

You will have seen by the papers what has been done here on the subject of Texas. This government may have been disposed to act with England, but the prudence of the King[3] and above all the anti English feelings of the people, are an effectual check to this tendency. All I fear is that France will join the efforts of England to indispose Texas herself to annexation. This is the quarter from which there is most to be apprehended; not war from this hemisphere, but European intrigue & influence upon the councils of Texas herself. I trust the effect of these exertions will be anticipated by the prompt action of the Congress of the United States. Postponement is replete with danger; everyday's delay renders success more uncertain.

There is one other subject upon which I will permit myself to make a few remarks. American character has suffered much abroad, from the defalcation of some of the states. Much error & prejudice prevail upon this subject, but it is not less the truth, that the national character & with it the republican cause, is affected by these partial shortcomings.

Europeans all express their surprise that the President, shows so little sensibity in the matter as to avoid urging the states to fulfil their obligations. They cannot understand that such advice would be improper & probably have a bad effect. I think however that something might be done with discretion & which would relieve the democratic party from the unjust suspicion or impression which prevails that it is indifferent to the fulfilment of these obligations. I suppose there may be some allusions in the message to the popular condemnation of assumption of state debts.[4] If this be the case, might not the states be gently stimulated to honorable exertions, by an expression of confidence in their fair intentions, & by repelling with something like indignation, the idea that they will prove faithless to their obligation? This could not offend; it might have a good effect; and it would at all events prove to our friends & enemies too, in Europe, that the democratic party is truly that of good faith & integrity, an opinion which I have always entertained, and which I have promulgated here with great confidence. I hope my dear Sir, you will excuse me for making this friendly suggestion, with all due diffidence & respect. I am solicitous for the character of my country & of my party. I have been annoyed at the unjust imputation which have been cast upon both, and I should be most proud & happy, should a return to payment by the delinquent states take place under a republican administration. I am, moreover, & in all sincerity, solicitous from personal grounds, for the character of your administration which I trust will prove *all* what your true friends, of whom I am proud to call myself one, desire. I will trouble you with no more importunate reflections at this moment. Should anything occur worthy of notice, while I am abroad I shall take the liberty of communicating it freely & respectfully. In the mean time I request you to present my most cordial congratulations & compliments to Mrs. Polk ....

J. L. MARTIN

ALS. DLC–JKP. Probably addressed to Washington City.

1. Martin served as secretary of legation at Paris from April 1844 until March 1848, when he was appointed chargé d'affaires to the Papal States. Although he died shortly after taking up his post at the Vatican, he earned the distinction of having been the first United States diplomat to be accredited to the Holy See.

2. Martin's biographical sketch in the Paris *National* is not identified further.

3. Louis Philippe, King of the French, 1830–48. Hailed as the "citizen king" after the Revolution of 1830, Louis Philippe ultimately lost the confidence of the French people for muzzling the press and refusing to broaden the suffrage to include working-class citizens. In the February Revolution of 1848 angry Paris crowds prompted Louis Philippe's abdication and English exile.

4. Reference is to Polk's inaugural address, which included the following passage on the questions of assumption and defalcation of state debts: "Although

the Government of the Union is neither in a legal nor a moral sense bound for the debts of the States, and it would be a violation of our compact of union to assume them, yet we can not but feel a deep interest in seeing all the States meet their public liabilities and pay off their just debts at the earliest practicable period." Richardson, ed., *Messages and Papers of the Presidents,* IV, p. 378.

## FROM WILLIAM C. CAMPBELL[1]

Dear Sir                          Springfield Mo January 28th 1845

I had intended to visit you & my other Friends & Relations in Tennessee Before your departure for Washington but circumstances of a Domestic character have precluded the possiblity of my doing so. I wish you to distinctly understand that I am not an aspirant for office but should like to have the Ear of the president in Relation to the pretentions of some of my Friends in the South West; you must know that although to some extent a private man, I participate largely with you & other friends & Relations in expressing unaffected joy at the Elevation of the pride of the Family to that distinguished Station where have sat *the* most renowned heroes & statesmen that Ancient or modern Times have produced; in reccommending my Friends I shall always make it a Test of qualifications that they are your *sincere friends* & that while I serve others I will augment the Glory & honor of your administration. From the Solicitude I have for the unexcelled prosperity of your administration I hope you will Pardon me for submitting some opinions about the Signs of the Times. This perhaps may raise a Smile on your cheek, but as it is the offering of Friendship I am sure I will find forgiveness in your generous nature. I dislike to see your administration getting into a Domestic War but if necessary, I should like to see you with your sling & your Pebbles marching against the mighty Goliath of Goth: Benton is your Bitter & Sworn enemy—he Had already upon various occasions Sounded the Tocsin, & sworn that upon a certain contingency, he Intended to Explode your administration. Does not confident Expression prove that he has *his* forces behind him & the Scattering & disappointed Remnant of the Vanburen Dynasty. It might be well for you to consider whether the accquiessence of Mr Vanburen in your nomination was seeming *or real*. I strongly conjecture that Lindenwold[2] will be the great central motion of motive so far as opposition to you is concerned. The article that lately appeared in the Missourian attacking you and the Nashville Union bears strange marks upon the face of it of a concerted movement.[3]

There is as you are aware *much* conjecture whether Mr Benton will truccle to your administration as he did to Gnl. Jackson. My own opinion is that he will not; if so it will be merely ostensible not Real. If he

Trucles it will be obvious. It will Render him Contemptible in the Eyes of the Sagacious & Philosophic & this alone will accomplish his over throw. My opinion is that he has taken the *Niaggra Express* & cannot Turn Back. He is therefore determined to give you a Battle & if so to use a homely Phrase it will be like butting his head against a *Black Jack* for Brief experience proves to me that administrations is a most potent *thing*. In the Language of the Father of his country, I was born free. [4] You must therefore indulge me when I speak freely of Benton, & not the least of Reasons in doing so is that he is akeing to disolate & Ruin my family. You have no doubt rept about Bentons remarks on the Baltimore Convention. [5] That too was significant. He talks about Fraud!! Frauds indeed yes there was a fraud but it was *Primary* not *Secondary*. It consisted in the Fact that a few Politicians of the old Dynasty had appointed Delegates not to Enquire who was the proper man for the Nomination!! but to Nominate *Mr Van Burren* & pave the way for the succession. The people saw all this & they Broke Loose Like the Damned up watters, they come Down Like an avelanche from the *Alps* & crushed the hopes of the Dictators. Yours was by acclamation Rather than Nomination. You understand the object of Mr Benton in Introducing his Bill [6] and the attitude in which the Democratic party stands Towards it. It is obvious to the whole South and If you Should Follow in his wake you will hear our deep Toned murmur from one End of the Continent to the other. It more than squints Towards abolitionism; and the South & west at a proper Time will assail the Fortress into which Mr Benton has thrown himself and *crush* his Lucifer like Disposition forever. He calls his Bill a compromise but it is a great compromise of the principles of Liberty & Equality for Political Reasons. The serviles of Benton may Promulgate their doctrine as much as they please but if I am not Lamentably Ignorant, they seem to go for him Because they conceive that he has power to control their political Existance but whenever your position is adverse to his They will flee from him as from the deadly [ ....] [7] It is stricly true that westward that the Star of Empire holds its course. This has Resulted from the Laws of necessity. It has been the course of centuries. Whatever a few servile Politicians may say Bentons Bill finds no favor with the people. The south & west will not suffer theirs to be desecrated with disguised abolitionism & before Texas will submit to Col Bentons Bill their Land will be Bristled over with Bayonets from the Banks of the Sabine to those of the Rio del Nort [8]; yea the deep mouthed cannon will be heard upon that soil which has been poetically Described as the Garden spot of the world. I have much to say to you that I no a Long political Letter is Irksome to a man in your Station. No[w] comes the Rub. General Samuel Hamilton Bunch a nephew of Gov Clays of Ala.

is an applicant for the office of Sub-agent for the osage Indians in the place of Maj Erdman the present Incumbent.[9] He is also a nephew of Col. Saml. Bunch of Tennessee.[10] But you will Reccollect that the former Bunch whose pretentions I am now Sustaining fought hard for you not only in the Late contest but when you was Batteling with Cannon[11] for the office of Gov of Tenn. Also Recommended to your favorable notice James H McBride[12] for Register of Lands at Springfield Mo & can safely say what you can Receive from numerous Sources that he is a man who will not only honour your administration but the Country & would be a valuable acquisition to any Land to which Providence might cast his destiny. Of the present Incumbent I will say but a few words. Suffice it he is the most unscrupulous scoundral that Ever disgraced Cristendom. I must also Insist that General Nicholas R. Smith[13] of Springfield Mo one of your old Constituents & Tenn. Friends should not be forgotten: I would Remind you that you never had a warmer friend, that he was the former Incumbent & was Removed through the influence of the Benton dynasty, merely to aggravate my Brother Jack & thwart him in his Political aspirations. He wants the office of Receiver at this place which is now filled by a non-Resident, an Envenomed & Imbitered Whig, George R. Smith. Nothing more but Remains....

Wm. C. CAMPBELL

ALS. DLC–JKP. Addressed to Washington City and delivered by the hand of Leonard H. Sims.

1. A son of John and Matilda Golden Polk Campbell, William St. Clair Campbell was born in Maury County, Tenn., as were his brothers, John Polk and Ezekiel Madison Campbell; the Campbell brothers moved to southwestern Missouri and in 1835 assisted in the formation of Polk County, where William laid out the town of New Market and subsequently served three years as clerk of the county court, 1835–38; John Polk Campbell, founder of Springfield, Mo., held the post of receiver of public moneys at that place from 1839 to 1842. The Campbell brothers were Polk's first cousins.

2. Upon leaving the presidency in 1841, Martin Van Buren returned to Kinderhook, N.Y., purchased the William Van Ness farm, and renamed it "Lindenwald."

3. Reference to the article in the St. Louis *Missourian* is not identified further.

4. Quotation attributed to George Washington is not identified further.

5. Reference probably is to Thomas H. Benton's letter of June 3, 1844, to the editor of the St. Louis *Missourian*, Ver Planck Van Antwerp. For the text of Benton's letter, see *Niles' National Register*, July 13, 1844.

6. On June 10, 1844, Benton introduced a bill authorizing and advising the president to open negotiations with Mexico and Texas for fixing by treaty a new international boundary west of the Nueces River and for annexing Texas to the United States. Benton's plan also outlined terms under which a portion of Texas,

not to exceed the size of the largest existing state, would be admitted to the Union and the remainder would be accorded territorial status, provided that the new territory's northern half would be forever free of slaveholding.

7. Two words illegible.

8. Misspelling of "Rio Bravo del Norte," commonly known in the United States as the "Rio Grande."

9. Samuel Hamilton Bunch, Clement Comer Clay, and Major Erdman. In 1838 Bunch resided in Madison Township of Polk County, Mo.; in 1842 won election to a two-year term as county sheriff and in 1845 served in the state constitutional convention. A lawyer and Alabama state legislator, Clay won three terms as a Democrat in the U.S. House, 1829–35; he also served as governor of Alabama, 1835–37, and as U.S. Senator, 1837–41. Erdman is not identified further.

10. Samuel Bunch sat in the Tennessee Senate, 1819–25, and in the U.S. House, 1833–37; he supported Hugh L. White's presidential bid in 1836 and subsequently lost his seat in the U.S. House to a Democrat, Abraham McClellan.

11. Newton Cannon, a Williamson County planter and supporter of Henry Clay, ran for the governorship of Tennessee four times; he won in 1835 and 1837 but lost in 1827 and 1839.

12. On December 29, 1845, Polk appointed James H. McBride register of the land office at Springfield, Mo., in place of Joel H. Hayden, removed; Hayden had served in that post since 1838.

13. John Tyler appointed Nicholas R. Smith receiver of public moneys at the Springfield, Mo., land office on August 31, 1842, in place of John Polk Campbell, resigned; Tyler removed Nicholas R. Smith and appointed George R. Smith in his place on January 16, 1844. Polk heeded Campbell's advice and on December 28, 1845, returned Nicholas R. Smith to his receivership.

## FROM AARON V. BROWN

Dear Sir                                        Washington City January 29th 1845

Nothing very material since I wrote you under charge to Mr. T. J. Read of Louisville.[1] Some rumor is prevailing now that Mr Stephenson[2] is to be in the *State* Department & that Govr. Wright has been importuning you to place him there on account of his relationship by marriage with Mr. Van Buren,[3] & that Govr. Fairfield of Maine is [to] take care of *the ships*. This *last rumor* I have no patience to listen to since he was so active in our house in the day of passing the Texas resolutions exhorting his representatives to go against it. The Morning news (of the Wright clique) of this morning[4] is *backing his oars* & we think it likely enough that both Senators from N.Y.[5] will go for the resolutions. I send you the N. York Herald marked, that you may read as you come up the river how anexation was received in that city.[6] Dr. Gwin is anxious for you to get here as early as possible so as to give time for a messenger to go to

Mississippi in time to commission *Walker's successor*. This is taking it for granted that W. will be one, which he does on his own responsibility & wish the express declaration that I knew nothing about it. I suppose he is very anxious to be Senator & I think he would make a very good & efficient one. He has a fine tact in such a situation.

A. V. Brown

ALS. DLC–JKP. Addressed to Cincinnati, Ohio.
1. Reference is to Aaron V. Brown to Polk, January 24, 1845. A staunch Jacksonian, Thomas J. Read moved from Nashville to Louisville in 1835 and became a wealthy commission merchant.
2. Andrew Stevenson.
3. Reference not identified further.
4. Reference is to the *New York Morning News*, founded in 1844 by John L. O'Sullivan and Samuel J. Tilden.
5. John A. Dix and Daniel S. Dickinson.
6. The enclosure has not been found; Brown's point of reference probably is to the *New York Herald* of January 26, 1845, which reported that despite the division of popular opinion on annexation, a large crowd of enthusiastic Democrats favoring Texas annexation rallied at Tammany Hall on January 24.

## TO GEORGE BANCROFT

My Dear Sir:                                    Nashville Ten. Jany 30th 1845
I seize a moment of leisure to acknowledge the receipt of your letter of the 1st Inst. I will leave here on the 1st Feby. (two days hence) for Washington. I will travel by the usual route and will make no delays, on the journey which can be avoided. I think I will be able to reach Washington between the 12th and 15th of February, and would be pleased to meet there about that time. I desire to have a personal interview with you shortly after I arrive, and hope it may be convenient for you to visit Washington, at that time. As regards the composition of my cabinet, I have received suggestions from many of my friends, but have kept my own councils and am wholly uncommitted. I know nothing of the cliques (if any such there be) of which so much is said in the newspapers, and will know nothing of them as such. When I reach Washington I will survey the whole ground, and make such selections, as in my judgment will be proper, & such as I hope may satisfy the country. Before I decide I desire to see and confer with you. Hoping to have the opportunity to do so.

James K. Polk

ALS. MHi. Addressed to Boston, and marked *"Private & Confidential."*

## TO MARTIN VAN BUREN

My Dear Sir:                                    Nashville Ten. Jany 30th 1845

On my arrival here on yesterday, on my way to Washington I was much gratified to receive your letter,[1] and thank you for the valuable suggestions which it contains. I will visit *Genl. Jackson* to day, and will leave for Washington on the 1st Feby. I will travel by the usual route, and will make no delays, on the journey which can be avoided. I think I will be able to be at Washington between the 12th and 15th Feby, when I shall be pleased to receive any additional suggestions which you may think it useful to make. I think it probable, that I may invite one of the gentlemen mentioned, to a place in my cabinet, but which one of them, I think it prudent to leave open until I reach Washington. Hoping to hear from you again, shortly after my arrival at Washington ....

JAMES K. POLK

ALS. DLC–MVB. Addressed to Lindenwald, N.Y., and marked "Confidential."

1. See Martin Van Buren to Polk, January 18, 1845.

# FEBRUARY

## FROM ANDREW J. DONELSON

Dr Sir,                                          New Orleans Feby. 1st 1845

I have returned to this place on leave of absence to settle some private business, and will have to go to Nashville to join my wife,[1] before going again to Texas.

A confidential letter from Genl Jackson met me here, making some suggestions in regard to my future connection with the public service. Of his views you are better advised than I am. So far as they relate to myself, I will say nothing until I see him, which I hope to do in seven or eight days, and after which I shall write to you.

As far as the action of Texas is necessary to secure the measure of re-annexation, there is no danger for the present, not even if our Congress does nothing this session. But if you should fail after making the honest effort expected of you by the people, the question must be lost.

I say nothing of what I have done. Of this you will of course be advised when you reach the city.

A. J. DONELSON

[P.S.] I hope you will not have decided on your Cabinet until after I have seen Genl Jackson, and can write you. AJD

ALS. DLC–JKP. Addressed to Washington City and marked *Private*.
1. Elizabeth Martin Randolph Donelson.

*80*

## FROM CAVE JOHNSON

Dear Sir                                    Washington 3 Feby [1845][1]

I was informed that the Democrats of this district would meet you probably at the Railroad depot & take you to your lodgings & would address you &c. I hinted to one of my friends that possibly you might like to see their address & have a little time to think of the reply. I have been furnished with it and enclose it.[2]

We have but little of interest here beyond the speculations of those interested in the question of who is to be uppermost. Each one speculates according to his own interests & wishes. Your silence upon these subjects gives great satisfaction to your friends both North & South. I doubt whether this division of the Democratic party can be reconciled. Texas you will see passed the House—14 of N.Y. demo's against it.[3] This arose from the fact, that there are Ten Districts (Congressional) in the State, in which the *abolitionists hold the balance*—voting for annexation threw[4] them on the side of the Whigs, which would loose us the State of N.Y.

We shall pass Oregon today.[5] Jas. Walker is here. Lucian Brown is here, pressing the removal of Winchester[6] at Memphis. I have thought it prudent to decline interfering & I believe AVB[7] also, for the reasons I have heretofore assigned.

C. Johnson

[P.S.] Wm.[8] will be confirmed before you receive this.

ALS. DLC–JKP. Addressed to Wheeling.
1. Johnson mistakenly dated his letter "1844"; corrected date has been identified through content analysis.
2. Enclosure not found. A Democratic reception committee met Polk at the Washington City railroad depot upon his arrival on February 13, 1845.
3. On January 25th the U.S. House passed a joint resolution for the annexation of Texas to the United States; New York Democrats divided ten for and fourteen against.
4. Syntax garbled. Johnson probably meant to write "would throw" in place of "threw."
5. The Oregon Bill requested that the president give notice to Great Britain that the United States intended to annul the 1827 convention regarding the Oregon Territory.
6. John Lucian Brown and Marcus B. Winchester. Brown, a Nashville lawyer, was active as a commissary officer in both the Mexican and Civil wars. Winchester had served as postmaster at Memphis since 1836.

7. Aaron V. Brown.
8. William H. Polk.

## FROM DUTEE J. PEARCE[1]

Newport, R.I. February 3, 1845

Pearce analyzes the presidential campaign in New Jersey and discusses patronage and party politics in Rhode Island. Disappointed by the election results in New Jersey, he attributes the Whig victory there to Stockton's prominent role in the campaign.[2] Because of Stockton's relationship to "the great corporation monopolies" in the state and his ties to Harrison and later to John Tyler, many New Jersey Democrats refused to follow his lead. Pearce attacks Tylerite office holders in Rhode Island and advises Polk on customs house appointments and candidates for collector of customs at Newport, R.I. He notes that recent turmoil has created new coalitions in state politics. At the beginning of the suffrage movement, about one-fourth of the Rhode Island Democrats left the party and joined the Whigs in forming "the *Law* and *Order* party."[3] By pursuing "a judicious and conciliatory course," the party could win back many of these former Democrats, but Pearce admits that there are "many rabid, crazy *Dorrites* in our ranks" who oppose this strategy.

ALS. DLC–JKP. Probably addressed to Washington City.

1. A Democrat and lawyer from Newport, R.I., Dutee J. Pearce won election to six terms in the U.S. House, 1825–37.

2. A supporter of William Henry Harrison in 1840, Robert F. Stockton backed John R. Thomson, his brother-in-law and Tyler Democrat, for the governorship of New Jersey and Polk for the presidency. Closely identified with canal and railroad interests in New Jersey, Stockton had invested heavily in the Delaware and Raritan Canal and in the Camden & Amboy Railroad. Better known for his naval service, Stockton received a midshipman's appointment in 1811; rose to the rank of commander while serving in the Mediterranean squadron, 1816–21; took an extended duty leave from 1828 until 1838; commanded the U.S.S. *Princeton* when in 1844 its gun, the Peacemaker, exploded and killed the secretary of state, Abel P. Upshur, and the secretary of the navy, Thomas W. Gilmer; directed sea and land operations clearing California of Mexican control in 1846–47; resigned from the navy in 1850; and won election as a Democrat to the U.S. Senate in 1851.

3. Popular dissatisfaction with suffrage restrictions led to Rhode Island's "Dorr Rebellion" of 1841–42. In late 1841 a popular but extralegal convention framed and ratified a "People's Constitution," which provided for white manhood suffrage and new elections; Thomas W. Dorr won the new constitution's gubernatorial election. The Rhode Island legislature, however, declared the new constitution illegal and sponsored a regularly scheduled spring election under authority of the colonial charter of 1663. Incumbent governor, Samuel W. King, gained reelection under the old charter. Both Dorr and King applied to John Tyler for military aid. Tyler backed King, but urged him to exercise conciliation

and restraint. On May 18, 1842, the Dorrites attempted and failed to seize the state's militia arsenal. As a result of the "Dorr Rebellion," Rhode Island's Whigs and many Democrats united against the more radical "Dorrite" Democrats in the 1844 campaign.

## FROM JOHN CATRON[1]

My dear sir                                    Washington, Feby. 4, 1845

I had the pleasure to receive your two last letters, acknowledging the procurement of lodgings, & on another confidential matter.[2] The dates not recollected—as they were read, & burnt—as all confidential letters are. Things are in statu quo[3] here and will so remain until you reach the City, I think to a certainty. The senate will not act on Mr Tyler's appointments in but few cases if any, and the two Houses are very much engaged, & absorbed with the Texas and Oregon bills—the first in the Senate from the House—the other fiercely contested in the House. I think it may pass, & hope it will. Some fretting took place at your *silence* on my first coming here. It has done you service. *The new generation,* are not in an attitude to prefer the claim of advisers, and are Jealous of the exercise of such a prevellege by those older and higher in name. At this time, there is more repose than I had hoped for two mo. ago. I have not noticed a bubble on the surface within two weeks. James Walker is here and concurs with my views that firm adherence to this course will in all probability be necessary for a week after you reach here. Bear in mind I am no politician, and may be mistaken: and that I speak from my own Judgment almost unaided. Of one thing I am absolutely certain, that you must begin as *absolute* master of your will, if this be possible, in forming your cabinet. *Strength* it must have, and men in it that will work in harmony: This done and you are perfectly safe, regardless of fretting for a brief space. The *old* dare not, as the young will overthrow them, and the young, set up no claim to such assumption.

Wednesday 5th. The Texas question is waxing fierce in the Senate. Col. Benton has moved to day, in a form adverse to the resolution before the Senate from the House by one of his own in truth much better[4]; he is seeking to be rectus[5]: though in bad temper generally on this subject he will not go off, as some of our friends have apprehended. They have looked to the turbulent and vigorous *will,* without duly appreciating the conservative, and conciliatory spirit lying beneath, personal enmities aside—terrible towards Presdt Tyler, & Secy Calhoun.

A word on ceremonies. To avoid the annoyance of petty committee arrangements, I think you had better come here at a time if it may be, not to be known certainly. By the Stoppages on the road, and answers

to inquires you may possibly escape. Gnl. Hunter[6] advises this. Your
appointments at Gadsby's—Coleman's[7] of course are ready. From 15th
to 20th is the time I name to Mr. Coleman, but the earlier time probably.
The very rough weather here may disappoint the anticipated speed, & I
think & very much fear will, if you have the like west.

You will find things some smoother here than I anticipated—or you
either I think.

You say you'l see me when you come; if you mean by this that with
me you are to dot your i's, I can only say, that my sole wish is a good
beginning on your own account, & that as a politician I am of very little
value. In regard to men, or self, *I have not a wish,* nor has anyone urged
at me to help him.

J. Catron

[P.S.] Say to Mrs. P. She is sure of ice for next summer. J.C.

ALS. DLC–JKP. Addressed to Wheeling, Va.
1. Appointed to the U.S. Supreme Court in the last days of the Jackson administration, John Catron was one of Polk's staunch political friends. A native
Tennessean, he helped the *Nashville Union* financially and occasionally wrote
editorials for it.
2. Polk's "confidential matter" is not identified further.
3. Latin phrase meaning "in the condition in which it was."
4. On February 5, 1845, Thomas Hart Benton introduced in the Senate a bill
for the annexation of Texas. Intended as a substitute for his annexation bill of
December 10, 1844, this new set of resolutions contained no mention of slavery
in the territory of Texas.
5. Latin legal term meaning "right."
6. Reference probably is to Alexander Hunter, who served as U.S. marshal for
the District of Columbia from 1834 until 1848.
7. Catron's reference is to the National Hotel, formerly Gadsby's Hotel, in
Washington City. Patrons of the hotel often referred to it as Coleman's, for the
proprietor Samuel S. Coleman.

## FROM NATHANIEL C. READ[1]

Dear Sir,                                   Cincinnati Feby. 4. [18]45
I am appointed to address you on your reception at Cincinnati.
I shall welcome you as president of the Whole *People*. I shall congratulate you and ourselves on your election, as having put in issue and settled
the following great questions, which we deem essential to the welfare if
not the very existance of our Free Institutions.
A strict construction of the constitution of the U.S. That the General
government and the State Governments have each their own sphere of

action and that the States are to be respected in all their rights, sovereign as well as guaranteed under the constitution and that the peculiar institutions of none shall be improperly interfered with. That there shall be no National Bank. No assumption of the State debts. No distribution of the proceeds of the public lands among the several states. That there shall be a Revenue Tariff only, with such incidental protection as may be fairly extended to Agriculture, Manufactures, Commerce &c., or may be done without injury to any particular class of the community, or that shall not operate unequally and oppressively upon any particular portion of the union. That Texas shall be annexed. That our right over Oregon be immediately asserted. That the Naturalization laws shall not be altered to extend the time of Citizenship,[2] but that our Country shall remain the asylum, and that the same liberal policy shall be extended, which has heretofor been pursued, towards the down trodden of the earth, who may seek an asylum our shores.

These were questions of direct issue. There are a thousand other great principles of human Liberty, benevolence and charity to man which are always reasserted in every triumph of Democracy. That government was made for man and not man for Government. That there shall be no special privileges, no monopolies but that all shall be protected alike. That Government is to protect men in what they acquire, in their rights and not disigned to build up classes and that it has not the power to make men rich, but only to give all an equal chance by protecting all and suffering an interference with none.

I shall refer to the great principles asserted in the Declaration of Independence that every people have the inherant right to Govern themselves, to alter and modify their government to promote their welfare, which I regard as having been violated in the case of Dorr.[3] I shall not probably mention Dorr, but only the principles which includes his case.

Having been engaged with us in the great struggle of truth and right, and by your firmness, your ability, your devotion to the cause of truth and free government having proven yourself worthy to be the leader in the great cause of free government and human rights, we welcome you with full and glad hearts.

My address will be brief of course.

Wishing you a safe and pleasant arrival ....

N. C. READ

ALS. DLC–JKP. Probably addressed to Louisville, Ky.

1. A Democrat from Hamilton County, Read served on the Ohio Supreme Court from 1842 until 1849.

2. In the 1844 presidential campaign the Whig party proposed to lengthen the residency requirement for naturalization from five to twenty-one years.

3. A lawyer from Providence, R.I., Thomas Dorr first served in the state legislature in 1834; became a leader of the Rhode Island Sufferage Association in 1840; won the 1842 gubernatorial election conducted under the state's new constitution; but failed to secure control of the state militia when the Whigs contested the new constitution and Dorr's gubernatorial election thereunder. In 1844 Dorr went to jail a convicted traitor, but the following year the state legislature passed a general amnesty and gave him his freedom.

## FROM JOHN F. RYLAND[1]

Lexington, Mo. February 5, 1845

After congratulating Polk on his election victory, Ryland emphasizes the need to use great caution in all dealings with Thomas H. Benton and reminds Polk that Benton has passionately attacked not only the actions of the Democratic National Convention but also "the movers and promoters" of the Nashville convention.[2] Noting that Benton gained control over patronage in Missouri during the Van Buren administration, Ryland claims that Benton's power to reward and to punish is the key to his influence in the state. He believes that Benton no longer enjoys the confidence of "the great mass of the people" in Missouri. Ryland adds that the Texas question "has shorn the locks of this political Sampson."

ALS. DLC–JKP. Addressed to Washington City.
1. Ryland, a lawyer from Lexington, Mo., served as a circuit court judge, 1831–48, and as an associate justice of the Missouri Supreme Court, 1848–57.
2. On August 15, 1844, a mass meeting of approximately 35,000 Democrats gathered in Nashville to support Polk and Texas annexation.

## FROM JOHN P. CAMPBELL

Col. Jas K Polk                    Sreave Port La February 6th 1845

Knowing that you will be crowded with communications, I will say, but a few words to you at this time, but will Explain to you when I visit washington which will be shortly as I have business there. Permit me in the first place to advise you to keep your Eye particularly on T H Benton, for assassin like, he has been stabing you in the back in Mo. and will continue to do so. Keep your Eye on the Executive of Mo. & his influence. For the Executive, the Legislative & Judicial influence will be used on you for the purpose of advancing the interest of a certain Junta in the State of Mo.[1] and prostrating all who are opposed to them. The latter are your real friends, and the former in reality your Enemies and T H Benton stands at their head. As Evidence of this fact I will refer you to his letter, addressed to Genl. Van Antwerp, Editor of the Missourian,[2] his organ, on the subject of your nomination. In which he says "that the procedings of the Baltimore convention (that nominated you) Nulified the choice of the people, the rights of the people & the verry principles of our government. But Mo. must go for Polk by Ten thousand votes not saying one word to the Democracy of the balance of the states."[3] I have a great many things to say to you but as before stated I will explain more fully when I see you.

JOHN P. CAMPBELL

ALS. DLC–JKP. Addressed to Washington City.

1. Reference probably is to the "Hards," a faction in Missouri politics which favored an all metallic currency and sought strict convertibility on bank-note issues. Their opposition, the "Softs," preferred generous issues of bank papers and easy credit practices during periods of business contractions.

2. Editor of the St. Louis *Missourian* from 1843 until 1846, Ver Planck Van Antwerp accepted appointment as receiver of public monies for the Territory of Iowa in 1846.

3. Campbell provides a loose paraphrase of Thomas Hart Benton's letter of June 3, 1844, to V. P. Van Antwerp. Benton's letter was published in *Niles National Register,* July 13, 1844.

## FROM ANDREW JACKSON

My dear Sir,                                        Hermitage Febry 7th 1845

Inclosed I send you the letter of the Revd. Mr. John D. Mathews[1] with the copy of Doctor Youngs letter to Mr. Mathews.[2] It exceeds all acts of tyrany & proscription I have heard of throughout all the political struggles we have passed. If it can be done with propriety, I hope Mr. Mathews May receive the appointment of chaplain to the Military academy. It is time that some care should be taken, to prevent the military academy from becoming the hot bed of aristocracy, and to prevent this the chaplain ought not to be a modern Whigg, which is synonimous to Federalism or aristocracy.

I think the case of the Revd. Mr. Mathews is one that demands notice & rebuke by all the democracy, and the interest of the Military academy will be benefitted by placing Mr. Mathews there, which I hope, if it can be done with propriety, may be done. We all salute you & yrs ....

ANDREW JACKSON

ALS. DLC–JKP. Addressed to Washington City.

1. A Presbyterian minister who had supported Polk in the 1844 election, John D. Matthews fell into disfavor with the Whigs and lost his bid to be elected chaplain of the Kentucky House of Representatives. In his letter of February 1, 1845, to Andrew Jackson, Matthews requested aid in securing the chaplaincy at the United States Military Academy at West Point. Matthews reminded Jackson

that the current chaplain "is, or was, a whig" and that the cadets were under undo Whig influence.

2. John L. Young, who was a Presbyterian minister and president of Centre College in Danville, Ky., wrote Matthews on January 8, 1845, and attributed his fellow clergyman's defeat to Whig intrigue.

## FROM MINER K. KELLOGG[1]

My dear Sir,                                              Constantinople Feb. 7. 1845

It gives me the greatest pleasure to congratulate you upon the result of the Presidential Election. The office has been conferred upon you emphatically by *the People*. I need hardly tell you how much I am gratified; you know so well my political sentiments which have not changed since I was at the Hermitage.

Your Election was a source of much surprize to the English, and they exhibit great ignorance of our people and government as well as their ill feelings towards them whenever they speak of the result of the late Election. When I was in Messina, on the island of Sicily I dined in company with several Englishmen at the Victoria Hotel. One of them took occasion to speak of American affairs and asked me if I did not think that our country would soon share the fate of all former Republics? Whether the people would not find it much better to have a King to rule over them as it was so difficult to elect a good and capable man as their President? I answered that I knew of no former Republic like our own and therefore could not exactly comprehend his meaning, but as far as I could judge of the feelings of our people, they were growing more and more averse to Kingly forms of Govt. and more jealous of the privilege they enjoyed of ruling themselves as they thought proper. "But" says he "they are not the best judges of what is good for them for they have just elected that Polk whom nobody knows in preference to Henry Clay who is well known in Europe and is one of the greatest men in the U. States." I gave him to understand that the American People knew very well who Mr Polk was and they did not choose their President from among those who were most popular in Europe because they believed themselves more capable of judging rightly in the matter than those who have always opposed and even villified their Republican Institutions; that it was probable Mr. Polk would be well known in England before the expiration of his term of office Etcetera. He was quite surprized to find a Polkite so far from home, as nearly all American travellers are of the Whig school.

I wrote you a letter last summer from Florence, after my return from Egypt Syria & the Holy Land.[2] I left Florence for this place last Decr and am pursing my profession in the hope of collecting much valuable knowledge. Our Minister Mr. Carr[3] is most kindly disposed towards me, and anxious to forward my wishes to the extent of his power. He can introduce me into many places where I have a great desire to go in search of novel and interesting subjects for my brush. If possible I will paint a portrait of the Sultan,[4] and thus introduce the first specimen of American Art into the Turkish Dominions.

Mr. Carr has made himself quite popular with the Turkish Govt. by his candor and good spirit. His course of diplomacy has given the Americans here good cause to rejoice that their minister is determined to place his Govt upon an equality with the "Five great Powers" who have so long held, as 'twere, the Sublime Port under their especial protection.[5] He demands for his countrymen "all the rights and privileges enjoyed by the most favored nations." If however, the office of Minister could be raised to that of Min. Plenipoy, there is no doubt in my mind but that our Country would find its reward in so doing. Everything with the Turk is governed by external appearances and the power and respectability of a nation is measured in a great degree, by the *rank* of the official personage who represents her interests at the Capitol. As this court has now become the principal arena of European Diplomacy, it is highly essential that we should be placed in such a position as the growing commerce of our Country in this part of the World so much requires. When I came here I had no idea it was so difficult for a stranger to make headway in his profession without the aid and countenance of the Legation of his country. Everything goes by favour and influence. Our yankee enterprize is sufficient to penetrate into the most remote countries, if it is only seconded and protected by our Government. If we only had the advantages afforded by other Powers to their citizens, our manufactures and inventions would soon rival those of any others in all the markets of the East. Even without this aid, it is surprizing how many American productions have found their way into these distant regions. As an instance, New England Rum, calicoes, and other articles, have been carried into the interior of Persia! and exchanged for the commodities of that country; and yet we have not even a Treaty with it, and of course not a single consular or other Government agent there to assist and protect our citizens in their commercial intercourse. Now with a country containing a population of upwards of 11,000,000 people, our manufactures and products might find a most extensive and valuable outlet if we could be placed upon an equal footing with the European Powers, all of whom have treaties with Persia. The English are deriving great advantages therefrom. I heartily wish that the honor of forming a Treaty with Persia could be placed to the credit of your administration.

I speak freely to you upon these subjects, knowing that whatever is of interest to our common country will be acceptable to you.

It is now more than four years since I left America and I feel anxious to see my native land again. I hope that I may return in time to visit you in the White House, and give you some account of the manner in which I have spent my time abroad, for I look upon you as having done much towards sending me out here.

Knowing the value of your time I cannot ask you to do me the honor of acknowledging the receipt of this, though it would give me much happiness. My address is Florence, Italy, where I still retain my studio.

I beg you to make my very best regards acceptable to Mrs. Polk.

With every wish for the health and happiness of yourself and Mrs Polk and for the honor and prosperity of our country under your administration . . . .

MINER K. KELLOGG

ALS. DLC–JKP. Addressed to Washington City.

1. American author, traveler, and artist, Kellogg painted portraits of Andrew Jackson, Martin Van Buren, and Polk in 1840. In 1848 he painted another portrait of Polk and one of Sarah C. Polk.

2. See Kellogg to Polk, July 17, 1844.

3. A Jacksonian Democrat, Dabney S. Carr served as naval officer for the port of Baltimore from 1829 until 1843, and as minister to Turkey from 1843 until 1850.

4. Abdul-Medjid I, sultan of Turkey from 1839 until 1861, was greatly influenced by Western-style reform advisors, as well as European diplomats.

5. Kellogg's reference is to the Straits Convention of 1841, which prohibited passage of warships through the Bosporus and Dardanelles in peacetime. Signatories of the Convention included the five great powers of the post-Napoleonic "Concert of Europe," Austria, France, Great Britain, Prussia, and Russia.

## FROM GORHAM PARKS[1]

Sir,                              Bangor Me. February 7th 1845

As the time is now approaching when you must make a selection of your cabinet, I presume to address you on that subject.

I suppose you will wish to take some one from New England as a member of it, and I doubt not that if any gentleman of suitable capacity and talents was offered from Maine, you would be pleased to reward the Democracy of our State, by taking one of her own sons for that distinguished station. Maine I understand has two of her Citizens offered to your consideration.[2] You must permit me to observe without further remarks, that I do not think any considerable portion of our party either desire or expect any cabinet appointment from Maine. Few men can refuse a recommendation for a friend whatever may be the expediency in their opinion of complying with their own request.

Going out of Maine, then whom have we from whom you can select. Messrs Woodbury of New Hampshire, and Henshaw Morton[3] and Bancroft of Mass. With Mr Woodbury you are well acquainted, and he needs no recommendation therefore to you. If you select him it would be satisfactory to a great many people and fully so to me, but I have supposed Mr. Woodbury did not desire the place. We come then to Mass. If I understand Mr Morton, his abolition tendencies ought to prevent his appointment. Mr Bancroft is not supposed to possess the least administrative talent, and if made a secretary where common labor and business talent was required would be found wholly incompetent. I look on Mr Henshaw as better fitted to fill the places of Secretary of the Treasury Navy or Postmaster General than any man in New England or in truth than any man I know in the Union. His habits of business are very great, his natural adaptation to it greater, his capacity his enemies have felt and acknowledged. What objection arises then. He has already been rejected by the Senate[4] and is a Calhoun man. What does the first amount to. Every one in New England knows that the secret charges preferred against Mr Henshaw were all untrue and would not bear the light an hour. Every Whig in Boston from Harrison Gray Otis[5] down would indorse Henshaws honesty, and so fixed is his reputation in that respect that his rejection did not injure him in the least. It was attacking him on a point where he was invulnerable. Then as to the second objection. You cannot but be aware what is meant in New England as a Calhoun man. It is an epithet bestowed by Mr Van Burens ultra friends on all who did not believe Mr Van Buren could be elected and who preferred their principle to a man. In fine it comprehends all your supporters in New England. No one supposed that if Mr Van Buren was laid aside Mr Calhoun could be taken up. We all knew (Mr Henshaw most certainly) that Mr Van Burens friends would never consent to have him laid aside and Mr Calhoun taken up. But those who did have the courage to state their honest convictions that Mr Van Buren could not be chosen, (a fact which no one now denies) ought not *at your hands* to be treated worse than those who were willing to sacrifice their party and their principles to advance one man, nor ought the friends and supporters of the annexation of Texas to be excommunicated by you from the Democratic political Church. I have stated all the objections that will be urged to Mr Henshaw. I do not know that Mr Henshaw wants the place; he has never directly or indirectly so intimated to me. I send this letter not to him but to one of his friends.[6] But I assure you in all the honesty *you know* I have, and in all the *sincerity* I used to you before your deserved elevation that Mr Henshaw is the only man I know of in New England excepting Mr Woodbury fit to go into your Cabinet and that of the two I should prefer Mr. H. If you appoint him you will find him no Calhoun Man no Van Buren man but the strong vigorous energetic honest and able supporter of your administration, bringing to the duties devolved on him a penetrating sagacity a capability to discover intrigue and frustrate corruption who with sterling integrity and laborious habits and powerful understanding make him [in] every way one of those men whom a President desires of the welfare of a great nation and of an economical administration of the Government would delight to call about him.

I feel Dear Sir, as if I had now done my duty by you, may your course be as glorious to yourself, as honorable to your country and as satisfactory to your friends, as even yourself in your most ardent aspirations can desire.

GORHAM PARKS

ALS. DLC–JKP. Addressed to Washington City.

1. A lawyer from Bangor, Maine, Parks won election to two terms in the U.S. House, 1833–37; served three years as U.S. marshal for the Maine district, 1838–41, and two years as U.S. attorney, 1843–45. Polk appointed Parks U.S. consul at Rio de Janeiro in 1845, and he served in that post for four years.

2. John Fairfield and Nathan Weston. An Augusta lawyer, Weston served on the Maine Supreme Court as an associate justice from 1820 until 1834 and as chief justice from 1834 until 1841.

3. David Henshaw and Marcus Morton. A successful Boston businessman and founder of the Democratic *Boston Statesman,* Henshaw held numerous state and federal offices: member of both the Massachusetts Senate, 1826–27, and House, 1839–40; collector of the port of Boston, 1830–37; and ad interim secretary of the navy, 1843–44. A lawyer from Taunton, Mass., Morton won election to two terms in the U.S. House, 1817–21, and to four terms as governor of Massachusetts, 1840–41 and 1843–44; he served as customs collector in Boston from 1845 until 1849.

4. The Senate overwhelmingly rejected Henshaw's nomination as secretary of the navy on January 15, 1844.

5. A wealthy and influential Bostonian, Otis held numerous local, state, and federal offices; once a staunch Federalist, he subsequently became an equally partisan Whig.

6. Parks apparently sent the letter to Nathaniel Greene, the postmaster of Boston, who then forwarded it to Polk stamped "Free" and bearing the postmark of February 12th. Greene, a protégé of David Henshaw, edited the *Boston Statesman* from 1821 until his appointment in 1829 as postmaster of Boston, a

position that he retained during the Jackson, Van Buren, and Polk administrations.

## FROM ANDREW JACKSON

My dear Sir,                                          Hermitage February 8th 1845
    I take the liberty of enclosing you a letter just received from the Honble Henry L. Pinckney So Carolina.[1] It will bring to your view the manner he was removed by Genl Harrison, & his wishes to be restored to the collectors office of Charleston, from which he was so unceremoneously removed. There is in this, a clear case, of retributive Justice to have him restored to the office. And I know when the time arrives for your action upon such cases, Justice will be done in this case.
    Since you left me my shortness of breath has increased. May god bless & guide you throughout yr administration is the constant prayer of yr friend.

                                                        ANDREW JACKSON

P.S. By letter from Mr Laughlin from Louisville[2] I am advised of your movements & incidents. Give him my respects, I cannot write him, and with all our kind salutations to Mrs. Polk, say to her how much we approve her conduct in putting down the desecration of the Sabath near Smithland.[3] Say to her carry this thro' your whole administration & god will smile upon you & her, and the whole United States will approve & rejoice. If Mr. Laughin would publish a short Journal of your trip with this incident it would relieve you from visits on the Sabath. When received, separate this P.S. from the letter. A.J.


    ALS. DLC–JKP. Addressed to Washington City.
    1. Pinckney requested Jackson's assistance in regaining the Charleston collectorship. Henry L. Pinckney to Andrew Jackson, January 29, 1845. ALS. DLC–JKP. Founder and one-time editor of the *Charleston Mercury*, Pinckney won election to several terms in the South Carolina legislature, 1816–32; sat for two terms in the U.S. House, 1833–37; served twice as mayor of Charleston, 1837–40; and headed the customs house in Charleston from 1840 until his removal two years later.
    2. Samuel H. Laughlin's letter to Jackson has not been found.
    3. Perhaps wishing to blunt Sabbatarian criticism of the inauguration party's traveling on Sunday, Sarah Polk refused to allow a musical performance on board the steamboat, which had stopped at Smithland, Ky., on Sunday, February 2. Anson and Fanny Nelson, *Memorials of Sarah Childress Polk* (New York: Anson D. F. Randolph & Company, 1892), p. 81.

## TO CAVE JOHNSON

Sunday night

My Dear Sir:                    Wheeling Virginia Feby 9th 1845

I reached here at dark to night, and will proceed on my journey tomorrow. I expect to be at *Cumberland* on wednesday night, and at Washington on thursday night. I will not go to Baltimore, but will change cars at the Relay-House and proceed directly to Washington. I have recd. your letter of the 3rd addressed to me at this place. During my journey, I have whenever I could do so, avoided meeting committees and responding to addresses, and would prefer to do so on my arrival at Washington. At Cincinati I was compelled to make a short response, but said nothing political.[1]

I saw your brother & *Mr Garland* & *Dortch* at Clarksville,[2] and learned from them that *Mrs. Johnson*[3] had been slightly indisposed, but was much better than she had been, and would soon be entirely well.

JAMES K. POLK

ALS. PHi. Addressed to Washington City.

1. In a brief response to a welcome address by Nathaniel C. Read, Polk repeated his intention to be president of the whole people, not just of those who supported his election.

2. Polk's reference is probably to Willie B. Johnson, Hudson Garland, and James N. Dortch. A Clarksville lawyer, Johnson sat in the Tennessee Senate for one term, 1835–37, and served for twelve years as attorney general for Tennessee's Seventh Judicial District, 1839–51. Garland, a native of Virginia, established a law practice in Clarksville, where he took an active part in local politics. Cave Johnson's brother-in-law, Dortch ran unsuccessfully for a seat in the Tennessee House in 1841.

3. Polk's reference is to Cave Johnson's wife, Elizabeth Dortch Brunson Johnson.

## FROM GEORGE BANCROFT

My dear Sir,                    Boston. Feb. 10. 1845

Deeply honored by the communication which I have just received from you,[1] I shall leave this city on Thursday morning, and hope to reach Washington on Saturday the fifteenth. I shall lose no time in joining in the welcome which the whole Democracy extends to its President Elect.

GEORGE BANCROFT

ALS. DLC–JKP. Addressed to Washington City.

1. See Polk to George Bancroft, January 30, 1845.

FROM LEVIN H. COE[1]

Dear Sir                                                        Memphis Feby 10. 1845

Your favor enclosing Deed came duly to hand and will be attended to as per instructions.[2]

We are making preperation for the struggle of next Summer. In Hardeman some collision is feared between Austin Miller & Edwin Polk.[3] I fear some harm from it.

Capt Roberts of Hardeman & Leavitt Lawrence of this place will both be applicants for command of the Snag Boats. Both are experienced Captains upon the river & men of energy. All things carefully considered I am of opinion the appointment of Lawrence would be the most judicious. The present incumbent[4] is a Harrison nominee & I understand the proof is in existence that he has turned off hands because they would not vote the Whig ticket.

I have read Nicholsons leader about removals published about 1st inst.[5] I thought the word "proscription" figured awkwardly & improperly in it. It cannot apply to the prompt removal of all the 2000 who were put in, in the beginning of the Whig reign. To turn them all out promptly is but even handed justice and is rebuking proscription.

H. Clay in his Lexington speech gave notice that all Democrats were if his party succeeded, to be removed.[6] All the Whig speakers I met in debate, when reminded of the doings of Jarnigan[7] boldly affirmed his acts and duly notified us if Clay was elected every Democratic office holder in America would be removed. Cave Johnson heard R. L. Caruthers[8] avow this. You have the map of the universal Whig party before your minds eye. You see it & judge it in all its parts but so far as my opportunities of Judging the animal extend, to show them favor, to give them power is but warming the viper. If the lash dont bring them in nothing will. For one I have full faith that all your acts will be with an eye single to our countrys prosperity in all its parts and that you consider the present and future ascendency of Democratic principles essential to that end. And if you deem it better to leave the patronage of the Government in Whig hands *so let it be.*

L. H. COE

ALS. DLC–JKP. Addressed to Washington City and marked "Care of Col. Joel L. Jones."

1. A popular lawyer and Democrat from Somerville, Coe sat two terms in the Tennessee Senate, 1837–41, and presided over that body as Speaker during the latter part of his second term.

2. Polk's letter has not been found.

3. Reference is to a possible contest for the Democratic nomination for the Tennessee House seat to be decided in the Tennessee state elections scheduled for the first Thursday in August 1845. A lawyer from Bolivar, Tenn., Austin Miller served as judge of Tennessee's Eleventh Circuit Court from 1836 until 1838, and won election as a Democrat to three terms in the Tennessee House, 1843–47 and 1861–63.

4. Not identified further.

5. Reference is to an editorial in the *Nashville Union* of February 1, 1845, which predicts Polk will use "prudence and caution" in his removal and appointment of government officials.

6. Reference not identified further.

7. Spencer Jarnagin studied law under Hugh L. White and practiced in Knoxville from 1817 to 1837, when he moved to Athens, McMinn County. A Whig presidential elector in 1840, he failed to win election to the U.S. Senate in 1841 but two years later achieved his goal and served in that body from 1843 until defeated for reelection in 1847.

8. A Whig lawyer from Lebanon, Robert L. Caruthers represented Wilson County for one term in the Tennessee House, 1835–37, and sat in the U.S. House for a single term, 1841–43.

### FROM MARTIN VAN BUREN

My dear Sir                                    Lindenwald Feby 10th [18]45

I recd. yours from Nashville, on your way to Washington, [1] this morng & would be happy to comply with your request by adding to the suggestions contained in my last, but can do but little beyond an expression of the confirmation which those have recd from subsequent reflection. The papers of last Eveng give additional weight to my thin anticipations in regard to the agency you are destined to have in the final settlement of the Texas affair [2] & in respect to which I have since been informd, Mr Butler goes farther with the friends of annexation than I then supposed, rending it quite certain to my mind, that no serious discrepancy of opinion upon that subject is at all likely to occur between him & yourself upon that point. That it would, under such circumstances, be vitally important to fill the Departmt of State from the north if you can, in other respects, be as well suited, is a position which I should suppose no enlightened & disinterested friend would be disposed to controvert.

The speculations of the best of us in regard to the future course of public events, which are so liable to be affected by unforeseen circumstances, will occasionally be at fault. Still we must, as the Yankee [3] would say, *guess,* & in some degree govern ourselves accordingly. I will give you an idea that has presented itself to my mind with imperative force, & you will let it pass for what it is worth. Until the administration of

Genl. Jackson the most exciting and difficult matters which every administration had to deal with were almost exclusively of Foreign origin. The dread of Foreign Governments to come in collision with him, looking upon him as I know they at first did, as one who preferred fighting as a matter of choice, & the overshadowing influence of the Bank question,[4] when just as he met it, changed this matter altogether, these questions in regard to our Foreign relations comparatively in the back ground, & made domestic questions those which occupied the attention of the administration & of its opponents, almost exclusively. In my opinion the course of affairs during your administration will fall back into their old channel. The reasons upon which this opinion are founded are by far too numerous to give in a hasty letter. I will refer to a few only, & first to begin with such as are of a merly factious character, which are least likely to be lost sight of. The Whigs are obviously making it a point to bring their first men into the Senate & will try to do the same in the House. When there they will want food to fatten their old grudges added to recent disappointment upon, & they, like all oppositions will prefer that which for the time being is of the most exciting character. This they will at this time hardly find in our domestic affairs. The Bank question, heretofore the most useful to them, & the parent of many others, wont do. It is defunct for your day. They know that it cant be carried (agt the veto) & their troops wont fight without a hope of success. They besides doubt at least whether their vote is at present the popular one, & many of their adherents are opposed to its farther agitation. You will therefore hear little upon that point. The remaining domestic topics, the public lands, the veto power, &c they have tried & have been beaten upon them. There is no novelty, nothing to assert attention in regard to them, & the same may to some extent, but by no means the same, be said of the Tariff. They will still work at that, but it is an old Story, & entered too deeply into the last canvass, to promise as much as they will desire for the next. The Treasury is full, & is likely to remain so, although I hope the Tariff will be greatly modified. An empty Treasury is a great lever by means of which designing & able men can stir up political bile in respect to almost every thing else. Of this they have had the full use but cannot have it again for some years at least. Where then can they go for matters through which to agitate if it be not to our Foreign Relations? & are they not in a condition to suit their purposes? It is not to be disguised that the Texas & Oregon affairs, after having been long subjects for popular declamation, have, as is usual on similar occasions, been carried to points where we must do more than talk. The administration which is charged with definite action in respect to them & which gives satisfaction to its constituents (or rather its friends for more than that is hardly to be expected) and at the same preserves the peace of the Country without detriment to its honor will have reason to regard itself truly fortunate. They are beyond all doubt beset with serious difficulties intrinsic extrinsic & accidental. It is in respect to them, & not to our domestic affairs, that the political battles of the next four years are to be fought. If it does not so turn out I shall be egregiously, but most happily deceived. I say happily, for there are many reasons why Foreign questions are most troublesome to an administration. I cannot therefore better comply with your request or evince the sincerity of my desire for your success than by conjuring you to look well & reasonably to every step you take in regard to all matters connected with this branch of the public Service, not overlooking of course any thing necessary to a safe & successful administration of our home affairs.

This letter is already longer than you will have time to read & I therefore conclude ....

M. Van Buren

P.S. I send this under cover to our friend Mr Blair.

ALS. DLC–JKP. Marked *"Private"* and *"Confidential."* Francis P. Blair delivered this letter to Polk on February 13. Blair to Van Buren, February 14, 1845. DLC–MVB. Extract published in Tyler, ed., *The Letters and Times of the Tylers*, III, 158.

1. See Polk to Van Buren, January 30, 1845.
2. In an editorial of February 9, 1845, the *New York Herald* speculated that the U.S. Senate would delay action on the House joint-resolution annexing the Republic of Texas and that Polk probably would call a special session of Congress in the summer to resolve the Texas question.
3. Transcription of the word "Yankee" or "Yonker" indeterminate.
4. Van Buren's reference is to Andrew Jackson's opposition to rechartering the Second Bank of the United States.

## FROM WILLIAM D. MOSELEY[1]

Tallahassee, Fla. February 11, 1845

After expressing his concern that his December letter[2] had presumed too much "upon our early acquaintance and friendship," Moseley discusses patronage questions in the territory and the prospects of statehood for Florida. Distressed at the thirst for spoils so pervasive among his fellow members of the territorial legislature, Moseley complains that he has been "excessively annoyed" by requests to recommend office seekers. He advises Polk to appoint only political friends to major offices; but in the case of "subordinate offices," Polk should not turn out a worthy officer for strictly political reasons. Moseley notes that he and his fellow Democrats unanimously support Florida's admission into the union during the present session of Congress. Some Whigs are opposed, but in

Florida they "are like Angels visits." [3] He believes that statehood would encourage the development of Florida and would eliminate not only problems "arising from foreign Legislation" [4] but also political corruption.

ALS. DLC–JKP. Addressed to Washington City and marked "Private."

1. Polk's classmate at the University of North Carolina, Moseley served in the North Carolina Senate, 1829–36, but lost his gubernatorial race in 1834. He subsequently moved to Florida, where he served in the territorial legislature; in 1845 he won election as the first governor of the State of Florida.

2. Letter not found.

3. Paraphrase of a line from Thomas Campbell's *Pleasures of Hope* (1799). Popular resistance to Florida statehood subsided upon conclusion of the Seminole War in 1842; Florida gained admission to the Union on March 3, 1845.

4. Moseley's reference probably is to Florida land grants made by the Spanish crown and left to be perfected by the United States government, as stipulated in the Adams-Onís Treaty.

## FROM MARTIN VAN BUREN

My dear Sir                    Lindenwald Feby 11th 1845

In my reply of yesterday [1] I strangely enough omitted a suggestion which was uppermost in my mind, & that is the great importance of having Major Donelson with you in some suitable situation. I was desirous of offering him a seat in the Cabinet, & was only prevented from doing so by his own modesty, and an apprehension on his own part that he would [be] regarded by the people of Tennessee as having been prematurely advanced out of favor to the Genl. [2] That consideration must by this time have lost its force, & I am very sure that there is not a man in the Country who could render you such varied, & such useful service. His talents are of the very highest order, his soul is the seat of honor, & he is by far too sagacious to be humbugged by the rouges, [3] whatever may [be] their calibre. It has not fallen to the lot of many to have better opportunities to become well acquainted with the real character capacities and disposition of the public men of the Country. He is always composed & firm, writes for all practical & useful purposes as well as any man I know & could make himself useful to you in a thousand ways; & the consideration I referred to in my first as applicable to an other worthy friend of yours would also apply with greatly increased force to Major Donelson. [4] But this is [ ... ] [5] carrying coals to New Castle, as I am treading on ground familiar to yourself, but even in such cases it is sometimes desirable to know that those for whose opinions we have respect think as we do. With kind regards to Mrs. Polk ....

M. VAN BUREN

ALS. DLC–JKP. Addressed to Washington City and marked "Private."

1. See Van Buren to Polk, February 10, 1845.

2. Andrew Jackson.

3. Probably a misspelling of the word "rogues."

4. In his January 18 letter to Polk, Van Buren discussed the selection of one of Polk's Tennessee intimates for a cabinet post.

5. Word or words obliterated by a tear in the manuscript.


## FROM DAVID PETRIKIN[1]


Danville, Penn. February 12, 1845

Confined to his sickbed for the past year, Petrikin nevertheless followed the campaign with great interest. After hailing Polk's election as a victory of "our Republican institutions" over Clay and "the British or federal party," he turns his attention to party politics and warns Polk about the intrigues of a set of men who have almost ruined the Democratic party in Pennsylvania. Petrikin attacks Ellis Lewis, H. B. Wright, Calvin Blythe, and J. B. Sutherland[2] for their ties to John Tyler and to the Whig party. Originally allies of David Porter, they deserted him when he refused to give them "as much of the plunder as they thought was their share." Petrikin believes that these men rose to positions of power in the party because the "laboring men and farmers" who form the majority of the Democracy lack the time to follow party intrigues. He urges Polk to rely on Henry Horn[3] and other honest and true members of the Democratic party.


L. DLC–JKP. Addressed to Washington City.

1. A physician, Petrikin won election as a Democrat to two terms in the U.S. House, 1837–41.

2. Ellis Lewis, Hendrick B. Wright, Calvin Blythe, and Joel B. Sutherland. A John Tyler supporter and two-term Democrat in the Pennsylvania General Assembly, Lewis served as state attorney general, judge in the state's eighth and then second judicial districts, and justice of the Pennsylvania Supreme Court from 1853 until 1857. Wright, who chaired the 1844 Democratic National Convention, won election to four terms in the U.S. House, 1853–55, 1861–63, and 1877–81. Blythe, a Democrat, served in minor state offices prior to his appointment by Martin Van Buren to the post of customs collector at Philadelphia; Polk removed Blythe in 1845. Sutherland, a Philadelphia physician and lawyer, sat five consecutive terms in the U.S. House, 1827–37; in 1836 he ran for reelection as a Whig and lost.

3. A Jackson Democrat and Van Buren loyalist, Horn sat one term in the U.S. House, 1831–33; in 1845 and again in 1846 Polk nominated Horn to be collector at Philadelphia but failed to secure his confirmation.

## FROM LAURA WILSON POLK TATE[1]

My dear brother           Morganton February 12 [1845][2]

I hope by this time you are in Washington City with your family in good health and happy. I was pleased indeed to learn of you in your letter to Dr Tate that Marshall[3] is a good boy and obedient, but I am very much grieved to hear that he is idle. Do my dear friend correct this great fault in him. Tell him positively that he shall not be idle. Convince him that it is sinful—that he is breaking God's commandments, and then I believe that he will do well. I always found this the best way to manage him. Tell Marshall that I will write to him next week. Give my love to sister Sarah[4] and say to her that I will write to her as soon as I feel in good health and spirits again. I love her very much and do sincerely hope that she may be happy in her new home. My dear brother I have always felt as if I was not capable of writing to you, but you may be sure that I feel very awkward when I know that I am addressing the President of these United states, so you must entirely excuse me for all blunders and mistakes. Dr Tate and all my little children are well. Dr James Tate of Mississippi[5] has written here to his friends several times requesting me to write to you something good of him. He wants an appointment. I do not know exactly what, but he is in Washington, and can tell you himself. I write this because I have promised to do so. Do not laugh at me for presuming to meddle in publick affairs, but I wish to secure to myself the friendship of his sister[6] a lady who I am desirous of not offending.

That God may bless you in all things is the prayer of your sincere friend.

                             LAURA TATE

ALS. DLC–JKP. Addressed to Washington City.

1. The widow of Marshall Tate Polk, Laura Tate married William C. Tate, her first cousin and a physician from Morganton, N.C.; James K. Polk served as executor of his brother Marshall's estate and as guardian of his nephew, Marshall Tate Polk, Jr.

2. Date identified through content analysis.

3. Letter not found.

4. Sarah C. Polk.

5. A prominent Lowndes county Democrat, James H. Tate went to Buenos Aires in 1845 as U.S. consul but resigned that post the following year.

6. Not identified further.

## FROM STEPHEN C. PAVATT[1]

Dear Sir                                   Huntingdon Febry 14th 1845

I wrote to Col Cave Johnson a hasty note a few days since stating I would be at Washington at Your Inorguration, but in my attempts to make arrangements for that purpose I most signally failed.

It would have given me great pleasure to have witnessed the Consumation of the end that Crow[n]s the hopes of the democracy in Tennessee particularly and I think throughout [the] Union. I should like to have seen the band of democratic soulders that won the battle of 44, but this pleasure I must forego. The political horizon here is now clear. I do not think there is a doubt of the success of our candidate for Governor and the prospects for a majority in the legislature is flatering. The best impression is, our two *great men* Foster and Bell[2] will both have to run a risk for office; that is Foster is to run for Governor and in getting a Whig Legislature to elect Bell to the Senate for the purpose of thwarting your Administration—to be a *sort* of a Clay in the Senate, as he will be from your own state and will make the opposition more coroding. The Whigs here knows the man and knows what he has done in times goneby. But the people has been deceived by them in the *White* affair and they reccolect it.[3] I therefore do not think they will succeed.

Poor Gustavus Adolphus Don Alfonzo De Malena Di Procida—Henry.[4] God knows what will become of him.

Our Chancery Court is just over and we have had a feast with the Whigs. Bullock[5] raves, and like a Grampus would snap at a pole if punched.

S. C. PAVATT

ALS. DLC–JKP. Addressed to Washington City.

1. A lawyer from Huntington, Pavatt served as a Democrat in the Tennessee House, 1833–37, and in the state Senate, 1851–53; he ran unsuccessfully for a seat in Congress in 1839, 1841, 1843, and 1853.

2. Ephraim H. Foster and John Bell. A lawyer from Franklin, Bell served a partial term as Speaker of the U.S. House, 1834–35, but lost his bid for reelection as Speaker to Polk in the next Congress; in 1836 he headed Hugh Lawson White's presidential campaign in Tennessee and subsequently became one of the state's most powerful Whigs. He served in the U.S. House from 1827 until 1841 and in the U.S. Senate from 1847 until 1859. In 1860 he ran unsuccessfully for president at the head of the Constitutional Union ticket.

3. Pavatt's reference is to Hugh L. White's break with Andrew Jackson in 1836, which led to the founding of the Southern branch of the Whig party. A

Knoxville lawyer, White began his career as private secretary to William Blount, served on the Tennessee Supreme Court, 1801–07 and 1809–15; won election to several terms in the Tennessee Senate, 1807–09 and 1817–25; sat in the U.S. Senate from 1825 until 1840; and ran unsuccessfully for the U.S. presidency in 1846.

4. Gustavus Adolphus Henry, a native of Kentucky and graduate of Transylvania College, served in the Kentucky House before moving to Clarksville, Tenn., in 1833; he failed in his bid to unseat Cave Johnson in 1842 but did carry the congressional district as a Whig presidential elector in 1840, 1844, and 1852. Pavatt's play on Henry's name is not identified further.

5. Elected to four terms in the Tennessee House, 1835–37, 1841–42, 1845–47, and 1857–59, Micajah Bullock ran as a Whig in his first three races and as a Know-Nothing in his last.

## FROM ANDREW J. DONELSON

My Dr Sir,                                                    At home Feby. 15th 1845

I wrote to you from New orleans a hasty note[1] growing out of some suggestions made to me by the Genl.[2] Since my arrival here I have had a full conversation with him, in which he has stated to me what will be your probable cabinet appointments.

It appears that without any knowledge or agency of mine some of my friends had suggested my name for the War office, and the Genl informs me your kind feelings disposed you to comply with their suggestion, but that he had made observations leading to a different result so far as I am concerned.

On this subject I have only to observe that I have no political aspirations, and certainly none that could lead me to consider the high office referred to as not demanding talents and experience greatly above mine. My only ambition is to repair now, by a life of economy, the mistakes of early years, and lay up, if possible, something for the education of my children, and the support of old age. This consideration and duty would induce me to accept public employment where it might aid this object, but not at the hazard of postponing the claims of others whose weight of character or greater efficiency would be a surer guarantee for the advancement of the public interest.

I shall remain here a few days and return by the way of my Mississippi plantation to New orleans, ready to execute any new instruction which may grow out of the legislation of this congress in regard to the annexation question.

Wishing you all the happiness, which, the complication of anxieties and cares, insuperable from the high station to which you are called, can spare to you; I offer the joint salutation of Mrs. D[3] & myself to Mrs Polk ....

A. J. DONELSON

ALS. DLC–JKP. On April 19, 1856, the Nashville *American Banner* published the text of a letter to Polk purportedly written by Donelson and dated February 14, 1845. Variances in both the argument and the language of the newspaper publication suggest its separate if not spurious writing.
1. See Donelson to Polk, February 1, 1845.
2. Andrew Jackson.
3. Elizabeth Martin Randolph Donelson.

## FROM ANDREW JACKSON

My dear Sir,                                           Hermitage Feby. 15th 1845
Since writing you on the subject of Capt Eastland, as a proper person for the Marshalsea of Neworleans, in which I informed you that Major A. J. Donelson had just reached home,[1] I have had a long *confidential* conversation with him. In which I have made known to him the provisions to be made in due time, for him. That is a full minister to some foreign court. The Major has had a severe attack of sickness, and wishes to be sent where health is promised. Spain, would suit his views, Brazil or Mexico, if that post become vacant. But will be content with Prusia or Austria. I believe Madrid in Spain would be the most congeneal climate for his constitution. The Major appears satisfied and will write you.[2] I have told him, that the suggestion of a foreign Mission in preference to any other that could be given him, came from me, and was cheerfully acquiesced in by you, and in due time he would receive the appointment. The Major is perfectly satisfied with this arrangement and by the mail that carries this will write you.

The Major will in a few days return to Neworleans where he will await despatches from the Government; and should the Joint Resolutions passed by the House of Representatives not pass the Senate, for the reannexation of Texas,[3] or some other for that object, he will resign as soon thereafter as he can make known to Texas, the wishes and desires of the Executive of the United States, agreable to such instructions he may receive. Major Donelson thinks Texas a sickly climate in the flat country near the Gulph.

Before this reaches you, you will have reached Washington, and I trust both you & Mrs. Polk in good health, altho you must be greatly fatigued. Myself & Houshold salute you & Mrs. Polk with our kindest wishes ....

ANDREW JACKSON

ALS. DLC–JKP. Addressed to Washington City and marked *"Confidential."*
Published in Bassett, ed., *Correspondence of Andrew Jackson,* VI, pp. 369–70.
  1. Letter not found. A New Orleans merchant and Democrat, Thomas B.
Eastland served as a quartermaster in the Mexican War with the rank of major.
  2. See Andrew J. Donelson to Polk, February 15, 1845.
  3. See Cave Johnson to Polk, February 3, 1845.

## FROM ALBERT G. JEWETT[1]

Dear Sir                        Augusta Feby 15, 1845
  I hope what I may now write will not be regarded by you as indelicate.
  During the Canvass of this State Mr Fairfield expressed to me a desire for reelection to the Senate; but informed me that he did not desire
a place in the Cabinet. I left the State after the September election to
Canvass other States, and on my return from Tennessee in Nov., Mr F.
informed me that he had changed his mind during my absence, and then
desired to go into the Cabinet; and that he had authorized his friends to
take measures for that object. Looking at Mr F's position and what had
there been done, I was unwilling that Maine should present a divided
aspect, & I therefore told him I would not be a candidate as I had intended to be, but would acquiesce in his movements for the place. And
therefore I do not desire now to do any thing to defeat his appointment.
But if from any circumstance you have definitely determined not to appoint him, I shall take the liberty to lay before you an expression from
this state which I doubt not will be entitled to your consideration; and
if entirely consonant with your views and feelings, I should indeed be
gratified to become a member of your Cabinet. The object of this note is
to apprise you of my position in relation to this matter, before I have the
honor of an interview with you at Washington for which place I intend
to leave Augusta in a day or two. Our state feels much solicitude upon
this subject and this and the circumstances before referred to must be
my apology for this letter.

                              A. G. JEWETT

ALS. DLC–JKP. Addressed to Washington City.
  1. A lawyer from Bangor, Me., Jewett campaigned in Tennessee in late October 1844. Polk appointed him chargé d'affaires to Peru in 1845.

## FROM JOHN L. O'SULLIVAN[1]

My dear Sir,                     New York. Feb. 15. 1845
  You are now in a position to realize, in the letters of your correspondents, more fully than ever you have done before, the truth of the maxim

that "brevity is the soul of wit."[2] I therefore will be as laconic as a Spartan, and state briefly the two points to which I desire to solicit your reflections. *The word "office" is not mentioned in the whole course of my letter.*

1. Suffer me to ask of you the favor to read the enclosed short article which I wrote in the Democratic Review in November, 1842.[3] I feel assured of your entire sympathy with the general spirit of the article, even though you may not perhaps deem it expedient to take up at all its suggestion in regard to the disposal of that most uncomfortable barrack of a residence in which you are condemned to live for the next four years. If ever to be acted upon, it would seem to be now. The two dynasties of the *Revolutionary Presidents* and the *Last-War Presidents* have both passed away, and you are the first of the younger class or dynasty. It would come with a good grace from you. Personal regard for an incoming incumbent must generally prevent others from making the movement, whether of his own or of the adverse party; so that it can only proceed from a President elect, at the outset of his administration. At the present juncture, the house is in a sad condition, with $20,000 about being appropriated to make it decent. That sum would nearly suffice to build a better house, for which I have no doubt that both you and Mrs. Polk would, on every personal ground, be delighted to exchange the old one. At the same time a building is precisely now wanted for the Smithsonian Institute.[4] If, therefore, you were to give it out as your wish, or as agreeable to you, I have little doubt that Congress would adopt it at once; while it would touch powerfully the whole popular heart, and make it swell towards you as indeed the truest Democrat ever in the Presidential chair. I think the whole land would ring with applause, and move deeply & warmly in sympathy with you, strengthening even the high and fine *morale* of your present *"national"* political position. It would also be (in my humble judgment) a noble record to stamp on the very first line of the history of your Presidency. You will, I trust, pardon the simplicity, & perhaps even boldness, of my present language. The deep earnestness of my love for those principles which are summed up in that noble word *Democracy,* alone prompts me to a freedom, which, rightly viewed, is indeed the highest tribute of personal respect, and confidence in your magnanimity, which I could pay you.

2. The other suggestion is as to the propriety of Congress restoring the local government of the District of Columbia to Virginia & Maryland. A tremendous Anti-Slavery agitation is just now beginning to ferment at the North. You can probably have little idea of the extent to which the proceedings of the last year in regard to this question have developed the Anti-Slavery feeling. The *national responsibility* for Slavery from

its existence in the central spot of the *national government,* is about now to afford the subject of a formidable contest; and I have been deeply alarmed at the numbers and characters (personal & political) of men whom, within the past few months I have heard declare themselves, not only prepared, but determined, to make this demand from the Federal Government. It is by no means unlikely that the Anti-Slavery sentiment may have strength to carry through the Congress to be elected in 1846 some strong act of legislation against slavery in the District. The consequences of such an act, or of its serious agitation, are fearful to contemplate. Under any circumstances we of the Democratic Party are going to have our hands full with Whiggism & Abolitionism in amalgamation together, and Tariffism to make up the triad of abominations. As the District is the great battle-ground of the Abolition agitation, this danger would be almost entirely parried by the *retrocession of the District,* in which act terms of compact could easily be made with the States covering all the purposes for which the District can be of any benefit to the Federal Government. The South would like it of course—indeed it has been rather a favorite Southern idea, since the Abolition agitation; and the whole Northern Democracy would be delighted to be thus rid of the question of slavery and slave-dealing under the shadow of the Capitol. The question has no embarrassments for me since yet the great bulk of the Democracy cannot draw the nice distinctions of Constitutional doctrine by which alone the present state of things there can be reconciled to the Northern sentiment; a sentiment already strong, and fast and formidably growing. Mr. Van Buren's declaration in his Inaugural[5] was very unpopular at the North—that he would peremptorily veto any bill abolishing slavery in the District. The point I desire to solicit your attention to, is, as to whether it is not worth while to throw out the suggestion of retrocession as a great tranquillizing and *national* act, in *your* Inaugural.

Excuse the length into which even the slightest statement of these two ideas leads me. I would have come on to Washington to state them verbally, and would indeed still do so, were it not for the manner in which I know you must be over-run with visitors. I spare you *one* in Washington, great as is the pleasure I should have had in welcoming you back there, under the present glorious auspices.

Being a mere volunteer suggestion, most diffidently advanced, and growing out of a zeal, of which the earnest sincerity must rescue it from the imputation of impertinence or officiousness, I beg you not to feel under obligation to give any of your time, or rather want of time, to the trouble of a reply.

J. L. O'Sullivan

ALS. DLC–JKP. Addressed to Washington City.

1. A New York City journalist, O'Sullivan joined Samuel D. Langtree in founding and editing the *United States Magazine and Democratic Review* in 1837. A strong advocate of American expansionism, O'Sullivan served one term in the New York legislature, 1841–43, and with Samuel J. Tilden founded and edited the *New York Morning News* from 1844 to 1846.

2. Quotation is from William Shakespeare, *Hamlet*, act 2, scene 2, line 90.

3. O'Sullivan argued that in a democratic republic the head of government should not reside in a mansion or make any ostentatious display of wealth while in public service. *United States Magazine and Democratic Review,* XI (November, 1842), pp. 539–42.

4. In December 1844 Congress had intensified its efforts to establish the Smithsonian Institution; in 1846 Congress would decide that the president, vice-president, chief justice, and cabinet members should take responsibility for implementing James Smithson's bequest of $600,000 "for the increase and diffusion of knowledge among men."

5. In his inaugural address of 1837 Martin Van Buren cited his campaign declaration that he would "go into the Presidential chair the inflexible and uncompromising opponent of every attempt on the part of Congress to abolish slavery in the District of Columbia against the wishes of the slaveholding States ...." Richardson, ed., *Messages and Papers of the Presidents,* III, p. 318.

### FROM WILLIAM WILSON POLK

Dr. Sir.                              [Phillips County, Ark.] Feby 15 1845

Having understood that a Son of mine[1] has applied to you for the Office of Receiver of Public money for the Land Office at Springfield in Missouri, & believing that he is worthy & well Qualified, possessing Integrity & Sober Steady business habbits & believing that the duties of the Office would be performed with correctness & fidellity, I would look on it (& feel It) to be a favor done to myself as well as to him were you to give him that appointment.

It would be unnecessary for me to say that I believe you will give him the appointment provided you can do So consistently with the many & Important duties you have to perform.

WILL POLK

ALS. DLC–JKP. Addressed to Washington City.
1. Reference is to Thomas M. Polk, youngest son of William Wilson Polk.

### FROM MARTIN VAN BUREN

My dear Sir                       Lindenwald Feby 15th [18]45

You have moved along with so much rapidity as to supercede in a great part the object for which this was intended to be written—that is to introduce to you my friend Genl. Dix of the Senate. I have before spoken to you of him & I now report that you will at all times & under all proper circumstances find him a sincere, discreet, intelligent, honest & firm friend. His political feelings are in perfect harmony with those of the Democratic masses of this State & I am very sure that he will under all circumstances be their true Representative. You will find him modest & reserved, but always ready to advise & act for the best when it becomes necessary & proper to do so. I am the more anxious that you should appreciate his merits from my knowledge of the extent to which many with whom you will have to act are immersed in personal intrigue & of his exemption from them. When he differs with you in opinion upon public questions he will be sure to tell you so honestly & frankly.

Every stage in the Commencement of a *new* administration constitutes an important era. From your election to your arrival is one in yours, & I feel that I can safely congratulate you on the success with which you have passed through it. The public mind has obviously been very favorably impressed. The next is the appointment and annunciation of the Cabinet, & the execution of that, will, I am very sure, be distinguished by the two qualities which our people like so much, & by which our good friend of the Hermitage[1] rendered himself so deservedly popular, viz promptness & stability. To the prompt it is by no means necessary to be hasty—a reasonable time to permit such friends as desire it to make their commendations & then a ready & unembarassed decision, anonced without reserve & adhered to with manly firmness & of all this we have the promise in the past. If only careful to avoid, as far as you can, just cause for dissatisfaction, you have nothing to fear from threats of disunion in the ranks of your party. Such bickerings are unavoidable & always witnessed at the formation of a new administration, here & every where. A profound observer gives to this occurence a simple & true origin. The active man in a Party, he says, although combining ostensibly, & for the most part sincerely for the promotion of the general cause, have, very generally, in view a separate interest of their own. While the contest rages you see nothing but Solicitude for the common cause. When it is over, & the battle won, each is thrown back upon his individual concern & as the objects of all cannot be gratified rivalry & contention take the place of harmony, & we witness such scenes as you are now in the midst of. If the battle is lost all private aspirations are concealed, & harmony reigns in the losing Party. This is I believe the true Philosophy of [the] matter. You are therefore dealing with troubles with the existence of which you need not reproach yourself—which are inseparable from the management of public affairs but which can be gotten along with if there is but steadiness & good intentions at the

Helm. Your reliance must be on the masses, & let them only see that the reins are in the hands in which they intend to place them, that they are steadily held, & their good the principal object in view & all will soon be well.

Excuse this hasty scrawl & believe me ....

M. VAN BUREN

ALS. DLC–JKP. Addressed to Washington City and delivered by John A. Dix.
1. Andrew Jackson.

## TO JAMES BUCHANAN

Sir                                    Washington City Feby. 17th 1845

The principles and policy, which will be observed and maintained during my administration, are embodied in the Resolutions adopted by the Democratic National Convention of Delegates assembled at Baltimore in May last,[1] and in the Inaugural address, which I propose to deliver to my Fellow Citizens,[2] on assuming the duties of President of the United States, and which is herewith handed to you for your perusal.

In making up my Cabinet, I desire to select gentlemen, who agree with me in opinion, and who will cordially co-operate with me in carrying out, those principles and policy.

In my official action I will myself take no part between gentlemen of the Democratic party, who may become aspirants or Candidates to succeed me in the Presidential office, and desire that no member of my Cabinet shall do so. Individual preferences, it is not expected or desired to limit or restrain. It is official interference by the dispensation of public patronage or otherwise, that I desire to guard against. Should any member of my Cabinet become a Candidate for the Presidency or Vice Presidency of the United States, it will be expected upon the happening of such an event, that he will retire from the Cabinet.

I disapprove the practice which has sometimes prevailed, of Cabinet officers absenting themselves for long periods of time, from the seat of Government, and leaving the management of their Departments to Chief Clerks, or other, less-responsible persons than themselves. I expect myself, to remain constantly at Washington, unless it may be, that no public duty requires my presence, when I may be occasionally absent, but then only for a short time. It is by conforming to this rule, that the President and his Cabinet, can have any assurance, that abuses will be prevented, and that the subordinate Executive officers, connected with them respectively, will faithfully perform their duty.

If Sir, you concur with me in these opinions and views, I shall be pleased to have your assistance, in my administration, as a member of my Cabinet, and now tender to you the office of Secretary of State,[3] and invite you to take charge of that Department.

I shall be pleased to receive your answer at your earliest convenience.
JAMES K. POLK

ALS. PHi. Addressed to Washington City. Published in John Bassett Moore, ed., *The Works of James Buchanan* (12 vols; New York: Antiquarian Press Ltd. reprint, 1960), VI, pp. 110–11. On the cover of an earlier draft of this letter Polk dated the document January 15, 1845, and endorsed it "Rough Draft of Letter, to be revised and corrected." AL, draft. DLC–JKP. On the cover of a copy of this letter, now dated "March 1845," Polk states that he sent duplicates of this letter to Buchanan, Walker, Marcy, Bancroft, Johnson, and Mason. L. DLC–JKP.

1. The Convention called for immediate annexation of Texas, termination of the joint occupation of Oregon, creation of an independent Treasury system, and economical administration of the general government; the Convention opposed restriction of the president's veto power, distribution of the proceeds of public land sales, creation of a national bank and/or a system of internal improvements financed by the general government, and revision of the states' rights to control their domestic institutions, as proposed by abolitionists and others. *Niles National Register,* June 8, 1844.

2. In the text of his draft of January 15, 1845, Polk had written "and in my Inaugural address this day delivered to my Fellow Citizens."

3. In the text of both his draft and the later copy Polk left a blank space to be filled in with the name of the specific cabinet office to be offered.

## FROM WILLIAM M. GOUGE[1]

Dr Sir                                          Washington Feb. 17 1845

It has been suggested to me that a succinct view of our existing laws, relative to the medium of public receipts and payments, might be acceptable to you.

By our first revenue act it was provided that public dues should be paid "in gold and silver coin only."[2] This provision has never been repealed.

By the joint resolution of 1814, it was declared that "nothing but gold and silver, treasury notes, and the notes of specie paying banks *ought*" to be received in payment of public dues.

The framers of the constitution evidently intended that the United States should have a *substantive* Treasury, *substantial* treasure, and a *real* Treasurer. The laws as they stand at present, render it practicable, though with some inconvenience, to carry that intention immediately into effect.

When the suspension of specie payments occurred in 1837,[3] there were various obstacles in the way. The Treasury Department was then living in lodgings; and but few of the public offices were supplied with proper conveniences for keeping the public money.

Now there is an excellent safety room in the new Treasury building. At Philadelphia, we have the building of Mr. Biddle's bank.[4] At New York and Boston, excellent Custom Houses supplied with all the conveniences for keeping the public money provided under the Sub-Treasury law of 1840.[5] All or nearly all the other custom houses, and, I believe, all or nearly all the Land Offices are provided with either fire proof vaults, or iron chests.

The chief difficulty, however, that existed in 1837, was found in the state of our laws which then afforded no remedy but a civil suit, in cases of public default. This has been removed by an act passed about the time the Sub-Treasury act was repealed. This new act makes it a criminal offence in any public offices whatever to apply the public money to private uses.[6]

I know of no law that *authorises* making deposits of the public money in banks, except one passed in the year 1809, and that extends to *disbursing* officers only, and to them only when they receive orders to that effect from the President of the United States.

I have ventured to submit these remarks to you, being convinced that the sooner the fiscal principles of your Administration are settled, the better it will be for yourself, and the better for the country. It is also of moment that you should have a cabinet who would agree with you on this important point. The embarassments to which Gen. Jackson was exposed, from his not understanding the views of Mr. Duane in relation to the deposits, were very great.[7]

I have no names to suggest to you as members of the Cabinet. I speak in the abstract.

There are many defects in our laws, in regard to the collecting, keeping, transferring and paying of the public moneys, but these can to a great extent be supplied by Executive orders. The chief difficulty would arise from no suitable provision having been made for the proper compensation of those who, by a strict construction of the Constitution and the laws, ought to have the charge of the public funds. Perhaps a statement of the difficulties you would have in carrying out these provisions of the Constitution and the laws which refer to the Treasury, might facilitate the passage of the present Sub-Treasury bill through the Senate.[8]

I enclose a copy of an essay written by me, and published in the Democratic Review in January 1840.[9] The passages having the most immediate bearing in the present position of affairs, are marked with black ink.

WM M. GOUGE

ALS. DLC–JKP. Addressed locally and marked "Private."

1. A hard money advocate from Philadelphia, Gouge served as a clerk in the Treasury Department from 1834 until 1841. An articulate opponent of the Bank of the United States, Gouge wrote extensively on United States fiscal policy: *A Short History of Paper Money and Banking in the United States* (Philadelphia, 1833); *An Inquiry into the Expediency of Dispensing with Bank Agency and Bank Paper in Fiscal Concerns of the United States* (Philadelphia, 1837); the *Journal of Banking* (Philadelphia, 1841–42); and the *Fiscal History of Texas* (Philadelphia, 1852).

2. Congress established the Department of the Treasury and provided for raising revenue by Act of September 2, 1789.

3. Reacting to the collapse of cotton prices, New York City banks suspended specie payments on May 10, 1837; most of the banks in the United States followed suit.

4. Nicholas Biddle, a Philadelphia native and president of the Bank of the United States from 1822 until its demise, secured a state charter in 1837 and continued to conduct banking operations as the Bank of the United States of Pennsylvania; he gave up control of the Bank in March of 1839.

5. The Independent Treasury plan, which excluded private banking industry from having custody and management of U.S. Treasury funds, became law on July 4, 1840; a Whig-controlled Congress reversed that decision the following year. The Independent Treasury system continued to function informally after its repeal for want of any other national banking system through which to conduct the general government's fiscal affairs.

6. Reference to the Act of August 13, 1841, which provided for fines equal to the amount embezzled, imprisonment for a term of up to five years, and repeal of the 1840 Independent Treasury Act.

7. A Philadelphia lawyer and Democratic operative, William J. Duane took over the Treasury Department in May of 1833; four months later Jackson dismissed him for refusing to remove government deposits from the Bank of the United States.

8. The U.S. House passed a Sub-Treasury bill on December 21, 1844; the Senate Finance Committee reported the bill on February 4, 1845; but Congress took no further action on it prior to its adjournment.

9. Enclosure not found. Language and ideas similar to Gouge's letter permeate an unattributed article, "The Fiscal System of the United States," published in the *United States Magazine and Democratic Review* of January 1840.

## FROM THOMAS RITCHIE

My Dear Sir                                    Richmond, Feby. 17, 1845

Excuse me for making one hasty Suggestion. I would respectfully advise you to keep your Cabinet to yourself as long as you can, until the great question of Texas is or is likely to be disposed of. To one of your Sagacity, I am sure, I need assign no Reasons. But one idea, I may trust is proper. I would not have you wound Mr. Calhoun in the slightest degree, if you can avoid it. And perhaps the settlement of the Texas question (and I begin to have new hopes of a favorable issue) may enable you to avoid giving him any cause of offence.

I shall have the pleasure of seeing you in Washington at the inauguration (after you have arranged your Cabinet) *provided* Texas be settld now *or* provided we fail in Congress am prepared the moment she is rejected to raise the standard, firmly yet prudently, and to rally all her friends, every where around the Cause, and to give confidence to the People of Texas, *that if she will not abandon us, we will not abandon her.*

Of course, my dear Sir I expect no answer to this hasty note, and I beg you sincerely, not to answer but only to excuse me for thrusting myself at this moment, upon your precious time.

I write for your own Eye only.

THOMAS RITCHIE

ALS. DLC–JKP. Addressed to Washington City.

## FROM WILLIAM C. BOUCK

Dr Sir                                        Fultonham Feby. 18. 1845

Feeling a deep interest in the success of your administration, I have taken the liberty of making a few suggestions, in reference to the state of New York.

It appears probable that the Texas question will not be settled by the present Congress; and it will necessarily be among the leading measures of your administration. The friends of this measure in this state, desire to be put in a position, that will enable them to exert a proper influence.

You are doubtless aware that a section of the democratic party in this State, are opposed to this measure, and will in all its stages embarrass its progress, if not directly oppose it. Bentons recent proposition in the Senate,[1] is I think, evidence of this design, and is supported by the Evening Post, the Morning News, Albany Atlas &c. &c. These papers are doubtless under the influence of the particular friends of Gov. Wright and speak their Sentiments.

If a member of your Cabinet should be taken from this State, and from this section of the party, it would dampen the ardor of the friends of this measure, and give this section a consequence, and influence, difficult to counteract.

The friends of this measure who compose a large majority of the democratic party, desire the appointment of one of its supporters. Such a course could not be regarded as proscriptive in so prominent an office. In lesser appointments I would not advise such a discrimination.

Senator Dickinson fully represents the wishes and feelings of the friends of this measure in this state, with whose suggestions they will doubtless be satisfied.

It is more than suspected, that a deep design is maturing to organize a Northern party, amalgamating democrats Opposed to annexation with Whigs but I sincerely hope this is not so. The prudent democracy of the North and South, have hitherto in a Spirit of forbearance, preserved the union. If this connection is broken, there is too much reason to fear the consequences.

Wм. C. Bouck

ALS. DLC–JKP. Addressed to Washington City and marked *"private."*
1. See John Catron to Polk, February 4, 1845.

## FROM JAMES BUCHANAN

My dear Sir,                                    Washington 18 February 1845

I feel greatly honored by your kind invitation to accept the Station of Secretary of State in your Cabinet; & I cheerfully & cordially approve the terms on which this offer has been made as they have been presented in your note of yesterday.[1] To prevent, however, any possible misunderstanding between us hereafter, I desire to make an explanation in regard to that portion of your letter which requires that any member of your Cabinet shall retire upon becoming a Candidate for the Presidency.

Before I had anticipated that you would do me the honor of inviting me to a seat in your Cabinet I had publickly presented my views on the subject of agitating the question of the next Presidency in the strongest colors.[2] Both patriotism & policy, the success of the party as well as that of your administration require, that we should have repose from the strife of making Presidents. I am, therefore, utterly opposed to the agitation of this question in any shape or form & shall exercise any influence which I may possess to prevent it both in regard to myself & others. Nay more, I think the welfare of your administration requires that in every prudent & appropriate manner this principle should be maintained by it and the patronages of the Government ought to be dispensed not to favor any individual aspirant; but solely for the good of the Country & the Democratic causes.

I do not know that I shall ever desire to be a Candidate for the Presidency. Most certainly I never yet strongly felt such an inclination; and I have been willing & should at this moment be willing to accept a station which would, in my estimation of what is proper, deprive me of any prospect of reaching that office. Still I could not & would not accept the high & honorable office to which you have called me at the expense of self ostracism. My friends would unanimously condemn me, were I to pursue this course. I cannot proclaim to the world that in no contingency, shall I be a candidate for the Presidency in 1848; nor in the mean time can I be held responsible for the action of occasional County meetings in my own or other states preceding general elections which, without my previous knowledge or consent, might present my name in connection with this office. I can answer for myself, that as I have never yet raised a finger, or stirred a step towards the attainment of this station; so I never shall make any personal exertions for that purpose, without your express permission, so long as I may remain a member of your cabinet. If, however, unexpectedly to myself, the people should, by a State or National Convention, present me as their Candidate, I cannot declare in advance that I would not accede to their wishes: but in that event I would retire from your Cabinet, unless you should desire me to remain.

I do not deny that I would be as much pleased to accept the Station of Secretary of State from yourself, as from any man living. I entertain a strong conviction, that under the controlling direction of your wisdom, prudence & firmness, I might be useful to you in conducting the Department of State: and I know, from your established character, so far as it is given to mortals to know any thing, that our social & personal intercourse would be of the most friendly & agreeable character.

If, under these explanations, you are willing to confer upon me the office of Secretary of State, I shall accept it with gratitude & exert my best efforts to do my duty to the Country & to yourself.

JAMES BUCHANAN

ALS. DLC–JKP. Addressed to Washington City. Published in Moore, ed., *The Works of James Buchanan*, VI, pp. 111–12.
1. See Polk to Buchanan, February 17, 1845.
2. Reference not identified further.

## FROM EDWIN CROSWELL[1]

Dear Sir,                                                    Albany, Feby 18, 1845
I am aware of the delicacy of any suggestion in relation to the Cabinet selections; & any thing I venture to say on that subject is said of course with a full reliance upon yr judgment, & the conclusions that, looking over the whole ground, you shall adopt.

It is in the event that you may deem it consistent with the general scope & course of yr. administration to select a member of yr Cabinet from this state, that I venture to represent the prevalent wish as to the individual. If the Treasury Department be thought the most in accordance with the position & interests of the state & country, under the present aspect of affairs, I am persuaded that no selection w'd give such general satisfaction & approval as that of Gov. Marcy.

It is perhaps unnecessary to dwell upon his qualifications for the place, by character, position, & long experience in public affairs. Aside from this, owing to the peculiar state of parties here & in the Union, I know of no one whose appointment w'd be more in accordance with public wish & expectation. So experienced in financial affairs, & a familiarity with all the public questions of the day, he unites enlarged & liberal views, & such as are in accordance with those of the Executive, I believe in every particular. While he w'd be acceptable to the North, he w'd be scarcely less so to the South; for on all occasions he has sustained the broad democratic policy which upholds the compromises of the Constitution, regardless of the clamors of fanatics or the designs of politicians.

EDWIN CROSWELL

ALS. DLC–JKP. Addressed to Washington City.
1. Croswell edited the *Albany Argus* from 1823 until 1854.

## FROM AMOS LANE[1]

Sir                                                       Lawrenceburgh Feby 18. 1845

I returned from Indianapolis last evening where I had been attending as a member of the State Board.[2] There were delegates from Every District in the state. Most of them Whigs. I was much gratefied to find them so well satisfied with your election, and so much pleased with the simple plain Republican manner in which you traveled to the seat of Gov.

I mentioned to you on the boat[3] that, it would not be convenient to leave home & could therefore not except of any office out of the State, and had no intention of visiting Washington. But from the importunities of your friends, Mr Calhoun & Genl Cass, I have been prevailed upon to be present at the Inaguration on the 4th of March. This movment has been induced from the fact of the discovery that self stated Leaders of the Old Van School, hangers on and office holders under him opposed to Texas, to your nomination, to Cass & Calhoun, and only came in to your support from necessity, are attempting to monopolize all the offices & influence in Indiana, and thrust your real, personal & political friends aside. Many of these men stated publicly, at meetings that they would rather fall with Van Buren than to succeed with any other candidate.

This was upon the nomination, and each of whom in 48, will be for a northern man with northern principles.

                                                              AMOS LANE

ALS. DLC–JKP. Addressed to Washington City.
1. A lawyer, Lane served three terms in the Indiana House, 1816–17 and 1839, and two terms in the U.S. House, 1833–37. He had urged Polk to name Lewis Cass secretary of state. Amos Lane et al. to Polk, December 10, 1844. LS. DLC–JKP.
2. Lane's reference is to Indiana's Board of Internal Improvements.
3. Lane joined Polk's inauguration procession along the Ohio River at Jeffersonville, Ind., and disembarked at Lawrenceburgh.


FROM JOSEPH HALL[1]


Dear Sir                                    Boston Massa Feby 21. 1845
Relying upon your courtesy and good will, I once more trespass upon your time by writing. I reached here on Tuesday the 11th inst, found my family and friends well, was much gratefied with my visit west, with the cordial reception and gentlemanly treatment extended to me, and also with the people and appearance of the country generally. Upon my return I ascertained that the Maine Legislature had reconsidered their resolutions relating to Texas, which, if you recollect had been previously laid on the table, and instructed their Senators and requested their representatives to vote for annexation in congress.[2] But the misfortune was that those resolutions were passed too late to effect the purpose desired. It is a source of regret that our friends in Maine should have been so much misled by certain prominent politicians at Washington & elsewhere, but that regret is fully balanced by the fact that the *people* are obliging those Democratic members of congress who voted against the cardinal principles of the late presidential contest to render an account of themselves.[3] Their course is not sustained. The question of annexation of Texas is so prominant a feature in the hearts of the people generally that those Democratic public servants who disregard their wishes will be judged severely.
A few days since I had the pleasure of meeting my old friend, A. G. Jewett Esq of Maine. I found him now as heretofore a consistant straightforward Democrat, and I learn that his course in relation to the Texian question has been firm and unweavering. Knowing Mr Jewett as I do, I am convinced that he is one of those staunch and fearless men who never falter or turn aside after deciding upon any important political subject. In New England, Mr. Jewett deservedly stands high with

that portion of the Democratic party who support measures rather than men.

Please accept for yourself and Lady my best respects.

JOSEPH HALL

ALS. DLC–JKP. Addressed to Washington City.

1. Hall served two terms in the U.S. House as a representative from Maine, 1833–37. From 1838 until 1846 he held the post of measurer in the Boston Customs House. He ran unsuccessfully in 1849 for the mayorship of Boston.

2. Maine's governor, Hugh J. Anderson, approved the Maine legislature's Texas and Oregon resolutions on February 4, 1845. Seven days later Hannibal Hamlin presented the Maine resolutions to the U.S. House to be read and laid upon the table. John Fairfield introduced the resolutions in the U.S. Senate on February 13, 1845.

3. On Janaury 25, 1845, the U.S. House passed a resolution for the annexation of Texas. With the exception of Shepard Cary, Maine's congressional Democrats, Joshua Herrick, Robert P. Dunlap, Benjamin White, and Hannibal Hamlin, voted against the resolution.

## FROM JOHN P. HEISS[1]

Browns Hotel
My Dear Sir, [Washington City] Feby 21st 1845

My object in desiring a half hour's interview this morning was, for the purpose of having some conversation with you in regard to the organ of *your* Administration. You very well know the feelings of a large majority of the Democracy, particularly of the South & West in regard to the "Globe," and whether it it would be policy for that paper to be the administration paper. You alone are best capable of judging.

I am backed by *Pennsylvania*[2] and many more of your strong friends in proposing to establish a "new press," to be under the *control of any true friend of yours* whom you may select, myself to be the business man of the concern, and organized *entirely* with the view of sustaining your administration.

Any amount of funds can be brought to my assistance for the purpose of establishing such a press in Washington City, and it was on this subject alone that I desired to call your attention to this morning.

JOHN P. HEISS

P.S. The Editor of the "Madisonian"[3] informed me this morning that his paper had been purchased and from what I could gather from him, I am led to believe the Globe is the purchaser.

ALS. DLC–JKP. Addressed locally.

1. A native of Bucks County, Penn., Heiss formed a partnership with Thomas W. Hogan in 1842 to publish the *Nashville Union*; he became the business manager of the Washington *Union* in May of 1845.

2. Heiss probably refers to Simon Cameron and Lewis S. Coryell, a wealthy Pennsylvania financier and supporter of John C. Calhoun.

3. John B. Jones.

## FROM PETER T. HOMER[1]

Colemans
My dear Sir,                            Washington 21 Feby 1845

If the suggestions of a private citizen who has not an interest to subserve beyond that which he shares in general with the whole Union, and who feels a deep desire that the policy of the incoming administration may be judicious and successful; can be of any moment, I shall be glad if those I personally made this morn may not be overlooked.

The policy of Genl. Jackson in opposing a great monetary central power as *anti* democratic, and in favoring the Compromise bill of 1833,[2] has always received my hearty support. The Bank question is silenced, and the great and leading issue for the future is to be, "a Revenue Tariff, or one of protection amounting to prohibition," for the Texas question is but transitory & will not long remain. In your speeches and letters you go for "a revenue tariff with *accidental* protection."[3] With that motto on our banners, we of Massachusetts went into the last campaign. I hope in developing your plans all other ideas will be *subordinate*.

A residence of ten years, out of the last twenty, in the Commercial & manufacturing districts of England has made me acquainted with the power of those interests to influence the policy of Great Britian, that I dare affirm that, a conciliatory Commercial policy on *our* part will relax the restrictions upon the importation of Bread Stuff in that country,[4] and increase the interest of the British & French population in an advancement as a powerful republic—a republic with Texas conjoined! The power of the Commercial interests of Great Britian was seen after we acknowledged the Independence of the republics of South America. A few years since I heard Mr Adams in conversation make this remark, "While the question of our recognition of the Independence was pending at Washington, Mr Munroe[5] and Mr Rush seemed to fear that a favorable decision would not be acceptable to the British Cabinet. I said to Mr Munroe, Sir, Great Britian is so dependant on her Commerce and interested in sustaining her commerical relations, that she will adopt the course we have at once, for she cannot afford to allow us any Commercial *advantages* by treaty or otherwise." His remark proved true and being in England in Decr 1825 I read Mr Canning's (foreign Minister) letter to Zea Bermudas (Spanish Minister)[6] in which he said, "personally he as well as other members of the Ministry were favorable to Spain holding on to South America as a Colony," but in a speech in the house of Commons, subsequently, he came out in support of their Independence.

The formation of a Cabinet pledged to liberal & *national* measures will unite & make stable our at present divided republic, do justice to its planting and agricultural sections, & no injustice to the manufacturing; increase our Commerce and Marine, keep the revenue steady and no longer frustrate the apparent designs of Nature & Providence.

PETER T. HOMER

ALS. DLC–JKP. Addressed locally.

1. A prominent Boston businessman, Peter T. Homer owned a part-interest in the import firm of Adams, Homer, & Co.

2. Homer refers to the Second Bank of the United States and to the Tariff Act of 1833.

3. See Polk to John K. Kane, June 19, 1844.

4. Great Britain's Corn Laws prohibited the importation of cheap foreign grain; Parliament repealed the Corn Laws in 1846.

5. James Monroe.

6. George Canning and Francisco de Zea Bermudez. Twice foreign minister, 1807–09 and 1822–27, Canning proved a strong advocate of Britain's recognition of the independence of Spain's rebellious South American colonies. Bermudez served two years as Spain's foreign minister, 1824–25.

## FROM JOHN W. EDMONDS[1]

Dear Sir                                        New York Feb 22. 1845

Having recently been elevated to the Bench & thereby withdrawn for some years to come from the strife of party politics, I can, without the imputation of selfish motives, take the liberty of asking your attention to some considerations, which are important to the success of your administration, the integrity of the party & consequently the welfare of the nation.

Mr Van Buren's defeat in the Baltimore Convention was not unexpected to the democracy of this State, but the ground on which it was placed, viz his opposition to the Treaty of annexation,[2] was calculated to produce immense mischief & to add to the disatisfaction growing out of Mr V.B's overthrow.

Immediately upon receiving the news of the proceedings at Baltimore, disatisfaction was apparent among some of our soundest & purest democrats; not the noisy, active ones, who generally take their cue from their leaders & follow it out fas aut nefas,[3] but the quiet, firm & disinterested ones whose votes have always been & will be necessary to our success.

That disatisfaction had two grounds. 1st that Mr V.B. was defeated. 2d that the party was to go into the contest upon the avowed grounds of extending the dominion of slavery.

The first ground alone would not have produced much mischief. Our people are too true to the cause ever to sacrifice it to men, however strongly attached to them.

But upon the other ground, the feeling was deeper & stronger than the shallow and unthinking had any conception of. And I can solemnly assure you, from the observations of 25 years active participation in the political struggles of the country, that there is among our people at the north a deep & a growing feeling of abhorrence to the institution of slavery & I anticipate that the time will come, when it will break out into a general & overpowering flame. When it will come or what shall happen to fire the train, no one can tell, but that it will one day come & with tremendous force cannot be doubted by any one who is an attentive observer of public feeling. My fear was that the false position on that subject in which the party was placed by the Baltimore Convention,[4] might be the match to that train or at all events work so far among our people, as in so close a contest as that was to be, to jeopard the result.

Having taken an open stand against Tyler's treaty of Annexation at the start, I was in a position to hear more of this feeling than any one of those who took part in the Baltimore Convention or who threw up their caps at its proceedings & I trembled for the result.

Something must be done to prevent the operation of this feeling, for we could spare none of those who complained.

Hence the celebrated "secret circular" was put forth.[5] It was signed by men who had never swerved a hair in their attachment to the party, who never stopped to count the cost to themselves of advocating its cause. And it was addressed not to rogues or the disaffected in our ranks, but to the wisest truest, best men of the party in the state, to those who could at once arrest the mischief if any had been intended by it or was likely to ensue from it.

Its object was simply & purely to throw off the Texas question from the strife & by a powerful appeal, to come from the leaders of the party, to incite all to unite, on the wonted grounds, in supporting the Baltimore nominations.

We knew that not a vote would be gained by our pro-Texas proceedings, while there was great danger of losing from that cause more than we could spare.

The intention was to follow up the circular by an address to the people in the same spirit & of all the answers we received from the leading men in all parts of the State, *only one* differed with us in opinion on the subject of annexation, while several urged the most prompt & decided action.

No farther action was necessary. The circular was published by some of our pro-Texas friends[6] & gave rise to a discussion which of itself produced all the effects designed by the movement originally. The Texas question was in, the minds of the disatisfied, divorced from the Presidential question & very many of those who had hesitated or avowed a decided hostility to the nominations, came in under our protest & gave them their support. Some however still stood out. In one county alone, Suffolk which has always been one of our most certain & reliable counties, our majority from this cause alone, fell off nearly 400.

A combination of causes operated to aid our purposes. The opposition of Mr V. Buren, & Mr. Wright to the Treaty, the nomination of the latter, the avowed hostility of the whole democratic press of this state to the Treaty, the stand taken in that circular, by many in the state, who in their individual circles defended it & by some of the party press who were open in sustaining it—all these causes tended to work in the minds of the people the convictions that the party had not identified itself with the Texas question.

If such a conviction had not been produced I tell you Sir we should have lost the State. As it was, we carried the State by a minority vote. The whigs & abolitionists outnumbered us by 10.000 on the Presidential vote. And there can be no doubt, that if our nominations had been fully identified with the pro-Texas feeling & our party regarded as fully sanctioning the Baltimore resolution on that subject,[7] the Whigs & the abolitionists would have united against us—nay more, very many of our friends, would not have supported our ticket & many of those, who, as it was, refused to vote at all for President, would have voted against us & we should have lost the State & with it the Union.

When that Circular was signed this state of feeling was well known to us & this disasterous result feared by numbers of our most sagacious men. It was true that the majority of our people were favorable to annexation but a strong minority was averse to it.

To save that minority from deserting us at that trying crisis, something must be done—somebody must throw themselves in the breach. And we did it with a thorough conviction that we should be rendered unpopular by it, but might, by our sacrifice save the party and the nation, and to leave no doubt as to our motives every one of us, were active & conspicuous during the whole contest, in supporting the whole nominations & thus set an example of fidelity, to those who agreed with us in opinion on that question.

I have taken the liberty of stating these truths to you, for two reasons:

1. Because as this question is to live to perplex your administration, you may understand the true condition of the feeling of the people who manage the matter as to save us from the disunion which may grow out of it.

2. Because a set of rogues who have no other claims than such as grow of their clamor upon the leading topic of the day have endeavoured to produce the impression that the signers of that circular were traitors, when in fact they deserve all honor for the bold & patriotic manner in which they threw themselves into the breach.

And *I* can say it to you in the hope of being beleived, because I can have no personal views to gratify. The position which I now occupy is one which I would not exchange for any one in your gift & necessarily withdraws me from the political field during your administration.

I am therefore disinterested in my representations to you & claim in behalf of my associates in the movement, the credit which is justly due to their praiseworthy conduct. It would indeed be lamentable, if such conduct should meet no other reward than the condemnation which the selfish & the untrue are so willing, for their own purposes, to visit upon it.

That you may be able to dispose of this very difficult matter in a manner, which shall redound to your own honor & the welfare of our common country, is the fervent wish of ....

J. W. EDMONDS

ALS. DLC–JKP. Addressed to Washington City.

1. A New York City penal reformer, lawyer, and state legislator, Edmonds served as a judge in New York's judicial system from 1845 until 1853; his appointments included terms on the state's First Circuit Court, Supreme Court, and Court of Appeals.

2. Reference is to Martin Van Buren's letter to William H. Hammet of April 20, 1844, in which the former president opposed immediate annexation of Texas by treaty. Van Buren's "Texas Letter" appeared in the Washington *Globe* on April 27, 1844. John Tyler submitted the Texas annexation treaty to the U.S. Senate on April 24, 1844.

3. Variant of Livy's phrase, "per fas aut nefas," which translates "by fair means or foul."

4. Edmonds' reference is to section seven of the Democratic National Convention's third resolution, which denied that Congress had power "to interfere with or control the domestic institutions of the several states" and denounced efforts of abolitionists to secure congressional interference in the slave question. *Niles' National Register,* June 8, 1844.

5. The Texas circular of July 1844 endorsed the Polk and Dallas ticket but rejected Texas annexation.

6. On July 24, 1844, the New York *Plebeian* published the "secret circular," along with an editorial denouncing its authors. The New York *Evening Post* published the circular later the same day and included an editorial supporting the authors.

7. Edmond's reference is to the Democratic National Convention's sixth resolution, which opposed ceding any part of Oregon to Great Britain and favored the immediate re-annexation of Texas. *Niles' National Register,* June 8, 1844.

## FROM ANDREW JACKSON

My dear Sir,            Hermitage February 22nd 1845

By the time this reaches, you will be inaugurated, and executing the great & important duties appurtaining to the office of President of the United States, surrounded by office seekers, and office recommenders. The object of this letter is to bring before you the characters of the number of individuals that will be pressed upon you for the collectors office at Mobile and as far as I am advised, to put you on your guard against those who now are presented by those who during the late struggle ran with the *hair,* and *cryed* with the *hounds,* [1] and are now pretending to be the Simon pures of democracy.

First I learn that Col Hogan [2] from ill health and debility is entirely incapable of performing the duties of that office, and that he is in the habit of intemperence. If this is true, however worthy otherwise, would bring down upon you censure to appoint him.

Then there is Mr Toulman, recommended by Mr. G. M. Gains [3] &c &c which will be well for you to enquire whether him, and his recommenders, have been zealous in the late struggle, or whether they have not been ranked with those who ran with the Hare and cryed with hounds. I learn Mr. Shields, ex. member of congress is at the city, [4] whom you know, and who can give you full information on the subject of the characters & fitness of all the candidates for the collectors office at Mobile.

I have been since you left me overun with recommendations from that state, all in duplicate, which I will not enclose you, as you will have the originals before you. But I sum them all up in this; that there are two prominant candidates for that office, one of whom ought to receive the appointment in the view of real democrats, one Mr. Sanders, and the other Mr. Andrew J. Crawford, who stand high as honest, capable, & fit men for this office! [5] Mr. Sanders I do not personally know. But Mr. Andrew J. Crawford I do, and will vouch that a more honest worthy man does not live, and one who has been a uniform democrat all his days, as was his revolutionary father[6] before him, who, in the revolutionary [war] did much good service, received severe wounds, which crippled him all his life, & rendered him incapable of providing for his family & all he had to leave them were, high character, for moral honesty, & english education. Mr. A. J. Crawford has a large family, to provide for, and if his claims are equal with Mr. Saunders, then I think in all such cases, it is due to the son of one of those revolutionary patriots, who risqued their lives, & freely shed their blood, in our glorious struggle for Independence should be preferred.

From those my feelings, I need scarcely say, that if Mr. Crawfords recommendations place him on equal ground with Mr. Saunders, *of which you are to Judge,* that it will afford me great pleasure to hear of his appointment. From the recommendations I have seen, I leave all others out of the question, altho there may be others who deserve well of their country.

We are all anxiety here, to see the result of the reannexation of Texas *now* before the Senate.[7]

The wiggs here have you in bad health at Wheeling. This, from advice from thence, we know is not true. But they had me a hundred times dead, but still I live; & it will be the way with you. We all salute you & yr. amiable Lady, and have no fear about your health, energy to administer your office *well,* and keep yourself clear of all influences of political cliques.

ANDREW JACKSON

P.S. I refer you to Mr. Shields, for correct information of the candidates fitness, & claims for the office of collector for the port of Mobile. A.J.

ALS. DLC–JKP. Addressed to Washington City and marked *"Private."* Published in Bassett, ed., *Correspondence of Andrew Jackson,* VI, pp. 371–72.
1. Variant of an early English colloquial saying, "to hold with hare and run with the hound."
2. John B. Hogan, a senator in the Alabama legislature from 1829 until 1835, served as collector of customs at Mobile from 1836 until 1841.
3. Theophilus L. Toulmin and George S. Gaines. A native of Kentucky, Toulmin served as a senator in the Alabama legislature from 1838 until 1844. In 1848 he accepted appointment as postmaster of Mobile and served until 1849. A native of North Carolina, Gaines sat for two terms as a senator in the Alabama legislature, 1825–26, and later served as president of the Mobile branch of the Alabama State Bank. In 1856 he moved to Mississippi and served one term in the state legislature in 1861.
4. An Alabama planter, Benjamin G. Shields served four terms in the Alabama legislature as a Democrat, 1835–38, before winning election to a single term in

the U.S. House in 1841. Appointed U.S. minister to Venezuela by Polk, Shields served from 1845 until 1850. Defeated in his bid for the Alabama governorship in 1851, he moved to Texas in 1854 and engaged in farming.

5. James E. Saunders and Andrew J. Crawford. Educator and Democratic politician, Saunders represented Lawrence County in the Alabama legislature in 1840; he moved to Mobile in 1842 to engage in commercial operations; and he received the appointment of customs collector for the port of Mobile in the fall of 1845. Crawford served as register of the land office at Demopolis, Ala., from 1833 until 1837.

6. Not identified further.

7. On February 27, 1845, the U.S. Senate passed joint resolutions for the annexation of Texas by a margin of 27 to 25.

## TO MARTIN VAN BUREN

My Dear Sir:                              Washington City Feby 22nd, 1845
I have received your several letters addressed to me at Washington,[1] and thank you for the information which you give me. When I wrote to you from Tennessee[2] it was my desire to look to N. York, for my Sec. of State or Sec. of the Treasury. Having subsequently made up my mind, to select the Sec. of State from another part of the Union,[3] I was still anxious to select a citizen of New York for the Treasury and came to Washington with that intention. Upon arriving here and taking a survey of the whole ground, I found great difficulties interposed. The South had in advance of my arrival very generally, united on a distinguished individual from that section of the Union, for that office.[4] *Indiana* and portions of some other of the Western States, had joined, them, in earnestly pressing the appointment of the same gentleman. I was not satisfied that it was proper to appoint him to that Post, but became convinced, that if I did not, great and extensive dissatisfaction would prevail, unless I could find, some individual in some other part of the Union who would be unexceptionable, to them & also to the North. Whether I have succeeded in this or not, time, only can determine. In your letter addressed to me in Tennessee,[5] you gave it as your opinion that *Mr Bancroft* of Massachusetts was qualified for any Department, and this opinion has been confirmed, by all the information which I have received from others. His appointment to the Treasury I have thought could not but be satisfactory to the North, whilst, those who urged the appointment of a Southern man, most strenuously, could take no exception to it. My present determination therefore is to call him into that Department. This being settled, and having made up my mind, as to the other places, except for the War and Navy Departments, I desire now to select a Secretary of War or of the Navy from New York. It would meet my present views

best to select a Secretary of War from that State. The reason for this, is, that the Cabinet will be a new one, unless, circumstances may exist to enable me to retain the present Secretary of the Navy, who is an old college associate and has ever been an intimate personal and political friend.[6] On this account I would be pleased to retain him, if I can do so with propriety and without giving offence to the other members of the retiring cabinet. Looking, then to New York for a Secretary of War, the question is, who is the proper man. *Mr. Flagg* and *Mr Cambreling* have only been mentioned in reference to the Treasury, and I presume would not be so well suited for any other Department. *Gov. Marcy* has been strongly recommended, and Mr *Butler* has been spoken of, but I have doubts from your letter whether the latter would accept. In this State of things, I sent for *Genl. Dix & Gov. Dickinson* last evening and had a *confidential* interview with them. They called this morning and united in recommending *Judge Jacob Sutherland* of Geneva for Sec. of War.[7] I am still left embarrassed. *Judge Sutherland* has I have no doubt a high reputation in New York, but he wants that nationality of charac- ter, which I think important to command the confidence of the country, at the commencement of the administration. And furthermore I have no knowledge that his opinions, upon the great questions, upon which the administration must act, would accord with my own. In short I have nothing upon which to rest, so far as *Judge Sutherland* is concerned, but the recommendation of *Genl Dix & Mr Dickinson*. If *Mr Butler* or *Gov Marcy* would either of them be satisfactory, to yourself and the Democ- racy of New York, I would have no hesitation in tendering the office to either. I know them *personally*. They have both public character, would be satisfactory to the public out of N. York, and give strength to the administration. Would *Mr Butler* accept? If he would I would be de- lighted to have him. Would *Gov. Marcy* accept? If he would I should be greatly pleased to have him. With either, I know I would have an able and safe man. These, are my present views given to you in the *strictest confidence* and for your *own eye alone*. Will you give me your advice in like confidence? Who ought to be selected? I have found your remark most true, that he knows but little of the difficulty of Cabinet making, who has never tried his hand at it.[8] Though I have great difficulties, in coming to satisfactory conclusions, the world knows nothing of them. I have kept my own secrets. I have heard opinions and suggestions from friends, scarcely any two of whom agree, but have communicated to no one, what my conclusions are. There never was a time when proferred silence, and secrecy as to the formation of a Cabinet was so important as at the present. My determination is not, to permit the names of the Cab- inet, to go to the public until they are nominated to the Senate. The City is crowded with visitors, and every hour gives rise to some new rumour as to the probable composition of the Cabinet. All I believe are now becoming satisfied that nothing can be known, and that the rumours which circulate cannot be relied on. I hope you will write to me by the earliest mail after you receive this letter. The time is short and I am most anxious to hear from you before I am compelled to act difinitively ....

JAMES K. POLK

ALS. DLC–MVB. Addressed to Lindenwald, N.Y., and marked *"Private & Strictly Confidential."*

1. See Van Buren to Polk, February 10, 11, and 15, 1845.
2. See Polk to Van Buren, January 4, 1845.
3. James Buchanan.
4. Robert J. Walker.
5. See Van Buren to Polk, January 18, 1845.
6. John Y. Mason.
7. Jacob Sutherland served as an associate justice of the New York Supreme Court from 1823 until 1836.
8. See Van Buren to Polk, January 18, 1845.

## FROM JAMES HAMILTON, JR.

My Dear Sir.                     [New Orleans, La.][1] Feby 23d 1845

As I am just from Texas, having left the seat of Government[2] a fortnight after Major Doneldson, I have thought before you went into power, it might not be unimportant to have the advices from that Country posted up to the period of my departure. Frequent intercourse with the Executive of that Country[3] & the officers of his Cabinet and still more intimate & frequent with Capt. Elliott[4] the British Chargé D'Affairs enable me to express some confidence in opinions, founded on facts, entirely within my own observation.

I violate no confidence when I say to you that I believe if the annexation of Texas to the United States is not consummated by the Autumn, that I entertain little doubt that on the single condition of non annexation and a reduction of her Tariff to 10 pr Cent ad valorem without a single concession on the Slave Question or single discrimination in favor of the commerce of G.B. the Independance of Texas will be guaranteed by the former together with a definitive Peace with Mexico. In fact Capt Elliott told me from what had passed between Lord Aberdeen & Dr Ashbell Smith the late Chargé D'Affairs[5] before he left London he felt satisfied these terms could be *immediately* obtained but that G.B. desired to see the final issue of the annexation settled which I have no doubt Mr. Packenham[6] has hitherto informed his

130    *Correspondence of James K. Polk*

Govt the Whigs with the disaffected Democrats were strong enough to defeat.

Should therefore the Measure be lost at the present session, I tell you candidly and sincerely that I believe its final success will depend on your reassembling Congress without delay and keeping the matter at *white heat* still on the anvil. Whether the objections to an *extra* Session outweigh the considerations which give value to the Union between Texas & this Country are topics which you are far more capable of forming a judgment than myself.

That 19/20th of the people of Texas are in favor of annexation is beyond all doubt, but it is equally true that the officers of Govt. and the ambitious Men who look to distinction beyond that which a subordinate State Govt can confer, are inimical to it. All they want is a *patent* to enable them to come *out*. At present they dread the omnipotence of public sentiment in favor of annexation.

I hope you received and will equally pardon the Letter I wrote you in favor of Mr Calhoun's being persuaded to remain in his present post.[7] I have since almost regretted the liberty I took, for if no public reasons can be found for his retention in the public service his friends ought to consult what belongs to himself in not arguing those of a private character. Dissmissing this subject with this remark under a conviction that Mr. Calhoun['s] public Reputation will always enable him to take care of himself you will allow me to say one word for two gallant & noble S Carolinians Col. R B Campbell Consul at the Havannah & Col. P. M. Butler Indian Agent.[8] Their social intercourse I assure you with Clay has never weaned them from their devotion & attachment to those principles which gave you your election and of which you are the powerful Exponent.

I beg your kind consideration of the claims which these gentlemen present not alone in being actual Incumbents but in their honor integrity & fidelity in their respective trusts.

Allow me in conclusion to wish you all the Prosperity & honor which can possibly attend an administration which I believe will be honest loyal & faithful to the public weal.

J. Hamilton

ALS. DLC–JKP. Addressed to Washington City, delivered by express mail, and marked "Private."

1. Hamilton mistakenly wrote "Washington City" on the dateline, but the letter was postmarked "New Orleans La. Feb 24."

2. Austin, Texas.

3. Anson Jones, a physician, served Texas as a member of Congress; as secretary of state, 1841–44; and as its last president, 1844–45.

4. Charles Elliot served as British chargé d'affaires to the Republic of Texas from 1842 until 1845.

5. George Hamilton-Gordon, Earl of Aberdeen, and Ashbel Smith. Aberdeen, a native of Scotland, was raised to the peerage of the United Kingdom in 1814; served as chancellor of the Duchy of Lancaster, twice as foreign secretary, and as secretary for war and colonies in the government of Sir Robert Peel; after 1846, he became the Peelite leader of the opposition in the House of Lords and subsequently formed a coalition government of Whigs and Peelites that lasted from 1852 until 1855. A graduate of Yale College and surgeon general of the Texas army, Smith served as Texas' minister to England and France from 1842 until 1844, and as secretary of state during Anson Jones's presidency.

6. A career diplomat, Sir Richard Pakenham served as British minister to Mexico, 1835–43; to the United States, 1843–47; and to Portugal, 1851–55.

7. See Hamilton to Polk, November 29, 1844.

8. Robert B. Campbell and Pierce Mason Butler. A South Carolina nullifier, Campbell served in the state legislature before his election to the U.S. House in 1823; defeated in his bid for reelection, he won a special congressional election in 1834 and a full term in 1835. Campbell filled consular posts first in Havana, 1842–50, and then in London, 1854–61. Governor of South Carolina, 1836–38, and agent to the Cherokees, Butler formed a South Carolina volunteer regiment to fight in the Mexican War and died in battle in 1847.

## FROM JOHN CATRON

Dr Sir,                                   [Washington City] Monday Feby 24 [1845][1]

1. Gnl. Harrison returned in person, the call of the Judges of the S.C.U.S.,[2] and my elder Brethren especially, expect the honour from you.

2. There is no law *requiring* the Ch. Justice to administer the inauguration oath to the Presdt. elect, and it is done by written request from the Presdt. elect to the Ch. Justice, and some days in advance of course.

I take the liberty to suggest these matters, because you might not recollect them, as I did not, until the Ch. Justice[3] stated it to me.

J. CATRON

ALS. DLC–JKP. Addressed to Coleman's Hotel, Washington City.

1. Date and place identified through content analysis.

2. United States Supreme Court.

3. A 1795 graduate of Dickinson College and member of the Maryland House for one term, 1799–1800, Roger B. Taney broke with the Federalist party over its opposition to the War of 1812; he subsequently served in Andrew Jackson's cabinet as attorney general and later as secretary of the Treasury. Whig opposition in the U.S. Senate denied him an associate's seat on the U.S. Supreme Court in 1835; however, the following year he went to the Court as its chief justice and served in that post until his death in 1864.

## FROM RUSSELL JARVIS[1]

Mrs Peyton's[2]

Dear Sir,                                    [Washington City] Feby 24, 1845

The following are the only additional suggestions which I wished to offer, founded upon a doctrine proclaimed in the Nashville Union; and I send them in writing, as a mode less obtrusive upon your time and engagements, than a personal interview. The Nashville Union says that no candidate for the Presidency will be admitted to the cabinet.[3] Though I take for granted that this highly respectable journal has no authority for proclaiming the opinions of the President concerning the construction of the cabinet, yet as the soundness of this rule will not be generally admitted, I rely upon your courteous acceptibility to any respectful suggestions against it, prompted by regard to the dignity of your administration, as essential to the honor and prosperity of the country.

My first objection against the rule is that, it must exclude the ablest men of the dominant party from the cabinet. Such men are usually candidates, their strength being the very reason for placing them in that position; and if that position excludes them, the President must be reduced to secondary men for his executive auxiliaries.

Another objection is that the rule is utterly indefinite, and therefore may be abused by rival portions of the dominant, and even by insidious portions of the defeated party. A man may recieve a nomination from a caucus of Congress or a State Legislature, a popular meeting, a self-constituted committee, or even a newspaper. Either invests him with the character of a candidate; and if such character must exclude him from the cabinet, any aspirant may thus exclude a rival of the same party, by procuring a surreptitious nomination. A self-constituted committee, or the editor of a newspaper, professed friends but real opponents of a prominent politician, may disqualify him for the cabinet by such nomination. And the division, faction or clique whose leader is thus insidiously ostracised, may return the compliment upon the leader of the division, faction or clique that has done the wrong; and thus may rival factions kill off the general officers of each other, till nothing is left for the cabinet but subordinates. And even the defeated party may thus exclude from the cabinet all the strong men of the victor party, by instigating enemies in the guise of friends, to *mark* them with nominations to the Presidency. A rule thus easily susceptible of abuse cannot be safe.

The only assignable reason for the rule, is the prevention of intrigues for the succession. But can they be so easily prevented by the President, within or without the rule? If men are excluded for this cause, the very exclusion makes them candidates still more conspicuously, and authorizes them to devise and prosecute plans for the succession. And these plans may be prosecuted beyond the cognizance of the President, and consequently beyond his power of prevention. Such men may feel justified in regarding the exclusion as a declaration of hostilities, and may therefore be prompted to annoy and embarrass the administration. But if such candidates are admitted to the cabinet, they cannot prosecute such plans without detection by the President; and if they be removed for such cause, the removal affectually destroys them with the people, who always regard as an abuse of office, the intrigues of a cabinet officer for the Presidency. Hence such candidates, out of the cabinet, are beyond the President's control, while his administration is not beyond their opposition; but in the cabinet, they are within his control, while his administration is beyond their opposition, which can merely injure or destroy themselves.

If then a President would most affectually protect his administration from the effective opposition of prominent candidates for the Presidency, he will place them in his cabinet.

I take for granted that the leaders of the dominant party who have ever been mentioned as candidates, would abstain from all indirect means for the succession, and in or out of the cabinet, would faithfully consult the interest of the country thro' the dignity and stability of their party; and hence the object of my remarks is to have the unsoundness of this rule, and not to intimate any thing concerning individuals.

It is proper to add that, although a partizan of General Cass before the Baltimore nomination, I offer these suggestions with no views to the succession. *That* should be left to the spontaneous action of the people, who will, I trust, in due time, assign it to the most worthy. In the mean time, it becomes every good citizen of our party to exert himself for the success of the administration, as essential to the honor and prosperity of the country.

Russell Jarvis

ALS. DLC–JKP. Addressed locally.

1. From 1825 until 1828 Jarvis joined Duff Green in editing and publishing the Washington *United States Telegraph*; in 1836 Jarvis established and edited the Philadelphia *Public Ledger and Daily Transcript.* Upon leaving the *Public Ledger* in 1839, Jarvis founded the Philadelphia *World,* an unsuccessful morning journal. Later he returned to the *Public Ledger* and also served as a correspondent for other journals.

2. Ann Peyton operated a boarding house at No. 1 Pennsylvania Avenue in Washington City; Polk kept rooms there from 1827 until 1832.

3. Jarvis probably refers to an article in the *Nashville Union* of February 1,

1845; the author of the editorial warns that "if any aspirant for the succession, or the friends of any aspirant have calculated upon obtaining the ascendency in his counsels, with the view of steering his administration to a given port, let them look to his wisdom, firmness, independence and energy as displayed under less trying circumstances, and they will abandon all such hopes."

## FROM JOEL B. SUTHERLAND

My dear Sir                         Philada 7 AM Feby 24th 1845

In the "Kensington *District*," at the recent election the *Natives* have only carried *one* out of 4 wards.[1] Things will do better *there,* hereafter than at the fall election. I was *invited* to 2 celebrations in Kensington on the 8th of January.[2] I could not conveniently attend them both on account of their *time* of meeting. I however sent a *Toast* to one & visited & *addressed* the other. I of course put some *fire* into the assembly before I left. The meeting was very large & I pressed union & harmony. The *recent elections* speak for themselves. Hugh Clark Esq. whose house during the *Kensington riots was gutted* & greatly injured has been elected *Alderman.*[3] He *held that office* at the time of the riot.

I was on Saturday invited to 2 public celebrations of the Birthday of Geo. Washington. Judge Blythe & Come Elliot[4] were also invited & were present. The celebrations were both of the *right character* although one was *military.*

We intend to celebrate Genl Jacksons Birthday. By occupying the minds of the people with proper subjects we cannot fail to do good.

I had an excellent letter from Genl Jackson *dated the 10th of Feby.*

Please remember me to Mrs P.

J. B. SUTHERLAND

ALS. DLC–JKP. Addressed to Washington City.

1. Kensington township, a northeastern suburb of Philadelphia, held local elections on February 21, 1845.

2. Sutherland's reference is to celebrations of the anniversary of the Battle of New Orleans.

3. Hugh Clark, a wealthy Irish weaver, served as a police magistrate in Kensington's Third Ward. In early May of 1844, armed conflict erupted between Protestant nativists and Irish Catholic immigrants; the riots resulted in several casualties and substantial property damage.

4. Calvin Blythe and Jesse D. Elliott. Elliott served with distinction in the War of 1812 and received command of the Philadelphia navy yard in 1844.

## TO BENJAMIN F. BUTLER

My dear Sir                                        Washington City Feb 25. 1845

The most important Duty which I will have to perform in the commencement and perhaps during my administration, will be the selection of my Cabinet.

For reasons which are satisfactory to myself I have determined to look to the State of New York for my Secretary of War. Among all her eminent citizens I have selected yourself in preference to any other for that office and now tender it to you. I do not doubt that your opinions and views accord with my own upon all the great questions now attracting the public attention and which will probably be the subject of action during the next four years. Your general political principles I Know are such as meet my full approbation. It may be proper to add that the principles & policy which will be observed & maintained during my administration are embodied in the resolutions adopted by the Democratic National Convention of Delegates assembled at Baltimore in May last and of which you were the author.[1] In the Inaugural address which I have prepared and which I propose to deliver to my Fellow Citizens on assuming the duties of President of the U States those principles are distinctly recognized & re-iterated with some amplification of course and are such as I have no doubt you will approve. That there may be greater certainty of this I will in the event of your acceptance submit the address to you for your perusal, before it is delivered. Having an anxious desire to compose my cabinet in a manner and of men that will be satisfactory to myself and to the Country I most sincerely hope that you will not hesitate to accept the office which I now tender to you. If you will do so I will be personally gratified & the Country I am sure will have the services of an able & efficient officer. I feel assured further that you will be satisfied with your associates in the Cabinet. I am surrounded as you may well imagine by many difficulties but can assure you that your selection is my own & that I prefer you to any other that has been named. The time is short between this & the 4th of March and I have to request that you will give me as early an answer as may be practicable. I have to request further that in the event of your acceptance (of which I hope there is no doubt) you will come to Washington at your earliest convenience that I may submit my inaugural address to you & confer with you about other important matters connected with the duties of my administration. It will be important for me to hear from you & if possible to see you before the 4th March & the earlier the better.

JAMES K. POLK

L, in the hand of J. Knox Walker. DLC–JKP. Addressed to New York City and marked "Copy" and "Private & confidential."

1. Butler served as the chairman of the committee that drafted the convention's resolutions. See Polk to James Buchanan, February 17, 1845.

## FROM GOUVERNEUR KEMBLE[1]

My dear sir,                                [Washington City] 25th feby [1845][2]

Mr. Buchanan spoke to me this morning in relation to the cabinet appointment from New York, and after a full consideration of all the difficulties, permit me to propose, that Mr. Butler should be nominated to the War Depart. If he refuse the office, which he probably will, you pay him and Mr Van Buren the compliment and you gain time—if then you consider Govr. Marcy the next most proper person to fill the office, he may be named with the concurrence of Mr. Wright, who would not I think refuse it. But governor Marcys appointment without such concurrence, is now rendered more delicate, for the reason, that the members of the Legislature who have just petitioned for it, are all of that section of the party opposed to the views of the governor.[3]

Excuse me from troubling you, but impute it I pray you to an anxious, and sincere desire to promote the harmony and success of your administration.

GOUV. KEMBLE

ALS. DLC–JKP. Addressed locally.

1. A New York cannon manufacturer, Kemble sat in the U.S. House from 1837 until 1841; he served as a delegate to the state constitutional convention of 1846 and to the Democratic National conventions of 1844 and 1860.

2. Date and place identified through content analysis.

3. On February 6, 1845, Andrew Billings and thirty other members of the New York House wrote Polk soliciting the appointment of William L. Marcy to the cabinet; on February 13, 1845, Calvin T. Chamberlain and twelve other members of the New York Senate urged Polk to appoint Marcy to a cabinet post. NsS. DLC–JKP. For the growing split between New York's Hunker and Barnburner factions, see Silas Wright, Jr., to Polk, January 21, 1845.

## TO MARTIN VAN BUREN

My Dear Sir:                                Washington City Feby 25th 1845

I wrote to you on the 22nd, giving you some account of my troubles in regard to the composition of my Cabinet and asking your advice. There has not been time for your answer to reach me. The time is very short, between this and the 4th of March, and I fear if I wait for your letter, that I will not have it in my power, to write again to New York, & receive an answer from any one whom I may determine to appoint. For this reason and because I feel assured, that the appointment of *Mr Benjn. F. Butler* could not fail to be satisfactory to yourself and the Democracy of New York, I have come to the conclusion to tender to him the office of Secretary of War. I have written to him, to day a strong letter, tendering the office to him and urging him to accept it. I am most sincerely desirous that he shall do so, & strongly hope that he will, not withstanding what you have written to me. I know Mr Butler to be one of the purest and best men on earth; and I have made a strong appeal to him for the sake of the country to accept it. With him near me I shall feel that I have a reliable friend as well as an able consellor. I hope you will exert your influence to induce him to accept. I am so occupied every moment with company, that I have no time to give you an account, of the perplexing troubles by which I am surrounded. If Mr Butler accepts, the greatest of these will be removed.

JAMES K. POLK

ALS. DLC–MVB. Addressed to Lindenwald, and marked *"Private & Confidential."* Van Buren's AE states that this letter was "Rcd after the affair was all over."

FROM WILLIAM H. HAYWOOD, JR.[1]

Wednesday morning

My Dear Sir [Washington City February 26, 1845][2]

Hon Mr Walker is not in his seat and how long he may be absent I cannot tell. You are at liberty to communicate to him what I reported to you if he should be at his rooms & of course in reach of a message from you.[3] I do not wish what I told you *written* to any one for the present.

WM. H. H. JR.

ALS. DLC–JKP. Addressed locally.

1. Haywood served several terms in the North Carolina House prior to his election as a Democrat to the U.S. Senate in 1843; he resigned his seat in 1846 rather than obey unacceptable instructions from the state legislature.

2. Place and date identified through content analysis. The Library of Congress has filed this letter at the end of 1838.

3. Haywood's point of reference probably is the Texas annexation compromise whereby the president of the United States would be given the choice of merging the two republics either by treaty or by articles of annexation.

## FROM WILLIAM H. HAYWOOD, JR.

Senate Chamber
Wednesday night
Dear Sir.                              [Washington City February 26, 1845][1]

As often happens high excitement has been created on account of Bagbey's speech.[2] It is just the time for patriots to keep cool. Temporarily there is peril. May it be only a storm preceding the sunshine of our harmony. I inform you of the peril that you may co-operate. How absurd. If Bagby *votes* with us what matters his speech. Exhort our friends to stand firm to the *Comp*[3] and all will be well. Rashness amongst even our humbler statesmen now may sacrifice all. The *Comp*: must not be abandoned. The still opposition to the House Resolution is a hostility of scruples honestly entertained and it *cannot* yield. If it could it would have been yielded long ago.

But a *panic* now will lose all and that is all I fear for. I write to you to keep you apprized. Bagby is solemly pledged to vote for the *Comp* & he will redeem it.

WILL. H. H. JR.

ALS. DLC–JKP. Addressed locally and marked *"Confidential."*
1. Place and date identified through content analysis.
2. A Democrat and an ally of Thomas H. Benton, Arthur P. Bagby served as governor of Alabama, 1837–41; U.S. senator, 1841–48; and minister to Russia, 1848–49. Reference is to Bagby's speech in the U.S. Senate of February 26, 1845, in which he questioned the constitutionality of the House's joint resolution for Texas annexation. Bagby, offering his support for an annexation bill tendered by Benton on February 5, 1845, noted that he favored the admission of Texas into the Union if it could be accomplished under the provisions of the U.S. Constitution.
3. According to Robert J. Walker's recollection Haywood suggested to him on February 24, 1845, that he introduce an amendment to the House resolution for the annexation of Texas; Haywood's suggestion, probably tendered with Polk's blessings, provided that the president of the United States would decide whether Texas' admission to the Union would be by joint resolution of Congress or by treaty. Assured that Benton's friends in the Senate would accept such a compromise, Walker consulted Calhoun's friends and then on February 27, 1845, offered the compromise as suggested by Haywood. Walker's amendment passed the Senate the following day by a narrow margin of 27 to 25. Robert J. Walker to Polk, November 6, 1848. LS. DLC–JKP.

## FROM CAVE JOHNSON

Dear Sir                                    Washington Feby 26th 1845

I had the honor of receiving yours of the 17th inst.,[1] inviting [me] to take charge of the P.O. Department & briefly suggesting, "the principles & policy" upon which you propose to administer the Government and have also examined your Inaugural address.

I concur most heartily with you in the principles set forth in your Inaugural address and in the Baltimore resolutions as well as the several suggestions in your letter as to the duty of your Cabinet officers.

I accept the position you have been pleased to assign me and shall enter upon its duties with zeal and a determination to use every effort to advance the common good of our country and to promote the success and glory of your administration.

                                                    C. JOHNSON

ALS. DLC–JKP. Addressed locally.

1. Letter not found. For the text of Polk's cabinet invitation, see Polk to James Buchanan, February 17, 1845.

## FROM JOHN TYLER

                              Wednesday morning. President's Mansion
My dear Sir,                     [Washington City February 26, 1845][1]

When I changed the day from Thursday to Friday to secure the pleasure not only of your company and Mrs. Polk's, but that of Mr. Dallas at dinner with us, it did not occur to me, that Friday was the anniversary of the very melancholy affair on board the Princeton, which involved in the same fate with others, Mr. Gardiner, the father of Mrs. Tyler.[2]

Will you, therefore, Dear Sir, permit me to substitute Saturday for Friday? when no circumstance will exist in the way of the full flow of pleasure and gratification.

                                                    JOHN TYLER

LS. Polk Memorial Association, Columbia. Addressed locally.

1. Date identified through content analysis.

2. Father of Julia Gardiner Tyler, David Gardiner was a supporter of John Quincy Adams and served as a New York state senator, 1824–27. Gardiner died in the explosion of the gun "Peacemaker" aboard the U.S.S. *Princeton* on February 28, 1844.

## FROM BENJAMIN F. BUTLER

My dear Sir,                                New York, Feby. 27th 1845

I have before me your letter of the 25th instant inviting me to become a member of your cabinet as Secretary of War. For this distinguished mark of your confidence, I beg you to receive my most grateful acknowledgments; and I very much regret that it is not in my power to give proof of their sincerity, as well as to manifest the interest I take in the success of your administration, by accepting the office proposed to me. This, however, I am prevented from doing by domestic and prudential considerations which forbid (except in a case of duty too clear and imperative to be mistaken) my removal to the seat of Government. The present does not seem to me to be such a case, and the objections referred to remain, therefore, in full and conclusive force.

While I will not affect to conceal that had you found it consistent with the public interest and proper in other respects, to tender to me the office of Secretary of State, or that of Secretary of the Treasury, I should have felt it to be my duty to make the sacrifices which my acceptance of either would involve. I beg you to be assured that in declining the station now proposed to me I have not been influenced, so far as any feelings merely personal are concerned, by any reference whatever to the relative importance of these offices. On the contrary, were my pecuniary condition favorable to a residence at Washington, I should unhesitatingly accept your present offer.

Though not requested, in the event of my non-acceptance, to make any suggestions in respect to the War Department, I avail myself of the occasion to say, that considering the present posture of things in this state, the appointment of Mr. Cambreleng, would I think, be highly judicious and acceptable. I am the more free to take this liberty because my engagements in this city will not permit me to visit Washington prior to the 4th of March, so that I shall have no opportunity of personal conference with you upon the subject.

Repeating the assurance of my high sense of the honor done me by your proposal, and most sincerely hoping that no serious embarrassment will result from this reply to it ....

B. F. BUTLER

ALS. DLC–JKP. Addressed to Washington City; delivered by John O'Sullivan and Samuel J. Tilden. Butler sent a copy of this letter to Martin Van Buren. L, copy. DLC–MVB.

## FROM BENJAMIN F. BUTLER

My dear Sir,                                        New York, Feby 27th 1845

Since writing the enclosed,[1] it has occurred to me, that contingencies may possibly arise in which you may wish to be informed, definitely & from myself, of my views as to the policy to be pursued by your administration in relation to Texas.

Considering the result of the late election as expressing the will of the American People in favor of the re-annexation of Texas at the earliest moment consistent with our national interests & honor, it will, obviously, be the duty of the new administration to devote itself, immediately & vigorously, to the accomplishment of this measure. How much will devolve upon it, and in what particular line it will be required to act, must, of course, depend on the posture in which the matter shall be left by Congress.

It will, in my judgment be your policy, as I doubt not it will be your inclination, to treat the subject in the same prudent, conciliatory & national spirit, in which it was presented to the country by the Baltimore Convention[2] & to deal with it on its true merits occupying no ground, and adopting no arguments of the last administration except such as shall be found to be just, tenable & wise.

In any shape in which the matter is likely to come to you, difficulties must be encountered; but if the object be pursued with wisdom and steadiness, I cannot doubt a successful issue—one that shall secure to the Union this important acquisition on terms honorable in themselves and pacific in their effects, and therefore acceptable to fair minded & reflecting men, of all parties, in all quarters of the Union.

The administration which shall effect such a result will merit, & receive, the lasting gratitude of the nation; and, in my judgment, no higher or nobler object of ambition can be set before an American President, than the glory of such an achievement.

In relation to the questions now pending in the Senate, I may mention, that although I have not deemed it useful, or so long as the composition of your cabinet was undecided, becoming, to obtrude my opinions upon the public, they have not been concealed from my friends. Considering the *last* bill of Col Benton,[3] as preferable in many respects, to any other form in which the subject has been presented, and especially so as likely to be more generally acceptable at the north than any other, I have advised, *first*, the adoption of that bill, if it could be carried; *secondly* the passage of the Joint Res. of the House[4] with the provisions of Col Bentons bill added as an alternative or in some other way consistent with the resolutions; *thirdly,* the Joint Res. of the House amended, by inserting the line of 100° W Long. from Col Benton's first bill,[5] or the line of 34° N Lat. from Mr. Haywood's bill[6]; and *lastly,* the Joint Res. of the House *as they stand.* A Letter embracing these points was addressed by me to Gen. Dix, one of the Senators from this state on the 24th inst. which should you desire it could be procured through my friend Mr. Tilden, for your perusal. No person now in Washington, but Gen Dix himself, knows of this letter (unless Gen. D. may have mentioned it) and for obvious reasons of delicacy towards him I should not, at present, speak of it to any person there but yourself.

B. F. BUTLER

P.S. Mr. Tilden is my personal & political friend & perfectly acquainted with my views & wishes. He may be freely spoken with, so far as may be necessary in relation to myself, with unlimited confidence in his integrity & honor. B.F.B.

ALS. DLC–JKP. Addressed to Washington City; delivered by John O'Sullivan and Samuel J. Tilden. Butler sent a copy of this letter to Martin Van Buren. L, copy. DLC–MVB.

1. See above, Butler to Polk, February 27, 1845.
2. See John W. Edmonds to Polk, February 22, 1845.
3. See John Catron to Polk, February 4, 1845.
4. See Cave Johnson to Polk, February 3, 1845.
5. For details of Thomas H. Benton's Texas Annexation bill of June 10, 1844, see William C. Campbell to Polk, January 28, 1845.
6. On January 14, 1845, William H. Haywood, Jr., introduced on the Senate floor a bill providing for the immediate annexation of Texas; however, Haywood's bill divided the question of annexation from that of acquisition: Congress would legislate in advance the terms for annexation and leave the mode of acquisition to be decided later, say by treaty or by resolution. Haywood's bill ran a free-slave dividing line west of the Indian Territory through Texas at the 34th parallel. Thus Haywood's bill would compromise the slavery question in the same fashion as the Missouri Compromise, although not on the 36.30 line; and it would separate and postpone the constitutional disputes over the mode of acquisition. Unless and until the two republics effected a territorial cession, the act of annexation would remain inoperative.

TO JOHN C. CALHOUN

Thursday morning

My Dear Sir:                    [Washington City] Feby 27 [18]45

I beg leave to introduce to you my nephew Col. Walker, who will hand you this note. I desire to have an interview with you, and request, that you will inform Col. W. at what time it will suit your convenience.

JAMES K. POLK

ALS. ScCleU–JCC. Addressed locally. Published in Clyde N. Wilson, ed., *The Papers of John C. Calhoun* (21 vols.; Columbia, S.C., 1959–93), XXI, p. 372.

## FROM MARTIN VAN BUREN

My dear Sir                                       Albany Feby 27, 1845

I recd. your letter last Eveng[1] whilst on the wing for this place. In that spirit of entire candour which has hitherto distinguished & ever shall our intercourse I must say to you that it has caused me considerable embarrassment, and not a little pain. If any honest and unbiased Democrat in the U. States had been asked in view of the circumstances of the late election from the nomination at Baltimore to the close of the contest, how the new cabinet ought to be formed, his first reply would be that what has hitherto been universally regarded as the first office in it might with entire propriety be taken from New York. Such I infer from the explanations accompanying your offer of the Treasury Department to Mr Wright[2] as were your own first impressions. Yet we could well consider that the condition of a great public question & the supposed adaptation of individuals to deal with it might well render it expedient & due to yourself to locate that officer elsewhere & therefore very cheerfully acquiesced in the suggestion of your letter to select the second place from here. But to find now[3] that the selection for this state is reduced to a lower point presents the matter in a very different light to those with whom a just state pride is stronger than the love of office, or the desire to obtain places for their friends. Still if any other state had happened to possess an individual so greatly superior in the proper qualifications to any which this could present as to make it due to a paramount regard to the public interest to select him we of New York would not have a word to say agt it. Conceding every thing to Mr Bancrofts capacities & admitting as I do that his appointment to the Cabinet affords me the greatest pleasure, still it is very certain that the decision cannot be put on that ground. But we are not left to conjecture upon this point as the statement contained in your letter clearly shows that it is a concession to a selfish influence proceeding from other quarters & directed agt New York directly & exclusively, & controuled by considerations which are easily understood but which you yet felt it your duty to make in the hope of avoiding the evils you describe. To give to the moment its most mortifying aspect it farther appears that it has recd its most efficient impulse from the same Indiana Delegation, with portions of those of Illinois & Michigan, who were the first & busiest actors in the field to unsettle public opinion before the Convention, & most active also in promoting a nomination which would have overthrown the Party[4] & which would have been made if New York had not promptly cast aside her own preferences to defeat it & thrown her great weight in favor of the movement which finally prevailed, & which she subsequently contributed so largely to make effectual. To a man of your sagacity & sound judgment it cannot in view of these considerations, when duly considered, be necessary to say that without even the knowledge of this latter circumstance, & most certainly with it, the honest hearted Democracy of this state will feel their pride severely wounded, & the recollection of past events painfully revived. Nor can it be necessary to say to you that those who give their sanction to such a state either by advice in its execution, or by their more direct agency in carrying it out, assume an undesirable & hazardous responsibility.

You will not I assume my dear Sir, for a moment, do me the injustice to suppose that I say this in a spirit of personal complaint agt your decision, or that I look upon your decision as evidence of a want of friendship on your part for Mr. Wright or myself or as a want of respect for the Democracy of this State. I am bound to say that too much has in my judgment been yielded to those who deem to look upon our State with an evil eye. I have at the same time the deepest conviction that you have done in the matter what you conscientiously believed to be for the best. You need no assurances to satisfy you that personal feelings or personal interests have had no weight with us. Mr Wrights & my own communications to you assured you abundant proof of this. You will recollect that I informed you in my first letter[5] that Mr Wright by allowing himself to be put in the breach & by which the election was secured had drawn out all opposition to his administration, for the moment not a little formidable but certain to go down in a very short time.[6] What those who compose it have done in regard to pressing the selection of any individual upon you for the Cabinet I cannot of course know, confident only that they would not be likely to bring forward anyone who would be the choice of Mr Wright *or* his friends. But we both know that no one has been pressed upon you by either of us. So far from having personal objects it is a fact that until this very day Mr Flagg was never informed, directly or indirectly, that either Mr Wright or myself had recommended him to you for any place, & I know that all the feeling either of us entertain upon the subject, beyond a sincere desire for the success of your administration, grows out of our desire that neither the character, pride, or interests of a State to which we both owe so much should suffer by any act of commission or omission on our parts.

Thus much for what is past & what we clearly perceive cannot be undone. Our course in regard to what remains to be done will be regulated by the same feelings which have forged it from the beginning—viz those of a deeply seated solicitude for your success in the truly difficult position in which you have been placed & a readiness to make all proper allowances for its embarrassments, which I can justly appreciate from actual experience.

There is not a better man in the State in all respects than Judge Sutherland, but my dear Sir the state of his health is such as to put it entirely out of his power to attend to the duties of the office of Secy of War. I was when I recd your letter upon the point of preparing letters for him to the South where he goes in the hope, I pray to god it may prove well founded, of saving his life. To shew that the Gentleman who presented his name[7] to you did so in my opinion at least very properly I need only state that I myself offered him a post in my Cabinet but which he for good reasons declined.

There is not time to consult Mr Butler but the exegencies of the case are such & the danger of your making a fatal mistake in this state so iminent that I take upon myself the responsibility of answering for Mr Butler that he will accept the War Department if it is tendered to him. He performed its duties under Genl Jackson & gained great credit in it. I shall however for my own protection send my son[8] to him by this days Boat to inform him of what I have done so that he may arrest it if he finds it out of his power to comply with our wishes for which there will be time, & in which event let me advise you by all means to take Mr Cambreleng.

[MARTIN VAN BUREN]

AL, draft. DLC–MVB. Addressed to Washington City; delivered by Smith Van Buren.

1. See Polk to Van Buren, February 22, 1845.
2. See Polk to Van Buren, January 4, 1845.
3. See Polk to Van Buren, February 22, 1845.
4. Van Buren's reference is to efforts to win the nomination for Lewis Cass.
5. See Van Buren to Polk, January 18, 1845.
6. For the growing rift between the Barnburners and Hunkers, see Silas Wright, Jr., to Polk, January 21, 1845.
7. Probably John A. Dix or Daniel Dickinson.
8. The fifth son of Martin Van Buren, Smith T. Van Buren occasionally served as his father's assistant and associated himself with the "Barnburner" faction in Albany.

## FROM MARTIN VAN BUREN

My dear Sir                                    Albany Feby 27th 1845

Your letter[1] did not reach me until last Eveng at the moment of my departure for this place. I have since my arrival here prepared a reply to your[2] questions with a view of the whole ground & when upon the point of committing it to the mail my son Smith has offered to guard agt. the contingencies of the mail by carrying it to you. He will leave here tomorrow & be with you as soon as possible & in person.

M. VAN BUREN

ALS. DLC–JKP. Addressed to Washington City.
1. See Polk to Van Buren, February 22, 1845.
2. See above Van Buren to Polk, February 27, 1845.

## FROM LEVI WOODBURY ET AL. [1]

Senate Chamber

Sir:                                    [Washington City] February 27, 1845

The committee of arrangements for the reception and inauguration of the President elect, on the 4th of March, and to apprize him of the same, have the honor to enclose copies of the programme of the arrangements for the occasion. [2]

The committee propose to receive the President-Elect at the Western gate of the capitol square opening into the Pennsylvania Avenue at a quarter before twelve o'clock M., and thence to conduct him to the Senate chamber. Should any other point of reception be more agreeable to you, the committee would be happy to learn your pleasure upon the subject.

LEVI WOODBURY

LS. DLC–JKP. Addressed locally.
1. This letter is addressed to Polk by a Committee of Arrangements and signed by Levi Woodbury, Sidney Breese, and Walter T. Colquitt.
2. Enclosure not found.

## FROM JOHN C. CALHOUN

My dear Sir                                    Washington [28]th Feb 1845[1]

Having been informed in the interview to which you invited me yesterday, of your determination to form an entirely new Cabinet, I deem it proper to apprize you of the fact, that I have resigned the office of Secretary of State to take effect, as soon as a successor is appointed & ready to assume its duties.

I regard it as not irrevalant[2] to the occasion to assure you, that the annunciation of your determination has caused, on my part, no dissatisfaction, nor abatement of the kind feelings, personal or political, which I have heretofore entertained for you. According to my opinion, it is the right of every President to select his Constitutional advisers, without giving any just cause of offense to any one.

In conclusion, I avail myself of the opportunity of expressing my sincere hope, that your administration may confer lasting honor on your self, & contribute to establish more firmly the liberty & prosperity of the country, by carring out in practice the great measures put in issue at the late election, & on which its success depended; by thoroughly reforming the government & restoring the Constitution to what its illustrious framers intended it should be; by preserving peace abroad, without sacrificing the honor or interest of the country; and by restoring & preserving brotherly feelings & harmony among the members of this mighty Union, in the only way it can be, by effectually discountenancing all attempts at interference with the institutions & internal concerns of each other, and equalizing, among the various sections, the burthens & the benefits of the government, especially in its fiscal operations.

J. C. CALHOUN

ALS. DLC–JKP. Addressed locally. Published in Wilson, ed., *The Papers of John C. Calhoun,* XXI, pp. 389–90. Polk's AE on the cover reads, "Hon. Jno C. Calhoun, S.C., Resignation as Sec. of State, Received March 1, 1845."

1. Calhoun misdated his letter "27th Feb"; correct date identified through content analysis.
2. Calhoun probably meant to write the word "irrelevant."

## FROM WILLIAM H. HAYWOOD, JR.

My Dear Sir                    W[ashington] City 28 Feb 1845
If you have it in contemplation to organize your Cabinet *excluding* a representative in it from N. York I beseech you to re-consider that point. I cannot conveniently call to night to say all I would upon this point & some others, but to guard you against surprise I send you the counsel of a friend, one who if not so *wise* is quite as *true* as any other. God prosper you.

WILL H. HAYWOOD JR.

ALS. DLC–JKP. Addressed locally and marked *"Private."* Published in Elizabeth Gregory McPherson, ed., "Unpublished Letters from North Carolinians to Polk," *NCHR,* XVI (October, 1939), p. 430.

## FROM ANDREW JACKSON

My dear Sir,                                    Hermitage Feby 28th 1845
When this reaches you, you will be amidsts of all that pressure of business which allways surrounds a president on entering on the duties of that office. Still aware of this my friendship for you & the real desire I have that you may go through your administration triumphantly concentrating the whole democracy in your support, & that no act of yours should be by implication or otherwise imputed to you, that would cause a split in the democracy.

I am just informed by Mr A Jackson Jnr,[1] that it is rumored & understood in Nashville, that our mutual friend Col Laughlin has gone on to Washington to become interested in the Madisonian, and that it is expected that the Madisonian is to become the organ of the administration. *Can this be so.* If so, surely the consequence cannot have been well considered. It will as certain as it is done, divide the democracy, and place you precisely in Mr Tylers shoes. It was his organ—*it has become yours*—and Col Laughlin accopanied you to the city. It will be by your enemies, ascribed to you that for this purpose you brought him on. Recollect that the papers because Mr. Tyler nominated your brother as charge de affairs,[2] at once came out charging you with bargaining with Mr. Tyler, for him to appoint your friends, & that you in return would pay the debt by appointing his to office.

When we see such vile slanders, as this, seized hold of to connect you with the Tyler party what may not be expected should you make the Madisonian the organ of your administration with Col Laughlin, in part, its Editor, your own good common sense will draw the conclusion.

What a spectakel would ensue. Pennsylvania New York, and all the democracy of the East would rise up against you & your administration on the ground that you had taken this step to aid Mr. Tyler to the succession.

I hope this rumor is not true. But if it is, I am sure Col Laughlin & all concerned have not reflected upon the result that must inevitably ensue, or have less judgment than I was in the habit of ascribing to them. I say to you as your real friend, & every good feeling for your success, that a more fatal or disasterous step to your administration could not be taken, and as your real freind without any other feeling or views but your success candour & friendship has induced me to bring the matter to your view. My dear friend look at the subject deliberately and then draw your own conclusions.

Major A. J. Donelson is now here, returned by the permission of the Sec of State,[3] leaves the 3rd, will await at New Orleans instructions from the Government, and when received will pass to Texas to carry them into effect. He had nearly lost his life in Texas, and will await your promise to send him [as] a full minister to some other station. Spain, Brazils, or Mexico, should Mr. Shannon[4] be recalled, or any other nation where health is promised. I assure him that he may rely in full confidence in your kind intention towards him—his pecuniary condition requires it.

Me & my whole household join in the kindest & best wishes to you & your amiable Lady, & pray for your entire success in the administration & that you may leave it with the united voice of the whole Union, well done thou good & faithfull servant.[5]

ANDREW JACKSON

P.S. I am greatly afflicted. When I attempt to walk, I am at once suffocated for the want of breath. A.J.

ALS. DLC–JKP. Addressed to Washington City and marked *"Strictly Confidential."* Published in Bassett, ed., *Correspondence of Andrew Jackson,* VI, pp. 372–73.

1. Andrew Jackson, Jr., the ex-president's adopted son, lived at the Hermitage with his wife, Sarah Yorke Jackson, and their three children, Rachel, Andrew III, and Samuel.

2. William H. Polk. See Cave Johnson to Polk, January 2, 1845.

3. John C. Calhoun.

4. Elected twice to the governorship of Ohio, 1838–40 and 1842–44, Wilson Shannon served as minister to Mexico from 1844 through 1845. He won election as a Democrat to a single term in the U.S. House, 1853–55, and then moved to the Kansas Territory, where he served two years as governor, 1855–56.

5. Jackson's last phrase is a partial quotation of Matthew 25:21.

# MARCH

## FROM BENJAMIN F. BUTLER

My Dear Sir,                                    New York, March 1. 1845

I have this day received letters from Mr. Van Buren and Gov. Wright, by which I learn, that they have been advised (through a letter from you to the former) of your intention to propose to me the office of Secretary of War, and by which they strongly urge me to accept it.[1] It also appears that Mr Van Buren has expressed to you the opinion that I would probably do so.[2] This seems to make it proper that I should say, that while the contents of these letters increase my regrets at the necessity which compelled me to make the decision announced in my letter of the 27th ult. and my anxieties as to the selection you shall make of a Cabinet Minister from New York, I do not find in them any ground for changing that decision, especially as I cannot know what action you may have taken on the subject since the receipt of my reply.

B. F. BUTLER

ALS. DLC–JKP. Addressed to Washington City.
1. See Polk to Martin Van Buren, February 25, 1845.
2. See Martin Van Buren to Polk, February 27, 1845.

## FROM JOHN P. HELFENSTEIN[1]

Dear Sir,                                    Washington City March 1. 1845

Rumor says that an effort will be made to place Samuel Madaira[2] of Ohio, at the head of the Post Office Department. As one of your warm and devoted friends, I will regret if it takes place, because it will be an act directly contrary to the wishes of your friends in that Section of the West in which a knowledge of Mr Madaira's political views are known. A great and powerful struggle has just pass'd away, and much depends on the selection you make of your constitutional advisers, to add strength to the good cause, and secure its permanency.

In 1840 Ohio was in the minority about 20,000. In 1842 the Democracy reduced that vote, and succeeded in Electing their candidate for Governor[3] by a majority of about 4000.

The cause of the defeat of the Democratic Party in Ohio in 1840 mainly arose from the high handed measures pursued by its then leaders, of which Mr Madaira was one of the Chief. Maney of the best Democrats of the state were discouraged, because the policy pursued by Mr Madaira and others would not relax—on the contrary, rather continued to persevere in their ruinous measures.[4] As one opposed to the measure then pursuing, I was fearful our nominee for Govr. would be defeated. A second defeat would not only ruin one of the best men (Govr. Shannon) but would destroy every prospect of regaining the State.

President Tylers United States Bank veto call'd from me a complimentary note.[5] In that note I pledg'd myself to give his administration my support, provided his acts continued in accordance to Democratic views. This note opened a Correspondence, and an understanding, between myself, the president, Govr. Shannon and prominent friends of Mr Tyler in Ohio. The sequel you know; success was the consequence, and again Ohio stood on the proud eminence of Democratic Victory.

In all this trial Saml. Madaira was the direct opponent, and if the negociation and arraingement had not been conducted with great prudence, and withheld from a Knowledge of Madaira and others, till near the election, defeat would have followed. The result was, the Election of the Govr., a majority in the Legislature, consequently a United States Senator.[6] These things are all fresh on the memory of the West. I now appeal to your Superior Knowledge and Judgment whether Mr Madairas appointment as Post Master General would be acceptable to the Democracy of the West.

You will recollect the astonishment created on the result of the Ohio election in 1842, and the great rejoicing of the Democracy on the un-

expected result, being the humble instrument then to bring about the
Union in Ohio. I had a fair opportunity of knowing men, and do with
confidence believe, if you nurse these men near your person, a favourable
opportunity will only be wanting to incumber your Administration with
dificulties, so as to give force and effect to their favourable measures.

To test the correctness of my statement, I appeal to Presdt. Tyler and
Govr Shannon, between whom I negociated the Union that resulted so
favourable in 1842. Letters are in my possession to sustain me.

The verry friendly manner you received me on introduction, taking
also in consideration your time, is the reason why I take this mode of
communicating to you.

                                        JOHN P. HELFENSTEIN

ALS. DLC–JKP. Addressed to Washington City and marked "Private."
    1. A native of Germantown, Penn., Helfenstein owned businesses in Lan-
caster and Carlisle before moving to Dayton, Ohio, in 1829. He ran for Congress
as a Jacksonian Democrat in 1832 and 1834 but lost both times to Joseph H.
Crane. From 1835 until 1841 Helfenstein served as land register in Lima, Ohio;
he moved to Wisconsin in the winter of 1843. The following year his son, J. Albert, received an appointment to the receivership of public monies at Milwaukee.
    2. Samuel Medary.
    3. In 1840 Harrison carried Ohio with a majority of 24,009; and Thomas
Corwin, the Whig candidate for governor, won the gubernatorial election by a
majority of 16,132. In 1842 Wilson Shannon, the Democratic candidate for governor, carried the state with a majority of 1,872.
    4. Helfenstein's reference probably is to Medary's hard money position on
banking reform in Ohio following the Panic of 1837.
    5. Helfenstein's letter has not been identified further; Tyler vetoed two Whig-
sponsored bank bills in 1841.
    6. The state elections of 1842 resulted in the election of Wilson Shannon as
governor, Democratic majorities in both houses of the state legislature, and the
subsequent reelection of Democrat William Allen in 1843 to the U.S. Senate.


## TO WILLIAM L. MARCY

My Dear Sir:                              Washington City March 1st 1845
    The most important duty which I will have to perform at the com-
mencement, and perhaps during my administration, will be the selection of my cabinet. For reasons which are satisfactory to myself, I have
determined to look to the State of New York for my Secretary of War.
I now tender to you the office of Secretary of War, and hope it may be
consistent with your views to accept it. I do not doubt, that your opinions and views accord with my own, on all the great questions now attracting the public attention, and which will probably be the subjects

of action during the next four years. Your general political principles I know, are such as meet my full approbation. It may be proper to add, that the principles and policy which will be observed and maintained, during my administration are embodied in the Resolutions adopted by the Democratic National Convention of Delegates, assembled at Baltimore in May last. In the Inaugural Address which I have prepared, and which I propose to deliver to my Fellow Citizens, on assuming the duties of President of the United States, those principles are distinctly recognized, and re-iterated, with some amplification of course, and are such as I have no doubt you will approve. I would be pleased to submit the address to you for your *perusal* before its delivery, but the time between this and the 4th of March is too short to allow of this. Not doubting that you will approve it, and having an anxious desire, to compose my Cabinet in a manner and of men, that will be satisfactory to myself and to the country, I hope you will not hesitate to accept the office which I now tender to you. If you will do so, I will be personally gratified, and the country I am sure will have the services of an able and efficient officer. I feel assured further that you will be satisfied with your associates in the Cabinet. I am surrounded as you may well imagine with many difficulties, connected with the responsible duties on which I am soon to enter, but shall meet them firmly and hope to be able to overcome them. I have to request that you will give me as early an answer as may be practicable, and in the event of your acceptance (of which I hope there is no doubt), that you will come immediately to Washington. I hope you may be able to reach Washington by the 5th Inst., on which day, I will probably make the nominations of the Cabinet to the Senate. I would prefer to make them all, at one time. If you come on, forthwith, and shall find it to be necessary to return to New York, preparatory to a permanent residence here, you could readily do so, after a few days, and when the administration would be fully organized.

JAMES K. POLK

ALS. DLC–WLM. Addressed to Albany and marked *"Private & Confidential."* L, copy in the hand of J. Knox Walker. DLC–JKP.

## FROM JOHN L. O'SULLIVAN AND SAMUEL J. TILDEN

Sat. morning
[Washington City. March 1, 1845][1]

Mr. Tilden & Mr. O'Sullivan of New York desire the honor of seeing the President, coming on behalf of Mr. B. F. Butler, & bearing a letter from him to be delivered to the President in person.[2]

N. DLC–JKP. Addressed locally. Polk's AE on the cover states that he had a personal interview with Tilden and O'Sullivan.

1. Date and place identified through content analysis.

2. Reference probably is to one of three letters from Benjamin F. Butler to Polk, February 27, 1845. ALS. DLC–JKP. Butler's letters of February 27th probably were enclosed under a single cover.

## FROM MARTIN VAN BUREN

My dear Sir                                    Albany March 1st [18]45

My Son Smith left me yesterday with a letter for you.[1] He was to see Mr Butler on his way down, or leave a letter for him from Mr Wright & myself, and I confidently trust that before this reaches Washington you will have been agreeably relieved from all embarrassment in regard to this State.

I arrived here at a moment when the honest portion of the Democracy were under a great excitement in consequence of a report brought by our friend Mr Tracy[2] direct from Washington that Mr *Woodbury* was certainly to be Secy of the Treasury, & that N York would in all probability be entirely passed by in consequence of a difference of opinion between Mr Wrights friends and those who had become his opponents in consequence of his permitting himself to [be] used as a Candidate for Govr. at the late election.[3] I had also before I sat down to write you, had before me the ingenuous & lamb-like countenance of Mr Flagg, insisting that his name should not be used for the War Deptmt. least it might continue your embarassment, although well understanding why he had been opposed, & conscious that those who dislike him solely on account of his straight forward & incorruptible character were rejoicing in his supposed defeat. Under these circumstances, & perhaps a little stimulated by your reference to the action of certain old acquaintances of mine from the West,[4] I wrote you, a longer, & I fear a more animated letter than should have been addressed to you under your present circumstances.

Although I took great pains to guard my feelings in the matter agt. misconstruction, and find upon a reperusal of its contents that as far as words could do so that was done, Still I am conscious that there was in it notwithstanding too much feeling expressed, having reference to your difficult & embarassing position. Being by habit & feeling most strongly opposed to any thing like sulkiness in such affairs and knowing how painful it is to one in your situation to receive complaints from those on whose friendship and forbearance he thinks he can place the greatest reliance, I cannot in justice to my own feelings suffer the matter to pass without removing from your mind any possible impression that Mr Wright or myself harbour the slightest feeling of unkindness towards yourself in consequence of what has been done or any other than that which was avowed—an anxious desire that the Democracy of the State should not believe that they had been slighted in this matter & that we had been wanting in our duty to them on the occasion. That I could not under the circumstances act further in the matter without consulting him will of course be at once apparent to you. You may then rest assured that so far as it is in his & my power & that of our friends to cause the selection of the Cabinet to be well recd. it shall be done. The agency of the auxiliary influence which was brought to bear upon the question,[5] & with the character & former practices of which we are much better acquainted than you can be, shall be cautiously concealed, & every thing done to give the new administration a favourable start. If it is constituted as we conclude it will be I am sanguine in my expectations of its general popularity. In Bancroft & Butler you will find what is of the greatest importance to one in your situation, men of kind feelings, cheerful temper & unfailing fidelity & firmness & if you succeed in making the retention of your old companion & friend[6] acceptable you will have another of like dispositions. No one can tell until he has experience how much the disagreeable feelings & vexations of all Kinds inseperable from the management of public affairs are alleviated by having the assistance & companionship of such men. I think I know Mr Mason well & esteem him most highly. Others will tell you that Bancroft is a literary man & not practical as they did me. But I know better. The troubles of the Custom Houses occupied a full third of our time & there was scarcely a day in which Mr Woodbury & myself were not closetd for hours in settling them. In respect to that at Boston whilst under Mr Bancrofts management[7] I do not recollect of a single difficulty occuring & I venture nothing in saying that no Custom House in this Country was ever better managed. The error consists in attaching to Yankees who are literary men, the same disqualifications for business which almost invariably attach to those of other races, but from which they & the Scotch are very generally exempt, wanting only opportunity, if they are fit for any thing, to qualify themselves for any thing. This affair being now finished you will not be harrassed with any more long letters from me & after expressing the satisfaction I derived from the scope, steadiness & self possession evinced in your last letter written under such trying circumstances,[8] I will only assure you of the unfeigned solicitude with which I will watch the course of events and hope for your success. Remember me kindly to Mrs Polk whose want of health I sincerely regret & ....

M. Van Buren

ALS. DLC–JKP. Addressed to Washington City and marked *"Private."* Van Buren sent this letter under separate cover to John A. Dix, and Smith Van Buren delivered it by hand to Polk on March 3. Van Buren's retained copy of this letter carries on its cover the following endorsement: "Mch 1st, 45. Both Mr Wright & John having expressed opinions that my letter of the day before was somewhat severe though very just, the enclosed was sent as an anodyne." L, copy in unidentified hand. DLC–MVB.

1. See Van Buren to Polk, February 27, 1845.

2. Van Buren's reference probably is to John Tracy. During the 1820's Tracy won election to four terms in the New York assembly. From 1832 until 1838 he served as lieutenant governor under William L. Marcy.

3. See Silas Wright, Jr., to Polk, January 21, 1845.

4. See Polk to Van Buren, February 22, 1845.

5. Not identified further.

6. John Y. Mason.

7. George Bancroft served as collector of customs for Boston from 1838 to 1841.

8. See Polk to Van Buren, January 25, 1845.


## TO MARTIN VAN BUREN

My Dear Sir:                                        Washington City March 1st 1845

I have waited anxiously for the last two days, in the hope that I would receive an answer to my letter of the 22nd ultimo, but none has come to hand. I wrote to you again on the the 25th informing you that I had invited *Mr Butler* to take charge of the War Department, and stating to you the reasons which had induced me to do so. I regret to say that I received *Mr. Butler's* answer to day, declining to accept it.[1] I am therefore at sea again, so far as that office is concerned. In my letter to you on the 22nd ult. I mentioned the names of *Mr Butler* & *Gov. Marcy* and in the order of their names, as the persons upon whom my mind was resting. They have both a national reputation, which would command the public confidence in advance, and this I think is important in the composition of my cabinet. I am fully sensible that I came into the office, not only at an earlier period of life than any of my predecessors, but perhaps, with less of the public confidence in advance than any of them. This being the case, I have thought it not only important, but perhaps indispensible to compose my cabinet of men, who had a public reputation throughout the Union, and who would give weight of character to the administration, the moment they were announced. It was for this among other reasons, that I desired most anxiously, to have Gov. Wright in the cabinet. Next to him I looked to *Mr Butler*. Both of these gentlemen have declined. *Gov. Marcy* stands, in reputation, out of New

York, next to Mr *Wright* and Mr *Butler*. He possesses undoubted talents and business habits, and as far as I am informed accords with me, in my political principles and views. Mr *Flagg* does not possess, a national reputation: and upon a view of the whole ground I cannot see, that the appointment of Gov. Marcy can be unsatisfactory, to my friends in New York. As I cannot wait another day, without being too late, for a letter to reach Albany and receive an answer by the 5th of March, on which day I will probably make the nominations of the Cabinet, I have determined to tender the office to *Gov. Marcy*, and will do so by the mail of this evening.[2] I hope his appointment may be satisfactory to you. If you were here, and could witness the difficulties by which I am surrounded, you could appreciate them, but not otherwise. I shall meet them firmly and I hope successfully.

In your letter to me in Tennessee,[3] you expressed the opinion, but with some doubt, that Mr *Butler* might possibly be induced to accept the office of Secretary of State, and that you were satisfied that he would not accept that of the Treasury. In *Mr Butler['s]* letter received to day, there is an intimation, that he might have accepted either. It is now however too late to tender either of them to him.

I have kept my own councils as far as it was practicable to do so, but still rumors, will circulate in the City. Among these the impression became general three or four days ago that *Mr Bancroft* was to be Sec. of the Treasury. This has brought down upon me, the N. Hampshire and Maine delegations in Congress, against his appointment, for the reason probably, that they had favorites of their own, whom they desired to have appointed. Some of these delegations have gone so far as to recommend strongly a Southern man, under the impression probably, that it would be better for *their* friends, to have a person, in that office, who would be a stranger to them in the dispensation of patronage, than one who would have his own friends in that section of the Union. Whatever the reason may be, I state to you the fact. I will not communicate to the public who my Cabinet will be until, they are nominated to the Senate. The City is crowded with strangers, a large majority of whom have their own personal & selfish ends in view. After the 4th of March I will cause it to be made known that I will make no appointments whilst they remain in the City. In this way I hope to disperse the crowd, when I can act deliberately, and understandingly, upon their applications.

JAMES K. POLK

ALS. DLC–MVB. Addressed to Lindenwald, N.Y., and marked *"Private & Confidential."*

1. See Benjamin F. Butler to Polk, February 27, 1845.

2. See Polk to William L. Marcy, March 1, 1845.
3. See Van Buren to Polk, January 18, 1845.

## FROM JOHN L. O'SULLIVAN

Dear Sir,                              [Washington City] March 2. 1845

After our conversation with you yesterday morning,[1] Mr. Tilden and myself concluded to write to Mr. Butler such representations as we thought would probably have the effect of inducing him to come on so as to reach here *on Monday Evening,* in season for a personal interview with you before the necessity of final action. We sent the letter by a private messenger, so as to ensure its delivery by 3 o'clock to-day; and unless he may have Engagements of business and duty of an absolutely insuperable character, we feel a strong hope and confidence that he will come on. The urgency of the public affairs, we thought, would justify even to him the necessity of starting on Sunday afternoon; or at any rate, by leaving on Monday morning, he could be here in the course of that night, so as to see you early on Tuesday morning. The former is, however, the more probable. Though regretting to intrude on you a note on the subject to-day,[2] it nevertheless seems proper that we should apprise you of what we have done and expect.

                                              J. L. O'SULLIVAN

ALS. JKP–DLC. Addressed locally.
1. See O'Sullivan and Tilden to Polk, March 1, 1845.
2. O'Sullivan's apology relates to his undertaking business affairs on Sunday.

## FROM SMITH T. VAN BUREN

My dear Sir                        [Washington City. March 2, 1845][1]

I am the bearer of a letter from my father which you expect to receive & which I wish to deliver personally.[2]

Will you oblige me by mentioning an hour when it will be convenient for you to receive it?

                                              S. T. VAN BUREN

ALS. DLC–JKP. Addressed locally and marked "Private."
1. Date and place identified through content analysis.
2. See Martin Van Buren to Polk, February 27, 1845.

### FROM JAMES WHITCOMB[1]

My Dear Sir,                                   Indianapolis, March 2d 1845

I am pained, as well on your own account as that of the Democratic party, to see so large a number flocking to Washington, ere you are well in your seat, in quest of office. My mortification only finds a partial alleviation in the belief, that had our opponents succeeded, the crowd would have been still greater. A sincere regard for the predominance of our party, its principles and measures, essential as I regard them to be, to the prosperity of the country, if not to the safety of our institutions, will, I hope, be viewed as a sufficient apology for my obtruding a suggestion in relation to this matter, (so far at least as Indiana is concerned) for your better consideration.

We trust that Indiana is now Democratic. And, as our majority of a little over 2000 in 1843,[2] has been followed by your majority of rising 2300 in Nov. last, we further trust that that majority is a sound one. Still, it is but a small majority in a State, the aggregate vote of which, at the last election, was above 140,000. The current however, is slowly setting in our favor and if no unlucky accident occurs, its force will, ere long, be such, as I hope will place us beyond danger.

The difficulty which I most apprehend would consist in the premature bestowal of offices, especially where rival applicants are numerous. Many have already gone on from this State to solicit offices. No little jealousy and crimination already exist among many of them and their friends. Within my own observation, the excitement in the community already prevails to a considerable extent. Each applicant of course feels, or professes to feel great confidence in the superiority of his own pretensions, and the tendency, I fear, will naturally be to detract from those of his rivals, if not indeed to misrepresent their standing and character. The appointment of one will certainly not strengthen the attachment of the others to the coming administration. The fear is that it will neutralize their exertions in a future canvass, if it does not turn them against us.

Similar affects of the numerous and sweeping appointments made by the party in power, within the first three months after they took the reins of government in 1841, was soon seen. They were manifested in their general defeat in the very next elections. In Maryland, when Harrison's majority had been from 4000 to 6000, the Democratic party carried their Governor.[3] These facts however, are familiar to you.

On the other hand, I am aware, that it seems to be expected, and indeed generally conceded, that changes will be made, especially in those offices from which our opponents ejected the incumbents solely on account of their political opinions. If it should be understood indeed, that no changes, or move of consequence, will be made, the effect I think, would not be less disastrous.

Under these circumstances, continued reflection has only strengthened my conviction that the better course would be, to *defer* making any changes, as far at least as this State is concerned, until after the next August election[4]; unless indeed it should become necessary by the expiration of the term of the incumbent. But let it be understood, that *time* is necessary for the purpose and that office will not be conferred on gentlemen while in attendance at Washington. This will also afford the necessary opportunity for mature deliberation as to the comparative merits of the applicants. For, the zeal with which an office is sought, the easily manufactured newspaper puffs, and the *number* of names brought to bear by an applicant, so far from being conclusive evidence of his superior pretensions, are generally the reverse. Inferior talent instinctively feels the *necessity* of extraordinary exertions; the modest pride of conscious worth will not stoop to them.

By deferring the appointments until after the next elections, every applicant will feel it his *interest* to recommend himself, in the meantime, by increased exertion. This is of the last importance in this State, for the next election, settles not only the political character of our delegation in the next Congress, but also that of our legislature which chooses a U.S. Senator, & which, if democratic, will rid us of the present unequal system of State representation fastened upon us by our opponents in 1840.[5]

Doubtless, you will have been fatigued with reasons of a contrary character to the views here expressed. The large majority of them visiting Washington at this time, are, I apprehend, desirous of office, and they can with difficulty see any reason in even a postponement of their wishes. The views of many, are too much circumscribed by a desire for present emolument for the requisite foresight, which regards our future ascendancy.

Although the publicity of these views would defeat their object yet they may be submitted to your constitutional advisors, if thought worthy of their attention, with the same injunction.

I hope, My Dear Sir, you will pardon this intrusion. My apology, I hope, will be found in a desire, amounting to a deep anxiety for the broad & continued success of your administration, deeply affected as it must be, by the policy pursued, at this, perhaps, its most critical period. As regards Indiana too, I am anxious, that my unremitted exertions to redeem the State ever since my dismissal from office at Washington, should not be rendered unavailing.

These reflections have doubtless crossed your own mind, but the situation of our affairs here, coming as they do, to a great extent under my own observation, makes me feel that I should be wanting in proper attachment to our principles, to our policy, & to you, upon whom, their success so eminently depends if I should withhold my views thus imperfectly expressed. I regard indeed, these principles and measures, as more directly in issue now, than they have been since 1800, & under fairer prospects, for we have not now a National Bank to struggle against.

Wishing you health happiness & a prosperous administration ....

JAMES WHITCOMB

P.S. The last intelligence we have from Washington leads me to hope that Texas is by this time a part of the U. States.[6] It is of the last importance to us in this State that it should be so.

ALS. JKP–DLC. Addressed to Washington City and marked *"Private"* and "Confidential." Polk's AE on the cover states that "Gov. Whitcomb of Indiana recommends that no removals be made in Indiana unless in case of vacancies until after the August election 1845."

1. A lawyer from Terre Haute, Ind., Whitcomb served as a member of the Indiana Senate, 1830–36, as commissioner of the General Land Office, 1836–41, and as governor, 1843–49. From 1849 until his death in 1852, Whitcomb sat in the U.S. Senate as a Democrat.

2. In 1843 Indiana held elections for the U.S. House, state legislature, and governorship. Democrats won eight of the ten U.S. House seats as well as majorities in both houses of the state legislature; James Whitcomb won the governorship.

3. A leading lawyer from western Maryland, Francis Thomas won five terms as a Democrat in the U.S. House, 1831–41 and then served as Maryland's governor from 1841 until 1844.

4. In August 1845 Indiana held elections for the U.S. House and the state legislature. Democrats won eight of the ten U.S. House seats as well as majorities in both branches of the state legislature. The legislature later appointed Democrat Jesse D. Wright to the U.S. Senate.

5. Reference probably is to a February 1841 bill reapportioning of senators and representatives for the state legislature.

6. Reference is to Walker's compromise bill of February 27, 1845, which allowed the president to choose between immediate annexation of Texas or continued negotiations with that republic.

## FROM GOUVERNEUR KEMBLE

My dear Sir                                        Monday 3rd March 1845

Mr. Smith Van Buren has stated to me that you had been guided in the selection of Govr. Marcy for the post of Secretary of War by my recommendation. You will recollect that in the short conversation which we had on this subject, while acknowledging the talents and capacity of Govr. Marcy to fill the station proposed, I stated, that although I considered him friendly, he did not stand in the same confidential relation with Govr. Wright that others did; and in the note which I delivered to you on Wednesday last,[1] I distinctly advised that he should only be called here with the approbation and concurrence of Govr. Wright. I did this because I was not fully informed of the personal & political relations of these gentlemen, and as I therein stated, because the members of the legislature who had asked his appointment, were known to belong to that section of the party whose views were opposed to the Governor.[2] Permit me now to repeat the advice which I then gave, that Mr. Butler be first nominated, and should he refuse, it will still be time enough to correspond with Govr. Wright—and I the more urge this upon you, because I now learn from Mr. S. Van Buren, and other Gentlemen recently arrived, that the appointment would not be agreeable to a large portion of the Democratic party in N York, and that if unsustained by Mr. Wright, it may lead to the most fatal divisions among us.

GOUV KEMBLE

ALS. DLC–JKP. Addressed locally.
1. See Kemble to Polk, February 25, 1845.
2. Reference is to recommendations from Andrew Billings et al., February 6, 1845, and from Calvin T. Chamberlain et al., February 13, 1845.

## FROM WILLIAM L. MARCY

Dear Sir:                                          Albany Mar. 3d. 1845
Your letter offering me the office of Secretary of War[1] has just been received, and I have concluded to accept it. I shall in compliance with your request leave immediately for Washington and hope to be there on the 5th or 6th instant.

I assure you that I duly appreciate the honor conferred on me by this selection to a place in your cabinet and shall endeavour to justify your favorable expectations. I anticipate a concurrence in our views upon all the great & important questions which may arise for your consideration during your administration, and it will be my earnest desire, as it will be my duty, to do, to the utmost of my ability, all that may appertain to my situation to bring about right results.

W. L. MARCY

ALS. DLC–JKP. Addressed to Washington City.
1. See Polk to Marcy, March 1, 1845.

## FROM JOHN Y. MASON

My dear Sir,                        March 3d 1845
The subject of our conversation last night had been presented to me for so short a time that, in my anxiety to promote your wishes in regard to your admn., and to retrive you from all embarrassment, I intimated an assurance, which the most mature reflection since has induced me to ask you to have the goodness to excuse me in asking to withdraw. I therefore respectfully ask that you will not make me the offer which you mentioned, as possibly to be made.
The considerations which prompt me to this course are purely personal, and I assure you, do not proceed from any want of sensibility for the kindness which you have evinced to me, or of ardent zeal for the success of your administration, and of your own personal happiness and prosperity.

                                             J. Y. MASON

ALS. DLC–JKP. Addressed locally, and marked "to be read when delivered." J. Knox Walker's AE states that Mason "asks that the President will not offer him a seat in the Cabinet."

## FROM JOHN Y. MASON

Sir.                             Washington. March 3rd 1845[1]
I have the honor to acknowledge the receipt of your esteemed favour announcing to me your desire to have my assistance in your administration as Attorney General,[2] and making known to me your views of the principles and policy which will govern you in the high office to which your country men have called you.
It gives me pleasure to assure you of my entire concurrence, of my anxious wish for the success of your administration, and for the advancement of your own personal Reputation. I accept the place which you are pleased to offer me, and if confirmed by the Senate shall enter on its duties, with a determination to devote myself to them, with the best of my poor ability, and with the assurance, that it will be my aim to meet your just expectations, and, if at any time, the most delicate sensibilities should make it desireable, to place my situation at your disposal.

                                             J. Y. MASON

ALS. DLC–JKP. Addressed locally. Polk's AE states that he received this letter on March 5, 1845.
1. The date "March 5th" has been written over to read "March 3rd."

2. Letter not found. For the text of Polk's form letter to his prospective cabinet members, see Polk to James Buchanan, February 17, 1845.

## FROM JOHN Y. MASON

Navy Department
Sir,                                        [Washington City] March 3d 1845
In the month of Novr[1] I apprized you of my intention to resign the office of Secretary of the Navy, in due season, to leave you wholly at liberty to fill it as to you might seem best. I have the honor to inform you that I have this day resigned my office, to take effect when my successor shall be appointed.

J. Y. MASON

ALS. DLC–JKP. Addressed locally.
1. See Mason to Polk, November 16, 1844.

## FROM HENRY E. RIELL[1]

Dear Sir                                    [Washington City] Mar. 3d [18]45[2]
Pray grant me a moments conversation relative to New York—if you cannot, pardon me for saying that you will find Marcy the most obnoxious to all honest men in the State. He will prove as treacherous as Foster and all the conservative Democrats of our State. In mercy's name save the Nation.

HENRY E. RIELL

[P.S.] Mr Brown knows my character.

ALS. DLC–JKP. Addressed locally.
1. A native of New York, Riell served as a gauger in the New York City Customs House in 1839; he held the post of weigher general in 1845.
2. Place and date identified through content analysis.

## FROM SAMUEL J. TILDEN AND JOHN L. O'SULLIVAN

Monday 2 pm
My dear Sir                                  [Washington City March 3, 1845][1]
Aware how oppressive your engagements are, I am extremely averse to intrude, even for a moment, upon your attention. But I feel that I should not acquit myself, according to my sense of duty, to parties to whom it is

only necessary to allude, if I did not *earnestly* solicit an interview with you at as early an hour of today as your convenience will allow.

S. J. TILDEN

J. L. O'SULLIVAN

ALS. DLC–JKP. Addressed locally and marked "Private."

1. Place and date identified through content analysis.

## TO MARTIN VAN BUREN

My Dear Sir:                                        Washington City March 3d 1845

Your letter of the 27th was handed to me by your son[1] at sun set on last evening. My letter to you of the 1st, will inform you of what has been done. If I have committed an error, I can only say it was unintentional. It pains me to think that you may suppose that I have acted unkindly towards yourself or your friends. I am surrounded now every moment, and have scarcely time to write this note. I must therefore postpone for a few days, that full explanation, of facts and circumstances here, which induced the course I have taken: only assuring you now that no influences, of which I have had any knowledge, which were of an unfriendly character towards yourself or Gov. Wright, have had any thing to do in controlling my course. The changes of position of the members of the Cabinet seemed to be imperative, upon me. I will write again as soon as I have leisure.

JAMES K. POLK

ALS. DLC–MVB. Addressed to Lindenwald, N.Y., and marked "Private." Van Buren's AE on the cover states, "the promised explanations have not been made."

1. Smith T. Van Buren.

## FROM SMITH T. VAN BUREN

My dear Sir,                                        Washn. March 3d 1845

I am so deeply impressed with the disastrous effects of the arrangement which was indicated in your communication to me this morning,[1] that I cannot omit one farther effort to avert those effects. The case in regard to Mr. Butler stands substantially thus: You wrote to my father[2] that if Mr. Butler would accept the War Dep't. you would be delighted to have him: before receiving an answer from my father you offered him (Butler) the appointment[3] and he declined it; upon receipt of this declension,[4] it was suggested to you that my father might induce him to accept notwithstanding his declension; and you assented to a delay of any definitive arrangement until you should receive my father's answer.[5] By the next mail after this understanding was had with the gentlemen who made that suggestion you offered the post to another.[6] On the next day you recd my father's answer[7] accepting for Mr. Butler; and you have not yet received an answer from the person[8] to whom the Department has been tendered.

Now, my dear Sir, in view of the deplorable consequences to the Party in the state of New York, of which I have sufficiently advised you, in view of the resulting influence on the success, honor and happiness of your administration & of the country, and also in view of the extremely awkward and embarrassing position in which my father & Mr. Butler stand, is it not entirely competent for you, is it not due to yourself & to the weighty considerations I have mentioned, that you shd.[9] appeal to the gentleman to whom you have last tendered the Department to restore you to the position in which you stood previous to your communication with him? Is not as much weight to be given to the state of your relations, on the subject, with my father & Mr. Butler, with the former of whom the question *was not closed* when you concluded to open it with another, as to the actual position of that other, from whom you have as yet no reply? It seems to me that these questions must be answered affirmatively. Can any honest friend to your administration insist on exposing you to the consequences of disregarding the delicate attitude in which the matter leaves the gentlemen with whom you first communicated? The delay of a day or two is not to be considered in comparison with the results of an unhappy decision at last. At all events I feel bound to make this suggestion, which is the only one that occurs to me as applicable to the case.

I regret to add to your troubles, or embarrassments, but I know that I am endeavouring to point out the shortest, safest & surest way out of them.

S. T. Van Buren

ALS, draft. DLC–MVB. Addressed locally, and marked *"Private."* Martin Van Buren's AE states that this was a "Draft proposed letter to Mr. Polk—not sent. Drawn up at the suggestion of O'Sullivan & Tilden."

1. Reference is to information communicated by Polk to Van Buren, who had called to deliver his father's letter to Polk of March 1, 1845.

2. See Polk to Martin Van Buren, February 25, 1845.

3. See Polk to Benjamin F. Butler, February 25, 1845, and Butler to Polk, February 27, 1845.

4. Van Buren probably meant to write the word "declination" here and below.

5. During a meeting with John L. O'Sullivan and Samuel J. Tilden on Saturday, March 1, regarding Butler's refusal of the War Department appointment,

Polk reportedly said that he "would wait a day or two longer in the hope of still hearing from you before making another selection." John L. O'Sullivan to Martin Van Buren, March 1, 1845. ALS. DLC–MVB.

6. See Polk to William L. Marcy, March 1, 1845.

7. See Martin Van Buren to Polk, February 27, 1845.

8. William L. Marcy.

9. Here Van Buren cancelled the words "for you to" and interlined the phrase "that you shd."

## FROM SILAS WRIGHT, JR.

My Dear Sir,                                                    Albany 3 March 1845

As this will not reach you until you will have entered upon the duties of your office, I write to discharge a duty I owe to one of the most faithful of friends, and worthy democrats. I refer to Ransom H. Gillet, whom you will recollect as a member of the House of Representatives with you for four years, I think from Dec. 1833 to March 1837.[1] He was from the Congressional District of my residence, was a law student in my office, and is now my neighbor, when at home. I know him as well as I can know any man, and, without brilliant talents, he is sound, industrious, practical, and faithful. He is a good lawyer, and has had extensive experience in the practice of the profession. He is a devoted friend of yours and has been as faithful to you, from the day of your contest for the Speakership to this hour. I am sure you will recollect him well.

He is an applicant for one of the $3000. situations at the head of the Beauro's, and especially wishes the place of Solicitor of the Treasury, for which he is most peculiarly qualified. He and I both know too well the duties and responsibilities resting upon you to urge you beyond reason in this matter, or to permit you to dream that any offence will be given to either, if you shall not be able to appoint him; but I feel as much anxiety on your account as on his that you should, if it be consistent, secure him near you. Without the least disposition to be intrusive, you would find Mr. Gillet sagacious, honest, fearless, and faithful, and as to all matters in this State, and at the North generally, as useful to you as any one can be, who can be placed in the Cabinet from the North. He knows men, and public opinion, as well as any such an one will, and he will do any thing you wish him to do, skilfully, faithfully and without noise. In short, if this place, or any Beauro situation can be given to any one from this State, I am certain you cannot offer it to a more competent, faithful, or useful man. In short, please to consider me as saying all I should say on behalf of Mr. Gillet, for I can say truly all that can be said of a good and worthy man.

A paragraph as to myself, and I will relieve you. I regret to see that some of our delegation at Washington seem to treat me as a Candidate for the Presidency, as your successor, and much more to be informed that other friends at home do the same thing, and have, as I am told, in letters to you, put me in that position. I beg you to believe me when I say that I am not such candidate in fact, in feeling, or in immagination, and I think I may safely say I never shall be a candidate for that office by my voluntary choice. My observations, during the periods of Genl. Jackson and Mr. Van Buren's administrations, have stripped that high place of all charms to me. I think the labour and care much greater than the honor and emolument, as is the fact, in my estimation, with the office I now hold. I freely admit that both are well worthy the ambition of those who feel sure they can administer them well for the Country, and satisfactorily to the people; but I can not bring myself up to a moderate degree of confidence that I can reach either of these points, and I have had, and have, no desire to try what I greatly fear I cannot accomplish. I was pleased with my place in the Senate, and while I was not very anxious to continue in it longer, I was not willing to exchange it for any other place than my private and quiet home. Circumstances, which I could not control, and which I thought I ought not to try to resist, forced me to change it for my present place.[2] I do not desire to remain in it beyond my present term of two years, even if my political friends and party should desire it, as I think they will not, and I do not desire any promotion beyond it. Like circumstances may, by bare possibility, be equally controlling, upon some future occasion, but nothing else will make what some of my too partial friends are willing now to consider me.

I say these things to you, not because I desire to publish them through you, but because I desire you should know them, and that you should not feel, or believe that I have selfish wishes, or hopes, or views, to be subserved by your administration, or by any selections you may make of persons to fill the offices at Washington, as elsewhere. If I know myself, no such feelings actuate me, either as to the formation of your administration, or in recommending the few persons I may recommend, as I do now our friend Gillet, to your favor.

I regret to have troubled you with so long a letter, when I know and feel how little time, or patience, you will have to read the letters thrown upon you. I will not repeat the infliction, and desire no answer to this. The part in reference to Mr. Gillet you will bear in mind, because you know him, and the residue of it is intended only for yourself, and then destruction by fire will be the most appropriate disposition of the communication.

SILAS WRIGHT

ALS. DLC–JKP. Addressed to Washington City and marked *"Private."*
1. In addition to his two terms in the U.S. House, 1833–37, Gillet served two years as register of the U.S. Treasury, 1845–47, and also two years as its solicitor, 1847–49.
2. See Silas Wright, Jr., to Polk, January 21, 1845.

## FROM GEORGE BANCROFT

Sir,                                           City of Washington. March 4, 1845
Concurring in the opinions and views, expressed in the letter which you did me the honor to address to me yesterday,[1] I shall enter on the office you tender to me with a singleness of purpose to justify the confidence you repose in me by my best and most assiduous exertions in the conduct of the department to be entrusted to me.

GEORGE BANCROFT

ALS. DLC–JKP. Addressed locally. Bancroft dated the draft of this letter "March 5. 1845." AL, draft. MHi.
1. The date of Polk's letter offering Bancroft the Navy Department is problematical. Polk signed the letter and wrote its inside address; the date line and text are written in variant, unidentified hands; and the date "March 5th" has been overwritten to read "March 3rd."

## FROM GEORGE M. BIBB[1]

Tuesday Evening
Department of the Treasury
[Dear Sir:]                              [Washington City] 4th March 1845
It is proper to make known to you that I did on yesterday Evening, tender to President Tyler, my resignation of the Office of Secretary of the Treasury, to take affect as soon as my Successor shall have been appointed & qualified to enter upon the duties of the office.
I avail myself of this Occasion to repeat, that which I stated in our friendly interview, that if you should find it convenient to retain as a member of your Cabinet, the Honle. John Y Mason, that it would be to me very gratifying, & I have good reason to believe that no member of the late Cabinet of Prest. Tyler would take any exception, or feel any unpleasantness, on that account. The cords of friendship between yourself & Mr. Mason knit in youthful association at Colledge,[2] & strengthened by the Scenes of manhood & eminent Considerations of talent & cultivation, are not to be slighted. The motives which shall prompt you to retain Mr. Mason, would be respected by all honourable men.

GEO. M. BIBB

ALS. DLC–JKP. Addressed locally.

1. A Kentucky lawyer and judge, Bibb served twice in the U.S. Senate, 1811–14 and 1829–35. An early admirer of Andrew Jackson, he broke with Jackson over the bank question. Bibb served as secretary of the Treasury in John Tyler's cabinet from July 1844 until March 1845.

2. Polk and John Y. Mason attended the University of North Carolina. Mason was graduated in 1816 while Polk took his degree in 1818.

### FROM DANIEL GRAHAM[1]

Dear Sir                              Nashville, Tenn 4 March [18]45

This has been a stirring day with you at Washington and we have had an interesting time at Nashville. Brown had more than three fourths of the Convention[2] on the first vote (viva voce). Stanton[3] the others. On the next vote they were unanimous for Brown and every one seemed to go in for him in the best spirit. They had a preliminary meeting at my house last night at which they settled the question of form, and suggested nominations. Fitzgerald & Dunlap were named from the district.[4] And Johnson & Rowles from E Tennessee C Johnson, Keeble & B. Martin[5] from Mid. but all were withdrawn except Brown & Stanton before they adjourned.

On the first vote today Davidson, Rutherford & Lincoln voted for Stanton, which may have been from a wish to conciliate the West, but my own inferences were that there was a disposition with some to keep down the claims of the district to the U.S. Senate if the demos should have the majority in next assembly. East Tenn went unanimously for Brown. The only objection made to him was that the Memphis people complained of his having procured for his cousin of Giles some appointment connected with the Memphis navy.[6] After the nomination, a committee reported a preamble & several spirited resolutions, which were unanimously adopted, opposing a Bank; supporting Texas and Oregon; recommending harmonious selection of Candidates &c &c. Speeches were then made by Nicholson, B Martin, Currin, Anw Ewing & Col Overton.[7] They then adjourned for more speeches tonight to be spoken by Jonas E[8] & others. Barclay, as usual, expatiated on things in general, applied some anecdotes pretty well, alluded to Foster by name as the expected competitor & handled the eleventh hour Texean conversion freely.[9]

I was at the Hermitage on Saturday. The Genl[10] is in regretted progression as you left him. When he takes medicine to relieve him of one affliction, the effect is unfavorable on another point. He takes great interest in the news from Washington and receives letters from Lewis and

Blair[11] regularly. I took up several letters from the Post office, amongst them a long one from Lewis which was read first of the packet. In it Lewis said that the rumor that day was that Tappan, Niles, Haywood and Bagby were said to be against Texas.[12] He also said something about the purchase by Laughlin of an interest in the Madisonian. The Genl seemed very anxious that the Globe should in no way be superseded.

Maj Donelson is here and has been home two weeks. He seems to be very anxious about things in general, and some say that he is not inclined to return to Texas, but that he would prefer going to Washington. If he does, I would apprehend that he is much influenced by the wishes of his wife[13] who appreciates city life. He is anxious that the Genl should say, or authorize to be said, something kind to Mr Calhoun. I advised him to suspend it until the Course of Calhoun & his special friends should be manifest in the reorganization of the government. He has also some undefined ideas of conciliatory words or deeds towards our New York friends.

A.A. Hall[14] has returned and will take charge of the Nashville Whig as soon as the proprietor[15] returns with new type &c for which he has gone. I have seen him more than once. He made a point to talk with me, & says he will be fair & candid towards you & the Admn. He goes fully for Texas. Wash. Barrow[16] is also here and tis said will go into the Banner office & perhaps into the Senate from Davidson. This is as much as you can afford to read at once, and I trouble you only with our own news without alluding to the Circumstances at the city, some of which we cannot comprehend. Armstrongs Case[17] &c &c.

DANIEL GRAHAM

ALS. DLC–JKP. Addressed to Washington City and marked "Private."

1. A resident of Murfreesboro, Daniel Graham became Tennessee's secretary of state in 1818 and served until 1830; in 1836 he moved to the post of state comptroller and served seven years.

2. Graham's point of reference is the Democratic State Convention, which selected Aaron V. Brown as its gubernatorial candidate in the state election scheduled for August 7, 1845.

3. A Memphis lawyer, Frederick P. Stanton served as a Democrat in the U.S. House, 1845–55, and as governor of the Kansas Territory, 1858–61.

4. William Fitzgerald and William C. Dunlap. Fitzgerald served as circuit court clerk in Stewart County, 1822–25; sat one term in the Tennessee House, 1825–27; and held the position of attorney general of Tennessee's Sixteenth Judicial Circuit before winning election in 1831 to a single term in the U.S. House. He moved to Henry County in the late 1830's and in 1841 became judge of Tennessee's Ninth Judicial Circuit. A lawyer from Bolivar, Tenn., Dunlap served two terms as a Democratic congressman, 1833–37, prior to his election as a state judge in 1840.

5. Andrew Johnson, George W. Rowles, Cave Johnson, Edwin A. Keeble, and Barkly Martin. A Columbia lawyer and Democrat, Martin served three terms in the Tennessee House, 1839–41, 1847–49, and 1851–53, and sat for one term in the Tennessee Senate, 1841–43. He won election to the U.S. House and served from 1845 until 1847.

6. Brown's cousin appointed to a position in the navy yard at Memphis is not identified further.

7. A. O. P. Nicholson, Barkly Martin, David M. Currin, Andrew Ewing, and Archibald Waller Overton. A Murfreesboro attorney, Currin ran as the Democratic candidate for elector in the Seventh Congressional District in 1844; he later moved to Memphis and served one term in the Tennessee House, 1851–53. Ewing, a Nashville Democrat, won election to a term in the U.S. House, 1849–51, but did not stand for reelection. A graduate of Transylvania University and a lawyer from Smith County, Overton served in both the Tennessee Senate, 1823–25, and in the Tennessee House, 1829–31; he ran unsuccessfully for Congress in 1815 and 1833.

8. Jonas E. Thomas.

9. Although the *Nashville Union* of March 6, 1845, covered the proceedings of the Democratic State Convention and the nomination of Aaron V. Brown, it did not publish the text of the convention's speeches or resolutions.

10. Andrew Jackson.

11. William B. Lewis and Francis P. Blair. A neighbor and longtime friend of Andrew Jackson, Lewis resided in the White House during Jackson's presidency and served as second auditor of the Treasury from 1829 until 1845.

12. Benjamin Tappan, John M. Niles, William H. Haywood, and Arthur P. Bagby. A lawyer in Steubenville, Ohio, Tappan served as judge of the Fifth Ohio Circuit Court of Common Pleas in 1816 and as U.S. district judge of Ohio in 1833; he won election as a Democrat to one term in the U.S. Senate, 1839–45.

13. Elizabeth Martin Randolph Donelson.

14. A native of North Carolina and resident of Nashville, Allen A. Hall served as chargé d'affaires to Venezuela, 1841–45; as assistant secretary of the U.S. Treasury, 1849–50; and as U.S. minister to Bolivia, 1863–67. In addition to his diplomatic duties, Hall served as editor and publisher of several Nashville newspapers including the *Republican Banner*, the *Nashville Whig*, and the *Nashville News*.

15. Formerly an associate editor of the Nashville *Republican Banner*, Caleb C. Norvell served as editor of the *Nashville Whig* from 1838 until 1845.

16. A lawyer from Tennessee and briefly a resident of Mississippi, Washington Barrow served as U.S. chargé d'affaires to Portugal, 1841–44; edited the Nashville *Republican Banner*, 1845–47; and won election to one term in the U.S. House as a Whig, 1847–49.

17. Graham's reference probably is to a rumor, circulated in the Nashville press, that Robert Armstrong would be offered the position of U.S. consul at Liverpool.

## FROM J. G. M. RAMSEY[1]

Mecklenburg, Tenn. March 4, 1845

After congratulating Polk on his inauguration, Ramsey passes on a request from A. R. Crozier,[2] the editor and proprietor of the *Knoxville Standard*. Crozier wishes to procure public printing contracts from either the Post Office or another government department. Ramsey reminds Polk of the upcoming state elections in Tennessee and that government aid is necessary to sustain a Democratic newspaper of "correct principles" in East Tennessee. With the income from public printing contracts, Crozier would be able to improve his newspaper and use it to "counteract to some extent the overwhelming influence of the opposition papers." Turning to personal matters, Ramsey notes that he has enlarged the scope of his "Annals of Tennessee" to include the period up to 1845. He adds that every moment that he can spare from "a very laborious & extensive country practice" is devoted to the completion of his history.

ALS. DLC–JKP. Addressed to Washington City.

1. A Knoxville physician, railroad promoter, and banker, Ramsey played a key role in the 1844 campaign by refuting charges that Ezekiel Polk, James K. Polk's grandfather, had been a Tory during the Revolutionary War. Ramsey also wrote one of the early landmarks in Tennessee historiography, *The Annals of Tennessee to the End of the Eighteenth Century* (1853). During the Civil War, Union troops burned Ramsey's residence and thus destroyed materials for a sequel to his history of Tennessee.

2. Arthur R. Crozier served as editor of the *Knoxville Standard* in 1845 and comptroller of Tennessee from 1851 to 1855.

## FROM HENDERSON K. YOAKUM[1]

Dear Sir,                                        Nashville March 4, 1845

Our convention has just nominated Hon A. V. Brown for Gov.

Some supported Mr Stanton on the ballot, on the grounds that Mr B. did not care for the place, & was withal wanted to defend our measures in Congress.

Supposing that just about now (3 o'clock) you have completed your inaugural and are quietly taking your first presidential dinner, you will be gratified to hear that matters were carried on & concluded most harmoniously by your friends here. This convention was the most numerous I have ever seen here of the representative kind.

There is a firm resolve among our friends to have no clashing in the different districts. You will see the proceedings, but I will merely add that if there were any points upon which our friends were particularly enthusiastic, they were the Texas & Oregon questions. Hoping you much success & happiness in discharging the high trust just confided to you ....

                                                                H. YOAKUM

ALS. DLC–JKP. Probably addressed to Washington City.
1. A graduate of the U.S. Military Academy, Henderson K. Yoakum served as mayor of Murfreesboro, 1837–43; won election to one term in the Tennessee Senate, 1839–40; moved to Texas in 1845; and authored a two-volume *History of Texas*, which was published in 1855.


## FROM RALPH I. INGERSOLL

My dear Sir                                          New York 5 March 1845
    I have read and re-read your inaugural address, with so much satisfaction that I cannot refrain from congratulating you upon it. It does your head and heart infinite honor. Not a sentiment or a word would I alter if I had the power. I have this morning been among friends and opponents— and the sentiments every where expressed would be most gratifying to you, could you hear them. Our political friends with one voice affirm— warmly affirm—and our political opponents, the more candid portion of them, speak of it as a document that does you great credit. Even the more bitter of them, know not how to find fault, and manifestly feel, that it tells upon the country most favorably for you.
    I am here in New York on business for a day or two, and shall return to Connecticut in a day or two more. I am so thoroughly concurrant with the feelings of the Connecticut and indeed the New England people, that I *know* the address will take in those regions, as well as you could wish.
    I write not this to flatter—far from it—it is the first gush of my own feelings—fresh and sincere it must pass for what it is worth.
    Your Cabinet, permit me also to say, is very judicious, and a strong one. Heaven prosper you and your administration.

                                                                R. I. INGERSOLL

ALS. DLC–JKP. Addressed to Washington City.


## FROM WILLIAM L. MARCY

[Dear Sir:]                                          Washington Mar. 5th 1845
    The suggestions of the 4th inst,[1] addressed to me in regard to the political and official conduct which you desire to have pursued by the gentlemen you have invited to a place in your cabinet, meet with my

entire approbation and I shall conform my course of action to them while I occupy the situation with which you have been pleased to honour me.

W. L. MARCY

ALS. DLC–JKP. Addressed locally.

1. The text of Polk's letter to Marcy of March 4, 1845, is almost identical to that sent to other cabinet nominees; Marcy received this letter upon his arrival in Washington City. LS. DLC–JKP.

## FROM SYLVESTER S. SOUTHWORTH[1]

My Dear Sir,                                    New York March 5, 1845

We received in this City, last night, the statesmanlike, dignified, and eloquent address, you delivered to the American People yesterday, on the occasion of your Inauguration.

The Address, reflects the highest honor, in your talents, and character, and will be acceptable to all of that portion of your countrymen, where good will or applause, is worth possessing. It was read here, by thousands last night; and I heard not one discontent voice, saving and excepting the murmurs that were indulged in by one or two eminent and deeply disappointed whigs—men who can never see anything aright, till Mr Clay, and his mad-cap doctrines succeed. Of course, they will never be satisfied.

The leading Whig paper here, the Courier & Enquirer,[2] of this morning, briefly reviews it, with some moderation and calmness; but its tone, will soon be changed to harshness; and the Administration will undoubtedly soon be seriously assailed. The leading Whigs, will not I think, suffer anything like pacification to be offered; and the High Tariff party, will be found rallying a force against you.

But let all these things take place. You are surrounded by a Powerful, a Patriotic, and an intelligent party, who will sustain you and defend the country.

On the commencement of your course, I congratulate you; and pray God to preserve your health, and to surround you with every earthly blessing.

S. S. SOUTHWORTH

ALS. DLC–JKP. Addressed to Washington City.

1. Employed as an inspector in the New York Customs House, Southworth wrote for the New York *Aurora* in 1844; formerly he had served as a Washington City correspondent for newspapers in Baltimore, Philadelphia, and Boston.

2. The *Morning Courier and New York Enquirer*.

## TO JOHN C. CALHOUN

President's Mansion
Dear Sir:             [Washington City] March 6th 1845

Feeling anxious to ascertain what action my predecessor has taken in regard to the Resolution to admit Texas into the Union,[1] I would thank you to transmit to me, by one of your Confidential Clerks, any dispatches on the subject which may have been sent to Mr Donelson.[2] I will thank you to send also the Resolution itself or a copy of it.

JAMES K. POLK

ALS. DNA–RG 59. Addressed locally.

1. For the terms of Robert J. Walker's compromise bill on Texas annexation, see William H. Haywood, Jr., to Polk, February 26, 1845. On Sunday, March 2, John Tyler called a cabinet meeting to consider what action if any he might take with respect to Texas annexation; the cabinet unanimously agreed that he should forego further treaty negotiations and offer annexation under the terms contained in the first two sections of the joint resolution.

2. On March 3, 1845, John C. Calhoun informed Andrew J. Donelson of Tyler's decision on Texas annexation and gave instructions on how to proceed in the matter. For the text of Calhoun's letter and the accompanying joint resolution of March 1, 1845, see Clyde N. Wilson, ed., *The Papers of John C. Calhoun* (21 vols.; Columbia, S.C.: University of South Carolina Press, 1959–93), XXI, pp. 398–402.

## FROM ANDREW JACKSON

My dear Sir,             Hermitage March 6th 1845

I now have the pleasure to congratulate my country on your now being, really, president of the United States, and I put up my prayers to the great Jehova, that he may conduct you thro your administration with honor to yourself, and benefit to our Glorious Union. "He does all things well."[1] And by continuing to take principle for your guide, and public good your end, steering clear of the intrigues & machinations of political clikes, that kind & overuling providence will crown your administration with a happy conclusion, both to yourself and our glorious Union.

I cannot forbear laying before you letters from Mrs. Linn widow of our Lamented Linn,[2] and one to my daughter[3] from Mrs. Forsythe widow of John Forsythe, Late Secretary of State of the United State.[4] It appears both families are left destitute, both deserves a better fate, and add my salutation to thiers that the humble boon asked for, may be bestowed, if it can be, with propriety. As to Mrs. Linn you have before you the united voice of the Democracy of the Legislature of Missouri. Mrs. Linn is perfectly competant to discharge the duties of that post-office, and it is a small boon to the memory of her worthy, but deceased Husband. May it be in your power to grant it.

Last night brought me the pleasing intelligence, one day head of the mail, that on Wednesday night the 26th the Senate passed the Joint Resolution from the House, with Col. Bentons bill moved by Mr. Walker as an amendment, for the reanexation of Texas to the United States. The letter from Mr. Thos. J. Reid, information from Mr. Jarvis[5] and says I may rely upon the fact. This my dear Sir, has aroused me altho, much more debilitated, than when you left me. I rejoice with all true american patriots, at this happy result. My family unite with me, in the kindest wishes to you and your amiable Lady, for your continued health & prosperity ....

ANDREW JACKSON

ALS. DLC–JKP. Addressed to Washington City.

1. Mark 7:37.

2. Elizabeth Relfe and Lewis F. Linn. A native of Kentucky and surgeon in the War of 1812, Linn represented Missouri in the U.S. Senate from 1833 until his death in 1843.

3. Jackson refers to one of his two daughters-in-law, Sarah Yorke Jackson or Elizabeth Martin Randolph Donelson.

4. Clara Meigs and John Forsyth. Forsyth served as a member of the U.S. House, 1813–18, 1823–27; as a U.S. senator for Georgia, 1818–19, 1829–34; and as governor of Georgia, 1827–29. He held the post of secretary of state under Andrew Jackson and Martin Van Buren, 1834–41.

5. Probably Russell Jarvis.

## FROM EDWARD J. MALLETT[1]

Providence, R.I. March 6, 1845

After alluding to "the agitation which has so long distressed this little State," Mallett emphasizes that Polk, through his use of patronage, could reduce the bitterness of party strife in Rhode Island. Although the Whigs are in a majority in the state, they do not expect a share of the offices; however, they do expect that Polk will exclude "those men who have been so ultra in their Dorr-ism as to peril the lives & property of our people." He warns Polk in particular about Welcome B. Sayles and Burrington Anthony.[2] Mallett notes that Sayles, a close associate of Thomas Dorr, left the state two years ago and subsequently in his political speeches has vilified the whole state government. Mallett adds that Anthony's house served as "the depository for arms & ammunition" at the time of the attack on the arsenal.[3] He stresses that the appointment of such men would anger the Whigs and weaken the party in Rhode Island.

ALS. DLC–JKP. Addressed to Washington City and marked *"Private."* Mallett's AES reads as follows: "I hope you will find time to read the within. It is written by the *request* of those who are deeply interested & it may save you some regrets."

1. A classmate of Polk's at the University of North Carolina, Mallett received the A.B. degree in 1818; he served as postmaster of Providence, R.I., from 1831 until 1845, when he moved to New York City.

2. Sayles presided over the lower house of the "People's Legislature" in 1842; Polk appointed him postmaster of Providence in December of 1845. Formerly U.S. marshal for Rhode Island, Anthony won election as sheriff of Providence County in 1842 on the People's party ticket.

3. See Dutee J. Pearce to Polk, February 3, 1845.


## FROM AARON V. BROWN

At Rooms
Dear Sir                                    [Washington City]March 7th 1845
After leaving you last evening, it occured to me & several other friends that Mr Thomas Ritchie was *the very* man to whom the mission to England should be offered.

A. V. Brown

[P.S.] Give him choice between this & that *other* arrangemt.[1]

ALS. DLC–JKP. Addressed locally.
1. Brown's reference is to Polk's efforts to recruit Ritchie for the editorship of the proposed administration newspaper, the Washington *Union*. See Brown to Polk, January 1, 1845.


## FROM AARON V. BROWN

Friday night
Dear Sir                                    [Washington City March 7, 1845][1]
I have today conversed fully with Mr. Calhoun who persists in the determination not to go abroad. He spoke of Mr Elmore in general terms of favor, but on my leaving the room he said to Judge Colquit[2] that he thought Genl Hamilton had higher qualifications to conduct & manage the questions pending with England, than any other person he knew of. This he said when Colquit had suggested that probably I might infer that you would prefer Mr Ellmore. On the whole I am convinced that *he* would think most favorably of Genl. Hamilton.

Mr Treasurer Selden[3] still thinks Ritchie (with whom he is in correspondence) would come here if thought best by you. By putting yourself or Mr. Cave Johnson in communication with him (Selden) the matter could be further investigated—or with Ritchie himself.

A. V. BROWN

ALS. DLC–JKP. Addressed locally.
1. Place and date identified through content analysis.
2. Walter T. Colquitt.
3. William Selden of Virginia became treasurer of the United States in 1840.

### FROM LEONARD P. CHEATHAM[1]

Dr. Sir:                                    [Washington City] March 7th, 1845

The inclosed letter is from Mr Mayfield the former Secretary of State from Texas.[2] From a conversation we had on our way from Vicksburgh, he wished to see you in person, & I presume he wishes you to see this letter, which you can return to me when I call to see you which will probably be to-morrow as I wish *verry* much to have a *20* minutes private conversation before I leave. Mr. Polk your uncle,[3] was present I think at our celebrated meeting at Wesly,[4] formed some attachment for me & has heretofore asked my advise, which has been renewed to day, as to the policy & propriety of his accepting any appointment from you: Such he says as would not last long, for instance the bearer of dispatches. I learn he was *verry* liberal in the last contest with his money. He owes some balance for his land, & although his friends intend to make him Sheriff next year, still if he could by some *minor* appointment be enabled to realize 10 or 1200 $ it would be of great benefit to him. I have said to him it would not be injurious to you or your party to confer on him any reasonable appointment. He is as you know a modest man & perhaps will scarsely mention it himself. I have written this in great haste & with a bad pen.

L. P. CHEATHAM

ALS. DLC–JKP. Addressed locally.
1. A lawyer and leading Democrat, Cheatham replaced Robert Armstrong as postmaster of Nashville in March of 1845.
2. James S. Mayfield represented Nacogdoches in the lower house of the Texas Congress and became that republic's secretary of state in 1841. On February 20, 1844, Mayfield wrote Cheatham warning of the dangers in delaying annexation and criticizing political intrigues in the U.S. Senate. ALS. DLC–JKP.
3. Probably Charles Perry Polk, who was elected sheriff of Hardeman County in 1846.
4. Cheatham's reference is to the Democratic mass meeting at Wesley, Tenn., on October 3, 1844.

## TO ANDREW J. DONELSON

My Dear Sir:                                     Washington City March 7th 1845

A despatch was transmitted to you by the late administration, on the 3rd Inst.[1] In two or three days another will be forwarded to you on the same subject by a special messenger. But five members of my Cabinet have as yet been confirmed by the Senate; the remaining member[2] of it I hope will be confirmed at the next meeting of the Senate. I write now to say, that I desire you, not to take any definitive action in pursuance of the instructions given in the despatch of the 3rd Inst. until after you receive the one which will be forwarded, in two or three days, and by which the instructions will probably be modified. I write you this informal note for the reason that *Mr Buchanan* the Secretary of State, has not entered on the duties of his office, and because I desire to have the Cabinet complete, before definitive action is had on my part.

JAMES K. POLK

ALS, draft. DLC–AJD. Addressed to Washington, Texas, and marked *"Private."* Donelson's AE on the cover states that he received this letter at New Orleans on March 19. Published in St. George L. Sioussat, ed., "Letters of James K. Polk to Andrew J. Donelson, 1843–1848," *THM,* III (March, 1917), p. 62.

1. See Polk to John C. Calhoun, March 6, 1845.
2. Polk's reference is to George Bancroft. On March 10, 1845, the Senate confirmed Bancroft's nomination as secretary of the navy.

## FROM AUGUSTUS BEARDSLEE[1]

Dear Sir                                     Little Falls N.Y. March 8/1845

Texas debt[2] ought to be pd by the Texas lands if worth anything and in any event Texas should *lay* a *small land tax*. This is the only way she can settle *land titles*. The immense and conflicting land titles there, will all but ruin her if she does not *settle them by tax sales*. Therefore let her own debt be in her own head so as to *compel her* to *levy a land tax*.

In no event consent to assume for the U. States any part, (even the smallest part) of her debt. If you assume one cent of the Texas debt, we, northern annexation men, will be prostrated by it. The abolition argument will be complete against us & we must sink under it.

I have not seen these points made in any of the speeches & I beg you to give them all consideration & full weight.

One other subject. We of the north, must be furnished with the tables (the most perfect that can be made) of all the articles and the value of them *manufactured in* the *Free States* and *marketed out* of the *Free*

*States* and what proportion are marketed & sold in the *Slave* States & what in *all* the *rest* of *the world*. And of the sales to the south, what amt is bad debt. I suppose that of the products of northern artizan labor sold out of & beyond the free states, three fourths, perhaps four fifths, are sold & marketed in the slave states.

The market in the slave states is immensely important to the northern artizan, but he is made to believe that it is nothing. We must have authentic facts to set this matter right.

The northern artizan is a good fellow but he thinks the southern markets are good for nothing and that the south have baulked him of that protection which is his *unalienable right*, or may hap, will yet do it; and strait way his pocket interest etherealizes, (unbeknown to him), into religion & philanthropy. He thinks he is Pure Benevolence when, being translated it reads thus: "If I can't have protection, by G-d, you shan't have niggers."

It is vastly important that we have these tables, however great the labor of making them up; that we have them ready against another session of congress and in a shape that can not be questioned or disputed. One of the Sovreigns of this country I earnestly, yet respectfully, submit these things, each of them, to your carefull consideration.

Accept my congratulations on your election & inauguration as President &c.

AUGUSTUS BEARDSLEE

ALS. DLC–JKP. Probably addressed to Washington City.

1. A New York lawyer, Beardslee received an appointment to Herkimer County's Court of Common Pleas in 1828 and again in 1843; he also won election to a single term in the New York Assembly in 1834.

2. The Texas annexation resolutions stipulated that Texas would retain both its public debts and its public lands; the Compromise of 1850 provided for the U.S. government's assumption of Texas' debts in exchange for the cession of a portion of Texas' western territory.

## FROM JAMES G. BRYCE[1]

Washington City. March 10, 1845

After alluding to his recent interview with Polk about Louisiana appointments, Bryce emphasizes that Polk's handling of federal patronage will determine "the future political complexion of the State." He notes that the four most important offices in the state are district attorney, marshal, surveyor general, and customs collector at New Orleans. Thomas Barrett, the present collector,[2] is very popular among "the creole and foreign population." During the campaign he corresponded with Bishop Hughes[3] and other prominent naturalized citizens in Baltimore, New York, and Philadelphia. Barrett's zealous support enabled the

Democrats to secure "the foreign vote" and win the state. Bryce warns Polk that the Native American party has many advocates in Louisiana. He adds that the Native Americans would point to Barrett's removal as evidence of Polk's secret support for their views.

ALS. DLC–JKP. Addressed locally and marked *"Confidential."*

1. A popular Democratic speaker during the 1844 presidential campaign, Bryce filled numerous engagements in middle Tennessee in behalf of Polk's candidacy.

2. An Irish immigrant and successful commission merchant, Thomas Barrett served as collector of customs at New Orleans from 1844 until 1846; Polk required Barrett's resignation in 1845 as the local consular agent for the Papal States.

3. An Irish native, John Joseph Hughes of New York headed the Roman Catholic hierarchy in the United States and vigorously defended Roman Catholic immigrants from nativist attacks.

## FROM JULIUS W. BLACKWELL

Washington City. March 11, 1845

Blackwell discusses patronage questions in Tennessee and reflects upon his upcoming reelection campaign. He informs Polk that he has written the secretary of state, the secretary of the Treasury, and the postmaster general[1] urging them to give their department's patronage in the area to the *Knoxville Standard*. He describes its editor, Arthur R. Crozier, as a true "Jeffersonian Democrat," and denounces James C. Moses, the editor of the *Knoxville Register*, as "a N. England Federalist."[2] Blackwell asserts that the *Register* throws stumbling blocks in the path of Polk's administration. Tomorrow Blackwell expects to leave for home. After observing that the district[3] contains a large majority of Whigs, he admits that his reelection campaign will be "worse than climbing mountains."

ALS. DLC–JKP. Addressed locally.

1. James Buchanan, William L. Marcy, and Cave Johnson.

2. A native of Boston, Mass., James C. Moses moved to Knoxville in 1838 and published the *Knoxville Register* from 1839 until 1849. Moses also served two terms on Knoxville's Board of Aldermen.

3. Blackwell's reference probably is to the Third Congressional District. In 1845 he lost to the Whig candidate, John H. Crozier.

## FROM ELIJAH HAYWARD ET AL.[1]

Washington City. March 11, 1845

Hayward warns Polk that during the past two or three years party factionalism has embarrassed the Ohio Democracy and diminished its strength. He criticizes in particular the soft money men who deserted Jackson, supported

Harrison in 1840, and subsequently turned to Tyler, Calhoun, Shannon, and Cass. Hayward blames these factions for the Whig victories in the state and presidential elections last autumn. Although these "trading politicians" represent only a small minority in the party, they form a very large majority of the Ohio applicants for federal office. He stresses that the future success of the Ohio Democracy depends upon Polk's appointments and the course of his policy decisions. Hayward names those Democrats best suited to fill the more important federal offices in the state, which include the posts of U.S. attorney and marshal, land receivers and registers, customs collectors, and postmasters.

LS. DLC–JKP. Addressed locally.
1. This letter is signed by Elijah Hayward, Joseph H. Larwell, and Rudolphus Dickinson. A Jacksonian Democrat and editor of the Cincinnati *National Republican*, Hayward served in the Ohio House from 1825 to 1828; he won election to the Ohio Supreme Court in January of 1830 but resigned later that year to become commissioner of the General Land Office, a post that he held until August 1835.

## FROM WILLIAM KENNON, SR.[1]

Dear Sir                                        St Clairsville March 11th 1845
I have from a Newspaper the following Sentiments "Who shall assign limits to the achievements of free minds and free hands under the protection of this glorious Union. No treason to mankind since the organization of society, would be equal in atrocity to that of him who would lift his hand to destroy it. He would overthrow the noblest structure of human wisdom which protects himself and his fellow man. He would stop the progress of free government and involve country either in anarchy or despotism. He would extinguish the fire of liberty which warms and animates happy Millions and invites all the Nations of the earth to immitate our example. If he say that error and wrong are committed in the administration of the government let him remember that nothing human can be perfect: and that under no other system of government revealed by heaven or devised by man has reason been allowed so free and broad a scope to combat error. Has the sword of despots proved to be a safer or surer instrument of reform than enlightened reason. Does he expect to find among the ruins of this Union a happier abode for our swarming millions than they now have under it. Every lover of his country must shudder at the thought of the *possibility* of its *disolution* and will be ready to adopt the patriotic sentiment *"Our federal Union—it must be preserved."*[2]
Whether the writer of the above sentiments had in his minds eye the North or the South, Massachusetts or South Carolina, abolition

or nullification or any man or set of men, the sentiments themselves are *worthy* of the Chief Magistrate of this *great nation*. He should not only entertain such opinions but upon all *Suitable* occasions *promulgate them* to the world. Who can tell what beneficial effect they may have upon the people of this country? Your Inaugral address will be read by *Millions* of people on this continent and if it has the same effect upon others which it had upon *me they* may *truly* say that they *felt* the fire of patriotism rekindling in their bosoms. All inteligent men know or think they know that if the liberty of the people of this Country shall ever be lost it will first commence by an attempted disolution of the Union; we shall fall by no foreign enemy. I am pleased with your whole address. The principles there avowed when carried out will have tendency to harmonize and strengthen the Union. The address has been read with interest in this section of Ohio and altho at this time there is collected here many lawyers of both political parties who converse freely on political subjects I have not heard a man find fault with it.

When I left Washington City all was speculation, no one pretended to know who would compose your Cabinet and indeed it was even doubted whether the president himself knew. Permit me in all candor to say to you that it seems to me under the circumstances in which you were placed no better or more popular selection *could* have been made. You have most judiciously avoided the leaders of aspiring *fractions* (not to say factions) of the Democratic party. It gives me great pleasure to know that the Hon Cave Johnson is post master General. He richly deserved some such appointment.

There are a few subjects upon which I would like say a word or two in relation your future course in administering the government and perhaps at some future time may trouble you with a letter; at present I shall only say that I most heartily congratulate you not only upon your election to what I consider the highest office in the world but also upon what I regard as a most auspicious and favourable commencement of your administration. My desire and hope is that you may so discharge the duties of your office that it may hereafter (a thing not impossible) be pointed to as a Model administration.

WILLIAM KENNON

ALS. DLC–JKP. Addressed to Washington City.

1. William Kennon, Sr., won election as a Democrat to three terms in the U.S. House, 1829–33 and 1835–37; he served as presiding judge of the Ohio Court of Common Pleas from 1840 until 1847.

2. Here Kennon quotes Polk's Inaugural Address, which included Andrew Jackson's "patriotic sentiment" offered as a toast at the Jefferson Day dinner

of April 13, 1830. Richardson, ed., *Messages and Papers of the Presidents*, IV, p. 376.

## FROM ALFRED BALCH

Dear Sir,                                    Nashville. 12th March [18]45

Your friends looked anxiously for your inaugural address and have read it with pleasure. I hazard nothing in saying that it has received their entire approbation. The Whigs are bitterly disappointed at not being able to detect any material errors in it of which they can complain and out of which they can make any political capital. For myself, I can say that all those doctrines which I have humbly advocated ever since I knew any thing of the principles of our constitution or the true policy of our Goverment are embodied in it and it has therefore my hearty and grateful approbation.

You have *forewarned* all those who may become the recipients of the public monies of the fate which will overtake them.[1] This is as it should be. The defalcations which were developed during Van Burens administrations[2] were fatal to his claims. I should be excessively distressed at any similar occurrences during your term.

I hope that you may be fortunate in the selection of your subordinate agents. There is a vast party in this country, hungry after place, who are led on by the eager desire of power and a keen appetite for *emolument*. Very many of them are mere *scamps*.

If there is any one quality, in my humble opinion, which distinguishes a great *Stateman* from the rest of the world, it is that power of intuition by which he reads the *characters* of those who press around him for office. More depends on the proper distribution of men, than on any thing else which a President can be called upon to do. The beau ideal of administrative government, consists in a kind of *instinct*, (synonimous with the most exalted wisdom), which enables a President and the members of his cabinet to station every man whom they may employ in the public service in that post which he is best fitted to occupy. But if he and they detach from the mass for any particular duties those who are dishonest or unequal to their performance, it is obvious that nothing but confusion can ensue, with perplexities and distress to him and them. When the elder Pitt was advised that Wolf was too young to lead the expedition against Quebec he replied. "I have talked with him." "He possesses all the qualities of a great commander therefore he is *not* too young."[3] With repects to Mrs Polk....

ALFRED BALCH

ALS. DLC–JKP. Addressed to Washington City.

1. Balch's reference is to the passage in Polk's inaugural address stating that "a strict performance of duty will be exacted from all public officers." Those officials failing to "account for the moneys intrusted to them," Polk promised, would lose their positions. Richardson, ed., *Messages and Papers of the Presidents*, IV, p. 382.

2. Balch's reference probably is to the "defalcations" of Samuel Swartout and Jesse Hoyt. Collector of customs for New York City from 1830 until 1838, Samuel Swartout embezzled over one million dollars in Treasury funds and fled abroad. His successor, Jesse Hoyt, accepted appointment as collector of customs for New York City in 1838; three years later he resigned following allegations that he had misappropriated over $30,000 in government funds.

3. William Pitt and James Wolfe. A member of the British parliament from 1735 until 1768, William Pitt served as secretary of state, 1756–61, and as wartime leader of the House of Commons, 1756–61; known as the "Great Commoner," he accepted the earldom of Chatham in 1768 and thereafter served as prime minister for two years. During the French and Indian War, Pitt marshaled Britain's military resources and ordered an attack against French strongholds in North America; his strategy yielded decisive British victories at Louisburg in 1758 and at Quebec in 1759. Only 31 years old at the time of his promotion to the rank of major general in 1758, James Wolfe commanded the successful British assault against Quebec in September of 1759. Mortally wounded in the attack, he survived long enough to learn of his victory over the French. Quotations attributed to Pitt have not been identified.

## FROM PHINEAS JANNEY[1]

Respected friend                    Alexandria D.C.   3rd Month 12th 1845

Annexed thou will please receive Invoice of 3 qr Casks of Wine as therein specified amounting to                    Dols. 311.75

which with the amount paid for 3 Brass Cocks Say                    1.50

makes the sum of

Three Hundred & Thirteen 25/100 Dollars                    Dols. 313.25

to thy Debt in a/c, payt in 6 mos or a Discount of 3 pct for Cash if paid within one month from date of Invoice.

The Wine now sent to thee was selected by thy worthy friend Judge Catron and I think thou will be confirmed (after tasting the Wines) in thy opinion of his being a good Judge. I have some superior Hygeia Champagne of my own Importation which I should like to send a few Baskets of to thee. Thou will see by the printed list of prices annexed that the price of my Champagne for Quart bottles is 13/21 pr Basket, but if Thou order a Dz Baskets I shall make a deduction of one Dollar pr Basket or on a half Dz 50 cn pr Basket.

PHINEAS JANNEY

[P.S.] At the request of my particular friend Hugh C. Smith I have taken the liberty to hand to thee, the Enclosed Card,[2] and of my own free will to say that the most implicit confidence maybe placed in his or the firm's representations. P. Janney

ALS. DLC–JKP. Addressed to Washington City.

1. An Alexandria wine merchant, Janney specialized in the importation of madeira, port, and champagne.

2. Enclosure not found. Smith was a prominent Alexandria porcelain merchant.

## FROM GOUVERNEUR KEMBLE

My dear Sir                      Albany 12th March 1845

Having been unavoidably detained at Philadelphia, and knowing your desire to receive an early answer from Mr. Flagg, I wrote to the Governor[1] communicating the offer of the collectorship of New York; and on my arrival here this morning, I found the enclosed letter, which agreeably to the desire of Mr. Flagg, I hasten to transmit.[2] I much regret that he should deem it proper to decline the office, because there is, in my humble opinion, no one so capable of cleansing it.

GOUV. KEMBLE

ALS. DLC–JKP. Addressed to Washington City. Polk's AEI on the cover reads as follows: "I did not intend in my conversation with Mr Kemble to authorize him to tender the office to Mr Flagg, but expressed to him my intention at a proper time to offer it to him, if on consultation with my friends it was thought proper to do so. I so expressed the opinion from what I had heard of him of Mr Flagg's eminent qualifications for the place. March 15th 1847. J.K.P."

1. Silas Wright, Jr.

2. On March 10, 1845, Azariah Flagg wrote to Kemble stating that in January last Aaron V. Brown, claiming to speak in behalf of the president-elect, had inquired of Lemuel Stetson whether or not his people in New York would be satisfied with the appointment of William L. Marcy to a place in the cabinet and Flagg to the customs collectorship of New York City. Flagg further stated to Kemble that upon receiving word from Stetson of Brown's conversation, he had replied to Stetson without delay and had expressed the view that the collectorship should go to some reputable merchant then resident in the City. Flagg concluded his letter to Kemble with the emphatic statement that he had not changed his opinion as previously communicated to Stetson and with an explicit request that Kemble forward this letter to the president. ALS. DLC–JKP.

## FROM JESSE MILLER[1]

My Dear Sir                                    Harrisburg March 12. 1845

We continue to feel the most deep interest in the appointment of Mr Welsh to the Collectorship.[2] We deem this appointment essential to the administration here and consequently to the democratic party. It is not a matter in my opinion that is susceptible of a well founded doubt & we cannot under all circumstances permit ourselves to entertain a doubt of the result.

Our democratic caucus for the nomination of a candidate to fill Mr B's[3] place in the Senate has just adjourn'd. All the Democratic members did not attend it—48 were present & 24 absent. Mr Woodward of Luzerne Co recd a majority of the votes present & was declared nominated.[4] The result of the Election is doubtful but I am inclined to the opinion Woodward will be elected. He is a talented man, tho' not a very able politician. Those who know him well say he is an honest man, which in these days is most desirable.

J. Miller

ALS. DLC–JKP. Addressed to Washington City and marked *"Confidential."*

1. Jesse Miller sat in both the Pennsylvania House and Senate prior to his election as a Democrat to the U.S. House, where he served from 1833 until 1836. He held the post of first auditor of the Treasury from 1836 to 1842; subsequently he received appointments as canal commissioner of Pennsylvania in 1844 and then as secretary of the commonwealth in 1845.

2. A Pennsylvania journalist and friend of James Buchanan, Henry Welsh won appointment as naval officer of the Philadelphia customs district in December of 1845.

3. James Buchanan resigned from the U.S. Senate on the day after Polk's inauguration.

4. A Wilkes-Barre lawyer, George W. Woodward presided over Pennsylvania's Fourth Judicial Circuit from 1841 until 1851. Polk nominated Woodward for an associate justiceship on the U.S. Supreme Court in 1845, but the U.S. Senate rejected the nomination.

## FROM AUGUSTUS C. DODGE[1]

Sir,                                           Washington March 13. 1845

About leaving for home, I take the liberty to address you a brief note relative to the political condition of Iowa, and the necessity of removals and appointments there. There are in the Territory which I represent, at least one hundred thousand Inhabitants, soon to assume the responsibilities of a State Government.[2] There are eight important Officers in the Territory of Iowa, who are appointed by the President of the United States.[3] The present incumbents are all Whigs, the enemies of the Democratic party, and your administration. They superceded honest and capable democrats, against whose personal and official character there never was the slightest objection, but they were the Sincere, but unobtrusive desciples of Jefferson and Jackson, and for this they were brought to the block. Not only are the present incumbents federalists, but most of them were foreign importations from some of the States, disgraced politicians at home, fastened upon us against our earnest remonstrance, who never had any interest or sympathies with our people. Justice, in my humble judgment demands their prompt dismissal from office, and the appointment of individuals residing among us, whose political principles are in accordance with a very large majority of the people of Iowa, who think that they have just reason to complain in having placed over them Officers of whom they had no knowledge or confidence, and to whom they were politically deadly opposed.

In the early formation of the Territory, when we were few in numbers the democratic administrations of Jackson and Van Buren, made most of the appointments in our Territory from our own Citizens. This wise and just policy, due to the pioneers of a new country, was totally reversed by the advent of Whiggery to power in 1840. Since the prostration of that party, and the triumphant assertion of Democratic principles in your election, we feel entire confidence that we may ask for a restoration of that liberal course towards us in the bestowal of Executive patronage which is so universally popular with the people of Iowa.

Having understood from a recent consultation with yourself, that my advice in local appointments would be desirable, and wishing to perform this most delicate and responsible duty, honestly and faithfully, I will after my return home, ascertain the wishes of the people I represent, and make such recommendations of those only, who are honest and capable & whose appointment, I sincerely believe, will best harmonize the popular feeling, and promote the public welfare.

A. C. DODGE

LS. DLC–JKP. Addressed locally.

1. The son of Henry Dodge of the Wisconsin Territory, Augustus Dodge served as registrar of public lands at Burlington, 1838–40; as congressional delegate from Iowa Territory, 1840–46; and as Iowa's first U.S. senator in 1848.

2. Created in 1838, Iowa Territory embraced the future states of Iowa and Minnesota and parts of North and South Dakota. By Act of March 3, 1845, Congress approved the admission of Florida and Iowa to the Union; however, the citizens of Iowa Territory rejected the terms fixed by Congress and insisted

upon the Missouri River as the western boundary of their future state. Congress relented and admitted Iowa to the Union on December 28, 1846.

3. On May 17, 1845, Dodge wrote to Polk noting that the most important federal officers in the Iowa Territory were the governor, the U.S. marshal, the secretary of state, the district attorney, the land registrars at Fairfield and Dubuque, and the receivers of public monies also at Fairfield and Dubuque. LS. DLC–JKP.

## FROM RICHARD M. JOHNSON

My dear Sir,                                    White Sulphur. Ky. 13. March 1845
I am just informed by the papers of the members of your Cabinet. This first Step is judicious. You have displayed judgement. You have made a selection of men who will do honor & service to the Country. I congratulate you, your friends & the Country. The task has been difficult & let no friend murmur or be dissatisfied, no matter what may have been his wishes & disappointment.

Your inaugural is well composed. Short, powerful, correct in principle & patriotic in sentiment.

We shall try & make your duty pleasant & profitable to the Country.
                                                    RH. M. JOHNSON

ALS. DLC–JKP. Addressed to Washington City.

## FROM THOMAS LLOYD[1]

Sir,                                           Baltimore March 13th 1845
Permit Me the pleasure of presenting you with one of they Hansomest Saddle horse in the United States, young Hickory. Six years old the Grand Son of Sir Charles, the Celebrated Horse Imported to this Country, he is perfectly gentle & admired by all gentlemen has Seen. Sir I wish you Many happy Days of pleasure with him.
                                                    THOMAS LLOYD

ALS. DLC–JKP. Addressed locally. Polk's AEI on the cover, dated March 15, 1845, states: "Thomas Lloyd offers to make a present of a horse. I declined to accept the present, and ordered the horse to be taken from my stable at the President's mansion where Mr Lloyd had placed him without my knowledge, and to be returned to him, at his stable in Washington. My Coachman *Terry* accordingly returned him on the same morning, the horse having been at my stable for 1/2 or 1 hour."

1. Appointed surveyor of the port of Baltimore by John Tyler, Thomas Lloyd served in that post from 1844 until 1845. Claiming that his reputation had been damaged by rumors that he was to be removed from office because of his gift, Lloyd wrote to Polk on March 22, 27, and 31, 1845, and asked for the chance to

resign from office. Polk removed Lloyd from the surveyorship in late March of 1845.

## FROM JESSE MILLER

My Dear Sir                                    Harrisburg [March 13, 1845][1]
I regret exceedingly to inform you that contrary to my hopes when I wrote you last evening[2] a combination of the Whigs & Native Americans, with Recreant Democrats has resulted in the election of Simon Cameron to the U.S. Senate. It is a most disgraceful & humiliating result to the Democracy of Penna. One of the means resorted to, was to make the Corrupt & trading rascals in the democratic party believe that Cameron could do more than any other man to obtain them offices & contracts from the general administration.
Little do these men know of your character.

J. MILLER

ALS. DLC–JKP. Addressed to Washington City.
1. Miller mistakenly dated his letter "March 12"; corrected date has been identified through content analysis.
2. See Miller to Polk, March 12, 1845.

## TO BENJAMIN F. BUTLER

My dear Sir.                                    Washington March 14. 1845
Genl Dix was kind enough to shew me your letter in answer to one written by him to you at my request.[1] I have authorized him to say that the office of Attorney of the United States for the Southern District of New York was not only unsolicited by you or any of your friends, but that you were voluntarily selected by me and the office tendered to you because of your eminent fitness to fill it. Your Nomination has been Sent to the Senate & will probably be confirmed to day.[2]
I have had great difficulties to encounter in the first days of my administration in selecting proper persons to fill the vacant places. More than Seventy nominations were unacted on by the Senate at the close of its late Session, which I have been compelled to fill during the Session of the Executive Session of the Senate.[3] In addition to these almost an equal number of vacancies have occurred in the early part of this month, by the expiration of the times of incumbents, for you will remember that four years ago Genl Harrison, made many vacancies & appointments for terms of four years. Without Knowledge of the proper persons to fill them I have necessarily relied upon such infor-

mation, as I could command and may in many instances have made mistakes.

Among others I was required to appoint a *Surveyor of the Customs & Navy Agent* in New York and an agent for purchasing materials to construct a dry dock at Brooklyn.[4] I was *not* satisfied fully with the information upon which I had to act in these cases. If however I find that I have made mistakes in reference to these or any other cases I will at an early day correct them.

I wish to have your advice *confidentially* of course in regard to the Collectorship & other Custom House Officers in New York.

1st Is it proper to make removals and if so when? If removals are made who should be Collector & who fill the other places? The Collectorship at New York where so large an amount of Revenue is collected is second in importance to no other Station in the Country. I wish to have a man in that office of high and known character, of unsuspected integrity and business habits! How would Mr Flagg do for that place. My mind is not settled upon any one, in the event it is decided to make a removal.

I ask your advice because I wish to get the best man, and to guard against the possibility of making any mistake. I know my dear Sir, that you may feel some delicacy in giving your opinion as between Gentlemen of equal or nearly equal merit but I must have such information from a reliable source to guide my action. Whatever you may say to me will be regarded *as strictly & sacredly confidential* and no one will ever know from me that I have ever written to you on the subject.

JAMES K. POLK

L. DLC–JKP. Addressed to New York; marked "Copy" and "Strictly Confidential."

1. Polk probably refers to Benjamin F. Butler to John A. Dix, March 8, 1845. In this letter Butler acknowledges the receipt of Dix's letter of March 6th and accepts Polk's offer of the office of U.S. attorney for the Southern District of New York. ALS. DLC–JKP.

2. Polk sent Butler's nomination to the Senate on March 12, and the Senate confirmed it on March 14.

3. Polk's reference is to the special session of the Senate, which lasted from March 4 until March 20, 1845.

4. Elijah F. Purdy, Prosper M. Wetmore, and Adam Pentz. A wealthy New York banker and powerful figure in Tammany Hall, Purdy served as acting mayor of New York in 1841 and later sat for three terms as president of the Board of Supervisors; Polk appointed him surveyor of revenue for the port of New York on March 13. A New York merchant and confidant of William L. Marcy, Wetmore was appointed naval agent for New York on March 13. Pentz was appointed purchasing agent for the U.S. navy's dry dock at Brooklyn on March 13.

## FROM JEFFERSON K. HECKMAN[1]

Sir                                                        Harrisburg March 14h 1845

I hope you will pardon my frequent communications[2] especially at a time when I have no doubt that you are overburthened with communications from your numerous correspondents, but as a democrat having the prosperity of the country and the success of the party deeply at heart I feel impelled from a sense of duty to inform you in relation to our defeat yesterday in the Election of a United States Senator, which was brought about by the union of Sixteen apostate Democrats with the Whigs and Natives. Mr. Woodward the democratic caucus nominee was defeated in a great measure through the influence of Senator Ross from Luzerne[3] the intimate and warm friend of Mr. H. B. Wright who circulated that he Woodward was a free tradesman. Senator Ebaugh and McKinley[4] from York County, were also two of the 16 apostates both of whom reside in the same County and are two of the intimate friends of Mr. Welsh. Rumour says that Mr. Cameran[5] has promised his influence in favour of Mr. Welsh. The excitement here amongst the members of the Democratic Party is very great. We intend this evening to hold a meeting for the purpose of placing ourselves right before the people of Pennsylvania.[6] I am the firm and decided friend of Mr. Wagener[7] and certainly would be highly gratified in his appointment, but if he should be disappointed I certainly hope for the honor of the party and for the perpetuity of correct principles that no person will be appointed from any County whose representatives have either in the whole or in part united with our political opponents in breaking down those old and wholesome usages of the party by our Country has so long prospered and flourished.

Mr. Cameron previous to his Election gave a written pledge to the Whigs that he would go against any reduction of the Tariff and in favour of the distribution of the proceeds of Sale of the public Lands.

JEFF. K. HECKMAN

ALS. DLC–JKP. Addressed to Washington City.

1. Heckman served one term as a state representative from Pennsylvania's Northampton and Monroe counties, 1842–43, and one term as a state senator from Northampton and Leigh counties, 1845–46.

2. Previous correspondence not found.

3. William S. Ross served as a state senator from Luzerne and Columbia counties, 1845–47, and as a state representative from Luzerne County in 1862.

4. Adam Ebaugh of York County won election to the Pennsylvania House in 1842 and to the state's upper chamber in 1844. Stephen McKinley served one term as a state representative from York County, 1844–1845.

5. Simon Cameron.

6. On March 14 a group of Democratic state legislators resolved to draft a public address denouncing the election of Cameron. Published on April 12, the denunciation included letters from George M. Dallas and James Buchanan, both of whom lamented the failure of party unity but refused to condemn Cameron's election.

7. A businessman and banker, David D. Wagener served in the U.S. House as a Democrat from 1833 until 1841.

## FROM JOHN P. HEISS

Sir                                    Browns Hotel March 14 [18]45
I cannot forbear, again bringing before you, the subject I some time since introduced to your consideration, in regard to your official organ. Although, knowing your duties to be so arduous, yet, I must beg of you to look at this matter in all its bearings, and give me an answer at the earliest practicable period.

If I can be honored with an interview of fifteen minutes, I can present before you many things that it might be important for you to know; and, I feel so confident of being successful in the publication of a Democratic paper in this city, that if you will *only consent to place it on an equality with the other democratic journals*,[1] I would undertake it immediately— said paper to be under the *entire control* of any gentleman who might be acceptable to you.

JOHN P. HEISS

ALS. DLC–JKP. Addressed locally.
1. Heiss probably refers to the Washington *Globe* and the Washington *Madisonian*; the Baltimore *Constitution*, formerly the Washington *Spectator*, published a congressional edition in Washington City during the 1844–45 session.

## FROM JESSE MILLER

My Dear Sir                              Harrisburg March 14. 1845
The enclosed slip[1] will shew the estimation in which the Whigs view the election of Genl Cameron, and every honest democrat regards it as a Whig Triump of the Worst Kind. Yet this man Cameron will come to you in the most plausible manner and profess friendship and willingness to aid you in your administration, for the purpose of getting some of the Scoundrels Who aided him in his election office to repay them for their services. It was openly avowed during the Canvass that Cameron could serve his friends better than any other man & must therefore be elected. You cannot distrust this man too much. He is as bad as Wright.[2] The

Whigs have disgraced themselves and the State in his election. He will no doubt occasionally recommend some worthy men, but his recommendations ought always to be distrusted. He can do us but little harm at home, if he is kept in his true position at Washington.

J. MILLER

ALS. DLC–JKP. Addressed to Washington City.
1. Miller enclosed an article, entitled "A Victory for the Tariff," that appeared in an extra edition of the Harrisburg *Intelligencer* of March 14, 1845.
2. Reference probably is to Hendrick B. Wright.

## FROM ROBERT ARMSTRONG

Dr Sir                                    Washington March 15th 1845
Allow me to give you a word of caution about your Louisiana appointments. There is much to look to in that business. Let me *urge* you by all means to give Col. Breedlove[1] a patient hearing. He will throw light upon the subject and it deserves your serious consideration. Col B will give you what I believe to be the facts in regard to those appointments and I beg also to remind you of what Gen Jackson said on the subject,[2] as to his views we none of us can for a moment doubt.

R. ARMSTRONG

ALS. DLC–JKP. Addressed locally.
1. A native of Virginia, friend of Andrew Jackson, prosperous banker, and leader of the Democracy in New Orleans, James W. Breedlove served as collector of customs for the Mississippi district of Louisiana from 1834 until his resignation in 1839; he regularly secured lucrative mail contracts for routes connecting New Orleans and Mobile.
2. Armstrong's reference has not been identified further.

## FROM HENRY HORN

My Dear Sir                                Philadelphia 15 Mar 1845
I enclose you a Whig Slip by which you will perceive that our party has been betrayed defeated and disgraced at Harrisburg,[1] and some of those who have recently been making great professions of friendship to you at Washington I believe have been instrumental in producing this deplorable result. I blush for Penna.

HENRY HORN

ALS. DLC–JKP. Addressed to Washington City.
1. Horn's reference is to Simon Cameron's election to the U.S. Senate. For identification of Horn's enclosure, see Jesse Miller to Polk, March 14, 1845.

## FROM THOMAS RITCHIE

My Dear Sir                                    Richmond March 16, 1845

It is with the utmost reluctance I once more address you on the subject of appointments. But I assure you, it is the last time that I will trouble you. I am impelled by a letter, which was received from Washington to-day, to break through a resolution, which I had almost held to be inviolable.

Mr. Stevenson has been named in the papers as among those who might go to London. Upon what grounds I know not. I confess it has suggested a scheme which I should be most happy to see realized. The relations between the two countries seem to require that our Minister at London should be at this time a strong Southern man. It is the Head Quarters of Abolitionism, and it seems to us of the South that our Minister should be enabled by his feelings and information to meet every question of this sort, which may be likely to arise, with an energy, which is suitable to the occasion. No man could have defended the rights of his country, with more vigor & force, than he did. None raised her name more abroad, as was stated the other day by Mr. Calhoun, and as I was but recently informed by one of the best informed, and accredited agents we have in Europe. The whole course of his Correspondence proves his ability, his public spirit, his acquaintance with the interests of the U States, and his devotion to them.

I beg leave, therefore, most respectfully to call him to your attention, assuring you that this is the last application I'll make for any man, and asking of you the favor that you will keep this Letter within your own bosom.

THOMAS RITCHIE

ALS. DLC–JKP. Addressed to Washington City and marked "*Strictly Confidential*." Polk's AE states that the letter was to be answered, but Polk's reply has not been found.

## TO JAMES BUCHANAN

My Dear Sir:                          [Washington City] March 17th 1845

Understanding that *Mr Senator Bates's* funeral[1] will take place at the Capitol at 12. O.Clock on tomorrow. It is usual and will be expected that the President and the Cabinet shall attend. At 1. P.M. tomorrow was the hour appointed, to see the Diplomatic Corps. I suggest a postponement until 1. O.Clock the next day (wednesday). If you concur with me, will you address, a note to each of the Diplomatic corps, explaining the reasons for the postponement, & saying that it will give me pleasure to see them on wednesday, instead of tuesday.

JAMES K. POLK

ALS. DNA–RG 59. Addressed locally.
1. A Massachusetts Whig, Isaac C. Bates served four terms in the U.S. House, 1827–35; he won election to the U.S. Senate in 1841 and served in that body until his death on March 16, 1845.

## TO ANDREW JACKSON

My Dear Sir:                                         Washington March 17th 1845
    I have been much gratified to receive several letters from you since I reached Washington. I have intended repeatedly to write to you, but have been almost overwhelmed with business and company. I know too that I had nothing special to communicate which you would not learn through other sources. Genl. Armstrong left for home last evening. I had a full conversation with him and he can give you some idea of the difficulties which I had to encounter in forming my cabinet and since that time. So far I am pleased with my cabinet. They are harmonious and united, and what is of great importance are I think, working men, and are devoting themselves to duties of their respective stations. I have as yet made no removals. The Senate will adjourn on tomorrow or the next day,[1] when I will have more time to deliberate upon the changes proper to be made. There must necessarily be many of them, but I must have time to examine each case well, and to be sure that when I make a removal, I put a better man in the place. I have had between one and two hundred nominations to make during the executive Session of the Senate to fill existing vacancies. In making them, I have been compelled to act upon very short notice & imperfect information, and it will be strange if I have not made some mistakes. If I have I will hereafter correct them. You will readily see how it happened that so many vacancies existed requiring immediate action. Near one hundred of Mr Tyler's nominations were not acted on by the Senate. The terms of many officers expired during the early part of this month, and were required to be filled during the Session of the Senate.
    The rumour which you heard, that *Col Laughlin* was to take charge of the Madisonian, and make it the Government organ, was without the slightest foundation.[2] No such thing was thought of. General Armstrong will explain to you the difficulties about a Government organ, as also my views and wishes. There is at present no paper here which sus-

tains my administration for its own sake. The Globe it is manifest does
not look to the success or the glory of my administration so much as it
does to the interests, and views of some certain prominent men of the
party,[3] who are looking to succeed me in 1848. The arrangement which
above all others I prefer would be that, the owners of the Globe,[4] would
agree to place it in the hands of a new Editor, still retaining the propri-
etorship of the paper if they choose. You may rely upon it, that without
such an arrangement, the Democratic party, who elected me cannot be
kept united three months. If *Majr Donelson* would take charge of the
Editorial Department, all the sections of the party would be at once reconciled and satisfied. If Majr D's[5] object is to make money, there is no
other position so desirable for him, for a year or two at least, as the one I
suggest. It is proper that I should speak plainly to you. If Blair continues
at the head of the Globe, and it shall be understood to be the Government
organ, it is certain that the administration will be in a minority from that
moment. Blair and his paper are so identified with certain men of the
party, and has increased the hostility of certain other men of the party,[6]
to such an extent, that it is impossible, for him to command the support
of the whole party. He would with almost certainty be defeated for public
printer in the next Congress,[7] though there might be a large majority of
Democratic members. I would not injure him pecuniarily or in any other
way, for my feelings are not unkind to him. If he looks to his true interest he would desire to make such an arrangement as I suggest, and yet
I fear he is disinclined to do so. If he will not, the safety and the success
of my administration, will in my judgment make it indispensible that I
should have a new organ, and that at a very early day. Majr *Donelson* or
Mr *Ritchie* are the only men in the country, who now occur to me that I
would be willing to have at the head of the Government organ. I cannot
go into further details or explain to you other difficulties which surround
the subject. I feel that my administration is at this moment defenseless
so far as the public press here is concerned. I find myself very much in
the condition which you were, early in your administration, when you
found it to be necessary to supercede the Telegraph by establishing the
Globe.[8] I refer you to Genl Armstrong for full information. As to the
*Madisonian* or *Constitution*, they are not to be thought of, for a moment
as the Government organ. Either the Globe must surrender the Editorial Department to another or a new paper must be established. What
Majr Donelson's inclinations might be I have no means of knowing. If
with a view to place himself in entirely easy circumstances pecuniarily,
he were willing to take the position here for two years, I could at the
end of that time probably gratify his wishes, in desiring to continue in
the Diplomatic service. I have heard within a day or two, a rumour that

Mr *Ritchie* might be willing to come here. It is probable that he would only agree to do so, upon a friendly understanding with Blair, as I know they are friends. My object is only to explain the state of things, and not harrass you or trouble you. I thought it proper that you should understand the difficulties. With my prayers for the continuance of your life and improved health ....

JAMES K. POLK

ALS. DLC–AJ. Addressed to the Hermitage and marked "Confidential." Published in Bassett, ed., *Correspondence of Andrew Jackson*, VI, pp. 382–83.
1. See Polk to Benjamin F. Butler, March 14, 1845.
2. See Andrew Jackson to Polk, February 28, 1845.
3. Polk probably refers to the inner circles of Thomas Hart Benton and Martin Van Buren.
4. Francis P. Blair and John C. Rives.
5. Andrew Jackson Donelson.
6. Polk probably refers to the followers of John C. Calhoun and Lewis Cass.
7. See Aaron V. Brown to Polk, January 6, 1845.
8. Polk's reference is to Jackson's decision in 1830 to replace the *United States Telegraph*, edited by Duff Green, with a new administration mouthpiece, the Washington *Globe*, edited by Francis P. Blair. Jackson's break with John C. Calhoun forced Green to choose sides, and as expected Green sided with Calhoun, his father-in-law and political mentor.

## FROM DANIEL T. JENKS[1]

My Dear Sir                    Newtown Bucks Co, Pa March 17th 1845
Being one of your devoted friends and haveing rendered all the service in my power to elevate you to the exalted position you now ocupy, and being very desirous that your administration should succeed in secureing the entire confidence of the *whole Democratic Party*, I therefore beg leave respectfully to address you in all frankness.
During the early part of the late contest, it was exceedingly doubtfull wether we could succeed in carrying the electoral vote in this state; hence it became a very important matter to secure for our Democratic Electoral ticket, that the friends of President Tyler, who numbered in the city & County of Philadelphia from 4 to 5 thousand voters. Besides haveing the largest Vote, they held *all* the Government Offices in this State; this power added to their vote, made them very formidable. Besides these advantages they combined a large amount of *tallent and great tact*; the truth is that, if we had not succeeded in obtaining the influence and suport of this body of voters it would of been impossible to have carried

our ticket in this state. At this great crises the venerable *Thomas Ritche* came out in his paper in favour of the *union* of President Tylers & your friends.[2]

The article of the Inquirer was coppyed by *all* the leading Democratic Papers of the country includeing the *Nashville Union*, and they commented on it with great approbation.[3] After the comment referred to had appeared Mr. Ritchee incorporated them all into an article, and he published them in *connection* with a "letter of *General Jackson*"[4] and the remarks of Mr R. were truly eloquent, and combined with the comments before refered to, it formed one of the most forceible appeals, that stands on record in our language.

The moment the friends of President Tyler saw the appeal of the Inquirer, they called a meeting of their friends, at the great saloon of the Museum in the city of Phila; and there defined their position and resolved to take ground in favour of the *Polk & Dallas Electoral Ticket*. Their was according to the opposition papers *5 Thousand* at the meeting, and it was found after the passage of the Resolutions and the speech of the Hon. Joel B. Sutherland, that a large number remained out side of the Hall, unable to get in. It was then on motion that the meeting adjoined to the Street and formed a *mighty* prosession with Banners Music &c. The procession called on *Mr Dallas* and he at 10 oclock at night addressed them from the courthouse steps. Vice President Dallas saw it *all*, and therefore I refer your excellency to him for the truth of my statement.

The great leaders, in this great and important maneuver of uniting the Party, was the Hon *Joel B. Sutherland, Hon. Calvin Blyth*, (he being president) and *William B. Whitacer Esq*[5] who organised the meeting, and *John O. Bradford*[6] one of your old friends and acquaintances. If I can lay my hands upon the proceedings as printed, I will send them to you.

My object in presenting these facts, was that you may be correctly advised as to how the electoral vote of this state was carried; I would sujust with great respect to your position that the plighted faith of the party, be kept toward our allies. By doing this we will secure the ascendency of the great Democratic Party throughout the country. I will also as soon as I can procure it send you the articles of the Richmond Inquirer; my frequent visits to Phila enabled me to attend the meetings and obtain these facts.

DANIEL T. JENKS

ALS. DLC–JKP. Addressed to Washington City. Polk's AE on the cover notes that this letter was "to be shown to Mr. Buchanan."

1. An ardent Democrat and former party worker in Bucks County, Penn.,

Jenks moved to Philadelphia in 1845 and secured an appointment as a clerk in the customs house in 1847.

2. Reference is to Ritchie's editorial in the *Richmond Enquirer* of August 20, 1844. Calling for a union of Tyler Democrats with the supporters of Polk and Dallas, Ritchie argues that a reconciliation of these factions would insure victory for the Democratic ticket against Clay and the forces of Whiggery.

3. Jenks' reference to the reprint of Ritchie's editorial in the *Nashville Union* has not been identified further.

4. Ritchie's article and the "letter of *General Jackson*" have not been identified further.

5. William B. Whitecar served as assistant appraiser for the port of Philadelphia, 1844–45.

6. John O. Bradford served briefly in 1837 as editor of the *Nashville Union*; the following year he went to Puerto Rico as U:S. consul at St. Johns. In March 1845, Polk appointed him to the post of purser in the navy.

## FROM HENRY OSBORN[1]

Respected Sir                                                 Troy, March 17 1845

I notice by the newspapers, that the notorious Isaiah Rhynders[2] is at Washington. He is represented as holding free, and confidential conversations with you, and particularly, and favourably noticed, by the members of your Cabinet. To me Sir, this seems *absolutely impossible*.

Rhynders, I have known from a boy—but a few years since, he was *Cook* on board one our river Sloops, then, a common hand before the mast, afterwards, promoted to the command of a small Sloop. He *purposely* got deeply in debt, failed, did not pay his creditors a farthing, removed to New York, became a *Bully* to a *Brothel*, and a *black leg*, in every sense of the word. He is more than suspected of obtaining money, in many ways *less* honest than *gambling*, has been imprisoned for Stealing Treasury Notes. He is, as you must have noticed, a rough, unpolished, ill-bred, and ignorant, rowdy & ruffian. His fathers family are *anything*, and *everything*, but respectable. His Mother is a prostitute, and his Sisters *no better than they Should be*.

Such a *creature*, so steeped in crime, and infamy, was used by the democracy of the city of New York last fall, to promote the election of the democratic candidate. And that *creature*, is said to be soliciting from you, some appointment as a reward for his faithful services to the party.

Sir, I am a democrat, and laboured hard to elect you, but rather would I see yourself, and the whole democratic party *annihilated*, than to see it *disgraced*, by the appointment of Rhynders to any office of honer or trust.

Henry Osborn

ALS. DLC–JKP.
1. Probably Henry Osborn, a clerk in Troy, N.Y.
2. President of New York City's Empire Club, Isaiah Rynders informed Polk on August 28, 1844, of his election to honorary membership. In 1849 Rynders participated in an anti-British riot in New York City that left more than a dozen men dead. Eight years later, James Buchanan appointed him U.S. marshal of the Southern District of New York.

## FROM JOHN C. RIVES

Sir:                                                    Washington, 17 March, 1845
I learned last night from good authority, that Levi D. Slamm, under whose name the New York Plebian is carried on,[1] had prevailed upon many editors, most of them Pennsylvanians, to recommend him to Mr Buchanan as a suitable person for Marshal of the Eastern District of New York. I told this to Mr Blair & Senator Allen last night, & they requested, me as I know Slamm personally, & know him to be a rascal to all & tell you what I know of him. I objected (or rather begged off) to doing so, solely for the reason that I did not like to trouble you now while you are so importuned for offices. But, this morning I concluded that it was due to you & to the democratic party, that I should see you & tell you in a few words what I *know* of Slamm. When I arrived in sight of your House I saw two carriages drive up to it, & I at once concluded that I would not trouble you in person, but would drop you a line. Now, in a word, I know Slamm's associations to be bad & I *know* him to be a bad man. I have no doubt but Rynders (who when I first knew him was called Rhinus) who is a professional gambler, a Fast dealer, was a better man than Slamm & would be more acceptable to the people of New York.
JOHN C. RIVES

ALS. DLC–JKP. Addressed locally.
1. A locksmith and labor leader, Levi Slamm served as a delegate to the General Trades' Union representing the Journeymen Locksmith's Society in 1835. In that same year and the next, he also served as a delegate to the conventions of the National Trades' Union. By the latter 1830's, Slamm associated himself with the Locofoco Equal Rights party. In 1840 he published the New York *New Era* and later the New York *Plebeian.* In 1842, he joined the Tammany Society.

## FROM CORNELIUS P. VAN NESS

Dear Sir                                          Washington March 17/[18]45
After my interview with you this morning I received the extraordinary letter (forwarded through a Senator) which I have the honor, herewith,

to send for your perusal. The writer, Dr Donovan,[1] held a situation in the Patent Office during the administration of Mr Van Buren, and was removed by Mr Webster in 1841. He remained without employment until I became Collector of New York, when I gave him a place in the Custom House, in order to furnish bread to his family. He has always been a devoted partizan & friend of Mr Van Buren and Mr Wright, and he feels grateful to me for a liberality I have shown to him & to Mr Van Buren's friends generally. The part he has acted at Albany, as detailed in his letter, has been without my authority or knowledge.

The object of my sending you the letter, is to show you the intense interest felt in a certain quarter to get possession of my office. There is no question made of my qualifications, nor any complaint of my official conduct, but there is, it is said, to be a constant *pressure* upon me which, it is supposed, I shall be unable to resist. But from whom is this pressure to come, except from the friends & instruments of the very persons spoken of? Then the party will be distracted, and the government harrassed with applications for my removal. Why should this be so if I am fit for the office, and perform its duties justly and impartially, the contrary of which is not pretended, or, at least, can not be shown? Indeed, would it not be for the very reason that the duties of the office are thus performed, and that a man is wanted who would have an eye solely to the interests of certain men, or of a certain *clique*? I have always been on friendly terms with Mr Van Buren & Mr Wright, and have treated their friends with great liberality. I have appointed men for Mr Wright, & he actually, in December last, wrote a letter to a friend of his in the Senate in favour of my confirmation. But I can not be made an instrument of, nor will I give up the control of the office to any *clique* whatever, or suffer it to be used for the interest or elevation of any individual. My political character is not impeached, and I am bold to say that for zeal & *consistency* in the support of the democratic cause, I do not fear a comparison either with Mr Van Buren or Mr Wright. Then why should the party be distracted more by me than by another, except upon the ground that the exclusive friends of certain Gentlemen constitute *"the party"*, and that a full *share* will not satisfy them, but that they must have the *whole*. Again, it will not be denied, but is notorious, that I am a cordial supporter of yours and of your administration, and if such support was the object of certain Gentlemen, why such anxiety to get me out of the way. I am no Calhoun man, no Cass man, no Tyler man, nor any body's man; but my whole object is to give a sincere and active support, as already stated, to you & to your administration. Is it not plain then that there is some object *at bottom*, other than a *true course* as it regards your administration and the interest of the *whole* party?

But it seems they consider me as entitled to *something*, and I suppose, they name the Mission to Spain because my wife's family [2] is there, and because they know I was successful there before, and also that I would prefer that place to any other, in case of my leaving my present position. I am, however, satisfied where I am, if it should please you to leave me there; but if it should, now or hereafter, be *your* wish to transfer me to another situation I shall be content; and if you should deem it *just* that I should be dismissed altogether, I shall endeavour to bear the stroke as becomes *a man*.

After having perused the letter referred to, I beg leave respectfully to request that you will let your Secretary enclose it to my address (at Washington) & send it to the Post Office.

C. P. Van Ness

P.S. I forgot to add, that before long, I feel sure, you will see it developed that not only the whole business community in New york is in my favour, but that a *majority* of the democracy of the City, when fairly expressed, and not through a few committees constituted for the purpose, *and* every member of which wants to get into the Custom House (having failed with me) is also in my favour.

ALS. DLC–JKP. Addressed locally. Polk's AE reads as follows: "Enclosed back to him as requested the letter of Thos Wash. Donovan addressed to him from Albany. Enclosed is addressed to Washington City, March 24th, 1845."

1. A native of Maryland, Thomas W. Donovan was an examiner in the U.S. Patent Office from 1839 until 1841, and he was appointed as a gauger in the New York City Customs House in 1844.

2. Van Ness' second wife is not identified further.

## FROM REUBEN M. WHITNEY

Dear Sir,                    [Washington City] Monday 17th March [1845] [1]

I find that I have been superceded in the office that I held for a short time. Misrepresentations I apprehend have been made to you concerning me. I will not now go further back than 1840, in which campaign I took no part whatever. At the Baltimore convention, I was a laborer out of doors for Commodore Stewart. [2] When your nomination was announced I went to Mr Butler and said to him, now we have a candidate whom we all can support.

On my return here from Baltimore, knowing that Mr Tyler must withdraw, I labored incessantly to bring about a union between his friends and your friends. To this the Hon Cave Johnson, Doctor Duncan and a number of others can testify. As soon as Mr Tyler withdrew, [3] I filled the editorial columns of the Madisonian, and continued it untill taken ill with articles in favor of your cause. I know that I acted zealously, how efficiently I leave others to Judge.

I deem it but an act of Justice to myself to make you acquanted with these facts, although I write in a sick bed.[4] I repeat, that I beleive some one has scandalized me to you, for it is in that only that I can account for what has taken place.

R. M. WHITNEY

ALS. DLC–JKP. Addressed locally.

1. Place and date identified through content analysis.

2. Charles Stewart commanded the U.S.S. *Constitution* during the War of 1812 and attracted minor support for the Democratic presidential nomination in 1844.

3. See Cornelius P. Van Ness to Polk, January 17, 1845.

4. On August 16, 1845, William Whitney wrote that his brother, Reuben, had died in May "from a cancer on the side of his face." ALS. DLC–JKP.

## FROM ANDREW J. DONELSON

Dr Sir:                                                New Orleans March 18th 1845

I reached here last night, having left home as soon as I heard of the vote on the annexation measure in the Senate,[1] and expecting to find here instructions from the Department of State. I see by the papers that communications for me have been intrusted to a messenger who was to pass by Nashville, under an impression that I would be there.[2] This was unexpected in as much as I had requested Mr Calhoun to forward to this point whatever additional views might be proper, after the passage of the bill.

The late papers from Texas, particularly the organ of the Govt, are opposing the House bill with a good deal of feeling, and on grounds that occur to me inconsistent with a sincere wish to consummate the measure of annexation.[3] I had Houston's express authority[4] for the belief that Texas was willing to pay her own debt, if the terms of union with us left her her domain; and he was also willing to leave to us the adjustment of the boundary with Mexico, either as a state or states, or as a Territory. It is true he did not except the public property or the minerals &c, but if this exception is the cause of the opposition now made in the paper devoted to his interests, it is disproportionate and unexpected to me.

Whatever may be the disposition of the existing Government, after it is placed in possession of the recent act of our Congress, I cannot doubt that of the people of Texas. They anxiously desire annexation, and I feel no doubt of the result whenever the question is submitted to them. But much may depend on the shape in which it may be presented to them, and hence it is important to secure the assent of their President[5] to the measure which will be presented to them either directly or through their agents.

On all these points I shall write to the Department fully, after I receive the instructions said to be in the care of Majr. Waggaman. As soon as I receive them, or as soon as a conveyance can be obtained to Galveston, I will lose no time in repairing to Washington in Texas, and shall request Houston to meet me there. It is upon him that I mainly rely to bring the question to the earliest practicable settlement.

I left the Genl[6] on the 8th intending to go by my plantation in Mississippi, but I was stopped by the high waters and obliged to turn my course down the Tennessee river by steam boat. From a conversation with him I anticipated that the New Yorker would be in the Treasury, & Mr Walker the atty Genl; but you were doubtless governed by circumstances which when understood will be found to be controlling with and satisfactory to all your friends.

The great measures of your administration are now the reduction of the Tariff of 42, and the occupation of Oregon, after the annexation of Texas. Your action in other respects will be rather *preventive* than *positive*, persuading the people to be content with the simple and legitimate operation of the Government, and to avoid all the schemes of the whigs in regard to the Bank, distribution &c, which are but modes of robbing labor and benefitting capital. That you may be successful is my fervent prayer.

I ought to say to you, as I do in the strictest confidence, that I have recd a letter from Genl Cameron, Genl Simon Cameron of Dauphine Penna (said to be an intimate acquaintance of Mr Buchanan),[7] which he says was written after consultation with your Brother in law[8] and other intimate personal friends, proposing to make me the editor of a new paper at Washington. I have not replied to it because I have thought the proposition was unknown to you, and ought not go further without your knowledge of it, and of its probable effect upon the present relations of the party. If made with the sanction of Mr Buchanan & the other members of your cabinet it ought to have been communicated by some one better authorised to approach me on a question of so much delicacy & importance.

As the matter stands, unexplained, and undefined as bearing on the Globe, which certainly could not be superceded without weakening the Democracy, I could not be made a party to it. And in any event I have too much distrust of my abilities to undertake a task of such responsibility, requiring a discipline and tact so foreign to my past pursuits.

If such a step is resolved on I would say by all means let it be so taken as to blend the Globe with whatever new organ may be started. If Mr Blair wishes to retire he can have no motive to mar the harmony so loudly called for by the great public sentiment which made you chief magistrate, and he would be, doubtless, among the first to make reasonable sacrifices for its attainment. These suggestions are made without consultation with any one. I will barely add that if the proposition referred to has been seriously entertained I hope you will take some occasion to explain to the friends suggesting it the grounds of my unwillingness to accept it. If however, it is unknown to you let it rest as it is.

My chief solicitude is now to repair the losses to which I have been subjected by a long connection with politics. In this respect my position has been unfortunate, borne along as you have been aware by circumstances from which I could not separate without apparent harshness to the Genl.

A. J. DONELSON

ALS. DLC–JKP. Addressed to Washington City and marked "Private & Confidential." Published in Bassett, ed., *Correspondence of Andrew Jackson*, VI, pp. 383–85.

1. Donelson probably refers to the vote on Robert Walker's compromise measure. See William H. Haywood, Jr., to Polk, February 26, 1845.

2. On March 3, 1845, Tyler dispatched to Texas his nephew, Floyd Waggaman, with documents necessary to effect Texas' annexation.

3. Reference is to the Washington (Texas) *National Register*, official organ of Anson Jones' administration.

4. Sam Houston, a former governor of Tennessee, won election to two terms as president of the Republic of Texas, 1836–38 and 1841–44. After Texas' annexation to the United States, he served as U.S. senator from Texas, 1846–59, and as governor, 1859–61.

5. Anson Jones.

6. Andrew Jackson.

7. Donelson wrote his identification of Cameron in the left margin of the fourth page of the letter.

8. James Walker.

## FROM ANDREW J. DONELSON

Dr. Sir,                                          New Orleans March 19th 1845

Mr Pickett handed me last night your private letter of the 7th advising me to defer action on the instructions of the 3d inst, until further instructed by the Department of State. I have not yet received the instructions referred to, and have done nothing but write a private letter to President Jones putting him in possession of the bill passed by our Congress[1] which I trust will induce him to convene the Congress of Texas without waiting for a formal communication from me.

From the tone of the National Texas Register I anticipate serious opposition from the existing Government to what is termed the House part of our bill. To escape this the wisest course for us will be to get the whole bill before the people of Texas, whose anxiety for annexation may be relied on to defeat a movement of the opposition founded on objections in detail. When the measure is once before the people its friends can assail British intrigue and interference and appeal with confidence to the friendship of the United States, as a guarantee that if the present bill takes too much from Texas, future Legislation will give it back.

It is on the people of Texas, as on those of the United States, that we must rely to defeat the intrigues of the British, and the interests of scrip-holding speculators.

I will write you fully when the instructions come, and can assure you nothing within my power will be omitted to give them effect in bringing to a speedy close the accomplishment of the great measure of annexation. The sooner this is done the better it will be for all the interests of our country.

A. J. DONELSON

ALS. DLC–JKP. Addressed to Washington City. Published in *Tyler's Quarterly Historical and Genealogical Magazine*, VI (April, 1925), pp. 235–36.

1. See Andrew J. Donelson to Polk, March 18, 1845, and William H. Haywood, Jr., to Polk, February 26, 1845.

## FROM JAMES REID[1]

St. Ignatius' church
Dear Sir.                                      Harford Co. Md. 19th March 1845

It may astonish you that so humble an individual as myself would thus address you without seeking an office or something else. I want no office higher than the one I occupy, which is certainly more durable than your own. I am a Roman Catholic priest, possessed of a Mission, under the venerable Archbishop of Baltimore.[2] I enjoy the highest honr. I could aspire to: 1st to be a priest and 2nd to be subject to so worthy a dignitary, as the Archbishop already alluded to, the perfect gentleman & scholar and a christian prelate presiding over the American church. But my motive in thus addressing you is this: I am a republican in politics. I was so, many years ago, in Kentucky, where I recd. my education. I have always been so. I am so yet. I was so rejoiced at the triumph of Democracy in your person that, altho' indisposed, I went to Washington to witness your inauguration. I was there unwell in the rain, but the worst of it was, altho' I heard you & saw you, I could not remain long enough to have the honr. of shaking your hand. I recd. a letter from Baltimore, when on the 5th Inst. I dined at Georgetown College, which called me back to attend to some business. I am quite conscious of the amount of executive business which must necessarily engross your attention at this time. Moreover, I could not expect a reply from your Excellency to so uninteresting a communication as mine. I only therefore wish to inform you that I hope in Apl or May to be at Washington for the express purpose of seeing you, in whom we have succeeded as astonishingly as did the Democracy of 1800. And, I hope that half a century will not reverse our present career. You will please to excuse this intrusion. And attribute it to a Zeal for the common cause of the Republic. Should you honr. me with a reply, you will please address the Revd. James Reid, *Hickory*, Harford Co. *Md.*

In conclusion, I thank God that the Texas Bill passed,[3] to check the north. And I hope that our legislative wisdom and prowess will retain Oregon from the fangs of british usurpation.

Wishing you every prosperity in your incipient undertaking. And above all, many blessings to our Republic ....

JAMES REID

ALS. DLC–JKP. Addressed to Washington City.

1. Ordained a priest in 1832, James Reid began his ministry in the Roman Catholic Church in the Diocese of Cincinnati; in 1839 he moved to the Archdiocese of Baltimore where he served as pastor of St. Ignatius parish; and in 1845 Reid took an assignment in the Diocese of Pittsburgh, where he became renowned for hearing confessions in Irish Gaelic.

2. The first American convert elevated to the Roman Catholic hierarchy, Samuel Eccleston served as the archbishop of Baltimore from 1834 until 1851 and during his ministry oversaw the rapid expansion of parochial schools in America.

3. William H. Haywood, Jr., to Polk, February 26, 1845.

## FROM JOHN F. H. CLAIBORNE[1]

My dear Sir:                         Washington 20th March 1845

As I wish to return home in a few days I beg to address you briefly in relation to an appointment in Louisiana, & you will perceive that I consider it in reference to the interests of the party & the country exclusively & not from favor or prejudice towards any of the applicants. In this view I ask your Excellency to read this long letter attentively. I address it to you confidentially, because being the editorial representative of the *whole* party I can take no active part in these matters.

For Marshall, I recommend *Mandeville Marigny* of New Orleans.[2] Mr. Slidell[3] concurs in this recommendation. When I first removed to N.O. I was induced to write a letter to you for Mr. Young,[4] an old personal friend, but as it became my business to study the state of the party, I soon found that the recommendation was improper. It is a point of the first importance to conciliate the *Creole* population. A little kindness & distinction will bring these enthusiastic people in support of your Administration. They have strong prejudices of *caste*, and sometimes vote for a popular man of their own number without regard to politics. They vote in masses, and from personal feelings. A more generous, high-toned and patriotic people never lived. Two of the grand divisions of the city, viz: the 1st & 2d Municipalities are occupied by them. They constitute the ruling population down the river to the Balize[5] & up to Point Coupee, and in the Sugar parishes west of the Mississippi. Even where less numerous than the American population, they are more formidable from the circumstance of their acting in unison. Ever since the cession of Louisiana, although sincerely Americans in feeling & principles, they have been jealous, and not without reason, of influence from abroad, and as often as they are passed over in the distribution of national favors, for men of recent citizenship, they feel that Louisiana is more like a conquered province than a sovereign state. Mr. *Marigny* belongs to this class. His father, Gen. Marigny,[6] a personal friend of Gen. Jackson, and of the Secretary of the Treasury,[7] is an eloquent and popular orator, and the acknowledged leader of the Creole democracy. His son, whom I recommend, was removed from the Marshalship, without cause or censure, merely to make room for a Virginian who happened to be related to an accidental President of the U.S.[8] He has always been an unflinching democrat, willing, at all times, to write, speak & pay for his party. The Louisiana delegation in both Houses protested against his removal. For his character as a man of integrity & as an untainted & honored gentleman, unconnected with any species of speculation, I refer to Senator Johnson,[9] who has known him from childhood, & Mr. Slidell, both of whom desire his appointment. The influence of his family is very great, and his appointment will rally to your support a powerful body of men. The young Creoles will declare for you at once, even many of those who are whigs. They feel in the unjust proscription of one of the most gifted of their number, that an indignity was put upon their *class*; and they look to you, the *President of the People*, the young Head of the New Movement, to do him & *them* justice. It is the only office probably, that you will fill with a French Creole. Nearly all the applicants before you are Americans.

Your Excellency, if I may judge from your appointments, has wisely prescribed to yourself the rule to preserve a rigid impartiality towards the whole party. You have retained some of Mr. Tyler's selections, where they are deserving. You have re-appointed some who held office under Mr Van Buren & were subsequently removed. You have appointed some who never held office before, but who established claims for themselves during the late canvass. Under this salutary rule the case of Mr. Marigny will fall. He was ejected on account of his democracy, or because a Whig relative of Mr. Tyler *from Virginia* desired to spend his winters in New Orleans, and now we most respectfully ask you to re-instate him.

A few words as to the other applicants. Col. Nicholas [10] is a clever gentleman, but nothing more. Accident some years since when there was little talent & little political organization in Louisiana, favored his election to the U.S. Senate, where he never opened his mouth. The circumstance of his being a sugar planter & therefore favorable to the sugar duty, induced certain whigs to support him. But he has since endeavored in vain to be elected to the Legislature & the Convention from his own Parish. He is a drone in politics, would transact all the business with *Virginia* deputies, and would not, and does not, weigh a feather in a political canvass. He is just about such a man as Powhatan Ellis, [11] good, amiable, respectable, but too hacknied, superannuated & lazy for the young Democracy of a new state. He is a political antedeluvian & besides holds a good sinecure office already. Mr. Buchanan, I understand, will urge his claims, because they were old bachelore together, but Mr. B. lives in Pensyla & I in Louisiana & I claim, with all respect, to know best what will conduce to the popularity of your administration there.

The objection to Mr *Eastland* is that he will bring into the office no political influence. Gen. *Dunlap* [12] & Mr *Young* are of too recent citizenship. Mr. *Dawson* & Mr. *Wagner* are both natives, [13] but they cannot pretend to have half the claims of Mr. Marigny; none of them have personal merits superior to him, and none of them but him belong to that powerful class, the *French* creole democracy which it is so important to conciliate. If he had consented to join the clamorous herd of office seekers who annoy your Excellency, half the state would have recommended him; but he merely requested me to present his name, saying that he would bow cheerfully to your decision.

New Orleans is divided into three Municipalities. Two of them are occupied chiefly by people of foreign extraction, the other by Americans. Remarkable jealousies exist between them. Every applicant before you, I believe, resides in the American division, save Mr. Marigny. Your Collectors, Surveyors, District Attorneys, Judges &c. &c. all live there. To succeed in our city elections we must preserve the balance of power between these rival divisions of sections & castes, and not confer favors solely on the Americans. In connexion with this, I will remark that we shall soon have an election for Governor & a Legislature, (which will choose a Senator) and the whigs, to secure the French influence, have nominated Gen. Dubuys,[14] one of the most popular men in the state. We shall require all the aid you can properly give us, and to this end as the best set-off to this movement of the whigs, I urge the appointment of *Marigny*. The district now extends over the whole state, & he will act by my advice in giving it an efficient organization & in the appointment of Deputies.

Finally, if it be not improper, if your Excellency satisfies yourself as to the integrity of Mr. Marigny, I ask his appointment as *a personal favor*. From the first time I ever saw you, in old Mrs. Burch's boarding house on Capitol Hill with Sam. Houston,[15] when I was a schoolboy here, I have been your *personal* friend. I corresponded with you before I was of age. You distinguished me with your favor when I came to Congress. I supported you for the Vice Presidency. When other democrats & even democratic papers in Mississippi & elsewhere attacked you, after your defeat for Governor, I defended you, and wrote an editorial, the *first* that ever shadowed forth your present position.[16] During the late canvass, I conducted two democratic papers for you unpaid; and excoriated to the bone Prentiss & his [ ...][17] whenever they assailed you. I have gone to New Orleans to labor in support of your Administration. My first fruit has been by my correspondence & conversations to bring thoroughly to your support a *whig* Senator, and now the only favor I ask of your Administration is the appointment of Mr Marigny, & I only ask it because I am sure it would be just, right & expedient for you to grant it.

I know your Excellency will decide from the best motives & be that decision what it may, I will support it.

JOHN F. H. CLAIBORNE

ALS. DLC–JKP. Addressed locally and marked *"Confidential."*

1. A lawyer, editor, and historian, Claiborne served two terms in the Mississippi House, 1830–34, before his election to the U.S. House in 1835. His bid for a second term in Congress failed when Sergeant S. Prentiss contested the 1837 election and the House voted to seat Prentiss. Claiborne edited the Natchez *Mississippi Free Trader* before moving to New Orleans, La., in 1844 and pursuing there his editorial work on the *Herald and Jeffersonian*, the *Louisiana Statesman*, and later the *Louisiana Courier*. He also wrote several historical works including a history of Mississippi.

2. Mandeville Marigny, descended from one of New Orleans' founding families, was graduate from the French military academy at St. Cyr and served as a lieutenant in the French cavalry. Returning to the United States he managed his family's sugar plantation and served as U.S. marshal for the Eastern District of Louisiana from 1839 to 1842.

3. A native of New York, John Slidell moved to New Orleans, La., in 1819 to

practice law. He served as U.S. attorney for the Eastern District of Louisiana, 1829–33, and won election to one term in the U.S. House, 1843–45. In 1845 Polk appointed Slidell minister to Mexico, but that government refused to receive him; he later served in the U.S. Senate from 1853 to 1861.

4. Claiborne's recommendation, probably of Charles P. Young, has not been found. Young, a resident of Madison Parish and a kinsman of Alfred M. Young of Young's Point, La., took an active interest in Democratic party operations in Louisiana's northeastern delta country as well as party patronage in New Orleans. His cotton business connected him with Madison Caruthers, Polk's brother-in-law and New Orleans cotton factor.

5. Reference is to a pilot village and fortification located half a mile above the mouth of the Mississippi River.

6. Bernard Xavier Philippe de Marigny de Mandeville inherited and squandered one of the largest fortunes in early Louisiana history; he served in both the Louisiana territorial legislature and state legislature from 1810 to 1838.

7. Robert J. Walker.

8. John Tyler appointed Algernon Sidney Robertson to the post of U.S. marshal for the Eastern District of Louisiana in 1842; Robertson's kinship tie to Tyler is not identified further.

9. A native of Virginia, Henry Johnson moved to the Territory of Orleans in 1809; won election to the U.S. Senate to fill the vacancy created by the death of William C. C. Claiborne, 1818–1824; resigned his Senate seat to become governor, 1824–28; sat two terms in the U.S. House, 1834–39; failed to win gubernatorial contests in 1838 and 1842 on the Whig ticket; and returned to the U.S. Senate in 1844 and served until 1849.

10. A Virginia native and major in the War of 1812, Robert C. Nicholas moved to Louisiana's Terrebonne Parish in 1820 and invested in sugar planting; he received an interim appointment to the U.S. Senate, 1836–41, and served as Louisiana's secretary of state from 1843 to 1846.

11. Ellis served two years on the Mississippi Supreme Court, 1823–25; in the U.S. Senate, 1825–26 and 1827–32; and on the U.S. District Court of Mississippi, 1832–36. Ellis went to Mexico as chargé d'affaires in 1836 and served there as minister plenipotentiary from 1839 until 1842.

12. Hugh W. Dunlap represented Henry and Weakley counties in the Tennessee House for one term, 1829–31; he subsequently removed to Madison Parish, La., and attempted to raise a volunteer regiment for service in the Mexican War.

13. R. G. Dawson and William F. Wagner. Dawson, son of John B. Dawson, is not identified further. Wagner served as U.S. marshal for Louisiana during Polk's presidency.

14. William Debuys, the Whig gubernatorial candidate in 1846, is not identified further.

15. Polk and Sam Houston boarded at the residence of Benjamin Burch during the first session of the 19th Congress, 1825–26.

16. Claiborne's editorial has not been identified.

17. Two words illegible.

## FROM HENRY HORN

My Dear Sir                           Philadelphia 20th March 1845

The rumours and counter rumours which continue to prevail here in reference to the appointment of Collector of our Port, are well calculated to shake the nerves of some of our sensitive friends. I am not however alarmed at such reports, especially as I know that my claims which are conceded here by every impartial man to be paramount to those of any of my competitors, are in the hands of an old and sincere friend for adjudication.

The reports from Washington which are received daily here produce great excitement. To day the stock of one of the aspirants rises on our political exchange, tomorrow it falls and the stock of some other is in the ascendant. These vibrations keep our friends in a state of continued alarm. And many of them are urging me to repair immediately to Washington to counteract any insidious movements that may be made there against me: can it be necessary that I should plant myself at the seat of government and like others who are there harass and annoy you by my personal importunities? I cannot believe it. I must indeed be much mistaken if your firmness and decision of character are not proof against any such appliances.

The only thing of which I have the slightest apprehension is that fraud and even forgery may be resorted to with a view to place me in a false position before you. Should this be the case I have only to ask at your hands that I may be afforded an opportunity to defend myself and expose the culprits who may assail me. My anxiety upon this subject may appear greater than it ought to be and the only apology I have to offer for it, is the incessant and pressing importunities of my numerous friends to ascertain something definite in reference to my prospects of success. And I trust I may soon be enabled to answer their enquiries in a satisfactory manner.

HENRY HORN

ALS. DLC–JKP. Addressed to Washington City.

## FROM SHADRACH PENN, JR.[1]

St. Louis, Mo. March 20, 1845

Penn discusses patronage in Missouri and criticizes the postmaster general's decision to give the *Missourian* the order for the publication of the list of letters for the St. Louis office.[2] Pointing out that the *Missourian*'s circulation is less than half of that of the *Reporter*, he adds that during the campaign the *Missourian* sustained Benton's attacks on the Baltimore convention and "the friends of immediate annexation." Unlike the *Missourian*, the *Reporter* faithfully supported Polk's nomination and Texas annexation. Penn warns Polk that Benton and his allies do not regard the annexation of Texas as a settled question. He has been told that Texas will not be admitted, "except on the principles Col. Benton has prescribed."

ALS. DLC–JKP. Addressed to Washington City.
1. A newspaper editor and publisher, Penn began his career with the Lexington *American Statesman* and then published the Louisville *Public Advertiser* from 1818 until 1841. At the request of Thomas H. Benton in 1841 he moved to St. Louis, where he edited the *Missouri Reporter* until his death in 1846. Penn broke with Benton politically in November 1842. The St. Louis *Missourian* became Benton's newspaper.
2. Penn's reference probably is to the post office's practice of publishing in a local newspaper the names of persons having unclaimed mail.


## FROM HENRY E. RIELL

Dear Sir                                            New York Mar 20th 1845
I was in Albany last Monday and was informed by Mr Flagg that he had declined your offer of the nomination of collector of our Port. Mr Wright was in hopes that you would select Mr C C Cambreling and I fully agreed with him in the selection, supposing that he would have been willing to serve. I was informed yesterday by his brother Mr Stephen Cambreling[1] that he would not accept this particular post under any circumstances. Should it meet with your approbation to nominate me to the collectorship, instead of the consulship at Rio, I would accept and can give the required securities. You have two of Mr. Van Burens letters which I presented to you,[2] stating his opinion of me fully and Mr Wright said if you desired to have his opinion also, he would immediately give it.

HENRY E. RIELL

ALS. DLC–JKP. Addressed to Washington City. Polk's AE on the cover reads, "My *note* on a letter received from Hon. *G. Kemble*, explains his mistake in supposing that the Post of Collector had been offered to Mr. Flagg. Says he would accept the office himself."
1. Riell probably refers to New York City lawyer, Stephen Cambreleng.
2. Letters not found.

FROM HENRY SIMPSON[1]

Dear Sir,                                   Philadelphia, March 20th 1845
I enclose you the proceedings, in part, of a celebration on the 8th January 1843, when as one of a Committee of Invitation, I insisted upon inviting you and toasted you for the high station you now fill, as one of Host Committee, and the letter and sentiment published from you,[2] had much to do with your nomination at Baltimore. Having had an agency in both matters, I now think it worth while to communicate the facts to you in hopes that you will have some regard for them and consideration for me.

When you addressed me in "private" 4th Jany 1843,[3] I made up my mind that if we could not nominate Mr Van Buren, we would nominate you at the Balto. National Convention of May last, and I was one of the first to go in for you, having had access to all the state delegations favorable to Mr Van Buren—indeed, your acquaintance and friendship with the leading *Van Buren men*, secured your nomination and election. It will be hard then, under the circumstances, to have all the friends of Mr Van Buren & Mr Dallas *proscribed* by your Secretary of State, who I understand swears he will do so. No doubt you intend to do what is strictly right, but the appointment of *Mr. Buchanan's friends* from the interior of this state, alarms every Democrat here. Genl Davis is from Bucks county, and Mr. Patterson from Montgomery county, Genl Keim, our Marshall, is from Berks county,[4] & our collector, Calvin Blythe, from Franklin county. The appointment of these men and the *continuance* of the practise will have this effect: It will make aspirants for offices *here*, in every county in our state, and completely dissatisfy the Democracy of this city and county containing near half a million of population, and *twenty thousand Democratic voters*. If Mr Buchanan's plans are to be carried out he will "rule or ruin,"[5] or both, one as regards the appointments *now*, and the other as respects our ascendency in 1848. I make thus free to communicate my views, because you once addressed me in the same strain and requested "to hear from me again." I know the politicians of this state well, but never supposed the *enemy* of General Jackson, Genl Davis, who headed an escort for Saml. D. Ingham in 1833,[6] would be appointed Surveyor of our port. Saml. D. Patterson is a partner with our state printer, Mr. Lescure,[7] and *by law* is not eligible to the office of navy agent, of this there can be *no doubt*, although, it might not be easy to prove it.

Our friend Henry Horn, is the choice of the people for collector of this port. I know this and am glad to communicate it to you, but he never blowed the trumpet for Mr. Buchanan, and says he never will. I ask you to make me *naval officer, Treasurer of the mint*, or *principal appraiser*, & believe that I have earned and deserve the *first*, and wish you could know my labors in the last campaign, you would cheerfully grant it to me, but I am willing to accept either of the two last, if it will aid and be a convenience to your administration. I sincerely hope you will take care of your own personal and political friends, without regard to the advice of any prejudiced person in or out of your cabinet.

HENRY SIMPSON

P.S. It would be far better for you to stand for a second term, than to allow Mr. B.[8] to build up capital for the succession, by the *patronage* of your administration. I know you do not, and cannot admit this, *if you know it*, but facts speak louder than words, and I refer you to the appointments already made from this state, of Messrs. Davis & Patterson, two most ardent friends of your Secretary of State for the next Presidency. HS.

ALS. DLC–JKP. Addressed to Washington City, and marked *"Private."* Polk's AE on the cover reads, "Pennsylvania politics—Important facts stated."

1. Henry Simpson, brother of noted Philadelphia editor and author Stephen Simpson, served as an alderman of Philadelphia, as well as a member of the state legislature. In the late 1830's he held the post of appraiser for the port of Philadelphia, but lost that position in 1841.

2. Simpson probably refers to a Philadelphia *Pennsylvanian* account of a meeting of Philadelphia Democrats who gathered on January 8, 1843, to commemorate the Battle of New Orleans. On January 2, 1843, Polk wrote the organizers of the celebration thanking them for their invitation and informing them that he would be unable to attend. Polk also sent a toast to be read. PL, Philadelphia *Pennsylvanian*.

3. Letter not found.

4. John Davis, Samuel D. Patterson, and George M. Keim. A merchant and farmer, Davis attained the rank major general in the Pennsylvania militia and won election as a Democrat to one term in the U.S. House, 1839–41; he served as surveyor of the port of Philadelphia from 1845 until 1849. Publisher of the Harrisburg *Reporter*, Patterson received an appointment as naval agent for the port of Philadelphia on March 13, 1845. Keim served as marshal of Pennsylvania's Eastern District from 1843 until 1849.

5. Paraphrase from John Dryden, *Absalom and Achitophel* (1680), I, 173.

6. Ingham served as a member of the Pennsylvania House and as secretary of the commonwealth prior to his election to the U.S. House in 1813. He won reelection to seven terms before joining Andrew Jackson's cabinet in 1829 as secretary of the Treasury, a post that he resigned in 1831 as a result of the Peggy O'Neale Eaton affair.

7. Not identified further.

8. James Buchanan.

## FROM DANIEL STURGEON[1]

Dr Sir                                   Washington City March 20th [18]45
    With regard to the proper adjustment of the offices in the city of
Philadelphia I feel very anxious and have given the subject much consideration.  I believe the Collector and Naval officer should be given
to Henry Welsh Esq and George F. Lehman Esq.[2] The situation each
should have is left to the determination of yourself and Cabinet on due
consideration of the merits and qualification of these Gentlemen.  Another party in the City I presume might be satisfyed by giving to John
Horn[3] the Treasurer of the Mint. I believe this arrangment would go far
in satisfying all parties. The three above named gentlemen are qualifyed
to discharge the duties pertaining to any & each of the situations named,
and I feel satisfyed would go far to allay any Jelousy or feeling that now
exists. I respectfully submit this view of the matter to your better Judgment, and repeat that my principal object in writing this note is to bring
about such a result as will be satisfactory to all interested. I also think
that the very earliest disposal of these offices will be the best.

                                                      DANL STURGEON

    ALS. DLC–JKP. Addressed locally.
    1. A Uniontown physician, Sturgeon won election to several terms in both
the Pennsylvania House and Senate, 1818–30; served as state auditor general,
1830–36, and as state treasurer, 1838–39; and sat two terms in the U.S. Senate,
1839–51.
    2. A Philadelphia physician and political associate of James Buchanan, Leh-
man lost his bid for a seat in the U.S. House in 1844, applied unsuccessfully for
the collectorship of Philadelphia, but did receive the postmastership of the city
in 1845.
    3. John Horn, the brother of Henry Horn, served as naval officer of Philadel-
phia from 1838 until 1841.

## FROM JAMES H. THOMPSON[1]

[Dear Sir:]                                   Nashville March 20. [18]45
    In connection with a matter of my own, I will write you a little share
of the news of *to-day*. As you are already aware this day was set apart
for the nomination of a Whig candidate for Governor. The delegates
met with a "beautiful diversity of opinions" in regard to *the* man, and
it was late in the day before they could be got together. When they
met, however, letters were read from Henry and N. S. Brown[2] declaring that it was utterly impossible for them to "come to tea," that they

could do more good elsewhere, that the determination of the Convention was theirs, &c. And lo! contrary to the expectations of Whigs and Democrats, Ephraim H. Foster was the only "available," and so, perforce he was *unanimously* nominated. But *such* "unanimity" won't begin to make a show. You have no idea how unpopular the nomination is among the rank and file. Foster made some twenty of the Delegates *put up* at his house the night before, but notwithstanding, several were heard to express their unwillingness to make him the nominee. Since your election Democracy is considerably above par in Tennessee, and more so since your Inaugural address has met with such universal approbation from papers of every hue.

Foster made a speech to-day, in which he gave you a good share of abuse, said that he would rather be a "noble Whig of Tennessee," doing his duty in a glorious but *baffled* cause than to be in the chair of that petty politician at Washington. (No applause—every body *knows* Foster.) As to the Texas question he stood upon his own *bottom*, that many rotten-hearted men who called themselves Whigs, would, no doubt, take that question as a loop-hole out of which to fire on their old associates, &c. but as for himself he would, as he had done throughout in this matter, "*stand* on his own *bottom*." [3]

"Yes," said a Democrat from Giles, "and the first thing you know our Brown [4] will throw you on your a ___ ." [Excuse me, sir, but it created so much mirth in the *Whig* convention that I must write it.] Such an uproar of laughter you never heard.

Every body is greatly pleased with Armstrong's appointment. [5] Great anxiety here as to the Post Office and Marshalship. The news of W.H.P.'s [6] confirmation reached us this evening, and for one, I say he is well suited for the office, and I'm very glad of it.

Now for myself. If I had have had money I wanted the inclination to dog you to Washington, even with the probability of receiving "patronage." From all I can learn, most of these hares have had enough that did go. Some amusing anecdotes are told of Harris, Stevenson [7] and others, and are laughed at "mightily." I am a poor devil, I know, have tried several times to make a start in the world but never could, on account of that fast friend of mine *Poverty*. I am willing, and have *worked* always for a living, but now I can scarcely get a chance to do that. I had an interest in the Gazette here, [8] but not sufficient to keep me there, so I was compelled to give up. It will be a sweet Whig paper in a short time, as they have the Whig editor from Murfreesboro [9] at the head of it.

I think I am capable of filling some place within your immediate gift or influence. If Gen Armstrong would take me to Liverpool, I *know* I could be of real service to him. Or if W.H.P. would give a man a shake, I would do there. If not myself, somebody else will go who will do no better, if half as well. Oh that I had some "long-tail kin" to help me, for I begin to feel *patriotic*, and more than willing to "serve my country."

A situation in the Custom house at N. York, or a copyist, or something like, in some of the clerks' offices at Washington.

If you *can*, please help me. If you *cannot*, why I can't help it, but remain ....

J. H. THOMPSON

ALS. DLC–JKP. Addressed to Washington City and marked "Private."

1. James H. Thompson edited and published the Columbia *Tennessee Democrat* from 1838 to 1841. Later Thompson published and, from January to October 1849, edited the *Nashville American*.

2. Gustavus Adolphus Henry and Neill S. Brown were possible Whig candidates for governor in 1845. On March 21, 1845, the Nashville *Republican Banner* reported that both Henry and Brown had "requested that their names should not be used before the convention." A Pulaski lawyer, Neill S. Brown represented Giles County in the Tennessee House, 1837–39; ran an unsuccessful race for Congress against Aaron V. Brown in 1843; won election as a presidential elector on the Whig ticket in 1844; served one term as governor of Tennessee, 1847–49; and went to Russia as U.S. Minister from 1850 to 1853. Joining the Know-Nothing party, he served one term as Speaker of the Tennessee House, 1855–57.

3. Reference probably is to an afternoon speech given by Foster on March 20, 1845, to the Whig party's gubernatorial convention. On March 25, 1845, the *Nashville Union* described the "equivocal" position of Texas annexation that Foster had adopted over the course of the past year. After noting that Foster had declared his support for annexation on several occasions, the *Union* then pointed out that he had voted against both the Texas treaty and his own joint resolution on Texas annexation.

4. Aaron V. Brown.

5. Reference is to Robert Armstrong's appointment as consul at Liverpool.

6. William H. Polk.

7. Probably J. George Harris and Vernon K. Stevenson. A wealthy Nashville merchant and railroad promoter, Stevenson proved instrumental in raising individual and institutional subscriptions for a Nashville railway line. In 1848 he became president of the Nashville and Chattanooga Railway Company and held that post until the end of the Civil War.

8. Thompson probably refers to the *Nashville Gazette*.

9. Probably Edwin J. King, a Whig editor who oversaw the Murfreesboro *Tennessee Telegraph* until its discontinuance in 1845.

## FROM JOHN S. BARBOUR[1]

Dear Sir,                                    Catalpa March 22nd 1845

I ought to have been more definite and explicit in my letter to you of the day before yesterday.[2] The restraints, which reluctance & delicacy often impose on us, in speaking freely, were upon my pen, and I see no reason why I should allow to them a stringent influence when the publick interest is in peril.

In Virginia our elections are at hand.[3] The Whig party are straining every nerve & bone & muscle to carry the state. Our Represented Voice in Congress is material to that party, & the choice of a senator is more sensibly felt by them in the mass, & by Mr Rives their leader individually, than any other interest now before the publick. If Mr Rives carry the state by carrying the spring elections of the next month, we shall be in bondage to the victors for years to come. To prevent this, we need the united power of the *whole* of the Democratic party. And if our cause & its principles (which make that cause) be worth exertion *at all*, it is worth—& *well* worth—our *undivided* exertion. The Globe is looked to as the organ of the Administration, & its denunciations as speaking the voice of the Administration.

Mr Calhoun has a strong interest in this state. That interest Mr Rives is trying to conciliate and if he succeed even in part, he will carry the state. And if so his revenge will spare nothing. With great wealth & talents, & with the whole power of the Whigs everywhere he is a most formidable & puissant adversary. The Tenth Legion[4] & Madison & Greene, gave us 4700 out of the 5800 of our majority last fall. When we look to the counties over which this 4700 is scattered they are small in number. And when we look to the further fact that in Madison, Greene and Albemarle, the personal, the commercial, (for his father was a merchant of much business),[5] the kindred & other influences of Mr Rives are most potent in action & will be most exerted, we have cause (ample cause) for uneasiness. And in those counties Calhouns friends are both talented & numerous.

In the contest with my kinsman Leake of Albemarle on our side & Irving on the Whig side for Congress, we have not a vote to spare.[6] And we shall have good fortune if we prevail. And there too we know no difference in the Democratic ranks. Its divisions are unfelt and unseen, if in reality any exist, and if they do not exist, why create them? These are matters I might with better propriety address Mr Blair. I fear they would not be taken by him as they are intended. I have no feelings to him, but those that are kind. And in the late canvass I have been so

often compelled to defend him, that the attachment which the execution
of such a duty of defence naturally breeds & fosters necessarily make me
kind to him. There are besides these other ties between us. Mrs Blairs
brother is my brother in law.[7] At a former time we were separated &
if I were to approach him on this subject, it might be misinterpretted,
and bruised feeling might be my only return. I regard the election of Mr
Rives to the Senate (with its quick concomitants) as one of those evils,
which ought not to be lightly considered, & which calls for all our energy
& prudence to avert. It is Union, Concord & Spirit, one and indivisible,
that can alone avert it.

The abuse & misapplication by Mr Rives of the letter of Mr Madison on
the tariff,[8] which I was the only living being, (by knowing all its accidents
& incidents) able to detect & expose, in the public discussions of last
summer, gave me an insight to the true character of his ambition & its
impulses, which make me look on him as one of the most mischievous &
unscrupulous men of the Republick.

If he prevails in his present views he will swell the strong current of
opposition in the Senate, and he will have that spot in the South for the
use of the Whigs, which Archimedes wished to put his machine upon for
moving the world.[9] Defeated now he is defeated forever.

Can you excuse this long explanatory epistle, & forgive my intrusion
with it, & on the time that must be precious in its use for your publick
duties.

J. S. BARBOUR

[P.S.] I do not expect an answer. My purpose is to possess you with our
views & our perils, leaving all else to your own judgement, and certainly
not to tax your time for replies. J.S.B.

ALS. DLC–JKP. Addressed to Washington City.
1. A veteran of the War of 1812, Barbour served a number of terms in the
Virginia legislature; sat in the state constitutional convention, 1829–30; and won
election to five terms in the U.S. House as a States' Rights Democrat, 1823–32.
2. Barbour's letter has not been found.
3. On April 24, 1845, voters elected members of the House of Delegates, one-
fourth of the Virginia Senate, and all fifteen congressmen.
4. Barbour's reference is to the Democratic stronghold of the Shenandoah
Valley wherein a large number of German immigrants resided near the village
of Tenth Legion in Rockingham County.
5. Reference is to Robert Rives, a native of Sussex County, and father of
William C. Rives.
6. Shelton F. Leake and Joseph K. Irving. A Charlottesville lawyer, Leake sat
for one term in the Virginia House, 1842–43; won election to two terms in the
U.S. House, 1845 and 1859; and served as lieutenant governor in 1851. Irving

ran for Congress three times as a Whig in Virginia's Fifth Congressional District, 1845–49.

7. Reference is to a brother of Eliza Gist Blair, either Henry Cary Gist or Thomas Cecil Gist; Barbour's sister is not identified.

8. Rives had produced a letter, attributed to James Madison and dated January 23, 1829, which refuted Democratic arguments that Thomas Jefferson had opposed tariff protection. *Niles' National Register*, August 3, 1844.

9. A paraphrase of Archimedes' statement regarding the lever: "Give me where to stand, and I will move the earth." Pappus of Alexandria, *Collectio*, book 8, section 11, proposition 10.

## FROM PETER V. DANIEL[1]

Richmond, Va. March 22, 1845

Daniel discusses patronage questions in Richmond and the situation in Texas. After attacking "the excess of political intolerance" that characterizes the Whig party in Virginia, he notes that this partisanship extends even to the appointment of night watchmen and embitters "social intercourse in all the ranks of life." Daniel also regrets to see in some of the Texas journals a growing opposition to annexation.[2] He blames British diplomacy for stirring up these feelings but believes that land and securities speculators and ambitious Texas politicians "who conceive that their own importance may be diminished by the transformation of that territory from a *primary* to a *secondary* position" have also encouraged these feelings. Daniel looks to the United States government to frustrate these selfish schemes.

ALS. DLC–JKP. Addressed to Washington City.

1. A native of Virginia, Daniel served as associate justice of the U.S. Supreme Court from 1841 until his death in 1860.

2. See Andrew J. Donelson to Polk, March 18, 1845.

## FROM JOEL B. SUTHERLAND

7 o'clock A.M.

My dear Sir                                            Philada March 22 1845

I send you enclosed the returns of the Election of yesterday, in the City & Liberties of Philada.[1]

In the *city* of Philada we have 2 Aldermen, 3 Natives & Nine Whigs.[2] The whigs, had *all* the Aldermen of the City *with them prior to the election*. In some parts of the County of Philada. our friends did very well. *Native Americanism* however seems still strong in some portions of the County. I hope during the coming year, we will be able to abate their strength somewhat by getting back to our ranks some of our *old* friends.

J. B. SUTHERLAND

ALS. DLC–JKP. Addressed to Washington City.

1. Enclosure not found.

2. On March 21, nine Whig, three Native American, and two Democratic candidates for alderman were elected; one additional Whig candidate ran unopposed.

## FROM CHARLES J. INGERSOLL

Dear Sir                                        Philad Mch. 23. 45

I flatter myself that you will take in good part my friendly suggestions. The following are submitted with no view but the prosperity of your admin and the country.

First. I send you a copy of my View of our foreign commerce which you probably have had hardly time to read.[1] The only great difficulty you have to overcome is a satisfactory arrangement of the Tariff: which may be accomplished, I think, without offending this State. But it must be done by extending the exports of the union. Cotton, coal, flesh, tobacco, timber, even grain may be disposed of in much larger quantities than at present by strenuous and judicious arrangement of our foreign relations.

Secondly. For this, the duties of our ministers must be performed very differently from their present discharge. All other countries make their foreign ministers mind their business. Ours, many of them, do anything else. They neglect all their duties and become mere men of pleasure and social intercourse. They write books, like Wheaton and Irving,[2] or do nothing like most of our Chargés d'Affaires. They should be required to write continually reports not only of the political but statistical, commercial, financial and other condition of the countries they inhabit. All other foreign ministers do so. You told me that yours shall be a *working* administration. Let it be so abroad as well as at home. Permanent foreign missions, doing next to nothing, are mere abuses.

Third. I suggested to Mr. Buchanan what you may consider a wild notion, to ask Mr. Clay to undertake the Mexican mission and make peace with that neighbor by paying her liberally for a new frontier including port Francisco. This by the same stroke settles our Oregon and Texas difficulties. If Mr. Clay consents he becomes your agent. If he refuses you have made a magnanimous offer which would redound to your present and to your historical renown.

Fourth. If I understand your policy as to removals from office, that is, not to make many arbitrarily, but let most commissions expire according to law, I cordially approve it. I recommended the plan to Mr Van Buren. It will make you some noisy enemies: but ten times as many sincere adherents. Mr. Tyler's proceedings in this respect were outrageous, ruin to any man and to any government.

Fifth. *Administrative* economy. The annual attempts of the house of representatives to cut down the enormous expenses of the army and navy, are clumsy and mostly absurd. The Executive may effect a saving of a million in each without the least reduction of the force of either. But this would require, like resistance to the phrensy for removals from office, a vigorous and unshrinking excision of many inveterate, tho' illegal and unaccountable official abuses.

I found a terrible state of things at Harrisburg, enemies to the Governor,[3] innumerable to his Secretary of the Com'th, Miller, and many more than I supposed to Mr. Buchanan. Democratic ascendancy is in danger in Penna, at the very next annual election.[4]

Tho' I witnessed close at hand all the scandalous intrigues by which a Senator was chosen yet I cannot put in papers, it wd. be too long, my own account of that affair. I am satisfied that I was preferred by the people of our party. The country papers every where by spontaneous effervescence showed that. But the politicians, particularly Miller contrived it otherwise.

The disappointment to me is unpleasant and the result very annoying. No one can regard the Penna. delegation in the next Congress without seeing that *I* am to hew all the wood and draw all the waters for your admin[5] with one dead weight and one counterpoise in Senate,[6] with scarcely any help in the house. Now that sort of drudgery and servitude I have borne, something like it so long that I am reflecting whether I will not withdraw, tho' I will not act precipitably.

Some of Mr. Buchanan's enemies impute this condition of things to him. I cannot believe it.

I owe it to the openness with which I always check with every one to add that I left Washington dissatisfied when I went to Harrisburg to be disappointed. Vain and selfish as we all are, I quite as much as others, I supposed that *I* almost made you president. Certainly I risked more than all your cabinet put together and did more than all except Mr Walkers, repudiating Mr. Van Buren, because I deemed his selection Mr. Clay's election, when I had assurances that in a Van Buren admin my position wd. be whatever I chose. Thus hazarding all for another choice and succeeding I imagined that my position wd. be at least as good. When therefore my colleagues and others proposed to you in my instance what I had not suggested, for I preferred the Senate, I confess I had no idea that it could be put by as if I had been a mere common applicant.

Still tho' dissatisfied, and then disappointed and even contemplating retirement, I trust the crude suggestions of this letter will prove that I am disposed whether in Congress or not to regard with best wishes the prosperity your admin.

                                                                    C. J. INGERSOLL

P.S. While writing this letter the enclosed Bedford Gazette has come to hand which I add as a specimen of the feeling aroused. [7] The Editor General Bowman [8] was one of the first and strongest of my supporters for the Senate, tho' we have no personal acquaintance. But Jesse Miller and his tribe deemed otherwise.

ALS. DLC–JKP.

1. Enclosure not found. Ingersoll probably refers to his U.S. House speech of February 19, 1845, on the Civil and Diplomatic Appropriations bill. The text of his speech appeared in the Washington *Congressional Globe* on February 21, 1845.

2. Henry Wheaton and Washington Irving. A jurist and historian, Henry Wheaton received an appointment as chargé d'affaires to Denmark in 1827, and in 1830 he secured a treaty of indemnity for American ships seized by Denmark during the Napoleonic period. Wheaton also wrote essays on Danish law and literature along with his *History of the Northmen* and began work on his *History of Scandinavia*. In 1836 Wheaton published *Elements of International Law* which aided in his promotion in 1837 to the post of U.S. minister to Prussia. In 1844 Wheaton negotiated with the German states of the *Zollverein* an agreement providing for the reduction of duties on American tobacco and rice and the free admission of cotton. He also arranged a series of treaties with various German states securing the rights of German emigrants who had become citizens of the United States. In 1846, Polk recalled Wheaton from Prussia. Washington Irving spent much of his adulthood living and writing in Europe. In 1842 he became U.S. minister to Spain and served in his post until 1846. While in Spain he worked on a biography of George Washington.

3. Francis R. Shunk.

4. Probably the Pennsylvania state elections of October 14, 1845. In those elections Democrat James Burns defeated his Whig and Native American opponents for the position of canal commissioner; Democrats also won five of the twelve Pennsylvania Senate seats open for election and sixty-eight of the one hundred places in the lower house.

5. Paraphrase of the quotation, "Hewers of wood and drawers of water." Judges 9:21.

6. Simon Cameron and Daniel Sturgeon.

7. Enclosure not found.

8. George W. Bowman bought the *Bedford Gazette* in 1832. He edited the newspaper until 1857, at which time he received an appointment from James Buchanan to edit the Washington *Union*.

## FROM ARCHIBALD YELL[1]

My Dear Sir.                              N. Orleans 23d March [18]45
    I reached this place on yesterdy (twelve days from Washington City).
Majr Donaldson arrived here a few days before me; and left on the 21st
for Mobile as I understand to transact some private business before his
departure to Texas.[2] Mr. Tylers Despaches reached him here on the 20th
as I am informed. Tommorrow Maj D. is expected back and will no doubt
proceed without delay to the seat of Government of Texas. On his Return I shall have an interview with him; and be governed somewhat,
in my movements, by his suggestions. I calculate, however, to proceed
with him to Texas, as was anticipated by the Department when I left
Washington, tho it was not supposed that I would be able to deliver my
Despaches short of Texas. Still I understand the wishes of the Secty of
State[3] and the principle object, in selecting *me* as the organ of communication & I shall on my part, endeavor to discharge that duty in such
way as is most likely to affect the object sought. As you might suppose
there is much anxiety felt here on the subject of Texas and all seem of
the same oppinion that the Texians must take, the *Resolutions* as they
are, and if they are not exactly to their notions that an Ordinance or
Compact can and would be entered into by our Govt. that would be *Just*
& *Liberal* and altogether sattisfactory to bothe nations. There is but one
oppinion in relation to the policy of opening a new negotiation & that is
that it would be fatal to our prospects. Of that fact however you are fully
apprised. I only mention, the matter to, apprise you that you are fully
sustained in your course by popular oppinion.
    Nevertheless there are very many inteligent Gentlemen here who are
not without their *fears*. Upon the passage of Browns Resolutions in the
Ho of Reps[4] some of the leading Texian papers came out furious and
intemperate against it. The leading Organ of the Admn the "*National
Register*" was very indignant and abusive. The "Civilian & Gazette"
with others of minor note and importance were also againt it. The "Galvaston News"[5] however is advocating the annexation, upon the lines of
the Resolution and it charges upon the other papers a Brittish interference, which I have no doubt is true as Holy Writ. That influence must
be over come, and put down, and it can be done by the potential arm
of the people. Public oppinion must & will prevail. I have the acquaintance of the Editors of the "Jeffersonian Republican" and the "Bulletin"
both strong (as you know) for the Annexation[6] and without betraying
any *Confidence* I have suggested the importance of meeting & settling
the question fully and boldly, and presenting the subject farely before

the people of Texas. *They will do it* and I have directed them to send to me at Washington for distribution a Doz papers from each office per week Until the matter is disposed of. Dont be alarmed. I pay the expense out of my "per diem" and it shall go as freely as the Quarterage I pay to my vilage parson. The Compensation you know was no part of the Consideration in my accepting the duty? And if I can farely, honorably, successfully apply it to the accomplishment of that great object (the annexation) no one I presume can or could complain! This part of my letter you will see at once is "Unofficial." I shall take care to have them distributed, judiciously and at the same time to keep myself in *"Cog."*

A steam packett will come in a few days for Galvaston; one is expected here to night from Texas. I will skan them and forward you the Papers if they are marked for their Hostility or flattering prospects. A few words on home affairs.

I find very many old acquaintances and have formed others, and from my acquaintance here I am fully able to correctly understand public oppinion.

Your Innaugural is remarkeably well received and your Cabinet appointments popular. Some prefer one portion & some another but all say that you have a *Talented & popular Cabinet*, and one, that will I venture to say give as general sattisfaction to the whole Country as any for the last quarter of a Century. Walker is very popular in the South West; he is [...][7] and on his exertions & activity, the friends of Texas have implisite confidence.

I may not find it necessary to trouble you again with a letter until I reach Galveston; from there you shall here from me.

A. YELL

P.S. 24th March/45 I have seen Donalson & we are off for Galveston this eveng at 6 Oclk PM. *Yell*[8]

ALS. DLC–JKP. Addressed to Washington City and marked "Private and Confidential." Polk's AE on the cover states that he received this letter on April 2, 1845.

1. A close friend of Polk, Yell practiced law in Fayetteville, Tenn., until his appointment as U.S. judge of the Arkansas Territory in 1832. He won election to several terms in the U.S. House, 1836–39 and 1845–46, and served as governor of Arkansas from 1840 until 1844. In 1845 Polk sent Yell to Texas to assist Andrew J. Donelson in his negotiations with the Texas government. Yell died at the Battle of Buena Vista in 1847 during the Mexican War.

2. See Andrew J. Donelson to Polk, March 18, 1845.

3. James Buchanan.

4. Reference is to Milton Brown's Texas annexation resolutions. See Cave Johnson to Polk, January 13, 1845.

5. Yell probably refers to the *Civilian and Galveston Gazette* and to the *Galveston News.*

6. Neither the editor of the New Orleans *Jeffersonian Republican* nor the editor of the New Orleans *Commercial Bulletin* has been identified further.

7. Three words illegible.

8. Yell wrote his postscript in the left margin of the fourth page of the letter.

## FROM GEORGE C. BECKWITH[1]

Sir,                                         New York, March 25, 1845

A knowledge of your character, acquired twelve or fifteen years ago through a mutual friend, leads me to presume that I may, without apology or offence, address you, even in your present high position, on any subject of interest to the cause of humanity.

You are doubtless aware, that philanthropists in both hemispheres have been at work for more than a quarter of a century, to supersede war by enlightening the community respecting its evils, & the possibility of obviating its necessity by acceptable substitutes. For the purpose of gaining a readier & more favorable access to the presses of our country on this subject, we desire the influence of your name, & if you approve the plan stated on the accompanying sheet,[2] & will signify your approval in a few words, returning the document to me, at *Boston*, at your earliest convenience, you will much oblige, along with others ....

GEO. C. BECKWITH

P.S. I have already obtained the approval of such men as the Hon. B. F. Butler & Hon. Theodore Frelinghuysen.[3] Permit me here to copy that of the former: "The interests of Peace are emphatically those of enlightened Liberty as well as of pure Religion, and, as the plan above proposed seems to me well adapted to promote them, it will give me great pleasure to see the popular press of our country devoted to its execution. New York, March 7th 1845. B. F. Butler."

ALS. DLC–JKP. Addressed to Washington City.

1. A Congregational minister and professor at Lane Theological Seminary, Beckwith served as secretary of the American Peace Society during the 1840's and edited the society's journal, the *Advocate of Peace.* He also wrote numerous sermons, pamphlets, and books for the antebellum peace movement, including *The Peace Manual* (1847).

2. Enclosure not found.

3. Selected by the Whigs as Henry Clay's running mate in 1844, Theodore Frelinghuysen of New Jersey served in numerous positions of public trust: state attorney general, 1817–29; U.S. senator, 1829–35; mayor of Newark, 1837–38; chancellor of New York University, 1839–50; and president of Rutgers College,

1850–62. Active in many private organizations, he served as vice-president of the American Colonization Society and as vice-president of the American Sunday School Union.

## FROM HENRY HORN

My Dear Sir                                    Philadelphia 25 March 1845
I beg leave herewith to enclose you a letter which I have cut out of the New York Herald of today, by which you will perceive that Mr Buchanan is represented as hostile to my appointment as Collector of this Port.[1] I do not rely implicitly upon statements emanating from such sources, especially as Mr Buchanan always greets me when we meet face to face in the most cordial and friendly manner, and as I am certain he can have no just ground of opposition to my appointment.

It is true in the late presidential canvass I prefered the claims of another[2] to those of Mr Buchanan for that high station. But I did it openly fairly and honorably and therefore I cannot suppose that a high minded and honorable man could find in that or in the idea that I might not be favourable to his claims for the succession four years hence any just cause of opposition to my appointment to a station which I pledge myself to prove that not only a large majority of the democracy of this district but of the state at large and of this commercial community ardently desire that I should occupy.

Mr Buchanan you must be aware resides not in this immediate vicinity, and with great deference I submit cannot be regarded as a fair exponent of the will and wishes of the people here, nor can I perceive what he has to do with the appointment in question. It is in no way connected with his department. My reliance however is upon the President himself and upon his characteristic firmness and decision, which I feel persuaded will resist all attempts at dictation or control in the just and rightful of his official duties.

                                                    HENRY HORN

ALS. DLC–JKP. Addressed to Washington City and marked "Private."
1. Enclosure not found. Horn probably refers to the letter of "Nous Verrons" that appeared in the *New York Herald* of March 25, 1845.
2. Martin Van Buren.

## FROM EZEKIEL STARR ET AL.[1]

Sir,                                    Washington City March 25th 1845
It is no ordinary feelings that induces the undersigned to address the President of the United States. Nothing but stern necessity and the pre-

carious situation in which they and their people are placed, induces them to do so now. We are the representatives of what is generally termed the "Treaty Party"[2] and flatter ourselves *our* petition will not be made in vain.

The history of the negotiation of the Cherokee treaty of 1835[3] & the cruel outrages subsequently inflicted upon the makers of that instrument, by the opposing party are too well known to you to require comment from us. The greivances of which we mostly complain are of recent date. Sometime since a Commission was instituted by your immediate predecessor consisting of Genl. R. Jones, Col R. B. Mason, U.S.A and Gov P. M. Butler,[4] who repaired to our nation for the purpose, as we understood of enquiring into the cause which have so long excited, and disturbed the peace and quiet of the two parties, and to make a report of the result of their investigations, preparatory to a final settlement of the difficulties complained of. A Council of the people was assembled for the purpose of taking into consideration this all important subject.

The plan suggested as being best calculated to produce so desirable a result, was a separation of parties and a division of Country propotionate to numbers. This plan (although in our opinion the only practicable one) did not receive a favorable consideration in their report.[5] Of the nature and character of the report (never having read it) it is not now our purpose to speak, except for the purpose of illustrating more fully what has since transpired. Soon after the adjournment of the Council we were appointed Delegates, with instructions to proceed to Washington, and urge upon the President of the United States the adoption of some measure by which we would be relieved from distress, oppression and ruin. But no sooner was the fact known than were our lives conspired against by the Ross party, and the night of our assassination and it is believed, not without the Knowledge and consent of John Ross.[6] This intelligence was immediately communicated to us by a lady of the Ross party, with a message begging us to leave the nation for safty. Thus were we without a moments preparation compeled to leave our families and homes, and travel by different routes to this city, where we arrived a few days since in safty. Shortly after we left we received information that had we not left at the time we did the bloody tragedy of the Ridges and Boudinot[7] would have been acted over again upon our persons, as the assassins at the appointed hour was seen in the neighbourhood of our dwellings. We learn also, that several persons who attended the Council and voted in favor of a division of the country, were compelled to leave their homes, and their property confiscated. This surely does not argue favorably for what has so often been repeated by Mr Ross and his friends that there was no dissension among the Cherokee people except those produced by a "few Renegades and outlaws." We throw back the insinuation, and say, could they have been free from the Councils of John Ross twenty years ago, anarchy and confusion would have been strangers, and peace, prosperity and happiness would have shown them forth to the world, a civilized and intelligent people.

For all the evils complained of we have no particular course to recommend, but leave it to your better informed judgment to point out the measure best suited to our case, and apply the remedy. We however confidently rely on a faithful execution of the Cherokee treaty of 1835, for in it protection is guaranteed to all and could one of your illustrious predecessors that venerable Sage and patriot of the Hermitage [8] have remained longer in the presidential chair, we should not now have cause of complaint, nor you the trouble of hearing this our petition.

E. STARR

L. DLC–AK. Addressed locally and marked "*Copy*."

1. Authorship of this letter is attributed to Ezekiel Starr, J. L. Thompson, and J. V. McNair, who represented themselves to be a delegation from the Treaty party of the Cherokee nation.

2. Factional splits among the Cherokees included the Old Settlers, who removed west of the Mississippi River prior to 1835; the Treaty party, who relocated following the signing of the Treaty of New Echota in 1835; the John Ross party, who resisted until their forced removal in 1838–39; and the North Carolina Cherokees, who remained in the Appalachian mountains.

3. Signed by the Treaty party on December 29, 1835, the Treaty of New Echota quieted all Cherokee claims to lands east of the Mississippi River, authorized U.S. citizenship for those choosing to leave the tribe, and provided 5 million dollars and 7 million acres of western land as compensation to the tribe for its relocation. Upon receipt of the draft treaty in Washington, the Jackson administration added five supplementary articles, one of which voided the option of taking U.S. citizenship and remaining in the East with preemption rights to 160 acres.

4. Roger Jones, Richard B. Mason, and Pierce M. Butler. A native Virginian, Jones joined the marines in 1809, switched to the army artillery in 1812, and served as adjutant general of the army from 1825 until his death in 1852. Mason, a native of Virginia, joined the army as a second lieutenant in 1817 and attained the rank of brigadier general in 1848; he served for a brief period as military governor of California, 1846–47. Tyler appointed the commission to investigate the factional divisions among the Cherokees in December of 1844.

5. For the text of the report, see Senate Document No. 140, 28 Congress, 1 Session. The Treaty party and Old Settlers had combined to ask that Cherokee land and remaining money payments be divided among themselves and the Ross party on a per capita basis, thus effecting a political separation of the two factions.

6. A Tennessee half-breed of Cherokee and Scot ancestry, Ross headed the Cherokee National Council from 1819 until its dissolution in 1826; assisted in

writing the constitutions of 1827 and 1839; led the eastern branch of the nation from 1829 until 1839; and following the removal westward served as chief of the united Cherokee nation until his death in 1866.

7. On June 22, 1839, John Ridge, Major Ridge, and Elias Boudinot, all three signatories to the Treaty of New Echota and leaders of the Treaty party, were murdered in separate acts of violence; the Treaty party claimed that the assassinations were part of a campaign of political intimidation by the Ross party.

8. Andrew Jackson.

## TO ANDREW JACKSON

My Dear Sir                                   Washington March 26th 1845

*Blair* called on me on the evening of the 24th and desired to know whether the *Globe* was to be considered the administration organ or not. I answered that no organ had as yet been selected. We entered into a full and as far as I felt or know a friendly conversation upon the subject. I explained to him the reasons which induced me to desire that he would if consistent with his views of propriety retire from the Editorial Department of the paper, retaining if he chose the ownership of the establishment, and of course deriving the profits. I suggested to him that such a man as *Majr. Donelson* (if he would accept) at the head of the paper would be acceptable to the whole party, North and South, and to every branch of it. I told him I had no unkind feelings personally towards him, but that it was a fact not to be concealed, that during his long career as Editor, he had rendered himself unacceptable to a considerable portion of the party, and from all I could learn, could not be elected public printer by either House of the next Congress, even though the Democracy might have a commanding majority in each.[1] The truth is his course on the Texas question has made him unacceptable to a large portion of the ardent friends of that measure. I told him that my deliberate judgment was, that if I were to take the Globe as the exclusive organ of my administration, I would find myself in a minority in the next Congress. I told him that the two great parties in the country were very nearly equally divided as was proved by the last election, and that if we expected my administration to be successful, and that the Democratic party to maintain its ascendancy, in 1848, the whole party must be united, that the slightest division would place us in a minority and defeat us. All I said to him was in a friendly spirit. He would not yield to any of my suggestions, and separated from me with the distinct understanding, that if the Globe was my organ, I must take it just as it was, and if I did not choose to that, I must take my own course.

In the *Globe* of the same evening (24th), an article on Texian affairs appeared of an exceptionable and mischievous character.[2] Whether it was written before or after our interview I do not know, but I presume afterwards. You will see that the tone of this article, as well as others which have recently appeared, is such as to justify *Mr Benton's* policy on the Texas question, (and of course to condemn mine) and to make my administration as far as a newspaper can make it, seem to support that policy. This is placing me in a false position and one which I am unwilling to occupy. The truth is, Blair is more devoted to *Col. Benton* than to the success of my administration, and his Editorial articles have already shown this, and will I doubt not continue to shew it, upon the greatest question, (the Texas question) now before the country. To be plain with you, I have a very strong impression, that *Mr Blair* expected to control me and the policy of my administration, upon this and other subjects. This I will not submit to, from any quarter. The inference I drew from the tone of Blair's conversation was, that he was acting on the belief, that I was helpless and defenseless without the *Globe*. I feel this, and am unwilling to remain in so defenseless a position. I must be the head of my own administration, and will not be controlled by any newspaper, or particular individual whom it serves.

*Mr Buchanan* informed me yesterday that Mr Blair had called on him, and held a conversation with him on the subject, in which he informed him that he had written to you, and perhaps, read a part of his letter or stated its contents to him. *Mr Buchanan* drew the inference that he would be willing to sell out the *Globe*, and retire. If he will do this, and a proper man could take hold of it, the whole party would be united, and I would have a bright prospect of having a successful administration. I assure you I have no unkind feelings towards Blair, and hope he may yet make a satisfactory arrangement. If he will not, I must act independently of him. If two Democratic papers are here, I will give both my countenance, but it would be infinitely better that there should be but one, if it were a proper one.

I dislike to trouble you upon the subject, but having told Blair that I had written to you some days ago,[3] and having learned that he had also written, I thought it altogether proper to let you understand the whole ground. Hoping that you may be spared by Divine Providence, to witness the success of your principles ....

JAMES K. POLK

---

ALS. DLC–AJ. Addressed to the Hermitage and marked "*Confidential*." Published in Bassett, ed., *Correspondence of Andrew Jackson*, VI, pp. 389–90.

1. See Aaron V. Brown to Polk, January 6, 1845.

2. Polk's reference is to the Washington *Globe* of March 24, 1845. Blair's editorial, suggesting that Benton's actions have been misconstrued, asserts that

Benton fully supported Texas annexation and labored to accomplish that goal through his legislative proposals.

3. Polk probably refers to his letter of March 17, 1845.

## FROM JESSE MILLER

My Dear Sir                                           Washington March 26. 1845

Owing to being a little too tardy, I did not get off this morning as I expected. I wish, that the appointments at Phila. may be delay'd, for some time. I will write you from Harrisburg on this subject. I never felt more confident in any opinion, than that it is the policy of the democratic party and of the administration, to make almost entire changes. Violent opposition men and go betweens ought to be removed, every where. Any thing else will be rank injustice to the honest democracy. But, these things ought not to be done hastily. Time is required to ascertain who are entitled, by their competency & merits as men and politicians to fill the places. The important offices at the seat of Govt ought certainly to be given to men of worth in the *States*. Men who have exerted their intellect & spent their money & time in promoting the cause of democracy. If they are given to droans and milk & watery creatures who are ready to fall in with the powers that be, no matter, whether Democrat Whig or mongrel it will afford but poor encouragement to integrity and honest political perseverance. In making these remarks I know I speak the sentiments of 99/100 of the democracy and I do not make them from any distrust of the sentiments of the administration, but merely to confirm, and strengthen what I believe to be the existing disposition.

I would not be understood as indicating the opinion that the democracy of the Country are guided in their political actions by a hope of reward in the form of Office. I believe they are governd by higher motives, but their patriotism is not of so self sacraficing a character as to induce them after a hard and severe Contest to prefer enemies, to hold places of honor & emolument, to friends.

Pardon me my Dear Sir for the freedom with which I write. It is a liberty, which we democrats are in the habit of taking with those in whom we repose entire confidence.

I forgot to mention the application of Genl Roumfort.[1] I do hope you may be able to do something for him. If you cannot give the situation he wants perhaps something else suitable may offer. I feel a deep interest in his success.

J. MILLER

ALS. DLC–JKP. Addressed locally.

1. A graduate of the United States Military Academy and brigadier general in the Pennsylvania militia from 1843 to 1849, Augustus L. Roumfort served as mayor of Harrisburg, Penn., from 1863 until 1866.

## FROM ARCHIBALD YELL

My Dear Sir                  Galveston Texas 26th March. 1845

I reached here to day after a boyestris trip from N. Orleans. On our arrivle at this place we found that a Brittish man of War had preceeded us two days with Dispaches to her Minister here. Emediatly on the Recept of this Dispach, the Brittish & French Ministers set sail for Washington[1] by express. Donalson[2] reached here to day & put off in a hurry after them, so we hope they may not be able to make many lasting impresions before he reaches Washington. The rumor here is that the B. minister has the notice of the Mixican recognition of the independence of Texas, and that that will, be followed up by a very liberal proposition on behalf of the Brittish govermnt in a commertial treaty etc etc, all of which may or may not be true. Of that fact you will be officially no doubt shortly advised.

On my arrivle here I fell in with my old acquaintance Gnl. M. Hunt, the former Texian Minister and through him made the acquaintance of Gnl McLade[3] the member of Congress from this District who I find to be a verry Talented & sagacious man, and devoted to the cause of annexation. Genl Hunt you know. From those gentlemen I have been able to learne much of the feelings of the people of Texas and to form a pretty correct estimate of the feelings of the leaders in Texas. Houston is looked upon as occupying a doubtful position, tho. Donalson has a letter from the old Chief[4] that he thinkes will settle that matter. If Houston is out & open for it so will the President be (in theire oppinon). If H. doubts, Jones will be against it, and may possbly refuse to call an Extra Session of Congress with a hope that it may be ultimately defeated, by the managemt of the opponants of the measure. Howevr of that fact I shall be able to inform you in the cours of 10 days. Should that obsticle present itself the friends of the measure will have the waite of the officials of the Govemnt and the Monied power to contend with. Our friends here are poor & have already exhausted their means and there is no money in the country except what is brought here by the Brittish party. I have already contributed $25 toward publishing some 2000 Extras, an Address to the Citizens of Texas etc.[5] I mention that to shew you how compleatly they are run out of funds. They are not dispirited tho they are poor and if *Jones* refuses to call Congress they will thin have a meeting and address a letter to all the Counties Calling upon the friends of annexation to meet and demand the Convention of Congress. In that event I shall make it convenat to go over to the Sabine Country. There we have for us cirtain K L Anderson the Vice President Genl Rusk & Henderson Greer & Scurry.[6] They will carry the Eastern Texas and no mistake. In the North & West they have Genl. Burlason Gov Reynolds Judge Lipscomb Col Hayes[7] and many other leading men, who I do not know. They think here that they will be able to force it upon the President & the anti annexation party. All this looks plauseable and may be so, but the thousand difficulties that the Admn. can throw in the way may finally defeat us if it should be attempted, which I hope, & rather believe will not be the case.

Many of the true friends of annexation are not exactly pleased with the *Resolutions*[8] but there will be no difficulty I apprehend on that subject if there is a Called Session. I shall remain if Congress convenes; if not, I see no necisity for my remaining long. I will bestow the last *might*[9] I have to spare & then make for Arkansas.

Upon consultation with Donalson, I concluded to remain here a week or ten days. By that time the Presidents determnation will be known. By remaing I shall be in *Case*. I may not have an other opportunty to write you short of a week but you know I am a good correspondent & will keep you advised of our acts & doings here. The most favorable simptum is, the people are in a perfect commotion & the frinds of the measure open & eloquent, tho in this city they are in a minority.

A. YELL

ALS. DLC–JKP. Addressed to Washington City and marked *"Private & Confidential."*

1. Reference is to the departure of Charles Elliot and Alphonse de Saligny for the Texas capital, Washington-on-the-Brazos. First sent to Texas in 1839 as a secret agent for France, Saligny served as chargé d'affaires to the Republic of Texas from 1839 to 1842 and from 1844 until 1845.

2. Andrew J. Donelson.

3. A native of New York City and graduate of the U.S. Military Academy, Hugh McLeod served as adjutant general of the Texas army in 1839 and as inspector general in 1840. He served two terms in the Texas House, 1842–43 and 1844–45.

4. Andrew Jackson.

5. Not identified further.

6. Kenneth L. Anderson, Thomas J. Rusk, James P. Henderson, John A. Greer, and either Richardson A. or William R. Scurry. A native of North Carolina, Kenneth L. Anderson resided in Bedford County, Tenn., before moving to St. Augustine, Texas, in 1837; he served as a member of the Texas House, 1840–42, and as vice-president of the Republic of Texas, 1844–45. A successful Georgia attorney, Thomas J. Rusk moved to Texas in 1835; organized a company of volunteers for the Texas revolution; and served as inspector general of the Texas

army from 1835 to 1836. A signer of the Texas Declaration of Independence, he served briefly as the Republic's first secretary of war in 1836; sat for one term in the Texas Congress, 1837–38; and served as chief justice of the Texas Supreme Court, 1838–42. Rusk represented Texas in the U.S. Senate from 1846 until his death in 1857. A brigadier general in the Texas army and an experienced lawyer, James P. Henderson served as attorney general, secretary of state, and agent to England and France for the Republic of Texas prior to his appointment in 1844 as a special minister to negotiate a treaty of annexation with the United States. Elected governor of Texas in 1846, he fought in the Mexican War with the rank of major general; later he served part of one term in the U.S. Senate, 1857–58. A native of Shelbyville, Tenn., John A. Greer served as a senator in the Texas Congress, 1837–45, and accepted appointment as secretary of the Treasury for the Republic of Texas in 1845. Lieutenant governor of Texas from 1845 until 1853, Greer died while campaigning for the governorship in 1855. An associate justice of the Texas Supreme Court from 1840 until 1841, Richardson A. Scurry served two terms in the Texas House, 1842–44, and one term in the U.S. House, 1851–53. William R. Scurry, an attorney and native of Gallatin, Tenn., moved to Texas in 1840 and served as district attorney of the Fifth Judicial District in 1841. He sat for one term in the Texas House, 1844–45; participated in the Texas Secession Convention of 1861; and served as a brigadier general in the Confederate army until his death in 1864.

7. Edward Burleson, Abner Lipscomb, John C. Hays, and Reynolds. A militia officer in Alabama and Tennessee, Edward Burleson moved to Texas in 1830; commanded a regiment at the Battle of San Jacinto in 1836; sat in the Texas Congress, 1837–39; served as vice-president of the Republic of Texas, 1841–44; and won election to three terms in the Texas legislature, 1846–51. A native of South Carolina and law student under John C. Calhoun, Abner Lipscomb served as chief justice of the Alabama Supreme Court, 1823–35; won election to one term in the Alabama legislature in 1838; moved to Texas in 1839; served briefly as secretary of state for the Republic in 1840; and sat on the Texas Supreme Court from 1846 until his death in 1856. John C. Hays, a native of Wilson County, Tenn., moved to Texas in 1837; served briefly as a surveyor for the Republic of Texas; assumed command in 1840 of a company of Texas Rangers; led a regiment of Texas volunteers during the Mexican War; moved to California in 1849; and served four years as sheriff of San Francisco County. Reynolds has not been identified further.

8. See William H. Haywood, Jr., to Polk, February 26, 1845.

9. Yell probably means "mite" in place of "might."

## FROM GEORGE M. DALLAS

My Dear Sir,　　　　　　　　[Philadelphia, Penn.] 27 Mar 1845

I have been requested by Col. Hubley to hand you the enclosed.[1] He felt extremely awkward at perceiving that a friendly recommendation in his favor has been referred to the very officer whom it was wished that he should supersede. Am I at liberty to say to him that the mistake was wholly accidental?[2]

The fermentation is great and on the increase. I have anxiously reconsidered the particulars of our last conversation, and remain convinced of the justice and expediency of the several appointments you then approved as, amid the very many applicants, the best for the public interests and character. As a whole, they will attest your solicitude to lift the character of offices, and to confide the public business to men universally recognized as competent and upright; while they will manifest to the democratic party your vigilant and unyielding preference. I sincerely hope, for the reputation of the Bar at which I have been at work for thirty years, that the only professional appointment in the gift of the Executive, that of the District Attorney, will not be conferred on the only unfit and incompetent person that has been pressed upon you.[3] Permit me to assure you, most sincerely and earnestly, that as far as respects this district and this State, you cannot make the appointments to which I have referred too soon.

Allow me to intimate that Mr. Gansevoort Melville,[4] whom I have seen on his return to New York, and whose hopes I endeavoured to fathom, has obviously a strong desire to be either Chargé at Vienna or Marshal in N. York, with a natural preference for the former post. The signal services he rendered in the canvass, (second only to those of Major Davezac,[5] whom I should like to see *en route* to Russia or Turkey) combined with the peculiarity of his position as to parties in the State of New York, would, I think, justify your early notice.

We who are outside of the magic circle of Cabinet mysteries speculate much on the probable effect upon your policy to be produced by the singular symptoms in Texas as to annexation, and the really bold swing of Sir Rob. Peel in his new financial projects.[6] The Tariff will soon engage attention, and its new attitude and relations are of extreme interest. Oregon, too, under the splendid and exact illustrations of an Exploring Expedition, assumes double importance.[7] I wish, with all my heart, you were quit of the perplexities of choosing men and had got into the wide and noble field of measures.

Indulge me, on behalf of a most meritorious partizan of your's in recalling to your recollection a memorandum from Messrs. Bailey & Kitchen of this place,[8] who wish, when your household is providing, to aid in furnishing silver & plaited ware &c. They are, in that line, certainly our most reliable men.

G. M. Dallas

ALS. DLC–JKP. Probably addressed to Washington City; marked *"Private."*
1. Enclosure not found. A Philadelphia Democrat, Edward B. Hubley sat two

terms in the U.S. House, 1835–39, and in 1846 served on the Cherokee Claims Commission authorized by the Treaty of New Echota.

2. Polk's AEI on the cover reads: "Mr Hubley's application for the office of commissioner of Indian affairs, referred to the War Dept, as Mr Dallas thinks by mistake. *Note*: I directed the mass of papers on my table relating to office and which I had not time to read, to be referred to the appropriate Executive Departments, and I suppose Mr Hubley's letter was among them. March 28th 1845."

3. Dallas probably refers to Benjamin H. Brewster. A Philadelphia lawyer and Democrat, Brewster served in 1846 on the Cherokee Claims Commission; he subsequently joined the Republican party and served as U.S. attorney general under Chester A. Arthur.

4. A New York Democrat, Melville went to Great Britain as secretary of legation in 1845.

5. Auguste D'Avezac, a creole emigrant from Santo Domingo, served as aide-de-camp to Andrew Jackson in the War of 1812; filled a number of consular posts during the 1830's; moved in 1839 to New York City, where he won election to the legislature in 1843; and served as chargé d'affaires to the Netherlands from 1845 until 1850.

6. Dallas probably refers to Sir Robert Peel's financial report delivered to the House of Commons on February 14; Peel proposed lower tariff duties on some imported goods, including cotton. The son of an industrialist, Peel began his service in Parliament in 1809; received his first ministerial appointment in 1828; and served as home secretary and chancellor of the Exchequer before becoming prime minister in 1841. His ministry lasted five years.

7. Dallas refers to John C. Fremont's *Report of the Exploring Expedition to the Rocky Mountains in the Year 1842, and to Oregon and California in the Years 1843–44*, which Congress published in March 1845. See House Document No. 166, 28 Congress, 2 Session.

8. Enclosure not found. On February 22, 1845, Dallas sent Polk information relating to the furnishing of the White House and praised Bailey and Kitchen for their support of the Democratic ticket. ALS. DLC–JKP.


## TO ANDREW J. DONELSON


My Dear Sir:            Washington City March 28th 1845

Your two letters of the 18th and 19th Instant were received this morning. The despatch of *Mr. Buchanan* left here on the 10th,[1] and will probably reach you as soon as that of which *Mr Wagaman* was the bearer.[2] The bearer of Mr B's dispatch[3] will have put you in possession of facts, which may aid you in affecting the object of your mission, and which could not be embraced in the despatch itself. You will at once recognize him as an old acquaintance and a gentleman of intelligence. Having proceeded directly from Washington, he will be able to inform you of the

disposition of the parties here on the Texian question; and of the determination of the Executive government to affect annexation by all honorable means, of which it can avail itself without compromitting the national honour. Recent information, received here will make it necessary
to send another messenger, with a dispatch to you in two or three days.
Hon. *Charles A. Wickliffe*, who designs visiting Texas, with a view to emigrate to it, will be the bearer of the dispatch. He has *my confidence* and
will be entitled to yours. He took a very active part in negotiating the
Treaty, last year,[4] and will be able to give you valuable information. He
will leave here on monday the 31st, will take his family to Kentucky and
after a very short delay, will proceed directly to Texas. Learning that the
bearer of this letter,[5] would leave here for Texas this evening on his own
private business, and in no way connected with the government, I avail
myself of the opportunity to address you this letter. I do not know him,
further than that he has been introduced to me as a Gentleman of good
standing.

The letter addressed to you by *Mr Cameron* was without my authority.
I heard of it a day or two after it was written. But though this is the case,
the subject to which it related had been one of anxious thought by my
friends, who with few exceptions concur in the opinion that a new organ
will be indispensible to unite the whole Democracy, and consequently,
for the success of my administration. In speaking of an organ to one or
two confidential friends, I had expressed the opinion that I would desire to have you connected with it, if it was consistent with your views,
and I suppose *Mr Cameron* had in some way heard this, when he wrote
to you. Since that time I have had full and free conversations with *Mr
Blair* and in good feeling frankly told him, that it was impossible for the
whole party ever to be united in support of the administration whilst the
Globe was regarded as the official organ, that I must have a new organ,
and that I desired you to be connected with it. Within the last forty eight
hours, the matter, has been brought almost to a head. Mr *Ritchie* has
been here. *Mr Blair* has reflected about it, and agrees as I learn willingly and cheerfully, to sell out his establishment, and retire; leaving Mr
R. and yourself to take charge of it as joint Editors if you can agree upon
the terms and you are disposed to do so. He wishes however to delay the
consummation of the arrangement until he can consult Mr Van Buren
and General Jackson. He says positively that if *Genl. Jackson* assents,
he will at once sell and retire. He is [ ...][6] and reasonable. I have written to the General[7] and hope he may assent. The business partner with
Mr *Ritchie* and yourself (not Mr Cameron) would advance the whole purchase money. Neither of you would be required to pay a cent. Your names
would go to the Head of the Editorial column, with a first rate business

man, to conduct the financial part of the establishment. There can be no doubt that with the printing of Congress, which you could certainly obtain you would make a fine fortune in a very short time and that without any risk except your time. Should the arrangement be made it will be a provisional one, reserving an interest for you if you choose to take it, otherwise for Mr *Ritchie* alone. If you go into it, after two or three years, I would be altogether inclined to gratify any other wishes you may have. I will desire to hear from you as soon as possible what your views are on the subject. A central organ headed by Mr R. and yourself, having the countenance of the Government, would be the most popular and powerful paper which this Country has ever had. Upon its establishment in my judgment, depends, not only the success of my administration, but of the Democratic party, in the choice of my successor in 1848. The Globe in its long career has created too many hostile interests, to make it possible for the party, to be ever united if it should be the organ. Upon this point there is not the shadow of a doubt. I most ardently hope that the arrangement now in progress, will be effected, but if it should fail I am still deeply convinced that it will be indispensible to have a new paper and I have so informed *Mr Blair*. Write to me by the first safe opportunity whether in the one contingency or the other you would be disposed to be connected with it. A new organ I must have. Without it I will be in a minority at the opening of the next Congress, and throughout my administration.

Reflect upon the matter and let me hear from you. In the mean-time remain at your post, in this most critical juncture of our affairs with Texas, when your services are so important. If you go into the arrangement here, the terms by the others in interest will of course be submitted to you for your assent, and after that assent is given, your successor in Texas, must on your application for leave to return, be appointed and be on the spot, before you can depart from Texas. I have written in great haste and have no time to copy.

JAMES K. POLK

ALS. DLC–AJD. Addressed to Washington, Texas, and marked "*Private and Unofficial.*" Published in *THM*, III, pp. 62–64.

1. On March 10, 1845, Buchanan wrote Donelson about John C. Calhoun's dispatch of March 3, 1845, and noted that on the question of Texas annexation Polk did not wish "to reverse the decision of his predecessor." Senate Document No. 1, 29 Congress, 1 Session, pp. 35–38.

2. Floyd Waggaman carried Calhoun's dispatch of March 3, 1845, to Donelson. See Andrew J. Donelson to Polk, March 18, 1845.

3. Archibald Yell.

4. Polk probably refers to the Texas annexation treaty, which was signed on

April 12, 1844, and submitted to the Senate ten days later. On June 8, 1844, the
Senate rejected the treaty.

5. Reference probably is to James Prentiss, a New York broker and financier
who invested in Texas land companies.

6. Word illegible.

7. Andrew Jackson.

## FROM ARNOLD S. HARRIS[1]

Sir                                        Smithland March 30th 1845

Gen Armstrong requested me to call your attention to the recommendations of Mr. Dibbrel of Nashville[2] for the situation of Superintendent
of Live Oak in Florida. Mr. Dibbrel will in a few days be out of employment. He is poor and in bad health. You will see by his papers[3] that he
is strongly backed.

I left Nashville yesterday. Gen A[4] and myself were at the Hermitage
the day before and found the old Chief[5] better than we expected. He sat
up all day and talked with his usual vigour.

Gen A recd a letter from you[6] on our return from the Hermitage. He
was to go up again yesterday after I left. I shall be in Washington with
the Gen and accompany him to Liverpool.

A. HARRIS

ALS. DLC–JKP. Addressed to Washington City.

1. Arnold S. Harris, a resident of Arkansas, was Robert Armstrong's son-in-
law.

2. Edwin Dibrell served as recorder of Nashville from 1828 until 1838.

3. Enclosures not found.

4. Robert Armstrong.

5. Andrew Jackson.

6. Polk's letter has not been found.

## FROM NATHANIEL P. TALLMADGE[1]

My dear Sir                          Taycheedah, W.T. March 30th 1845

I have read with much interest your Inaugural Address, and it gives
me great pleasure to say, all its positions receive my most cordial approbation. There are two or three topics, in relation to which I will venture
to make a few suggestions. I have long entertained the opinion, that
a Tariff for revenue sufficient for the economical wants of the Government, with such discrimination as to give incidental protection to the
domestic industry of the country, was all that could be desired by any
portion of the people. And I see no reason why that question should

continue to agitate the country, unless it be for mere political and party purposes.

On the subject of the annexation of Texas, I think your views entirely correct. I voted against the Treaty in 1844, on the ground that we had not the proper evidence that the people of Texas assented to the annexation. I held that, in a Republican Government, the Executive and Legislative power could not give consent to annex to, or merge their Government in, another. That consent must come from the People, in their primary capacity, in Convention. Although I had reason to believe, that the people of Texas desired to be annexed, to our Union, still there was not such evidence of it, as I deem necessary to consummate such an act. The Joint Resolutions recently passed by Congress require their consent in Convention.[2] With such consent, I see no obstacle, to the annexation. The introduction of steam boats & locomotives, with the recent invention of the electro-magnetic telegraph have removed all the objections which were formerly made to the extension of our Territory. When the annexation of Texas shall have been perfected, there will remain one other thing which, in my judgment, ought to be done, namely, the purchase of Upper Calafornia. Our Government must negotiate with Mexico for the settlement of the boundary of Texas. At the same time we ought to negotiate for the cession of Upper Calafornia from the western boundary of Texas, on the 37th parallel of latitude, to the Pacific Ocean. This would include the harbor of San Francisco, which is said to be, the best in the world, and which is so much needed for our whalers, and our trade in those seas. In due time we might anticipate a steam boat and rail road communication from that port to the Rio del Norte, and thence by steamboat to the Gulph of Mexico, and thus open a direct trade to China & the East Indies. The harbor at the mouth of the Columbia river is so obstructed by shifting sand bars, that it will never answer the anticipations which have heretofore been formed of it. Hence the greater necessity of that of San Francisco, not only for our own convenience, but to keep it out of the hands of a Foreign power. This proposition was entertained by Genl Jackson in 1835, and I submitted to the Senate a Resolution to the same effect, during the pendency of the Texas Treaty in 1844. The territory, thus to be acquired, would be north of what is called the "Missouri Compromise line," (36° 30') and whenever it should come into the Union, it would come as a free state.[3] This *prospect* would go far towards reconciling, at the North, the opposition to Texas. In regard to slavery, I am content to leave it to the wisdom of Providence. It has been permitted for wise purposes, and will be disposed of by the same wisdom that permitted its existence. I have long been of opinion that the annexation of Texas instead of increasing will tend to diminish slavery, and the purchase of Upper Calafornia would tend to allay all excitement in relation to it. A liberal price might well be paid for it; and it could be paid by offering, in whole or in part, as the case might be, the amount due from Mexico to our citizens, and which may, perhaps, be the only mode in which it can ever be paid. This purchase would reach to latitude 42°, the Southern boundary of Oregon, and then, with the settlement of our northern boundary with the British Government, and extending with Texas to the Rio del Norte, we should want no more Territory. The question of Territory would be forever settled at the South, and the time is, probably, far distant when such a question of extension will be agitated at the North, unless in case of war, with Great Britain. Then the annexation of Canada may be agitated.

There were one or two other topics, which I designed to touch upon. But, my letter may have already extended beyond the time you can devote to its perusal, and I will, therefore, omit for the present any farther remarks.

Standing, as I do, in an official relation to you, it may not be improper to say, that every thing is going on prosperously in this Territory. I found on my arrival here, that the people had been much distracted by the bitter personal and political quarrels between the Legislature & my predecessor.[4] It was my first effort to endeavor to restore peace and quiet to the Territory. I am happy to say, that in this I have been entirely successful. We had a most harmonious session of the Legislature. I have devoted myself to harmonise the Democratic party. In this I have also succeeded, and there is not a single act or a single appointment during my administration to which any member of that party can take exception. There was an effort made by one member, at the commencement of the session, to make difficulty. But, it was more the result of the *habit* of warring on the Executive, than from any other causes. He was, however, discountenanced by the great body of the discreet & sober portion of the party, and his movement abandoned, and we all separated with good feeling. This state of things will continue unless unforeseen causes should make it otherwise, which I do not anticipate.

Mrs. T unites in kindest regards to yourself & Mrs P whom she remembers at Washington.

N. P. Tallmadge

ALS. DLC–JKP. Addressed to Washington City and marked *"Private."*

1. A lawyer from Poughkeepsie, N.Y., Tallmadge served in the U.S. Senate from March 1833 until June 1844, when he resigned to become governor of the Wisconsin Territory. Polk removed Tallmadge from office on May 13, 1845.

2. Tallmadge refers to the first and second articles of the Joint Resolution for the Annexation of Texas. 5 U.S. Stat., 797–98.

3. The Missouri Compromise of 1820 prohibited slaveholding in all new states created from that part of the Louisiana Purchase territory lying north of the 36 degree 30 minute parallel; Tallmadge proposed to extend that restriction to any territory acquired from Mexico.

4. A New York lawyer and land speculator, James D. Doty moved to the Michigan Territory, where he served as judge of the Northern District from 1823 until 1832; as territorial delegate to the U.S. Congress from the Wisconsin Territory from 1839 until 1841; and as governor of that territory from 1841 until 1844. He won election as a Free-Soiler to two terms in the U.S. House, 1849–53.

## FROM BENJAMIN F. BUTLER

New York, N.Y. March 31, 1845

After apologizing for the delay in answering Polk's letter of March 14th, Butler discusses patronage in New York City. He emphasizes that Polk needs to replace the collector, Cornelius P. Van Ness. A Tyler appointee, he proved to be a source of "mischief and dissension" during the late campaign. Since Polk's election Van Ness has removed many useful officers and has appointed in their places a sorry collection of "pothouse brawlers, bullies, & other low characters." No reform, political or moral, is possible as long as Van Ness remains in office. Azariah C. Flagg would be the ideal choice for collector, but unfortunately Flagg believes that it is his duty rather to remain in Albany "with his small salary of $2500, than to come to New York, with a *certainity* of $6000 & a *chance* of something more." At present Butler will not mention names for specific appointments but promises to send Polk detailed recommendations by the end of the week.

ALS. DLC–JKP. Addressed to Washington City and marked "*Private.*" Polk's AE on the cover states that he received this letter on April 2, 1845.

## FROM SAMUEL H. LAUGHLIN

[Washington City] March 31, 1845

Following up on an earlier conversation with Polk, Laughlin discusses patronage matters. He urges Polk to remove William J. Anderson, a clerk in the Quartermaster General's Office.[1] Anderson, a John Bell appointee, is "a scribbler, and vindictive meddler" and a constant correspondent of the Nashville junto. During the campaign he worked with Willis Green's committee and sent "thousand of libels" into the Mountain District.[2] Such men must be removed for the good of the Democracy, for "the Whigs, federalists, pimps, and spies" who remained in office during Van Buren's administration played a crucial role in his overthrow. Laughlin informs Polk that he will continue to collect information on all the incumbents in the Land Office.

ALS. DLC–JKP. Addressed locally and marked "*Confidential.*"

1. A native of Tennessee, Anderson served as a clerk in the Quartermaster General's Office from 1841 until 1845.

2. A Kentucky Whig, Willis Green served three terms in the U.S. House, 1839–45, and supervised Whig committee activities in Washington City during the 1844 presidential campaign. Laughlin's reference is to the charge that Green distributed bundles of anti-Polk pamphlets and handbills during the campaign.

# APRIL

## FROM JOHN FAIRFIELD

Dear President,                                        Saco April 1. 1845

After the interview which I had the honor of having with you just before leaving Washington, I informed, confidentially, those who were personally interested, and some other friends here, in what offices changes
were to be made, and *who* were to receive the new appointments. As
*usual* in such cases, the information was not long in reaching the *public* ear; and I have now the satisfaction of assuring you that the proposed appointments will be *universally acceptable*, except to the little Calhoun, Tyler clique who now have the offices.  Our friends in
the Legislature, now in session, have been particularly gratified at the
prospect, and have been anticipating great political advantages from
such a course.  All at once however they have become alarmed, and
have just sent a Senator to confer with me upon the subject.  The appointments, not having been made or either of them as they anticipated,
Parks & Jarvis [1] remaining at Washington after my return home, a general mustering among the members of the clique here, and the principal men among them having started for Washington, in addition to certain flying rumors, have all conspired to awake fears that some change
may have been wrought in your purposes.  I have assured them that
their apprehensions are entirely unfounded, but have yielded to their
earnest solicitation to address you again upon the subject.  I have deemed

*248*

it necessary to state these facts as an apology for troubling you with this letter.

It is not strange that a good deal of solicitude should be felt by the prominent political men in the State, for, all see, that the consequences of permitting the Tyler appointments to stand, would be serious if not *disastrous* to us. Our party is a party of *principle*. We have faith in man, and do not believe it *right* or *necessary* to resort to intrigue or management of any sort, to accomplish our purposes. Offices we regard as created for the public good, and not as mere prizes or objects for contention among political speculators and gamblers. Created for the public they should be filled in accordance with the public will. The man who has by *trick* or *management* obtained an office against the will of the people (and the *majority* are the people) is as guilty of wrong doing as he who has gotten the pocket book of another. These are the notions entertained by the *honest* masses of the democracy, those who have elevated you to the Presidency. And shall these notions be shocked by our seeing the tricks & cheating by which the present incumbents obtained their offices upheld and rendered successful? I trust not. *Immediately* after our September election, when it began to be apparent that the corrupt crew who had got possession of the government were about to be hurled from their seats of power by an indignant people, Virgil D. Parris, [2] knowing that the honest democracy of the State would not confer the office of Marshall upon him, hastened to Washington and stealing a march upon the democracy obtained it at the hands of Tyler. Kingsbury, the editor of a factious paper accompanied him, [3] & in the same way procured An office of Surveyor of the Port of Portland. *After* the elections were all over, and the people had pronounced condemnation upon Tyler and all his works, A. I. Stone and Benj. Wiggin, [4] procured the resignations of the federal incumbents of the collectorships at Bath and Belfast, and repairing to Washington obtained these offices of Tyler, against the wishes of the democracy of our State, and when they well knew they could not obtain these offices from you. Now shall they be permitted to keep *possession* of offices thus *wrongfully obtained*?

For many years we have had a little faction in this State, whose ranks are kept good by the annual contributions of disappointed office seekers. Their number is small, but this is made up for, in their activity virulence and boastfulness. They are regular grumblers, and will be satisfied with nothing short of having all the offices. Nevertheless they *generally* go with the main party at elections, because this party could succeed without them. They are a sort of "waiters upon Providence," [5] live upon accidents, flourish but when the party is in tribulation, catch every stray plank as it floats by to keep themselves afloat. They went for Wingate for Governor when Parris was the *regular candidate*.[6] They went for Adams, when the true democracy were for Crawford.[7] They supported Sam Smith for Governor agt. Dunlap[8] regularly nominated. They were for Calhoun when the party were for Van Buren.[9] They did not oppose my election as Governor because they saw it would be of no effect. They did oppose my election and reelection to the Senate, though in the Legislature there was hardly enough of them to count. They are now opposed to your making any changes in the offices of this State. If this faction is to succeed, and now to prevail over the true democracy of the State, woe betide us.

By reading in a letter of Mr. McIntires you will find that we agree.[10] He thought that if Parks and Bradbury, Collector of Eastport,[11] should remain undisturbed it was all that the faction ought to ask for. John Anderson[12] is not one of them. He did not *seek* the office he holds. It was *proffered* to him & accepted by my advice and that of many others.

I ought to apologize for detaining you so long, but I felt a desire to give you a birdseye view of the state of things here, and to furnish some apology for the solicitude which our friends manifest in regard to the appointments in this State. Before closing let me urge you to make our appointments *now*. Delay will do no good, but may do harm. Let them come in a batch. The sooner the better. The gentlemen whose names I gave you, and who are so strongly recommended, are capable, faithful, honest and well deserving the favor of your administration.

JOHN FAIRFIELD

ALS. DLC–JKP. Probably addressed to Washington City; marked "Private."

1. Probably Gorham Parks and Leonard Jarvis. A Democrat, Jarvis served as a representative from Maine, 1829–37, and as navy agent for the port of Boston, 1838–41.

2. Virgil D. Parris served as assistant secretary of the Maine Senate in 1831; as a member of the Maine House, 1832–37; and as a U.S. congressman, 1838–41. In 1842 he returned to the Maine Senate where he won election as president pro tempore. In 1844 John Tyler appointed Parris to the post of U.S. marshal for the District of Maine, and he served in this capacity until replaced the following year by Augustine Haines.

3. Appointed by John Tyler in 1844, Benjamin Kingsbury, Jr., served in the 1840's as surveyor for the district of Portland and Falmouth and inspector of revenue for the port of Portland.

4. Alfred I. Stone and Benjamin Wiggin. In 1844 John Tyler appointed Stone collector for the port of Bath, Me., and Wiggin collector for the port of Belfast, Me. In 1846 the U.S. Senate rejected Polk's nomination of Amos Nourse to replace Stone; subsequently Polk nominated and the Senate confirmed John C. Humphreys. In 1845 the Senate rejected Polk's nomination of Nathaniel M.

Lowney to replace Wiggin; and the following year Polk nominated and the Senate confirmed Alfred Marshall.

5. Quotation not identified.

6. Joseph F. Wingate and Albion K. Parris. Prior to Maine statehood, Wingate served in the Massachusetts House, 1818–19; he received the collectorship of the port of Bath in 1820; and in 1827 he won election to the first of two terms in the U.S. House. Parris served a single term in each house of the Massachusetts legislature, 1813–14; he won election to two terms in the U.S. House and served from 1815 until 1818, when he resigned to become judge for the U.S. District Court of Maine. Returning to the political arena he served as governor, 1822–27, and as U.S. senator, 1827–28. He resigned to take a seat on the Maine Supreme Court, a post that he held from 1828 until his appointment in 1836 as second comptroller of U.S. Treasury.

7. John Q. Adams and William H. Crawford were the only two candidates on the Maine presidential ballot in 1824. Crawford, a Georgia lawyer, served as U.S. senator, 1807–13; U.S. minister to France, 1813–15; and secretary of the Treasury, 1816–25. He ran unsuccessfully for the presidency in 1824 as the candidate of the radical republican wing of the Democratic party.

8. Samuel Emerson Smith and Robert Pinckney Dunlap. Smith served as a Democrat in both the Massachusetts and Maine legislatures, 1819–20; as judge of various Maine courts, 1821–30; and as governor for three terms, 1831–33. Dunlap served as a Democrat in both houses of the Maine legislature, 1821–33; won election to the governorship in 1834 and 1836; and sat in the U.S. House from 1843 until 1847. Polk appointed him collector of customs at Portland in 1848, and Franklin Pierce named him postmaster of Brunswick in 1853.

9. Fairfield wrote this sentence in the left margin of the fourth page of the letter.

10. Rufus McIntire, a member of the Maine House in 1820 and prosecuting attorney of York County, won election to the U.S. House to fill the vacancy caused by the death of William Burleigh in 1827; he subsequently won reelection as a Jackson Democrat to three additional terms. In 1845 Polk appointed him U.S. marshal for Maine.

11. Gorham Parks and Bion Bradbury. In 1844 Bradbury received the customs collectorship for the Passamaquoddy district of Maine; in 1849 and again in 1862 he won election to the legislature.

12. A Portland lawyer, Anderson sat four terms in the U.S. House, 1825–33; became mayor of Portland in 1833; served as U.S. attorney for Maine, 1833–36; and twice held the post of customs collector for Portland, 1837–41 and 1843–48.

## TO THOMAS RITCHIE

My dear Sir                                    Washington April 2, 1845

Mr Blair called to see me on yesterday and again this morning. He informed me that Mr Rives had returned, that his friends had yielded their cordial assent to the arrangement contemplated.[1] No obstacle now exists to its accomplishment, but to adjust terms & details. Mr Heiss I understand is now at Philadelphia, but is expected to return this evening. As soon as he arrives, Mr B is ready to make the arrangement desired with him. This he does cheerfully in the most perfect good temper. I write in much haste, simply to inform you, of the exact state of the business, & will write again, as soon as any thing definite is done.

JAMES K. POLK

LS. DLC–FP. Addressed to Richmond, Va., and marked "Confidential."
1. Reference is to the purchase of the Washington *Globe* and establishment of the Washington *Union*.

## FROM ALEXANDER JONES[1]

Dear Sir                                            New York April 4th 1845
As the period for our charter election[2] approaches it is rendered more certain that we shall elect our Democratic Mayor & probably a majority of the common council.

I never have known as little excitement to prevail on the eve of an election in New York, as that now witnessed. The whigs make some little stir, as well as the natives, each indulging in some invective, one against the other, while the Democracy stand united cool and determined. As the result of a charter election is more or less local, its canvass ordinarily cannot be expected to give rise to as much excitement, as when mixed up, more extensively, with national and state politics. Many local questions enter into charter elections, which have no weight in general elections, such as the reduction of city Taxes, the planing & execution of city improvements &c.

Owing to the enormous cost of the introduction of the Croton Water,[3] which amounted to from 12 to 13 million of dollars, the city Taxes are very high, being at the present time about 80 cents on the one hundred dollars worth of property, real and personal. It is believed by many without the strickest economy is observed, the Taxes will have to be increased from 80 to 100 cents on the hundred dollars.

The town of Williamsburg, on the opposite side of the east River, above Brooklyn, this week, elected a full Democratic Ticket of Mayor & Aldermen over both the Native and Whig tickets.[4] The town of Schenectady in this state, has just elected a Democratic Mayor, the first for many years, the place having long been a strong whig hold.[5]

Your administration thus far meets the approbation of all moderate and intelligent men, of all parties. That none will be found to complain, or that you will ever succeed in satisfying all, is not to be expected. To

please all, is beyond human skill or effort. You have the great body of
the people with you, & they will sustain you in all your just and honorable endeavours to administer the Government (as the President of
the United States) on the broad & elevated principles of public good,
national justice, honor & peace.

The importation of foreign goods this spring has been less than during the same period of 1844, which has caused a corresponding reduction in the receipt of Revenue. The most prosperous interest at the
present time, is that of the manufacturers. Many of their largest companies, are amasing immense fortunes. At Lowell the stock of many of
their chartered companies, has advanced to 22, 30, & 38 per cent above
par.

With the present high duty on iron, & its great advance in England,
the article will soon reach an enormous price to the consumers, and for
many purposes, have a tendency to exclude it from market. When the
news of its advance reached New York, several of our largest houses withdrew their stock from market, to await higher prices.

Our trade with China is steadily on the increase, & will soon reach a
degree of importance it has never before attained. We have secured their
market for Lead. It is said they prefer the Lead from the United States
to that from other countries, as it is more soft, or ductile, and better
adapted to the lining of Tea chest &c.

We also supply the market with a large amount of heavy piece Cotton
Goods.

The weather in New York continues exceedingly fine.

I see a Lady by the name of Story in Greenville S.C. has given birth
to three children, two daughters and a son. She has named the latter
James Knox & a daughter Elizabeth Polk, while the other daughter is
called Rebecca Dallas. She ought to have called the daughter Sarah instead of Elizabeth. I imagine from this time forward, you & Mr. Dallas
will have almost as many name sakes, as you have had applicants for
office. There is no better sign of popularity than this, of having lots of
the rising generation named after you. An unpopular man, never leaves
namesakes behind him. Senates decree Statutes, but the people give
names, and cherish the memory of those they loved & admired.

ALEXR. JONES

ALS. DLC–JKP. Addressed to Washington City.
1. A native of North Carolina, Jones practiced medicine in Mississippi before
removing permanently in 1840 to New York City, where he wrote regularly for
the *New York Journal of Commerce.* Quick to grasp the use of the telegraph in
news distribution, Jones organized a cooperative press among several American
cities and served as the first general agent of the New York Associated Press.

2. New York City held its municipal elections on April 8, 1845; the mayoral contest included the Native candidate and incumbent, James Harper; the Whig candidate, Dudley Selden; and the Democratic candidate, William F. Havemeyer.

3. Completed in 1842, the Croton Aquaduct supplied water for New York City, extended some 40 miles in length, and cost in excess of $10 million.

4. In local elections held on April 1st, Democrats swept the Williamsburg electoral slate, including town supervisor, town clerk, justice of the peace, and superintendent of the common schools.

5. John I. DeGraff won election in the Schenectady mayoral contest by a majority of seven votes; the Democrats also won 6 out of 16 aldermanic posts.

### FROM THOMAS HAGUE[1]

11h. 21m. A.M.

Mr. President.                                Washington City. April 5th 1845

After the Baltimore Convention; it being publicly known that Jas. K. Polk, & Henry Clay were the candidates for the chair of state; I lost no time in examining your nativity, & his, and comparing them with the Horoscope of this great Republic. Having satisfied myself that the chair of state was destined for you, I boldly published my astrological judgment thereon, ten days previously to the 1st of November last, a copy of which was forwarded to you by myself.[2] The result of the last Presidential election fulfilled my prediction.

My object in addressing you in this manner and at this time is important, as regards my interest, and fame. I would just say, that after the "Horoscope" for Novr last appeared, Joel B. Sutherland, Calvin Blythe, Mr. Whitaker, Judge Bradford, lawyer Harris, & others who formed a committee for the purpose of sustaining the Democratic ticket[3] sent a carriage by express to my domicile, and a message requiring my presence at the Custom House. I appeared accordingly & was introduced to Mr. Sutherland & the Comee.: S. informed me that my "Horoscope" had been shown to him and the members of the committee: They said that my prediction ought to be known throughout the states of Penna, & N.Y. as soon as possible, for if known it would have a great influence in electing Jas. K. Polk President of the U.S. I was asked what I would give a thousand or two thousand copies for, & spread them myself, according to the best of my judgment. I answered, for $3. per 100; which they agreed to give me, and other expenses that might arise during my journey through Lancaster Co. & little Delaware. Accordingly I distributed nearly 2000 Copies: Not an editor in the Union to my knowledge, missed getting one. Even the farmers and labouring men as well as store keepers & lawyers were furnished with copies to the extent of my means. I was present in Lancaster City & County several days, previous to the election; doing all in my power to fulfil my engagement with the gentlemen above named. The Hon. Jas. Buchanan knows this to be a fact, as I made his house my home whilst in Lancaster. The expenses I incurred in the distribution of the "Horoscope" amounted to $68. After the election was over the result known, I presented my bill, but have only received $20. The rest is still due to me.

I have called on them until tired. They refuse to fulfil their engagement, & I therefore have determined to communicate the facts of the case to you, & request your aid in causing justice to be done towards me by the persons I have mentioned above.

Whilst in Washington I have seen Sutherland, Blythe, Whitaker, & Bradford, but did not wish to trouble them again before seeing you. Such men, whether they now satisfy me or not, are unfit to hold any office of honour or trust in this republic.

That this petition may have its due influence & effect with you ....

THOMAS HAGUE

LS. DLC–JKP. Addressed locally.

1. A Philadelphia astrologer, Thomas Hague published several works on astrometeorology, including *Hague's Christian Almanac* (1846) and *A Narrative of the World: Astrotheologically and Naturally Told ...* (1873).

2. Hague's letter to Polk has not been found.

3. Joel B. Sutherland, Calvin Blythe, William B. Whitecar, John O. Bradford, and S. Harris headed Philadelphia's Democratic Invincible Legion. S. Harris has not been identified further.

## FROM J. GEORGE HARRIS

My Dear Sir,                              Nashville April 6. 1845

I arrived here a week ago yesterday evening.

I am glad to learn that Blair & Rives have expressed a willingness to dispose of the Globe. If their price is not exorbitant it will be an establishment of great value to its owners and if no aspirant to the succession has too much to do with raising the purchase money it cannot fail to be of great service to your fame and to your administration. You have learned, ere this, of Gen Jackson's disinclination to have Maj. Donelson connected with it, and yet I know not how the Maj. can decline an editorial association with the veteran Ritchie. Texas papers received here to night state that the Ho. Res for Annexation will be acceptable to that country.[1]

J. GEO. HARRIS

ALS. DLC–JKP. Addressed to Washington City.

1. Harris probably refers to the joint resolution on Texas annexation introduced in the U.S. House; see Cave Johnson to Polk, February 3, 1845. The *Nashville Union* of April 8, 1845, carried a report of a March 21st meeting of Galveston citizens and their support for resolutions in favor of annexation.

## FROM ROBERT ARMSTRONG

My Dear Sir                                            Nashville 7 April 1845

I am this moment from the Hermitage. I found the Genl[1] much more feeble and indisposed than I expected. I fear he will last but a short time, he thinks so himself. I will return in the morning with Doct. Robertson.[2]

Your two letters of 27 & 28th March[3] recd on Saturday night by the same mail changed entirely the whole Globe affair. As soon as the Genl understood that Blair was willing to sell, he readily gave his consent and wrote you and Mr Blair by the mail of to night,[4] & saying that perhaps they were the last letters he would ever write, requesting me to say to you what a deep interest he felt in every thing that concerns you. He says that he advised Blair shortly after your election to sell out. He was fearfull of divisions and difficulties and has some letters recently from Pensyl, in relation to *Cameron* that induced him to fear that there was a party forming to injure you &c. All this is now quieted and he is satisfied to any *sale* or *transfer*. He says he cannot say any thing for Majr Donelson's acceptance &c of a place as editor. As to Majr Lewis' *case* he said but little.[5] He has been long satisfied of Lewis' course on the Bank and in the contest of 40.

I would I think make but few removals in Tenss at the present. Let the marshal remain on *awhile*.[6] All is going well here. Nicholson & myself got out a ticket for Donelson on Saturday.

McIntosh for the Senate.

Joe Horton & Col Shelton for the House and

Majr Turner for Congress.[7]

He will make Payton[8] behave himself and probably beat him.

Your whole course since your *election* and at Washington has had a most powerful influence on the whigs (I mean the rank & file). They are satisfied and their leaders cannot keep hundreds of them from a support of Brown who I think will make easy work of Foster. They commence the campaign to day at Clarksville.[9] In haste ....

R. ARMSTRONG

ALS. DLC–JKP. Addressed to Washington City; marked *"Private."*

1. Andrew Jackson.

2. Son of James Robertson, Nashville's founder, and Jackson's physician, Felix Robertson served as mayor of Nashville in 1818, 1827, and 1828; during the 1844 election campaign he headed the Nashville Democratic Central Committee.

3. Letters not found.

4. See below, Jackson to Polk, April 7, 1845; see also Jackson to Francis P. Blair, April 7, 1845. ALS. DLC–AJ.

5. Armstrong's reference is to the removal of William B. Lewis as second auditor of the Treasury. Although Jackson expected Lewis to play a role in the new administration, Polk replaced him with John M. McCalla.

6. Benjamin H. Sheppard served as U.S. marshal for the Middle District of Tennessee from 1842 until 1846.

7. On April 8, 1845, the *Nashville Union* published the Democratic party's ticket for Davidson County. John McIntosh held a clerkship at the Tennessee State prison in Nashville during the 1830's. Joseph W. Horton, sheriff of Davidson County from 1822 to 1829, worked as cashier of the Bank of Tennessee's Nashville office. W. G. Shelton has not been identified further. Robert B. Turner, a Nashville attorney, headed the Democratic party's militia companies known as the Texas Volunteers and organized by Turner during the 1844 presidential election.

8. Joseph H. Peyton, a Sumner County physician and Whig, served one term in the Tennessee Senate, 1841–43, before winning election to the U.S. House in 1843. Although elected to a second term, Peyton died in November of 1845.

9. Reference is to the April 7th gubernatorial debate in Clarksville, Tenn., between Aaron V. Brown and Ephraim H. Foster.

## FROM EDMUND BURKE

Sir                                    Newport, N.H. April 7. 1845

During the interview I had with you on the morning previous to my departure from Washington, I hastily suggested that a vacancy would probably occur on the Bench of the U.S. Court, by reason of the resignation of Judge Story.[1] And I farther suggested the name of the Hon. Levi Woodbury as his successor. On my way through Boston, in conversation with some of the friends of Judge Story, I learned that the idea of his early resignation was familiar with them. It is anticipated that the event may occur during the present spring, or the approaching summer.

If Judge Story should resign I have strong reason to believe that the office, thus vacated, would be very acceptable to Mr Woodbury. And I think I can with truth add, that his appointment to the Bench of the U.S. Court would be very gratifying to the Democratic party of New England at least, and I believe, of the whole country. I need not say that the distinguished honor would be duly appreciated by his native state.

Of the general talents, soundness of principle, and high personal character, of Mr Woodbury, I need say nothing. But it will not be out of place to add, that Mr Woodbury is esteemed as one of the ablest lawyers whom this State has ever produced; and that in early life he, during several years, filled the office of Associate Judge of the highest judicial court in this State, the duties of which he discharged with distinguished ability.

If Judge Story should resign there would seem to be no man in New England whom public opinion would more generally designate as his successor, than Mr Woodbury if he would accept the place.

His friends in this State are not unaware of the importance to the country, and to the Democratic party, of retaining the benefit of his experience and ability in the Senate. We know that he has none but the kindest feelings towards yourself personally, and that if he should remain in the Senate, those feelings would be manifested by a faithful and cordial support of your Administration. And I think I can assure you, that Mr Woodbury is confident that the feelings which he entertains towards you personally, are reciprocated by you, and that he has the confidence and friendship of yourself and Cabinet. And whatever conclusion you may form in regard to the successor of Judge Story, will of course make no difference in the conduct of Mr Woodbury in respect to yourself personally, or to your Administration.

I might add a few words on the importance of placing upon the Bench of the U.S. Court, a man of Mr Woodbury's soundness, and indomitable firmness, of principle; but I feel that it is unnecessary.

In conclusion allow me to say by way of apology, that I reluctantly obtrude my communications upon your patience, and your invaluable time.

EDMUND BURKE

ALS. DLC–JKP. Addressed to Washington City.
1. A lawyer and scholar from Salem, Mass., Joseph Story received his appointment to the U.S. Supreme Court in 1811 at age 32. He gained prominence for his legal opinions and commentaries, many of which were published, and held a professorship at the Harvard School of Law. He had planned to leave the bench to devote more time to the law school but died in September 1845.

## FROM BENJAMIN COWELL[1]

Sir                                                      Providence April 7 1845
I sought an interview with you at Washington a few weeks since, for the purpose of having some conversation about our recent difficulties in this State, and you were kind enough to say that if I would call the next day you would endeavour to grant me a few minutes but the crowds which surrounded you prevented me.

I had never taken a very active part in our late troubles but when the "peoples constitution" so called[2] was adopted by a majority of the people I thought it was the Supreme law of the land according to the doctrines of the Revolution, and I voted for Gov Dorr under it.[3] For doing this I was accused of improper conduct and to defend myself I wrote our late Governor King a letter giving my views which was published & a copy of which I have now the honor to send you.[4]

For publishing this letter, however, strange it may seem, I was driven into exile & kept out of the State, during the existence of Martial law.[5] A Sergeants gard was sent to my house, under a pretence for searching for arms, but in reality to arrest me as I was afterwards informed. This may seem to you incredible in this land of liberty, but it was strictly true and it was but one specimen of that tyranny which the old Charter Party exercised towards individuals. I was kept in exile over two months, before I was allowed to return to my family. As I had been instrumental in getting Gov Dorr *into* prison, I have always since then felt it my duty to help git him *out* and it was upon this subject I wished to converse with you at Washington.

We have recently held a State election & have elected a "Liberation Governor."[6] But the Governor under our present constitution has not the pardoning power. It is vested in the Legislature; what that body will do, it is impossible to determine.

As respects myself I deem it not improper to say that a few years ago I left the Bar for the station of Chief Justice of this County. This station I held until the whigs gained the ascendency in 1838, when a whig Legislature, who had under the Charter Government, the appointing power, at the annual election of officers appointed another to fill that office, contrary to the wishes, I have the satisfaction to say, of the members of the Bar. They all desired my reappointment. But my political principles defeated their wishes. Since that period I have been in private life. Should you at your leisure read the enclosed you will see how I have stood in our recent difficulties.

BENJA COWELL

ALS. DLC–JKP. Addressed to Washington City.

1. A Providence lawyer, Cowell became collector of the port in 1848. Two years later he published a history of Rhode Island during the Revolutionary War entitled *Spirit of '76 in Rhode Island.*

2. See Dutee J. Pearce to Polk, February 3, 1845.

3. See Nathaniel C. Read to Polk, February 4, 1845.

4. Enclosure not found. Cowell authored *A Letter to the Hon. Samuel W. King, late Governor of . . . Rhode Island* in 1842. A surgeon and veteran of the War of 1812, King served as governor from 1839 until 1843.

5. Cowell's reference is to the 1842 rule of martial law declared during the Dorr Rebellion.

6. In state-wide elections set for April 2, 1845, a coalition of "liberation" Whigs and Democrats had campaigned for a general pardon for the Dorrites. Charles Jackson, a lawyer, manufacturer, and state legislator won the gubernatorial contest and issued a general amnesty for the Dorrites.

## FROM L. W. GOSNELL[1]

Sir,                                                                    Balt. 7 April 1845

From the conversation I had the pleasure of holding with you on Saturday evening upon the subject of political affairs in Balto. I am induced to take the liberty of presenting some general views, which I hope may afford you some light in making your appointments for Balto.

In the onset allow me to assure you, that I have nothing to ask for myself; neither have I any particular interests to serve. My sole object and desire is to render my mite to preserve the ascendancy of the Democratic party.

I look upon it that our victory is not yet entirely complete. I deem it of importance to the success of your administration that our majority in the House of Rep. of the next Congress should be a decided one, and to the Democracy of Balto. it is of vital importance that we should carry the 3d congressional district (now rep. by Mr. Kennedy) at the coming fall election,[2] in order to secure to us the ascendancy in the City hereafter: *This can only be done by keeping the party united*, as far as it is possible to do so, and much, very much indeed, I feel assured will depend on giving us such appointments as will be most acceptable to the working portion of our party.

Our legitimate majority cannot be over 400, or 500 votes, all told, a portion of which, (but what portion cannot be correctly estimated) we shall undoubtedly lose at the next election upon the Native American question: Our position therefore is inevitably this, that any further defection from our ranks, than we shall suffer from this question would be fatal.

As I remarked to you on saturday evening, our strength in Balto. lies almost exclusively in the hands of the mechanics and working people. When they can be united, success with us is always certain; displease them and defeat is equally certain.

I am in a more favorable position perhaps, to learn the feelings and sentiments of the great mass of our voters, than any other gentleman in the City who is not himself a mechanic; having one brother who is a practical builder, and in constant communication with every branch of mechanics and labouring men connected with the building business, and another who is a partner in a large merchant Tailoring establishment— both firm and uncompromising Democrats,[3] and I speak with entire confidence when I say, that all this portion of our friends are unanimous in their *expectations* and *desire*, that in the appointments for Maryland, the "working man" will not be overlooked by their President. By the term working man, I mean Mechanics, Farmers, &c, including all except the learned professions. I have no feelings of hostility to the learned professions myself, but allow me *particularly to impress* it upon you to save us from the appointment of gentlemen of the Bar except it be to such situations as where a knowledge of their profession is necessary to the correct performance of their official duties: They are but few in numbers compared with mass, and generally manage to obtain a very large over proportion of the public offices, notwithstanding, from some unaccountable cause, they are exceedingly objectionable to the great mass of our people.

The doctrine of rotation in office has become a favourite theme with our party here, so much so, that I am fully satisfied that the appointment of gentlemen, who have heretofore enjoyed the favour of either the State or General government would meet their decided disapprobation. This feeling does not stop here, but it is expected that not only our opponents, but those of our friends who have been in for a long time, will be removed to make place for those who have never yet enjoyed any public favour.

In conclusion permit me to assure you that although I did, some weeks ago, give letters to two gentlemen who had heretofore held stations under the government, publice feeling in the democratic ranks has so fully disclosed itself, that I am now entirely satisfied that the appointment of ex-office holders and gentlemen of the Bar would be sufficiently offensive to the great body of the Democracy of Balto. to lose us not only the election in the 3d Congressional district next fall, but in my judgment, would greatly endanger the election of a democratic Mayor in 1846: To this general rule perhaps Mr. Vansant might be an exception because he is a practical working man.[4]

Hoping this may be received in the same spirit of kindness I write it ....

L. W. GOSNELL

ALS. DLC–JKP. Addressed to Washington City. ·

1. In the 1840's L. W. Gosnell owned a dry goods business in Baltimore.

2. Maryland held state and congressional elections on October 1, 1845. A Baltimore lawyer and Whig, John Pendleton Kennedy represented Maryland's Fourth Congressional District for three terms, 1838–39 and 1841–45; he served as secretary of the navy from 1852 to 1853.

3. Gosnell's brothers, Philip and Talbot, are not identified further.

4. Joshua Van Sant, a journeyman hatter from 1817 to 1835, enjoyed a long and varied career in Baltimore's public service: postmaster, 1839–41; state legislator, 1845; finance commissioner, 1846–55; U.S. congressman, 1853–55; mayor, 1871–75, and comptroller, 1876–81.

## FROM J. GEORGE HARRIS

My Dear Sir,                                              Nashville April 7. 1845
    Since I have learned of the willingness of Blair & Rives to withdraw from the Globe, thus removing the main obstacle to the arrangement so much desired by yourself & friends, and have heard that Maj. Donelson will in all probability decline a connexion with the editorial department of the new paper, it has occurred to me that Mr. Ritchie will scarcely be disposed to conduct it alone, and that some other person will be associated with him.
    Now, my dear sir, if you are still of the opinion that my *residence in Tennessee*, altho' a native of Connecticut & a resident of New England for nearly 30 years, precludes the possibility of your giving me an eligible and profitable position abroad at an early day, how would it do to have *me* associated with Mr. Ritchie? Would there be any great objection to my occupancy of the position which you had intended for Maj. Donelson in that establishment?
    The truth is, I am at this moment exceedingly anxious to be engaged in something lucrative, and I feel assured that if you cannot lend me a helping hand in one way you will in another.
    Please remember me to your amiable family ....

                                                          J. GEO. HARRIS

ALS. DLC–JKP. Addressed to Washington City.

## FROM HENRY HORN

                                                          Fullers Hotel
My Dear Sir,                              [Washington City] April 7 1845
    I beg leave to enclose you a letter from our mutual friend the Hon. John Galbrath[1] which I hope you will do me the favour to read as I believe it speaks the sentiments of every honest and unprejudiced democrat in our State.
    As my longer continuance here cannot be useful and may be troublesome to you I shall leave in the morning. In the mean time I beg that you will make my apology to Mrs Polk for anything that might have appeared distant in my demeanor to her on the evening of the 5th. Be pleased to

assure her that it was the result of an innate diffidence which always overwhelms me when ever I am suddenly thrown into the presence of a lady for whom I entertain the most exalted consideration especially when I have reason to believe I am not recognised. And allow me to say that you are not entirely blameless in omitting the ceremony of an introduction.

HENRY HORN

ALS. DLC–JKP. Addressed locally.
1. John Galbraith's letter to Horn has not been found. A Pennsylvania lawyer and judge, Galbraith won election as a Democrat to the U.S. House, where he served three terms, 1833–37 and 1839–41; subsequently he presided over the bench of Pennsylvania's Sixth Judicial District from 1851 until his death in 1860.

## FROM ANDREW JACKSON

My dear Sir,                                             Hermitage April 7th 1845
    Genl R. Armstrong has this moment reached me & presented for my perusal your two confidential letters to him of the 27th & 28th ultimo.[1] I have read them & given them all the consideration my sickness and great debility would allow. I have wrote Mr Blair to sell out; indeed it is the only way left him, unless he was to abandon his democratic principles, which he will never do, or submit to degradation, which I have long known, he will never do. Therefore to sell out is the only mode left him without doing your administration & the democratic cause much injury which are I well know opposed to his principles & feelings.
    Who are to be the purchasers ought by you to be well considered. If such men as Cameron is to have any interest in, or controll over its columns, the democracy will be split to pieces, and instead of that smooth and pleasant road that opened to you, at the commencement of your administration will become thorns & briars. The very change of the Globe as the organ, you hazzard the loss of the support of the democracy of the Eastern States, & N. York & split up Pennsylvania, for I repeat as I stated in my confidential letter to you, that the Globe has the confidence of more of the democratic members of Congress than any paper in the Union.[2]
    But it appears the die is cast, and I hope for the best. But it behoves you to take care of who are the purchasers, least it give rise to the belief that the tools of some of the aspirants for the succession are concerned in the purchase. You may depend on one thing, that your course with regard to the Globe & Blair has & will sour the minds of many firm democrats. With my prayer that you may get thro this difficulty without

injury to yourself & the democratic cause. We all salute you & your amiable lady ....

ANDREW JACKSON

ALS. DLC–JKP. Addressed to Washington City and marked *"confidential."* Polk's AE states that he received this letter on April 14, 1845.
1. Letters not found. See Robert Armstrong to Polk, April 7, 1845.
2. Jackson probably refers to his letter to Polk of February 28, 1845.

## FROM JESSE MILLER

My Dear Sir                                            Harrisburg Apl 7. 1845
Nothing but the great importance of the appointment and the most entire conviction of my Judgement that the selection of Henry Welsh will best subserve the public interests and those of the democratic party could induce me again to trouble you in relation to the Collector at Phila. The Governor[1] and myself feel more than an ordinary interest in the question, and it is upon the most mature reflection and the fullest confidence of the propriety of our course that we ask that Mr. Welsh may be appointed. Dr Leyman & Mr Horn[2] are both good men but I feel confident there is such opposition in the City itself that the appointment of either will be more offensive then there than that of Mr Welsh. Besides neither of them understand the politics of the State any thing like as well as Mr. Welsh and as to the performance of the duties of the office I do not believe there is an applicant before you his superior. I do not speak this lightly, but because I know the truth of what I state and for which I am willing to be held responsible.

The idea of retaining Mr Blythe ought not to be entertained for a moment. He has descended from a once respectable position to the *nadir* point of political degradation and now caters to the interested purposes of the worst and meanest of political trimmers.

Mr Rush's name has been incidentally suggested. Mr Rush is as we all know a gentlemen, but has as little knowledge of the men of the present day as can well be imagined. He many years since lost caste with the Democratic party in consequence of the course he took on the Anti-Masonic question. He in some degree retreved himself afterwards on the Bank question,[3] but I solemnly believe his opinions and writings have no more influence now in Penna. than that of any other intelligent man. I have no unkind feeling to him but I have no hesitation in saying *emphatically* he *ought not* to be appointed and in this opinion I know I would be sustained by 99/100 of the genuine democracy of the State.

In urging the appointment of Mr Welsh I have no earthly object in view but the promotion of the public good and the interests of the democratic party as *a whole*. I have no wish to advance or oppose the interests of any man who may have any ulterior honorable purposes in view. Should Mr Welsh be appointed I know he will act with fairness to all and will not prostitute the influence of his situation to any.

We are now in a most singular and critical position in this state. We have a more corrupt state of things than any man who does not see & feel the influences that are at work can begin to immagine. The election of Cameron was a most unfortunate result and will inevitably be productive of incalculable mischief and the extent will just be in proportion to his influence or *supposed* influence with the Genl Administration. He started as the friend of Welsh and in consequence of this fact and 2 of the York County members voting for Cameron, Welsh became suspected by some with conniving at Cameron's election & it gave some trouble to put down the suspicion.

Now I would not be disappointed if Cameron and his friends would either openly or covertly oppose Welsh and go to retain Blythe, or form some other combination to defeat the appointment of Welsh. He will sustain no man who will not sustain his interested and selfish purposes and will change his position instanter and bargain with any man or set of men who will promote his interests.

In view of every thing and especially of the peculiar position we are now in Welsh ought to be appointed and I trust will be. If we are forsaken here by the Genl administration & from any misapprehension of the true condition of things its influence should be unintentionally thrown against us the party must be prostrated in Penna. at least for a time.

J. MILLER

ALS. DLC–JKP. Addressed to Washington City and marked *"Confidential"* and *"Private."*

1. Francis R. Shunk.
2. George F. Lehman and Henry Horn.
3. Richard Rush, a prominent Anti-Mason, declined to run for president on that ticket in the election of 1832; Rush strongly opposed the rechartering of the Bank of the United States in 1832.

## FROM BENJAMIN F. BUTLER

My Dear Sir,                                      New York, April 8th 1845

I returned, this morning, from the north, and having consulted freely with political friends here, as well as there, am prepared to fulfill the promise made to you in my last.[1] Under all existing circumstances, it is our opinion, and we accordingly so recommend, that *Jonathan I.*

*Coddington*, of this city, should be appointed Collector, and *Michael Hoffman* of Herkimer County in this state, Naval Officer of this port.[2] Mr. Coddington's name is before you for reappointment to the office of Postmaster; and nothing need be said in regard to his integrity or worth as a man, or his merits as a politician. He will not be so expert and ready as some others, and he has not the legal qualifications of which I spoke as desirable; but we cannot find any lawyer of our party *who will take the office*, and whom, upon the whole, we think it proper to name; but then he has excellent business habits, enjoys the entire confidence of the whole community, and will take good advice in the execution of the office, in all legal matters with which he is not personally familiar. His experience as a merchant, too, is of the most favorable character; because he has been so long out of active business, that he is free from any undue commercial bias, while he will yet enjoy the benefits of a long and diversified business in that department.

Mr. Hoffman was known to you, I believe, when a member of the House of Reps. from this state. He is a man of high order of talent; of the most unblemished reputation; a professor (& one who adorns his profession) of religion; a great favorite with a large portion of the Democracy; and altogether, one of our most estimable citizens. His efforts to restore the credit and pecuniary character of the state, in the sessions of 1843 & 1844,[3] were of the highest value; and though some object to him, that like other men who have given their minds very intensively & exclusively, to a single measure, he has come to regard that measure with undue solicitude; yet in the place for which we propose him, there is no room for any such criticism. He will be a most valuable, I might say, an *invaluable* adjunct to the Custom House; because he will render the Naval Office, what the law intends it should be, *a check on the Collector*; while he will perfectly harmonize with Mr. Coddington & be ready, at all times, to give him the aid of his extensive legal knowledge whenever required. I will only add that in the case of Gov Throop, appointed to this office by Gen. Jackson in 1833,[4] we have a precedent for conferring it on a distinguished citizen from the interior of the State; & I can promise you, I am sure, not only a ready assent, but a most cheerful response to Mr. Hoffman's appointment from the great mass of the Democracy of the city. In the interior of the state, it will be hailed by acclamation; and I may add, by withdrawing Mr. Hoffman from the limited scenes & the particular sphere, in which he has lately moved, will contribute not only to the success of your administration, but have a tendency to calm those internal dissensions of which you have been obliged to hear too much.

I have not time to enlarge, but will add, that Mr. O Sullivan who goes this evening to Washington, has been made acquainted with the matters here stated—(he does not know that you had written to me)—and that I have stated to him my reasons for knowing that Mr. Hoffman will accept, if the office be conferred on him. As to Mr Coddington, he has also the like knowledge.

B. F. Butler

ALS. DLC–JKP. Addressed to Washington City and marked *"Private."*
1. See Benjamin F. Butler to Polk, March 31, 1845.
2. A Barnburner and lawyer from Herkimer, Hoffman won election to four terms in the U.S. House, 1825–33; served two years as canal commissioner of New York, 1833–35; sat in the New York House for three terms, 1841–44; and held the post of naval officer of the port of New York from 1845 until his death in 1848.
3. Butler probably refers to Hoffman's role as the radical anti-bank, anti-state debt leader of the Barnburners in the New York state legislature. A firm believer in limited liability for state corporations, especially banks, Hoffman supported the "stop and tax" policy for funding state internal improvements and led Barnburner opposition to a canal improvement bill debated during the 1844 session of the state legislature.
4. An Auburn lawyer, Enos T. Throop was elected to one term in the U.S. House in 1814; was appointed circuit court judge in 1823; was elected lieutenant governor of New York in 1828; served as governor upon Martin Van Buren's resignation to become secretary of state; was appointed naval officer of the port of New York in 1833; and served as chargé d'affaires to the Kingdom of the Two Sicilies in 1838.

## TO FRANKLIN H. ELMORE

My dear Sir:                    Washington City 8 April 1845
I shall regard it to be my duty to appoint at an early day an Envoy Extraordinary and Minister Plenipotentiary to Great Britain to succeed Mr Everett[1] and I now tender to you that important mission.

In the event of your acceptance, it is desired that you will enter upon your duties at as early a period as your convenience may permit. Mr Everett in a letter of the 3d ultimo[2] anticipated his recall and adds, "it would be agreeable to me that my successor should be named as soon as it can be done with due regard to the public service in order that I may be able to remain at my post till his arrival, (which I think desirable both on his account and that of the public) without my being delayed till the season of the year is too far advanced for a safe and comfortable passage across the Atlantic." In selecting you for this distinguished station I gratify my own personal feelings, while the Country will have a guaranty in your well known patriotism & ability that the public interests confided to you will be safe in your hands.

I request that you will inform me at your earliest convenience whether you accept or not. If in your answer you signify your willingness to accept, a commission can be immediately signed and the necessary instructions prepared.

My impression is that it will be necessary for you to sail in the course of a few weeks, say in all the month of May.

JAMES K. POLK

L, copy. DLC–JKP. Addressed to Charleston, S.C., and marked "*Private*" and "*Copy.*"

1. A Unitarian clergyman, Edward Everett served five terms as an Independent in the U.S. House, 1825–35; won election as governor of Massachusetts in 1835 with the backing of Whigs and Anti-Masons; went to the Court of St. James in 1841 as U.S. minister and remained in that post until 1845; returned to the United States to serve as president of Harvard College; served as secretary of state under Millard Fillmore, 1852–53; won a seat in the U.S. Senate in 1853; and ran as the vice-presidential candidate with John Bell on the Constitutional-Union ticket in 1860.

2. Polk's reference is to Everett's letter of March 3, 1845.

## FROM GEORGE S. HOUSTON[1]

Sir:                                                        Athens 8 Apl [18]45

Dr Parrott[2] who is in one of the bureaus in the Navy Dept (Provisions & Clothing I think) wants to go to Mexico with your new minister if you make a change at that *court* as secretary or whatever it is called. Dr P. is a Kinsman of Mrs Houston[3] & I should like to see him promoted. I think too he is a clever sensible man, & a very superior officer, but as I dont want you to rely upon my statement I will not say much but ask you to learn of his capacity integrity &c & I have no fear of the results. You will find him a very superior man & well qualified in every way for the office. If however you make no change of ministers & he fails to go to Mexico, & there should be a vacancy in the head of the bureau in which he is chief clk. I would like you to promote him to the head of it &c. I have no fear in saying he is well qualified & a gentleman.

GEO. S. HOUSTON

ALS. DLC–JKP. Addressed to Washington City.

1. George S. Houston of Athens, Ala., served nine terms in the U.S. House, 1841–49 and 1851–61, and two terms as governor of Alabama, 1874–78; he won election to the U.S. Senate in 1879, the year of his death.

2. A native of Virginia and a trained dentist, William S. Parrott engaged in Mexican business operations that subsequently led him to file indemnity claims against the Mexican government; on March 28, 1845, Polk appointed Parrott to

serve as a confidential agent of the United States in Mexico; Parrott later held the post of secretary of legation in Mexico before and after the war years.

3. Mary Beatty Houston.

## FROM CHARLES S. JONES[1]

Washington City April 8, 1845

Describing himself as "an humble Democrat and a mechanic," Jones writes Polk on behalf of the Democrats of the District of Columbia and discusses how "proscription in all its varied forms" has been used against the Democracy. He claims that the municipal authorities, the courts, the banks, the insurance companies, and "other chartered Institutions" refuse employment to local Democrats. He notes that a "vast majority of the citizens of the District are bitterly against us, and in addition to corporate proscription, individual proscription is brought to bear powerfully upon us in our business, and is even carried into the social walks of life." Jones adds that the Whigs also hold three-fourths of all the government situations. Having mentioned that the Democracy here quickly raised "the glorious banner of 'Polk, Dallas, Texas, and Oregon'" and vigorously supported the ticket during the campaign, Jones requests that Polk appoint Charles P. Sengstack, "the body and soul of the *working* Democracy of the District," to the office of commissioner of public buildings.[2] Jones raises charges of corruption against the current office holder,[3] who has repeatedly denied employment to members of the working Democracy strictly on the grounds of partisan politics. Jones emphasizes that the appointment of Sengstack would be "a tribute of respect to the mechanic interests."

ALS. DLC–JKP. Addressed locally.

1. An ardent Democrat and son of Richard Jones, an inspector of the penitentiary in Washington City, Charles S. Jones applied to Polk for a position at the Capitol but did not receive the appointment.

2. Secretary of the local Democratic Association, Charles P. Sengstack received an appointment as warden of the penitentiary at Washington City in 1848. In 1847 Polk appointed Charles Douglas to serve as commissioner of public buildings.

3. William Noland served as commissioner of public buildings from 1834 until 1846.

## FROM ROBERT ARMSTRONG

Dear Sir                                                   Nashville Aprl 9th 1845

Genl. Jackson is something better, his feet hands and face are very much swollen and I think his present suffering is from Dropsy. It is getting up in the chest, and if not releaved, he will soon die. Carroll[1] you recollect was releaved and lived some months.

To day he seemed better and is well pleased at the transfer or sale of the Globe believing that it will give you ease and quiet and that your administration will move on without difficulty. The Establishment of a *new* paper he thought would endanger our party, and tend to division. With Lewis's retirement he is satisfied.

Every thing moves on here well and Brown will succeed with ease. I am satisfied that the rank and file cannot be roused up. I know Jarnagins feeling toward Foster. He will cripple him in East Tenness. Bell is Soured & Dissatisfied and has not weight or influence. Think of T J Reid[2] as PM at Louisville. I assure you he is the man to appoint there. Say to William Polk that I will leave in a few days after my *mail robber* is tried,[3] and want to sail by 15 May that he promised to wait for me and I hope he will do so as I wish to go out with him.

Turner will give Peyton great trouble in this Congressional District and our County Ticket brings out *all* our force for Brown. With kind respects to Mrs. Polk ....

R ARMSTRONG

ALS. DLC–JKP. Addressed to Washington City.
1. William Carroll, an elder statesman of the Tennessee Democracy and state governor for six terms, 1821–27 and 1829–35, remained active in party affairs until his illness and death in 1844.
2. Thomas J. Read.
3. Armstrong's reference is to the prosecution of George Gould, a clerk at the Nashville post office, for theft of $5 from a letter deposited at the post office.

## FROM JOHN F. H. CLAIBORNE

Dear Sir,                                              Washington, April 9th 1845

I beg to unite with many other friends of your Excellency in presenting the name of Col John A. Rogers of New Orleans, for the office of Cherokee Commissioner.[1] It would be superfluous for me to speak to your Excellency of his personal merits, integrity & peculiar qualifications for the office. His appointment would be very gratifying to your friends in Louisiana & Mississippi, where he is well known & highly appreciated.

I beg also to observe that, in my humble opinion, the present Commissioners[2] are totally unqualified for the places they occupy. Champagne drinkers and gentlemen of leisure from the Atlantic cities, are not the men to settle Indian affairs. We have intellect & information enough for such duties west of the mountains.

Besides I know at least one of those gentlemen to be a violent federal partisan, & if it be true that Gov. Butler has borrowed money from John Ross, he ought to be, I humbly submit, *removed.*

There has never been any branch of the Government so shamefully & profligately managed as the Indian department under the late Administration; & nothing could be more ridiculous than the sending of a dandy officer like Gen. Jones to report on Cherokee affs.

I believe there is a wide field in which yr Excellency will harvest glory & fame by the correction of these abuses, and by a searching enquiry into the monstrous frauds that, have been sanctioned under the late Administration, & which must assuredly attract attention at the next session of Congress. If these are not now arrested by your intervention, the Whig party, ever vigilant, will themselves take up the matter with wonderful effect. The whole Indian Bureau & its proceedings at *this present moment*, requires overlooking.

It is because I believe Col Rogers free from all connexion with these frauds & know him to be honest & capable, that I have recommended him to your Excy.

JOHN F H CLAIBORNE

ALS. DLC–JKP. Addressed locally and marked *"Private."* Polk's AEI on the cover states that he received this letter on April 12 and that "He will *not* be appointed."

1. A native of Hawkins County, Tenn., Rogers won election as a Whig to three terms in the Tennessee House, 1827–28 and 1835–38, before removing to New Orleans.

2. See Ezekiel Starr et al. to Polk, March 25, 1845.


## FROM J. GEORGE HARRIS

My Dear Sir,            Nashville, Tenn. April 9. 1845

Since it is known that Blair & Rives will withdraw and that the Globe will be "the official" under the editorial management of Mr. Ritchie and another, I have thought deeply of your suggestion that I might be a partner in the concern. For it seems to be rendered quite certain here in the private circle of our friends that Maj. Donelson cannot be persuaded to be the associate editor; and as he is expecting "something better abroad" than the position which he now occupies you would scarcely be able to serve both him and myself in that capacity as hailing from this State. Therefore I have thought that if it be perfectly acceptable to yourself and Mr. Ritchie, you might perhaps be disposed to give me the associate-editorship with the profits and prospects thereof as tendered to Major Donelson and at the same time be able to do for him what Gen. Jackson so much desires. I laid this same proposition before you in my letter of the 7th, that you might entertain it about the same time that you were apprised of Major Donelson's probable declination.

When you kindly suggested that I might be one of two fiscal partners in the new concern—while the two editors would also be partners—the opinion seemed to prevail that the Globe could *not* be purchased and that Blair & Rives would *not* withdraw—thus leaving it exceedingly doubtful whether the new rival establishment could be made to yield a living profit to four such partners. The withdrawal of Blair & Rives, the consent of the veteran Ritchie to be the chief editor, and the prospect of an *immediate arrangement*, entirely changes the scene and gives it a more favorable aspect.

I have no personal acquaintance with Mr. Ritchie, but I presume that I am not entirely unknown to him as an editor in times past both at the Northeast and Southwest. I have often had the pleasure of seeing my promotions for the *original* Bay State Democrat and the Nashville Union, represented to the People of this country through the Richmond Enquirer. I have never offended any portion of the democratic press, have uniformly supported the republican party, and have a good many fast and influential democratic friends at the Northeast, West and Southwest.

No man has a higher opinion of Mr. Ritchie than myself. If associated with him, to his longer experience and superior judgment I should always defer. I feel that it is not egotism in me to say that having had nearly fifteen years experience in the detail of editorial management, I could as *junior* editor render as much service to him, to the press, to the party, and to the administration, as almost any other person. How far I might be able to render you personal service, you are of course the better judge.

You know how very unpleasant it would be to make a retrograde movement voluntarily, and therefore can appreciate my disinclination to be a fiscal partner *merely*. I am very desirous of a business position where I can be mending my fortune; and if at the same time I can advance a step by an editorial association with the Nestor of the American press, I shall be the better satisfied.

If it should be your pleasure to place me in the position intended for Maj. Donelson, and it becomes necessary to make the new arrangement forthwith, Mr. Ritchie will be perfectly at liberty to use my name wherever he uses his own, and proceed in all things as though I were present and giving assent.

If you think well enough of this proposition to consult my friends Bancroft, Johnson &c, and to have it suggested to Mr. Ritchie in a proper manner, assuring him that I am capable of making myself useful and agreeable to him in the proposed connexion, I shall feel very grateful.

I had hoped ere this to have received a letter from you. If you have not yet written, I pray you give me a line when it is perfectly convenient. Especially let me hear what you think of this proposition.

Please remember me to the members of your family & believe me ....

J. GEO. HARRIS

[P.S.] Gen Jackson is yet in very feeble health, and cannot last long. He is very much gratified to learn that Blair retires from the Globe cheerfully, and gives his full consent to the transfer.[1]

ALS. DLC–JKP. Addressed to Washington City and marked *"Private."* Polk's AE on the cover states that he received this letter on April 17, 1845.

1. Harris wrote his postscript in the right margin of the final page of his letter.

## FROM ALEXANDER JONES

Dear Sir                                                    New York April 9h 1845

You will perceive the success of the Democratic charter nominations has been most triumphant. We have carried our mayor by a large vote and the Aldermen in every ward of the city but two![1] Some days before the election it became evident that the result would prove as it has turned out. We have, however, rather exceeded our own expectations. We have carried more wards than we expected, and run in *Havenmeyer*[2] by a heavier vote than we had reason to suppose.

To the *"native party,"* this election has proved a perfect "waterloo defeat." They have been routed "horse foot and dragoons." *They have not elected a solitary member of the common council.* This defeat will probably terminate the existence of this party in the United States. Here, it had its rise, progress, & temporary success, and here it has been most signally defeated and overthrown.

Some of our friends think our success has been almost too good, that coming in so very strong may beget indifference among our city representatives with regard to necessary reforms, and the energetic administration of city affairs. Large majorities are also calculated to engender divisions.

Our new mayor is a native of the city, of German extraction, and much respected by men of all parties. He is a man of long established and sound Democratic principles. He is also a man of large property, and deeply interested in the proper Government, and prosperity of New York.

Some anxiety prevails here, with respect to Mexican news, which is now daily looked for. Under the apprehension that it may prove unfavourable to peace, state securities are very heavy on change; many sober and reflecting men, however, think we have nothing to fear from that quarter.

ALEXR. JONES

ALS. DLC–JKP. Addressed to Washington City.

1. In the New York City municipal elections of April 8, 1845, Democratic candidates won fifteen of the city's seventeen wards. Democratic mayoral candidate William F. Havemeyer secured a majority of nearly 7,000 votes over his Whig and Native American opponents.

2. A native of New York City, William F. Havemeyer served as a Democratic presidential elector in 1844 and won election to three terms as New York City mayor, 1845, 1848, & 1872.

## FROM JAMES HAMILTON, JR.

My Dear Sir,                                         Charleston April 10th 1845

As I am recently from Texas and I believe as well acquainted with the public sentiment of that Country in relation to the question of annexation as most persons in the U.S. I am very desirous of making to you a suggestion or two which I think might have a very favorable influence on the decision of Texas on this highly important subject. I could convey them to you in this Letter but anticipating visiting Washington between the 15th & 20th of this Month on my way to New York I will reserve my communication for the pleasure of a personal interview.

In the mean time My Dear Sir be assured of my best wishes for the success of your administration and of the high personal esteem ....

J. HAMILTON

ALS. DLC–JKP. Addressed to Washington City and marked *"Private & Confidential."*

## FROM JOHN N. MARS[1]

Honerable Sir                                   Salem, Mass. April the 10th 1845

In looking over your Inaugural Address I find it contains two or three Sentences that I must confess that I do not understand and as I am a lover of truth and a seeker after the same, I take this humble method to just inquire of your honour for a short explanation, on those two or three points or Sentences. And the first is, You Say, All distinction of Birth or rank have Been Abolished. Now, Dear, Sir, I was not aware of that fact—if a fact it is. I would to God it was so. And if it is so I have thus far of my life bin kept in the dark. Do Sir give me light on this greate Subject. Did you mispeake, or did you speake what you ment? This is a point of greate Interest here in this region of Cuntry. The Second is, you say, that All Citizens whether native or adopted, are placed upon terms of precise Equlity. Now Sir as a candid man Bound to the Bar of God I ask is this so? You Sir will confer a greate favour on me if you will just explain this point also. The third is, you Say that, All are intitled to Equal rights and Equal protection.[2] Sir is this a fact? If so, why Sir will you not proove it By letting my Brother and my Sister come out of your own prison house of Bondage to injoy the rights that God has given them? And this is done, then and not untill then, can I believe that you ment what you there asserted. Now Sir, I ask for an explenation on those points. Justice demands it, truth demands it. And if you will please give it to me, I will be much Obliege to your honour. I have not maid these inquires out of any impure motive, you Sir may Be ashured for I hate Slavery as bad as I do the *Devil*, and mean By the help of God to live and die a bold advocate of Equal rights to all ranks and Conditions and Colours. Pleas to answer this and Oblige a friend. I remain yours for God and Equal rights.

J. N. MARS

ALS. Polk Memorial Association, Columbia. Addressed to Washington City.

1. A Methodist clergyman, John N. Mars joined the New York Conference of African Methodist Episcopal Zion Church in 1829 and served various communities in New York and New Jersey. In the 1840's he removed to Salem, Mass., where he assisted a white minister. In 1850 he received an appointment from the African Methodist Episcopal Zion Church to serve in Springfield, Mass. An advocate of resistance to the fugitive slave laws, Mars attended the New England Colored Citizens Convention of 1859 and urged blacks to settle in the West. During the Civil War he received a chaplain's commission in the Union army's regiment of North Carolina Colored Volunteers.

2. In his inaugural address Polk devotes a long paragraph to a discussion of "the inestimable value of our Federal Union." Near the end of the paragraph, he states: "All distinctions of birth or of rank have been abolished. All citizens, whether native or adopted, are placed upon terms of precise equality. All are entitled to equal rights and equal protection." See Richardson, ed., *A Compilation of the Messages and Papers of the Presidents*, IV, p. 376.

## TO JAMES BUCHANAN

Sir                                      Washington City, April 11th 1845

In executing the laws there is no duty which appears to me more imperative, than to take care that officers who receive the public money shall promptly and fully perform the duties for which the law appropriates their respective salaries. Justice to the public and a proper regard for the clearly expressed will of Congress require that this shall be done. Those who come to the seat of Government on public business should not be unnecessarily delayed by the negligence or inattention of Heads of Bureaus or clerks connected with the Executive Departments. I therefore invite your attention to the thirteenth section of the Act of Congress approved on the 26th of August 1842, entitled "An act legalizing and making appropriations for such necessary objects as have been usually included in the general appropriation bills, without authority of law, and to fix and provide for certain incidental expenses of the Departments and officers of Government, and for other purposes"; and to the 12th section of the "Act to reorganize the General Land Office," approved on the 4th of July 1836.[1]

I desire that you will cause the monthly reports required by the Act of 1842 to be regularly made, and that you will transmit them to me.

The law contemplates that the distribution of labor amongst the clerks shall bear a fair proportion to their compensation, and it is unjust that the meritorious and faithful should have to perform the duties of such as may be found to be negligent, idle, or incompetent. To prevent this injustice, it is essential that each clerk shall attend regularly in his office, and discharge his own appropriate duties. It is desired that each head of a Bureau shall cause to be kept a daily statement, showing the absence of each clerk from his duty, during office hours, the causes of each absence as far as he may be able to ascertain them, and that this statement accompany the monthly reports.

I also desire that you will accompany the monthly reports with a statement of any complaints which may be made to you of any clerk in your office, who may have contracted debts since his appointment and does not pay them agreeable to his contract. Disclaiming any right to interfere with the private affairs of officers of Government, I am yet unwilling that they shall be embarrassed in the performance of their public duties, by the just importunities of disappointed creditors, who trusted them on the faith of their compensation from the Treasury.[2]

Believing that the duties required of the officers and clerks employed in the several Executive Departments are by no means unreasonable, and impressed with the importance of a prompt and efficient despatch of the public business, I desire that you will take measures for the due execution of the laws, to which I have called your attention.

JAMES K. POLK

LS. DNA–RG 59. Addressed to Washington City. On the cover of his draft of this letter, dated April 11, 1845, Polk wrote the following notation: "Copy of a letter addressed by the President to the Secretaries of *State, Treasury, War,*

*Navy*, and the P.M. Genl. relating to the faithful execution of the laws, by the heads of Bureau & clerks in their respective Departments. J.K.P." ALS, draft. DLC–JKP.

1. Section 12 of "An Act to reorganize the General Land Office" states that the "Departments of Treasury, War, Navy, State, and General Post Office, shall be open for the transaction of the public business at least eight hours each and every day, except Sundays and the twenty-fifth of December; and from the first day of April, until the first day of October, in each year, all the aforesaid offices and bureaus shall be kept open for the transaction of the public business at least ten hours in each and every day, except Sundays and the fourth day of July."

2. At this place in his draft Polk started a new paragraph and then canceled the following phrase: "Intending to devote my whole time to the dispatch of my public duty." DLC–JKP.

## FROM HENRY HORN

My Dear Sir                                    Philadelphia 11th April 1845

Although I endeavoured to keep my visit to Washington a secret I found on my return home that it had become extensively known. And many of my friends called upon me immediately after my arrival expressing great anxiety to know the result of my mission. I of course communicated but little except that I had reason to believe that great influence from our state authorities and others connected with them had been brought to bear in favour of the appointment of a collector of our port from the country.[1] This information produced much excitement. They denounced the influences of a most malign character calculated to blight and blast everything within its reach, declared that the twenty thousand democrats within this city and county would not tamely submit to it, and expressed a determination to make a demonstration against it. I however discouraged any such action as premature, assuring them that the President could not be deceived by any such false lights as his secret enemies at Harrisburg might thow up to mislead him, and that no unhallowed connection between the state and general government would be formed by which the rights of the democracy of this county which gives tone to the whole state would be bartered away to subserve the views and promote the sinister ends of a miserable faction at Harrisburg. I have in a spirit of friendship deemed it my duty to make you this communication.

Please present my sincere respects to your amiable lady ....

HENRY HORN

ALS. DLC–JKP. Addressed to Washington City.

1. Horn probably refers to the efforts of Francis Shunk and his inner circle to secure the appointment of Henry Welsh as collector.

## FROM ANDREW JACKSON

My dear Sir,                                    Hermitage April 11th 1845

My disease has assumed an alarming type of dropsy; how soon this, with my other combined afflictions, may take me off, that all wise god who holds us all in the hollow of his hands only knows. I am ready to submit to his will with calm resignation.

I am in the receipt of Mr. Blairs letter of the 1st instant in which he says, "I have handed over to the president the Globe that he may place it in such hands as he chooses." This imposes great responsibility upon you and, as perhaps, this is last tribute of friendship I can bestow, I from this principle alone venture to suggest a few things to you. Let the Globe fall into none but perfect solvant hands, and those who will alone look to the success of your administration & the carrying out of those great principles set forth in your inagural. Let none be proprietors that might secretly & elicitly turn it to the advantage of any political clique who will be seeking to promote some friend to the succession. There will be not few of these. I have, & do still regret that this, what I view not only a useless but ill timed & dangerous to the union of the great democratic party, and this, altho, I hope for the better, without great prudence and circumspection in you, in the arrangement injury will be, I fear, the result. Why, as you were entering on your administration with such unanimity & pleasure to all the democracy why not let things alone, at least for a while. If you, with Blair & the Globe had found it necessary to make a change you could then have done it as I did with Duff Green.[1] But my dear friend this movement was hasty, and as I think badly advised and I pray my god that it may not result in injury to the perfect unity of the democracy. You will I fear find great heartburnings in many places. But the thing is done, and you must act with great decision with your Cabinet to prevent evil growing out of it.

I regret that Major Lewis has been dismissed from office, but I regret more the manner than the thing. The Major writes that his successor[2] was appointed on the 31st of March to take possession of his office the next day & at 9 oclock p.m. of the 31st March he had not been informed, officially, of his dismissal. I regret to see it stated in the Madisonian, that you consulted me upon this removal and that I was agreed to it. This my dear friend, have contradicted, as the first intimation I had of your intention to remove him was thro your confidential letter to Genl Armstrong laid before me the 4th instant,[3] & in mine to you of the 4th I referred to it.[4]

But I must close. All the inmates of the Hermitage join in good wishes to you & Mrs. Polk and prayers for your successful administration ....

ANDREW JACKSON

P.S. I see it stated in the N. Union that Mr. Richie & Mr. Hise[5] are to be the Editors of the Globe & the administration organ. The first is experienced and talented, the second I fear not competent to the task, & may become a supporter of some looking up to the succession. *Keep on him a steady eye.*

ALS. DLC–JKP. Addressed to Washington City and marked "*Confidential.*" Published in Bassett, ed., *Correspondence of Andrew Jackson*, VI, pp. 399–400.
1. See Polk to Andrew Jackson, March 17, 1845.
2. John M. McCalla.
3. Polk's letter to Robert Armstrong has not been found.
4. Jackson's letter to Polk has not been found.
5. Thomas Ritchie and John P. Heiss. Jackson's reference is to a story in the *Nashville Union* of April 10, 1845, which reports that Ritchie and Heiss would serve as editors of the Washington *Globe*.

## FROM JOHN Y. MASON

Attorney Generals Office
Sir                                                                 11th April 1845
I have had the honor to receive your communication of the 10th Instant,[1] requesting my opinion, whether there be any authority of law to make payment of Twenty seven Hundred and thirty seven Dollars and eight cents, to meet the expenses of recasting cannon &c, as a present to the Imaum of Muscat[2] and if there be such an authority, from what fund appropriated by Congress, can the payment be made?

The papers accompanying your letter shew that the present has been made in return for one made by the Imaum to the President of the United States.

In the intercourse of our Government with the semi-barbarous Nations of Asia and Africa, it seems to have been the practice from the earliest period of our history to interchange presents. And it has been a question for the President in his discretion to decide how far the public interests would be injuriously affected by declining to receive the presents offered, and to make others in return. While the Constitution denies to him the right to appropriate them to his own use it has been deemed important not to decline them, and they have been deposited in the public offices or sold by order of Congress, without any disapprobation of the Executive conduct in receiving them.[3] Annual appropriations have been made without change of terms, for the Contingent Expenses of Foreign Intercourse. The objects of expenditure under this Head of Appropriation have never been enumerated or defined in the Act appropriating or in the Estimates from the Department. The Contingent Expenses of Foreign Missions have not been chargeable on these appropriations, but on others specifically made in the same Act for that object. With the Imaum of Muscat an interchange of presents was made in 1834, and in 1840. The presents received by the President were in each case disposed of agreeably, to a Resolution of Congress,[4] and those sent to the Imaum in return, were purchased under the direction of the State Department and charged to the Appropriation for Contingent Expenses of Foreign intercourse.

The President is charged with the conduct of our Foreign Relations. To enable him to perform this duty this appropriation is placed at his disposal. If in its performance he shall be of opinion that the public interests will be promoted by returning a present, which he has deemed it proper not to decline, I am of opinion that he has the power to make such present, and to defray the expense, resort may be had to the Appropriation for Contingent Expenses of Foreign Intercourse. He cannot exceed the amount so appropriated, but within that Amt. his power is full.

If I had doubts on the subject the uniform practice of the Executive and the continued annual appropriations by Congress, with a knowledge of the objects of expenditure to which they have been applied without disapprobation or modification would have great influence in removing them.

The papers transmitted with your letter are returned.

J. Y. MASON

LS. DLC–JKP. Addressed locally.

1. Polk's letter has not been found.

2. Said bin Sultan reigned as Imam of Muscat and Oman from 1804 until 1856.

3. Reference is to a clause in Article I, Section 9 of the U.S. Constitution, which stipulates that "no Person holding any Office of Profit or Trust under them, shall, without the Consent of the Congress, accept of any present, Emolument, Office, or Title, of any kind whatever, from any King, Prince, or foreign State."

4. Joint Resolution No. 13, signed by Andrew Jackson on February 13, 1835, provided for the disposition by the president of a lion and two horses received by the consul of the United States at Tangier, from the Emperor of Morocco. U.S. House, *Journal*, 23rd Congress, 2nd Session, p. 367. Joint Resolution No. 16, signed by Martin Van Buren on July 20, 1840, provided for the disposition by the president "in such time and manner as he shall see fit, of all such of the

presents to the Government of the United States as have been sent from the Imaum of Muscat, or the Emperor of Morocco, and cannot conveniently be deposited or kept in the Department of State and cause the proceeds thereof to be placed in the Treasury of the United States. U.S. House, *Journal*, 26th Congress, 1st Session, p. 1246. The Imam's gifts included two Arabian horses, a box of pearls, a bale of Persian rugs, and sundry other articles of considerable value.

## FROM HERSCHEL V. JOHNSON[1]

My Dear Sir: Milledgeville April 12th 1845

The intelligence has just reached me through the public prints of the appointment of my brotherinlaw James Polk naval officer for the port at Baltimore.[2] And though I have not the vanity to suppose that my expressed wish availed a feather's weight with you in the selection, yet I will not forego the satisfaction of expressing my unfeigned gratitude for the bestowal. Knowing him to be needy & with all, no drone, no mere sucker at the "public tite," I could but feel from my relationship to him the deepest interest in his successful application.

Next to him, I believe I feel most concern for Mr. Josiah F. Polk of Washington.[3] I think from my acquaintance with him, that he is among the most amiable, unassuming, intelligent & pure men, I have ever known. And what is most admirable, he is devoted to his three maiden sisters[4] & thinks no sacrifice too great to promote their happiness & support. He has been a long time in office, & I think without even a suspicion against him, uttered by the foul tongue of slander. But you know him better than I, and doubtless join me in believing that what I have said is scarcely a compliment. I know not what may be your peculiar views in reference to extending too much favour to those of your own name. To my mind there is really no impropriety in it, though it may excite the sneers and jeers of the Whigs. But they would find fault with a celestial being if one should be permitted to preside over the affairs of this "great people." If however it should consist with the public interest & your sense of justice, I know nothing that would gratify me more, than to see our friend & kinsman, Josiah, elevated. He has long been a faithful subaltern; I presume he would feel flattered at promotion. I make these remarks with an eye to the Commission of the Bureau of Indian affairs. I am not advised that he is an applicant, but I think his qualifications for that office are of a high order. If he should desire it, I feel confident that he would render most valuable service to the government.

I hope you will pardon the liberty I take in addressing you so freely on matters in which it may be impertinent for me to say a word. While expressing my thanks for your kindness to my brother-in-law, I thought I would not give offence, if I should indicate my concern for Josiah, who I know is indispensible to the support of his three sisters.

In this state so far as I learn the Democracy are pleased with the opening of your administration, and the Whigs are stricken almost with silence, because they can find so little to condemn. Their effort South, will be to embitter and array, if possible, the friends of Mr. Calhoun against the administration. This is their principle hope. On the subject of Texas they are in "a stew." They are afraid to denounce Mr. Stephens, [5] (for that would indicate hostility to annexation which they are anxious to conceal) & yet they hate him as a viper. In proof of it, You do not hear a syllable of condemnation against Mr. Berrien. [6] Things are working finely in Georgia. The Democracy are zealous & united if nothing unfortunate arises we shall carry the state triumphantly next October. [7]

Mrs. J. [8] begs to be remembered to yourself & lady. With great esteem & friendship . . . .

H. V. JOHNSON

ALS. DLC–JKP. Addressed to Washington City and marked "Private."

1. A Milledgeville, Ga., lawyer and 1844 Democratic presidential elector, Johnson served as U.S. senator, 1848–49; as judge of the Superior Court of Georgia, 1849–53; as governor of Georgia for two terms, 1853–57; and as senator in the Confederate Congress, 1863–65. In 1860 he ran unsuccessfully for vice-president on the Democratic ticket with Stephen A. Douglas.

2. James Polk received an appointment as naval officer for Baltimore, Md., in 1845.

3. Proprietor of the Washington City boarding house, "Polk House," Josiah F. Polk served as chief clerk in the office of the Second Auditor of the Treasury.

4. Not identified further.

5. Alexander H. Stephens, an attorney from Crawfordville, Ga., served both in the Georgia House, 1836–41, and in the Georgia Senate, 1842; from 1843 until 1859 he held a seat in the U.S. House, initially as a Whig and later as a Democrat. During the Civil War, he served as vice-president of the Confederate States of America. He was elected to the U.S. House in 1866, but was denied his seat. In 1872 he returned to the U.S. House and served in that body until 1882, when he was elected governor. Stephens served in that post but a few months prior to his death in 1883.

6. A Savannah lawyer and judge of the Eastern Judicial Circuit of Georgia, 1810–21, John M. Berrien served in the U.S. Senate as a Democrat, 1825–29, and then as a Whig, 1841–52. He also held the post of attorney general in Andrew Jackson's cabinet, 1829–31. An opponent of the resolution annexing Texas, Berrien declared in the U.S. Senate that the measure constituted "an open, palpable violation of the Constitution."

7. Johnson's reference is to the gubernatorial election of October 1845.

8. Ann Polk Johnson, born in 1809 in Somerset County, Md., married Johnson in 1833; she was the daughter of William Polk, who served as a judge on the Maryland Court of Appeals from 1806 until 1812. The kinship ties among the Tennessee, Maryland, and District of Columbia Polks have not been further identified.

## FROM DANIEL BROWN[1]

Sir                                                    Newport April 14th AD 1845

There is very strong solicitude in the minds of the democratic party in this district respecting the appointment of Collector for this Port. The Present incumbent Mr. Ennis[2] has put himself at the head of about twenty men in this Town who stile themselves abbolitionest, whose pockets are always filled with a paper known by the name of Emancipator[3] whose collumns is always filled with slander against the best men that ever lived only because they happened to be born in a slave state. These men are a travvelling all over the state circulating the most infamous slanders against the friends of your administration. Among the many there is one that when the Honble. Dutee J. Pearce visited Washington that you would not suffer him in your presence and that any paper bearing his signature cannot receive any favourable consideration at your hands. Genl. Wilbour[4] was recommended by a large Majority of the democratic party of this district and they desire his appointment and they believe it would give general satisfaction to all parties except the abbolition clique. And if Mr. Pearce is not popular with you, you will not suffer that to Prejudice your mind against Genl. Wilbour. I hope and trust that the stories they circulate are not true for Mr. Pearce addressed meetings in your favour previous to your election in this state Massachusetts Connecticut and Maine and we sincerely believe that he is the most usefull and tallented man belonging to the democratic party in RI, and his friends here are entirely at a loss to conjecture how any conduct of his should have met your displeasure and men who did all they could against you retain your confidence to the exclusion of your friends. His friends here consider his claims for an appointment to be greater than any man in the south part of the state or the north part. There has been no man with the exception of Govr. Dorr that suffered half so much as Mr. Pearce. If [it] had not been for Mr. Pearce the democratic Party would have been entirely Broken down. When Govr. Dorr left the state the burden fell on Mr. Pearce. I hope that if your mind has come to an unfavourable conclusion as to the appointment of Genl. Wilbour you will give the appointment to Mr. Pearce who I have no doubt will accept the appointment rather than our custom house should be the rendevous for abbolitionests and abbolition meetings. Mr. Pearce has refused for several years Past to be a candidate for any office but I have no doubt if you will respect the feelings and wishes of his friends so much as to appoint him he will accept it merely if for nothing else to keep out of the Custom house Abby Kelly and her particular friends[5] and save the democrats of this district from deep disgrace which will follow the continuance in office of Ennis and the appointment of his gang. One word as to myself. I was the first man in RI that was indicted for treason against the state in company with Govr. Dorr and Mr. Pearce. I was under Indictment three years. I have suffered every thing rather than give my democratic doctrine. I want no office at your hands but I do most earnnestly but respectfully solicit your aid in removing from office these men who has so sorely persecuted us and opposed your election.

DANIEL BROWN

ALS. DLC–JKP. Addressed to Washington City.

1. Brown represented Newport in the People's General Assembly in 1842. Arrested under a warrant from the charter government for treason on May 4, he gained his release on a five-thousand-dollar bond. Brown, Dutee J. Pearce and three others signed an address that denounced the military activities of both the Dorr supporters and the charter government and that supported a call for a new constitutional convention. A Newport County grand jury returned an indictment for high treason against Brown on August 25, but the case did not go to trial. Brown later served four years as an inspector in the Newport Customs House, 1853–57.

2. William Ennis, a Tyler appointee, served from June 1844 until his removal in December 1845.

3. Brown probably refers to the Boston *Emancipator and Republican*, edited by Joshua Leavitt.

4. A Newport banker, Edwin Wilbur was nominated for the collectorship in 1844, but was rejected by the Senate; Polk appointed him to that position in 1845.

5. A Massachusetts Quaker and teacher, Abigail Kelley began lecturing in the abolitionist cause in 1837 and served on the executive committee of the American Anti-Slavery Society in 1840. She married Stephen S. Foster on December 31, 1845.

## FROM JOHN N. ESSELMAN[1]

Dear Sir,                                                    Nashville 14 Apl, 1845

I reached home on the 9 Inst. and imidiately called to see Genl. Armstrong, and learned that all was right respecting the sanction of General Jackson relative to the sale of the Globe. However Genl. Armstrong & myself visited Genl. Jackson last evening, and found him quite indisposed. He has become dropsecal or Anasarcous which is confined to the extremities. He thinks himself near his disolution; however it is my opinion he will live some time. I prescribed for him and Andrew Jackson [2] was in town to day and says he is very much better this morning; though the General was very feeble he talked freely respecting politics, and especially on the subject of the change in the government organ. He said he had readily given his consent to the sale of the Globe, but did not appear to be aware of the necessity for a change. I endeavoured to explain to him the reasons why it had become actually necessary that there should be a change in the government organ. He agreed if these reasons I advanced did actually exist, that it was all right & proper that there should be a change. He said he indorsed your political principals to the democracy of the country from Maine to Louisiana, and had nothing to fear in so doing and had the fullest confidence that all would be well, but requested me to say to you, to be careful who you let have an interest in the new paper, as fifty thousand dollars was quite a large sum of money to be responsible for. He stated he had received a letter from Mr. Blair, saying that he had handed the Globe over to *You* on the 1st Inst. I learn from Andrew Jackson Jr. that W. B. Lewis is constantly writing to the Genl. and most likely does not present things in their most favourable aspect, since his *decapitation*; he did not mention Lewis during our stay, but I learn from Andrew that Lewis complained most bitterly to the General respecting his dismisial, and most probable will pry into every act of your administration & give the worst colouring he can to every thing. The canvass for Governor is fairly opened. The candidates met at Clarksville on the 7th inst. where I learn Brown bested Foster.[3] Well, there is but little excitement here as yet; nor do I think there will be; however the Whiggs will endevor to git up one as it is their only chance of success. Maj. Graham has moved to his place in the country. He was in my office this morning. I explained to him the reasons why he was not called to Washington. They appeared to be entirely satisfactory. He is much pleased with his new home, draped in homespun, saddlebags on arm, looked quite rustic as well as democratic. You will please remember me to your family & accept for yourself my best wishes for your health & prosperity.

JNO. N. ESSELMAN

P.S. If you should find a leisure moment that you can devote to small maters, I shall be much gratifyed to have the honour to receive a letter from you. E.

ALS. DLC–JKP. Addressed to Washington City.
1. A well-known Nashville physician, Esselman was married to Anne Campbell, sister of George W. Campbell.

2. Andrew Jackson, Jr.

3. See Robert Armstrong to Polk, April 7, 1845.


## FROM ROBERT H. MORRIS[1]

71 Cedar Street

My Dear Sir.                               New York April 14th 1845

You have seen the result of our city election.[2] One effect of this change in our city government will be a thorough change in all the subordinate officers of the City government. This will bring out *Thousands* of applicants from among the Democratic masses. Thousands must be disappointed because there are not places for them.

If you intend making removals in any or all of the Government officers of this city, then I suggest it should be done before the city government go into operation, that the officers you may appoint may make the selection of their subordinants before the immense number of applicants to the city Government, who must be disappointed, can be turned off to the United States officers for appointments. Notwithstanding the immense pressure for office which I saw upon your Excellency when I was in Washington, still I can assure you you can have no conception of the rush and importuning for office in this city, where the applicants all live, and where they can all see the appointing power in the same line, unless the crowd should be so great, which it frequently is, as to prevent access to the individual sought. This picture strong as it is, I can assure you, does not exceed the reality. I have experienced it, when mayor, frequently. The conviction that great trouble, vexation and disappointment will be saved by the course I have suggested is my excuse for thus obtruding upon your notice.

There is also another reason why the Post Master[3] should be speedily removed. After July next, the post office as regards its compensation to the incumbent will be an experiment. Then the new Bill goes into operation[4] and it is very questionable wither the increase of matter forwarded through the mails will be sufficent to make up the decrease of the postage so that the percentage will pay the expenses and the salary of the Post Master. If so, then the recpts between this and July would be very important to whoever may receive the appointment. It would give him something to live on until the meeting of Congress.

Confident that you will truly appreciate the motives that induce me to make this communication ....

ROBT. H. MORRIS

ALS. DLC–JKP. Addressed to Washington City and marked "Private & Confidential."

1. Morris, a lawyer and Democrat, served three terms as mayor of New York City, 1841–44; Polk appointed him postmaster in December 1845.

2. See Alexander Jones to Polk, April 9, 1845.

3. John L. Graham, a lawyer, held the office of postmaster of New York City from 1842 to 1845 and served as one of John Tyler's chief patronage dispensers in that city.

4. By Act of March 3, 1845, Congress approved postal reform measures effective July 1, 1845; the new regulations lowered postage rates on letters, eliminated postage on newspapers mailed within thirty miles of the place of publication, and outlawed private express mail services.

## FROM FRANKLIN H. ELMORE

My Dear Sir                               Charleston April 15. 1845

A temporary absence from the City at the time of the arrival of your letter of the 8th inst (postmarked on the 10th) prevented my receiving it as early as it reached here. I was not altogather unprepared for its contents, as from friends & the public press I had received some intimations of the probability of such an event. I had therefore to some degree taken the matter into consideration. But still I felt it due to the great importance of the subject, both as it bore upon the interests of the Country & also to myself & family, & most especially as due to you My Dear Sir for the very kind & complimentary manner in which you have tendered to me this distinguished mark of your confidence & friendship that I should again deliberate & review the whole subject. I have therefore taken some days to do so, and after the most careful consideration, controlled by a sincere wish to conform to your desire, I feel compelled to forego the acceptance of the appointment. I am free My Dear Sir to say that in doing so I do it with unfeigned reluctance. That no Mission & no Station in the Government has in itself so much to attract me & that my course is dictated purely by a stern necessity which I cannot control. It grows out of the situation of my private affairs which would render as early an absence impossible & one as protracted as this promises to be, utterly ruinous. I feel it due my Dear Sir to your kindness & friendship that I should speak freely & without disguise on this point, that you may be not for a moment, under misconceptions. My situation is the result of circumstances produced mainly by others; & I have, without any thing to charge myself with except too much confidence, to shoulder business & obligations on which hang the fortunes of my own family, of the family of an Elder Brother who educated me & was as a Father,[1] & of other friends who are very dear to me. To these duties I sacrifice all personal ambition, & nothing short of some great national good, which none other could do as well, would justify me to myself, for abandoning the prospects now seeming to open themselves to me for redeeming our lost fortunes. I have not the vanity to suppose that there are not many of your friends who will not be able to do this service with at least equal ability & fidelity. The public service can therefore receive no detriment from my declining.

Allow me now my Dear Sir to express the deep sense I shall ever entertain for this distinguished mark of your regard & friendship as a man and of the confidence & trust it implies as the Head of this great People. I fully appreciate the distinction & in foregoing its fruition, I shall retain as lively & abiding a sense of your kindness as I could have done had the honor & all its enjoyment been accepted.

With my warmest wishes for yourself personally & for the honor of your Administration & the welfare of our Country under your guidance, by the promotion of which alone will the former be secured....

           F. H. ELMORE

ALS. DLC–JKP. Addressed to Washington City. Polk's AE states that he received Elmore's declination of the mission to England on April 18, 1845.

1. A graduate of South Carolina College, Benjamin T. Elmore commanded a company in both the War of 1812 and the Seminole War of 1836; served two terms as state comptroller-general, 1823–26; and ran unsuccessfully for governor in 1838. He died in 1840.

## FROM AUSTIN MILLER

[Sir]            Jackson Ten April 15th 1845

I am here attending the Supreme Court. Messrs. Brown & Foster addressed the people here on yesterday[1] and left here to day, tomorrow they speak at Trenton. Brown evidently got the advantage here. Foster spoke first. The time they have agreed upon to speak is an hour & a half, and a half hour in reply. Foster led off by eulogizing the principls of the great Whig party told of his devotion, his willingness to die for their principls. He was a Captain that had fought a hundred battles for the party and was all over covered with scares. Consumed about a third of his time in this Kind of general rant, with out producing any applase, from his Whig friends which he was evidently trying to ellicit. He spoke of the United States Bank as one of their great principls, of the Tariff, and distribution, and defended [h]is course on the Texas question.[2] He succeeded towards the latter part of his speech to get some of his friends to take the hint and shout, but it was more for affect than from feeling. He agreed to occupy his time for reply while up and spoke about t[w]o hours and set down nearly exhausted.

Upon the whole he made but an indifferent speech not such a one as we expected. Still he made a good many heavy licks, and a speech that I thought somewhat dificult to answer, and felt fears that Brown would not be able to meet him at every point. But in this I and all our friends was most agreeably disappointed. There is no man in the state so will calculated to answer him. He lashed him from the word go, and done it in an easy a gentlemanly manner. He was often times applauded and every democrats countenance looked bright. The Whigs admitted that Foster had met with his match. I am informed that Brown has gotten the advantage of him in every contest they have had. At least all the Democrats that have heard them whom I have seen say so and the Whigs do not claim the victory. It is the opinion of the Democrats here that Browns majority will be from 5 to 10 thousand, and as from what appeard yesterday it would seem to be a reasonable calculation. Still I think it by no means certain. Foster has a great many personal friends. There is a good many officers and candidates whose political success depend upon the success of their party and Foster by runing for governor will so identify himself with the party that his success is the parties success. The Whigs who were or at least pretended to be violently opposed to the annexation of Texas, are now beginning to excuse Mr Foster for his course on that question. They say that the Majority of the American people had decided in your election in favour of annexation. That the Whigs of Tennessee never oppose the will of the majority, that annexation had to come and they prefer the manner adopted by Foster & Milton Brown[3] to that of the Democrats, that it was right for them to try to have it done in the manner most acceptable to their party, and are trying to make an issue between Browns resolution & Walkers amendment[4] rather than put Mr Foster on a defence of his course. And when we consider how easy it was for them to change last spring against Texas after Mr Clays letter[5] came out we can not expect them to have much scruples of concience upon this matter. They can be for, against, half for & half against or any way that may suit best to hold their party together. For my part I predicate my hopes of success more from the zeal and uninimity of the Democrats than from the disaffection of the Whigs to Mr Foster.

Mr Ash[6] is no longer a candidate for Congress. He has declined and The Revd. P. T. Scruggs[7] has announced himself in his place. I will not have any opposition in Hardeman. Candidates for senator & f[l]oater in our district are not out. The Whigs have no candidate for senator as yet. Col Kyle of Jackson & Mr Harris former Senator both Whigs are candidates in the districts composed of Madison Haywood &c for the Senate.[8] I hear of no dificulty about candidates on the democratic side in the W District except in Weakly. I am informed there are four or five out but it is thought here that matters can be settled. We have had a cool and dry spring until a few days past; it is now warm and some light showers quite favorable for cotton. The small grain looks well and farmers are very forward in their preperation for their crops.

AUSTIN MILLER

ALS. DLC–JKP. Addressed to Washington City.
1. The gubernatorial debate at Jackson on April 14th featured Aaron V. Brown and Ephraim H. Foster.
2. See James H. Thompson to Polk, March 20, 1845.
3. See Cave Johnson to Polk, January 13, 1845.
4. Miller's reference is to Milton Brown's Texas resolutions and Robert J. Walker's compromise bill.
5. Henry Clay's Raleigh letter appeared in the Washington *National Intelligencer* of April 27, 1844, and set forth a series of arguments opposing the annexation of Texas.
6. John B. Ashe.
7. A former Methodist Episcopal clergyman, Phineas T. Scruggs practiced law in the Western District, first in Fayette County and later in Shelby County.
8. Gayle H. Kyle and John W. Harris. A Tipton County lawyer, Harris represented Haywood, Lauderdale, Madison, and Tipton counties in the Tennessee Senate from 1843 until 1847. Kyle, a Madison County farmer and merchant, sat for the same district from 1847 until 1851.

## FROM JOHN NORVELL[1]

Detroit, Mich. April 15, 1845

Seeking to secure the post of U.S. district attorney for Michigan, Norvell challenges Lewis Cass' opposition to his appointment and defends his record as a "uniform friend to the South" and as a supporter of "right measures against sectional prejudices." He points to his involvement in every important movement in the state and notes that "General Cass is neither the state nor the democracy of Michigan, and that he was in Washington, and in Europe, when the democratic party of that state was organized." Referring to the state constitution, Norvell takes credit for its liberal extension of the franchise to immigrants and its exclusion of "blacks from the right of voting."[2] Since then he and his friends have maintained the provision excluding blacks from the franchise against "the most pertinacious efforts" of the Whigs and some Democrats. Norvell adds that while he was in the Senate, he never presented any abolitionist memorials or petitions. On the subject of Texas annexation, he claims that he led the way in mobilizing support in Michigan and points to his role as organizer of a pro-Texas meeting at Detroit in March 1844. Norvell charges that prior to this meeting Cass had opposed annexation.

ALS. DLC–JKP. Addressed to Washington City.

1. John Norvell served as postmaster at Detroit, 1831–36; as U.S. senator from Michigan, 1837–41; and as U.S. district attorney, 1846–1849.

2. In the Michigan Constitutional Convention of 1835 Norvell and his political associates supported franchise provisions requiring but two years residency in the country and six months residency in the state; he and his friends led the opposition to black suffrage.

## FROM CORNELIUS P. VAN NESS

Dear Sir                                                          New York April 15/45

I rise from a sick bed to write you a few lines. It is currently reported here by my opponents that I am to be immediately removed from office by you, and some say that it has been done already. I was in hopes, Sir, that if any doubts existed in your mind of the propriety of continuing me in my present position, the late election in this City would have effectually removed them.[1] That election was carried by the money raised in the Custom House (and to which I contributed liberally) and by the activity and tact of Custom House officers, and especially, by that portion of them who are my personal friends.[2] This can be abundantly proved. I understand that all sorts of reports are circulated by my opponents at Washington, & that O'Sullivan, the Editor of the Morning News is very busy and boisterous, and he is backed by Mr Butler, as is reported. I will not enter into any recriminations in this letter, but I hope I shall be allowed an opportunity to remove any complaints, and to refute any charges, that may be brought against me. You will, doubtless, remember that you had the kindness to say to me at Washington that I *should* be allowed an opportunity to defend myself if any thing was alledged against me. You may rely upon it, Sir, I have been faithful to the public interest, and I have been *true to you*. It would mortify me, as well as my family & connexions, to be unceremoniously removed at this time, and by a President who has no better or truer friend in the country than I am, and than they are. But, Sir, if you *have* determined, or *should* determine, to remove me, I hope you will give me until the 1st of July, by which time I might make some preparation to go into some other business. I leave my case, Sir, in your hands, still relying upon your justice & friendship.

C. P. Van Ness

P.S. Pardon me, if you please, Sir, for adding that if you should deem it expedient to deprive me of the office I now hold, but should, at the same time, consider me worthy of some consideration, I have no hesitation in declaring that I would prefer any other honorable situation under the government, either at home or abroad; for this office has been a very laborious and vexatious one. I would prefer either of the other three offices in this City which have not been changed as yet. But, Sir, I repeat what I said in a former letter, that if you should determine that I am to be wholly turned off, I shall endeavour to bear the blow as becomes a *man*.[3]

2nd P.S. To my utter astonishment, I have just heard that my enemies are charging me at Washington with some improper conduct in regard to our City election. Now, Sir, if any charge or complaint of this character is made, I beg of you, as a matter of strict justice, that you will give me time to confound the accusers, & to show their malice & the total destitution of truth in what they say. The Custom House raised about $1000 (perhaps more, but I do not know the exact sum) and the money was delivered to a committee of 3 persons, the chairman of which, & who actually took the money, was Dr Vaché, a most respectable man, belonging to the Van Buren portion of the democracy.[4] This money was used principally in the doubtful Wards & with the utmost good effect. All this can be most clearly proved. The real truth is, the very men who make, or insinuate, this charge, actually wished the election to be lost, in order to cast the blame on me, as they did the loss of your election last fall, in order to be able to say it was because Mr Van Buren had not been renominated. I understood this perfectly, and put forth my whole strength in the election, and the result ought to justify me in the fullest manner. I court the most scrutiny on this subject, & only ask a chance to show my side of the case.

ALS. DLC–JKP. Addressed to Washington City and marked "*Private*."
1. See Alexander Jones to Polk, April 4 and 9, 1845.
2. According to copies of Van Ness' letters to Alexander F. Vaché of April 4 and 7, 1845, certified as authentic by the recipient, Van Ness contributed $50 to the Democratic candidates in the city elections; other customs house officers contributed a total of $500; and Vaché further certified that he received an additional $450 from the same sources. LS. DLC–JKP. Van Ness sent these certified copies in his letter to Polk of April 16, 1845.
3. See Van Ness to Polk, March 17, 1845.
4. A New York City physician, Alexander F. Vaché took an active part in managing Democratic party operations in the Sixth Ward.

## FROM JAMES WALKER

Dear Sir                                       Columbia, April 15, 1845
I reached home in due time, and found all well, except Jane, who was not so well as [s]he had been but is recovering from the spell.[1]

·I had a long confidential conversation with Genl Pillow since I reached home, and find that he was deeply mortified that he did not get the Consulship to Liverpool. He spoke much of the disinterested character of the services he rendered to you, and of the convsations he had had with you on this subject. I told him what General Armstrong had said to you in relation to his wish that he (Armstrong) should get the appointment. To this he replied that if Armstrong had got the appointment from Tyler he would have been perfectly satisfied, but he thought you ought to have written to him before you acted upon what Armstrong said &c. To this I replied that you had no time, that the vacancy existed, and was obliged to be filled immediately. When our convsation closed I thought he was tolerably satisfied, but not entirely so. Under all circumstances I wish you could find some position for him that would be satisfactory as he did render important services & looks pretty high, speaks of having spent $1000 in the canvass.

The Whigs here are still bitter & ferocious. As a little instance of their malice I had scarely got home before I was warranted for a little corporation tax of the present year.[2] They appeared in a special hurry, lest I might have the power to pay it without the annoyance of being warranted. Such is the contemptible character of Columbia Whiggery. They think it would never do to allow our family to feel the gratification of your elevation without imposing all the petty vexations in their power.

It is highly important to Sam & Pickett[3] that Pickett's appointment should be made as early as *it is proper*, that they may, make their business arrangements for the keeping up the New Orleans house &c.

I need not tell *you* to burn this letter.

JAMES WALKER

ALS. DLC–JKP. Addressed to Washington City.
1. Walker's reference is to his daughter, Jane Clarissa Walker Barnet, who was married to Isaac Newton Barnet.
2. Walker's reference is probably to the annual city property tax. Columbia was incorporated in 1817.
3. Samuel P. Walker and William S. Pickett.

## TO EDMUND BURKE

My Dear Sir:                                     Washington City April 16th 1845
Shortly after my arrival in Washington in February last, some of your friends in Congress, expressed to me an earnest desire, that you should be appointed *"Commissioner of Patents,"* and placed in my hands, a written paper to that effect.[1] Although you have never intimated to me, such a wish, yourself, yet I presume that what was done by your friends, was

not without your knowledge and approbation. Presuming that it will be agreeable to you, I now tender, to you the office of *"Commissioner of Patents,"* and in the event of your acceptance I have to request that you will repair to Washington at an early day, prepared to enter upon the duties of the office. *Mr Ellsworth,*[2] the present Commissioner has given notice of his intention to resign, as soon as a successor shall be appointed, and be ready to take charge of the office.

I have to request that you will give me an early answer. In the event of your acceptance, I desire you to inform me at what time you will be in Washington.

JAMES K. POLK

ALS. DLC–B/R. Addressed to Newport, N.H., and marked *"Private."*
1. Letter not found.
2. A Connecticut lawyer, farmer, and merchant, Henry L. Ellsworth won appointment in 1832 to the post of chief commissioner to the Indian tribes south and west of Arkansas; he served as commissioner of patents from 1836 until 1845.

## FROM LEVIN H. COE

Dear Sir                                      Jackson 16. Apl. [18]45
On monday Brown & Foster met at Phillippi.[1] There can be no mistake as to the result. The impression made was all for Brown. Foster has fallen much in the estimation of his Whig friends. In this end of the state all things will run smooth and we must gain. Staunton[2] to Congress & two at least to the Legislature.

I find many of our leading Democrats dissatisfied with some of your appointments and I think it will be the means of curbing their zeal in the approaching elections. Passing over such men as Mjr Turner for L. P. Cheatham, who is looked upon by many as faithless and treacherous in his business matters is complained of.[3] Also the appointment of Cargill[4] is particularly opposed as well as the fact that your appointments from this state are almost confined to Nashville & the neighbourhood. To gratify Cheatham, his creditors & securities by passing him to higher office & to give J. G. Harris an office will do us damage.

I write this in no spirit of fault finding. I care not for my part who fills the offices of the Country. I have no personal objection to Cheatham to Harris or any other person. I have no relation to be favored, no obligation of private friendship to pay, Desire no office from President or people to myself. My only care is that our old ship may avoid breakers and quicksand.

L. H. COE

ALS. DLC–JKP. Addressed to Washington City.
1. Aaron V. Brown and Ephraim H. Foster held a gubernatorial debate in Jackson on April 14. Coe's Philippi reference alludes to an incident in Polk's 1843 gubernatorial campaign. See Polk to Sarah C. Polk, April 4, 1843.
2. Frederick P. Stanton.
3. Coe refers to the Nashville postmastership. Robert B. Turner and Leonard P. Cheatham both sought the position.
4. Coe probably refers to Henry A. Cargill, who was appointed deputy collector of the New York City Customs House in 1845.

## FROM ALEXANDER JONES

Dear Sir                                        New York April 16th 1845
The Great Western arrived this morning, bringing 21 days later news. She sailed from Liverpool on the 29th ult.
The news by her in a commercial point of view is not very important. Cotton was some duller, with a shade lower prices, than those received by the Queen of the West.
You will perceive the English papers have indulged in some censure, on that part of your Inaugural Address, which relates to the Oregon question.[1] This is a matter of Small moment. You can afford to put up with what they say about you, when it is considered how severely they handle Mr Tyler's special message in reference to the Slave Trade.[2]
So far, I have not seen any contradiction in the English papers, of the charge made against the Government, of its intrigue with Santa Ana[3] for the purchase of California.
The Resolutions of Congress in favour of Annexation are much commented on by the English Press. When the news of their final passage reached London, English Consols declined from 100./2 & 100./4 to 99./4 or fully 1 per cent; but has slightly rallied again. I have not had time yet to receive the Letters I am usually in the habit of receiving by the Steamers.
Although general business in New York seems large and active, yet I am informed by some of our most respectable merchants that it is by no means so extensive as it was at the same time last year.
In polilitics, things since the late charter election,[4] have settled down into a quiet state. Much conversation prevails with regard to expected future appointments in this quarter under your administration. We have a rumour that Mr Codington, late Post Master of this city, is to supercede Gov. Vanness in the Collectorship.[5] As far as I know anything of the opinions entertained by our principal merchants of Mr Codington, they are favorable. It is believed he would make a good and efficient officer.

I have a kind of general knowledge, either personal, or indirect, of our leading or prominent men of every shade of politics in New York, and have no other interest in them, or in their appointment to office, than a desire, to see you select, (for your own satisfaction, & for the best interest and honor of the country), those most, *honest capable* and *industrious*, which, I sincerely hope you and your cabinet may succeed in doing.

After a long dusty dry spell of weather a north east wind, has set in, accompanied with rain.

It is now ascertained that probably about 40 Lives were lost bye the sad accident to the Steam boat Swallow; 13 bodies, from this number, have been recovered.

News from Mexico is daily expected to reach this city, by a vessel now due from the port of Vera Cruz which, our business men await with much anxiety.

My best respects to all the members of your family, not forgetting "My fellow citizen of North Carolina by Nativity" Master Marshall Polk.[6]

ALEX JONES

ALS. DLC–JKP. Addressed to Washington City.

1. The British press echoed the concerns expressed in both houses of Parliament over Polk's statement in his inaugural address that the United States would make good as soon as possible on its "clear and unquestionable" claims to the Oregon territory.

2. On February 20, 1845, Tyler sent a message to Congress criticizing the role of British agents alleged to have engaged in an illicit slave trade to Brazil and protesting Britain's failure to repatriate Africans discovered on captured slave vessels. The British government and press angrily denied any failure to enforce their policy on the slave trade.

3. A general in the Mexican army, Antonio López de Santa Anna often headed the central government during the period from 1833 to 1855; he commanded Mexican armies in the Texas rebellion and in the Mexican War with the United States.

4. See Alexander Jones to Polk, April 4 and 9, 1845.

5. Jonathan I. Coddington and Cornelius P. Van Ness.

6. Marshall Tate Polk, Jr.

# FROM JACOB L. MARTIN

My dear Sir. Paris 16th April 1845

I seize a moment before the departure of the steamer to congratulate you upon the auspicious commencement of your presidential career and to say what pride & pleasure were felt by the friends of American republicanism when they read your able & patriotic message.[1]

The most unfriendly here could not find a pretext in it for censure or even criticism. It has however raised a storm in England which nobody anticipated. Ill will at the success of the annexation bill was the true cause of this hostile demonstration. Oregon is made to bear the brunt of Texas. The declaration of the Ministers[2] were not so hostile as the unanimous acclamations with which they were received in Parliament, & the offensive and defying tone of the public press. Depend upon it there is much ill will against us in England, which has been growing for years. Our silent growth & formidable future excite the jealousy if not the fears of our old enemy, who would gladly check our progress by any means which would not cripple herself too much. It is stated that a fleet has been sent to Oregon to fortify the British posts in that country & which have been established in violation of good faith under the convention of joint occupation.[3] So bold a step & one so contemptious of the faith of treaties, it is hardly endurable, yet there is but little doubt, that a fleet has been sent to that quarter with no very friendly purpose. I trust as I believe that our attitude will be firm & fearless. Fortunately our people are well united upon this question, and will present an almost undivided front. When the English see our calm but resolute bearing, perhaps they will hestitate before advancing further. Much as a war may injure us it has great evils in store for them. The loss of Canada, the moody discontent of Ireland, financial difficulties, palsy of manufacturing industry, interruption of commerce, are not considerations to be neglected. I only wish we were better prepared, especially that we had a good system of harbor defence & that we had a sufficient number of efficient war steamers, which are the most reliable means of offence possessed by England. The storm may & I hope will blow over but we should be prepared for the worst & when it is seen that we do not fear that result it will be the less likely to happen. The rejected Texan minister here Gen Terrill,[4] a worthy man but a decided opponent of annexation, thinks that if Mexico declares war upon us it is an undoubted indication that she is stimulated thereto & will be secretly supported by England. As he was in frequent cordial consultation with Lord Aberdeen, & evidently expects anxiously some decisive action on the part of Mexico, I think it is well for me to call your attention to the circumstance especially as the English papers speak of our folly in inviting a war with Mexico & England together. The French people sympathize with us but the govt. does not. Louis Philippe is devoted to England, though he is anxious to preserve peace & will do any thing in his power to prevent hostilities. The English accuse us of robbing Mexico of a province which is lost to her forever, in the same breath with which they acknowledge that they are ready, provided the young republic remains separate to guarantee her independence against Mexico! What consummate impudence. Unfortunately we have no private hand this time for dispatches, which cannot be sent through England safely by mail so I send you this hasty scrawl, which I enclose by way of precaution to Mr. Selden, Treasurer. Be good enough to present my kindest & most respectful regards to Mrs. Polk & accept to yourself the best wishes of ....

J. L. MARTIN

P.S. Mr. King[5] has read & approved this hasty note. He send[s] his best compliments.

ALS. DLC–JKP. Addressed to Washington City. Polk's AE on the cover states that he received this letter on May 8, 1845.

1. Martin probably refers to Polk's inaugural address.

2. On April 4, 1845, the British Parliament debated the Oregon territory and Polk's assertion that the United States' claim to that territory was "clear and unquestionable." The Earl of Aberdeen, addressing the House of Lords, declared that Polk's inaugural remarks did not call for legislative action and predicted that the agreement for joint occupancy would continue. He expressed hope that the two nations could avoid war over the issue but insisted that Britain would protect her rights in the Oregon territory. Lord John Russell and Sir Robert Peel, addressing the House of Commons, likewise doubted that the United States' claim to Oregon was "clear and unquestionable" and expressed regret that Polk's remarks might jeopardize negotiations. Arguing that British claims to the territory were stronger, Russell added that the foreign policy of the United States "tends toward territorial aggrandizement." Hansard Parliamentary Debates, 3rd series (1845), Vol. LXXIX, p. 178.

3. Martin's reference is to the Convention of 1818 by which the United States and Great Britain, having settled the boundary of the Louisiana Purchase to the Rocky Mountains, agreed to joint occupation of Oregon. In 1827 the two nations had renewed the agreement.

4. George W. Terrell served as attorney general of Tennessee under Sam Houston and in the Tennessee legislature from 1829 to 1836. In 1837 he moved to Texas where he served briefly as secretary of state in 1841 before accepting an appointment as attorney general of Texas. From 1844 to 1845 Terrell served as chargé d'affaires to France, Great Britain, and Spain.

5. William Rufus King served as U.S. senator from Alabama, 1819–44 and 1848–53, and as U.S. minister to France, 1844–46. Elected vice-president of the United States in 1852, he took his oath of office in Cuba and died shortly after returning to Alabama in early 1853. Martin wrote his postscript in the left margin of the final page of his letter.

## FROM JOHN P. CAMPBELL

[Dear Sir]                                   Springfield Mo. April 18th 1845

On ariving at home and becoming familiar with the state of affairs here, I am still of opinion, that it would be impolitic to remove *Silas Reed Esq.*[1] from the Genl. Land office in this state. So far as I have had means of assertaining in St. Louis & through out the state generally, he has given general satisfaction to all, except the Benton faction and the whigs who oppose him for the reason he was appointed by Mr. Tyler, and fought manfully in the Democratic Ranks in 1844; and here permit me to reassure you that Benton, nor none of the leaders of that faction, are your true friends.

I am sorry to learn that the "Missourian" has been made the government organ in this state, & it has produced a great deal of dissatisfaction here, for the reason that it is well known here that the "Missourian" is owned by Benton.

Col. S. Penn has fought long & hard for democratic principles, while Benton has been furnishing the whigs with amunition, through his orgain here, to shoot Democrats with.

Joel H. Headon[2] should be removed, from the land office here, as a large portion of our Democratic friends here have no confidence in his political or moral honesty. It is an Every Day Enquiry, why Headen is not removed!

JOHN P. CAMPBELL

N.B. Morton, Register at Clinton, should be removed.[3]
[Addendum] I concur in the above. L. H. Sims[4]

ALS. DLC–JKP. Addressed to Washington City. Polk's AE on the cover states that he received this letter on May 7, 1845.

1. Reed served as surveyor-general of Illinois and Missouri from 1842 to 1845.
2. Joel H. Hayden.
3. Abraham B. Morton held the post of land office register at Clinton, Mo., from 1844 to 1845.
4. Leonard H. Sims, a Missouri Democrat, won election to one term in the U.S. House, 1845–47. Sims wrote his addendum below Campbell's postscript.

## FROM ROBERT H. MORRIS

My Dear Sir,                                   New York April 18 1845

During my interviews with you I was induced to believe that it would be your desire, if removals should be made among the officers of the U.S.

Government in this City, to give me some one of the places of honor and
profit in your gift. Public opinion afterwards indicated me for the Collectorship. I now, however, find that Benjamin F. Butler Esqr. and General
Dix have selected Mr. Coddington for that position and inform the public
here that he will be appointed and that Mr. Hoffman from the interior
of the State, whom they have also designated, will be appointed Naval
Officer. I also learn that Mr. Butler and General Dix have determined,
for some reason, that I shall not be appointed to any public station.

Knowing that an Executive who is not personally acquainted with a
City like New York must in a great measure be influenced in his appointments by the representations and advice of others, and knowing your
high estimation of Mr. Butler as exhibited by your giving him an office
which he did not ask for [1] and also fully appreciating the influence of the
character and official station of General Dix, and they having made (substantially) the statements above alluded to, I presume the appointments
they have indicated will be made and that I shall be left a private citizen.
Most probably all this will have been done before this can reach you.

Notwithstanding this convinction I have determined to write you
frankly that you may see the effects which may result from the advice
of the gentlemen I have referred to. Such letter to some men might
prejudice me in their estimation. My knowledge of human nature has
made me judge differently of you. I believe the honest truth, frankly
stated, cannot prejudice its author in your mind. This risk, however, I
am willing to run in the performance of a duty which I feel I owe to the
Democratic party.

You are aware that the Democratic party in this City numbers about
24,000. The energy and force of it are among the young men who also
constitute the great majority of its members. For years we have been
governed, as regards appointments among us, by the central power at Albany. Nearly every prominent appointment has been made either from
gentlemen in the country who have been sent to us or from those who
came from the country but shortly before their appointment, and indeed I may say we have been ruled with an iron hand by them in their
denunciation of us for our progressiveness. They have proscribed us for
originating the very measures which afterwards they were compelled to
adopt as Democratic principles. This conduct of theirs has frequently
broken us up, caused dissensions and divisions, frequently caused our
defeat and accounts for the appearance of instability among the Democratic masses of the City. Mr. Van Buren sent Mr. Butler among us as
District Attorney; Mr. Butler, before he went to Washington, was a resident of Albany, out of the Southern District of New York. From his
office he received over $100,000. He entered into speculations with his

brother[2] for the purpose of increasing his wealth, lost it all and incurred a large debt.

Mr. Coddington, then very much embarassed in his circumstances, was appointed Post Master. At that time, that office was very lucrative. He realised a large fortune from it, has prudently taken care of it, and is now wealthy. We ran Mr. Coddington for Mayor last spring and he obtained only 20,000 votes and was beaten.

I have been elected by the People twice to our State Legislature and three times Mayor, in every instance running above my ticket. The last time I was elected by nearly 6,000 majority, having polled over 25,000 votes. I never was nominated, that I was not elected. These offices made me poor, not as poor as Mr Butler because my debt is a very small one and incurred not by speculation, but by expenses indispensably necessary for the office of Mayor.

You, for satisfactory reasons, appointed Mr. Butler to the office which I asked for, and he did not, and out of which he had before received so much. The people desire I should be appointed Collector. Mr. Butler, thus favored by you probably to my detriment, designates Mr. Coddington who was already rich from office and who had been defeated before the People; and I, with such evidences of popular favor am set aside at the instance of Mr. Butler. This the people here consider the act of the central power at Albany and that both Mr. Butler and Mr. Coddington are restored to office. Again as to Mr. Hoffman, (a man for whom I have the greatest respect and admiration) he is brought from the interior of the State out of the Southern District of New York, to the exclusion of one of our own citizens, Mr. Moore, who is a great, very great, favorite with the mass of the Democratic party.[3] And thus both of us are to be excluded from any appointment and that too by the same central power.

The consequences of such refusals and appointments upon a population like that of the City of New York, any reflecting minds may appreciate. The party in its principles is Democratic to the core. It is however, as a party, composed of men of warm feelings, ardent attachments and great self respect. To have their favorites overlooked will certainly disappoint them, but to have their wishes thwarted by a central power that has frequently tyrannised over them will wound their self pride and must hereafter sway them against that power. In the contest against men principle may be lost by our common adversaries coming in between the division of our friends. At all events I fear the consequences. I fear leaders cannot prevent it and I write this thus early that should it occur the cause may be known.

ROBT. H. MORRIS

LS. DLC–JKP. Addressed to Washington City and marked "Private."

1. Polk appointed Benjamin F. Butler to the post of U.S. attorney for the Southern District of New York.

2. Morris probably refers to Charles Butler.

3. A journalist and trade union leader in New York City, Ely Moore served two terms in the U.S. House, 1835–39. From 1839 until 1845 he presided over the board of trade and served as surveyor of the port of New York; in 1845 Polk appointed him U.S. marshal for the Southern District of New York.

## FROM ASA WHITNEY[1]

Sir                                      Washington 18th April 1845

Will you permit me to ask your attention to a memorial praying for a grant of the Public Domain to construct a railroad from Lake Michigan to the Pacific & which I had presented to the last Congress & by the Committee recommended to the next Congress & to the people[2] & will you also permit me to give an explanation of the plan by which I propose to carry into effect the project.

I have asked of Congress to grant to me 60 miles wide of the Public Domain from Lake Michigan to the Pacific, the proceeds & avails of said lands to be applied exclusively to the building & completing the said road. And in order fully to attain such object I would have commissioners appointed, the same as our judges now are, whose duty it should be to dispose of said lands with my consent, they holding the avails thereof subject only to the building said road, responsible & bound to report to each Congress, they not having power to dispose of land without my consent, nor I power to use the lands or their avails without their consent, thus being a check, upon each other. Having friends who have offered to me means which I think adequate to the commencement of the work & believing that its commencement will draw to it so much enterprise, that it cannot fail of success, gives me full confidence.

From Lake Michigan where I propose to commence, to the Missouri river a distance of about 650 miles making about 25 millions of acres, through which I learn from good authority that a road can be built with great facility. I also learn that the land is all good & would be likely to sell & settle quite as fast as the road can be built, that the road will facilitate the sale & settlement cannot be doubted.

I estimate that the road will cost about $20,000 per mile for its complete construction, thus for 650 miles would cost $13 millions, the 25 millions of acres at $1 1/4 (the government price) would be $31 millions leaving a surpluss of $18 millions or equal to build 900 miles beyond the Missouri river.

From all accounts from those who have passed over the country & particularly that given me by Ramsey Crooks Esqr[3] the lands from the Missouri to some distance beyond the mountains, are very poor not producing enough to sustain there animals, generally covered with a wild sage & nothing else therefore but little could be realized from them.

The whole length of the road with its windings will probably be 2400 miles, the lands from the Lake to the Missouri providing for 1550 will leave 850 miles to provide for out of the poor lands from the Missouri to beyond the mountains & what good lands there may be between the mountains & the ocean.

The estimated cost of the road is $50 millions, not producing any returns till its full completion, would require $15 millions more to keep it in repairs & operation.

I learn from Capt Fremont (whose report is to be published by order of Congress)[4] that to build a railroad, through the Rocky Mountains is not only possible, but offers a more favorable rout, than any we have known or read of in any part of the Globe, that the entire rout from the Missouri to the Ocean can be built, in a grade of about seven feet to the mile so that it would seem nature has given it to us for this very purpose. Considering the poor quality of the lands from the Missouri onward for a long distance, & considering the magnitude of the enterprise, I do not feel that I have asked for too much.

The value of the lands from the Lake to the Missouri & their undoubted increase in value from the building of the road, through them, their avails *all* of which to be applied to the continuance of, I consider a sufficient guarantee to the government that the road will be completed.

It is my intention to pass over examine & partially survey 7 or 800 hundred miles of the rout the coming summer.

The reasons for commencing from Lake Michigan are many & obvious. First, as the road is to be built from the lands, it is necessary to commence at a period when they are unappropriated & when there is sufficient time for its construction; secondly the great necessity for a cheap & easy water communication from the important Atlantic cities to transport settlers, laborers & materials directly to the road; and last tho not least, the great importance of the commerce of England, with the vast coast of South America & Mexico, with China, Australia & India. England could make her depot at Montreal or some point in Upper Canada, use the Lakes, then the railroad to the Pacific, & then her own Vessels again thus for a small toll for the use of the railroad, would enjoy its great benefits.

The great saving in time so all important to the merchant of far greater consideration than any reasonable cost of freight, would force Commerce through this channel and this road would have a great advantage over others in the cost of freight, having no interest or cost of construction to provide for. Merchandise may be transported upon it for less than a half cent per ton per mile, costing from Oregon to Lake Michigan less than $12 per ton weight & one ton weight being equal to 2 to 2 1/4 tons measurement of Teas or such like merchandise, it would cost less than $6 for the transportation of one ton measurement of Teas from the Pacific to the Lake. And it would make a saving of more than six months in time on all the business of both England & the United States with China &c. For instance a Vessel sails from the United States or from England, in from March to May (later will not do on account of the monsoons in the Chinese seas) arrive in China from June to September & must there wait to November or December for the Tea Crop, return, arrive in England or the United States in March to May, about 10 to 12 months. The sales of American & English manufact. goods take place in China in September to January, their Tea Crop coming into market from November to January so that merchandise or other funds may be sent by this rout to meet the market there as also the Tea Crop for a return & save full six months & often much more.

I have given my reason for commencing from the Lake which you will fully understand & agree in its importance. It will also be seen that this road must force the opening & completing all the veins of communication from all the Atlantic Cities from Boston to New Orleans, to it; when we shall have a direct line of railroad, rivers & canals from each & all the Atlantic Cities to the Pacific, which can be traversed in 8 days, look at the picture & where is the man who can withhold his voice & hand required without effort for this great work.

I believe that the granting of the lands which I ask for, & the commencing the work will open such a field for industry & enterprise, as the world has never known & that the wealth & enterprise of the world must be attracted & drawn to it by an irresistable force & where is the man amongst us who may not expect benefit. Here is a vast region of country, a wild, a waste, a delightful climate suited to the people of the north of Europe & to those of our own states much of it a beautiful country, the soil rich & fertile upon this road through it. It unites the two great oceans of the world. It becomes the great thoroughfare of nations subject to a toll so small as to be almost free. It will be as a new found world. The overpopulation of Europe must & will flock to it.

The magnitude of this work appears startling at first view, but it is small compared with what we have already done comparative with our population. We are now 20 million, having doubled in the last 22 1/2 years, we have now 5000 miles of railroads in operation, built in the last

15 years, & built from means drawn from the people; in 22 1/2 years more our population will be 40 millions, & this road completed without asking means from the people, but will itself supply its own means, drawn mostly from Europe, will add to, rather than take from, our own people; or in other words that which is now valueless becomes the most important part of the Globe yielding not only the means which creates & builds up its own importance & value but spreads its influence & thus its wealth over our whole country.

It appears to me that we now have the power & means (means which costs us nothing but will be exchanged for a valuable consideration, an industrious productive people) of accomplishing a work greater than has been done by men or nations, the results of which must change the whole world. We are now at one side, the extreme of the Globe; build this road & we are in the center, with Europe on the one side & Asia & Africa on the other. You Sir can see, you can read what must then be our destiny. We can then traverse the vast Globe in 30 days. We bring all the vast world together as one nation, as one family & what must be the result, it will harmonize, it will civilize, it will christianize, it will do more than all mankind before us have done, & where is the man who will not say, let it be done.

I believe that this work will bring our vast country so directly together as one family, that all the sectional jealousies, differences & interests will harmonize, each state & section left to manage their own domestic affairs in their own way, as was intended when our Compact was formed. The scale will be so grand & interests so diversified, that no one shall predominate; the agricultural by its extended influence must harmonize all, while it does not seek legislative protection, can never require the subjection of any other interest to its own.

I have devoted much time & attention to this subject. I think I do not exagerate, the expected results, but believe they must far exceed even my imagination. I believe the work not only practicable but perfectly plain & easy of accomplishment. I know how much you are occupied & how much the crowd press themselves upon your attention & therefore feel that I may be an intrusion. My only apology is my strong desire that you may investigate this as I think important subject, for I know that if you see it as I do your powerful influence will ensure its success. Therefore if I am not asking too much, I shall feel myself greatly honored & obliged if you will permit me to see you for a few moments, when I may be able to explain more fully than I can now write.

A. WHITNEY

ALS. DLC–JKP. Addressed locally. Polk's AE on the cover states that he received this letter and enclosure on April 21, 1845.

1. A New York City merchant, Whitney's extensive travels to Europe and China led him to formulate his plans for a transcontinental railroad. Frustrated by congressional inaction, he later wrote and spoke widely on the subject in an effort to build public support for his project.

2. Polk's AE on the cover states that Whitney enclosed "a memorial to Congress praying a Grant of Public Land, to construct a Railway from Lake Michigan to the Pacific Ocean." Polk retained an offprint of Whitney's memorial to Congress of January 28, 1845. Senate Document No. 69, 28th Congress, 1st Session.

3. A Scotch-born fur trader, Crooks had headed the American Fur Company since 1822 and thereby had gained extensive knowledge of the Oregon Territory.

4. John C. Frémont attended Charleston College before receiving at the behest of Joel R. Poinsett an appointment as a mathematics instructor aboard the U.S.S. *Natchez*. Resigning from the navy, he joined the Topographical Corps as a second lieutenant and assisted in surveying a projected route for the Louisville, Cincinnati and Charleston railroad. He married Jessie Benton in 1841 and thus gained another influential patron in her father, Thomas Hart Benton. Frémont shared Benton's vision of westward expansion and published two highly popular reports on his western expeditions of 1842–43 and 1843–44. He conducted a third western exploration in 1845 and the following year undertook without written orders the reduction of Mexican authority in California. Appointed by Robert F. Stockton to serve as civil governor of the territory, Frémont refused to obey the orders of Stockton's replacement, Stephen Watts Kearny; arrested for insubordination, Frémont lost his case before a court martial and resigned from the army in 1848. Frémont later served as a U.S. senator from California and as the Republican presidential nominee in 1856.

## FROM DUTEE J. PEARCE

Newport, R.I. April 20, 1845

Stressing the need to appoint a sound Democrat to the position of collector of customs at Newport, R.I., Pearce argues that the people look to this appointment with deep interest. After warning Polk to beware of *"new converts,"* he recommends Edwin Wilbur and explains the importance of the position. Although the emoluments of this collectorship amount only to about seven or eight hundred dollars, the patronage of the office is considerable. Pearce notes the collector superintends the eight lighthouses in the state and exerts great influence in appointing their keepers and in hiring laborers and mechanics to repair and maintain the lighthouses. The collector also nominates the surveyor, inspector, and boat-man at each of the four ports of delivery. Pearce reminds Polk that in many towns and villages there is "as much interest and feeling manifested, in the appointment of a boat-man, or a tide-waiter, as in the Election of a President." Encloses extracts of his February 3rd letter concerning the customs officers at Newport.

ALS. DLC–JKP. Addressed to Washington City. Polk's AE on the cover states that he received this letter on April 25, 1845.

## FROM ABIJAH MANN, JR.[1]

Dear Sir                                    New York 21st April 1845

I hope you will not deem me as improperly intruding by expressing a very earnest desire that our friend M. Hoffman to whom (it will not be saying too much) the people of our State are as much indebted as to any other man, may be appointed to the naval office in this city. I am confident that the "young democracy" the sound Interests of the State—the sound men of the State would respond to any appointment which you might confer upon him and which he could accept. There exists I am confident towards him deep feelings of enthusiastic kindness which no other name excites. I need not testify to you in his favor. I am aware also that the speculating and prodigal interests are not his friends. The sound democracy, the men who must be relied upon if this state is secured through your administration are in favor of Hoffman. It is known that he is poor by misfortune, that he is honest, capable and faithful and men of every class desire his welfare. He cannot become an office begger & haunt your house like some of the bawling trading men, who are at Washington to get their pay for services rendered, though of little virtue.

I am confident I am not mistaken in believing that as far as may be in your power you will sustain the true interests of the democratic party and its true principles & true men. I am not however insensible to the difficulties which beset your path nor to the necessities which sometimes controul. Among the evils of life false friends are most to be derided and I cannot avoid the apprehension that you may be in some danger in this respect as well with "your advisers" as with politicians at large. I cannot, but time will explain. For the present charge this apprehension to my unregulated Jealousy.

You are aware that I am so far withdrawn from active politics as to be a mere observer & "looker on in Venice"[2] though I will not confess any indifference about results because I have the same strong desire for the prevalence of the democratic principle and consequent animouses that I have always possessed.

I could find fault with several details in the new arrangements, but it does not follow that I could propose new twists to better them by any means. Your task is most difficult and if you can succeed in retaining the support of the northern democracy for two years you will under the circumstances deserve and gain a political immortality next to miraculous.

I confess that the removal of Blair (without knowing any causes or circumstances) has given me more alarm than any other event,[3] since the inference drawn here by many good men is that *some* members of the Government considered that he was not a tool they could use and wanted one whose fortunes pecuniary and political rendered him more suitable to their purposes. That Blair had faults need not be denied, but he had redeeming qualities making full compensation, and it remains to be shown that his successors will obtain the measure of confidence reposed in him by the democracy at large. They will I fear be under the disadvantage at least of having it to gain and acquire against some prejudice at the north. Tendencies are towards Geographical divisions and parties and a prudent forecast is required to counteract them. This is not a new feature in our affairs and will be I doubt not regarded & weighed by the advantage and lights of experience.

I had sometime designed to express myself in respect to the Two offices of Collector & Post master here[4] but perhaps I had better not say more than that the present Incumbents are not entitled to my respect or confidence in any measure politically or otherwise. If they are permitted to remain in office justice will remain cheated.

A. MANN JR.

ALS. DLC–JKP. Addressed to Washington City and marked "Private."

1. A New York merchant, Abijah Mann, Jr., served two terms in the U.S. House as a Jackson Democrat, 1833–37.

2. Paraphrase of a quotation from William Shakespeare, *Measure for Measure*, act 5, scene 1, line 315.

3. See Aaron V. Brown to Polk, January 1, 1845.

4. Cornelius P. Van Ness and John L. Graham.

## FROM JOHN Y. MASON

Attorney General's office

Sir                                                21st April 1845

I have the honor to acknowledge the receipt of the papers transmitted by you this day, and your written request,[1] that I would give you my opinion on the legality of a transfer of a part of the appropriation made for the Quarter Masters Department of the Army, under the Head of Incidental Expenses, to the Head of Barracks Quarters &c, and to that of Transportation of Officers Baggage.

In an opinion given by Mr. Attorney General Legaré[2] on the 3d November 1842, he reviewed the provisions of the various laws bearing on this power of transfer of appropriations made for the Army in the following words:

"The Act of the 3d March 1809, is a general enabling Statute. The

President and Secretary might make transfer of portions of appropriations, subject to one restriction only, that they must have been made within a particular Department of the service: e.g. war or navy.

The Act of the 3d March 1817, restricted this discretion, even within the War Department, so far, that money appropriated to fortifications &c, could not be transferred to any other object of expenditure within that Department; that is as I construe it, to objects of any other class.

Then came the Act of 1820 which though affirmative, ends with a repealing clause and alters very materially the previous state of the law on this subject. This Act enumerates all the branches of expediture in the War and Navy Departments, from which transfers might be made to other branches. This provision carries still further the policy of the Act of 1817 in regard to fortification &c. It protects all other branches of expediture (except those enumerated), from the discretionary power vested in the President by the Act of 1809, and no transfer could from that time be made from any of those branches to any other not enumerated. It did not of course restrain the Presidents discretion within the same branch of expenditure."

By the terms of the Act of 1820 the Presidents power of directing a transfer was limited, so that he could direct a portion of the moneys appropriated, for any one of the following branches of expenditure in the military Department, to wit, for the subsistance of the army, for forage, for the medical department, for the Quarter Masters Department, to be applied to any other of the before mentioned branches of expenditure in the Said Department. It protected all other branches of expenditure except those enumerated, from the discretionary power vested in the President, by the Act of 1809. It did not of course restrain the Presidents discretion within the same branch of expenditures. At the date of the Act of 1820, and for many years preceding, the appropriation for the Quarter masters Department was in gross, as "For the Quarter Masters Department $150,000" to be applied to the various objects of expenditure within the range of its duties, at the discretion of the Department of War. In the Act of the 3d of March 1821 the first attempt at specification by law, of the items to which the appropriation should be applied, was made. The specification has become more minute, and in the Act of 17th June 1844 there are six branches of appropriation under the control of the Quarter Masters Department. Is it competent for the President to direct a transfer from one to the other? The Act of 1820, which contemplated the appropriations for the Quarter Masters Department, as one gross appropriation, has been modified since its passage in that aspect but in one instance. The Act of 1817 forbade transfer of appropriations made for forts, arsenals, armories, custom houses, docks, navy yards or buildings of any sort, to be applied to any other object. The Act of the 2d July 1836 modified this law so far as concerned fortifications, authorizing the President to direct transfer from one head of appropriations for fortifications to that of another for a like object. By the Act of 31st of August 1842, the power to authorize transfers of appropriations for the navy was taken away, the power in regard to those made for the army remaining. It does not appear to me that the specification of the items of expenditure in the appropriations Acts restrains this most necessary power of the President, but that his power may be exercised under the Act of 1809 and 1820, in the same manner as if the appropriations for the Quarter Masters Department, were now in the form in which they stood then, subject only to the restrictions imposed by the Act of 1817. This Act does not affect the subject now under consideration.

I am therefore of opinion, that the President may if he deem it conducive to the public interest, direct the transfer of the sum asked, from the branch of expenditure of Incidental expenses of Quarter Masters Department, to the other branches of Barracks Quarters &c, and of Transportation of officers baggage.

                                                        J. Y. MASON

LS. DLC–JKP. Addressed locally.
1. Letter not found.
2. Hugh Swint Legaré, founding editor of the *Southern Review*, 1828–32, served as attorney general of South Carolina, 1830–32; went to Belgium as U.S. chargé d'affaires, 1832–36; and sat one term in Congress as a Union Democrat, 1837–39. Appointed to John Tyler's cabinet in 1841, Legaré served as attorney general of the United States until his death in 1843.


## FROM DAVID PETRIKIN

                                          Danville, Penn. April 21, 1845
Noting that he enjoys at present a remission in his illness, Petrikin dictates a letter to Polk about late political movements in Pennsylvania and discusses in detail the legislature's recent U.S. senatorial election. After attacking Woodward as an unprincipled demagogue and tool of Shunk's clique, he praises Thomas Bell[1] as the best candidate but adds that Bell had been a warm friend of H. A. Muhlenberg, "an unpardonable offence in such little minds as Gov. Shunk & Co."[2] Although Petrikin denies that he had supported Cameron, he believes that Cameron is "as much superior to Woodward as Genl. Jackson is to Henry Clay." He points out that Cameron, like Bell, had been an ardent supporter of Muhlenberg. Petrikin attributes the present clamor in Pennsylvania over Cameron's election to Shunk's hostility toward Muhlenberg's friends and argues that the real reason for Shunk's victory in the gubernatorial election was the Democracy's fear of losing the state in the presidential election. Turning to

national politics, he regards the change in the editorial department of the *Globe* as a useful move and remarks that Blair had made many enemies "by acting without sufficient reflection and often persevering obstinately in it."

L. DLC–JKP. Addressed to Washington City.
1. A West Chester lawyer, Thomas S. Bell served six years as president-judge of the Chester-Delaware District Court, 1839–46; he sat on the Pennsylvania Supreme Court from 1846 until 1851.
2. Henry A. P. Muhlenberg, a Jacksonian Democrat, won election to five terms in the U.S. House, 1829–38; declined offers in 1837 to be named secretary of the navy or minister to Russia; but served as minister to Austria from 1838 to 1840. A friend to both Andrew Jackson and Polk, Muhlenberg headed the Democratic state ticket in Pennsylvania in 1844 but died on August 11th prior to the election. In 1835 he had opposed the incumbent Democrat, George Wolf, for the governorship and thus had divided the party between the "Mules" and the "Wolves."

## TO FRANCIS W. PICKENS

My Dear Sir:                                    Washington City April 21 1845

I deem it to be proper to appoint a successor to *Mr. Everett* as Envoy Extraordinary and Minister Plenipotentiary to Great Brittain, and now invite you to accept that station. In selecting you for this important mission, I feel assured that the country will have a guaranty in your well known character and ability, that the important interests which may be committed to your care, will be safe in your hands.

*Mr. Everett* in a letter of the 3rd ultimo,[1] anticipates his recal and adds, "it would be agreeable to me that my successor should be named as soon as it can be done with due regards to the public service, in order that I may be able to remain at my post till his arrival (which I think desirable both on his account and that of the public) without my being delayed till the season of the year is too far advanced for a safe and comfortable passage across the Atlantic."

I request that you will give me an answer at your earliest convenience. If you signify your willingness to accept, a commission will be immediately signed, and the necessary instructions prepared. In that event it is desired that you will sail, by the first of June, and earlier if you can conveniently do so.

JAMES K. POLK

ALS. ScU–SCL. Addressed to Edgefield Court House, S.C., and marked "Private."
1. Polk's reference is to Edward Everett's letter of March 3, 1845.

FROM JEREMIAH TOWLE[1]

Dear Sir,                                          New York April 22/45
    I think it proper your Excellency should be informed that signatures
to petitions for my office have been procured by applicants, and their
friends, *on their assurance that it would be the policy of this adminis-*
*tration to remove from office, indiscriminately, all persons appointed by*
*President Tyler*, without regard to their uniform republican principles
and long services in the democratic ranks, and of course that the Naval
officer must fall under this rule.
    I understand that Mr. Eli Moore has given out amongst the subordi-
nates of the Custom House, that he is absolutely to be appointed Naval
officer thus doing great injury to the public service by creating a spirit of
unsubordination among my clerks. Until recently I have never had the
slightest apprehension for my position under the government believing
my whole political life to be too well known to need any explanation from
me.
    It may not be improper for me to say that I was appointed to office,
two years since, at a time when it was intended by Prest. Tyler to de-
mocratize his whole administration, and our democratic journals haild
my appointment as an evidence of that intention.
    Before my appointment I was assured by President Tyler, himself, that
it was not his wish or intention to raise a third party.
    After his nomination by a mass convention,[2] Alderman Hatfield the
chairman of the Genl. Committee at Tammany Hall[3] called on me and
expressed a desire that we should do something to unite and harmonize
the republican party so as insure its success in the approaching election.
    I said to him that I had no doubt Mr. Tyler would with pleasure with-
draw his name from the canvass, provided he could be placed in a position to do so without discredit to himself. And I suggested that a letter
should be addressed to Gen. Van Ness inviting him, and some of the
friends of Mr Tyler to a conference with such of the members of the
Genl. Committee as were favorably disposed.
    A meeting was accordingly convened and resolutions adopted approv-
ing of Mr Tyler's democratic measures. I was one of a committee who
presented him with these resolutions, which were promptly responded
to by a withdrawal of his name from the canvass.[4]
    I subjoin an article from the Plebeian[5] as the most concise & authentic
way of presenting the facts in regard to my appointment and solicit the
attention of your Excellency to the enclosed copy of a letter from Mr.

Spencer, the late Secretary of the Treasury, as an evidence of the faithful discharge of my public duties. [6]

JERH. TOWLE

ALS. DLC–JKP. Addressed to Washington City and marked "Private." Polk's AE on the cover states that he received this letter on April 24, 1845.

1. A New Hampshire native, Towle moved in 1822 to New York City, where he became involved in municipal activities; he served as naval officer from 1843 until his removal in 1845.

2. Towle probably refers to a New York City mass meeting called to ratify Tyler's nomination in July 1844.

3. Abraham Hatfield served as alderman from the Eleventh Ward from 1840 until 1844, and won election to one term in the New York House in 1852.

4. See Cornelius P. Van Ness to Polk, January 17, 1845.

5. Enclosure not found.

6. Towle's reference is to John C. Spencer's letter to Moses G. Leonard, June 11, 1844. L. DLC–JKP. A former legislator, congressman, and secretary of state of New York, Spencer served as U.S. secretary of war from October 12, 1841, until March 3, 1843, when he became secretary of the Treasury. He resigned from the latter post on May 2, 1844.

## FROM WILLIAM ALLEN

My Dear Sir                                    Chillicothe 24 April 1845

Col. Medary, the Editor of the Ohio Statesman, will be in Washington in a day or two, on his way East. You are already somewhat acquainted with him and know something of his character and standing. But as he is a much more important man than he is generally known to be at a distance, I will say a word or two to you about him; as I am particularly anxious that you should rightly appreciate him, and *attach him to you*. He is a man of strict honesty and truth, talented and prudent, radical and firm in his opinions, free from selfishness; and exerts great influence with the party in the State, and indeed, in the whole Northwest. Allow me to ask you to receive him with the utmost kindness. He is a man with whom you can speak fully and in confidence; and upon whos word, with regard to men and things in this state, you may fully and confidently rely. From his great services to the party and his influence in it, he very naturally feels that he is entitled to be considered worthy of consideration and confidence, and you will, therefore, greatly gratify him, and *strongly attach him to you*, by manifesting your good will toward him, and your just appreciation of his services and character.

W. ALLEN

ALS. DLC–JKP. Addressed to Washington City and marked *"Private."*

## FROM ROBERT B. REYNOLDS[1]

Sir:                              Washington City D.C. April 24th [1845][2]

I called on Tuesday afternoon to see you, but was denied admittance; nor would your door-keeper[3] hand you my card. This was unexpected to me.

I was anxious to see you in relation to matters in Tennessee & only wanted a few minutes conversation. *I did not come to seek an office for myself.*

I wished merely to know if the Government intended to remove the remnant of Cherokees, now residing in N. Carolina to a home west of the Miss.[4] If so I wished to bring before you the name of Geo. W. Harris Esqr of Knoxville, as a Suitable person to visit them & Enrol them to go west.[5] *They are willing to emigrate.*

For the purpose of sustaining a Democratic press at Knoxville I wished to procure the patronage of the government so far as to get the printing of the laws from the Secretary of State, and the Advertising of the Land sales in the columns of the Standard.[6] I want to make a vigorous fight for Brown & the Legislature when I return & if we had but a small portion of government patronage we could fight better & faster & harder. I do not want it for myself, though I have involved myself for the cause. I shall make suitable arrangements to extricate myself by & by. In former times, I served the cause to the best of my ability & I am not less zealous now. I do not demand pay for past services; but I do wish government patronage bestowed on the Standard so far as it is compatible with the public interest. Our party being too poor to sustain a press at Knoxville, without foreign aid.

It would be but just that the Postmaster General should change the *Distributing* Post office from Cumberland Gap to Knoxville. A great number of Post roads terminate at Knoxville; the Cumberland Gap office gets the emoluments & the Knoxville Office has the labor to perform. This change ought to be made, because of the justice of the case, and because it would add popularity to the Department to do it.

I shall remain in Washington a few days longer to see if the East Tennesseans can obtain these few favors from the Government.

R. B. REYNOLDS

ALS. DLC–JKP. Addressed locally.

1. Reynolds, a lawyer and key member of the Knoxville Democratic Central Committee, served as attorney general for Tennessee's Second Judicial District from 1839 until 1845.

2. Date identified through content analysis.

3. Not identified further.

4. See Ezekiel Starr et al. to Polk, March 25, 1845.

5. A noted humorist and author of the *Sut Lovingood Yarns*, George W. Harris served as captain of the steamboat *Knoxville* from 1835 until 1838. From 1838 to 1839 he captained the *Indian Chief* and employed his vessel in the removal of the Cherokees westward. Apprenticed as a young man to Samuel Bell, a jeweler, Harris opened his own shop specializing in engraving as well as the production of jewelry and silverware. He served as postmaster of Knoxville from 1857 until 1858.

6. See Julius W. Blackwell to Polk, March 11, 1845.


## FROM FRANCIS R. SHUNK

Dear Sir,                                                         Harrisburg April 25th 1845

There are several rumors in circulation here respecting the appointment of Collector for the Port of Philadelphia. I expressed to you in a former letter my reasons of preference for Mr. Welsh.[1] The course of events and subsequent reflection have strengthened these reasons of preference. His discriminating mind and sound discretion well enable him, with his industrious business habits, satisfactorily to execute the duties of the office and make the best practical distribution of the patronage belonging to it. I must confess that in regard to the patronage I feel peculiar anxiety. The few offices I had to bestow in Philadelphia were sought by numerous applicants who are of course not pleased by their disappointment. A collector who understands my political relations may in a measure relieve me from the false position in which I am placed, while he makes the best possible selections. My relations with Mr. Welsh will enable me without reserve to communicate with him upon this subject and his knowledge of city and country will direct him to strengthen his own hands, while he strengthens the party and softens the unkind feelings towards me which have been provoked by overlooking several hundred applicants many of whom are very worthy men. I know I may in this respect be chaged with selfishness. But it must also be remembered That the moral worth, the intelligence, industry and purity of Mr Welsh present unquestionable claims to your Confidence.

FR. R. SHUNK

ALS. DLC–JKP. Addressed to Washington City and marked "*Private.*" Polk's AE on the cover states that he received this letter on April 26, 1845.

1. Letter has not been found.

## FROM ALFRED BALCH

Dear Sir,                                              Nashville 26th April 1845

I am rejoiced to learn that my old friend Ritchie is about to take
charge of the Globe. He is a virtuous man, a safe counsellor and an
able writer. He got wrong on the question of the sub-treasury; but
when he saw his error he acted magnanimously as I happen to *know*
for I was specially deputed by Mr Van Buren to proceed to Richmond
to settle that difficulty and succeeded after Mr Wright, who had pre-
ceded me, had utterly failed.[1] Ritchie you may rely upon it will stand
by you through good and through evil report. I (in common with our
whole community) am pleased at the removal of my quondam brother
in law William B. Lewis. His whole life has been a life of hypocrisy
and servility. He now knows "that thrift does not *for ever* follow
fawning"![2]

The prompt dismission of Lt Hurst has extorted the decided approbation of every right thinking man in the Nation.[3] Our General election
which is to come off in August has excited, as yet, but little interest.
The truth is, that our people have not yet recovered from the exhaus-
tion of their tremendous effort in November last. They are satisfied
with their success and are therefore somewhat apathetic. Brown altho
a pleasant respectful and conciliatory speaker imparts no *enthusiasm* to
the crowd whilst Foster's incoherent raving is all syllabub and "leather
and prunella."[4] Bell is looking on, apparently with indifference, but his
disappointed ambition is devouring him. If the Whigs can secure success he will then make a desperate struggle to reach the senate. Little
Dickenson having dismounted, Jones and Gentry[5] are each striving to
vault into his saddle. I wish the rogues would quarrel and then honest
men would have some chance to get at their own. I perceive that justice has been done upon that treble traitor Talmadge.[6] When in 38 he,
Rives and Garland[7] were secretly banded together to oppose the Democracy whilst they were making treacherous professions of regard for it, I
was authorized by Mr V Buren to adjust all matters depending between
them. I acted in perfect good faith; they declared that they were satisfied
and instantly violated their solemn pledges and gave in their adhesion
to the enemy. Mr Talmadge has now gotten his reward & I trust that R.
will follow suit.

We have here the finest prospect for a crop of cotton I have ever seen.
The stand is perfect. If Providence only sends us grateful and seasonable
showers throughout the spring and summer and the frost does not injure
us in the fall we shall prosper even altho the price of this great staple

should continue low as it certainly will. With respects to Mrs Polk I remain ....

ALFRED BALCH

ALS. DLC–JKP. Addressed to Washington City.

1. In 1837 Thomas Ritchie joined other conservative Democrats in opposition to Martin Van Buren's efforts to establish an independent treasury. A year later Ritchie dropped his opposition.

2. Paraphrase of a line from William Shakespeare, *Hamlet*, act 3, scene 2.

3. William D. Hurst joined the navy as a midshipman in 1829 and won promotion to lieutenant in 1841. Involved in a duelling incident with a midshipman, Hurst lost his command of the brig *Truxton* at Polk's direction on April 12, 1845. On January 31, 1846, Hurst wrote Polk explaining his part in the controversy and gained reinstatement. ALS. DLC–JKP.

4. Paraphrase of a quotation from Alexander Pope, *Essay on Man*, epistle IV, part 1, line 204.

5. David W. Dickinson, James C. Jones, and Meredith P. Gentry. A Murfreesboro lawyer, Dickinson served in the Tennessee House, 1831–33; in the U.S. House as a Democrat, 1833–35; and in the U.S. House as a Whig, 1843–45. A Whig presidential elector in 1840, Dickinson died on April 27, 1845. Jones, a Wilson County farmer and one-term member of the Tennessee House, 1839–41, defeated Polk in the Tennessee gubernatorial elections of 1841 and 1843. In 1850, Jones moved to Shelby County and became president of the Memphis and Charleston Railroad. He won election as a Whig to one term in the U.S. Senate, 1851–57; following the collapse of the Whig party in 1854, he joined the Democrats and supported James Buchanan for the presidency in 1856. Gentry, a member of the Williamson County bar, served as a Whig in the Tennessee House, 1835–39, and won election to several terms in the U.S. House, 1839–43 and 1845–53. He ran unsuccessfully for governor in 1853 on the American party ticket.

6. Balch's reference is to Polk's removal of Nathaniel P. Tallmadge as governor of Wisconsin Territory.

7. Nathaniel P. Tallmadge, William C. Rives, and James Garland. Balch refers to their break with the Democratic party in 1837 over the independent treasury. A lawyer from Lovingston, Va., Garland served one term in the Virginia House, 1829–31, and three terms as a Democrat in the U.S. House, 1835–1841. An unsuccessful candidate for reelection in 1840, Garland moved to Lynchburg, sat on the corporation court from 1841 until 1882, and served as the city's commonwealth attorney from 1849 until 1872.

FROM LEWIS CASS

My dear Sir,                                    Detroit April 26. 1845

I have this instant read your kind letter,[1] and cannot delay a single instant without telling you how greatly I am obliged to you for it.

Pressed as you are with the concerns of this great nation, I appreciate highly the favour, you have done me in explaining the affair of Mr Norvell.[2] It is all perfectly satisfactory, and you have done right, and as soon as Mr Norvell returns I will have a full conversation with him, and I doubt not we shall bring him to harmonize with all the party. At any rate my efforts shall not be wanting to produce this result. I again repeat, we shall be satisfied, because it is our duty to be so.

I am greatly obliged to you for your views, respecting my son.[3] It was with the utmost reluctance, that I ever suffered his name to be mentioned, in connection with a foreign appointment. He argued strongly and I yielded, for it is difficult to resist the importunities of an only Son. I would drop it altogether, but his application is known here, and I should therefore dislike an ultimate failure. But, my dear Sir, I know how you are beset, and I know how to make allowance for the position. My son had preferences respecting positions in Europe, but he would accept any station of Chargé there, which may become vacant. If the publick interest should permit you to send him there, I should be highly gratified, and I feel sure he would be found competent to his duties. Should it not, I shall be entirely content, well knowing it would not be for any want of disposition on your part to gratify me. You would still find me, as ever, your true and sincere friend personally & politically.

I thank you for the appointment of Mr Ten Eyck.[4] I doubt not you will find him worthy.

Mrs Cass[5] joins me in the tender of our best regards to Mrs Polk.

LEW CASS

ALS. DLC–JKP. Addressed to Washington City.

1. Polk's letter has not been found.

2. See John Norvell to Polk, April 15, 1845.

3. Lewis Cass, Jr., served as a major of the Third Dragoons during the Mexican War and accepted appointment in 1849 as chargé d'affaires to the Papal States. Promoted to minister resident in 1854, Cass remained in Italy until 1858.

4. A native of New York, Anthony Ten Eyck moved to Detroit, Mich., in 1835 to practice law. In 1841 Ten Eyck accepted an appointment as a commissioner to Hawaii and served until 1843, when he returned to Detroit to become clerk of the Michigan Supreme Court. A Cass delegate to the 1844 Democratic National Convention in Baltimore, Ten Eyck served as U.S. commissioner to the Sandwich Islands, 1845–49; as deputy postmaster at Detroit, 1860–61; and as major and paymaster of volunteers during the Civil War.

5. Elizabeth Spencer Cass.

## FROM DANIEL T. JENKS

My Dear Sir          Newtown, Bucks Co. Pa. April 26th 1845

It is said to be one of the established principals of your administration, that the question of the sucession, shall be wholly excluded from it. And I can say without fear of contradiction that the great body of the Democracy of the nation most heartily approve of the exclution of "The *succession.*" And therefore when those who see the wheels in motion by the rivals, who are playing for the *succession*, it becomes the friends of the Administration to let the President see the *machinery working* for 1848.

Mr Buchannan has at this time his bosom friend an Editor Mr Forny of Lancaster Couty[1] *Deputy* to John Davis, Surveyor for the Port of Philadelphia. This Deputyship was not of course an *accidental affair*. It is said too, that *he* is to establish a paper in the city of Philadelphia. Mr Buchannan has also two very warm friends, that he wishes to hold the *other* posts in the custom House. Viz. Dr Leman of Phila,[2] and Henry Welsh of York County. They are both as devoted friends of Mr Buchannan as any two men in the Country.

Should he succeed in haveing them, *he* will have then, all the important places in the custom House, in the hands of his friends, and will use their influence for the *succession* in 1848. I might also say that S. D. Patterson, the new Navy Agent is the ardent friend of Mr Buchannan. I am not opposed to Mr Buchannan; on the contrary I am friendly to him, should he not grasp at what I conceive to be too much. But it does appear to me, that neither *he* nor *any other member of the Cabinet*, should have *their* friends appointed to fill the offices of the Country. Indeed I feel convinced, that if *no succession* was in view, your Excellency would not be urged so much to make changes, *at this time*.

In my letter of the 22nd instant[3] I said that the retaining of the present officers, was the only safe course to sustain a Polk Administration, clear of *Cliqueism*. I have in my possession eulogistic articles upon members of the cabinet, taken from the papers of the country. All showing that there is no office for them *now to fill, except*, that of President of the U. States. I have also some to show that they ought to be candidates for 1848.

When I see your Excellency again I will present them to you; I send you this now, to apprise you of the object of certain removals. I will not extend this letter, but I deemed it my duty, to say before I conclude that of all *the candidates* up for the offices in Pennsylvania, there is not one who is not now pledged or understood to be favourable to the Vice President or some *cabinet* candidate for 1848.

Whereas the incumbents *know*, as I wrote the other day, that if they are retained, they are *kept in* by the President himself. It would seem most adviseable therefore to refuse to change, and immediately to let every one know that his case will be considered, when the present terms expire. The question to be settled is then wether the President is to *give in*, to the applicants, or the applicants, to wait the Presidents own good time.

DANIEL T. JENKS

P.S. This letter of course is sent confidentially for your own personal perusal, not out of any hostility to any one, far from it, but solely for the good of the Democratic party, and to sustain, your Excellency's Administration. D.T.J.

ALS. DLC–JKP. Addressed to Washington City and marked "Confidential."

1. A native of Lancaster County, Penn., John W. Forney began his journalistic career with the Lancaster *Intelligencer* and subsequently became part owner of the Philadelphia *Pennsylvanian*; a partisan of James Buchanan, he won appointment as deputy surveyor of the port of Philadelphia in 1845. Elected clerk of the U.S. House in 1851, he continued writing for Democratic journals until the eve of the Civil War, when he joined the Republican party in support of the Union cause.

2. George F. Lehman.

3. On March 22, 1845, Jenks wrote that the support of John Tyler's friends in Pennsylvania had proven crucial in carrying the state for Polk and urged that the Tylerites not be proscribed from office. ALS. DLC–JKP.

## TO ANDREW JACKSON

My Dear Sir: Washington City Apl 27th 1845

I was much concerned to learn from your last letter,[1] as well as from other sources, that your afflictions continued, and that your health was worse that it was when I parted with you. As the warm season approaches I most naturally hope that it may be better.

My labours have been thus far so great, that I have had scarcely a moment of time, to attend to my correspondence. The change of the *Globe* has not, as far as I know, affected in the slightest degree, the good personal relations existing between *Mr Blair* and myself. He has acted well in the matter. In the course of his long career as an Editor, he had necessarily incurred the displeasure of a portion of the Democratic party, and this together with the reasons which I have already given you, made the change necessary, if not indispensible, to the harmonious Union and harmony of the party. As soon as he found that such was my settled opinion he yielded, and has since acted well.

One or two matters of minor importance which you mentioned to me will be attended to. One of them is the restoration of *Mr Taggart*,[2] to the place from which he was removed by Mr Blake.[3] It has been delayed for the reason that Judge *Shields* of Illinois[4] who succeeds Mr Blake as Commissioner of the Land office, did not arrive and enter upon the discharge of his duties, until a few days ago. Say to Mrs. Jackson that he shall be restored in a few days. I have seen *Thomas Donelson*[5] since he came to Philadelphia, who informed me that he preferred a place in the Custom-House at Philadelphia to a Clerkship in Washington. I told him he should be gratified, as soon as a change was made in the Collectorship. I have had great difficulty in making proper selections for the Philadelphia and New York appointments, but expect to act upon them in the course of this week. As soon as I do so, Mr Donelson shall have the place which he desires. You see I have done justice to our old friend *Majr Davezac* by restoring him to his old place as chargé to the Netherlands.

Much of my time has been occupied recently in relation to our Foreign affairs. The arrogant tone of defiance, and of menace held by the British Press, and Ministry on receiving my inaugural address, has not disturbed my nerves.[6] My position upon the Oregon and Texas questions will be firmly and boldly, but at the same time, prudently maintained. I have no fear of War, but if contrary to my present impressions it should[7] be forced upon us, because we assert and maintain our just rights, let it come. You may rely upon it we will not recede, from our ground.

Majr. Donelson's last dispatch was of the 3rd Inst.[8] We have private letters from others as late as the 10th. I am satisfied that President Jones is opposed to annexation, and there is too much reason to believe that, the intrigues and influence of the British and French ministers in Texas, have had some effect, upon the Executive Government, and upon other leading men. Houston up to my last accounts, held a mysterious silence on the subject. If he were to take ground for annexation the question would be settled in a day. If he unites with *Jones*, against it, my information is that the people, a vast majority of whom are for annexation, will take the matter into their own hands, and carry it through. The policy of President Jones, is, I am satisfied, to delay action, until the British Government can consummate their plans. *Asbel Smith*, the Texan Secretary of State, left Texas, immediately upon hearing of the passage of the Resolutions by our Congress.[9] He is now in the U. States, and we have information that he will probably sail for England in the

Boston packet, which will leave on the 1st of May. He has not been at Washington. *Majr. Donelson* has been instructed to press the subject to an early conclusion.

From Mexico, I think there is but little danger of any hostile movement. We have taken the precaution however, to have a strong naval force off Vera Cruz, and in the Gulf, ready, promptly to protect our citizens and commerce, should any hostile movement be made. We adopt your motto, to ask from other nations nothing but what is right, and submit to nothing which is wrong.

With my prayers for the continuance of your life, and that you may have improved health ....

JAMES K. POLK

ALS. DLC–JKP. Addressed to Washington City and marked "*Private.*" Published in Bassett, ed., *Correspondence of Andrew Jackson*, VI, pp. 402–03.

1. See Andrew Jackson to Polk, April 11, 1845.

2. James B. Taggart, husband of Jane York Taggart and brother-in-law of Sarah Yorke Jackson, held clerkships in the General Land Office, 1837–43, and in the Treasury Department, 1845–46.

3. A lawyer from Terre Haute, Ind., Thomas H. Blake won election to one term in the U.S. House as a National Republican in 1826 and served three years as commissioner of the General Land Office, 1842–45.

4. An Irish-born lawyer from Kaskaskia, Ill., James Shields held a number of state offices, including a place on the Illinois Supreme Court in 1843. He served as commissioner of the General Land Office, 1845–47; as a general officer in the volunteers during the Mexican War; as governor of the Oregon Territory, 1848–49; and as a U.S. senator, 1849–55. Shields removed to Minnesota and won election to a partial term in the U.S. Senate from that state, 1858–59; he commanded a regiment of Union volunteers in the Civil War.

5. Thomas Jefferson Donelson, twin brother of Andrew Jackson, Jr., obtained a minor post in the Philadelphia Customs House in 1845.

6. See Jacob L. Martin to Polk, April 16, 1845.

7. Polk cancelled the following word, "happen."

8. Polk's reference is to Donelson's diplomatic dispatch of April 3, 1845, to James Buchanan. Awaiting an official response by the Texas government to Congress' joint resolutions on annexation, Donelson mentioned rumors of British and French intrigues intended to impede annexation. Senate Document No. 1, 29th Congress, 1st Session, pp. 51–52.

8. Polk's reference is to the joint resolutions on Texas annexation.

9. Polk paraphrases a passage from Jackson's second inaugural address, "To do justice to all and to submit to wrong from none has been during my Administration its governing maxim ...." Richardson, ed., *A Compilation of the Messages and Papers of the Presidents*, III, p. 3.

## FROM DANIEL S. DICKINSON

My Dear Sir                                    Binghamton April 28 1845

There is much anxiety and no little jealousy prevailing among our friends lest you should be induced, unwittingly to sanction a "restoration." It is not to be denied that with all the excellent qualities of Mr Van Buren his patronage run in very narrow channels in this state and there had long been a half suppressed muttering among the most efficient men of our party. Much as the party is attached to Mr Van Buren his defeat & your nomination at the Baltimore convention brought high gratification to many of his best friends, not that they had got rid of Mr Van Buren but that they were rid of a clique of perpetual & professional office holders and in the belief that new interests and a younger class of men would be heard. I deem it due to frankness to say that any restoration of this class of men is looked upon with decided disfavor by the mass of the party and by all *your* active supporters.

These gentlemen have been so long on the tapis that they understand perfectly every avenue to preferment and can manufacture public opinion so perfectly than none but a *New Yorker* can detect it. They are generally clean active men and understand well their business.

I understand they are now moving at our most prominent post offices and also at the New York city patronage with renewed vigor, alleging that all Mr Tylers appointees should be displaced. I need not say I suppose that I am very strongly opposed to this policy and think nothing could be more injurious. Your nomination & election was a new era in political parties to some extent and I could name many if I should try, who are now very squeamish about party adherence who failed to countenance your nomination until after the August elections[1] when they saw you were to succeed.

I cannot omit to repeat what I have before said that I think you may repose great confidence in the integrity & sagacity of Govr Marcy and I feel assured that he not only will understand our people and our condition but that his whole object will be to build up the party as a whole and not seek to create, perpetuate or reward cliques.

I hope you will not deem me intrusive in this hasty & ill digested note for I have no object to answer but a common one and write that you may be aware of the feeling which is awakened at the many "rumors" which are, doubtless idly circulated.

D. S. DICKINSON

P.S. The appt of our friend Melville to some place within his ambition is expected by his friends & the party generally & would be highly acceptable.

ALS. DLC–JKP. Addressed to Washington City and marked *"Confidential."*
1. Dickinson probably refers to the August 1844 state elections in Alabama, Illinois, Indiana, Kentucky, Missouri, and North Carolina.

## FROM HENRY HORN

My Dear Sir                                    Philadelphia 28th April 1845

From a conversation I had this morning with Mr Kane I regret exceedingly to find that you are still embarrassed in relation to the appointments for our city. And were it in my power to relieve you from the difficulty without a sacrafice of my honor and standing in this community which are far dearer to me than the honors or emoluments of office I would most cheerfully do so.

For the first time in my life after an ardent and devoted service to my party of more than thirty years during which time I have suffered in a pecuniary point of view to the amount of many thousands and withstood the slanders detractions and persecutions of our political opponents to an extent perhaps greater than any other individual in our state I find myself a candidate before you for an appointment to which no disinterested man of either party here or elsewhere will deny my just, nay my paramount claims over any of my competitors for the station either of whose claims will be *more than requested* by any of the subordinate stations here.

To recede then from the ground I have taken that another less worthy and less competent may occupy it would be dishonorable alike to myself and the friends who support me. It would be a course that I am sure you as my sincere friend could not advise me to pursue.

My name is before you for a place designated by my numerous friends as one for which I am especially qualified and one to which I am in their judgment eminently entitled. Should you think otherwise (for it is to you alone that I appeal) I must submit to my fate with the best grace I can.

In the mean time believe me to be sincerely and truly ....

HENRY HORN

ALS. DLC–JKP. Addressed to Washington City.

## FROM JOHN K. KANE

My dear sir,                                                    Phila. 28 Apr. 1845

I saw Mr. Horn this morning, and after some conversation on general topics passed to the question of the appointments here, the difficulty of making selections among friends, etc. etc., taking care, without committing you in any degree, to express the highest degree of confidence on your part in him, and to convey to his mind the idea that, while it was impossible for me to imagine what would be your determination in regard to the Collectorship, I had no doubt whatever that either of the other places was perfectly accessible to him. I added that I felt an anxious wish to bring about such action as might consolidate rather than distract our party here, and that I should be glad to find him willing to accept the post office or the Naval Office. He replied at once, that his views were well known in the whole matter, that he had been nominated to you by friends without his personal agency, and that he could not withdraw his name as a candidate for the only place for which it had been indicated. And in a word, expressed a determination, such as I had already heard, in rumours, not to vary his position before you. He spoke of having written to you already on the subject, and said he might very probably do so again. [1] On the whole my visit was unsatisfactory as to its result, though altogether definite in character.

I do not know that there is anything for me to say farther on the subject of this appointment. I may be wrong in my judgment of party policy, for I feel that, with Mr. Buchanan on one side and Mr. Dallas on the other, it is scarcely probable that the middle course can be approved. But I will still repeat that I consider Mr. Welsh as preferable to either; and were other reasons absent, I should choose him as the middle man.

Let me however say one word as to the Post Office, on the assumption that it is not to be filled by Mr. Horn. The right man I assure you is Col. Page, notwithstanding his former tenure of the place. [2] He is right honest, patriotic, and *very popular*. No other appointment would be, as I think, equally well received, certainly none that I have heard talked of.

We have called our Oregon meeting for thursday, as you have seen. [3] We hold a preparatory caucus tonight, and hope to make the movement a decided one. The news from Mexico, which we have just received, explains the meaning of Sir Robert Peel, and makes it in my view certain that we are to be precipitated into a war. [4] I look upon the crisis with a feeling of interest, disproportioned altogether to any responsibility which can rest upon any detached individual like myself; but without alarm or doubt. I have the confidence of absolute certainty in the patriotic energies of our people; and feel that, come when it may, the war can neither be inglorious to our Country nor unprofitable to the World.

J. K. KANE

ALS. DLC–JKP. Addressed to Washington City.

1. See Henry Horn to Polk, April 28, 1845, and Horn to Polk, May 1, 1845.

2. James Page served as postmaster of Philadelphia from 1836 until 1841. Following the U.S. Senate's rejection of the nomination of Henry Horn on June 24, 1846, Polk appointed Page collector of customs at Philadelphia.

3. Kane refers to a public meeting called by supporters of George M. Dallas for May 1st with a view of sustaining Polk's Oregon policy. Fearing such a display on Independence Square might give Dallas' supporters an advantage in the dispensation of patronage in Philadelphia, partisans of James Buchanan issued their own call to gather at the same place on the same day. The two factions battled to control the platform and address the crowd of several thousand citizens; the meeting yielded two sets of resolutions, both of which criticized recent pronouncements by British ministers on the Oregon question, underscored public support for Polk's position as stated in his inaugural address, and asserted the United States' claim to "absolute sovereignty" over Oregon. Both factions also emphasized a desire for peace with Great Britain but added their determination to defend the United States' claims to Oregon.

4. Kane probably refers to Sir Robert Peel's address to the House of Commons on April 4, 1845, and to news of Mexico's suspension of diplomatic relations with the United States. See Jacob L. Martin to Polk, April 16, 1845.

## FROM FRANCIS W. PICKENS

My dear Sir                                    Edgewood 28 April 1845

I recvd yours of 21st inst: yesterday, and return you my thanks for the distinguished honor you are pleased to tender in offering me the appointment of "Envoy Extraordinary & Minister Plenipotentiary to Great Britain."

Highly important as I know the position to be in the present juncture of our affairs and gratifying as it might be personally to me, yet under existing circumstances I most respectfully decline the appointment.

There are questions of grave import connected with the future policy of our government which I fondly hope and believe will be adjusted under your Administration so as to give *permanent justice*, equality, and protection to all,[1] but until these are settled I could not (unless in the contingencies of war) accept any office consistently with the feelings of allegiance I bear to my own State.

F. W. PICKENS

ALS. DLC–JKP. Addressed to Washington City. Polk's AE on the cover states that he received this letter on May 2, 1845.

1. Picken's reference probably is to the Tariff of 1842; he regarded this tariff as an unjust burden on the southern states and demanded a readjustment. See Francis W. Pickens to Polk, December 5, 1844.

## FROM HENRY WELSH

Dear Sir.                                                York, Penna. Ap 28/45

As you will probably soon take up the Philada appointments, I beg to say a few words on that subject. All my information from there goes to show that there is nothing, really, in the objections made by the Philadelphians to my appt as Collector, in consequence of my not residing there *now*; these objections, I am assured, proceed more from interested motives, than a desire for the welfare of the party. If I believe my appt would have the least tendency to injure the party, I would not ask it, nor would I hold it a single day. If it were likely to have that tendency, surely Govr Shunk, Secretary Miller, Atty Genl Kane and Judge Laporte, the Surveyor Genl of the State, *that is to be*, would not so anxiously desire it.[1] The State Admn has much at stake, and its salvation depends upon the union of the party. It is not the single appt. of Collector, which creates the feeling in Philada; it is the patronage connected with that office; and that patronage almost exclusively dispensed in the City &c, as I would dispense it, were I appd., would, I have no doubt, satisfy them. My residence there, for several years, gave me a tolerably correct knowledge of the divisions and subdivisions of the party; *and, being entirely free from clique or faction there, and elsewhere*, I could cooperate with Mr Secry Walker, in the selection of subordinates, solely in reference to *competency, business qualifications, and moral and political integrity*. I would steer clear of the miserable horde of trading politicians, who hang like an incubus upon the party, and who have been one of the main causes of bringing it into the almost hopeless minority in which it now is, in the City and Co. The truth is, had the counsels of the Philada politicians prevailed, we would, long since, have been in a minority in the State also. I could have had recommendations in abundance from Philada, but I did not wish to place myself under any seeming obligations to the politicians there, so that I would be left entirely free to select subordinates in reference alone to the best interests of the Government, and the union and harmony of the great republican party.

In conclusion, I will only add that this is my first application for any office, and that I would be much pleased to succeed; but, should you think it best to confer the appointment upon another, I will not murmer, nor shall such event, in the least, change my warm personal regard for you, nor my devotion to the Democratic party, with which I have always acted, and in whose success and prosperity are involved the best interests of the Country.

HENRY WELSH

ALS. DLC–JKP. Addressed to Washington City.
1. Francis R. Shunk, Jesse Miller, John K. Kane, and John Laporte. Born in Asylum, Penn., Laporte served several terms in the Pennsylvania House, 1828–32; won election to two terms in the U.S. House, 1833–37; sat on the bench of the Bradford County Court, 1837–45; and held the post of state surveyor-general from 1845 to 1851.

## FROM HENDERSON K. YOAKUM

Dear Sir,                            Memphis Tennessee April 28. 1845
The Candidates for Governor[1] spoke here to day. Supposing you would be glad to hear what they are doing, I drop you a line.

When the nominations were first made, I felt some misgivings as to the result, but I feel none now. Brown triumphs every where they meet. Such was asuredly the case to day, for I was an eye witness. The whole current is with us. The betting democrats are making large offers here, but get no takers up. The excitement on the Texas question is growing. I think there is no doubt of at least five thousand majority for us.

It is not my business, but I think if you knew the moral standing of the postmaster here,[2] you would give a tone to public virtue by turning him out. I have it from the best men in Memphis that he has been living in open adultery with a mulatto woman, and actualy keeps one of his children, by her, in the post office.

I am on my way to the great west. Trusting that yourself and lady are in good health ....

H. YOAKUM

ALS. DLC–JKP. Addressed to Washington City and marked "*Private.*"
1. Aaron V. Brown and Ephraim H. Foster.
2. Marcus B. Winchester.

## FROM GEORGE M. DALLAS

My Dear Sir,                        [Philadelphia, Penn.] 29 April 1845
I avail myself of a trust-worthy private opportunity to write to you. The Post-office is, at present, not to be relied upon.[1]

I saw Mr. Henry Horn, agreeably to your request, this morning, and I spoke to him with entire candour and friendship. I assured him of your wish to manifest your kindness and respect for him by an appointment, but that the Collectorship was not the place as to which you were entirely free from embarrassment: that he ought frankly to relieve you from all difficulty, by consenting to take another post: and that in my own opinion the Treasurership of the Mint was, in every respect, as honorable, and better suited to him. The result, after a conversation of some length was that he declared himself content to forego the office of Collector and to accept that of Treasurer at the Mint, provided a person were appointed Collector to whose acknowledged character for capacity and standing he might defer without personal disgrace or depreciation. He told me he had written to you yesterday,[2] though he had not gone perhaps as far as with me.

If this course be taken, it will hardly be possible for you to do for Mr. John Horn, the brother, what you had intended; and you will be free to select for your Naval Officer, either Mr. Welsh, Dr. Lehman, Mr. Schnabel, Dr. Skerrett or Mr. John T. Smith.[3] Of all these, I should, on the whole, be bound to indicate Mr. Welsh as the one to be preferred, tho I really have no strong choice. They are all worthy men, honest, and of moderate capacity.

I find, on enquiry, that Mr. Rush never was on any *Clay* Electoral Ticket, and that you have been misinformed. In 1824, he was on our *Crawford* Electoral Ticket—put there while he was abroad. In 1828, he was on the *Wirt* Electoral Ticket.[4] He was always opposed to *Clay*: and indeed that gentleman regarded his consenting to be on the Wirt, or antimasonic, ticket in 1828, as an act of hostility. He never said a word or penned a letter against Genl. Jackson: but on the contrary was an ardent admirer, and the General early recognized him as a friend who had been temporarily embarrassed by his associations.

Rest assured, my Dear Sir, that I speak with the sincerest conviction, after the most careful reflection, when I say that in designating Mr. Rush, Mr. Welsh & Mr. Henry Horn to the places mentioned, you must receive the entire approbation of our community, barring only those who must be removed.

A popular movement has begun as to Oregon, and a Mass meeting will be held in Independence Square on thursday next.[5] The purpose, as communicated to me, is to reply to Sir Robert Peel and Lord Aberdeen, and to express a firm determination to stand by the Administration.

G. M. DALLAS

ALS. DLC–JKP. Addressed to Washington City and marked "*Private.*"
1. Dallas probably refers to the political reliability of James Hoy, Jr. Ap-

pointed postmaster in 1844, Hoy had previously served as deputy surveyor of the port of Philadelphia, 1841–44.

2. See Henry Horn to Polk, April 28, 1845.

3. Henry Welsh, George F. Lehman, Ellis B. Schnabel, probably David C. Skerrett and John T. Smith. Schnabel was a Philadelphia attorney; Skerrett was a Philadelphia medical doctor. A Philadelphia native, Smith served one term as a Democrat in the U.S. House, 1843–45.

4. A Virginia lawyer and author, William Wirt served as attorney general of the United States from 1817 until 1829. He headed the presidential ticket for the Anti-Masonic party in 1832. In 1828 Richard Rush ran as the vice-presidential nominee on John Q. Adams' ticket.

5. See John K. Kane to Polk, April 28, 1845.

## FROM AARON V. BROWN

Dear Sir                               Somerville April 30th 1845

Allow me to say that so far my canvass has progressd very satisfactorily. At Clarksville, Paris, Jackson Brownsville & Memphis our triumph was evident & admitted. Friends every where satisfied of an increased vote in August. Foster begs off from anecdotes & every thing like fun in our discussions & to day proposes that we shall address a note to the public calling in all our appointments, issue a circular letter & close up the Canvass. I am inclined to do it, but our friends are divided here on the policy, so I shall take some days, perhaps till I reach Nashville to give him an answer. He is worsted considerably whilst I am in fine voice & general health. The published account of our meetings, in the Union are not exagerations for effect; they fall rather below than above the true mark. He is the most vulnerable man I ever saw.

I say nothing about general matters & only take time to congratulate you on the Ritchie arrangement.[1] I have not received a letter from you or Johnson since I left.

In great haste & with my best respects to Mrs. Polk....

A. V. BROWN

ALS. DLC–JKP. Addressed to Washington City.
1. See Aaron V. Brown to Polk, January 1, 1845.

# MAY

## FROM HENRY HORN

My Dear Sir,                                    Philadelphia 1st May 1845

My friend Magee[1] after expressing to me the many obligations he felt
for the very Kind and cordial reception he received at your hands communicated a portion of the conversation he had with you in reference to
myself, from which it appears that you have not read the sealed letter of
which he was the bearer from me. I therefore deem it necessary lest the
original may be lost or mislaid to give you the following extract.[2]

"I regret exceedingly to find that you are still embarrassed in relation
to the appointments for our city, and were it in my power to relieve you
from the difficulty without a sacrafise of my honor and standing in this
community which are far dearer to me than the honors and emoluments
of office I would most cheerfully do so.

For the first time in my life after an ardent and devoted service to my
party of more than thirty years during which I have suffered in a pecuniary point of view to the amount of many thousands, and withstood the
slanders detractions and persecutions of our political opponents to an extent perhaps greater than any other individual in the State I find myself
a candidate for an appointment to which no disinterested man of either
party either here or elsewhere will deny my just, nay, my paramount
claims over any of my competitors, either of whom would be more than
requited for all the services they have rendered by an appointment to

*331*

any of the subordinate places here. To recede then from the ground I have taken that another less worthy and less competent may occupy it would be dishonorable alike to myself and the numerous friends who support me. It would be a course which I am sure you as my sincere friend could not advise me to pursue.

My name is before you for a place designated by my friends in truth I may say by nearly the whole community as one for which they believe I am especially qualified and one to which I am in their judgement I am eminently entitled. Should you think otherwise (*for it is to you also that I appeal*) I must submit to my fate with the best grace I can."

And here allow me again to assure you that there is nothing on earth consistent with my own sense of honor that I would not do to serve you, and had fortune reversed our relative positions, the machinations of your enemies I am sure never would have been permitted for a moment to shake my confidence in you or to have made me halt or hesitate in my purpose to serve you.

I do not however ask you to do that for me through private friendship which public opinion will not justify, God forbid that I should.

HENRY HORN

ALS. DLC–JKP. Addressed to Washington City and marked "*Private.*"
1. James Magee, a member of the Philadelphia Democratic Hickory Club, is not identified further.
2. See Henry Horn to Polk, April 28, 1845.

## FROM ANDREW JACKSON

My dear Sir,                                      Hermitage May 2, 1845
Weak & debilitated as I am I could not resist endeavouring to wade through the debate in the English parliament & comments on your inaugural as it relates to oragon.[1] This is the rattling of British drums to alarm us, and to give life to their friends in the United States, such as the Hartford convention men, the Blue light federalists[2] & abolitionists, and to prevent if Britain can, the reannexation of Texas, by shadowing forth war & rumors of war, to alarm the timid, & give strength to the traitors in our country, against our best interests & growing prosperity. This bold avowal by Peel, & Russell[3] of perfect claim to oragon, must be met as boldly, by our denial of their right, and confidence in our own, that we view it too plain a case, *of right*, on our side to hesitate one moment upon the subject of extending our laws over it & populating with our people. Permit me to remind you that during the canvass, I gave a thousand pledges for your energy & firmness, both in *war* & in *peace*,

to carry on the administration of our government. This subject is intended to try your energy—dash from your lips the council of the timid on this question, should there be one in yr council. No temporising with Britain on this subject now, *temporising will not do.* Base your acts upon the firm basis, of asking nothing but what is *right* & permitting nothing that is *wrong.* War is a blessing compared with national degradation. The bold manner of Peels & Russels announciation of the British right to oragagon, the time & manner requires a firm rebuke by you in your annual message, and has opened a fair field to compare their claim to orgagon with their right to the Territory claimed by Britain on our north East boundery,[4] & which we were swindled out of, there being on file in archeives of England the map on which was laid down our boundery agreable to the treaty of 1783,[5] which Lord Browman said in Eulogy of Lord Ashburton, shewd that England in her claim to that territory *had not a leg of right to stand upon.*[6] Just so with oragon, & Peel & Russle both well know it. Still, now, a perfect right to oragon is claimed. Make a note of this, & in your annual message expose Englands perfidy to the whole civilized wor[l]d. To prevent war with England a bold & undaunted front must be exposed. England with all hear Boast dare not go to war. All Europe knows she has no right to oragon nor never had. You will pardon these my friendly suggestions. The Whiggs have held you forth to England as feeble & [un]energetic, & would shrink at the threat of war. I am sure you will meet this with that energy & promptness that is due to yourself, & our national character.

From a letter just received from Mr. Thos. J. Donelson, it appears, that he is without employment, and has the whole of the expence of his wife & family on his hands, and also the expence of his sick mother-in-law,[7] who is too penurious to afford herself support or to aid her daughter who she induced to sacrafice her property here to go to her, being her only daughter. If Mr. Donelson should be disapointed in getting an office for a few years, will be reduced to perfect want & his family.

My dear daughter Sarah is in a gloom fearfull that the intrigue of Blake, who turned out Mr. Taggart out of office & put in his nephew may prevent Mr. Taggart from being reinstated. Blake is an artfull deceiptfull man, and well calculated to get the ear of Mr. Walker Secretary of the Treasury, & if you leave the case there without your own enquiry, injustice will be done Taggart. Now I hazzard the assertion that there was no good cause for turning out Taggart but to make way for Blakes nephew,[8] a Tyler Whigg, & if you investigate the matter you will find this true. *I say to you, in the most confidential manner*, that I regret that you put Mr. R. J. Wa[l]ker over the Treasury. He has talents, I beleive honest, but surrounded by so many broken speculators, and being greatly himself encumbered with debt, that any of the other Departments would have been better, & I fear, you will find my forebodings turn out too true, and added to this, under the rose, He is looking to the vice presidency, and you will find that there is not that cordial good feeling between him & Mr. Buchannan as ought to exist. He belongs to what is now called the Dallas party. The real old democratic party of Pennsylvania—the Leapers,[9] the Horns, the Kanes, the Duane party &c. &c. &c. I write you this that you may have your eyes open, & whilst you have confidence that you may descover whether it is well placed. You may look out for a severe attack upon Walker by the Whiggs soon & by vigilence over that Department, you may be able to shield the Executive from it. The Revd. Mr Mathews[10] visited me a few days ago. He is looking out for a place to settle himself & family. Still hopes you may be able to send him to West Point. There is wanted, *really*, a change there. If he can get that appointment get Genl McCalla to write him that he may cease looking elsewhere. If he cannot get it then Genl. McCalla might intimate that to him. My dear sir, do not let Sarah be disappointed by neglect of Taggart. Her sister Jane *Mrs. Taggart*, raised Sarah hence the great attachment, & Mr. Weatherale[11] was a father to her. My complaint has assumed a high dropseal type. I am swollen from the toes to the crown of the head. I suffer much. May god preside over yr. administration & crown it with success is the united prayer of all its inmates.

ANDREW JACKSON

ALS. DLC–JKP. Addressed to Washington City and marked *"Confidential."* Polk's AE on the cover states that he received this letter on May 9, 1845, and answered it on May 12, 1845. Published in Bassett, ed., *Correspondence of Andrew Jackson*, VI, pp. 404–05.

1. See Jacob L. Martin to Polk, April 16, 1845.

2. Prominent New England Federalists elected by the legislatures of Massachusetts, Connecticut, and Rhode Island met in Hartford, Conn., on December 15, 1814, to coordinate opposition to the war, commercial restrictions, and westward expansion. Although delegates recommended constitutional amendments to curb Southern political power and protect New England's commercial interests, many Americans condemned the Hartford Convention as treasonous. During the War of 1812 Federalists reportedly signalled to the British fleet with blue lights to indicate that Stephen Decatur was preparing to run their blockade at New London, Conn.

3. A member of the British House of Commons from 1813–55 and 1859–68, Lord John Russell served as prime minister from 1846 until 1851 and from 1865 to 1866. Raised to the peerage in 1861, Lord Russell proved an outspoken proponent for the repeal of the Test and Corporation acts and played a key role in the passage of the Reform Bill of 1832.

4. The Webster-Ashburton Treaty, ratified by the U.S. Senate in 1842, settled

the Anglo-American dispute over the border between Maine and Canada and improved relations between Britain and the United States. The compromise settlement, which established the present boundary line, proved controversial because Britain claimed and received a sizable portion of the disputed territory.

5. Jackson's references are to the Treaty of Paris, signed in September 1783, through which the United States formally concluded the struggle for independence, and the map employed by British and American negotiators to determine the boundary between Maine and Canada. The map, a subject of controversy in negotiations for the Webster-Ashburton Treaty, reportedly included a red boundary line, drawn by Benjamin Franklin during the 1782–83 peace talks, which confirmed the United States' claims to territory in Maine.

6. Alexander Baring, first Baron Ashburton, and Henry Brougham, Baron Brougham and Vaux. Lord Ashburton served in the British House of Commons from 1806 until 1835, when he was raised to the peerage. He represented Britain as a commissioner to the United States in 1842 and negotiated the Webster-Ashburton Treaty. A proponent of electoral and judicial reform, as well as an outspoken supporter of Britain's anti-slavery movement, Lord Brougham served in the House of Commons, 1810–12 and 1815–31. He received his peerage in 1831. Jackson's reference is a paraphrase of a portion of a speech by Brougham in the House of Lords on April 7, 1843. While praising Ashburton's diplomatic skills, Brougham noted the existence of two official contemporary British maps that verified the red boundary line claimed by the United States as the Maine-Canada boundary in 1783.

7. Thomas J. Donelson married Emma Farquher, a cousin of Sarah Yorke Jackson. Donelson's mother-in-law was Eliza Yorke Farquher.

8. Not identified further.

9. Jackson probably refers to William J. and George G. Leiper.

10. A Presbyterian minister from Lexington, Ky., John D. Matthews was dismissed from his church for supporting Polk in the 1844 presidential election. Matthews applied unsuccessfully for the chaplaincy at West Point and in 1847 secured a clerkship in the General Land Office.

11. Reference probably is to Samuel M. Wetherill, brother-in-law of Sarah Yorke Jackson.

## FROM NICHOLAS P. TRIST[1]

[Sir:]             (Near) Havana May 2. [18]45

A late vessl from New York brought a letter from Mrs. Meikleham, a sister of Mrs. Trist just established in that city,[2] casually mentioning an incident which *may* have *something at the bottom of it*. Mrs. M. had sent to the counting house of Mr. Codwise,[3] for shipment to Havana, some trunks belonging to members of my family, which she judged would be acceptable on the occasion of our removal. They were there seen by an officer of the customs, whose attention being attracted to the name *Trist*, this gave rise to some enquiry or remark, which led Mr. C. to say that the family were about returning to the United States, and that he supposed Mr. T. was to receive some appointment. Hereupon the officer (his name or grade not mentioned, but Mrs. M. says "a staunch locofoco") observed, "Mr. Polk will not *dare* to give him an office."

Now, this may have been mere idle talk; or, at most, the expression of individual opinion or feeling. On the other hand, it may be that this opinion or feeling is a more or less general sentiment of the northern mind with respect to me: one not confined to those who are actuated by party views or prejudices. On this point, you possess ample means of informing yourself. I mention it with a view to your doing so; and in the wish, that, having done so, you will act in regard to my appointment or non-appointment with the same freedom exactly as if the subject were now for the first time presented to your mind. This, I wish you to do, not merely with reference to your own individual opinion as to whether I am "honest, capable & faithful"; but with reference to Public opinion also, and to the degree in which it may appear to yourself necessary or important, that, as a matter of mere party policy, you should be governed by public opinion on this point.

It is true, that the duty of filling the offices of the country (in itself by far the most difficult of those which attach to your post) *cannot* be discharged to the satisfaction of every body; and this would be true still, if you acted under the guidance of an Archangel, intuitively gifted with full & perfect knowledge of all men & all things. Even under this supposition, no appointment you could possibly make could fail to be attended in a greater or less degree, according to its importance, with disapprobation: even within the ranks of the party, beyond which it would be futile to look to public opinion in regard to matters of appointment. I speak not here of the feeling of disappointment in those directly or sympathetically interested; but of conscientious disapprobation, either positive or relative, in minds altogether free from any such bias. This cause of party discord cannot but have its activity awakened by every single step you take in the discharge of this branch of your duties. Here, it is unavoidable that you should be incessantly doing that which (to say nothing of its operation upon & through individual selfishness & individual partiality) weakens *confidence*, the only good ingredient in the cement that binds party together, the one thing indispensable to that concert of honest hearts, wherein consists the very existence of party, as a tangible thing, as an efficient cause; and which, by weakening confidence, does therefore to the same extent endanger the preponderance of the principles to which those honest hearts are devoted, but devoted to no purpose unless the causes which tend to disturb harmonious action upon points of no moment in themselves be kept under.

This is inevitable. But what follows? That you should disregard this effect, which, do what you may, you must at every moment be giving rise to? No: that it should, on the contrary, be your constant aim to keep it at its minimum; so far as this may be compatible with the just weight of other considerations. That this is your duty, I am fully sensible; and I have no wish that you should lose sight of it in regard to me. I wish the reverse. So far as I know myself, I am incapable of ever harbouring the desire—be the circumstances of my position what they may—that any sentiment sufficiently strong & extensive to demand respect, as a matter of party policy merely, however erroneous the grounds upon which it may have arisen, should be *braved*, for the sake of àny personal advantage to me or mine.

If therefore, upon full consideration, you should be of opinion that the nature of the case is now such, and the probable result of its agitation would be such, that there would really be any "daring" in appointing me to office, let the thought be dismissed from your mind.

Do not suppose that I have any apprehension on the subject; that I dread *any* ordeal, to which, in the event of my appointment to office, I may be subjected. There is one thing which I do dread; which is so revolting to me, that nothing short of the weighty motive which alone makes office of any kind acceptable to me could have power to overcome the disgust: the toil & trouble, the *waste of my time* that would be involved in such an ordeal; or rather, in the *preparation* necessary to secure my triumphant passage through it. This further waste of my life—too great a portion of which has already been thrown away upon this worthless subject—I do dread; but it is the only dread I have, and this dread is overcome by the weighty motive just referred to: the comfort & well being of my wife and children & others connected with me. From what I had learnt from a variety of quaters, from expressions of esteem and good feeling which have spontaneously come to me, I had been led to suppose that a very extensive reaction had taken place against the misconception of my character occasioned by the assaults to which it has been exposed.[4] (That a *strong* one has take place, in individual minds, I know to be a fact. I do not mean *here*, because here those assaults have always been impotent, every man *knew* that they arose from malice & had nothing but falsehood & misrepresentation to rest on; but at home, among people to whom I was personally unknown, and who could judge of me only by means of information obtained from those whom they knew they could rely upon) I had, I say, been led to suppose that a very extensive reaction had taken place; and very possibly the remark thus casually reported to me may not be any evidence of the contrary. But if the state of the case be otherwise, let it be as far otherwise as it may, I meet it, in all that regards myself, *with defiance*. If "a dead set" is to be the consequence of my receiving an appointment, then I say, so far as regards any bearing it may have upon *myself* (as contradistinguished from the bearing & influences it may have within the party) *Let them come on*. Let John Quincy Adams be the leader of the band, and let his malice be more viperous than ever it showed itself to be. I defy him, and it, and all the "et ceteras" (to borrow his own phrase) that can find room in his train.

This is my feeling, so far as the bearing of the question is upon me, or upon the *result* of any such ordeal. Upon this point, I entertain no doubt, I am perfectly certain. What it is my wish, that you should now consider, is, not the *result* of any ordeal in the senate, (for on this point the grounds for judgment are not within your reach) but the effect of the *appointment*; the effect of this, within the party & upon the party, owing to any sentiment which may *now* prevail with regard to me.

[NICHOLAS P. TRIST]

L, fragment. DLC–FP. Marked "Copy of part of my letter to James K. Polk Esq. President of the U.S."

1. Trist married Virginia Jefferson Randolph, a granddaughter of Thomas Jefferson; studied law under his father-in-law; and began his career in public service in 1827 as a clerk in the State Department. Andrew Jackson appointed Trist consul in the port of Havana, Cuba, in 1833; John Tyler recalled him in July 1841; and Polk appointed him chief clerk of the State Department in 1845 and then special agent to negotiate a peace treaty with Mexico in 1847.

2. The tenth of twelve children of Martha Jefferson and Thomas Mann Randolph, Septimia Anne Randolph married David Scott Meikleham in 1838.

3. Trist probably refers either to Charles F. Codwise, a New York City iron merchant, or to David Codwise, a New York City lawyer.

4. In August 1839 New York City shipmasters and shipowners petitioned the President and Congress for Trist's removal as consul to Havana. Trist had earned the enmity of the mercantile community and press by refusing to resist Spanish authority prosecuting crimes committed by American sailors on U.S. ships in Havana harbor. In separate cases Spanish officials imprisoned a captain of the U.S. brig *Kremlin* for severely beating a crewman and convicted six crewmen of the *William Engs* for mutiny against their captain. Trist explained that his investigations of these incidents verified the Americans' guilt and that international law gave jurisdiction in these cases to the Spanish authorities. The House Committee on Commerce investigated Trist's conduct and in July 1840 reported that they found no grounds for action against him. House Report No. 707, 26th Congress, 1st Session, pp. 1–2, 11–17, 443–475.

## FROM JAMES BUCHANAN

My dear Sir                                    [Washington City May 3, 1845][1]
Allow me to suggest to you most kindly & respectfully the propriety of not deciding on the appointment of minister to England until Monday. Since I came home I have been so impressed with the importance of the movement that I have ventured to make this suggestion. The appointment will I fear separate from us the friends of Mr C.[2] & although they may not be very numerous their talents & energy give them weight. I have no objection in the world, personal or political to Mr V.B.[3]

JAMES BUCHANAN

ALS. DLC–JKP. Addressed to Washington City.
1. Date and place identified through content analysis.
2. John C. Calhoun.
3. Martin Van Buren.

## FROM RANSOM H. GILLET

My Dear Sir,                                    Washington May 3. 1845
Before leaving for the Banks of the St. Lawrence, I take a few moments to follow out the conversation of yesterday. I have reflected fully on the subject of retaining Mr Van Ness as Collector, & am clear in my convictions that he should not be retained. He is but a new comer in NY from Vt, & is not looked upon as a New Yorker. Last year he opposed us, as long as he had hopes, & then faced about & asks to be retained in the most responsible office in the state. He has sought to sustain himself by appointing the relatives of leading men to office under him. You may rely upon it, that those who urge his retention have their *friends provided for under him*, except perhaps Southern men in your cabinet. To retain him will be to disappoint the friends of *all* other candidates & chill their feelings. They *all* agree he should go out, & they make the mass of the democracy in that city. The offer of the office to Mr Flagg has transpired to the public, & furnishes the evidence that you thought VN ought to go out. I cannot immagine a reason that can be put before the public, for a change of views. To say he *promises* to *behave well*, is what every man will do. If he promises to employ under him true democrats, who can judge of that question? Turn out the present set, & *they* will be as clamorous for his removal, as they now are for his retention. What reason can be assigned for his changes? It will not do to say, it is because he promised to do so to retain his office. Still it will be

so considered by the public. Why displace the subordinates who agree with him in all things, & leave the head! It would be unjust to allow the idea to prevail that changing his cause, after it was necessary to do so, to save his office, should effect the question of his continuance. Few of the sterling democrats of our state would ask him for office, or recommend their friends, when they know, that at heart, he is the same man he was when singing the praises of Tyler & denouncing you & Mr Dallas, & Wright & Gardiner.[1] His hostility to the latter still exhibits itself in Slam's[2] Plebian. I can see no possible way of retaining him & placing your administration in that high position which I so ardently desire. Your *real* friends should be allowed a preference over those who are not so, & when opponents send you glowing *promises*, you may well *think*, if not *say*, "I fear the Greeks though bearing gifts."[3] In this matter, you have a duty to perform & in my judgement, the sooner it is done the better.

As to successor, I have no anxiety, other than the one you so sensibly feel—that of getting the right man. I have no personal knowledge of the vorius[4] names before you, except Hoffman & Moore, both of whom you know &, so far as my judgement goes, properly appreciate. H. should be naval officer, beyond dispute. I have entire confidence in the judgement of Messrs Butler & Dix. Though it is said Coddington is inferior in talents to some others, still, my experience has taught me, that the highest talents do not always afford the best business qualifications. This you saw every session of congress. It is to be seen every where. This, I think an answer to the objection to Coddington. He is certainly a more *discreet* man than Morris. Coddington should be made P.M. if not Collector. Moore is strong with the rank & file, being a mechanic, & if his position is such as I suppose it to be, may well be made Marshall—but of this, I am less confident, than of the other suggestions, I have made.

I hope you will pardon this long letter, as you will appreciate the motive which has dictated it. In communicating with those whose motives as pure as your own, I may be said to be *thinking aloud*, rather than studying what I shall say. Hoping you may be entirely successful in your desire to do what is best ....

                           R. H. GILLET

ALS. DLC–JKP. Addressed locally and marked "Confidential."

1. Addison Gardiner served as lieutenant governor of New York, 1844–47, and as a judge of the New York Court of Appeals, 1847–55.

2. Levi D. Slamm.

3. Paraphrase of a line from Virgil's *Aeneid*, Book Two, line 49.

4. Probable mispelling of the word "various."

## FROM JOHN F. H. CLAIBORNE

My dear Sir,                                              New Orleans, May 4, 1845

I have taken some pains to review my recommendation of *Martin Duralde*[1] since my return to this city, and I am firmly persuaded that his re-appointment would be one of the wisest acts of your administration. The very fact that he is the son in law of Henry Clay, and that you spared him out of delicacy & respect for your great rival, would have, throughout the Union, a vast moral effect, particularly when it would be observed that he was the *only Whig* retained in the public service. The magnanimity of the act would strike even your most bitter enemies. Office seekers may represent things differently, but there is something dear to your own fame & this, I think, would be a rich contribution to it.

One effect of such a course would be to keep the Whig senators in good temper, and thus stay a factious opposition to your favorite nominations. Mr. Duralde's relationship to Mr. Clay gives him great importance.

Aside from all this, he is an excellent officer & no partisan. He voted for his father in law, (as I should do for mine, under the same circumstances) but he is a Texas man, and if Mr. Clay be not the candidate of the Whig party, the course of your Administration on the Texas and Oregon questions will bring him into the democratic ranks, and with him will come 500 Creole whigs.

The very circumstance of Mr. Duralde's being retained by you will neutralize his whole family connexion, including numerous voters & some of the most influential men in the state.

For these reasons I recommend his re-appointment and no man in the state has a greater personal interest than myself in making recommendations exclusively with a view to the perpetuation of the party.

JOHN F. H. CLAIBORNE

ALS. DLC–JKP. Addressed to Washington City and marked "Confidential."

1. Naval officer at New Orleans from 1841 until 1845, Martin Duralde, Jr., married Susan Hart Clay, daughter of Henry and Lucretia Hart Clay. Duralde's sister, Julie, married Henry Clay's brother, John Clay, Jr.; another sister, Clarissa, married William C. C. Claiborne, uncle of John F. H. Claiborne.

## TO BENJAMIN F. BUTLER

My Dear Sir:                                          Washington City 5th May 1845

Having decided that it was proper to recal Mr *Everett* from England, and that for reasons which it is unnecessary to state, it was decided that the Mission should be filled by some gentleman in the South, I have tendered it to that section of the Union, and it has been declined. The importance of the mission at this juncture of our relations with England, has been greatly increased, since the receipt of the news brought by the last steamer.[1] In the existing state of these relations, my opinion, now is, that we should be represented at the English Court, by the ablest man in the country, without reference to his geographical position. I made a remark to this purport, on saturday last, in the presence of *Mr Bancroft*; *Mr Bancroft* thereupon related a conversation which he held with you, shortly previous to the 4th of March last, in which you expressed to him, your opinion that *Mr Van-Buren*, might be willing to accept a Mission to some of the principal Courts of Europe. *Mr Bancroft*'s recollection of the opinion expressed by you is, that you thought a Mission abroad was the only public station which an Ex President could with propriety accept, and that *Mr Van-Buren* might do so. I immediately expressed to *Mr Bancroft* my regret, that he had not before given me the information, for that above all men in the country *Mr Van-Buren*, was best suited for such a mission, and that if I thought he would accept it, it would give me the greatest pleasure to tender it to him. I have seen *Mr Bancroft* again to day, and after holding a conversation with him, resolved to address you on the subject. If *Mr Van-Buren* will accept the mission, I will feel honored by it, while the whole country, will have a sure guaranty in his iminent ability and acknowledged patriotism, that the important interests entrusted to his care will be safe in his hands. I now address you for the purpose of learning your opinion whether it would be acceptable to *Mr Van-Buren* to have the Mission tendered to him. I address you rather than *Mr V.B.* fearing that possibly he might not receive the suggestion kindly, and supposing too, from your intimacy with him, that you may be able to communicate to me his views. I would on no account do any thing which might by possibility give him displeasure. If you shall be of opinion that he would accept the mission, or that he would receive the tender of it, in the kind spirit in which it would be intended, you are authorized to inform him, that it will give me sincere pleasure to confer it upon him. It is important that *Mr Everett's* successor should be appointed immediately, for though considerable progress was made in the negotiation upon the Oregon question during the last administration, a negotiation which will be received here shortly, yet there are great and important interests, requiring the presence an able minister at London. *Mr V.B.'s* appointment and acceptance would be hailed with joy and general satisfaction in every part of the Union. I have to request that you will do me the favour to give me an answer at the earliest practicable moment, after you shall be able to give me satisfactory information. I hope you may not be mistaken in the opinion you expressed to *Mr Bancroft*. If you are not I will make the appointment immediately. If he declines to accept, I must select some other person without delay. In either event an early answer is desired.

It is scarcely necessary to say that if I had been possessed of the information given me by *Mr Bancroft* two days ago, I should have made this communication some weeks since.

JAMES K. POLK

ALS. DLC–MVB. Addressed to New York City and marked "Private & Confidential."

1. See Jacob L. Martin to Polk, April 16, 1845.

## FROM GEORGE M. DALLAS

My Dear Sir,                                  [Philadelphia, Penn.] 5 May 1845

The enclosed note[1] will be more interesting to Mrs. Polk, than to yourself. Its writer certainly does furnish the wares of which she speaks of a beauty and quality not easily surpassed. I have so long known and dealt with her shop, that I cannot refuse to recommend it as it really merits.

The Texian Proclamation[2] relieves us from all anxiety. The day of session might well, to be sure, have been fixed some weeks sooner, but it is early enough, if, as cannot be doubted, the popular sentiment be resolved. The matter has in fact, by an act of Congress alone, ceased to be under the controul of the Executive: the ball has got its impulse, and must now roll to its destination in spite of corrupt or crusty officers. I most sincerely congratulate on the prospect.

G. M. DALLAS

ALS. DLC–JKP. Addressed to Washington City.

1. Enclosure not identified further.

2. Dallas probably refers to Anson Jones' April 15 call for a special session of the Texas Congress on June 16 to discuss the U.S. Congress' joint resolutions on Texas annexation.

## FROM ROYAL R. HINMAN[1]

Hartford, Conn. May 5, 1845

Recalls that prior to his removal as collector of customs at New Haven, he warned against proscribing the Tyler office holders in Connecticut. He urges Polk to support those who sustained and voted for him during the late election and to avoid the clique of politicians who "dilantly & slyly opposed you" during the campaign. Hinman argues that men like Niles and Welles[2] will lend the administration no real strength. They ruled the party under Andrew Jackson and Martin Van Buren "with a rod of iron," but now their power is gone. He has heard that the hunker cliques in New York and Pennsylvania create similar party divisions. In his postscript Hinman adds that the appointment of an avowed Tyler Democrat would strengthen the position of the administration, for he concludes that the Tyler Democrats hold the balance of power in Connecticut.

ALS. DLC–JKP. Addressed to Washington City.

1. A lawyer and author, Hinman served seven years as Connecticut's secretary of state, 1835–1842, prior to his appointment to the collectorship at New Haven in 1844; during his service in state government he compiled several volumes of colonial and revolutionary era records and edited two volumes of the public laws.

2. John M. Niles and Gideon Welles. A Hartford journalist, Welles won election to several terms in the Connecticut legislature, 1827–35; headed the Hartford post office for five years, 1836–41; and under Polk held the chief clerkship of the navy's Bureau of Provisions and Clothing, 1846–49. Later he helped found the Republican party and served as navy secretary from 1861 until 1869.

## FROM JESSE MILLER

My Dear Sir                                  Harrisburg. May 5th 1845

The recent proceedings in Phila. at the meeting call'd to sustain the Administration in the Independent and correct attitude assumed in your Inaugural address is rather mortifying to the Pride of a true Pensylvanian.[1] The great body of the democracy however of the City as well as County are right on all questions touching our National rights and Honor and if any emergency arises will be found ready to give the administration an efficient support not in words but in actions. It seems that the leaders of the opposition from fixed principles or from the force of habit invariably go wrong on all the great questions involving National honor and if our friends would but act prudently and avail themselves of the errors of their opponents, would have every thing to gain and nothing to lose in the discussions of such questions. The great body of the people of all parties are honest and patriotic and when things assume an aspect where they can clearly perceive the right and wrong a majority of them will always be found on the side of their Country.

I have already said so much about the appointment of Collector at Phila. I am almost afraid to refer to it again, lest you may think me too importunate.[2] The Interest however which we feel in it must be the apology. Permit me by the way to observe that Governor Shunk and myself must feel as deep an interest in the success of the democratic party in this State as any other gentlemen can do. Our own success and to some extent our personal honor and interests are intimately connected with it. With those feelings and interests we have felt a deep solicitude for the appt. of Mr Welsh as the one among all the persons named best calculated to strengthen us. If you will appoint him we care comparatively little about the other appts. I have my preferences to be sure but we have no right to ask you to consult our wishes in all the appts.

The recent proceedings alluded to, in Phila. have strengthened our convictions in reference to the appointment of Welsh. He will identify himself with no *Clique*. My opinion is that the appointment of Welsh to the Collectorship, Henry or John Horn, Doct Leyman[3] & James Page to the other offices would be as well recd as any you can make. I hardly know who are the applicants for the District Atty. Brewster I know is one and I confess I dont like him. I do not think he has the proper temper and discretion to fit him for the place. Besides he is *Cameronian*. I know Mr Buchanan is for him but as high a regard as I have for B's talents I think he is frequently mistaken in reference to the selection of men.

I look upon Brewster McCully Alexander Cummings, all as *Cameronians* and that they are a rule or ruin clique.[4] I care not what Cameron's professions may be, or how he may act in the Senate. I feel as confident as I do of my own existence that he & those who act with him are determined to break down our State administration if they can. They are essentially dishonest and as they know they cannot have the confidence of the State administration they will produce a division or Join the opposition to break it down if they think they can succeed, and all they gain in appointments or influence at Washington is so much gained for our destruction.

In conclusion let me again say I hope Welsh will be appointed. I cannot suffer myself to doubt on this question and I am clearly of opinion, for many reasons the sooner the Phila. appts are made the better.

J. MILLER

[P.S.] Judge Pettitt would make a very excellent Dist. Atty.[5]

ALS. DLC–JKP. Addressed to Washington City and marked *"Private"* and *"Confidential."*

1. See John K. Kane to Polk, April 28, 1845.

2. See Jesse Miller to Polk, March 12 and April 7, 1845. On March 29 Miller again wrote about the Philadelphia appointments and mentioned that his opinions had not changed since his interview with Polk. ALS. DLC–JKP.

3. George F. Lehman.

4. Benjamin H. Brewster, Thomas McCully, Alexander Cummings, and Simon Cameron. McCully, a member of the Pennsylvania legislature, 1841–1843, chaired the May 1 meeting in Independence Square. Cummings, a Cameron supporter from the Northern Liberties, represented Philadelphia County in the Pennsylvania House in 1855.

5. Miller wrote his postscript in the left corner of the last page of the letter.

A Philadelphia jurist, Thomas M. Pettit served as deputy attorney-general of Pennsylvania, 1824–30; sat on the district court of Philadelphia, 1833–45; and held the post of U.S. attorney for the Eastern District of Pennsylvania, 1845–49.

## FROM ARCHIBALD YELL

My Dear Sir                                        Galveston Texas 5th May 1845

Maj Donalson[1] and myself reached this place a few days since, where I expect to remain until I return to Arkansas, which will be in 8 or 10 days, without I see more necesity for my remaining than I now do, or receive some news by the steamer N. York (whis is due in 4 or 5 days) to change my determination.

Every thing that was necessary to consumate the object so much desired has been done by our worthy and talented Charge D'Affaires. No other man in the Union could have affected so much. His pecular relation to the Old Hero of the Hermitage as well as the Hero of *San Jacinto*,[2] and his acquaintance with the members of Congress of Texas, as well as the temperment of the people and the various cliques and factions, give him the power to do more than any other man could have done.

In ordinary Cases, any Gentleman could acquit himself well enough. But when the Executive and his Cabinet was *disinclined* to say the least of it,[3] it required more than ordinary address, to bring the Executive to terms just as he desired them, and to place *others* in a *position*, from which they willingly retreat. Since the issuence of the Proclamation, convening Congress[4] every thing goes on well. The people are full of enthusiasm and there will be but one voice either in Congress or with the people! Even Unconditional Independence, recognized by Mexico, will not materially change the result.

But the last accounts from Mexico the 15th April does not indicate a disposition to make peace with Texas. That however was before Capt Elliott's despaches, reached the City of Mexico.[5] The intercision or interfearence of the British govermt may induce them to take the alternative, *Independence*, rather than annexation. Upon all those subjects you are much better advised than we can be here. You may now rest assured, that nothing but a Providential interfearence can prevent Annexation, so far at least as Texas is concerned.

Yesterday, President Houston reached this place on his way to the Hermitage. The position he heretofore *assumed*, has been communicated by Maj Donalson. He now seems willing to have the matter succeed, at least he will not oppose it, nor is he disposed to be considered in opposition. *He is now safe* and no apprehensions need be feared from that quarter, and He is "the Power behind the Throne, greater than the Throne itself." All dissensions and opposition in Texas will now cease and nothing can make a change but a proposition more favorable from some foreign govermt, which is neither to be feared or antisepated.

In effecting this great work, there are many worthy & talented Gentlemen who have devoted their time and money to accomplish it. They desirve the thanks of their country, but as it was not a part of my business here to interfear in appointmts to office, I shall leave that to the proper Departmt.

Allow me in conclusion to return you my acknowledgemts, for the expression of your kindness and confidince in intrusting in a small degree the great question now pending before the people of Texas, and I only regret I have not had it in my power to render more sirvice, for I will not attempt to even share a portion of the credit which is wholy due to our Minister Maj Donalson.

I go emediatly to Fayettville Ark where I hope to hear that some of my frinds in Arkansas have not been forgotten by you. I beg you to say to Mr Buchannon [6] I will settle my account next faul when I reach Washington.

A. YELL

[P.S.] Mr. Wickliffe reached here yesterday in good health. Y. [7]

ALS. DLC–JKP. Addressed to Washington City and marked "Private."

1. Andrew Jackson Donelson, United States chargé d'affaires in Texas.

2. Andrew Jackson and Sam Houston. On April 21, 1836, Texas troops under the command of Sam Houston attacked and routed Santa Anna's army at San Jacinto, Texas. Captured in the battle, Santa Anna signed an armistice in which he agreed to remove his armies from Texas.

3. Despite growing popular support in Texas for annexation, Anson Jones maintained diplomatic channels to Mexico through Charles Elliot, the British chargé d'affaires in Texas.

4. See George M. Dallas to Polk, May 5, 1845.

5. Lord Aberdeen instructed Elliot to pursue Mexico's full recognition of Texas independence and Texas' agreement not to join the Union.

6. James Buchanan.

7. Yell wrote his postscript in the left margin of the final page of the letter.

## FROM BENJAMIN F. BUTLER

My dear Sir,                                    New York, May 6th 1845

I am favored with your letter of the 3d [1] and have written to Mr. Hoffman expressing the earnest hope, that he may accept the office you have tendered him. This appointment does honor to your administration, and is a just tribute to a worthy citizen and useful public servant. There is always some discontent here; when a person from the interior is appointed to what our citizens think a local office[2]; but there will be less in the present case than is usual, and none deserving of consideration.

I regret, exceedingly, that you should have hesitated on the other point. And from those who are connected personally, or by office or the desire of office in his gift, with the present Collector, I know of no sound Democrat who doubts the propriety or necessity of a change. Speaking generally, I believe the sentiment to be universal among the sound Democracy of the city & state. In my former letter, I stated the grounds of this sentiment.[3] I do not wish to go over them; but I must assure you, that I believe them to be all well founded, and that I could give you many illustrations to confirm them on every particular. The general expression of this feeling, has been kept back by various causes. In the first place, no person has made *himself* a candidate; who was deemed, by our most worthy & judicious men, altogether fitted for the place; and they were therefore unwilling to commit themselves to the appointment of any such candidate. In the next place, immediately after your inauguration, well authenticated assurances were received here, that a new Collector would be appointed as soon as a candidate uniting the deliberate judgment of those friends in this State whom you honored with your confidence, should be named to you. The fact soon after made public, that the office had been tendered to Mr. Flagg, confirmed the impression before existing that a change was resolved on; and thenceforward the only question with the great mass of the party, was, as to the fittest person to succeed the present incumbent.

The confirmation by the Senate, under the circumstances, was a thing very much of course; and this fact, as well as the other considerations referred to in your letter, existed and had the same force, when the office was proposed to Mr. Flagg, which can be ascribed to them now. I owe it to truth and frankness to say, that I do not believe they will reconcile the mass of the party in this city & state, to the retention of Mr. Van Ness. After all that has happened, and with the perfect certainty, that the whole power & influence of the Custom House, so long as he is at its head, will be wielded by unworthy men & for purposes of mischief, they will regard such a measure with the deepest regret & dissatisfaction. Those who honestly entertain these views will, of course, freely express them; compliments on this head will beget distrust & division; and thus at the very outset of your administration, the harmony of the party in this state will be fatally disturbed, and the good feeling of many of your best friends cooled, and in the end (for such is the invariable course of such things) displaced by other sentiment. I am, therefore, constrained to say, and I esteem it the office of friendship not less than of duty, that in my Judgment, you will do great injustice to the sound democracy of this city & state, and much injury to yourself & to important public interests, if you decide to retain this gentleman in his present place.

If it be thought best to allow him to remain in office until the end of a *year* from his entrance on official duty, which, I believe, was about the 20th of June, no particular harm would result, provided a new appointment be immediately announced to take effect from that day. To prevent unnecessary fermentation & excitement, and the pernicious consequences which would follow, as well as, to relieve yourself from further annoyance on the subject, the decision to make the change (if such it shall be) should be announced without delay. I most earnestly hope that you may concur in this view. In regard to the fitness of Mr. Coddington for the place, you have misapprehended the tenor and design of my letter,[4] if you think I have any doubts as to his capacity to perform its duties with safety to the Government & credit to himself. He is not a lawyer and therefore has not some qualifications which I think desirable; nor is he a man of as much quickness and facility of execution, as some others. But he is a thorough man of business, an intelligent merchant; possesses excellent common sense; and is most faithful & exemplary in the performance of any trust he assumes; and when his inflexible political integrity, his perfect acquaintance with the city, and his safety in other respects are taken into the account, I feel satisfied, that he will make an excellent Collector, and that such will be the public judgment the moment his appointment is announced. He was, as all agree, the best Postmaster we ever had in this city; and I may mention as illustrating the character of the man, that during the five years & a half he held the office he was not absent from it a *single day*. On the other hand, it is notorious, in this city, that Mr. Van Ness has no particular capacity for the duties of the office of Collector, and that he leaves matters very much to his deputies & clerks, and especially to one of the latter who is called, at the Custom House, the Assistant Collector. You may infer, from his long attendance at Washington in the months of February & March last, that he does not deem his personal presence in the office absolutely essential, and that he relies largely upon others. Taking his habits in this respect, into consideration, and I feel perfectly justified in saying, that I deem Mr. Coddington, on the score of capacity, fully the equal of Mr. Van Ness; while in every other respect he is incomparably superior. You may be sure, also that while his administration of the appointing power will be liberal & just to all sections of the party in this city, he will give a decided and faithful support, to yourself, and make the interests of the Government and the public, the constant object of his pursuit.

I wish to make some further inquiries before writing as to the Appraisers & Assistant Appraisers, but will endeavour to do so before the end of the week.[5] From my own experience, and more especially from my observation of the experience of others, I can readily comprehend how much difficulty, solicitude & vexation you must find, in the exercise of the appointing power. After the first six months, you will, however, be greatly relieved; and during that period as well as afterwards, you will find in this as in every other part of your arduous & harassing duties, in pure intentions and earnest desire to promote the public good, your solace and reward.

B. F. BUTLER

ALS. DLC–JKP. Addressed to Washington City. Polk's AE on the cover states that Butler "Insists on the Removal of Mr Van Ness, as Collector at N. York."
1. Polk's letter has not been found.
2. Butler's reference is to the appointment of Michael Hoffman as naval officer.
3. See Butler to Polk, March 31, 1845.
4. See Butler to Polk, April 8, 1845.
5. On May 10, 1845, Butler wrote Polk about the subordinate offices in the New York Customs House; he reviewed the responsibilities of the three appraisers and four assistant appraisers and made several recommendations. ALS. DLC–JKP.

## TO ANDREW J. DONELSON

My Dear Sir:                              Washington City 6th May 1845
I enclose to you a letter from *Mr Ritchie*,[1] now the Editor of the official organ here, under the title of *"the Union."* I send also a few copies of his paper, containing an article, setting forth the views of the Executive government, towards Texas,[2] if she consents to accept, the terms of annexation offered to her under the two first of the joint Resolutions of Congress. I have no hesitation in expressing to you the confident opinion, that if Texas shall accept the proposition as made to her, and thus puts the reunion between the two countries beyond danger, that the U. States, will afterwards, adopt such measures, as will meet all her just wishes. Her extensive domain is valuable, and may be purchased at a price, which will enable her to pay all her debts, and take her stand in our Union unembarrassed. More liberal terms I have no reason to doubt would have been proposed by the last Congress, but for the peculiar state of parties, and that action upon the subject was to be had almost immediately after an exciting Presidential election. Every day adds to the strength of the policy of annexation in the United States, and opposition to the measure will hereafter be nominal rather than formidable.

It will be mainly confined to the Federal leaders. The elections which have already taken place show that the Democratic majority in the next House of Representatives, will be large and commanding. There is as little doubt but that there will be a Democratic majority in the Senate. As the Senate now stands the parties are equal, the Vice President having the casting vote. There are three vacancies, one in Virginia, one in Indiana and one in Tennessee.[3] The late Virginia election shows a Democratic majority of 32 on joint ballot in the Legislature, thus assuring the election of a Democratic Senator in place of *Mr Rives*.[4] In Indiana we have no doubt a Democratic Senator will be chosen, & our chances in Tennessee are more than equal.[5] In addition to this *Iowa* and *Florida* were by an act of the last Congress admitted into the Union.[6] They are both Democratic, and will be represented by four Democratic Senators next winter. Upon the Texas question we will command the votes of several Whig Senators in favour of the measure. Not a doubt remains therefore, that their will be in both Houses of the next Congress, a strong and decided majority favourable to Texan annexation, and the public sentiment of the country is now such, that there can be as little doubt, that full justice, will be done Texas, and all her reasonable wishes gratified, if she will now come into our Union; so far as I am concerned, and in this I have the united concurrence of my Cabinet, the whole power of the Executive branch of the government will be exerted, to extend to Texas, liberal and satisfactory terms. We desire most anxiously that she will accept the offer as made to her, and if she does she may rely upon our magnanimity and sense of justice towards here. We will act in a way which will satisfy her. I hope her people and government will not hesitate. Nothing could give me more pleasure personally, and nothing I am sure would give a vast majority of our people more pleasure, than to see my old friend *Houston* bearing her Constitution in his hand as one of her Senators, take his seat in the Senate of the U. States next winter. Surely he will not, cannot hesitate. Make my kind respects to *Houston* and tell him, that I hope soon to welcome the young Republic of which he was the founder, into our confederacy of States: and to see him the representative of her sovereignty in our Senate.

I wrote to you by Mr *Prentiss*, that I desired that you should be one of the Editors, of the administration organ here.[7] Under the uncertainty which existed, whether it was a situation, which would be agreeable to you, or which would be accepted by you, Messrs *Ritchie* and *Heiss*, purchased the *Globe* establishment in *their own right*, and are the sole proprietors. Should you desire to become interested in it after the termination of your mission, I think it probable that such an arrangement, could be readily made. It will not however do for you for a moment to think of leaving your post in Texas, until the object of your mission is consummated. It would be disastrous to change our Representative to Texas, at the present critical juncture of affairs, and it will be expected that you will remain at your post, until the object of your mission is consummated. Should you not become interested in the *"the Union,"* I hope it may be in my power during my term, to gratify the wishes of your friends in other respects. We have great anxiety to hear from you, by every opportunity, the actually existing State of things in Texas, and hope you will write by every Steamer which may leave Galveston for New Orleans. As I have marked this letter *unofficial*, I have written freely and in haste, and have no time to revise or copy.

When I last heard from *Genl. Jackson* he was declining in his health and strength. I hope he may live, to see the last earthly object of his wishes consummated, the annexation of Texas to our Union, and what would be still more consoling, to the closing hours of his life, to shake by the hand his old friend *Houston* as the Senator elect from the new State of Texas.

JAMES K. POLK

P.S. Mr *Ashbel Smith* has not been at Washington. It is now well understood that he is on a mission to England and France. The English policy is undoubtedly to procure delay, from the Texian government, in their action on our proposition, with a view to induce Texas to decline, but with the ultimate object of making Texas in truth and in fact a dependency of her own. You will of course be at the seat of government when the Texas Congress convenes on the 16th June. Early action on the part of that body is, our policy and should be urged, whilst, it will undoubtedly be the object of the Brittish Minister[8] to interpose any obstacle, and hold out any inducement which may produce delay, and gain time, with a view to defeat the object which we have so much at heart, both on account of Texas and of our own country. J.K.P.

ALS. DLC–AJD. Addressed to Washington, Texas, and marked *"Private & Unofficial."* Published in *THM*, III, pp. 64–66.

1. Letter has not been found.

2. Polk probably refers to an article in the Washington *Union* of May 3, 1845. The author urged Texas' swift acceptance of the United States' annexation proposal and warned of the dangers of Texas making alternative arrangements with Great Britain to guarantee its independence and extend its government a loan of $10 million.

3. In the fall the Virginia legislature would replace William C. Rives with Isaac Pennybacker; the Indiana legislature would choose Jesse Bright in place of Albert White, who did not seek reelection; and the Tennessee legislature would

elect Hopkins L. Turney to fill the seat vacated by Ephraim H. Foster, who had resigned to run for governor.

4. See John S. Barbour to Polk, March 22, 1845.

5. Indiana held its state elections on August 4, 1845; and Tennessee, on August 7, 1845.

6. Polk refers to the Act for the Admission of the States of Iowa and Florida into the Union, passed on March 3, 1845. Iowa held a plebiscite on April 7, 1845, to decide the statehood question; Florida accepted statehood without a popular vote and proceeded to announce state elections to be held on May 26, 1845.

7. See Polk to Donelson, March 28, 1845.

8. Charles Elliot.

## FROM JAMES HAMILTON, JR.

My Dear Sir.                                    Charleston May 6th 1845

On my arrival in this place, I met the accounts from Texas, by the last Steamer, which are quite decisive of the popular sentiment, being in favor of annexation, and that the Govt will be unable to resist it. I have written to Mr. Buchanan & submit to yourself, whether it will be at all expedient, to send Govr Lamar[1] into the Country more especially. As for expences he may find it necessary to incur, I am sure being a Texian, he will accept no compensation. I will however urge him to write a public Letter, which will serve to check anxiety & compel Houston, to keep no longer in the dark.

Having disposed of this subject, I hope you will pardon my adverting to another.

The friendly confidence with which you spoke of the Mission to England, induces me to address you in a spirit of equal confidence.

When you were pleased to say that but for my once having occupied a diplomatic appointment, from the Republic of Texas you would after the tender of this Mission to Mr Calhoun you would have offered it to me before the profer to Mr Elmore & Mr Pickens, that possibly with a sentiment of considerate kindness and tenderness towards me, you were assinging a secondary or plausible reason for an act to which you had been impelled by more valid considerations. In a word My Dear Sir, I have apprehended that some person very inimical to me, and having his own ends to answer, urged as an objection to my appointment, & induced you to prefer my Juniors for a most distinguished post, accorded to our State, on the ground of my having dedicated a portion of the Bonds of the Jas. River & Kanawha Company, to the service of the Republic of Texas when I was acting under a fiscal appointment from its Government as well as that Company. And that it would never do for you to give this high office to one who had been held up as a defaulter. It is not with the view of inducing you to reverse any decision you have made as to the Individual you deem best qualified for the British Mission at this interesting crisis because I have distinctly informed you, that my circumstances did not permit me to accept the office of Resident Minister at any foreign Court, but to lay before you my entire acquital by the President & Board of Directors of the Jas. River & Kanawha Company which is contained in the enclosed Resolutions.[2] For this intrusion you will find my apology, in the fact that I do not desire to be excluded from your entire confidence, on any mistakened grounds of culpibility.

The long & short of the version of a circumstance which gave me more pain than any other misfortune of my whole Life is briefly this. That at a moment when I had the pledge of the french Govt for the guarantee of the Texian Loan of 5 Millions of Dollars, and had made a Contract with the House of Laffitte, I used for a temporary purpose, to meet engagements for the Republic of Texas, $50.000 of the Bonds of the Company, with a contingent benefit to themselves of great value on the Moment the former Loan was realized. By a perfidy almost unexampled the french Govt. violated its pledge, and I *was stranded with the amt myself to shoulder*. I beg you to pardon the sensitiveness, which induces me, to trouble you with this explanation. But I have feared you have never seen my vindication, by the Company, and that prejudiced in your confidence I *may have suffered*. The best thing we have in this world is a good name, and the best we can leave behind us.

Before I conclude let me say one word on another point. With all possible candor then allow me to remark: because Texas by a Joint Resolution of her Congress made me a Citizen without calling on me to renounce my allegiance to the U.S. and gave me Commissions to the four principal powers of Europe to negotiate for the recognition of her Independance I do not think I ought to be disfranchised from my rights & privileges as a Citizen of the United States, or that my signal success with the Govt of her Britannic Majesty in a case in which all others had failed ought to constitute a valid objection to my being employed where I have made so many friends among the most influential public men of that Country. I say this with the sincere declaration which I made to you in person that it was impossible for me to accept the Mission as *Resident Minister to St James*, however willing I might be on any special occasion to strike speedily & decisively an important blow for the interests of the Country & my own Reputation. For such a service if Mr Calhoun had remained in your Cabinet I believe he would respectfully have recommended me to your consideration. But as it is I am well satisfied that things have taken the course they have and that in my most gratifying interviews with you at Washington I had an opportunity of assuring you of the cordial esteem with which I am ....

J. HAMILTON

P.S. In the course of two or three Days, I will address you on the subject of a pacification with Mexico, which I believe can be effected thro the influence of the Bankers of that Govt. in London. If you should have any immediate occasion to address me be so kind as to direct to Savannah Geo. *Strictly confidential.* I hope & believe Pickens will accept the mission; if he however declines & it should not again be pressed on Mr Calhoun. Let me earnestly urge you My Dear Sir to tender it to your friend Stevenson. I was a witness of his ability & the many friends he made in England. I tell you in confidence he feels a little sore as Genl Jackson wrote a friend to inform him that he would be in your Cabinet. This suggestion of mine is as sincere as it is disinterested.

ALS. DLC–JKP. Probably addressed to Washington City. Marked "Private & confidential."

1. Mirabeau B. Lamar, a native of Georgia, edited the *Columbus Enquirer*, 1826–35, and fought under Sam Houston in the Battle of San Jacinto; Lamar succeeded Houston as the second president of the Republic of Texas, 1838–41.

2. According to the enclosed resolutions signed by W. B. Chittenden, secretary of the James River & Kanawha Company, James Hamilton, Jr., appeared before the directors on June 20, 1842, and gave satisfactory explanations of his failure to sell company bonds in London and Amsterdam. The directors also found that Hamilton had acted in their interest in diverting a portion of the proceeds of a loan from Determeyer, Weslinger & Sons of Amsterdam; the board further resolved to continue Hamilton as their financial agent abroad. DS. DLC–JKP.

TO ROBERT J. WALKER

Sir:                                                          Washington 6th May 1845

This note will be handed to you by *Mr James B. Taggart*, the gentleman of whom I spoke to you. He desires to be restored to the clerkship, from which he was removed, by Mr Blake. He is the brother-in-law of *Andrew Jackson Jr*. Will you see him, this morning.

JAMES K. POLK

ALS. NjMoHP–LWS. Addressed locally.

## FROM CHARLES A. WICKLIFFE

D Sir                                          Galveston, Texas. May 6. 1845

I have requested Mr Buchanan to hand you my letter to him of this date[1] that I may thereby be saved the labour of writing again the same things to you.

I shall leave this in a few days and proceed to other parts where I shall see some friends. Van Zandt and Henderson[2] are at work in the right way in Eastern Texas.

Indeed Sir there is now no division, upon this question. In my future communications, I may confine myself more to a statement of facts in relation to the physical and other resources & advantages of this country, under a belief that when I tell you that Texas will accept the terms & thus promptly & that she will have on the 1st Monday in Dec. next knocking at the doors of Congress two Senators & two Representatives with a good Constitution in their hands, I have told you all on this subject which you desire to hear.

C. A. WICKLIFFE

ALS. DLC–JKP. Addressed to Washington City and marked "Private." Polk's AE on the cover states that he received this letter on May 18, 1845.

1. Wickliffe's letter has not been found.

2. Wickliffe probably refers to Isaac Van Zandt and James P. Henderson. Born in Franklin County, Tenn., Van Zandt migrated first to Mississippi and then to Texas, where he practiced law. He represented Harrison County one term in the Texas House, 1840–42, and served as chargé d'affaires to the United States from 1842 until 1844.

## FROM BENJAMIN F. BUTLER

My Dear Sir,                                   New York, May 7th 1845

I have just received your letter of the 5th and as I feel well assured that Mr Van Buren will receive the proposal contained in it, in the spirit in which it is conceived and expressed, I have thought it a fit exercise of the discretion entrusted to me to enclose it to him by this day's mail. It is due to each of you, and to the subject, that the explanations in regard to time should be before him when considering the matter and I know of no way of accomplishing this end so proper as by the transmission of your letter.

I should add, that Mr. Bancroft has correctly recollected the substance of my remarks, though I was very careful to say, that the suggestion was *exclusively my own* and to venture no opinion as to the probability of its being acceded to, in any event, by Mr Van Buren. It was made, *very casually*, in some such way as this: I said, "that were I at Washington, I should propose to you, without consulting Mr. Van Buren or any of his friends, to propose to him the embassy to England, that it was the most commanding post in the foreign service of the country, that it was specially important at this juncture, that it was a position which an Ex-President, in my judgment, might fill with perfect propriety as he would be withdrawn from local differences and represent the *whole nation*, and from the distinction he had enjoyed in his own country, possess great consideration & proportional means of usefulness, and that as Mr Van Buren had been unhandsomely recalled from this service by a factious Senate,[1] I thought that it would be a happy vindication of his own & his country's honor to send him, with the full sanction of the nation, which he could now receive, to complete the service then so rudely terminated."

I still entertain these views; and though they may be liable to some objections, I trust they will not be deemed by Mr. Van Buren entirely without weight. Should he communicate with me, you shall hear from me at once.

B. F. BUTLER

ALS. DLC–JKP. Addressed to Washington City and marked "Private."

1. Butler refers to Martin Van Buren's rejection as U.S. minister to Great Britain. In June 1831 Van Buren accepted Jackson's appointment and sailed for England; in January 1832 the Senate rejected Van Buren's nomination. On that occasion the president of the Senate, John C. Calhoun, cast the tie breaking vote.

## FROM ROBERT H. HAMMOND[1]

Sir,                                     Milton Penna 8th May 1845

I am very desirous to have a situation in the Army, either in the Inspector or Paymasters department, those being, as I understand the only offices in the Army to which a citizen can be appointed. I think I have some claims to a military office. I served seven years in the army in the early part of my life & resigned with evidence which I could easily produce of having served faithfully & honorably. Ever since I left the army I have been engaged more or less every year at considerable sacrafice of time & money in organising & training the militia of our state. Besides being elected to various minor offices in volunteer corps, I have held by election the office of Brigadier Genl. for the last 16 years & I know that I would give you abundant evidence that I have during all that time rendered much service in the disciplining & training our militia & volunteers. I have done my duty too, faithfully in the ranks of Democracy ever since I had a vote.

I therefore hope that when favours are dispensed I may not be forgotten.

R. H. HAMMOND

ALS. PHi. Addressed to Washington City.
1. A two-term congressman from Pennsylvania, 1837–41, Robert H. Hammond served as a lieutenant in the army from 1814 to 1820; he accepted a commission in 1846 as paymaster with the rank of major. Wounded in the Mexican War, Hammond died en route home on sick leave in 1847.

## FROM EBENEZER KNOWLTON[1]

Respected Sir                              Philadelphia May 8th 1845

As a freeman and Citizen of this Republic, and one that derives his existence from the blood that was spilt on Bunker Hill, on the Paternal side, and on the Maternal also, yet disdaines to be called, or associated with the party termed Native American, therefore as an American citizen I presume to address you, trusting that my observations may receive your notice.

There is in this, and other Cities of the United States men in the employmt of the Goverment, who are not naturalized; a stranger arriving on our shores, immediatly receives the approbation, and appointment to office, he, willing to succumb, to the caprices of the donor, under any, and all circumstances. Is this right? I suggest to your Excellency whether it would not be more discretionary and just, as also true, to the interest of this Republic, that all Citizens not born on the Soil, should hold office under the United States.

The appointment of foreigners to office has caused turmoil, war, and murder, in this our City, and other Cities of the Union, and because Why? that the goverment upholds emigrants from Europe in places of power. Whereby in such place of power, ignorant of our institutions and laws they become insolent, then arrogant, knowing that they have a licence under the law of the United States. The horribale outrages which pervaded this City,[2] was in part occasion by foreigners occupying the Civil and Military orders of the City, and if thus, our Public and General United States Institutions are to be governed by foreigners, our Republic quakes. Great Britan can do no better, than send her paupers her. They are a powerful army. More so, than Bayonets, and the paupers are the first to receive appointment, for the reason that they will sacrifice their lifes for the Ballot Box.

With these considerations I have the honor to be....

EBENEZER KNOWLTON

ALS. DLC–JKP. Addressed to Washington City.

1. A Philadelphia scrivener, Ebenezer Knowlton applied to James Buchanan on May 10, 1845, offering his services as a secret agent to monitor the activities of "foreign influences" in the city. ALS. DNA–RG 59.

2. Knowlton refers to the May 1844 riots in Philadelphia.

## FROM WILLIAM B. LEWIS

Sir,                                    Washington 8th May 1845

I learn from a private source that you have intimated that my removal from office was rendered necessary, because the position I occupied was dangerous to the government, in as much as it would enable me to impart information to a foreign power to the disadvantage of my own Country.[1]

I hope there is some mistake in this. You had the right to take my office from me, but not my reputation. I beg, therefore, to be informed whether you have made the imputation against me to which I have referred.

W. B. LEWIS

ALS. DLC–JKP. Addressed locally. Polk's AE on the cover states that the letter was "Handed to me by Majr *John H. Eaton* in my office on the 13th May 1845."

1. On April 10, 1845, Andrew Jackson wrote Lewis that Polk had determined to remove him as second auditor of the Treasury; Jackson explained that he had learned of the decision from a letter Polk had written to Robert Armstrong detailing the reasons and asking the same be communicated to Jackson. ALS. NN–Ford Collection. In an April 15 letter to the Washington *National Intelligencer*, Lewis included extracts of three earlier letters from Jackson expressing the former President's high regard. On July 9, 1845, the *National Intelligencer* published Jackson's April 10 letter to Lewis along with Lewis' letters to Polk of May 8, 18, and 19, 1845. Lewis anticipated that publication of these letters would offset rumors suggesting that he had compromised his office through overly close associations with Alphonse Joseph Yves Pageot, the French Minister to the United States and husband of Lewis' daughter, Mary Ann Lewis Pageot. During the closing weeks of Tennessee's 1845 state election campaign the *Nashville Whig* gave prominent coverage to Lewis' continuing complaints against Polk and suggested that Polk's dismissal of Lewis proved Polk's disloyalty to Jackson.

## FROM HENRY WELSH

Dear Sir.                                   York, Penna, May 9th, 1845

I received notice that you have been pleased to appoint me Naval Officer, for the District of Philada. For this mark of your confidence, I most heartily thank you. I can only now promise, to the best of my ability, an honest, faithful and vigilant discharge of the duties of the office.

The recent outrageous proceedings in Phila. on Oregon, have inflicted a deep disgrace upon us, and made us the sport of our political opponents.[1] We, *Country people*, look upon it as an insult to the Administration to *agitate*, when we want *repose* and the whole energies of the party to enable you, satisfactorily, to adjust the great questions of the Country, Texas, Oregon and the Tariff. The truth is, however, we can trace all our political difficulties, in Penna. to factious movements in Philadelphia. In the country, the party is united on the Oregon question. We have, in this County,[2] 2 English and 3 German newspapers, all manfully sustaining you. These papers go to the fireside of every Democrat in the County, and thus, afford a most substantial kind of support. The fact is, the true hearted Democracy of the interior of Penna. *is always to be found on the side of the Country*; it was that noble Democracy that brought out, elected, and sustained Gen Jackson; it was that Democracy that saved the State in the recent contest; and, it is to that Democracy we must look, for the future; it can always be relied upon, at the ballot box and elsewhere.

HENRY WELSH

ALS. DLC–JKP. Addressed to Washington City and marked *"Private."*
1. See John K. Kane to Polk, April 28, 1845.
2. York County.

### FROM RUFUS McINTIRE

Parsonfield, Me. May 10, 1845

After alluding to rumors about Joseph Story's imminent resignation from the U.S. Supreme Court, McIntire discusses the political ramifications of Polk's prospective Court appointment. He emphasizes the crucial role of the Court in deciding political controversies that deal with "constitutional questions & those involving the rights of the states." Referring to John Marshall's selection by John Adams,[1] McIntire maintains that this appointment did more to disseminate "Federal doctrines" than did all the other political acts of Adams' administration. He notes that the subject of Story's successor already evokes speculation and that most people assume the choice will go to someone from New England. Among the prominent figures mentioned are Marcus Morton, Levi Woodbury, and Ether Shepley. McIntire describes Shepley as a man with a legal mind of the first order and assures Polk that Shepley's political and constitutional principles are sound.

ALS. DLC–JKP. Addressed to Washington City.

1. A native of Fauquier County, Va., John Marshall served as a captain of Virginia volunteers during the American Revolution, sat for several terms in the Virginia House of Delegates, and won election to the U.S. House in 1799. Appointed secretary of state in 1800, Marshall went to the Supreme Court bench the following year and presided over the Court until his death in 1835.

## FROM DAVID PETRIKIN

My Dear Sir,                                        Danville Penna. May 10. 1845

I have seen the announcement of the appointment of Messrs. *Horn, Petit, Welch* and *Lehman* to office in Philadelphia[1] and I do assure you that you have made good selections and that the old steady Democrats will hail such appointments as the earnest of Penna. continuing a Democratic State. You might have found as good men as those appointed but I doubt much if you could find the superiors of Henry Horn and Dr. Lehman any where. If such unprincipled Demagogues as H. B. Wright Ellis Lewis Joel B. Sutherland Geo. M. Keim and others of the same caste had been permitted to fill the prominent offices under your administration the Democrats in Penna. would have been disheartened and their energies destroyed; the reverse now will be the case & if Gov. Shunk will cease his prosciptive course all will be right.

Pardon me for my intrusion and be assured that I am induced to make this effort altho suffering great pain from a wish to give you correct information as you cannot rely on newspapers; every faction and clique has its newspaper and the party but very few; for instance there are seven papers *called Democratic* in this Congressional district[2] and not one which is not in the pay of some faction. I hope you will go on with the good work give us new men and genuine Democrats no time servers or *Cow Boys* who have been acting with the enemy or engaged in producing factious divisions and dissensions in the Democratic ranks.

The course adopted by you relative to Texas and Oregon is universally approved of by men of all parties except a few British Federalists. But one opinion prevails with all Democrats and patriots respecting Oregon that is War in preference to yielding one acre of that territory to the British and any man who would propose such a measure as compromising by a division would be held up as a traitor to his Country.

The people are a good deal excited on this question as they consider the honor of the Country involved in it independent of all considerations of value or convenience. You may rely upon it that this is the universal feeling throughout Northern Penna.

That you may enjoy health and strength to enable you to discharge the arduous duties of your station is the sincere prayer of ....

DAVID PETREKIN

L. DLC–JKP. Addressed to Washington City.
1. Henry Horn, Thomas M. Pettit, Henry Welsh, and George F. Lehman.
2. Pennsylvania's Eleventh Congressional District encompassed Columbia, Luzerne, and Wyoming counties.

## FROM BRIGHAM YOUNG ET AL.[1]

Hon: Sir                                                   Nauvoo, May 10th 1845

Suffer us, Sir, in behalf of a disfranchised, and long afflicted people, to profer a few suggestions for your serious consideration, in hope of a friendly and unequivocal response, at as early a period as may suit your convenience, and the extreme urgency of the case seems to demand.

It is not our present design to detail the multiplied and aggravated wrongs that we have received in the midst of a Nation that gave us birth. Most of us have long been loyal citizens of some one of these United States, over which you have the honor to preside; while a few only claim the privileges of peaceable and lawful emigrants, designing to make this Union our permanent residence. We say we are a disfranchised people. We are privately told by the highest authorities of this State, that it is neither prudent, nor safe for us to *vote* at the *polls*; still we have continued to maintain our right to vote, until the blood of our best men has been shed, both in Missouri and the State of Illinois, with impunity.[2]

You are doubtless somewhat familiar with the history of our extermination from the State of Missouri[3]: wherein scores of our brethren were massacred; hundreds died through want and sickness occasioned by their unparalleled sufferings, some millions of our property were confiscated or destroyed, and some fifteen thousand souls fled for their lives, to the then hospitable and peaceful shores of Illinois; and that the State of Illinois, granted to us a liberal charter, for *"the term of perpetual succession,"* under whose provision, private rights have become invested, and the largest City in the State has grown up, numbering about 20,000 inhabitants.[4]

But, Sir, the startling attitude recently assumed by the State of Illinois, forbids us to think that her designs are any less vindictive than that of Missouri. She has already used the Military of the State, with the Executive at their head, to coerce and surrender up our best men to unparalleled murder,[5] and that too under the most sacred pledges of protection and safety. As a salvo for such unearthly perfidy and guilt she told us through her highest Executive Officer that the Laws should be magnified and the murderers brought to justice; but the blood of her innocent victims had not been wholly wiped from the floor of the awful arena, when the citizens of a Sovereign State pounced upon two defence-less servants of God, our Prophet, and our Patriarch, before the Senate of that State rescued one of the indicted actors in that mournful tragedy, from the Sheriff of Hancock County, and gave him an honorable seat in her Hall of Legislation, and all others who were indicted by the Grand Jury of Hancock County, for the murder of generals Joseph and Hyrum Smith, are suffered to roam at large, watching for further prey.[6]

To crown the climax of those bloody deeds, the State has repealed all those chartered rights,[7] by which we might have lawfully defended ourselves against aggressors. If we defend ourselves, hereafter against violence, whether it comes under the shadow of law or otherwise (for we have reason to expect it both ways) we shall then be charged with Treason, and suffer the penalty; and if we continue passive, and non-resistant, we must certainly expect to perish, for our enemies have sworn it. And here, Sir, permit us to State that General Joseph Smith, during his short life, was arraigned at the bar of his country about 50 times, charged with criminal offences, but was acquitted every time by his Country, his enemies, or rather his religious opponents almost invari-ably being his judges. And we further testify that as a people, we are law abiding, peaceable, and without crime, and we challenge the world to prove the contrary. And while other less cities in Illinois have had special courts instituted to try their criminals, we have been stript of ev-ery source, of arraigning marauders and murderers, who are prowling around to destroy us, except the common Magistracy.

With these facts before you, Sir, will you write to us without delay, as a Father and Friend and advise us what to do? We are all members of the same great confederacy. Our fathers, nay, some of us, have fought and bled for our Country, and we love her Constitution dearly.

In the name of Israel's God, and by virtue of multiplied ties of Country and kindred, we ask your friendly interposition in our favor. Will it be too much for us to ask you to convene a Special Session of Congress, and furnish us an Asylum, where we can enjoy our rights of conscience and religion unmolested?

Or, will you in a special message to that body, when convened recom-mend a remonstrance against such unhallowed acts of oppression and Expatriation, as this people have continued to receive from the States of Missouri and Illinois?

Or, will you favor us by your personal influence and by your official rank?

Or will you express your views concerning what is called the *"great Western* measure" of colonizing the Latter Day Saints, in Oregon, the north Western Territory, or some location remote from the States, where the hand of oppression shall not crush every noble principle, and extingish every patriotic feeling?

And now, Hon. Sir, having reached out our imploring hands to you, with deep solemnity, we would importune with you as a Father, a friend, a patriot, a statesman, and the head of a mighty nation; by the constitution of American Liberty; by the blood of our fathers; who have fought for the independence of this Republic; by the blood of the Martyrs, which has been shed in our midst; by the wailings of the Widows, and orphans; by our murdered Fathers and Mothers, Brothers and Sisters, Wives and Children; by the dread of immediate destruction from secret combinations now forming for our overthrow; and by every endearing tie that binds men to men, and renders life bearable; and that too, for ought we know, for the last time that you will lend your immediate aid to quell the violence of mobocracy, and work your influence to establish us as a people in our civil and religious rights where we now are, or in some part of the United States, or at some place away therefrom, where we may colonize in peace and safety as soon as circumstances will permit.

We sincerely hope that your future prompt measures, towards us, will be dictated by the best feelings, that dwell in the bosom of humanity, and the blessings of a grateful people, and of many ready to perish, shall come upon you.

                                                    BRIGHAM YOUNG

P.S. As many of our communications, postmarked at Nauvoo, have failed of their destination, and the mails around us have been intercepted by our enemies, we shall send this to some distant office, by the hand of a special messenger.[8]

LS. DLC–JKP. Addressed to Washington City.

1. This letter was addressed to Polk by a committee in behalf of the Church of Jesus Christ of Latter-day Saints at Nauvoo, Ill., and signed by Brigham Young, Willard Richards, N. K. Whitney, and George Miller. A native of Windham County, Vt., Brigham Young joined the Mormons in 1832; achieved recognition for his missionary work; assumed the leader's role following Joseph Smith's murder in 1844; and supervised the Mormons' move to Utah upon their expulsion from Nauvoo, Ill. He served as Mormon president from 1847 until his death in 1877.

2. References are to the expulsion of Mormons from Missouri in the late 1830's and to the murders of Joseph and Hyrum Smith. A native of Windsor County, Vt., Joseph Smith founded the Church of Jesus Christ of Latter-day Saints in Seneca County, N.Y., in 1830 and in that same year published *The Book*

*of Mormon*, for which writing he claimed divine revelations. Hyrum Smith, one of the principal organizers of the Mormons served as patriarch from 1841 until his death in 1844.

3. The Mormons settled first in Kirtland, Ohio, and in 1833 moved to Jackson County, Mo. Subsequent persecutions forced Smith and his followers to relocate to Daviess and Caldwell counties, but the Missouri government, supported by the governor, Lilburn W. Boggs, ordered the Mormons to leave the state in 1839.

4. The Mormons moved to the small town of Commerce, Ill., and established the city of Nauvoo. Granted a city charter by the Illinois legislature in 1840, the prosperous Mormon community at Nauvoo grew rapidly and by 1845 had become the largest city in the state with approximately 12,000 inhabitants.

5. By June 1844 threats of violence prompted both sides to organize militia units; armed conflict appeared imminent. The arrest of Joseph and Hyrum Smith offered hope for a peaceful resolution of the crisis; but on June 27, 1844, an angry mob murdered the two leaders in the county jail at Carthage, Ill.

6. Those charged with the murders of Joseph and Hyrum Smith included J. C. Davis, Mark Aldrich, William N. Grover, Levi Williams, and T. C. Sharp, editor of the Warsaw *Signal*. Tried in May 1845, the five defendants won acquittal.

7. In January 1845 the Illinois legislature repealed the Nauvoo charter, which had given extensive authority to the Mormon-controlled city government.

8. The cancellation on the cover of the letter reads "New York, May 27."

## FROM ANDREW J. DONELSON

Dr. Sir,                                                New Orleans May 11 1845

Govr. Yell will explain to you among other things the grounds of our wish to do something for Mr. Miller, who is the particular personal friend of Genl Houston,[1] and the individual made somewhat prominent as the editor of the *"National Register"* in opposition to the act of our Congress providing for the admission of Texas into the Union.[2] He was misled by the Government.

If the troops are ordered to the Sabine he would be a good person to supply them, as a suttler or special commissary. He is intelligent, honest, and indefatigable—the best clerk I ever saw. His appointment would be gratifying to Ex President Houston.

A. J. DONELSON

ALS. DLC–JKP. Addressed to Washington City and delivered by Archibald Yell. Polk's AE on the cover indicates that he received this letter on May 19, 1845.

1. Co-editor and publisher of the Washington *National Register* (Texas) from 1843 until 1845, Washington D. Miller served as Sam Houston's private secretary in 1841; as secretary to the Texas Seventh Congress, 1842–43; and as Texas' secretary of state from 1845 until 1848.

2. See Donelson to Polk, March 18, 1845.

## FROM ANDREW J. DONELSON

My Dr Sir,                        New Orleans May 11th 1845

Governor Yell, who has been with me, the greater part of my time at Washington in Texas, has agreed to take charge of this letter and a dispatch to Mr Buchanan.[1] He is familiar with my correspondence and views, and will be prepared to answer all your enquiries respecting the progress of the annexation question and the difficulties that were thrown in its way by the President[2] and his cabinet. In my judgment no more obstacles can hereafter arise. Yet there may be some, and I shall therefore return in time for the meeting of Congress on the 16 of June, for the purpose of controlling as far as possible any immediate movement arising out of the local parties.[3]

I have been greatly vexed at the course of Houston who has controlled the President and all his cabinet. Looking, however, at the difficulties which might have been produced if the people had taken as they were disposed to do, the Government into their own hands, I have hazarded much to save the administration, and to keep Houston connected with the interests of annexation.

Your letter by Mr Prentiss[4] was received just as I was starting from Washington. No certain conveyance of an answer would have been ahead of the present, and I have therefore reserved it until now.

I cannot sufficiently express my thanks to you for the kindness which has prompted your suggestion in regard to my connection with the public service. Although personally unacquainted with Mr Ritchie, no one has placed a higher value than I have on his useful and fine career as an editor and politician. Associated with him therefore in a paper which will aim at the advancement of the doctrine of Va,[5] and the exposition of those Republican principles by which we hope to give the fullest weight to the blessings of Representative Government, I would feel honoured. But am I fitted for so imposing an association—would it be right for one so unused as I am to an exercise of this kind to share its responsibility and reward with him who will bring into the field so much more experience and wisdom? My answer would be no, yet not without a willingness to obey the command of those who may think me capable of promoting the work of my country and party in such an undertaking.

I would make other suggestions in relation to your assurances on this subject. Cannot the matter be left open until I return to my family, say about the 8th or 10th July, when the Texas duty will be over, and I may see what are the arrangements which will best suit my private affairs?

I could then see and consult with Genl Jackson and my wife[6] and take the course recommended by prudence.

At all events I would take it as a favor to be allowed to leave Texas as soon as Congress accepts the proposals of our joint Resolution. My private business requires my return home: and it is a great sacrifice I make to go back. No foreign ministers have ever remained more than a day or two at a time at Washington even in the winter. It is probably the sickliest place in Texas and without any of the comforts of life.

Mr Buchanan may very well state to me on the information which he will possess after the receipt of my dispatches to this date, that seeing no necessity for my longer continuance in Texas I am at liberty to close the business of the legation and take leave of the existing Government. If this cannot be done I must ask you to accept my resignation for nothing could induce me to remain at the seat of Government after the 1st of July.

Desiring to be kindly remembered to Mrs Polk, I remain ....

A. J. DONELSON

ALS. DLC–JKP. Addressed to Washington City, marked "*Private*," and delivered by Archibald Yell. Polk's AE on the cover indicates that he received this letter on May 19, 1845.

1. In a letter to James Buchanan dated May 11, 1845, Donelson reports sources having sighted British warships thought to be bound for Havana. He speculates that this fleet may be part of an arrangement with Mexico preparing for war with the United States over Texas annexation. Donelson advises the reinforcement and readiness of U.S. troops stationed on the Red and Arkansas rivers as measures needed to secure the Texas border in case of war. Senate Document No. 1, 29th Congress, 1st Session, pp. 57–58.

2. Anson Jones.

3. Donelson refers to the June 16, 1845, special session of the Texas Congress called to consider the question of annexation.

4. See Polk to Donelson, March 28, 1845.

5. Donelson probably refers to the Virginia Resolutions of December 24, 1798.

6. Elizabeth Martin Randolph Donelson.

## TO ANDREW JACKSON

My Dear Sir:            Washington City 12th May 1845

I have received your two letters of the 30th ult. and 2nd Instant, the former enclosing one from *Mr Marshall* of Kentucky.[1] I will attend to M's request, as soon as a vacancy, at West Point occurs. I saw *Mr Taggart* two days ago. He had been offered a place in the land office by the Secretary of the Treasury from which he was removed by *Mr Blake,* and had without my knowledge declined it, prefering as he said to be attached to some other Department. I told him he had acted, precipitately, as there was no certainty that a suitable vacancy would occur in any other Department. The Secretery of the Treasury happened to come in whilst he was with me. *Mr Walker* promised him, to give him, a suitable place on the 1st of June, and you may rest satisfied that he will be taken care of. Say to Mrs. Jackson[2] that it shall be so. *Thos. Donelson* who was here a few days ago, prefers a place in the Philadelphia Custom House. I made known your wishes as well as my own to *Mr Horn* the new Collector, two days ago, and be assured sir that he would give *Mr Donelson* the place he desired. Before the late news, from England, I had tendered the Mission to that Court to the South, believing from sound considerations, that the Minister should come from the slave-holding section of the Union. It was declined in that quarter,[3] leaving me free to make another selection. Fortunately I learned from a friend[4] a few days ago that Mr *Butler* of N. York, had expressed the opinion, that *Mr Van-Buren* would probably accept the Mission, if it was offered to him. Instantly upon learning this, I did not hesitate to write to *Mr Butler*, authorizing him to say to Mr *Van-Buren*, that it was my anxious desire, in the present juncture of our relations with England, to avail myself of his services & that it would give me the greatest pleasure to appoint him, if he would accept.[5] *Mr Butler* writes me[6] that he had written & made known my wishes to *Mr V. Buren*, but had not received his answer. I expect an answer in a day or two. I hope he may accept, as we want at this moment the ablest man in the country, to represent our interests at the *Brittish* court. If I had had the slightest idea that *Mr V. Buren*, would have accepted, I would have offered it to him in the first instance in preference to any man in the Union. You need have no uneasiness about the course of the administration on the Oregon question. The blustering, rumours and tone of defiance, of *Sir Robert Peel, Lord John Russell* & others in the Brittish Parliament, were intended probably to test our nerves.[7] We stand firmly and boldly on our rights. We prefer peace if it can be preserved consistently with the national honour and interests, but if it cannot we are resolved to maintain our rights, at any hazard. I have myself no serious apprehensions of War. *Packenham*[8] has since the debate in Parliament reached this country, manifested some anxiety to re-open the negotiation, and is manifestly anxious to settle the controversy amicably. Mr *Buchanan* is firm, and is ready to meet, him, in a proper spirit. The negotiation will probably be re-opened very soon.

With my kind regards for your household, and my prayers for a continuance of your life.

JAMES K. POLK

ALS. DLC–AJ. Addressed to Hermitage and marked *"Confidential."* Published in Bassett, ed., *Correspondence of Andrew Jackson*, VI, pp. 405–06. AE by Andrew Jackson at the bottom of the fourth page of the letter states that he answered the letter on May 26, 1845.

1. Thomas F. Marshall's letter has not been found. On April 24, 1845, he wrote Jackson and asked him to recommend Charles William Field for a West Point appointment. ALS. DLC–AJ. A Kentucky lawyer, Thomas F. Marshall served in the U.S. House from 1841 until 1843.
2. Polk's reference is to Sarah Yorke Jackson, the wife of Andrew Jackson, Jr.
3. Polk had already offered the position to John C. Calhoun, Franklin H. Elmore, and Francis W. Pickens.
4. George Bancroft.
5. See Polk to Benjamin F. Butler, May 5, 1845.
6. Polk probably refers to Butler's letter of May 7, 1845.
7. See Jacob L. Martin to Polk, April 16, 1845.
8. Sir Richard Pakenham.

## FROM JOHN LAW[1]

My Dear Sir                    Terre Haute Indiana May 12th 1845

I am just closing at this place my Judicial labours for the Circuit, ending here, and have had an opportunity of becoming acquainted with the feelings and opinions of the democracy in this section of Indiana in reference to the new administration.

It affords me much pleasure in saying, that there is but one opinion here, and that an entire satisfaction with the Executive action since your elevation to the Presidency. On the Oregon, and Texas questions you will find the democracy of Indiana united to a man. Our title, our whole title, our right our whole right, to the Country beyond the Rocky Mountains they will maintain with the last drop of their blood, the last dollar of their treasure's, and they fully sustain the bold manly and American view of the question taken in the Inaugural Address. Many of our people are preparing to emigrate to the Oregon, and many have gone. And if ever the contest should come between us and Great Britain, relative to our respective rights there, a contest certainly not to be sought by either party, but not to be avoided when our rights are invaded, the latter will find more Western rifles on the banks of the Columbia, than they ever dreampt of seeing in that quarter. The fact is, that nothing can, and nothing will stop our people from wending their way Westward. "The Star of Empire"[2] points in that direction, and no threat from abroad, no legislative action at home, can prevent our population from reaching the shores of the Pacifick. Ere four presidential terms have rolled around, not only Oregon, but *California* will be populated by American enterprise, and who shall stay their progress. And what human power can say, "Thus far Shalt thou go and no farther."[3] Well did the individual reply to Mr Packenham[4] last winter at Washington, when the former said in reference to the annexation of Texas "Your countrymen (The Americans) seem to have a most grasping ambition." Sir said he, "You forget our Anglo Saxon descent."[5] It comes with an ill grace from an Englishman, to charge us with a spirit of Territorial Acquisition.

Each party is making preparation for the approaching contest in August, our state Election. I am a pretty good judge of political prospects, and if there is any truth in the assertion "that coming events cast their shadows before them"[6] democracy will be triumphant in the Hoosier State. We shall have a majority on joint ballot in the Legislature, shall elect a United States Senator, and carry eight out of the ten districts for Congress. This is the only doubtful one (Wright's). The Whigs have a majority, but they are so split up and divided. I may also add, so apathetic, that I should not be surprised if we carried it. Wright will run again, he was only elected by *three* votes at the last election. In my own district Davis[7] will get the nomination and probably run without an opponent. You know, we claim to be, and are the Banner District of the State. At least 1500 majority, and the party was never more united.

Present my best regards to Mrs Polk....

JOHN LAW

ALS. DLC–JKP. Addressed to Washington City.

1. An Indiana lawyer and legislator, Law served as a delegate to the 1844 Democratic National Convention, as a judge for the Seventh Circuit Court of Indiana, and as a two-term member of the U.S. House, 1861–65.

2. Paraphrase of "westward the star of empire takes its way" from John Q. Adam's *Oration at Plymouth* (1802).

3. Paraphrase of the scriptural verse, "Hitherto shalt thou come, but not further: and here shall thy proud waves be stayed." Job 38:11.

4. Sir Richard Pakenham.

5. Reference probably is to John C. Calhoun.

6. Quotation is a paraphrase of "coming events cast their shadows" from Thomas Campbell's poem, *Lochiel's Warning*.

7. An Indiana Democrat, John W. Davis served four terms in the U.S. House, 1835–37, 1839–41, and 1843–47; he presided as Speaker during his last term.

## FROM HENRY HORN

My Dear Sir　　　　　　　　　　　　　　　　Philadelphia 13 May 1845

I had a private interview with Mr Dallas yesterday which was the first I could obtain since my return home when I communicated to him the substance of the conversation I had with you in reference to the Mint. He says he has no wish to express upon the subject, and manifests a total indifference as to the removal of a Majr Roach[1] or the appointment of Mr Rush. Our conversation however was then interupted by the entrance of several persons into the office when I left him with an invitation to call and see him again. Should anything transpire at our next meeting which it might be serviceable to you to know, it shall be communicated. I think however from the apparent tone of his mind he will not be likely to indicate his preference for any one.

Mr Miffen[2] and Mr Simpson are both anxious to receive the appointment of Treasurer of the mint and the selection of either of them would give general satisfaction should you determine to remove the major and not to appoint Mr Rush.

HENRY HORN

ALS. DLC–JKP. Addressed to Washington City and marked "*Private.*"

1. Isaac Roach was treasurer of the U.S. mint from 1841 until 1847.

2. Probably Horn refers to Benjamin Mifflin, editor of the Philadelphia *Pennsylvanian*; Polk appointed Mifflin to the post of weigher at the Philadelphia Customs House in June 1845.

## TO HENRY HORN

My Dear Sir,              Washington City 13th May 1845

I informed you in the conversation which I held with you a few days ago, that I did not interfere, with Collectors in the appointment of subordinate officers of the customs. I do not now design to do so, but under the peculiar circumstances attending the late appointments at Philadelphia, I feel it to be no departure from this rule, to make to you such suggestions, as I may deem useful to you. I am informed then, that a person named *McCully*[1] now holds a subordinate place in the Customhouse, and it is apprehended he may be removed. He is represented to be a Democrat, and much anxiety is expressed in a letter now before me that he should be retained.[2] Another letter expressed great anxiety that a *Mr Ford* now an Inspector,[3] and who is the brother-in-law of the Editor of "The Spirit of the Times"[4] should be retained. Of course I can know but little of these persons, but feel that it is proper to give you the information, and to repeat to you what I said in conversation, that in the dispensation of your patronage, justice, should be done to every branch of the Democratic party. My rule is, to proscribe no part of the Democracy, to know no cliques, but as far as possible to harmonize and unite the whole party. I am aware that you are surrounded by embarrassing circumstances, but I am sure that you will carry out this rule, as far as it may be practicable to do so. You will I know properly appreciate my motive for making to you these suggestions. I have been expecting to hear from you in relation to the *Treasurer* of the mint. I have not acted in the matter and will not until I have further information.

JAMES K. POLK

ALS. NjP. Addressed to Philadelphia and marked *"Private."*

1. A Philadelphia boatbuilder, James McCully was appointed an inspector of customs in 1843.

2. Letter not found.

3. On May 10, 1845, John S. Du Solle wrote Polk on behalf of his brother-in-law, Robert Ford. ALS. DLC–JKP. Ford was appointed an inspector in the Philadelphia Customs House in 1842.

4. Editor of the Democratic Philadelphia *Spirit of the Times* from 1837 until 1849, Du Solle also published a collection of *Letters from Europe* in 1846.

FROM ANDREW J. DONELSON

My Dr Sir,                                 New Orleans May 14 1845

Your private letter of the 6th inst, has just reached me, and also that from Mr Ritchie, with the several numbers of his article in the Union of the 3rd on Texan Affairs.[1] Having but Twenty minutes after the receipt of these papers before the return mail closes, I have only time to acknowledge their receipt, and to ask you to say to Mr. Ritchie that I shall answer him tomorrow.

Govr Yell left here on Monday last. He will satisfy you that annexation is safe beyond the possibility of defeat. Neither Houston, nor the executive of Texas, nor all the Diplomacy of Europe can throw a moments doubt about the decision of the people in its favor. Congress and the people in Convention will ratify our proposals without the change of a letter.

I stated to you in my letters by Gov. Yell[2] that I would return to Texas a few days before the meeting of Congress, but that I should wish to return home as soon as Congress accepts our proposals.[3] There will be no necessity for my waiting after that period.

I sent you some correspondence between Houston & myself, which I fear did not reach you,[4] as you have not alluded to it in your letter. Another letter since received from him authorises the declaration that he will not be an opponent of the measure. That letter will reach you the day after this, as I have just heard of the vessel to which it was entrusted.[5]

Your letter by Mr Prentiss,[6] and that just received, will be noticed more particularly tomorrow. I may say to you, however, that all your suggestions in regard to the liberality of the ensuing Congress of the United States, so far as Texas may wish to correct what she deems objectionable in our proposals, have been anticipated and stated in various letters to prominent men in Texas. But the truth is Texas is satisfied with the terms, and could not be pursuaded out of their ratification *just as they are.* The power she has over the public domain, the creation of new states, and the Indian occupancy, places the United States in a position somewhat dependent upon her, and her intelligent citizens know it, and will make the most of it hereafter.

I have a letter from Mrs D[7] dated the 26th. Genl Jackson was then better.

A. J. DONELSON

ALS. DLC–JKP. Addressed to Washington City.
1. See Polk to Donelson, May 6, 1845.
2. See Donelson's letters to Polk, May 11, 1845.
3. Donelson refers to the June 16, 1845, special session of the Texas Congress called to consider the question of annexation.
4. Correspondence not found.
5. Letter not found.
6. See Polk to Donelson, March 28, 1845.
7. Elizabeth Martin Randolph Donelson.

## FROM ANDREW J. DONELSON

My Dr Sir,                                    New Orleans May 14th 1845

Seeing that the address of Mr Ritchie's letter to me[1] was in your handwriting, I send the answer under cover to you,[2] and without being sealed, in order that you may read it.

There is nothing of much interest in New Orleans. I wished to go to my plantation but was afraid to run the risk, of being out of the touch of direct communication with the Govt, if any thing important arose. At this point I can do more good, until the meeting of Congress in Texas, than I could at Galveston. But there is now but little to be done if Houston comes in the next boat. If he does not I will go back to see what he is about.

You must excuse my anxiety to be at home, which is greatly increased by the accounts we get of the Genls[3] declining health. For the neglect of my family and private business too, I feel that the little public good I can do is but a poor excuse.

A. J. DONELSON

ALS. DLC–JKP. Addressed to Washington City and marked "*Private*." Polk's
AE on the cover states that he received this letter on May 22, 1845.
1. See Polk to Donelson, May 6, 1845.
2. Letter not found.
3. Andrew Jackson.

## FROM DUFF GREEN

My dear Sir                                    New York 15th May 1845
   I enclose you an article from one of the New York papers[1] and can say
that I believe the commercial interest of this City are decidedly in favor
of the appointment of Mr Calhoun to England, & that I have a letter from
Col Elmore in which he expresses the opinion that Mr Calhoun could be
induced to accept the appointment.

                                                        DUFF GREEN

ALS. DLC–JKP. Addressed to Washington City.
1. The article, clipped from an unidentified newspaper and dated May 15,
1845, recommends the appointment of John C. Calhoun as U.S. minister to Great
Britain and argues that Calhoun would prove most qualified to protect the interests of the nation and the South.

## FROM CHARLES S. JONES

Respected Sir.                              Washington May 15th 1845
   A few weeks since I had the honor of addressing you a communication relative to certain official misconduct of the present Commissioner
of Public Buildings.[1] I again respectfully take leave to address you on
the same subject, and beg your patient attention to what I say. If ever
there was a removal from public office called for by every consideration
of justice to the workingmen and to the Government it is that of Mr
Noland from the office of Commissioner of Public Buildings; and the
great wonder with men of both parties *who know the man*, is that it has
not been done before this. There is every reason to beleive that he has
been concerned indirectly in almost every contract given out from under
his hands for the last 10 years. Such is the general opinion, in some instances there is the strongest evidence in the world to sustain it. Besides
this, there is the strongest positive proof of his dishonest speculations on
the hard earnings of workingmen. I will cite an instance to you. Messrs
McCauley, and Dickson[2] entered into a contract to lay water pipes along
Penn Avenue, for which they were to receive $8000. They performed the
work, but the Commissioner took the Government draft for the amount
which was equivalent to specie, sold it for Virginia money (at that time

10 per cent under par); compelled McCauley and Dickson to receive the Virginia money, and pocketed the proceeds $800 himself. If you have any doubts of this McCauley, and Dickson (both Whigs) are prepared to appear before you at any time, and testify to it.

Mr Noland attempted the same thing with Mr Sengstack, and because that gentleman resisted, and refused to receive any thing but gold, and silver for his work; he became his violent enemy, and persecutor. Indeed the whole course of conduct of this man Noland seems to have been his own aggrandizement at the cost of the workingmen, and the Government. It was with a full knowledge of the man, and his acts that the Democratic workingmen of the District, took the matter in hand, and determined to try whether a change could not be effected upon the accession of your Excellency to the Presidency. With unanimity, and enthusiasm they settled upon that faithful old sentinel on the Democratic watchtower, Mr C P Sengstack as a candidate for the office of Com of Pub Buildings. The announcement of his name checked the aspirations of all our friends, because all are anxious that he, and he alone should have it. Your Excellency then is at no loss on this score. Charles P Sengstack stands alone before you as a candidate for the office of Com of Pub Buildings, backed by a host of friends of whom any man might be proud. Shall we succeed in getting this glorious appointment or not? With you Mr President rests the answer. If you would still subject us to the insults, taunts, and sneers of our political opponents, and indelibly impress on our minds the idea which *they* have as yet in vain endeavored to convey—that we are looked upon with contempt by the present Administration—then will you refuse to give it to us. But if on the other hand you would cause our hearts to swell with gratitude, and indelibly impress on them the idea which we have all along so fondly cherished— that there *is* something more in Democracy, than the name—then I say you will confer upon our worthy champion the appointment we ask for him. Should such be the result of your deliberations, we will send forth a shout from this District that will be heard from Maine, to Texas, which will be *felt* in the contest of 1848, and which will cause many a hardhanded, warm-hearted workingman to thank God for the day which restored the Democratic party to power in the persons of James K Polk, and Geo M Dallas. For that this appointment would be popular with the workingmen there can be no doubt. It would be giving practical evidence of that which our opponents accuse us of only professing in theory—respect for the working classes.

CHARLES S. JONES

P.S. I am the son of Richard Jones, whom you have just appointed Inspector of the Penetentiary in this City.[3] I thank you kindly for the appointment you have given my father. I shall take pleasure in calling on you in a few days, and in the meantime respectfully refer you for any information in regard to my character &c to the Hon Amos Kendall, Hon Wm J Brown, Judge Dunlop, James Hoban, Major H C Williams, Genl J M McCalla, and others.[4] C. S. Jones

ALS. DLC–JKP. Addressed to Washington City. Polk's AE on the cover states that he received this letter on May 19, 1845.
1. See Charles S. Jones to Polk, April 8, 1845.
2. McCauley and Dickson are not identified further.
3. Richard Jones is not identified further.
4. Amos Kendall, William J. Brown, James Dunlop, James Hoban, Hampton C. Williams, and John M. McCalla. An Indianapolis lawyer, Brown served as a member of the Indiana House, 1829–32 and 1841–43; as state prosecuting attorney, 1831–35; and as Indiana's secretary of state, 1836–40; he won election to two terms in the U.S. House, 1843–45 and 1849–51; and held the post of second assistant postmaster general during the Polk administration. An inspector at the U.S. penitentiary, 1831–35, and a criminal court judge for Washington City, 1838–45, Dunlop received an appointment as assistant circuit judge for Washington City in 1845. A Washington City lawyer, Hoban served briefly as U.S. district attorney for Washington prior to his death in January 1846; he was the son of James Hoban, the architect who designed the White House.

## FROM WILLIAM R. McDOUGAL[1]

Sir                                           Washington May 15th 1845
The peculiar embarrassment under which I am placed by contingencies unavoidable on my part, compels me to make one more appeal to you. I am aware of the ardent nature of your duties, the many and important considerations that crowd themselves upon your mind and the fatigue and lassitude that daily result from them; and let me assure your Excellency, that urged as I am by the most imperious necessity, it is with the greatest reluctance that I consent to add a moments reflection to those which already harrass and perplex you. The frequency of my applications to you, and the apparent importunity with which I saught your favor, may induce you to believe that I am a stranger to every sense of modesty or propriety. But believe me, nothing can be more humiliating to my sense of pride and propriety, than the scene through which I have just passed. Not that I esteem the least office in your gift as insignificant, on the contrary I would place the highest estimate on the least token of your regard. But the very fate that compels me to become an applicant for public favor, together with my own conflicting emotions between pride and necessity, are more hu-

miliating to me, than all the untoward circumstances of my life combined.

In becoming an applicant to you, I was aware of your disposition to serve your friends. Nor was I insensible to your partiality in my behalf. Your disposition to serve me and your power to execute your purposes together with your kind assurances that I should be provided for, gave me the utmost confidence in my ultimate success. Hence it was that I so frequently applied to you during three months of abortive efforts to procure a place which I believe you were anxious to bestow. Nor would I intrude myself upon you now, if I were not conscious that I have sustained an injustice, which is in your power to remedy. I allude to the premature decision Mr. Washington[2] made in relation to my qualifications for a clerk, which he has since withdrawn. I recently exhibited to him some specimens of my hand writing with which he expressed his entire satisfaction and assured me that he would express the same opinion to Mr. Walker. I told him in person that I thought his conduct towards me was premature and that it had met with the disapprobation of all who were acquainted with the circumstances. I feel no disposition to impugn the motives of Mr. Washington or analyze his conduct, but I beg leave to say that he is extremely unpopular in his office, and a large majority of his clerks are not only about to petition for his removal, but intend to prefer charges against him, that would disqualify him for office. These statements were made to me by persons, upon whom reliance can be placed. I think Mr. Walker is my friend and would have reappointed me if he had not supposed that it would have implied a censure upon Mr. Washington, and now, that every alleged objection is removed I feel assured that you will not permit me to suffer, when it is in your power to make reparation.

After my abortive attempts to secure even a clerkship and the mortification of a failure on the grounds of incompetency, I should have returned to Tennessee without another effort, to retrieve myself from the injustice I had sustained, from Mr. Washington. But the assurance you gave me that I should not be neglected and that endorsed by Mr. Walker induced me to remain here under the confident expectation that I would soon be able to realize the emoluments of an office. Relying upon these assurances I have remained in Washington until I have exhausted my means to leave it. I am a stranger here, and I know no one on whom I could with propriety call for assistance. I had informed my friends and family that I had received an appointment and with what grace could I return to them, the slander of incompetency would not fail to reach them, and I would be met both by your enemies and mine, with the most tantalizing reproaches.

On a former occasion I intimated to you that I had not the most remote intention of becoming an applicant for office, until I found that
the course I had taken to secure your election had so much impaired my
prospects in a county where my patronage depended upon the Whigs,
that I was compelled to abandon it.[3] Having no resources except those
which depend upon future contingences, only one of two alternatives
presents itself, either to prosecute my profession with no prospect of
success surrounded by political enemies of the most relentless character or throw myself upon your generosity for temporary relief. I choose
the latter, and now, after the fraternal reliance which I place in you,
and the more than filial regard which cherish for your welfare, shall
I be repulsed? I have a family, a wife who holds your Excelency in
the highest estimation, and whom I have taught during my recent absence to look upon you as her benefactor. I have a son too, a child I
first taught to lisp your name, and to cherish and revere your memory.[4] Now what shall I say to them? I have repeatedly told them that
you were my friend, and that you had expressed the kindest solicitude
in my behalf, but will they believe me when I tell them that you have
no power to afford them relief. I do not wish to appeal to your sympathies. I did hope to be spared the pain of acquainting you with my circumstances, and even now, no extremity however direful, could urge me
to confess the humiliating picture, was mine, if the happiness of those
whom I hold more dear than my own, was not inseperably linked to my
fortunes.

W. R. McDougal

ALS. DLC–JKP. Addressed to Washington City and marked "Private." Polk's
AE on the cover states, "To be shown to Mr Walker Sec. of the Treasury. 16th
May 1845."
1. A lawyer from Lebanon, Tenn., William R. McDougal claimed to be unable to pursue his profession and support his family due to the dominant Whig
influence in Wilson County.
2. Peter G. Washington served as Treasury auditor for Post Office accounts
from 1845 until 1850.
3. See Polk to A. O. P. Nicholson, June 2, 1845.
4. Neither his wife nor his son is identified further.

## FROM WILLIAM D. MOSELEY

Dear Sir                                    Tallahassee May 16. 1845
I send you the Floridian of this date, and have marked several passages for your particular attention.[1] You will perceive that during the
last Presidential Campaign my honorable competitor,[2] wrote letters to

Georgia to influence the freemen of that state, to aid in elevating your great rival[3]: not only by the most unqualified exagerated assertions, as to his superiority, but by attempting to underrate your worth, in the estimation of those would be called upon to cast their suffrages for the one or the other. This certainly was his priviledge. But that those who supported you here at that time, should now be misrepresented at Washington, (I allude particularly to Mr Levy[4]) and that this same gentleman and his partisans who went out of their way, to speak of you in the language of the quotation in the Floridian, should seek for admission into the Democratic ranks, under the plea that they agree with you politically is hypocresy of the lowest order. I know the manner through which these misrepresentations are made; and only regret that it is so. Geo K. Walker,[5] a cousin of my competitor, I understand, expects shortly to visit Washington. I will give you a short biography of him. He is the relation and friend of Call, and has the most sense decidedly. He has the reputation here of being a cunning shrewd man, of good address and generally succeeds in making a favorable impression at the first interview, but which disappears after a more intimate acquaintance. He and I were political opponents last year for a seat in the senate for Middle Florida. He the Whig and myself the Democratic Candidate. He electioned through the district, which had hertofore been Whig. He was well known in the district as a lawyer, yet in this district I beat him about 200 votes, and that too in a district before that time decidedly Whig. I met him but once on the stump. The burthen of his speech was fulsome, disgusting eulogies of Mr Clay, and political abuse of you, underating you as a man of no talents, and one whom Tennessee had twice buried, and that the Democrats were now seeking to raise you a third time. Sir I dislike the idea of writing thus as to a political opponent because it may have the appearance of a secret recusation and therefore be improper. I certainly feel myself justified in this matter, first because I understand others have been misinformed at Washington, and secondly because I know the man and the whole party here, and know that you had not in any part of these United States more bitter, disgusting filthy mouth, undignified opposition, than these same Florida whigs gave you, at the head of whom, was R. K. Call and Geo. K. Walker. Now Polk, you know me, you know also whether or not I have ever dec'd you, whether or not I am capable of doing so. It is for you to believe me, or to believe those who make different representations of the state of things in Florida. If I have misrepresented them I certainly feel responsible not only to them, but to a higher tribunal, and expect to be held so, at the "great day for which all other days were made."[6] The object is not to injure them therefore but to put you on your guard. They say now, that they agree with you on the tariff, since the publication of your inaugural. Yet the same political opinions were published by you, I think to Mr Kane,[7] not after which you were denounced by them as I have stated, and as the extract hereby sent, shows you. Mr Long I understand is your personal & political friend.[8] He is not the political friend here, of those who supported you, and who have always been found on the side of the Democracy, and opposed to Federalists. Call was ejected by Mr Van Buren from the office of Gov. purely upon the ground of his being totally unfit for the office. From that time to present, he and his friend Walker have headed the most bitter opposition in Florida, that Democracy ever had, and even in his speech a few days since, he vented his still bitter spleen against Mr Van Buren; and ridiculed him, as the tricky Dutchman &c. That however had a very unhappy effect for his speech, as there were a good many Dutchmen present, who were not a little excited by his unprovoked attack upon the Dutch. This letter is entirely confidential.

W. D. MOSELEY

ALS. DLC–JKP. Addressed to Washington City and marked *"Private."* Polk's AE on the cover states that he received this letter on May 27, 1845.

1. Enclosure not found.

2. Richard K. Call fought as a lieutenant under Andrew Jackson in the War of 1812 and in Florida. A brigadier general of the militia from 1826 until 1842, he served as Florida Territory's congressional delegate, 1824–25; as receiver of public monies for West Florida, 1829–36; and twice as territorial governor of Florida, 1836–39 and 1841–44. Call split with the Democracy over his replacement as governor by Martin Van Buren in 1839. In elections for state offices on May 26, 1845, Call lost the gubernatorial contest to Moseley.

3. Henry Clay.

4. A St. Augustine lawyer, David Levy Yulee served as Florida's territorial delegate, 1841–45; as a member of the state constitutional convention in 1845; and as U.S. senator for two terms, 1845–51 and 1855–61.

5. A native of Kentucky, George K. Walker shared a legal practice with Medicus A. Long in Tallahassee. Walker served as U.S. attorney for West Florida, 1831–34 and 1835–40, as well as secretary for the territory, 1834–35.

6. Quotation not identified further.

7. See Polk to John K. Kane, June 19, 1844.

8. A lawyer from Nashville, Medicus A. Long published several newspapers, including the Nashville *Union* from 1835 until 1836. He won election to one term in the Tennessee House as a Democrat in 1841. Long moved to Florida in 1843 and married Ellen Call, the daughter of Richard K. Call. Long had a law partnership in Tallahassee with George K. Walker.

## FROM JOHN F. H. CLAIBORNE

Dear Sir,                                        New Orleans, 17th May 1845

I have the honor to enclose you a letter from the Collector of this Port.[1]

It is very true that he has been acting as Consul for the Papal states, an office that brings in no revenue, but which is attended with some personal influence. This influence had better be in the hands of a democrat than a whig. It was exercised for our benefit during the last canvass. Look at the vote of our Catholic population.

Mr Barrett held this office without reflecting on the constitutional incompatibility. A person who had been removed from the Custom House made the charge against him at the Treasury Department, & perhaps, accompanied it with the hint that no man could be Consul for the Pope, without being hostile to the liberties of this country! It was like the old story raised against Mr Van Buren in 1840, who was set down as a Catholic because he wrote a diplomatic letter to His Holiness.[2] When Mr Barrett heard of this charge, he submitted the matter to Mr Bibb, then Secretary of the Treasury & awaited his decision. Receiving no reply, the inference was, that the Secretary found precedents to justify the case, and at all events did not consider it cause of censure or removal. Upon my suggestion however, Mr Barrett has resigned the appointment, & I only hope it may fall into the hands of one who may use it as efficiently for the good of the Republic. We have some Catholic whigs here, who with that appointment, could influence the course of men in New York, Boston & Charleston, as well as in this community.

If you deemed the two offices incompatible, & the Collector knowing your scruples, declined to resign the consulship, it would be just cause of removal; but I submit it to your justice if the resignation does not remove the objection?

If he has erred by holding the Consulship, it was from want of information on that point & the belief that the practice was common among commercial men.

The charge of neglect of duty, I pronounce *false*, on my personal responsibility. A more attentive & punctual man I never saw, & I have occasion to visit the Custom House twice a week to collect statistics of trade for my paper. If the records of the Treasury Department do not show Mr. B. to be a faithful & prompt officer, I will write in requesting his dismission.

But it is charged that Mr Barrett is no democrat.

Not so. He was an original Jackson man, but like many others he refused to support Mr Van Buren & took no part in the contest. He came out promptly, and decidedly for you & to my own knowledge contributed more to aid our friends & exerted more personal influence by an extensive co[rres]pondence with distinguished Catholics [in] other states, than any five men in this city. It may as well be charged against Messrs Caruthers & Prieur (who are applicants for the office) that they are not democrats.[3] Mr. Caruthers was a whig of 1840, but a democrat of 1844. Mr. Prieur was a democratic Van Buren man of 1840; but if he made any exertions in 1844 for the Baltimore nominations, I am yet to hear of it. If Mr Barrett will be removed because he did not vote for Mr Van Buren, the same principle would exclude 1/3 of the members of our party as at present organized.

But Mr. Barrett is a foreigner! Here I plead guilty. He is by birth an Irishman, but came *here* when a *boy*. He married into an extensive & powerful democratic Creole family which has been located here for 200 years. The Irish population feel that his appointment is a compliment to themselves. He is President of our Hibernian Society & Repeal Association,[4] & has just dissolved the latter in consequence of the course pursued by O'Connell.[5]

In conclusion, Sir, allow me to say that, in my opinion, the removal of Mr Barrett will be attended with no good. Petitions for his removal have gone on, but that is nothing. One half who sign such documents are disappointed applicants for Custom House appointments. Others are the partisans of the several aspirants for the office & others are men who will sign any memorial which has a few respectable names on it.

I can in one week get 500 names to a Memorial to one to remove or even to *hang* your whole Cabinet.

JOHN F. H. CLAIBORNE

P.S. I have mailed this letter *privately*, but I beg you to refer to Mr. R. J. Walker to corroborate many of the facts contained in it.

ALS. DLC–JKP. Addressed to Washington City and marked *"Private."*
1. Claiborne refers to Thomas Barrett's letter to Claiborne of May 17, 1845. ALS. DLC–JKP.
2. Reference is to Gregory XVI, who reigned from 1831 until 1846. Claiborne's reference to Martin Van Buren has not been identified further.
3. Madison Caruthers and Denis Prieur. A former resident of Columbia, Tenn., and briefly Polk's law partner, Caruthers moved to New Orleans in the 1830's and became a partner with Adlai O. Harris in a cotton brokerage firm. After the death of his wife in 1836, Caruthers moved to Memphis and continued his commercial pursuits. Mayor of New Orleans from 1828 to 1838, Prieur campaigned unsuccessfully for the Louisiana governorship in 1838; he accepted an appointment as collector of customs for New Orleans in 1845.
4. New Orleans' Hibernian Society, founded in 1818 by James Workman,

functioned as a social organization for the port's more prosperous Irish citizens and provided charitable aid to indigent immigrants. The society also funded construction of the Hibernian Hospital. The Irish Repeal Association of New Orleans, supporting the work of Daniel O'Connell, advocated repeal of the union between Great Britain and Ireland.

5. Known as the "Liberator," Daniel O'Connell championed the cause of Irish nationalism. Elected to Parliament, he served for many years before being arrested and sentenced to prison in 1844 on a charge of creating discontent and disaffection. Upon appeal his judgment was reversed, and he was released from prison. Claiborne's reference probably is to O'Connell's public condemnation of slavery and its extension through Texas annexation.

## FROM WILLIAM E. CRAMER[1]

Albany Argus Office
President Polk                                     Albany May 17th [1845][2]

It is generally rumored here that a new appointment is soon to be made in the office of first comptroller of the Treasury.

If any change is to be made, the numerous friends of Chesselden Ellis[3] of this State are looking forward with the hope that the President will confer this office on him. His reputation and abilities are not unknown to you, while his unshrinking fidelity to his friends and his Party justly entitle him to the confidence of the chosen Head of the Democratic Party.

It is not my habit to press any one for office, unless convinced that his character gives every evidence that the Appointing Power will receive not less benefit than the favor conferred.

WM. E. CRAMER

P.S. The Legislature closed its session yesterday. Though our friends were divided on some important measures, I trust the pure air of the country will scatter some of the gloomy forebodings with which they left.[4] We shall have a warm election in the fall.[5] The Whigs will come out with vigor and animation some of our most sagacious friends think that they (the Whigs) will carry the State. I feel differently. The Oregon question may be so directed as to become the absorbing issue. On this, we could carry the State with a *sweep*. Its popularity is so deep and pervading that many of the Whig papers have already been forced to take the strong and high American ground of your Inaugural. The very word Oregon rouses every chord of the popular heart. Your Commanding Position on that question will give the Democratic Party an immense advantage in every political contest they may wage. *The attack of Sir Robert Peel*[6] *was all that was wanted* to fix your position as *the Head* of the most important as well as the most popular question that has agitated our country in thirty years.

ALS. DLC–JKP. Addressed to Washington City and marked *"Private."*

1. William E. Cramer, son of Polk's former colleague in the U.S. House, John Cramer, had been associated with the *Albany Argus* since March 1843.

2. Date identified through content analysis.

3. Chesselden Ellis served as the prosecuting attorney of Saratoga County, N.Y., from 1837 to 1843. He won election in 1843 as a Democrat to the U.S. House but lost his seat in the 1844 election.

4. Cramer probably refers to Silas Wright's veto of the internal improvements bill of that session.

5. Cramer refers to state election scheduled for November 4, 1845.

6. See Jacob L. Martin to Polk, April 16, 1845.

## FROM AUGUSTUS C. DODGE

Burlington, Iowa Territory May 17, 1845

After alluding to his interviews with Polk at Washington, Dodge discusses patronage in the territory and prospects for Iowa statehood. Noting that John Chambers, the governor,[1] and most of the territory's officeholders are bitter opponents of Democratic principles, he reminds Polk of his pledge to remove all Federalists and to appoint sound Democrats. Dodge claims that two-thirds of the voters in the territory are Democrats. Under the Jackson and Van Buren administrations, resident Democrats filled most of the offices in Iowa, but that policy changed after 1841. Determined to ensure that Iowa would be "federalized" before it entered the Union, Whigs removed all Democrats and replaced them with "representatives of Messrs. Clay and Webster" and a host of "political hacks and broken-down politicians" from outside the territory. Dodge observes that in the act for Iowa's admission into the Union, Congress reduced the size of the state.[2] Citizens of the territory then voted on the question of adopting a constitution and accepting statehood under the conditions of the act of Congress. He notes that since Iowa citizens voted down the constitution, Iowa will remain outside the Union longer than anticipated.[3] Pointing to Whig efforts to turn this situation to advantage, he urges Polk to remove them from office as soon as possible.

LS. DLC–JKP. Addressed to Washington City. Polk's AE on the cover states that he received this letter on May 29, 1845.

1. A Kentucky Whig and governor of the Iowa Territory from 1841 until 1845, John Chambers served as aide-de-camp to William Henry Harrison in the War of 1812; won election to the Kentucky House four times, 1812, 1815, 1830, and 1831; sat two years on the bench of the Kentucky Court of Appeals, 1825–27; and filled a partial term in the U.S. House, 1828–29, and two full terms in his own right, 1835–39.

2. See Dodge to Polk, March 13, 1845.

3. In a popular vote on April 7, 1845, Iowa refused to enter the Union under the terms of legislation signed on March 3, 1845; citizens of Iowa Territory objected to the proposed western boundary of the new state.

## FROM JACOB L. MARTIN

My dear Sir. Paris 17th May 1845

The Steamer of the 1st May is in but we have not yet received the despatches which are first sent to the Legation in London. This is to be regretted, as before writing to you, we should have been pleased to have authentic intelligence with regard to the critical questions at issue. The public mind in England has been *much* calmed by the Late news from America. We now observe that war is deprecated in England, notwithstanding the language of the ministers & its echo in Parliament.[1] But that language is to be regretted, because it may yet kindle a flame in America which may make it difficult to settle the Oregon question in a rational manner. I suppose our people would be satisfied with no arrangement which should not preserve to us the Columbia throughout its course. The line of 49° prolonged to the sea, & then following the coast, so as to give to England all the bay of Fuca[2] has been strongly recommended by a fair & sensible article in an English paper which has attracted no little attention. I think Mr. King has written on this subject to Mr. Buchanan, and perhaps suggested a similar arrangement. I content myself to simply stating what has been suggested by others. If our warlike means were equal to the spirit & strength of our people, at this moment, the questions at issue would be promptly settled & without war. I trust that this will prove a lesson to be better prepared, hereafter. The boldness of the British govt. proceeds chiefly from its confidence in its formidable means of offence, especially its steam-navy, greater than that of the world besides.

From what we see in the papers, we are not a little uneasy about Texas. Every day's delay increases the danger. It is now obvious, what I always believed, that the principal persons in the government of Texas are hostile to annexation & will leave nothing untried to prevent it. Conversations with the late Chargé, General Terrell, convinced me, that he looked earnestly to England for means to prevent a measure to which he is fanatically hostile. Ashbel Smith, is equally so, though not quite so openly. We were sure of this before he left Europe, and not the less so, from the aversion he affected to entertain for Lord Aberdeen, at a time when they were acting in earnest concert. It seems to us, that Jones would scarcely resolve upon so conspicuous a step as sending his Secy. of State to England, without some reason to hope that his intrigues would prove successful. The British govt. will do much to promote the objects of these men, with whom it has a perfect understanding. I trust that means will be taken to expose these unworthy intrigues to the people of Texas, that their pride will be stimulated & their indignation excited. Will the people of Texas calmly look on, and permit themselves to be betrayed & sold to the aims of old England, by these two New England schoolmasters, Jones & Smith? I trust not. I trust that the people will promptly teach these men, that they are their servants not their rulers.

The threats of Mexico give us very little uneasiness, unless they are significant of the hostility of England. Mexico will hardly venture to engage with us single handed, & if she did, the contest would be ludicrous. To revert to the Texas question, it makes me indignant to see our government accused in the English papers of a rapacious desire to rob Mexico, of one of her fairest provinces, at the very time when it is admitted that England & perhaps France, are willing to gurantee the independence of Texas, provided she consents to maintain her separate existence, which would certainly be robbing Mexico just as effectually of Texas, as the annexation. The true objection is not to taking Texas from Mexico, but adding it to the U. States. The plan of Jones is obviously by any subterfuge & pretext to stave off annexation, in order to get time for his intrigues with England to operate. I hope the people of Texas understand or will be made to understand this. Money, promises, flattery, nothing will be spared, to defeat this great measure. God grant, that these men may not prove successful, as they will probably be, unless strongly & promptly counteracted.

Permit me before I close, to say a word in behalf of my worthy friend, Mr. Blackford Chargé d'affaires to Bogota.[3] If he can be saved it will make me happy. He is an able & excellent man & rendered me great service in times gone by. I congratulate you & the D. party upon the Virginia election.[4] Be pleased to present my kindest & most respectful compliments to Mrs. Polk ....

J. L. MARTIN

ALS. DLC–JKP. Addressed to Washington City.

1. See Jacob L. Martin to Polk, April 16, 1845.

2. Martin refers to conflicting U.S. and British claims to the territory between the 49th parallel on the north and the Columbia River on the south. The Strait of Juan de Fuca is located just south of the 49th parallel.

3. A native of Frederick County, Md., William M. Blackford moved to Virginia and edited the Fredericksburg *Political Arena* from 1828 until 1842; he served three years in Columbia as chargé d'affaires at Bogota, 1842–45.

4. See Polk to Andrew J. Donelson, May 6, 1845.

## FROM WILLIAM H. HAYWOOD, JR.

My Dear Sir                        Raleigh 19 May 1845

I hope, and as a yankee might say, I "calculate" that a Minister to England may be found *outside* of South Carolina after three ineffectual attempts to saddle that honour upon one of her statesmen.[1] Mr Cheves's celebrated letter I recollect advised that none of them should accept offices under your administration[2] and so far they have pursued that course—if they were not following that advice "aut Caesar aut Nullus."[3] I venture to write this to you because in thus expressing my own wishes, I do but give shape and form to the sentiment of all your friends as they utter & feel it throughout the circle of my association.

It is passing strange that our sagacious and patriotic(?) Fed Editors should have failed to detect the folly and ill manners of the Inaugural until it had been re-shipped to them across the Atlantic! Before the English Premier[4] gave them to understand (by a ship kept in port for the purpose) how incensed he was at it not a single one of them had perceived the monstrous political blunder of our President!

Funny enough is it not that *three english words* of your Inaugural should have frightened John Bull? Lord Robert directly confessing the day after he had shipped off his wrath that he was bidding for Irish help to whip Jonathan. A very "small cloud" had brought him to offer the Maynooth College Gift as a placebo to Irish disloyalty for fear of the U.S.[5] And what a bounty! How immense the loyalty that could be purchased with £20.000 to £30.000! The whole thing as enacted in Parliament would be a broad farce & so it will seem to everybody in a little while unless our friend Mr Ritchie releaves it by giving more long columns to the subject in the "organ."

Speaking of the Organ I must remark that the removal alias the retirement of our friend Blair or whatever else if was has all been a mystery to me. No one explained it before hand. It is certain that the published articles do not disclose it to my dull apprehension. I hope it was done with such real good feeling all around as may not divide our party in the choice of a Printer for Congress. For independent of the injury to the party it would be a cruel misfortune to defeat Mr R thereby to ruin his personal fortunes. It should be remembered that the excellent old gentleman is one of these sanguine mortals who may be misled by his own temperament in such a matter as this and there is safety in being cautious. I write all this as I do the whole of my labor for *you* and for your eye only. Presumptious as he might think it I should not like the Organ less if the Editor would write less of himself—too many "*We &*

"Us." Too much appearance of the *Admn* being supported by "the Organ" instead of "the Organ" being established & supported by & for the Admn. A little too patronizing to express it by a single word. This criticism is not entirely original with me. Leaving these things and a total silence on Sub-Treasury I think our friends are pleased with the *Union*.

By the way in connexion with this subject of Sub Treasury I remark that it is published in N. York (democratic) papers that the public Deposits are to be made with *Banks* who are to pledge the amount in Govt Stocks. Can this be so? Is it not virtually paying the Banks 5 & 6 per cent for keeping the money? If you deposit with me 1000 Dollars to hold subject to your check upon condition that I buy in your *note bearing interest* 5 per cent and that note is put with you in pledge as a security the Interest still accruing and we settle the account at the end of a year how does it stand? I pay your check for £950 & take back the note out of pledge will it not close the transaction in substance & effect? What is this if it is not allowing me the *Interest* for taking your money to keep? I am not very vain of my Financial learning but really the thing looks so to my plain knowledge of figures.

The subject of Texas is one upon which you know my opinions so well that I should be making it a *bore* to write much on it.

The choice of alternatives having been made by you, probably upon information about wh. I know nothing; to speak my mind of what is thus past recall would be idle & unnecessary.[6] Without meaning therefore to express either my concurrence or non concurrence I have misapprehended the state of your feelings to me if you can take it amiss in me to say that I have strong fears of *our own* Congress. Very probably however your experience last winter of how easy a matter it was to be deceived on such a subject where leading politns acted upon mere *conjectures* in respect to the vote of senators suggested the policy of ascertaining with *certainty* what might be the end of the course taken, before others were *excluded*.

Should Texas form a Constn and that is laid before the next Congress for her admission *as a state* and yet the next Congress shall refuse to *admit* Texas, the embarrassments to Texas, to the Union, & to your Admn. would be very great, not to say very perilous. And yet with the lights *before me* I am obliged to say I apprehend there is no little danger of it, if the subject is presented *out* & *out* in the form of the Resolns called Browns or the House Resolns.[7] I recollect that my fears were considered unworthy of notice last winter until it was almost too late. I remember & you know the circumstances which arrested our progress toward defeat. I cannot shake off the dread of imminent perils ahead of this measure (in the form proposed). It is by no means my intention to *croak*. But to alarm into vigilance by the humble warning of a friend your forethought &c against the dangers of a false security & nothing more. If my judgment did not approve of the act and my public station as well as my personal relations make it a duty to do at least so much *you* can very readily understand why I could have preferred to say nothing on this subject.

I see that my friend Col Stevenson of N. York[8] in whose behalf I became so warmly enlisted failed to get the station of *Naval officer.* From the name "Naval" I hastily assumed that the appointment belonged to the Navy Depart., carelessly omitting to recur to its duties I overlooked the fact of its being an office in *Treasury* Department. Had I known that Mr Morris the next most conspicuous and active agent in exposing the *Infamous pipe laying frauds*[9] would be appointed Post Master I should have urged Col. S. claims upon Democrat party even more strongly. But *"n' importe."*[10] Though sorry for it I am not disappointed.

If in the multitude of your engagements you should find time and feel inclined to write you know it will give me pleasure to receive your letters. I should have reminded you of this long ago by an earlier compliance with your parting request that I should write you. But the fact is I feel a great reluctance at obtruding my crude opinions so freely & every day convinces me more and more that *I ought to quit political life.* Still I beg you to understand once for all that at any time & at all times I am ready to serve you, if you should think I can serve you by doing any thing for your Admn. consistent with the obligations of a Patriot & a christian gentn, and I am *sure* you would not ask me to sacrifice those of the one or the other.

This is the first letter I ever wrote to a *Prest* and you will perceive that by turns I have forgotten & then again recollected that I was addressing a *President of the U.S.*!

Any way you will please consider the whole letter as one of confidential scribbling to a *friend*.

My best respects to *Madame* if you please.

WILL. H. HAYWOOD JR.

ALS. DLC–JKP. Addressed to Washington City and marked *"Confidential."* Polk's AE on the cover states that he answered this letter on August 9, 1845; Polk also notes on the cover, "Copy forwarded to Mr Haywood at his request: Sept 21, 1846." Published in *NCHR*, XVI, pp. 435–38.

1. Haywood refers to John C. Calhoun, Franklin H. Elmore, and Francis W. Pickens.

2. Haywood probably refers to Langdon Cheves' letter to the editor of the *Charleston Mercury*, reprinted in *Niles' National Register*, September 28, 1844. A Charleston lawyer, Cheves served in the South Carolina House, 1802–10; won

election as a Democrat to the U.S. House, 1810–15; succeeded Henry Clay as
Speaker in 1814; sat as a justice on the South Carolina Court of Appeals, 1816–
19; resigned to become a director and president of the second Bank of the United
States, 1819–22; and held the post of chief commissioner of claims under the
Treaty of Ghent, 1822–29.

3. Latin phrase meaning "either a Caesar or a nobody."

4. Sir Robert Peel.

5. Haywood's reference is to an editorial in the Washington *Union* of May 12,
1845, which contained an excerpt from a speech by Peel on April 18, 1845, closing debate on the Maynooth Grant Bill. The controversial measure granted an
increased annual subsidy of £26,000 to Maynooth College, an institution dedicated to the education of the Catholic clergy in Ireland. Ritchie claimed that the
Maynooth Bill was Peel's attempt to pacify the Irish preparatory to a possible
conflict with the United States over Oregon.

6. Haywood refers to the president's choice of alternatives under Robert J.
Walker's compromise bill on Texas annexation. See William H. Haywood, Jr., to
Polk, February 26, 1845.

7. Haywood probably refers to Milton Brown's Texas resolutions and the U.S.
House joint resolution on Texas annexation.

8. A native of New York and colonel of the militia, Jonathan D. Stevenson
represented New York City in the state assembly in 1846. During the Mexican
War he commanded a regiment of New York volunteers and served as military
commander of the southern district of California in 1848. Following the war,
Stevenson remained in California and prospered as a San Francisco real estate
agent.

9. A few weeks before the presidential election of 1840, a Whig operative
named "Glentworth" was arrested and charged with voting frauds alleged to
have been committed in the 1838 New York gubernatorial election. According
to Thurlow Weed in his *Autobiography*, Glentworth had received the office of tobacco inspector as compensation for having recruited gangs of Pennsylvania laborers to lay water pipes between Lake Croton and New York City; Glentworth's
out-of-state pipe layers only worked on election days and in such places as their
illegal votes could be counted with safety. Legislation designed to prevent election fraud came to be known as "anti-pipelaying" bills.

10. French phrase meaning "it's no matter."

## FROM WILLIAM B. LEWIS

Sir,                                             Washington 19th May 1845

Having waited a week and received no reply to my note,[1] I am authorised to believe that you have decided not to answer it, from which I
infer that the intimations therein referred to, as having been made by
you, are true, or you would have availed yourself of the opportunity thus
afforded to disavow them. I think proper, therefore, to inform you that

I propose leaving tomorrow morning for Tennessee, and shall there determine upon the time and mode of vindicating my character against the aspersions which you have attempted to cast upon it.

W. B. LEWIS

ALS. DLC–JKP. Addressed to Washington City. Polk's AE on the cover states that "This letter was brought to my office with other letters on the night of the 21st May 1845."
1. See William B. Lewis to Polk, May 8, 1845.

## FROM J. G. M. RAMSEY

Mecklenburg, Tenn. May 19, 1845

After stressing the need to secure federal patronage for the *Knoxville Standard*, Ramsey discusses Polk's choice of Thomas Ritchie as the editor of the administration's newspaper, the Washington *Union*. He believes that the selection of Ritchie meets with "unqualified approbation" among Polk's friends. Praising Ritchie as the wisest and safest guide on questions of foreign policy as well as domestic issues, Ramsey claims that he combines "the best elements that distinguished Jefferson & Jackson." He also notes with approval Polk's decision to select the minister to the Court of St. James from the South.[1] On the subject of the fall elections in Tennessee, Ramsey mentions the lack of "a common head to suggest, arrange, converge, & control" the campaign but acknowledges Brown's efforts to make "a good fight." He notes that the Whigs are apathetic and adds that "the menacing tone of England" strengthens the Democracy.[2]

ALS. DLC–JKP. Addressed to Washington City.
1. Ramsey refers to Polk's efforts to appoint a South Carolinian as minister to England.
2. See Jacob L. Martin to Polk, April 16, 1845.

## FROM JOEL B. SUTHERLAND

Dr Sir                                                        Philada May 19th 1845

I recd a day or two ago a note from the Comptroller Mr McCulloh[1] requesting me to deliver over to Henry Welsh Esq the books of entry &c, as he had been appointed naval officer in my place. I had previously seen in the *Union* the appointment of Henry Welsh in the place of Joel B Sutherland *removed*. I frankly confess that I did not expect to be *removed* for the 18 or 19 months, that I had to serve. After I recd Genl Jacksons letter *a copy of which I forwarded to your Excellency*[2] I certainly thought I had a right to expect that I would have been *notified* of the intended *removal*, in which event I would *have certainly resigned*. It may be a weak conceit, that I have, but I confess that after having been

in Congress for some 8 or 10 years with you & a host of other competent men, throughout the Republic I feel my sensibility greatly wounded,
*daily* in seeing my *name* going the *rounds* of the Press with the word *removed attached* to it. It was but yesterday, that I saw an Alabama paper
with my *removal* in it. It will go *over every hill valley lake & river of the
nation*. The other *gentlemen removed* had no *congressional* reputation
& cannot of course feel, the *publication* as keenly as I do.

I cannot believe that you entertain any personal hostility toward me
or I would not send you this, for during the campaign I kept you most
minutely advised of every thing that was important. I *helped* carry over
the Tyler party, that I think was necessary to secure the vote of Penna
for the Democratic Candidate. At my own personal expense, I printed
hand bills &c & spent two nights with the ships carpenters of Southwark
& Kensington & thus reduced the majority against us in the county of
Philada in the Novr election. Night and day I gave a very large portion
my time up to our cause. I am quite sure I addressed from 3 to 5000 Tyler
men assembled in the great Chinese Museum & wrote the resolutions &
raised with that force the *first great procession* in your favor in Philada. [3]
Some of the men who have since the election been *up for office*, said to me
during the campaign, that their party could not *begin to hold a meeting
with us*. Besides I spent from 6 to 800 dollars in printing and other
expenses incident to the contest. We had five meetings in the Chinese
Museum, 20 dollars a night. *I* paid 70 dollars to one paper for publishing
proceedings &c at one time, & 200 to another. We met sometimes at the
Assembly rooms, which had to be paid for. We have *here* to *pay* for a very
large portion of our newspaper articles.

In the House of Representatives, we were together so long that I
thought I had a right to a *notice* that I might *resign*. I had a just right
to think that a good fellowship existed between us when I left Congress
as I had on one occasion so satisfactorily sustained one of your decisions
as to receive your personal thanks. [4] Besides during the campaign, you
were pleased to request me to continue my letters. [5] I could have cut out
both Lehman & Welsh from the support of Mr Buchanan, I think if I had
gone in for the *succession*. On the contrary at our great meeting on the
8th of Jany in the Assembly rooms, we drank the following toast "The
succession. Those who start *early* in this race, will be trodden under foot
long ere, the meeting of the convention to name a candidate for 48'." [6]
We also drank "The Polk administration & nothing else," or words to
that effect. This was based upon an *idea* that I sent your Excellency in a
letter immediately after you were elected, [7] as the best mode of keeping
clear of the rivals for 48. Mr Buchanan complained of our toasts, as not
being strong enough for him. We said that we were not for any Presi-

dential candidate then, that we neither wanted Buchanan, Dallas, Cass, Walker nor Wright, but that we wished for a Polk administration clear of all cliques. I did not *then* tell why I was not for either of the candidates, but I may say here, *now, that I am removed from office,* that I then firmly believed that the party could not run any body against Mr Clay, who I saw in advance was getting ready for the race again, except Young Hickory *Nolens Volens.*[8] I repeat if I had been an open mouth'd champion of Mr Buchanan I feel sure, he would have been as strong for me, as for Mr Welsh or Mr Lehman. I have recently read, what "the Union" says is the principle upon which your Excellency makes the appointments. It is, that you examine all *the papers* presented & then conscientiously make up your decision.[9] It ought however to be kept in mind, that the Tyler men in Penna had no Representatives either in the state or the national legislature. It was impossible *therefore*, that they should or could get the assistance of either, particularly where most of the Congressmen, *whose terms had expired* were busily engaged in *providing for themselves or their friends* directly or indirectly. Besides as Govr Shunk, could not provide for all that he *wish'd*, he was interested in pushing his neglected friends upon the U. States Govt for places. But although the Tyler men could not, or did not get the legislature state or national, yet they were *immensely valuable as a body of men in carrying the President* & are necessary to keep the State of Penna in Democratic hands. I think I may say, that I am *nearly* as well acquainted with the Politics of Penna as any *one* residing in it—my letters to your Excellency will settle that matter. Now, great reliance is placed at Washington in the Judgment of Mr Buchanan, & yet this same Mr Buchanan, told me in Mrs Ronkendorffs Ice Cream House in Washington City[10] in the presence of 2 or 3 other persons that Mr Van Burens Majority would be 20.000 I think in June before the election of 40.

I, then told him the vote, would run down more likely to *hundreds*. I mention this to show how little *he* knew about *Penna*. It is true he came to Philada & traversed the western part of the state on that occasion, but he could not carry the state for Mr Van Buren. The Democrats always receive what B. says with grains of allumen as he was *once* the leader of the Federal party and has never yet been able to get the true *hang* of the Democracy in Penna. Hence he could not get the vote of Penna in the national convention. In forty I foretold the result or what would likely be the result in Penna. In '44, I did the same thing. While men, who are near relatives of persons *now in office* in Philada did not believe we would *carry* at the time I wrote your Excellency we would. I repeat upon my knowledge of the state, that without *our* Tyler assistance here the Polk ticket would not have carried, & yet we are *re-*

*moved*. The Aspirants for '48 are at the bottom of my removal. I *accepted* the office, as my private affairs *then* required me to do so. But I repeat if I had thought I was to have been removed I would most gladly have resigned. While writing I will say one word or so more. An *office holder* labors under many inconveniences. He cannot leave his post, or he is charged with negligence of his duties. While an office hunter can way lay the path of the Executive continually, one on the ground *near* the President has a thousand advantages over persons at a distance. Cabinet meetings on appointments are not only not necessary but absolutely prejudiced. Hence, you see daily *laudations* upon *each* member of the cabinet, & *their* presses going for a single term, which necessarily puts the Executive in the back ground. They have their Dallas Clubs & Balls. Buchanans paper announced 3 months ago the proceedings of a meeting recommending him for '48.[11] While *all* go to the death for a *single term*, which necessarily *whittles away* the *Polk influence daily*. In the Sentinel here,[12] I from time to time wrote articles in favor of a Polk administration. Because I thought it was the true mode of keeping matters harmoniously together. But Aspirants never copied them, & although you said no *Aspirant* should use the influence of the Govt for himself yet, such is the present arrangement of matters, with the Aspirants, that a search warrant, would hardly find a *Polk* man in office in any of the states except Tennessee. I believe if the Sentinel has not published Polk articles, the cabinet ministers, would not agree to certain removals. The views of the *succession* were hostile to my continuance. It is easy enough to find Wright Men Dallas Men Buchanan Men & Walker Men in office. Each Candidate uses, as is *natural*, all his power to get his men *into place*, to back him up for '48.

I am quite confident you had not a truer friend in office in the wide Union than myself.

What also looks strange here is, that others who have been in office much longer than I have been in Penna have not been removed.

J. B. SUTHERLAND

ALS. DLC–JKP. Addressed to Washington City and marked *"Private."*

1. Head cashier of the Baltimore branch of the Bank of the United States in 1819, James W. McCulloh won election to one term in the state House of Delegates from Baltimore County in 1825, served as an Adams presidential elector in 1829, and became first comptroller of the Treasury in 1842.

2. On April 1, 1845, Sutherland wrote Polk and enclosed a copy of Jackson's letter of March 21, 1845, assuring him that Polk was aware of his energetic support during the campaign and would not remove him without just cause. L, copy. DLC–JKP.

3. Sutherland probably refers to the June 1, 1844, rally and march called to confirm the Baltimore Convention nominations.

4. Reference not identified further.

5. Sutherland wrote this sentence in the left margin of the second page of the letter.

6. Sutherland's reference is to the January 8, 1845, meeting of Philadelphia party leaders on the anniversary of the Battle of New Orleans.

7. Sutherland probably refers to his letter to Polk of November 12, 1844.

8. Latin phrase meaning "willing or unwilling."

9. Sutherland's reference is to the May 13, 1845, Washington *Union* editorial entitled "Appointments by the President."

10. Ronckendorff, who ran a confectioner's shop on Pennsylvania Avenue, is not identified further.

11. Sutherland possibly refers to the Lancaster *Intelligencer*.

12. Philadelphia *American Sentinel*.


## TO LEVI WOODBURY

My dear Sir.             Washington City 19 May 1845

Having determined at an early period after the commencement of my administration to appoint a Successor to Mr Everett as Minister Plenipotentiary and Envoy Extraordinary to Great Britain and that for reasons which it is unnecessary to state, it was desirable that the mission should be filled by some Gentleman in the South, I tendered it to that section of the Union and it has been declined. The importance of the mission at this juncture of our relations with England has been greatly increased by the late proceedings in parliament[1] & my opinion *now* is that we should be represented at the English Court by the ablest & most prudent man in the Country who may be willing to accept it, without regard to his residence or Geographical position. I have selected you for this important mission & now tender it for your acceptance in the sincere hope that you may be willing to undertake the important trust. Your acceptance I am sure, would be hailed by the Country with general approbation. Your established public reputation & well known ability & patriotism would inspire general confidence, that the great interests entrusted to you would be safe in your hands. In the event of your acceptance (of which I hope there may be no doubt) I may add that the duration of your continuance abroad, will be left very much to yourself. Unless by your own voluntary choice your absence need not be of the usual duration. Of this however you would yourself decide. Mr Everett anticipates his recall & in a letter addressed to me he says "it would be agreeable to me that my successor should be named as soon as it can be done with due regard to the public service, in order that I may be able to remain at my post till his arrival, (which I think desirable both on his account and that of the public) without my being delayed till the season of the year is too far advanced for a safe and comfortable passage across the Atlantic." [2]

In selecting you for this distinguished station I gratify my own personal feelings & in the event of your acceptance will I am sure, serve the best interests of the country.

I have to request that you will give me an early answer. If in your answer you signify your willingness to accept, a commission will be immediately signed & the necessary instructions prepared.

With my Kind regards to Mrs Woodbury .... [3]

                                                      JAMES K. POLK

LS, draft. DLC–JKP. Addressed to Portsmouth and marked "*Private.*"
1. See Jacob L. Martin to Polk, April 16, 1845.
2. Quotation from Edward Everett's letter to Polk of March 3, 1845.
3. Elizabeth Williams Clapp Woodbury.

## FROM JOHN CATRON

Dr Sir.                                           Nashville, May 20, 1845

I have been at home two weeks and can only give, 'the Signs of the times,' by speaking of negatives. Party animosity seems hardly to exist in this part of Ten. The Whigs are not only quiet, but passionless. In the Election to come on in Augt. less interest is felt, than I had thought possible. Foster is free from all excitement, and weary of contest. Brown does not wish it, as his party is supposed to be in heart, and on the gain, and the other the reverse. So Stevenson thinks, and that a state of repose is best for the Dem. side. What the result of this course will be, I have no means to judge.

Bell is entirely silent so far as I have heard; indeed his private business requires his time, and he is very tired of political effort, I feel very sure.

Dr. Jenning's [1] spirits have flagged, by again running Dr. Peyton for Congress. He is silent and pursuing his profession. All attempts to generate bitter feelings so far made by the whig press, (Banner & Whig,) have met with no response. If the British Government should by further indiscretions [2] arouse a war feeling it will nearly obliterate party lines; as the Whig *Young* men will resent any British assumption as readily as the other side, and the enfeebled condition of the old leaders is such as to leave no efficient controll in their hands—on this head they are powerless. Half a dozen well written Oregon articles in the newspapers, free from all party allusions, would run down all opposition, but this should not be attempted pending a negotiation. The materials are in abundance, so far as the American side requires advocacy: not but that a fair case, & plausible claim, can be made for the British side also, founded on discovery, or occupancy by the fur companies, Hudson's Bay, & No. West, on conquest during the last war, coming in aid of previous possession.[3] This question is "a bone to knaw"[4] and excuse for war measures founded on the consideration that this Young Eagle had as well have a wing cropped to keep her out of Texas, California, and the ancient palaces of Mexico. There it is, England seeks the footing she has long had in Portugal & Spain,[5] and she is making masterly work of it, and has near you a diplomat transferred from Mexico to Washington because of his enlarged experience in the affairs of our Sister republic.[6] At least so I have supposed. The Texas annexation spirit here, & in the west generally, is calm for the reason that the thing is looked on as a *settled* matter; any attempt to defeat it would raise a storm of more violence than a dozen Oregon questions. The extent of public attention, and purpose to settle in Texas on its admission, is greater than anything of the kind that you or I have ever witnessed.

Your administration so far has been more approved than you had any just grounds to anticipate. Faith in its *prudence* and *vigor*, exists with your opponents, and among your friends, in pretty much an equal degree. You have fewer personal enmities to contend with than I believed you had when you went into office. I find nearly all the men of wealth, who want nothing but protection to their goods & lands, are perfectly content, & will support the administration, regardless of any whig preferences they may have had. They speak of you in the kindest terms, and all laud Mrs. Polk, no small matter by the way in that White House, that text for gossips, where a silly son or two may ruin a presdt, & where the democrats have always held since Jefferson's day that a wife is a *bad* thing.

Our friend Genl. Jackson is very much afflicted, has been swollen all over, & is some yet. He is exceedingly emaciated, & cannot last long, not through the summer I think, and so does he. I was there on friday. He for an hour and more conversed with me as usual & especially about Penn. men recently appointed, & put out—told anedotes of Dr. Sutherland &c, laughed heartily. Gave his views of our position with England; of men & things that now were in power, and seemed to have all the memory and strength of mind usual to him at any time within ten years. But it exhausted him. He lay on a couch & could not leave it alone. His breath leaves him very soon on the least exertion. He has nothing left but the head. He is the picture of extreme age, & feels & knows it to be so well as I do. On the subject of his approaching end, we conversed as on an indifferent subject, & as of a 3d person. We have done so for years however, which made it not remarkable. Death must come, & in the condition of our friend he ought not to be a *dread* messenger—little is left of life to loose. Genl. J. is still alive & excited about the coming in of Texas, & was anxiously awaiting Houston's first assenting speech, being obviously well advised of what it was to consist. It is a great curiosity to see a man with the look of ninety years weighing him down, physically feeble as a young infant, wielding the power of a country; a foreign land, in aid of an object, greater than almost any History records as having been accomplished by peacible means, and treating of it with a sagacity & *boldness*, that would have done no discredit to Frederick or Bonaparte. Then he turns over in his mind the contemplation of what he could do with our present *material* of war, on the plains of N orleans if he was 40 years younger.[7] How the rush down the Mi wd be made, the marchings, & fighting John Bull round the Gulf &c, totally forgeting he could not stand alone.

My old friend Edwin Dibrell wants to be inspector, & protector of live oak in Florida. I told him that so many were applying on the spot or near it in the *New State*, that I feared you was not in a situation to oblige him, but I would say to you, he was well suited to it, as he is.

Then again my frnd. Kenneth Mackenzie of St. Louis[8] wd like to be consul at Glasgow Scotland, as wd his wife Mary[9] like to be *Consuless* still more, *I think*. I know, no man in America better qualified. He is high toned; & as a dealer in & with mercantile affairs is a man of the first class, & very high experience in Europe itself. In will, & integrity, he resembles Armstrong very much, but is highly skilful as a man of the world on a large scale. Being at the head of the Fur company for twenty years, or nearly so, he has had nothing to do in politics, but said to me last summer he should have gone for Clay had it not been for his wife's family, & their wishes, & had he not come to Tene. during the canvass. He is rich, & free from every taint of avarice, lives some better than *you* or I could afford, & I take it he and Mary would grace the consulship with good cheer, whether much come into the toll-dish, or little, from that source. Whether there is any place to fill, or one worth filling, I do not know, nor much care. Still, I like him very much, as do my Missouri friends, & shd be very well pleased if he shd be gratified.

The country is healthy and prosperous. Friends generally well.

                                                              J. CATRON

ALS. DLC–JKP. Addressed to Washington City. Polk's AE on the cover states that he received this letter on May 29, 1845.

1. Catron probably refers to Thomas R. Jennings. A Nashville physician and member of the medical department of the University of Nashville, he served as a Whig member of the Tennessee Senate from 1839 until 1845. In 1844, he

won election as a Whig presidential elector for Tennessee's Eighth Congressional District.

2. See Jacob L. Martin to Polk, April 16, 1845.

3. British claims to the Oregon Territory derived from the discoveries of Sir Francis Drake, James Cook, and George Vancouver; the Nootka Convention with Spain in 1790; a treaty with Russia in 1825; and the activities of the Hudson's Bay and North West fur companies.

4. Paraphrase of "He ... gave them a bone to gnaw." William Fulbecke, *The Pardectes of the Law of Nations* (1602), p. 69.

5. During the Napoleonic Wars Britain and France fought a series of military campaigns for control of Spain and Portugal. With the defeat of France Britain sought to maintain a controlling influence over the Iberian peninsula and the Spanish and Portuguese colonies in the New World; to that end Britain maintained a strong military presence on the Tagus River and Gibraltar during the following decades.

6. Sir Richard Pakenham.

7. Catron refers to the Battle of New Orleans on January 8, 1815. The battle had taken place thirty, not forty, years before.

8. A fur trader and merchant from Scotland, Kenneth MacKenzie came to North America as an employee of the North West Company and became a citizen of the United States with the founding of the Columbia Fur Company at St. Louis in 1822. His company merged with the American Fur Company in 1827. Removing to Europe in 1834 he engaged in the commission mercantile trade in foreign liquors. MacKenzie had extensive land holdings in Missouri, Illinois, and Minnesota.

9. Mary Marshall MacKenzie.

## FROM MICHAEL HOFFMAN

Dr. Sir,                                              New York, Tuesday [May 20, 1845][1]

The Letter of the Comptroller of the Treasury[2] of the 5th inst. notifying me of my appointment to the office of Naval Officer of this District, was not received until yesterday. By the mail of to day I have informed the Department of the causes of the delay, my acceptance of the place and expressed my thanks for the favor. I prefer to get my bail[3] from the country rather than in the city. The Collector[4] is absent and if I had the Bail I could not take the oath of office until his return and by the present rule the Bail & oaths must preceed the commission. The short future delay can I believe work no mischief.

The offer of this place by any president would merit hearty thanks. We were intimate acquaintances for a long series of years and that acquaintance ripened into an ardent friendship. I witnessed with great satisfaction your industry in business, your devotion to duty and the principles for which we contended. After the lapse of years and varied fortune, the frank expression of your confidence esteem and good wishes, by my appointment to the responsible place in question, recalls the past with warm affection, cheers the present, and excites the most ardent desire for your perfect success. The least return I can make will be to discharge the trust confided to me in a manner not unworthy of your friendship.

After a short apprenticeship to learn details and after the usual scramble for the patronage of the office, I shall have some leisure that can be devoted to subjects of general interest. Among these I regard as important, such a modification of the Tariff of federal taxes as will permit commerce to reward production and thus make it possible for the Debtor States to proceed in the work of payment. Any assistance I can give on this or any other subject you may freely command. Since 1841 my position has obliged me to study the condition, wants and progress of the State,[5] the causes of past defeats and the means of Democratic success, and I can scarely forbear after our wonted manner in conversation to attempt details. After a long, often violent and some times desperate struggle the victory of Democratic principles, of economy in expenditure, payment, and a sound currency, of moderate & equal taxes state & federal, over expenditure, Debt, irresponsible banking and grants of monopoly and special privileges, is, by means adequate and sufficient rendered as certain as any thing human can be. We may therefore well hope for a really Democratic administration in this State, and for all the support that a successful Democracy here can give to that of the Union.

MICHAEL HOFFMAN

ALS. DLC–JKP. Addressed to Washington City and marked "*Private.*"
1. Hoffman misdated his letter "May 21."
2. James W. McCulloh.
3. Archaic use of the word "bail" to mean "bond."
4. Cornelius P. Van Ness.
5. Hoffman represented Herkimer County in the New York Assembly in 1841, 1842, and 1844.

FROM DUFF GREEN

Dear Sir                                  New York May 22nd 1845
I have been much annoyed by the articles in the Herald,[1] and more by an article in the Union which has just fallen under my notice from which it appears that I am suspected of communicating with or prompting the Herald.[2] I believe I know the sources through the Washington corre-

spondent of that paper gets much of his news (Heart of the Constitution & Dr Jones the late postmaster)[3] but I have not directly or indirectly communicated with the Herald or written an article for a paper since I returned to the United states except one now before for the Union on our relations with England.

I have been to Albany and have heard and seen much. The old Regency are quarrelling & I have seen a correspondence which casts a flood of light on the intrigues by which Van Buren & his faction ov[er][4] threw the democratic party, & I have heard much that it behoves you to know.[5] I will be in Washington in a few days when I can satisfy you that your confidence has been most grossly abused.

DUFF GREEN

ALS. DLC–JKP. Addressed to Washington City and marked "*Private*."

1. Green probably refers to a series of editorials in the *New York Herald* between May 13 and 20, 1845. Drawing on information from a correspondent with the "best means of information," those editorials reported that Polk probably would offer John C. Calhoun the mission to England with authority to settle the Oregon question, as well as other commercial matters; the editorials also claimed that Thomas Ritchie and some members of Polk's cabinet favored Martin Van Buren's appointment.

2. Reference possibly is to a Washington *Union* editorial of May 14, 1845. Ritchie rebuked the authority of the *Herald*'s "private and well-informed correspondent" and denied any action by the administration offering the British mission to either Calhoun or Van Buren at that time. The editorial also denied any factionalism or favoritism on the part of the administration or the *Union*.

3. John Heart and William Jones. Heart, who had written for the Washington *Globe* and Washington *Spectator*, published a special campaign newspaper, the *Young Hickory*, devoted to securing Polk's victory over Henry Clay. Following the election Heart edited the Baltimore *Constitution* until it ceased publication in December 1845. Jones served as postmaster of Washington City from 1836 until his removal in 1845.

4. Part of this word has been obliterated by a tear in the manuscript.

5. On June 1, 1845, Green wrote Calhoun and described the correspondence that he had seen in New York. After noting the circulation of several Jackson letters that were "very offensive" to Polk, Green discussed the discovery of a collection of letters between Van Buren and other leaders of the Albany Regency. Filed with records in the New York Customs House and dating back to 1824, the letters dealt with elections, "combinations and intrigues for office," and party politics. "Some of the copies," Green added, "have been exhibited to the President & he now understands, that he has every thing to fear and nothing to hope by identifying himself with that clique." PL, in Wilson, ed., *The Papers of John C. Calhoun*, XXI, pp. 580–81.

## TO ANDREW JACKSON

My Dear Sir:                                    Washington City 22nd May 1845

Recent dispatches from *Majr. Donelson* and information brought by *Gov Yell* of Arkansas, who arrived here two days ago as bearer of despatches from Texas,[1] puts the annexation question upon the terms proferred by the U. States beyond doubt. *Texas* may now be regarded as a part of our country.

In the existing state of our relations with England, rendered the more important, by the late blustering and menacing proceedings in Parliament,[2] made it, in my judgment important, that the U.S. should be represented at that Court by the ablest man in the country. I accordingly tendered the Mission to *Mr Van-Buren* through Mr *Butler* of N. York.[3] Mr *Van-Buren* in a very kind letter, and I think with some hesitancy declines.[4] I should have been most happy to have availed myself of his services at this junction of our relations with England. Upon receiving his declination I immediately addressed a letter to Mr *Woodbury* tendering the mission to him.[5] There has not been time as yet to receive his answer.

It was thought best, immediately after the commencement of my administration that this mission should be filled by some gentleman in the South, and it was accordingly offered to that section of the Union and was declined. The late news from England makes it much more important, than it was at first believed to be. I have no hesitation in saying that had I been in possession of the information, which I now have, the mission would have been offered to Mr *Van-Buren* in the first instance. This was explained to Mr *Van-Buren*.

My public duties continue to be very great. The pressure upon me by office seekers, has scarcely diminished since I came into office. I have however made public that I will appoint no man who comes to Washington seeking an office, whilst he remains here, and the effect, has been to diminish the number of personal importunities upon me.[6]

From your last letter I have great solicitude concerning your health.[7] I hope it may have improved. I have procured a copy of *Sully*'s fine portrait of you in your military costume taken many years ago.[8] I have it in my office. The contrast between your appearance then and now is very great.

Say to *Mrs. Jackson*[9] that *Mr Taggart* will have his place on the 1st of June. Mr *Horn* the new collector, promised me to appoint *Thos Donelson* to the place he desired in the Philadelphia Custom House, and I suppose has done so. I have entire harmony in my Cabinet and hope the administration is getting on well. We hear occasional Complaints from some former office-holders, whom I have deemed it to be my duty to remove, but this I suppose is natural enough. With most sincere wishes for your welfare, in this world and in that which is to come.

JAMES K. POLK

ALS. DLC–AJ. Addressed to the Hermitage and marked "*Private.*" Printed in Bassett, ed., *Correspondence of Andrew Jackson*, VI, pp. 407–8.

1. See Andrew J. Donelson to Polk, May 11 and 14, 1845.
2. See Jacob Martin to Polk, April 16, 1845.
3. See Polk to Benjamin Butler, May 5, 1845.
4. Polk probably refers to Martin Van Buren to George Bancroft, May 12, 1845. ALS, draft. DLC–MVB.
5. See Polk to Levi Woodbury, May 19, 1845.
6. On March 29, 1845, *Niles' National Register* ran an article on Polk's policy towards office-seekers. Polk sought to direct all applications and supporting claims to the appropriate cabinet departments, and the cabinet heads then would be responsible for presenting the candidates for a given position to the president.
7. Polk probably refers to Jackson's letter of May 2, 1845.
8. Polk probably refers to a copy of Thomas Sully's 1819 portrait of Jackson, painted by Thomas Sully, Jr. See John H. Wheeler to Polk, April, 1845. NS. DLC–JKP. A native of England, Thomas Sully was among America's finest portrait painters of the Romantic school. He maintained his studio in Philadelphia. His son, Thomas Sully, Jr., also achieved renown for his portrait painting.
9. Polk refers to Sarah Yorke Jackson, the wife of Andrew Jackson, Jr.

## FROM LEVI WOODBURY

Dear Sir,                              Portsmouth, N.H. 22d May 1845

I feel greatly obliged by the proposal you make to send me minister to the Court of St. James.[1] On the arrival of your kind letter I was preparing to visit Portland, where Mrs. W.[2] has been for some time with her parents[3]; and, before my return early next week, I will endeavour to give a final answer to your invitation.

Allow me to say now, however, that no situation abroad could be so agreeable as this, did I look in a diplomatic direction for spending a few years more in the public service. But not having, for some time, formed any expectations for that kind of life, in consequence of the situation of my family, I am not sure it will be in my power to overcome the difficulties, which still grow out of that situation.

But be assured, Sir, that my disposition to oblige you and in any station assigned to me by the partiality of my friends, to contribute all I am able to sustain the high principles involved in our relations with England, will call forth my best efforts to remove those objections, which have heretofore proved insuperable in the way of my accepting any foreign mission.

With great respect & regard to Mrs. Polk as well as yourself....

Levi Woodbury

ALS. DLC–JKP. Addressed to Washington City. Polk's AE on the cover states that he received this letter on May 25, 1845.
1. See Polk to Levi Woodbury, May 19, 1845.
2. Elizabeth Williams Clapp Woodbury.
3. Her parents were Asa and Elizabeth Clapp.

FROM AARON V. BROWN

Dear Sir                                   Nashville May 23rd 1845

I enclose you a letter from our friend Ramsey & a note from Crozier, shewing his necessities.[1] They desire my assistance in appealing to the Departments for some help. Also no doubt expect some contribution from my private resources. If much reliance is placed on this last idea, it cannot be realized beyond a hundred or two dollars as I have had already to help out several of our small establishments in that way. Be good enough to look into the case early & if any thing can be done cause some *words of comfort* to be written to Crozier in time. You will see in the paper I send you that Foster and myself have remodeled our appointments.[2] His Wish & proposition was to close the Canvass altogether. This I refused but consented to the pretermission of the main Democratic portions of *middle* Tennessee. Here was our strength & it would naturally grow *per se* & I could see no advantage in opening it to Foster for experiment on it. In my old district & Jones & Culloms,[3] no Whig was running for Congress who could defend F.[4] & on my return the appointments had me through the greater portion of Peytons. In the 3 or 4 days left I can go to Robeson[5] Davidson & Rutherford *if then thought adviseable* for at present I averted the policy of *rousing* up the *passions* of his friends to provoke them into the fight. I cannot give him *easy* battle. His *lies* have been great & his punishment must be great. I draw *blood* every day from him & the sight of that would make his relations & friends raise the *Howl* & rush to the rescue. I remember you lost 150 or 200 votes in Davidson alone by making a *great* speech at Nashville. I am not likely you may say to perpetrate *that* blunder any where. In the 20 Counties canvassd, I feel that I had the advantage *every day* & at Clarksville Paris, Jackson Brownsville Memph[is] & Bolivar gained great *victories* over him. The War in E. Tennessee shall be bloody enough. I will spare him no where, taking it for granted that there is no danger of creating much sympathy in that quarter in his behalf. The counties canvassd by me last fall, will receive me I doubt not kindly. Beside those in E. Tennessee I made speeches in Warren, Coffee, and Bedford, which increased my willingness to pretermit in our arrangement the counties in that quarter. Would it do no good for *you* to write a confidential letter to Brookins Campbell? or to Blair[6] & a few others to interpose in that difficulty. You can judge best what to do in the case & I therefore only name it to you. I venture no prediction yet about results but will do so when I have circled a little through E. Tennessee. But I never saw our party so *confident* before. They have dismissed their fears that Fost[er][7] [cou]ld *laugh* & *joke* me out of the case. I ha[ve] [gene]rally no talent in that line but *he* would provoke the D___l to be retortative sometimes—there's a Word for you! Every day is a day of personal *torture* to him from which he would most willingly escape.

Present my best respects to Mrs. Polk, with the assurance that I try hard on my field labors not to disgrace my "illustrious predecessor."

A. V. BROWN

ALS. DLC–JKP. Addressed to Washington City and marked *"Confidential."* Polk's AE on the cover notes that he received this letter on May 30, 1845.

1. Letter and note not found.

2. Enclosure not found. The *Nashville Union* printed the revised schedule of appointments, along with an open letter from the candidates, on May 20, 1845.

3. Brown refers to the Sixth, Fourth, and Fifth Congressional districts. A native of Virginia, George W. Jones followed a saddler's trade in Fayetteville, Tenn. He served two terms in the Tennessee House, 1835–39, and sat one term in the Tennessee Senate, 1839–41. An unsuccessful candidate for presidential elector on the Van Buren ticket in 1840, Jones first won election to the U.S. House in 1843 and served as congressman until 1859.

4. Ephraim H. Foster.

5. Misspelling of "Robertson" County.

6. Brookins Campbell and John Blair. A lawyer from Washington County, Campbell served five terms as a Democrat in the Tennessee House, 1835–39, 1841–43, 1845–47, and 1851–53; he won election to the U.S. House in 1853 and served until his death in December of that year. A merchant, manufacturer, and lawyer in Washington County, Blair served as a Democrat in the U.S. House from 1823 until 1835; he lost his bid for reelection in 1834 to William B. Carter.

7. Manuscript torn here and below.

## TO MICHAEL HOFFMAN

My Dear Sir:                              Washington City 23d May 1845

I was gratified to receive your friendly letter of the 21st Instant.[1] I have performed no duty I assure you, since the commencement of my administration, which gave me more pleasure than your appointment to the responsible office, which you inform me you have accepted.[2] I knew you personally and intimately, and was not therefore compelled to rely on information derived from others, which in some instances misleads and deceives the appointing power. I have had great difficulty, in determining what I should do in reference to the New York collectorship, and now desire, in the frankness of our old friendship to say a word or two to you on the subject. Most contradictory and inconsistent representations have been made to me, and from sources seeming to be entitled to credit, in regard to the propriety of removal of the present incumbent and in that event of the person who should succeed him.[3] I sought information from some friends in N. York, but certainly I did not at any time understand myself to stand pledged to conform to their views as I learn they understood me. I sought the information, to enable me to form *my own judgment* & act understandingly. If that judgment accorded with their views, of course I would act accordingly: if not they could not expect me to do so. I had information, which I supposed to be reliable from other sources, which led me to doubt, and I have postponed action. Being responsible, to the public, I must be *myself* satisfied before I act. I regret to say, that the postponement, of my action, in removing the collector, has induced two or three of those whom I had regarded as my best friends, to address me letters, manifesting, I must say unnecessary, impatience, and not acting thus in the friendly spirit I had a right to expect. Indeed they wear something the appearance of a dictatorial spirit, giving me to understand, by the intimations they carry, that unless I do as they direct, many of my friends will become *cool* and that this feeling may hereafter induce them to oppose the administration.[4] And this too because of one solitary appointment and because I was acting cautiously and deliberately in reference to it. I have deemed it proper to communicate these things to you, in the confidence of the old friendship between us &, to which you have alluded in your letter. This I do for yourself alone, and with no view, that what I write shall be communicated to others. I am free to receive advice from my friends, and to give it the proper weight but in my present position, as in all others of responsibility which I have held, I cannot yield to dictation from any quarter, not even from friends, though they may intend well. I hope the language used by some of my correspondents, has not been weighed and its import deliberately considered. I have not yet made known what I will do in regard to the collectorship. The inclination of my mind in taking a view of the whole ground has been and is, that a change may be proper and necessary. If a change be made, it may not occur until near the close of the present quarter. In that event who the successor shall be is a question of great importance. I confess I am not entirely satisfied with those who have been named. Some of my friends in New York, who have written me on the subject, had at first some doubts of the entire fitness of one of them, whose appointment they now urge making and as I learn censure me for not making.[5] In this state of things I have looked abroad in the State, to see if I could find some qualified man, whom I knew personally as I did you and of whom I could form my own judgment. *Cornelius W Lawrence* has occurred to my mind, as one who was favourably, known to me when he was in Congress. He has filled high trusts in N. York, is an old merchant, a man of responsibility, of undoubted integrity and I suppose him to be qualified. I mention his name to you, in strict confidence. He has not applied for the office, nor has he been recommended, or presented by his friends. If I were to select him, it would be my own voluntary choice, based upon what I know of him personally, and what I learn of his qualifications and character. I am glad that you are in New York, and that I can have a free communication with you in relation to this and other matters, relating to the public interests.

[JAMES K. POLK]

AL, draft. DLC–JKP. Addressed to New York City and marked "copy." Polk's AE at the head of the first page reads: "To Michael Hoffman appointed Naval Officer of N. York: This rough draft may not be a *literal* copy, but it is substantially a copy of the letter sent." Polk's ALS, not found, probably bore the date of May 27, 1845; in replying to this letter on June 2, 1845, Hoffman cited the later date.

1. See Hoffman to Polk, May 20, 1845.
2. Polk refers to Hoffman's appointment as naval officer of the port of New York.
3. Cornelius P. Van Ness.
4. Polk probably refers to Ransom H. Gillet to Polk, May 3, 1845, and Benjamin F. Butler to Polk, May 6, 1845.
5. Jonathan I. Coddington.

## FROM SHADRACH PENN, JR.

Washington City. May 24, 1845

Penn discusses party politics and patronage in Missouri and warns Polk that the state of things there requires his close attention. He argues that the best way to harmonize the Missouri Democrats is to do justice to Polk's "real friends." Penn complains that no Democrat who zealously supported the Baltimore nominations and Texas annexation has been appointed to federal office. The new appointments have gone to "men who ascribed the action of the National Convention to intrigue and management, and contended, with their leader, that disunion was at the bottom of the Texas movement."[1] He cautions Polk about recommendations from Missouri congressmen in favor of Benton's friends and asks that Polk reward the Democrats who answered Benton's denunciations and Whig misrepresentations during the campaign. Penn mentions that one way to strengthen Polk's "real friends" would be to give the *Reporter*[2] the printing patronage for the executive departments. On the subject of the St. Louis Post Office, he believes that the appointment of Linn[3] would give general satisfaction and would silence all clamor.

ALS. DLC–JKP. Addressed to Washington City. Polk's AE on the cover indicates that he received this letter on May 29, 1845.
1. Thomas H. Benton led the Martin Van Buren faction in Missouri.
2. St. Louis *Missouri Reporter*.
3. Penn's reference is to Elizabeth Relfe Linn, the widow of Lewis F. Linn.

## TO ANDREW J. DONELSON

My Dear Sir:                       Washington City 26th May 1845

I have received your several letters, addressed to me from New Orleans.[1] Your public despatches have been received at the Department of State, and *Mr Buchanan* has forwarded to you a despatch addressed to New Orleans, which will probably reach you before you leave that City.[2] *Gov. Yell* has been here and has given us all the information in his possession. I fear you may be too sanguine, about the assent of *Texas* to our terms of annexation, though *Gov. Yell* concurs with you in opinion. There is danger I think that the friends of the measure may be lulled into a false security. There can be no doubt that the combined efforts of the *Brittish French* & *Mexican* authorities will continue to be exerted to prevent it, as long as there is the slightest hope of success. Whilst this is the case, it is well known that many leading men in Texas, are secretly opposed to the measure and are only restrained from making open resistance to it, by, the popular opinion of the masses. I see too that some of the leading men of Texas favourable to annexation are in the U. States, resting securely in the belief that the matter is settled. Two of these *Mr Archer* & *Genl. Green*[3] called to see me ten days ago, and expressed their intention not return to Texas until the autumn. In your letters you express a desire to leave your mission and return to the United States as soon as the Texian Congress, which will meet on the 16th June, shall have given their assent to our proposition.[4] I do not think it will be safe or adviseable for you to do so. The assent of the existing Government when given, will be but the initiatory step, in accomplishing the object of your mission. It will not be consumated and put beyond danger, until after the Convention of the people, shall have been chosen and given their assent.[5] In the progress of the measure it may be very important that the minister of the U. States should be on the spot, ready to counteract any influences or intrigues which may be brought to bear upon the measure to defeat. I know your anxiety to return to your family, but you must remember that this is *the* great question of the times, and that no vigilence on our part, should be omitted, and nothing left to chance or accident. By remaining too you can aid the friends of annexation much, and can induce them, to call their convention at the earliest possible day and to act speedily. I urge you therefore to remain in the country until annexation is consumated by the Texan authorities. If you fear your health, may be affected at the Seat of Government, you could retire for a time to some more healthy spot, but still be in the country and ready to act as circumstances may require. I am so deeply impressed with the correctness of these views, that I cannot too strongly urge their observance upon you. I had intended to write to you about other matters alluded to in your letters, but am called off to attend to other matters. I will write to you again in a day or two. You will of course keep us advised by every opportunity, of every thing of interest which occurs, after the Texian Congress convenes.

*Genl. Armstrong* reached here on yesterday on his way to Liverpool. He left the Hermitage on the night of the 15th & states that *Genl. Jackson* was extremely feeble. Your family were in good health.

JAMES K. POLK

ALS. DLC–AJD. Addressed to New Orleans and marked *"Private & Unofficial."* Published in *THM*, III, pp. 66–67.

1. See Andrew J. Donelson to Polk, May 11 and 14, 1845.

2. Polk probably refers to James Buchanan to Donelson, May 23, 1845. Senate Document No. 1, 29th Congress, 1st Session, pp. 40–41.

3. Branch T. Archer and Thomas J. Green. Born in Fauquier County, Va., Archer studied medicine in Philadelphia, returned home to practice, and won election to two terms in the Virginia House of Delegates. He moved to Texas, and with Stephen F. Austin and William H. Wharton served as a commissioner to the United States to secure support for Texas' struggle for independence. A member of the first Texas Congress, Archer served as Speaker of the Texas House during its second session. A native of North Carolina and a graduate of West Point, Thomas Jefferson Green served in the legislatures of North Carolina and Florida before removing to Texas in 1836. Commissioned a brigadier general in the Texas army, he recruited volunteers in the United States before winning election to terms in the Texas House and Senate. He published his *Journal of the Texian Expedition Against Mier* in 1845; four years later he moved to California, accepted a commission as a major general of the state militia, and served one term in the California Senate.

4. See Andrew J. Donelson to Polk, May 11 and 14, 1845.

5. The U.S. joint resolution required the people of the Texas republic, "by

deputies in convention assembled," to draw up a constitution for the proposed state of Texas. On May 5, 1845, Anson Jones issued a proclamation calling for statewide elections to select convention deputies on June 4, 1845. The convention was scheduled to assemble at Austin on July 4, 1845. See Charles A. Wickliffe to Polk, June 4, 1845.

### FROM ANDREW JACKSON

My Dear Sir,                                    Hermitage May 26th 1845
   In due course of mail I received your letter of the 12th marked confidential, and sincerely thank you for it, & Sarah[1] begs to thank you for your kindness to Mr. Taggart. I have also received yr letter[2] by Mr LaBranch. I wrote Major Donelson by him & I am sure the Major will serve him in any way he can. Texas comes into the union with a united voice, and Genl Houston, as I knew, puts his shoulders to the wheels to roll it in spedily. I knew British gold could not buy Sam Houston. *All* safe & Donelson will have the honor of this important Deed. But my Dr Col, the sacrifice to his private affairs has been great, and you must provide for him a situation that will aid him in regaining the sacrifice of his property that he has been compelled to have made to meet his pecuniary engagements. I rejoice to be informed how well you have got through with your Philadelphia appointments. With *care* you will get well thro all of them, *I hope*.
   It would be a fortunate thing for your administration and the country could Mr Van Buren be got to go to England. But my Dear friend, would not the precedent be one of humilation to our Republic that one of its presidents should go abroad, not to meet the King or Emperor, to arrange national matters, but to meet a subordinate agent. I think this idea will prevent you from getting the services of Mr V.B. You must have a man to send to England of the highest standing and one whose principles are well known to be firm in the southern feeling, a man of strong integrity who will not temporise with England on any of the great principles in dispute. My Dear Friend I have wrote thus far gasping for breath. I am swollen from the toes to my abdomen & in bandages to my hips. My whole system a jelly. You can run a finger half an inch into the limb and the impression will remain for minutes. Added to this I have a bowel cramp upon me, a dificulty in urinating & a severe attack of piles. I am unable to cross my room without help. You can judge of my situation & capacity for writing. What my affliction may end in god only knows. I am truly resigned to his will whatever it may be. He does all things well[3] & I rejoice to see your administration succeding as well. May a gracious providence preside over & aid you in your administration and may you

pass thro it & retire thru the plaudits of your country, with *well done good & faithfull servant*,[4] is the prayer of your sincere friend. We all salute you & your amiable Lady ....

ANDREW JACKSON

ALS. DLC–JKP. Addressed to Washington City. Polk's AE on the cover states that he received this letter on June 4, 1845. Published in Bassett, ed., *Correspondence of Andrew Jackson*, VI, pp. 411-12.
1. Sarah Yorke Jackson.
2. A planter and member of the Louisiana House, 1831–33, Alcée Louis La Branche served as chargé d'affaires to Texas, 1837–40; won election as a Democrat to one term in the U.S. House, 1843–45; and received an appointment as naval officer at the port of New Orleans in 1847. Polk's letter to Jackson by La Branche has not been found.
3. Mark 7:37.
4. Paraphrase of Matthew 25:21.

FROM CHARLES S. JONES

Respected Sir.                                     Washington May 26th 1845
Knowing that your time is precious I shall waste no words in the letter I now address you, if you will only give me your attention a few minutes. And although I address your Excellency individually, I can assure you that I speak the sentiments of the Democracy of this District. We have learned with surprise, and regret that exception is taken to a single paragraph in some Circular issued by the Wash Dem Association during the late canvass,[1] and that some of our friends Mr Walker among them consider it indiscreet and calculated to cause the rejection by the Senate of Mr Sengstack's nomination for Com of Pub Buildings. We are inclined to beleive that there was nothing "indiscreet" about it, and our friends in some of the States agree with us in opinion, for in Penn, and Geo and perhaps other states the Circular was reprinted, and circulated by thousands. On the contrary, we beleive that it was instrumental in a great measure in effectuating the glorious triumph we achieved at the ballot box; and we think it hard that *Mr Walker* who is now enjoying the advantages derived in part from this circular, should attempt to cast odium upon the signers of it. Besides if any odium is to be attached to it, Mr Walker must come in for his share of it. These Circulars received his endorsement. He requested them of us, and sent them through the Country. But no odium can attach to it. If Mr Walker's name had been vulnerable on this point, it would have been attacked when *his* nomination was before the Senate. And as for its preventing Mr Sengstack's confirmation, it is all imagination. Surely, retribution will not be vis-

ited on our heads by our own political friends in the Senate for an act
which we conceived, and carried out for the benefit of the party. Even
if such should be the case we would still have the present satisfaction of
knowing that the Democratic Administration had done its duty to the
Workingmen of the country by responding to their urgent request in appointing Mr. Sengstack. Admitting the excepted sentence in the Circular
however to have been wrong, ought not all good Democrats to look upon
it as one of those excesses consequent upon the excitable nature of the
contest in which we were engaged, and the desperate means resorted to
by our opponents to sustain their sinking cause? Were there not other
acts of indiscretion besides this committed during the late canvass? Was
not Mr. Walker himself guilty of indiscretion in sending to the North
his tract called "the South in danger," whereby we have every reason to
beleive the States of Ohio, Connecticut, and perhaps others were lost to
the Democracy?[2] Can any one point to a single vote that was lost by our
Circular, and does it not speak volumes in our favor that out of the millions of pages of Documents circulated by us, but a single sentence in a
*private* Circular is open to objection? Is it just that Mr Walker should be
encircled with the robes of office, and at the same time the finger of scorn
pointed at us as men who gloried in dishonesty? Are not our characters
as dear to us, as Mr Walker's to him? Are we to be eternally harassed
either by the injuries, and persecutions of political enemies, or what is
worse the insults, and treachery of political friends? Are broken down
aristocrats to monopolize all the situations under government? Are men
to be preferred for political advancement who have spent a competency
in debauchery, over those who have spent their lives in virtue, and all
their little means in sustaining Democratic men, and measures?

Are the hardhanded, warmhearted working men of the Democratic
party, worthy of nothing—fit for nothing? These interrogatories are put
in no spirit of unkindness to your Excellency. Far from it. On the contrary we know that your heart's best wishes are with us, and we can but
love, honour, and respect you for the kindness, and urbanity with which
you have always treated us. But at the same time we *know* that every
effort will be made to supplant Mr Sengstack in your estimation by attempts to impress on your mind an idea of his incompetency, and thus
secure the situation of Commissioner of Pub Buildings to some milk,
and water Democrat who would have been as brisk in dancing attendance upon Mr Clay, did he occupy the Presidential Chair as upon your
Excellency. We beleive that the objection which has been made to the Circular is all humbug, and that the grand objection is that Mr Sengstack
is a *Mechanic*. Knowing these things as we do, is it not natural that we
should think, and feel deeply on the subject. If *we* had any *doubts o*

Mr Sengstack's competency for the situation, we should have too much respect for your Excellency, for the Democratic party, and for ourselves to press him on you in the manner we do. In conclusion then I feel authorised to state that the Democracy of the District are willing to run the risk of Mr Sengstack's nomination before the Senate: if any blame is attached to the Circular, they will publicly exonerate Mr Walker from it: if the duties of the Office are not discharged to the satisfaction of your Excellency, it will be resigned by Mr Sengstack at any time: if it is necessary we can bring the approving voice of twenty thousand Democrats here from all parts of the country, to sanction the appointment, and call for its confirmation by the Senate.

CHARLES S. JONES

P.S. We have not the least disposition to hurry your Excellency in this matter; but there is an under current working out of doors having for its object the withdrawal of Mr. Sengstack. This his own sense of honor, and self-respect forbid him to do. He considers the matter in the hands of his friends, and with them he leaves it. Mr Towles [3] states to me that if his withdrawal will secure Mr Sengstack appointment, he will cheerfully do it. CSJ

ALS. DLC–JKP. Addressed locally and marked "Confidential." Polk's AE on the cover states that this letter was "Not for the public files. May 29, 1845."

1. On September 25, 1844, James Towles and Charles P. Sengstack sent a circular letter detailing a "Plan of Organization" to get the Democrat militiamen to the polls in the forthcoming presidential election. In the cover letter the writers suggest that the Democrats should "take all the money they can get of the Whig corruption fund, and then vote their sentiments." For the text of the plan and the cover letter, see the Washington *National Intelligencer*, October 17, 1844.

2. Jones' reference is to Robert J. Walker's pamphlet, *The South In Danger! Read Before You Vote: Address of the Democratic Association of Washington, District of Columbia*. The *Niles' National Register* of November 2, 1844, carried the text of Walker's essay.

3. A Washington City carpenter and builder, James Towles chaired the Democratic Association of Washington during the presidential campaign; he had applied for the office of Commissioner of Public Buildings and warden of the U.S. Penitentiary.

FROM BENJAMIN PATTON [1]

Dear Sir                                          Pittsburgh May 26, 1845

I have recently had the pleasure of perusing a letter addressed to a friend by Dr. Brown, President of Jefferson College at Canonsburg. [2] It afforded me so much gratification that I felt prompted to take from it an extract, of which the following is a copy. I have thought that to be conscious of winning golden opinions from such men as Dr. Brown, would be to yourself a source of no small degree of satisfaction. "I have seen the President. I like him. I met Mr. Buchanan there. Had a very pleasant interview—am almost persuaded to be a loco-foco. I took the liberty to say to the President that the religious community were much gratified by his testimony in behalf of the Sabbath. He made a beautiful reply. "Sir, I had a pious mother.[3] She carefully instructed me in the principles of Christianity. The impressions thus made, have never been erased. I always have and, I trust, always shall venerate the sabbath."

I had a great mind to manufacture out of this a little newspaper paragraph: and nothing but an apprehension of taking too much liberty with yourself and the writer will prevent me from doing so.

I have observed in the Washington Union a favorable notice of the action of the General Assembly of the Presbyterian Church (at Cincinnati) on the subject of slavery.[4] Judg. Grier[5] was one of the delegates from this quarter. He had other engagements, but postponed them for the purpose of attending as a delegate. And this he did wholy with reference to the adjustment of that question. I talked with him before he started. I know this to be the case. I know also that no one contributed more than he did to the happy result that proceeded from the deliberations of the assembly on that exciting topic. It was entirely satisfactory to the southern delegates. The first principle laid down was that in the relation of master and slave there was nothing anti scriptural or sinful *per se*. &c. &c. This question being disposed of Judge Grier obtained leave of absence, and left before the assembly adjourned.

BENJN. PATTON

[P.S.] Mrs. Patton[6] comes into my office, and, finding that I have taken the liberty of addressing a letter to the President, tells me I must put in a good word for her brother, J. A. K. Helfenstein the Receiver of the Land office at Milwaukie, Wisconsin.[7] Permit me on this subject to repeat the request that he may remain undisturbed. I have already written to you on the subject.[8] He and all his family have been democrats all their lives, and were amongst your most active friends. No complaint has been made as to the manner in which his official duties have been discharged. He is a Pennsylvania German Democrat, and it is important to have a german in that office. His Father, his Brothers, and himself command an invaluable influence amongst the German population of that Territory.

ALS. DLC–JKP. Addressed to Washington City and marked "*Private*."
1. Benjamin Patton, a lawyer and Jacksonian Democrat, considered establishing his practice in Nashville, Tenn., but chose to settle in his native state

of Pennsylvania. He served as U.S. district attorney for the Western District of Pennsylvania, 1837–39; and as a judge on the Court of Common Pleas during the 1840's. He moved to Ohio in the 1870's and sat in the state legislature from 1880 until 1883.

2. A native of Pennsylvania, graduate of Dickinson College, and Presbyterian minister, Matthew Brown served as president of Jefferson College in Canonsburg, Penn., from 1822 until 1845.

3. Jane Knox Polk. During their trip to Washington for the inauguration, Sarah Polk had refused to allow a musical performance aboard their steamboat on Sunday, February 2. In Washington the Polks declined to receive company on Sundays.

4. Patton's reference is to a Washington *Union* article of May 28, 1845, outlining the proceedings of the May 21 meeting of the Presbyterian Church. The Presbyterian General Assembly, having received numerous memorials condemning the institution of slavery, passed a series of resolutions noting that the church could not condone the mistreatment of slaves and the oppressive laws regulating the institution. The Assembly declared, however, that the existence of slavery in the South "is no bar to Christian communion" for slaveholders. Presbyterian leaders also denounced efforts to divide southern and northern members of the church over the slavery issue.

5. A Pennsylvania attorney and president judge of the district court of Allegheny County from 1833 until 1846, Robert C. Grier served as an associate justice of the U.S. Supreme Court from 1846 until his death in 1870.

6. Matilda Helfenstein Patton.

7. J. Albert Helfenstein.

8. On April 30, 1845, Patton wrote Polk on this subject. In his letter Patton mentions that J. Albert Helfenstein, his father, and his brothers are political friends of Lewis Cass. ALS. DLC–JKP.

9. J. Albert's father was John P. Helfenstein. Two of his brothers, Charles P. and William Helfenstein, played key roles in the development of the anthracite coal fields of western Pennsylvania

## FROM LEVI WOODBURY

Dear Sir,                                      Portsmouth, 26th May 1845

I have spent two days in efforts to overcome the difficulties of a domestic character, alluded to in my former letter[1] and which still stand in the way of my going abroad. But I have found it entirely impracticable and, therefore, feel compelled to decline the mission you offer to my acceptance.

This is done, however, let me assure you, with a grateful sense of your kindness in proposing an honour so distinguished, though, with less regret, from a conviction, that some other gentleman, more able to vindicate the public interests, may be found, whose family may not be in a position, which interferes with his inclination to gratify the wishes of his friends.

Levi Woodbury

ALS. DLC–JKP. Polk's AE on the cover states that he received this letter on May 29, 1845.

1. See Levi Woodbury to Polk, May 22, 1845.

## TO LOUIS McLANE[1]

My Dear Sir:                                    Washington City 31st May 1845

I shall at an early day, deem it to be proper to recall *Mr Everett* as Envoy Extraordinary and Minister Plenipotentiary to Great Brittain. The late proceedings in Parliament,[2] and the existing State of our relations, with England, give to that mission great and unusual importance. In my judgment the United States, should be represented at that Court, not only by one of our ablest citizens, but by one possessing experience, in the Diplomatic Service, as well as full & minute information, upon the important questions at issue between the two countries, and which remain to be adjusted. You have once represented your Country at that Court, and possess in an eminent degree, the experience and information, which would enable you to render most important services to your country. I know that you have prefered for several years past to retire from public life; still I indulge the hope that you may be willing to accept this important mission, which I now tender to you. Your acceptance I am sure would be hailed by the country with general approbation. Your established reputation and well known ability and patriotism would inspire general confidence, that the great interests entrusted to you, would be safe in your hands. In the event of your acceptance (of which I hope there may be no doubt) I will add that the duration, of your continuance abroad, will be left very much to yourself. Unless by your own voluntary choice, your absence need not be of the usual duration. *Mr. Everett* anticipates his recall. In a letter addressed to me he says, "It would be agreeable to me that my successor, should be named, as soon as it can be done with due regard to the public service, in order that I may be able to remain at my post, till his arrival (which I think desirable both on his account and that of the public) without being delayed till the season of the year is too far advanced for a safe and comfortable passage across the Atlantic."[3]

I have to request that you will give me an early answer, or if it shall suit your convenience, that you will visit Washington, that I may confer with you personally on the subject.

With very kind regards to Mrs. McLane .... [4]

JAMES K. POLK

ALS, draft. DLC–JKP. Addressed to Baltimore and marked *"Copy"* and *"Private."*

1. A lawyer and Democrat, McLane served five terms in the U.S. House, 1817–27, before winning election to the U.S. Senate in 1827. He served twice as minister to Great Britain, 1829–31, and 1845–46; as secretary of the Treasury, 1831–33; and as secretary of state, 1833–34. After his resignation from the Cabinet, McLane became president of the Morris Canal and Banking Company in New York; in 1837, he moved to Baltimore to become president of the Baltimore and Ohio Railroad Company.

2. See Jacob Martin to Polk, April 16, 1845.

3. Polk refers to Everett's letter of March 3, 1845.

4. Catherine Mary Milligan McLane.

# JUNE

## FROM MICHAEL HOFFMAN

Dr. Sir,                                      New York June 2, 1845.
    After receiving your kind favor of the 27th ult.[1] while I employed every proper opportunity to obtain information as to the capacity and fitness of the Gentleman you named to serve in the difficult and responsible trust you refered to, I did not meet him personally to observe his health and activity until too late to write yesterday.[2]
    I have not enjoyed the advantages of his personal acquaintance. I saw him at Albany in the winter of 1842. From other recent kind and most useful service, he had contributed to render me, I was predisposed to form the most favorable opinion of him. I did so of his moral character and amiable courtesy; but from some cause not easily explained he did not appear to be distinguished for promptness activity and decisive action. His character here corresponds with the opinions I had formed with the favorable opinion I had formed of his amiable good qualities, but does not enable me to predict that he would by decided action meet and overcome the difficulties in the place refered to. He is much engaged in his bank, receives a good salary and would not probably be disposed to exchange his personal quiet for the perplexities of patronage & power. His health however appears to me to be good and he seems to possess more firmness and activity of body and mind than he exhibited in 1842.

It is not easy to decide on the wisest course of action in relation to the great contiguous & therefore excitable mass that constitute our great cities. After considering the matter as well as circumstances will allow it appears to me that the true course is, to insist in strong distinct terms that the candidate should be a man of unquestioned good moral character, and of known vigor decission and activity of mind. Thus secure the Government & community an able efficient officer. In addition to these the leaders and masses of the party to express a purely decided & united preference for their man; and by this unanimity you make it the interest and duty of the party & its leading men, not only to aid the appointed they have solicited but to defend him and the appointing power against unjust reproaches & calumnies. This course appears to me not only proper, but almost indispensibly necessary in the case of an officer with large patronage located in a populous city.

MICHAEL HOFFMAN

ALS. DLC–JKP. Addressed to Washington City. Polk's AE on the cover reads: "Hon. Michael Hoffman, N.Y. Concerning the collectorship at N. York. *Private & Confidential.*"

1. Polk's letter of May 27, 1845, has not been found; for the draft of that letter, see Polk to Hoffman, May 23, 1845.

2. Hoffman probably refers to Cornelius W. Lawrence and the collectorship of the port of New York.

## FROM ELY MOORE

Dear Sir,                                            New York, June 2, 1845

A rumour has just reached this City, that Ex Gov Bouck is to receive at an early day, the appointment of Collector of this Port. I sincerely hope, and in this I am prompted by a desire to preserve the harmony and welfare of the Dem. party in this City and State, that the report in question is unfounded. I have not consulted with an individual on the subject; but from my knowledge of the position of affairs, in this section, I can with perfect safety, hazard the opinion that such appointment if made would be very unsatisfactory to the great mass of the party in this city and state. It would, I am well persuaded, be alike unsatisfactory both to the friends of Govr Wright, and to the radicals and Constitutional reform portion of the party, and which constitute a large majority.[1]

If I am not much deceived, Mr. Butler, and, indeed, all those inimical to the present Collector,[2] would prefer his retention in office, to the appointment of Govr Bouck. Be that however, as it may, one thing is certain, at least in my judgment, and that is, should the bald question be submitted to the democracy of this City whether Govr Van Ness should be removed and Govr Bouck substituted in his stead as Collector, the proposition would be rejected by a majority of *two* to *one*.

In expressing this opinion, I do not mean to be understood as taking sides either for or against any man, whether as it regards the present incumbent, or those aspiring to supplant him, nor do I intend to mix myself up with such matters. I know my position too well to act the part of a *mere partizan* or *Clique-ite*. At the same time however, I regard it as a duty which I owe to the Executive, and to the Democratic party to express my views to the appointing power, at this important conjuncture, frankly and without reservation and having done so, I will close this hasty communication, by expressing the hope that you will excuse the liberty which I have taken in thus obtruding my opinions upon you in this matter.

ELY MOORE

ALS. DLC–JKP. Addressed to Washington City and marked "*Private and Confidential.*"

1. Moore refers to the radical Barnburner faction of the Democratic party and to those party members who supported the calling of a constitutional convention. In April and May 1845, the two houses of the state legislature passed a constitutional convention bill; on May 13, 1845, Silas Wright, Jr., gave his approval.

2. Cornelius P. Van Ness.

## TO A. O. P. NICHOLSON

My Dear Sir:                    Washington City 2nd June 1845

Mr *McDougal* of Wilson County Tennessee,[1] came to this City in February last with the expectation of obtaining public employment here. I have entertained friendly feelings towards him, and would have been pleased to see him in some situation, which would suit him. Of my desires in this respect he is himself sensible. In the midst of the crowd of persons who have been here seeking places, and owing to circumstances, which I need not state to you, but which he may communicate to you, it has been found to be impossible to gratify his wishes. Among other obstacles which have stood in his way, is the objection made in some quarters, that Tennessee (my own State), had already received her full share of the Government patronage. Though I do not think this objection altogether well founded, yet a proper deference to the opinions of those who have made the objections, has constrained me, not to give additional force to it, by making *at the present time*, more appointments from the State.

As I learn from Mr *McDougal* he has been advised by *Genl. Armstrong*, & *Col. Laughlin* to return to Tennessee and procure, if he can, a situation connected with the *Union Office.*[2] If you can aid him in this, I think he would be useful, and at the same time be able to make a decent support for his family. He is very poor, and I cannot help feeling some sympathy for him. Hoping that you may be able to further his aims.

JAMES K. POLK

P.S. Why do you not write to me more frequently? Give me your opinion of our prospects, in the pending political contest in the State.[3] J.K.P.

ALS. NHi. Addressed to Nashville and marked *"Private."* Published in Joseph H. Parks, ed., "Letters from James K. Polk to Alfred O. P. Nicholson, 1835–49," *THQ*, III (March, 1944), pp. 75–76.
1. See William R. McDougal to Polk, May 15, 1845.
2. Nicholson at this time edited the *Nashville Union*.
3. Polk refers to the August gubernatorial, legislative, and congressional elections.

## TO CORNELIUS W. LAWRENCE

My Dear Sir:                                   Washington City 3rd June 1845
  I have been for some weeks as you are aware subject to great importunity upon the subject of a change in the Collectorship at New York. Many letters have been addressed to me, some in favour of retaining, the present incumbent[1] & a still greater number in favour of his removal. I see too from the newspapers, that your City has been agitated by public meetings and otherwise in reference to it. With the information in my possession and upon a view of the whole ground, I mentioned to *Gov Marcy* some days ago, my conviction that a change would become proper and necessary, and that in that event my mind was made up to tender the appointment to you. This I did from my own personal knowledge of you, and because I preferred you to any candidate who had been named. You had made no application for the place, nor had your name been presented by your friends. You were my own voluntary choice. I believed you to be eminently qualified for the office, and that your appointment would be satisfactory to the Democracy and useful to the Country. Gen. *Van Ness* had intimated some weeks before, my conversation with Gov. Marcy, that he would be willing to give up the office, about the 1st of July, if it was thought that the interests of the country as of the Democratic party, would be promoted by it. I am now advised by a letter addressed by him to a member of my cabinet, that I may expect his resignation in a day or two, to take effect on the 1st day of July next.[2] *Gov. Marcy* has placed me in possession of the correspondence which he had with you after I had communicated to him the necessity of a change and my purpose

to appoint you. And now My Dear Sir: my object in writing to you, is to inform you, that it is my intention to appoint you Collector of the Port of New York, to take effect on the 1st of July. Your established reputation and high qualifications for the place, will I have no doubt give general satisfaction, not only to the Democratic party, but to the public generally, and especially to all those having business with the Custom House. Your appointment will be announced as soon as I am officially advised of the resignation of the incumbent; which I cannot doubt will be in a day or two. Relying upon what you said in your last letter to Gov. Marcy, and believing it to be necessary for the interests of the country and of the Democratic party that you should accept and not doubting and that you will do so, I will not delay for any further communication with you, but will make the appointment, as soon as the resignation is received. If no resignation should be possitively be forwarded, still you may calculate on serving the appointment at the time named the 1st July.

For reasons which I deem it unnecessary to state I desire that you will regard this letter as *private* and intended for *yourself alone*. It will avoid useless speculation to say nothing about it until the appointment is actually made and announced to the public.

James K. Polk

ALS, draft. DLC–JKP. Addressed to New York City; marked "*Copy*" and "*Private & Confidential*."

1. Cornelius P. Van Ness.
2. Polk refers to the correspondence between Robert J. Walker and Van Ness on the question of the latter's resignation. See Cornelius P. Van Ness to Polk, June 10, 1845.

## FROM CHARLES A. WICKLIFFE

Dear Sir                                       Galveston June 3rd 1845

I refer you to my note to Mr Buchanan of the 30th Inst. in reference to the return of Mr Elliot and the preliminaries of a treaty or basis of negotiation with this Republic proposed by Mexico.

Upon his arrival at this place on Friday evening, a gentleman of this place with whom Mr Elliot is very intimate spent some time with him and learned the particulars &c which I have condensed in the letter to Mr Buchanan.[1] Com. Stockton and myself started down the coast as intimated in my former letter in company with the gentleman upon whom I relied to obtain information from the Rio Grande.[2] We encountered very heavy head winds, and this man and myself became so extremely sick that my own safety in the opinion of Com. Stockton required that I should be landed, and return.

We arranged with the captain of the Texas Revenue cutter to proceed and take Mr Jones a member of congress[3] who undertook to obtain all the information he could from the Brassos Santiago and Rio Grande, to see Col. Kinney[4] and request that he would return in the cutter to Galveston when and where we expect to hear through Genl Sherman[5] the views and wishes of President Jones. Col Kinney has not yet arrived, neither have we heard from Genl Sherman.

Fortunately Col Donalson[6] arrived on Saturday evening, and we will be governed in this matter by his advice. It is my opinion, however that Prest Jones will discountenance the movement, under the impression that the United States will have the right, and will be bound to remove the Mexican military from east of the Rio Grande after annexation takes place. Would not this be an act of War upon Mexico by the United States?

Will you allow me to submit a remark or two which may be of service, as to the points to be occupied by the United States troops in Texas, whenever it is deemed advisable to remove the troops across the line, and the mode or route of their march.

Corpus Christi at the mouth of the Nueces is the most westwardly point now occupied by the Texan troops. This point is on the west side of that river. The Brassos Santiago is the only point near the mouth of the Rio Grande on the east side which can be occupied near the Gulf: and this, as I have before said, is in possession of the Mexicans, at which place they have a custom house, and about 150 soldiers as reported about 60 days ago. When the United States assumes the defence of this country, one or both of these points must be occupied. Not more than 500 soldiers with a suitable proportion of artillery are necessary, unless the Mexicans are in greater numbers than is believed here. Dragoons in this part of the country I think would not be required, particularly if Capt Hays' Rangers, of the Texas government, be retained as I think they should be by all means.

The Infantry and Artillery companies can not reach these points overland at this season of the year under three months, if at all, owing to the nature of the country the want of water, and the extent of prairie over which they would have to march. It would at this season of the year kill over half the men.

The troops I understand, are stationed at Fort Jessup, between the Red River and the Sabine.[7] These troops can not, now, owing to the stage of water in Red river, and the raft be brought in boats to New Orleans. Upon enquiry, I am satisfied that whatever of Infantry you order to the points I have designated, as well as Artillery, should be marched by land from Fort Jessup to the mouth of the Sabine and there take shipping for the point to be occupied. If they are compelled to march, the beachs on the gulf from the Sabine to this place, and from this place to Corpus Christi is the only road over which they can march. It is a fine hard sand beach only obstructed by the mouths of rivers at which there are ferries. Along this beach waggons and artillery could be conveyed and beef driven for their supply. This route would require some thirty or forty days march, whereas vessels would perform the trip in 6 or 7 days. It will not do to attempt to march these troops through the country crossing the Sabine at Gaines' ferry. This route would upon the map to a person not acquainted with the country seem to be the proper one, but rest assured, I am well advised when I say to you, it will not be one at this warm season of the year over which troops on foot can be marched.

What route the cavalry should take I am at a loss to advise. It would seem to me that their destination or location should be on the north of Texas, and west from Fort Towson.[8] In no part of Texas can corn or oats be had for horses now. That which is used for bread commands one dollar per bushel and very scarce at that. The only subsistence for horses in the whole republic now is the wild grass, and if the Dragoons are stationed on the north in the counties of Red River or Nacogdoches the horses might be sustained on grass and if wanting in western Texas they could by moderate marches be transported across the country towards San Antonio.

I am of opinion that 200 or 300 Rangers mounted under the command of Capt. Hays on the horses of their country would be more effective as a defence than the whole corps of cavalry mounted on horses unused to living on grass alone.

It would be well, I think, to give orders to march a portion of the troops now at Fort Jessup to the Sabine, where they could be as well and as cheaply rationed, if not more so, than at Fort Jessup.

Maj Donalson will no doubt give you full information in reference to his interview with Capt Elliot.

I shall leave here on Wednesday for Austin. My object is to see Capt Hays who commands the Rangers to see if I can get him to clear the country west of the Nueces of the Mexican military.

C A WICKLIFFE

[P.S.] By the rout I propose the whole distance is about 400 miles; by the rout crossing the Sabine at Gaines Ferry it is at least 600 miles and on a rout for troops on foot almost impossible at this season of the year. Wff.

LS. DLC–JKP. Addressed to Washington City.
1. Wickliffe probably refers to his letter to James Buchanan of May 31, 1845. In this letter Wickliffe summarizes Elliot's conversation: "Capt Elliott says he

has obtained for Texas all he promissed and what the President assured him in April last would be satisfactory to the Government of Texas, Viz. 'an agreement by Mexico to acknowledge by treaty the Independence of Texas upon the sole condition that she will stipulate never to annex herself to the United States The question of boundary to be hereafter settled.' " PL, in William R. Manning, ed., *Diplomatic Correspondence of the United States: Inter-American Affairs, 1831–60* (12 vols.; Washington: Carnegie Endowment for International Peace, 1939), XII, pp. 421–22.

2. Wickliffe probably refers to his letter to Buchanan of May 20, 1845. Thomas F. McKinney, Wickliffe's traveling companion and former Sante Fe trader, settled in the Austin Colony in 1828 and with his partner, Samuel M. Williams, played a prominent role in the transportation of troops in the Texas revolution, loaned funds to the new Republic of Texas, and operated a banking house in Galveston from 1837 to 1841. In his letter, Wickliffe claimed that McKinney enjoyed a close friendship with Mariano Arista. PL, in Manning, ed., *Diplomatic Correspondence*, XII, pp. 412–15.

3. Augustus H. Jones, a planter and stockman, migrated from Georgia to Texas in 1835; a veteran of both the Texas revolution and the Mexican War, he represented Gonzales in the Texas House for one term, 1844–45.

4. Henry L. Kinney, a rancher and merchant, came to Texas in 1838 and settled in Corpus Christi. He won election to one term in the Texas Senate, 1844–45; and during the Mexican War served on the staff of the Texas volunteers.

5. A native of Massachusetts, Sidney Sherman pursued business operations in Boston, New York City, and Cincinnati before going to Texas in 1835 as colonel of a Kentucky regiment of volunteers. Appointed a colonel in the Texas army, he settled in Harris County, which he represented for one term in the Texas House, 1842–43; the following year he won election as a major general in the Texas army.

6. Andrew J. Donelson.

7. Fort Jesup was established in 1822 in Sabine Parish, La., on the road between Natchitoches and Nacogdoches, Texas.

8. Fort Towson, in the Indian lands that became the Oklahoma Territory, was established in 1824 along the Red River to guard the frontier with Mexico and the Choctaw Indians.

## FROM CHARLES A. WICKLIFFE

Dr Sir                                                      Galveston June 4th 1845

On last night Genl Sherman returned from the seat of government after having seen Prst. Jones & his cabinet. He explained to them the object of his vissit, immediately on his arrival. They all and at first President Jones concurred on the propriety of removing the Mexicans west of the River Rio Grande. Genl Sherman was directed to call next morning for a final decision. He did so and the President informed him that tho he saw the propriety and admitted the necessity of the movement which Genl. Sherman proposed yet he was so situated that he could not issue a proclamation, but hoped that in the course of four or five days he could do so with out doing violence to any understanding which existed. [1] When pressed harder upon this subject, he at once said he expected to hear in a few days from Mexico as to her final determination and until he heard from her he could not without violating his pledge authorise any movement on the Frontier. He talked figuratively and said this question of annexation was a sensitive plant that tho there seemed to be evidence that it was settled by the opinion of the people, yet it had to go before congress the convention and finally before the congress of the United States and that circumstances might so change as to alter the face of things &c &c. A few days however would determine every thing.

In the midst of the cabinet counsel and express arrived from San Antonia with a communication from Capt. Hays the commander on the Frontier with information of the state of things there.

Capt. Hays writes that he had information which he had no doubt was correct that the mexican forces on the Frontier had been collected to the amount of 7,500 at the following places. At Monteray 4000, at Saltillo 1000, at Camargo 1500, at Laredo 300, At Presidio Rio Grand 500, [...] [2] 500. These added to the lowest estimate heretofore at Matamoras and the Brassos Santiago 500 constitute a force exceeding 8,000 troops. Capt Hays also said in his letter that he had assurance that a body of troops of 100 have marched to a point called Rio Frio on the Newesus and that he should the next day with fifty men start for the purpose of giving them battle.

Genl. Sherman then urged upon the President the propriety of his being directed at once to reinforce Capt Hays and of increasing the force under his command if they were not permitted to move upon the Mexican forces east of the Rio Del Norte. This Prst. Jones sd could not be done without a violation of the understanding which existed. In fine he said he must await the return of Capt. Elliott which he said would be in three or four days. Genl. Sherman then remarked to him that he must be aware of the power vested in him Genl. Sherman by the act of Congress to call out the militia to defend the country without waiting the orders of the President. He replied he was but that he would esteem it as a personal favour if he would not act and that he might not assume events in a few days would remove all obstacles against prompt action and co operation on the part of the Executive, and that he might expect to hear from him in a few days. Genl. Sherman says he does not believe that the cabinet concurred with the President at least one of them told him he did not.

Genl. Sherman on his return to this place met Capt. Elliott at Houston who in great haste hired a conveyance and was to travel all night until he reached Washington. Capt. Elliott did not hesitate to speak of the object of his visit to Mexico to the citizens of the Republic; said that *he had obtained* their Independence but he regretted to learn upon his return that a majority of the people were for annexation and that he felt for them who opposed it, that Mexico would declare war instantly. The United States would Blockade the ports of Mexico but that the British Government would not submit to it consequently there would be war for 20 years and he would advise his *friends* in Texas to leave the country.

This is *modest* I admit in the Representative of Great Brittain, certainly kind if not respectful to the Government and people of Texas!

I give you the substance of the Report made by Genl. Sherman to Col Donalson[3] Com Stockton & myself last night.

What do these facts prove if they be true and I assure you they are believed here.

They prove at least one thing that my opinions and suspicions of Prest. Jones and those who control him were correct. They also prove that he had entered into a scheme with Elliott to defeat annexation at a time when popular sentiment had not (without division) developed itself. That he was pledged to Elliott to prevent all military opperations on the part of Texas on the Frontier until the result of his mission to Mexico could be known and that no call of congress would be made until its regular session in Nov. That when he was forced to convene congress by the people he fixed the day to meet that Elliott could have time to return before the day.[4]

It is however needless for me to speculate upon the motive objects or fidelity of the parties in this Drama. What is to be done is the question which most concerns me.

I have no doubt Elliott will dispatch an Express from Washington to Monteray to inform Arista[5] that the offer of Mexico is rejected and immediately I have less doubt the whole force of Mexico on the Frontier will cross the Rio Grande and invade this Republic before they have decided to accept the terms.[6]

Will it be just and right for the United States to stand by and witness this, waiting for the final decision of the convention when deliberations at Austin may be interupted by an invading army?

I have ever been of opinion that an attempt to invade this country by Mexico pending the question of annexation imposes upon the United States the obligation to repel such act. You may rely upon it the *people* of Texas are ready to do what ever is required of them to defend their homes but they have very few resources save their indomitable courage. They have Rifles without powder and pockets without money.

C. A. WICKLIFFE

[P.S.] The steam boat is about to be off & I have not time to copy this off in a better hand or to correct mistakes. Wff

ALS. DLC–JKP. Addressed to Washington City and marked "*Private*." Polk's AE on the cover states that he received the letter on June 14, 1845.
1. Reference probably is to Anson Jones' "understanding" with Sir Charles Elliot. See Archibald Yell to Polk, March 26, 1845, and May 5, 1845.
2. Word illegible.
3. Andrew Jackson Donelson.
4. On June 16, 1844, a special session of the Texas Congress convened to discuss the United States' annexation proposals.
5. A participant in Mexico's struggle for independence and general in the Mexican army, Mariano Arista served as secretary of war under José Herrera in 1848. Elected president of Mexico in 1851, he served until 1853.
6. Syntax garbled. Wickliffe's meaning is that Mexico may take military action before the Texans accept the United States' terms of annexation.

## FROM WILLIAM L. MARCY

My Dear Sir:                                    West Point 5 June [1845] [1]

I remained one day in the City of New York and from what I learned there, am satisfied that you have come to the right conclusion in relation to the removal of the Collector. If it had been a simple question as to which of the two V. Ness or Codington [2] should have the office, it is far from being clear that a change would be expedient. The individuals who have taken into their hands the cause of Mr. C. are much more unpopular than he is. He is objectionable upon the ground that those who have busied themselves in his behalf would have the complete controll of the patronage. I found that the persons who had talked with you on this subject had spoken quite too freely of promises & commitments and extended them further than to the office of collector. [3] Bleecker, the candidate for Marshall, [4] says that a promise was given by you to the same persons who allege a commitment as to the collectorship, that he should be marshall &c. I felt authorised to say that you had not made the alleged promises & if certain gentleman had so understood you they were *mistaken*. I had an interview with Mr C. W. Lawrence and find he will accept the office of collector & I am still more firmly convinced that the selection will be satisfactory—more—that it will be quite popular. It is not supposed he would take it & his name had not been much brought into view, & I did not use it even by way of speculating upon what you might do in case you saw fit to make a change. To one person only, who is well acquainted with the position of things in the city & upon whose judgment I place great reliance, I said in confidence that I heard you had remarked to my Tilden when asked by him who you would select that you should be guided in it by your own knowledge of the man, of his fitness, his character, his responsibility &c. It was possible I remarked that you might have had in your mind *Cornelius W. Lawrence*, as you were in Congress with him & was particularly acquainted with him. The person observed that it would be an excellent appointment & would give very general satisfaction. It would be one to which no fair exception could be taken even by those who sought an occasion to find fault; but he concluded by expressing an apprehension that Mr. L. would not accept the office.

Of one thing I am well satisfied & it is that the gentlemen who came to Washington to inform you of the wishes of the democratic party are not the fair exponents of these wishes, they are not in high standing in the party, they are really unpopular, and particularly so since they have assumed to be its oracles and organ of communication with you & to complain of the nonfulfillment of promises &c. Mr. Tilden as I am informed tried his fortune with the new common council & failed of getting a respectable support for the office of attorney and for that also of counsel. The opinion prevailed in the City that they are not at heart well disposed towards your administration, and that nothing will please them short of having the privilege of controlling the appointments & by *having it known* that they have this controll.

I am informed that they beset Hoffman to make the removal of Van Ness a condition of his acceptance of the naval officer but he replied that would be a poor return to you for having bestowed the office unsolicited upon him. It is due to Gov. Wright to say that he disapproved of this suggestion in regard to the course which was strenuously urged upon Mr. H. Upon the whole I am satisfied with the public judgment upon your administration. I will write you again before I leave this place.

W. L. MARCY

ALS. DLC–JKP. Addressed to Washington City and marked "*Private.*"
1. Date identified through content analysis.
2. Cornelius P. Van Ness and Jonathan I. Coddington.
3. Marcy probably refers to Samuel Tilden and John L. O'Sullivan.
4. A New York City auctioneer, Anthony J. Bleecker served as U.S. marshal for the Southern District of New York, 1840–41.

## FROM DAVID T. BALDWIN[1]

Respected Sir.                                    New York June 6/45

It is unqualifiedly asserted by Messr Dix & Butler that you gave them *your word possitively*, that you would appoint the man to the Collectorship of this City who they should approve, & they mentioned Mr Coddington whom you said *should be* the man, & now sir it is said that Mr Lawrence is appointed to that office. If this is true sir you will be no longer entitled to the confidence of the party who elected you. But sir I represent a class who are unwilling to believe that such is the case. Mr. Lawrence is known here as a man very cool in the last Presidential election & when called upon to contribute to defray the expenses of the election he positively declined *giving 1 Cent*. Mr Lawrence is a respectable citizen, but not a *respectable democrat*, having been rather whigish in his ideas since 1840, & it is also asserted that he has men employed in the Bank with him,[2] whom he says he is going to take into the Collector's office, who voted for Genl. Harrison in 1840, & it is also asserted by the inspector of elections in his ward, that Mr. Lawrence voted also for Genl. Harrison & *in your election he did not vote at all*. Consequently no man would be more obnoxious to the Democratic party & no man less entitled to its confidence. This is the state of things here sir, appoint any good Democrat sir but if you have the best interest of your party at heart, pray dont disorganize us here, or it will be felt throughout the Union. It is said that Mr. Marcy has been instrumental in this appointment as he owns stock in Mr. Lawrences bank and is anxious for the deposites. Mr. Marcy sir is known to represent a very small faction in this state & to give that faction all the patronage will cause an immediate breach in the party. Mr. Marcy has made the appointments of Messr Morris & Moore & those are certainly all he is entitled to. Please let the public know if what Messr Dix & Butler assert is true or false.

                                                    DAVID BALDWIN

ALS. DLC–JKP. Addressed to Washington City.
1. Baldwin owned a partner's share in the firm of Baldwin and DeKlyn.
2. Cornelius W. Lawrence headed the Bank of the State of New York.

## TO SAM HOUSTON

My Dear Sir:                          Washington City 6th June 1845

It gave me sincere pleasure I assure you to receive your kind letter of the 26th ultimo, written at New Orleans.[1] It could not fail to revive, pleasant recollections of our early and intimate association, in public as well as private life. I am glad that you are on your way to the Hermitage and hope you may see our venerable friend[2] before he sinks to the tomb. I know he bears for you an ardent personal affection, and the meeting will be as gratifying to him as it can be to you.

I congratulate you upon the *certainty*, of which you give assurance, that Texas, will accept the proposition for annexation made to her by the U. States,[3] and that she may in effect be now regarded as a part of our Union. If the terms proposed in our Resolutions are not so liberal to Texas, as the ardent friends of the measure in the U. States desired or as Texas expected, you should remember that parties were very, nearly equally balanced in our last Congress, and that it was with very great difficulty that any proposition could be passed. We have now however the certain prospect of a decided majority favourable, to annexation, in both Houses of the next Congress, who will, I have no doubt be ready, and willing to do the full measure of justice, which the citizens of the new State can reasonably desire. I think it very important that Texas, should accept the terms offered without change or alteration. If she accepts unconditionally, the great measure, of the re-union of the two countries, will be placed beyond danger and may be regarded as consummated, for the next Congress as a matter of course will redeem the National faith and admit her into our Union. Let this be done and I have no hesitation in saying to you that you may safely rely, upon our magnanimity and justice, to do all which your citizens may reasonably ask or desire. I will recommend the most liberal policy, and have every confidence that I will have the cooperation of Congress, in carrying it out. You may have no apprehensions in regard to your boundary. Texas [was] once a part of the Union,[4] and we will maintain all your rights, of territory, and will not suffer them to be sacraficed. I mention the question of your boundary, because you allude to it in your letter, and to assure you that it will be my duty as it will be my pleasure to guard your interests in that respect with vigilance, and care. I hope the Texas Convention, which I see is to meet on the 4th of July,[5] may be able without delay to form a Republican Constitution, and that Senators and Representatives under it may be here at the meeting of our Congress in December next. I shall be rejoiced to see you as one of her *Senators*, bearing her Constitution in your hands, ready to introduce the Young Republic (whose Independence you have contributed so largely to establish), into our Union, upon an equal footing with her sister States.

I will not fail to remember your wishes in regard to your friend *Mr Miller*, and will when the proper time arrives, gratify your wishes and his.

I hope My Dear Sir: to hear from you often during your stay at the Hermitage, and after your return home.

JAMES K. POLK

ALS. TxGR. Addressed to Nashville and marked "*Private.*"
1. Letter not found.
2. Andrew Jackson.
3. Polk refers to Robert J. Walker's "compromise" version of the joint resolution on Texas annexation. See William H. Haywood, Jr., to Polk, February 26, 1845.
4. Polk's reference is to U.S. claims to Texas based on the Louisiana Purchase Treaty of 1803. By the terms of the Adams-Onís Treaty of 1819 the United States gave up its Texas claim. The Adams-Onís Treaty fixed the United States' western boundary with Spain at the Sabine River extending from the Gulf of Mexico north to the 32nd parallel, thence north to the Red River and along same to the 100th meridian.
5. See Polk to Andrew J. Donelson, May 26, 1845.

## FROM ANDREW JACKSON

My dear Sir,                                           Hermitage June 6th 1845

Your letter of the 12th ultimo, (*confidential*) has been *received.*[1] Be assured my friend that it is truly gratefull to learn from you, that you have a united & harmonious Cabinett. May it so continue to exist thru your administration, is the prayer of your friend. Sarah[2] is truly grateful to learn from you, that her friend Mr. Taggart will be provided for as you promised. We all salute you & Mrs. Polk with the kindest good wishes.

My dear Sir, I wish you to recollect the caution I gave you about the Treasury Department. Here you are to be assailed, and without great vigilence & energy in yourself, your administration wounded deeply, and in the strictest confidence as your real friend, draw your attention again to it. I was well advised, and by Mr. Walkers friends, that Mr Walker would be pressed for this office by all those who were interested in those choctow fraudulent claims,[3] & by those deeply interested in them, and in their origination. There never was a greater fraud attempted & committed than in these claims and when properly investegated will throw shame & disgrace upon all concerned. The passed acts by Congress on this subject, you cannot repeal, but look well to the future. Scrip has been issued upon those fraudulent claims to the amount of $1,500,000— this is now worth 50 cents on the dollar for entering land. The great aim of those Speculators are to get Walker as Secretary of the Treasury, by a circular, to place this scrip upon the same footing as the U. States, and at once to raise 100 pct, putting $750,000 in the pocketts of these fraudulent speculators. Look to this my friend, let the scrip rest on its own basis where congress has placed it. Do you not believe that such an act in the Secretary of your Treasury would blow you & your administration sky high.

But again, I am informed thru a channel in which I have a right to confide, and is a man of much truth himself, That the late ex Secretary of the Treasury,[4] for the short time he was at the head of it, made ninety thousand dollars, by arangements with the two brokers Banks, of New York where large sums of the Public money was deposited, & other deposit Banks in N. York. Enquire cautiously amongst the clerks in the city of Washington, by which you will find a key that may unlock the door to a proper enquiry. But an enquiry by the Whiggs, one prepared for you should Mr. Walker have the folly to have any thing to do with either of these abominable projects, I say to you put yr veto upon them both, or you & your Secretary will be blown sky high. And what cares those corrupt speculators for yours, or his character if they can get hold of the cash. I can write no more—friendship has aroused me to make this attempt.

ANDREW JACKSON

ALS. DLC–AJ. Addressed to Washington City and marked "*Confidential.*" Printed in Bassett, ed., *Correspondence of Andrew Jackson,* VI, pp. 413–14. Polk's AEI on the cover states: "Genl Andrew Jackson, written June 6th 1845, two days before his death, and the last which he ever wrote to any one. This letter was not received by me until this day, the 24th of Oct 1845. The cause of delay is explained by the accompanying letter of Andrew Jackson Jr., in which this letter was enclosed. J.K.P." On October 10, 1845, Andrew Jackson, Jr., enclosed his father's letter to Polk and explained that it had been misplaced. ALS. DLC–AJ.

1. Jackson probably refers to Polk's letter of May 22, 1845. Jackson's AE on Polk's letter of May 12, 1845, states that he answered that letter on May 26, 1845.

2. Sarah Yorke Jackson.

3. Jackson's reference is to speculations on former Choctaw lands in Mississippi. The lands had been ceded to the United States by the Treaty of Dancing Rabbit Creek in 1830, when most of the Choctaws removed west. The remaining Choctaws received Mississippi land grants, which speculators then bought and issued scrip upon in hopes that the federal government would purchase the land.

4. George M. Bibb.

## FROM WILLIAM H. POLK

My Dear Brother                                   Liverpool June 6th 1845

We arrived last evening, the 5th, after a passage of seventeen days. I will leave in the morning for London, where I will remain two or three days—thence to Paris and tarry two or three weeks, for the purpose of acquiring some slight knowledge of the French language, which will be of great advantage, in making my way to Naples. I will write you from London, more fully. Please *write to Mother*,[1] and let her know of my *safe arrival*.

Write me, and make such suggestions as should mark my course at Naples. It is a new field of action for me and any assistance will be acceptable. I write in haste.

WILLIAM H. POLK

ALS. Polk Memorial Association, Columbia. Addressed to Washington City.
1. Jane Knox Polk.

### FROM DAVID T. BALDWIN

Sir.                                              New York June 7 [18]45
Since I wrote you yesterday[1] I have heard something to substantiate my assertion concerning Mr. Lawrence. Mr. Theopilus Peck[2] a merchant in this city & the Treasurer of the general committee at Tammany Hall tells me he called on Mr. Lawrence to solicit a contribution towards the election. Mr. Lawrence replied that he would not give one cent as he was unfavorable to the Texas issue & Mr. Jas. Colton[3] the inspector of elections of Mr L's ward told Mr. Peck that Mr. L. did not make his appearance at the polls *at all* during the day of the election Novr. 5/44. Facts are stubborn things & if you have any regard for the Democratic party in this vicinity to whom you are entirely endebted for your election, you will not appoint this wavering conservative, but will choose a man who has the confidence of the party or retain Mr. Van Ness, for I can assure you, that the removal of Mr. Van Ness to make room for Mr. L. would tend more to our disorganization here than the retention of Mr. V.N. who is admitted to have ardously supported your election. But to Mssr Butler & Dix you are doubly endebted, particularly the former to whom you owe your nomination[4] & sir a large majority in this state composed of the so called "Van Buren, Wright clique" whom you are now deserting, have done & would do everything in their power to support your administration. Is it right, is it honorable after what Messr Dix & Butler assert for you to be guided by the dictation of Messr Walker & Marcy rather than Dix & Butler, in making the nominations for this city. But sir I have dwelt too long on a deed thats done & past redemption, but I cannot but think that there was some condition in your promise to Messr Dix & Butler of the appointment of Mr. Coddington; if there was the people should

know it, for it is thought here that you have broken your honorable promise & Mr. Butler speaks of resigning his present situation in consequence; how simple, how noble would have been your acquiescence to their request. The idea of a bankman filling the office of Collector for this Port is disgusting to all radical democrats; you forget the discourteous manner of Mr. L. when you was here some years. He mentioned it to me, saying that you intended returning good for evil, as he supposed that he was the last man in N.Y. that you would have chosen.

But the appointment will probably be officially announced before you receiving this. There will be a breach in the party here that nothing can repair, & the whigs will triumph in 1848 in consequence. You would be aware of this if you knew the influence of the N.Y. Custom House; I am a merchant here who has always been a democrat, & never held an office & never will. I am not personally acquainted with Mr. Coddington but he has an unrivalled reputation here for honesty integrity & industry, & was the best government officer while in the Post Office that ever N.Y. had. This was admitted by the whole community & no appointment would have given such universal satisfaction to our merchants as that of Mr. C. to the Collectorship. A president is public property & as such I have taken the liberty to address you. Please excuse the warmth of my opposition to the appointment of Mr. L., of whom I have been & am now a strong personal friend, but not his political friend as I think the party in power should appoint men to office from their own ranks & not men who are ready to leap on the other side of the fence, at the prospect of personal aggrandizment. Mr. Lawrence contemplates retaining his two other offices viz. city treasurer & Prest. of the Bk. as he owns half the stock in the bank & will improve it by giving his bk the deposits.

DAVID BALDWIN

ALS. DLC–JKP. Addressed to Washington City.
1. See Baldwin to Polk, June 6, 1845.
2. Theophilus Peck is not identified further.
3. James Colton is not identified further.
4. Baldwin's reference is to Butler's role at the Democratic National Convention in May 1844. On the ninth ballot Benjamin F. Butler encountered difficulties convincing his fellow delegates from New York to support Polk; for the first time Butler disclosed that prior to the convention's meeting he had received from Martin Van Buren a letter authorizing him to take such action as might be necessary to bring the meeting to a harmonious decision; at length the New York delegates agreed that Butler could withdraw Van Buren's candidacy.

## FROM CORNELIUS W. LAWRENCE

My Dear Sir                                    New York 7th June *1845*

I have to tender to you my sincere thanks for your communication of the 3d (of course) after my letters to Gov. Marcy. I shall accept the office referred to, if it shall continue to be your wish; but if upon further reflection or information you shall come to the conclusion that another would be more satisfactory to our friends & the public I beg of you to feel no hesitation in giving the appointment to that other.

You have in your letter given to me evidence of your consideration & confidence which can never be forgotten.

C. W. LAWRENCE

ALS. DLC–JKP. Addressed to Washington City.

## FROM SAM HOUSTON

12 o'clock, night
My Dear Sir:                                Hermitage, June 8, 1845

In deep sorrow I address you this hasty note. At 6 o'clock this evening Gen. Jackson departed this life. He retained his faculties to the last hour. I lament that I was denied the satisfaction of seeing him in his last moments. I was unfortunately delayed in ascending the Mississippi, so that I did not reach Nashville till half-past six this evening. I immediately procured a conveyance, and came out with my family [1]—having understood that the General's health was exceedingly precarious, and being anxious to administer, if I could, some comfort in the closing scene of his eventful life. On my way, a few miles from the city, I met the family physician,[2] who informed me that the General was no more.

About three hours before his departure he conversed for some time with his family, and took an affectionate leave of them, as also of his domestics. His physician represents the scene as most affecting; and remarks that he departed with perfect serenity of mind, and with full faith in the promises of salvation through a Redeemer.

I have seen the corse since my arrival. The visage is much as it was in life.

The funeral will take place on Tuesday next, at 11 o'clock, a.m. A nation will feel this loss, as a nation has received the fruits of his toils during the best years of his life.

SAM HOUSTON

PL. Published in the Washington *Union*, June 16, 1845.

1. Margaret Lea Houston and Sam Houston, Jr.
2. John N. Esselman.

## FROM ALFRED BALCH

No. 170. Bleecker Street
Dear Sir, New-York 9th June 1845
On my arrival here ten days ago I found a company of friends who were on the wing for West-point and who insisted that I should go along. That institution is admirably managed by Major Delafield.[1] The cadets exhibited themselves at the Black-board to great advantage.

When I reached the point I was thrown into the midst of a large crowd of politicians by whose speculations I was much amused. The whigs generally and the protectionists particularly, learning that I was from Tennessee and a personal acquaintance of yours were very kind, soft and *liberal* alledging that as yet they had found nothing in your public acts worthy of censure, that every thing *depends on your annual message of next winter* and that they hope to be able to support all your measures. I thought to myself what a pack of hypocritical rascals you are!

The appt of Lawrence to the Collectorship is well received. He certainly maintains a very elevated character in this great city.

I would have called at Washington on my way to this point to see you; but I could have told you nothing which Genl Armstrong had not communicated. After visiting *Kinderhook* and seeing some valued acquaintances in this quarter,[2] which can be done in the next ten or twelve days I shall return to the west as rapidly as steam and horse flesh can carry me.

ALFRED BALCH

ALS. DLC–JKP. Addressed to Washington City.
1. An 1814 graduate of West Point, Richard Delafield served twice as superintendent of the U.S. Military Academy, 1838–45 and 1856–61. He commanded the Corps of Engineers from 1864 until 1866 and retired from service with the rank of major general.
2. Balch probably refers to Martin Van Buren, who lived at Lindenwald, his estate located near Kinderhook.

## FROM J. GEORGE HARRIS

My Dear Sir: Nashville Te. [June 9, 1845][1]
Gen. Jackson is dead. He departed this life at the Hermitage yesterday at or near 6 oclock p.m. He had full possession of all his mental faculties up to the last moment, and conversed much and freely with the members of his family and with his numerous servants even after he had lost his

eye-sight. He will be interred beside the remains of his wife[2] (in his garden) to-morrow (Tuesday) morning at eleven o'clock.

Gen. Houston arrived at the Hermitage a few moments after the Old Hero breathed his last. He grasped the hand of his old friend, but it was cold in death. On coming into town this evening I learn that a meeting called by the Mayor[3] has just been held at which Gen Houston made very happy remarks appropriate to the mournful occasion.[4]

J. Geo. Harris

ALS. DLC–JKP. Addressed to Washington City.

1. Harris misdated this letter "June 8, 1845." Harris corrected the date in his letter to Polk of June 10, 1845.

2. Rachel Donelson Jackson.

3. Reference is to Powhatan W. Maxey, who served as mayor of Nashville from 1844 until 1845.

4. Responding to the request of the mayor and board of aldermen, a meeting of Nashville citizens convened on June 9, 1845, to make preparations for the June 10 funeral of Andrew Jackson. After short speeches by Andrew Ewing and Sam Houston, the meeting passed resolutions calling on all citizens of Nashville to attend the funeral and requesting local businesses to close for the occasion.

## FROM WILLIAM H. POLK

Dear Sir                                          London June 9th 1845

Enclosed I send a letter to Mother,[1] which you will please forward to her. I reached London last evening. Mr Everett has been very kind. I dined with him to day. From considerations of a pecuniary character I have concluded not to remain in London longer than to day. Mr Everett very kindly proposed to introduce me to Court, and to the leading characters of the Government; but to have accepted would have forced me to purchase a costly English wardrobe, which would be of no use to me on the continent, the fashion being so different. I leave in the morning for Paris, where I will remain one or two weeks.

William H. Polk

ALS. DLC–JKP. Addressed to Washington City. Polk's AE on the cover states that he received this letter on July 7, 1845.

1. Jane Knox Polk.

## FROM RANSOM H. GILLET

My Dear Sir,                                 Washington June 10 1845

I enclose you the leading edition of the Morning News of yesterday. It rejoices at the expected removal of Van Ness, & says nothing against or for Lawrence. It tends to confirm the opinion I expressed to you yesterday—to wit: that some will be disappointed & those who had expectations for themselves or friends will feel & occasionally express their disappointment. But that Mr Lawrence will conform to the Morning News rule, of *making the Custom House mind its own business*, & that in three months the public will be quite satisfied with the appointment. Mr Coddingtons immediate friends will feel disappointed. Mr Lawrence can easily *salve the wound* by pursuing a proper course toward him & them, which perhaps ought to be suggested to him in a proper way.

R. H. GILLET

ALS. DLC–JKP. Addressed locally.

1. Gillet refers to an article in the Van Burenite *New York Morning News*. The article, entitled "Collectorship of the Port," predicted that Polk's replacement of Van Ness would be applauded by the Democracy of New York and accused Van Ness of using the patronage of the collectorship to persecute the supporters of Martin Van Buren and Silas Wright, Jr.

## FROM J. GEORGE HARRIS

My Dear Sir:                                        Nashville June 10. 1845

My letter of yesterday should have been dated the 9th and not the 8th inst.[1]

I have just returned from the Hermitage, where I attended the funeral of Gen. Jackson. It was estimated, fairly I think, that from 2500 to 3000 persons were present. There were rising two hundred carriages in attendance to say nothing of horses, which as fastened to the boughs of the trees in front of the Hermitage yard literally filled the woods. At 11 o'clock a.m. Rev. Mr. Edgar[2] took position in the porch, front of the front parlor, and pronounced a most appropriate prayer happily alluding to "this great and distinguished man of our nation, who had lived as a patriot and Christian," and invoking the blessings of Heaven to sustain and comfort, the bereaved. A psalm was sung next to the tune of "Old Hundred" commencing,

> "Why should we start & fear to die,
> What timorous worms we mortals are" &c. &c.[3]

Mr. Edgar's sermon was the best that I ever heard fall from his lips. He endeavored to do full justice to the high public and private character of Gen Jackson, and he came much nearer to the accomplishment of his object than I had expected he could. His text was from a passage in the Revelations: "These are they which came out of great tribulation and washed their robes white in the blood of the Lamb."[4] The sermon was nearly an hour in length. A hymn was then sung, another prayer offered; and then the body was removed from the front parlor where it had remained during service to the hearse and borne down outside the garden as far as the burial place where the fence had been removed that it might be brought through to the grave. There was some little difficulty in lowering the body into the vault, in consequence of the too large dimensions of the box which contained the coffin, but this was soon overcome, and then Mr. Edgar made a series of well chosen remarks admirably suited to the place and the occasion. The entire service closed by a "favorite Psalm" of the General's which Mr. Edgar said was often spoken of by him when living.

I have never witnessed a funeral occasion of half the solemnity. Every man woman & child seemed to be conscious that mankind had lost one of their greatest & best benefactors.

It was his request, as I learn, that little or no pomp or parade should be observed at his burial; nevertheless the Nashville Blues were present in uniform and were permitted to fire three or four times over the grave. [5]

The family seems to be resigned. Mrs. Jackson [6] is almost inconsolable, her little children [7] are scarcely sensible of their loss. His adopted son (And. Jackson) manifests a keen sense of his bereavement. I have thus given you a few particulars which I had thought might not be destitute of interest.

J. Geo. Harris

ALS. DLC–JKP. Addressed to Washington City. Polk's AE on the cover states that he received this letter on June 17, 1845.

1. See J. George Harris to Polk, June 9, 1845.
2. Nashville civic leader and editor of the *American Presbyterian*, John T. Edgar served as pastor of the First Presbyterian Church from 1833 until his death in 1860.
3. Quotation from Isaac Watt's hymn, "Why Should We Start & Fear to Die."
4. Paraphrase of the scriptual verse "these are they which came out of great tribulation and have washed their robes, and made them white in the blood of the lamb." Revelations 7:14.
5. The Nashville Blues were a volunteer militia company.
6. Sarah Yorke Jackson.
7. Harris' reference is to Rachel, Samuel, and Andrew Jackson III.

### FROM CORNELIUS P. VAN NESS

Dear Sir                                            New York June 10th 1845

On the 28th of last month I received a private letter from Mr Walker, the Secretary of the Treasury, informing me, that you had "deemed it necessary to change the Collector at New-York," and advising me, as a friend, to send on a letter of resignation, *by return of mail*, to take effect on the first day of July next.

Within an hour after the receipt of this letter, I wrote to Mr Walker, saying that I would, within three days, address to him such a letter as he had advised. On more mature reflection, however, I had doubts as to the propriety of a resignation after I had been informed that you had already determined to remove me; and especially since the world would probably understand that my resignation was a forced one. I, however, prepared such a letter, and sent it by Mr Bogardus,[1] who was going to Washington, with directions to deliver it to you, or not, as certain friends of mine there might determine; and it appears the letter has not been delivered, in consequence of my friends, generally, being opposed to my resigning.

But having been your sincere friend, and being so still; and relying fully upon your professions of friendship towards me; I have determined, upon my own responsibility, to send to you, herewith, a duplicate of the letter withheld,[2] and to leave the matter entirely with yourself.

C. P. Van Ness

ALS. DLC–JKP. Addressed to Washington City and marked "*Private.*" Polk's AEI on the cover states: "Hon. C. P. Van Ness. Accompanying his letter of resignation of the Port of New York to take effect on the 1st day of July 1845. Recd. 12th June 1845. Cornelius W. Lawrence was appointed Collector of New York on the same day (12th June 1845) to take effect on the 1st July 1845. J.K.P. *Private.*"

1. Cornelius S. Bogardus served as assistant collector from 1844 until 1845, and Polk appointed him naval officer of the port of New York in 1848.
2. Letter not found.

## FROM J. GEORGE HARRIS

My Dear Sir,                                                 Nashville June 11. 1845

Aware of the deep interest which you must feel in everything appertaining to the last hours of Gen. Jackson I continue to take the liberty of addressing you unreservedly on the subject. Ten days before his death he sent me word that he would like to see me and requested that I would visit him on the next day if convenient. It afforded me pleasure to comply with his request, and I had an hour of uninterrupted conversation with him concerning national affairs and matters connected with them. As on all former occasions he made me the repository of his confidence and expressed his hopes his wishes his feelings with great earnestness and fervor. He did not seem to be feebler than he was the week previous, and I thought it quite probable he would continue a month longer. Notwithstanding he expressed to me his belief that in about *ten days* his health would improve or he would at that time take his departure for another and a better world. How prophetic was the language. I came to Nashville on Saturday the 7th to go to the Hermitage; but on learning here that he had on the 5th or 6th written you a letter on the subject of national affairs, I concluded that he must be improving, and deferred my visit, determining to visit him on Tuesday. On Monday I heard of his death, and instead of having the pleasure of taking him by the hand on Tuesday, as I had contemplated I rode to his funeral.

On the day before his death he franked a letter to the Hon. Th. F. Marshall of Ky. which had been written under his direction by his adopted son[1] in reply to anxious inquiries concerning the state of his health. His last letter in his own hand was that which he wrote to you on the 5th or 6th instant.[2]

He seemed to be conscious that his time had come on Saturday evening, for he intimated as much to his physician[3] by saying "My life is drawing rapidly to a close, and I shall expire in the hope that the liberties of my country may endure forever, and that my enemies, if I have any, may find peace," or something of this substance. I give it you, as it is given me.

At the breakfast hour of the morning on which he died, he swooned away, and the household became very much alarmed, white and black rallying to his room in tears; but he revived in a few moments and as he opened his eyes met the glance of his adopted daughter[4] at his bedside saying: "do not weep; it is true my sufferings are great but they are not so great as were those of Christ upon the acursed cross. I shall soon be relieved." He then called up the members of his family respectively and addressed each of them in the kindest language of love and affection. He missed his two little adopted grand-children[5] and inquired for them. He was informed that they were at Sunday-School. He requested that they should be sent for—in a few moments they came in and received his prayer and blessing. He then called in all his servants and exhorted them to embrace the religion of Christ, giving them the most wholesome advice. The scene was painfully affecting, for he now seemed perfectly conscious that he could last but a few hours longer.

He had directed Mrs Jackson[6] to send for Maj Lewis as soon as it should be discovered that he was dying, and the Majr was accordingly now sent for, remaining throughout the day. Until ten or eleven o'clock he conversed with usual freedom, on the subject of religion altogether; and afterwards made only an occasional remark up to 6 p.m. the time of his death. Two or three minutes before his last breath he asked his adopted son to adjust the pillow beneath his head. Up to the very last moment he maintained the most unshaken reliance in a blissful immortality a certain re-union with his beloved wife [7] and all his Christian friends in Heaven. Clearly, clearly, he was *ready to die.*

Mr. Edgar pronounced a most admirable sermon at his funeral, detailing all his private and social virtues, and giving an account of his conversion to which he (Mr. Edgar) was a witness, some six or seven years ago. I am told that this sermon will be printed in pamphlet, [8] certainly it should be preserved, for the truths which it set forth concerning the spotless life of the General in his retirement will fill a bright page in history.

I presume that other friends have given you more interesting details than any which I have been able to gather, but I believe you will receive none from sources more reliable than [ ...] [9] which I have derived mine—members of the family.

I had forgotten to notice a scene of the funeral [ ...] I would give much to see preserved on canvas. You [ ...] situation of the burial, spot which the General had chosen in the [ ...] beautiful flower garden. On the 10th of June all the beds of [ ...] flowers with which it abounds were in full bloom and it looked to me like some spot of which I had read in fairy tales but never before witnessed. It was truly enchanting. His corse was borne over and through a portion of this "wilderness of fresh flowers" to the place of interment, quietly and without the least pomp or parade. Painful and melancholy as was the service, yet a delightful charm was given to the scene by the freshness and fragrance and beauty of that perfect flower garden matured by the taste and watchfulness of his adopted daughter, the accomplished Mrs. Jackson.

I have written more than I had intended, more than will be interesting to you, I fear, but I love to tell of the old Hero, for you know he was my friend.

J. GEO. HARRIS

ALS. DLC–JKP. Addressed to Washington City.

1. Andrew Jackson, Jr.
2. Harris refers to Andrew Jackson's letter to Polk of June 6, 1845.
3. John N. Esselman.
4. Sarah Yorke Jackson, the wife of Andrew Jackson, Jr.
5. Of Sarah Yorke and Andrew Jackson's three surviving children, Rachel, Andrew III, and Samuel, the two boys were the youngest.
6. Sarah Yorke Jackson.
7. Rachel Donelson Jackson.
8. Not identified further.
9. This word and those on succeeding lines have been obliterated by a tear in he manuscript.

FROM J. GEORGE HARRIS

My Dear Sir                                      Nashville June 12. 1845

I continue to enjoy the liberty already taken of addressing you freely on the subject matter of Gen. Jackson's demise. In my last, I gave the substance of a patriotic sentiment expressed by the General on the evening before his death.[1] Dr. Esselman tells me it was occasioned by his entering the room, on the physician's last call, and on seeing a letter (the letter to Marshall) on the table with the General's frank upon it, and anxiously inquiring if he had been *writing* the General replied: "I have only given my frank to this letter which was written by my direction. I shall probably write no more letters. I am fully aware of my condition and my last wish shall be liberty and prosperity to my country; and peace to my enemies, if I have any." This does not vary in substance from the sentiment as given in my last, although I now give it in the exact language as nearly as the Dr. can recollect.

As I have before said the last day of his life was devoted to language of religious exhortation addressed to both the white and black members of his family affording a theme on which Dr. Edgar dwelt with force and affect in his funeral sermon. The Dr. used the General's old Bible and Psalm book which had been literally worn out by the veteran's own hands; and deduced therefrom one of the most powerful arguments in favor of Christianity that I have ever heard. He said that on one occasion the General whom he had found engaged in reading this bible held it up in his right hand and said: "Dr., this book, sir, is the bulwark of our Republican institutions, the anchor of our present and future safety." The Dr. repeated many other remarks strikingly characteristic of that great and good man all which, no doubt, will appear in the printed sermon.[2]

Most of the elder citizens of Nashville, regardless of all differences of opinion which had existed, were present on the funeral occasion; and all appeared to be equally sensible that a great and good man had fallen. Had it been possible to give one day more of notice between his death and burial the concourse at the grave would have been ten times as great. There seems to be but one feeling & one sentiment. All parties, sexes, conditions, and colors seem to be alike sensible of the loss which they and their country have sustained. Truly may it be said "we are in tears."

Gen. Houston, his lady and son, were at the funeral,[3] after which they repaired to the house of Maj. A. J. Donelson where they are now stopping You would scarcely recognize Gen H. for instead of the large and fleshy man which he was six years ago he is a spare, tall, and thoughtful-looking person, rather pale, and more reserved than formerly in his intercourse with the masses. Albeit it is possible that this difference, in my view, may have been occasioned by the melancholy circumstance under which he has appeared in public since his arrival here.

He protests that no European Government has acted in any other than the most open and fair spirit towards Texas, and avows that Texas has not connived at any intrigues like those of which Pres. Jones has been suspected. So far as my judgment goes of what Gen. H. says, he is of the opinion that Texas, while attempting to dispose of her sovereignty had the right of a young girl to play the coquette a little, but that she would have fought again and again for her own independence before she would have been annexed either directly or indirectly to any other power than the U. States, and he seemed to be deeply affected by the death of Gen. Jackson; and was constantly expressing his regret that he had not arrived a few hours earlier to receive the last blessing of the patriot.

I had supposed that when Gen. Houston arrived at Nashville all parties would be ready to greet him with the plaudit: "Well done, good and faithful servant," [4] for although he had been absent from home for years yet he did not return in the light of a "prodigal son." [5] On the contrary, the "talent" which his native country had given him he had not buried, but had "gained five other talents," [6] and certainly he deserved a general welcome. But it really seems that those who have politically opposed the annexation of Texas have determined to discountenance the measure even after it shall have been successfully consummated in obedience to the expressed will of a majority of our people.

One word in conclusion of this too long letter concerning our State affairs. The contest now pending is the quietest I ever witnessed in the State. It seems to be the mutual wish of parties that there shall be no excitement. The gubernatorial candidates [7] have entirely passed over Middle Tennessee in their discussion, the section in which you know lies all our strength. We hope and trust and believe that we shall elect a democratic Governor and Legislature, but, really, the result would be doubly certain if the battle were fought out more fully as in former days. *We*, you know, have always depended on the strength of our principles and power of our arguments—*they* on management, which is most successful in quiet times. However, the influence of a Tennessee President and his very acceptable Inaugural, cannot, I think fail to give us the victory in August.

J. GEO. HARRIS

ALS. DLC–JKP. Addressed to Washington City.
1. See J. George Harris to Polk, June 11, 1845.
2. Not identified further.

3. Reference is to Margaret Lea, whom Sam Houston married in 1840, and to Sam Houston, Jr., born in 1843.

4. Paraphrase of Matthew 25:21.

5. Harris refers to the parable of the prodigal son. Luke 15:1–32.

6. Paraphrase of Matthew 25:20.

7. Aaron V. Brown and Ephraim H. Foster.

## FROM LOUIS McLANE

My dear Sir,                                           Baltimore June 12. 1845

I have experienced great embarrassment in coming to the conclusion I am now to announce in regard to the mission you have been pleased to place at my disposal.[1] Nevertheless, as I deem the present crisis in our relations with England to be of the utmost importance to the Country and to the success of your administration, and as you think that my services may be useful in contributing to the adjustment of the difficulties, I do not feel at liberty to withhold them. I will therefore, accept the mission, and make my arrangements as early as possible, to enter upon its duties.

I have taken this step, however, without consultation with the Board of which I am President, and without ascertaining their disposition to leave the place, I am to vacate, open for my return. Certainty upon this point could not be had previously to my acceptance with proper respect to you or to myself; and I must therefore count this among the other risks of the enterprise I am about to enter upon, and trust to events.

Under these circumstances I take the liberty of asking two things: first, that the public annunciation of my appointment may be delayed for a short time, to afford me an opportunity of dissolving my present connections with the least possible disappointment; and second, that in the selection of the Secretary of Legation, at present vacant, I may be allowed the share always accorded to our Public Ministers by Genl. Jackson, and usually by his Predecessors. I am satisfied, from my own experience, that the importance of proper character in the Secretary, and of harmonious & indeed cordial public & personal relations, with the minister cannot be over estimated; and I presume if the selection be in all respects *fit* on public grounds, you would see no reason to interpose objections.

Louis McLane

P.S. Perhaps, you may state to my son[2] who will hand you this letter your own view as to the time you deem it important I should embark for London?

ALS. DLC–JKP. Addressed to Washington City. Polk's AE on the cover states that he received this letter on June 12, 1845.

1. See Polk to Louis McLane, May 31, 1845.

2. An 1837 graduate of West Point, Robert M. McLane served in the army until 1843, when he resigned to practice law in Baltimore. He won election to four terms in the U.S. House, 1847–51 and 1879–83; served as a Democratic presidential elector, 1852; represented the United States as a commissioner to China, 1853–54; and served as governor of Maryland from 1883 until 1885. Resigning the governorship in 1885, he accepted appointment as U.S. minister to France and held that position until his removal in 1889.

## TO ROBERT J. WALKER

My Dear Sir:                                        Washington 12th June 1845

Have you heard any thing from New York? If Mr *Bogardus* has returned he has not called on me, and I have received no letter. *Mr B.* asked delay until this morning & no longer. Would it be adviseable to make the appointment to day, or postpone it until tomorrow, and write to Mr Lawrence this evening, that he may have a day's notice, to prepare to enter on the duties of the office *immediately*? I am better to day but am too feeble to go to the office.

JAMES K. POLK

ALS. NjP. Addressed locally.

## FROM ROBERT J. WALKER

Dear Sir                                        [Washington City] June 12. 1845

I send you the resignation of Mr. Van Ness to take effect on 1st of July next.[1] I also send the commission for Mr Lawrence to go into effect at the same period.

I think Gov. Van Ness deserves additional credit for this act, from the fact, that he has done it against the advice of many indiscreet friends. I have learned enough to convince me, that in justice to him, his friends here ought to have delivered his resignation to you more than one week since.

I feel it due to him now to say to you, that Mr Van Ness has conducted the business of the office with consummate ability. I have no dout that Mr. Lawrence will make a most able & faithful officer, & that the appointment will give general satisfaction. It is not to be disguised that the *removal* of Mr Van Ness might have created serious agitation, & I congratulate you on the fact, that the administration has now passed safely through all the whirlpools of N. York politics.

R. WALKER

ALS. DLC–JKP. Addressed locally. Polk's AEI on the cover states: "Transmitting the resignation of *C. P. Van Ness* as collector of the Port of New York, to take effect on the 1st July 1845. Recd. this letter and the resignation 12th June 1845. Cornelius W. Lawrence was appointed collector of New York on the same day (12th June 1845) to take effect on the 1st July 1845. J.K.P."

1. See Cornelius P. Van Ness to Polk, June 10, 1845.

## FROM GEORGE BANCROFT

Sir,                                        Navy Department June 13, 1845

I have the honor to submit for your consideration a letter addressed by me on the 6th inst. to the Secretary of War,[1] proposing a transfer of Fort Severn, Annapolis, Maryland, to this Department, to be used as a Naval school.[2]

The Secretary of War and Major General Scott[3] concurring in opinion that the transfer may be made without detriment to the military branch of the public service, I have the honor to solicit your authority for such transfer, if the plan meets your approbation.

GEORGE BANCROFT

L. DNA–RG 45. Addressed locally.

1. William L. Marcy.

2. Built in 1808 on the south side of the Severn River, the fort was formally transferred on August 15, 1845, for the establishment of the United States Naval Academy.

3. A Virginia native, Winfield Scott practiced law in Petersburg before his commission as a captain in the artillery in 1808. A decorated major general and popular hero at the conclusion of the War of 1812, Scott later supervised the removal of the Cherokees in 1838, encouraged arbitration to settle the Maine boundary dispute of the same year, and commanded operations in the southern theater of the Mexican War, 1847–48. Nominated for president by the Whig party in 1852, he won promotion to lieutenant general in 1855 and retired six years later.

## TO EDWARD EVERETT

My Dear Sir:                            Washington City 13th June 1845

In your letter of the 4th of March last[1] you seem to have had a just appreciation of the circumstances in which I was placed, and which might induce your recal as minister to England. In coming to the conclusion that it was proper to relieve you from the duties of that station, I beg to assure you, that I entertain for you the kindest personal feelings. Though always differing in our views, upon many subjects of public policy, I yet remember with pleasure that our long association in public life, was of an agreeable character. Having tendered the mission to the *Honble. Louis McLane* of Baltimore without his solicitation, it was not until yesterday that I received his letter of acceptance.[2] I learn from *Mr McLane* that he will be ready to leave the United States about the middle of July, and you may therefore expect him at London about the first of August. I should have given an earlier answer to your letter but that I was unable to inform you, who your successor would be, and at what time he would be ready, to enter upon the duties of the station. I was much gratified at the tone and spirit of your letter, and hope it may suit your personal convenience to remain, in the discharge of the duties of the mission until his arrival.

JAMES K. POLK

ALS. MHi. Addressed to London.
1. Polk probably refers to Everett's letter of March 3, 1845.
2. See Louis McLane to Polk, June 12, 1845.

TO ANDREW J. DONELSON

My Dear Sir:                    Washington City 15th June 1845
Your Despatches of the 2nd and 4th Inst. were received at the Department of State last night.[1] I received also letters of the 3rd and 4th from Mr Wickliffe.[2] The threatened invasion of Texas by a large Mexican army, is well calculated to excite great intrest here, and increases our solicitude concerning the final action by the Congress and Convention of Texas, upon our proposition for annexation.[3] In view of the facts disclosed by you, not only as regards, the approach of an invading Mexican army, but of the open intermeddling of the Brittish Chargé d'affairs,[4] with the question of annexation: I have lost no time in causing the most prompt & energetic measures, to be adopted here. I am resolved to defend and protect Texas, as far as I possess, the Constitutional power to do so. The despatches which will be handed to you by *Genl. Besancon*, who will leave here to night,[5] with instructions to convey them to you with least possible delay, will acquaint you with what has been done. An express messenger will leave at the same time (to day), for Fort Jessup, bearing orders for the troops, to march immediately to the mouth of the Sabine, to be there in readiness to act as you may direct, under the instructions from the Department of State. The fine steam ves-

sel, (*The Spencer*, one of our revenue cutters) a small but most effective War Vessel, with her guns mounted, has been ordered to proceed at once from New York where she now is, to Galveston, and report to you. An additonal Naval force will be ordered to the Gulph, to day or tomorrow.

I suggest to you that it will be very important that the *Convention* of Texas, should on the day they meet, pass a general Resolution accepting our terms of annexation. The moment they do this, I shall regard Texas as a part of our Union; all questions of Constitutional power to defend and protect her, by driving an invading Mexican army out of her Territory, will be at an end, and our land and naval forces will be under orders to do so. Let the Convention pass this general Resolution on the 4th of July, and they can then proceed in their deliberations in forming their State Constitution, whilst we will protect them against their Mexican enemies, stimulated & excited as these enemies have been by Brittish intrigue & influence. The assent of the Convention is all we want. Let that assent be given, and we will not wait for the tedious, process, which may occur in forming the new Constitution, but will feel ourselves fully warranted to act without that delay.

In the contingency mentioned in Mr *Buchanan*'s despatch,[6] viz, that a Mexican army should cross, the Rio-Grande, after the Congress of Texas have given their assent to annexation, but before the Convention have done so, it is submitted to your discretion to judge, of the propriety or necessity, of ordering our army and navy to repel the invaders of Texas. If that invasion, in this stage of the action of Texas, shall be in your judgment calculated to over-awe, or shall in fact interfere with or disturb, the free and peaceful deliberations of the Convention, then in my judgment, the public necessity for our interposition, will be such, that we should not stand quietly by, and permit, an invading foreign enemy, either to occupy or devestate any portion of the Texian Territory. Of course I would maintain the Texas title to the extent which she claims it to be, and not permit an invading enemy, to occupy a foot of the soil East of the *Rio Grande*. I hope however that there will be no necessity to consider of what it may be proper to do under the contingency supposed. Our troops at Fort Jessup, cannot reach the mouth of the *Sabine*, before the 4th of July, (the day the Texan Convention convenes), and if the assent of that body is promptly given, no question of our power, to expel the Mexican army from her soil will exist, and it will be promptly and efficiently done.

The Post Master General[7] here, will to day issue orders, to employ three steamers, to carry the mail three times a week each way between

New Orleans and Galveston, which will greatly facilitate the transmission of information to and from Texas. You will of course keep us regularly advised of all that occurs in Texas. You will be expected to remain in Texas, as you were informed by *Mr Buchanan* in his last despatch[8] until after the Convention shall adjourn.

I write you this private letter, in addition to the Public despatches which you will receive by *Genl. Besancon*, not that I deemed it to be absolutely necessary to do so, but to express to you in this informal manner, my determination to stand by Texas, and defend her in this crisis to the utmost of my Constitutional powers. The people of Texas, may be assured too, as I wrote you in a former letter,[9] that when she becomes a member of our Union, we will not only defend her but do her full and ample justice. I have written in great haste, but as my letter is *private* and not *public*, I need not transcribe it or take time, to put it into better form.

JAMES K. POLK

P.S. *General Besancon* the bearer of despatches is a very intelligent gentleman, and can give you more in detail, the public anxiety now prevailing in the U. States for the success of the measure of annexation. The Whig party seems with but few exceptions to have given up their opposition to the measure. The Genl. will return immediately, and will if you desire it be the bearer of despatches from you to the Government here. J.K.P.

P.S. Just as I had finished this letter *Mr Eldridge* of Texas,[10] arrived direct from the *Hermitage*, bringing the melancholy news of the death of *Genl. Jackson*. He died at 6. O'Clock P.M. on sunday the 8th June. President *Houston* arrived at the Hermitage two hours after he expired. J.K.P.

ALS. DLC–AJD. Addressed to Washington, Texas, and marked "*Confidential*." Published in Sioussat, ed., *THM*, III (March, 1917), pp. 67–69.

1. Polk refers to Andrew J. Donelson's letters to James Buchanan of June 2 and 4, 1845, published in Senate Document No. 1, 29th Congress, 1st Session, pp. 64–67. On June 2, Donelson reported that Charles Elliot had arrived in Texas with a British treaty guaranteeing Texas independence. Donelson speculated that this British maneuver would result in a war with Mexico following Texas' acceptance of the annexation resolution and that Texas was willing to fight. On June 4, Donelson reported Mexican troop movements on the Rio Grande and indicated his belief that an invasion of Texas would follow immediately upon Texas' ratification of the annexation resolution.

2. See Charles A. Wickliffe to Polk, June 3 and 4, 1845.

3. See Dallas to Polk, May 5, 1845; and Polk to Donelson, May 26, 1845.

4. Charles Elliot.

5. Born in New York, Lorenzo A. Besançon moved to Mississippi, and founded the Natchez *Mississippi Free Trader* in 1835. Named president of the state bank commission in 1837, he moved to New Orleans in the early 1840's and later served as a captain in the Louisiana mounted volunteers during the Mexican War.

6. Polk refers to James Buchanan's letter to Donelson of June 15, 1845, published in Senate Document No. 1, 29th Congress, 1st Session, pp. 42–45.

7. Cave Johnson.

8. Polk refers to James Buchanan's letter to Donelson of June 3, 1845, published in Senate Document No. 1, 29th Congress, 1st Session, pp. 41–42.

9. See Polk to Donelson, May 6, 1845.

10. Born in New York City, Joseph C. Eldridge moved to Texas in 1837; Sam Houston appointed him general superintendent of Indian affairs in 1843; and three years later Polk appointed him a purser in the navy.

## FROM DANIEL T. JENKS

Philadelphia June 15, 1845

In his discussion of Philadelphia appointments Jenks emphasizes the important role of the Irish in city politics. He informs Polk that the Irish Repeal Association has selected Robert Tyler as its president[1] and recalls that its leaders had supported John Tyler's candidacy in 1844. Noting that Sutherland and Whitecar have great influence with Irish voters, he claims that their removal from office has displeased "our *Irish friends in Philadelphia*." Jenks adds that the appointment of Little, a Native American, has proven offensive.[2] He states that the repeal Irishmen regard the Native American party as "the most desperate politicians in the country" and take the appointment of a Native American as "a very serious affront to them personally." Jenks alludes to the lack of knowledge about Philadelphia politics on the part of Polk's cabinet minister from the interior of Pennsylvania[3] and stresses that the Democratic party in the city relies on Irish voters. Without their support, the Democracy will experience serious difficulties in the upcoming elections.

ALS. DLC–JKP. Addressed to Washington City.

1. Robert Tyler, eldest son of John Tyler, served in the Land Office at Washington during his father's tenure as president. Later he practiced law in Philadelphia, served as register of the Confederate Treasury, and edited the Montgomery *Daily Advertiser*. The Irish Repeal Association of Philadelphia advocated dissolution of the union between Great Britain and Ireland.

2. Jenks refers to the appointment of William Little to the post of assistant appraiser in the Philadelphia Customs House.

3. James Buchanan.

## FROM J. GEORGE HARRIS

My Dear Sir,            Nashville Tenn. June 17. 1845
     The simple inscription on the slab that covers the remains of Jackson, will be

"Andrew Jackson"
"Born March 15. 1767"
"Died June 8. 1845"

It has been currently reported that his property was to be settled on the wife and children of his adopted son.[1] This is not true. His adopted son And. jr.[2] is sole heir to all he possessed with the exception of a few small presents made to family connexions.

     I have seen several sketches of "the last scene at the Hermitage," as drawn from descriptions by members of the family, all which substantially agree with that which I have given you in previous letters.

     Gen. Houston is still here. On Saturday (28th inst.) a public dinner (barbecue) will be given him by the Democracy of Nashville, the whigs *refusing* to join.[3] He is vastly improved in his habits & bearing. In two weeks he proposes to visit his friends in E. Tenn. I understand he aspires to, and will probably be elected to, the U.S. Senate from Texas.

     The crops in this section are flourishing; our political campaign is the quietest I ever witnessed; both parties seem to be reposing; yet we firmly believe we shall be able to carry the Governor & Legislature.

J. Geo. Harris

ALS. DLC–JKP. Addressed to Washington City.

1. Harris refers to Sarah Yorke Jackson and her three children, Rachel, Samuel, and Andrew III.

2. Andrew Jackson, Jr.

3. On June 17, 1845, a group of Nashville citizens, representing both the Democratic and Whig parties, invited Sam Houston to attend a barbecue in his honor on June 28. The invitation, published in the *Nashville Union* on June 19, suggested that Houston would use the occasion to provide "an account of the past and present condition of Texas." Accepting the invitation, Houston attended the barbecue and addressed an enthusiastic crowd for two hours on the subject of Texas. He traced the course of Texas history, enumerated the advantages of annexation to the United States, and declared popular support in Texas for union to be a "fixed fact." *Nashville Union*, July 1, 1845.

## FROM JOHN CATRON

My dear sir.                                        Nashville, June 19th 1845
    I wrote you a note on Genl. Jackson's death,[1] and ere this you have
learned all the particulars. One conclusion I would mention—it is, that
ordinary public meetings and eulogies are out of place in memory of the
deceased. He now stands as a man of History, & 2d probably in the
annals of the U.S. His prominent acts belong to history proper, (not to
ephemeral eulogy,) and now is not the time to present them to the world.
Death and time, must do a good deal before the policy and acts of removing the Indians west, and of overthrowing the money power, & policy of
Mr. Hamilton,[2] can be *Historically* presented: and the same may be said
on minor heads. From the familiar and free associations of Genl. J., re-
curring to a credulous degree, among very inferior men, there is danger
if any newspaper excitement was not got up. The Whig papers would
teem with certificates and pretended memories partly true, but mainly
false, injurious to the fame of our decd. friend—things that when living, a word, (& that sure to come,) from him, wd. have dissipated. It
is idle to open any such door to men smarting under raw and rankling
wounds, near starving for bread by exclusion from the public chest, in
fact or fancy, (it matters not which,) and this inflicted as they supposed
by Genl. J. It is a state of things time can best deal with: Time, will
effectuate the policy (Texas inclusive) devised, & cure the spite at the
same rate. Village parade is beneath the man's character, & out of taste,
if nothing more cogent existed to the contrary. Hence I have thrown cold
water on all attempts of the kind. Then again, there are very many who
would have immolated Genl. J's principles for years past, who are now
seeking to be chief mourners; who would thrust themselves in the van,
of any meeting that might be called, and become accredited witnesses
afterwards to the prejudice of Genl. J's fame, under the garb of especial
& confidential friends. This is a small aspect, but one with which I have
been troubled, and thought worthy of being guarded against. But not a
word have I said on this head save to yourself, and in strict *privacy* here.
    To Gnl. Houston a barbacue will be given,[3] where all can be, & hear,
and where he can explain the reasons of the first Texas rovolt, the *"Act"*
of declaring Independence, the onward progress of the Republic, *his*
course during Mr. Van Buren's administration in regard to annexation:
His course during Mr. Tyler's administration, & since: And his intercourse with Genl. Jackson on the Subject, How he (H.) conceded, and
his visit to the Sage of the Hermitage,[4] an hour too late. Not a bad
text for a peroration in such hands, you will allow. Houston is strictly

temperate, & though a little feeble from affliction of stomach when he came here, will in ten days be as stout as I am. He did me the honour to say, any suggestions I would make would oblige him—in regard to topics and heads he meant no doubt—and the arrangement of the matter to suit public opinion in the U.S. His thoughts will be settled in a few days, when I will try to aid him. If—'I the vein,' few men can match him in the execution, at a Barbecue, & to such a crowd. He is sore on the charges of "land robbers," &c.

J. CATRON

ALS. DLC–JKP. Addressed to Washington City.
1. Not found.
2. Alexander Hamilton.
3. See J. George Harris to Polk, June 17, 1845.
4. Andrew Jackson.

FROM WILLIAM McLAIN[1]

Colonisation Rooms

Sir                                        Washington City 19 June 1845
    I take the liberty of inclosing to you a copy of a letter from Stephen A. *Benson*, a citizen of Liberia, to Gov. Roberts, & also a letter from Gov. Roberts to me,[2] relating to the Seizure by a British Man of War Cutter of the Colonial Schooner "John Seys" belonging to said Benson.[3] I also inclose a printed copy of the letter of Com. *Jones*,[4] referred to, together with a letter from Mr. Ellsworth & one from myself explanatory of certain circumstances connected therewith.[5]
    From a full consideration of all the facts before us, this appears to be a most wanton attack by British authority upon the strugling, young Republic of Liberia. And although the Government of the U. States has no direct connection with, or control over Liberia, yet as the patrons & friends of colonisation, having important interests at stake there, we as citizens of the United States would most respectfully ask the council & assistance of our own Government, in whatever way it can be consistently rendered.
    It has occurred to us that it would be competent for the United States Government to act as a *Mediator* between the Government of Great Britain & the Commonwealth of Liberia.
    Commander *Jones*, in his letter to the Gov. dated Sept. 9, 1844, (a copy of which is referred to above) denies the right of the Liberian Government to impose duties, regulate commerce, or perform any other act of Sovereignty: and to justify himself in the premesis, he says that the Sovereignty of Liberia has not been acknowledged by the United States.

And now, it seems he is, reducing his doctrine to practice, "vi et armis," in the fullest extent.[6]

Cannot the present Executive of the U. States, recall to the mind of the British authorities, the fact, that the (tacit) recognition of the Sovereignty of Liberia by the former has been *officially* communicated to the latter, in the Correspondence of Mr. Upsher with Mr. Fox, & of Mr. Everett with Lord Aberdeen?[7] And could not the United States as a friendly power distinctly request the British Government to make a similar acknowledgment, & for the Sake of humanity, for the Sake of the colored race & the last hope of Africa, to allow Liberia to remain unmolested, & to enact and execute any laws (not inconsistent with the "law of nations") which they might deem necessary for their internal peace & welfare.

If the Government of the United States would say to Great Britain, "We consider Liberia as an independent political community, having a right to enact & enforce such laws as those in question, & we request you to do the Same," would any public interest of the U. States be compromised, and might not much good result to Liberia.

I inclose an article which was lately published in the African Repository Showing on what grounds we claim that the Sovereignty of Liberia is founded.[8] The ground is undoubtedly tenable & the facts set forth establish the claim.

You will please to pardon me for laying these documents before you and asking for these suggestions your distinguished consideration, at your earliest possible convenience.

W. McLain

ALS. DLC–ACS. Addressed locally.

1. William McLain served as a traveling agent for the American Colonization Society before becoming treasurer in 1843 and corresponding secretary in February, 1844.

2. Enclosures not found. Stephen A. Benson and Joseph J. Roberts published their letters in the July 1845 issue of the *African Repository*. A Maryland-born free black, Benson arrived in Liberia in 1822. He served as a member of the Commonwealth legislature from Grand Bassa County, 1842–47; won election to the vice-presidency of Liberia in 1853; and served as president of Liberia from 1856 until his death in 1865. A Virginia-born free black, Roberts went to Liberia in 1829. He won election to the lieutenant governorship of the Commonwealth in 1841; served as its last governor, 1842–48; and became the first president of Liberia in 1848.

3. The British West African Squadron commander had ordered British merchants not to pay any anchorage or harbor fees to the unrecognized Commonwealth of Liberia. Accordingly, the captain of the British merchant vessel *Little Ben* refused to pay harbor fees at Bassa Cove, and the collector seized enough

goods to pay the fees. On April 15 the British man-of-war *Lily* seized the *John Seys* in retaliation. The incident provided a catalyst for the creation of an independent nation of Liberia.

4. Enclosure not found. The *African Repository* of July 1845, carried a printed copy of the letter dated September 9, 1844, and signed by "Captain W. Jones." Jones is not identified further.

5. Enclosures not found. Henry L. Ellsworth served on the executive committee of the American Colonization Society. McLain's explanation below is similar to his article in the *African Repository* of April 1845, entitled "Sovereignty of Liberia."

6. Latin phrase meaning "by force of arms."

7. In his article in the *African Repository*, McLain refers to the official correspondence between Abel Upshur and Henry S. Fox, September 25, 1843, and between Edward Everett and Lord Aberdeen, December 30, 1843. A justice of the Virginia Supreme Court, 1826–41, and secretary of the navy, 1841–43, Upshur succeeded Daniel Webster as secretary of state on July 24, 1843. A British diplomat, Fox held ministerial appointments as minister plenipotentiary to Argentina in 1830, Brazil in 1832, and to the United States in 1835. He assisted in the Webster-Ashburton negotiations. Replaced in 1843, Fox continued to reside in Washington City until his death in 1846.

8. Enclosure not found.

## FROM J. GEORGE HARRIS

My Dear Sir                                         Nashville June 21. 1845

After watching the two or three last mails with unusual solicitude I am glad to learn of your recovery from your late illness as chronicled in the "Union."[1]

Gen. Houston's reception here is, perhaps a matter of some consequence. Donelson was exceedingly anxious that he should not fall into the hands of the "whigs." At first all the whig leaders declined signing the invitation given him to a free barbecue, but, on a second thought, Dr. Shelby & the Mayor (Maxey) signed it, thus depriving the affair of an exclusive democratic character.[2]

At a public meeting held in the Court Ho. to-day, Dr. *Shelby* presided, our friends feeling anxious that the barbecue should have no party *caste*.[3]

I have just received a letter from R. B. Reynolds of E. Tenn. who says Brown and Foster are producing some sensation there. Robt J. Chester from the West. Dist[4] says there will be a large demo. gain beyond the Tennessee River. Mr. Nelson (Rutherford whig)[5] opposes Col. Gentry for Congress. Gen. Trousdale made a speech (his first) at Gallatin last Monday, so says Gen. Donalson.[6]

There is no political excitement here. Each party seems to strive with the other as to which shall keep the quietest. All our friends believe Brown & a demo. Legislature will be elected.

J. GEO. HARRIS

ALS. DLC–JKP. Addressed to Washington City.

1. According to the Washington *Union* of June 11th, Polk became "slightly indisposed" on June 9th, did not go to his room at the State Department, nor "see company at his quarters at Coleman's." On June 12th the President, though feeling better, had not recovered from his indisposition; on June 13th he rode out "for a short time"; and on June 14th he met his cabinet at the State Department and "attended to his usual duties with his usual spirit."

2. See J. George Harris to Polk, June 17, 1845. A Nashville physician and army surgeon under Andrew Jackson during the Creek War, John Shelby served as postmaster of Nashville from 1849 until 1853.

3. Reference is to a meeting of Davidson County citizens called for the purpose of designating a location and soliciting contributions for the June 28 barbecue in honor of Sam Houston.

4. A Carthage merchant and friend of Andrew Jackson, Robert J. Chester moved to Madison County following the Panic of 1819. Contractor, land speculator, and lumberman, he served as postmaster of Jackson, 1825–33, and as marshal for the western district of Tennessee, 1838–49. Chester County was named in his honor.

5. A Rutherford County Whig, Charles L. Nelson ran unsuccessfully for the U.S. House in 1845.

6. William Trousdale and Daniel S. Donelson. A native of North Carolina and veteran of the War of 1812, Seminole War, and Mexican War, Trousdale represented Sumner and Smith counties for one term as a Democrat in the Tennessee Senate, 1835–36. An unsuccessful candidate for Congress in 1837, 1839, and 1845, he served one term as governor of Tennessee, 1849–51, and accepted an appointment as U.S. minister to Brazil in 1853. A West Point graduate and Sumner County farmer, Donelson won election to three terms as a Democrat in the Tennessee House, 1842–43 and 1855–59.

## FROM DANIEL T. JENKS

My Dear Sir                 Philadelphia June 21st 1845

From all I can learn, I think it likely that there will be much opposition shown to Mr Horn's appointment as collector in the interior of Penna. on the 4th of July. This opposition is mosetly from the friends of Mr Buchannan's.[1] You no doubt recollect Mr Wilmot[2] makeing the complaint that Mr Horn would not appoint none of the Secretays friends. This was said in my pressence when I last visited your Excellency.

I will however write you on this subject, again before the 4th. It will require all our skill to keep Penna. on the right tack. From present prospects, I have great fear for 1848. All the Tyler men of any consequence have been *removed from office.*

The impression is general here, that they were *absolutely* necessary to carry the election of '44. Mr Sutherland is a hurt of himself. Dont therefore add to further difficulties, by declining to reappoint his son, in Wisconsin.[3]

DANIEL T. JENKS

P.S. I was much pained at hearing of the death of your old friend Gen. Jackson. Could his life of been prolonged a little longer, to of heard of the final consumation of the annexation of Texas, it would of been very pleasing to all his friends. It may be truly said, that a great and good man has fallen.

I am trying to get a letter that was published since John Davis was appointed in this city where he is published as a whig, and his letter against Jackson.[4] There is much opposition to him I find, I am often warted on about it. I tell all you have been deceived, and time will make all right. I understand he is on at Washington. D.T.J.

ALS. DLC–JKP. Addressed to Washington City and marked *"Private."*
1. James Buchanan.
2. A lawyer from Towanda, Penn., David Wilmot served three terms in the U.S. House as a Democrat, 1845–51; gained prominence as a Free Soil Democrat in 1847 and 1848; played a leading role in the founding of the Republican party in 1854; served as presiding judge of the Thirteenth Judicial District, 1853–61; filled a partial term in the U.S. Senate as a Republican, 1861–63; and sat on the U.S. Court of Claims from 1863 until his death in 1868.
3. Thomas W. Sutherland, son of Joel B. Sutherland, served as U.S. attorney for the Wisconsin Territory, 1841–45, and as U.S. attorney for Wisconsin, 1848–49.
4. Not identified further.

FROM MARSHALL TATE POLK, JR.

Dear Uncle                    Colemans Hotel June 21. 1845
I have thought a great deal of the opportunity you have offered me of improving my education, and I acknowlege my error in not before this studying more your pleasure, as well as my own interest. If it be agreable to your wishes now, I will most gratefully accept your kind offer of sending me to the Georgetown College. I will go cherfully and beg that you will forgive the reluctance I have shown in doing that which you thought best for me and I promise that in the future I will exert myself

all that I can to advance myself in my studies with as little expence as possible, and as little trouble to you.

MARSH T. POLK

ALS. DLC–JKP. Addressed locally.

### FROM MEMUCAN HUNT

State of Texas
Dear Sir,                                        Galveston, June 25th 1845

Commodore Stockton left our coast on the 23rd with the view to reach Washington City as early as practicable with the gratifying assurance that the Congress of Texas has *unanimously* concurred in the first and second sections of the Joint Resolution of the Congress of the United States offering to Texas admission as a State, of the U.S.A.[1] Least some unforeseen cause should prevent the Commodore from arriving at Washington as early as is expected I do myself the gratifying honor and pleasure of transmitting to your Excellency a Gazette containing the result of the deliberations of the Texian Congress, in consumating, as far as it can, this great measure.[2]

MEMUCAN HUNT

ALS. DLC–JKP. Probably addressed to Washington City.

1. On June 21, 1845, the Texas Congress adopted joint resolutions consenting to the terms of annexation offered by the United States and calling for a convention to adopt a state constitution.

2. Hunt probably refers to the *Civilian and Galveston Gazette*. The enclosure has not been found.

### FROM JOHN LAW

My Dear Sir                          Vincennes, Indiana June 26th 1845

You have learnt no doubt ere this, that we have nominated Davis for Congress in this District (the 6th). There was some difficulty at first in settling the rival pretensions of some of our other friends, but these have been satisfactorily arranged, and he has a clear field, so far as the democratic party is concerned. His opponent is a Methodist clergyman by the name of Farmer, who is out "on his own hook."[1] The Whigs utterly deny having anything to do with his outcoming and many of them will not support him. Davis's majority will not be much short of two thousand—our majority in November was 1498—and we have added to our strength since then. We shall carry the State easily in August.[2] In my own County[3] where the Whigs had a majority last fall of two hundred and fifty eight, we have every assurance of electing a democratic senator; indeed I think there is little doubt we shall do so. We shall elect seven members of Congress certain, possibly eight. Wrights district is uncertain. So is Samples (Whig).[4] If we loose in both, we shall loose one member. If we gain in either, we shall stand as we did last session— eight democrats, two Whigs. I deem Cathcart's (democrat)[5] chance in Samples district a good one. While I fear the result in Wrights, where the Whigs have a majority of one thousand. We Shall elect a democratic senator next winter, I think beyond all doubt from present appearances, having a very fair prospect of a decided majority in both branches of the Legislature. So much for the political aspect of things in this quarter.

A friend at Philadelphia occasionally sends me files of English papers, and I have been not a little amused with Peels bluster on the Oregon question.[6] It formed a most beautiful episode in a debate on the *grant to Maynooth College*! It was evidently however a part of the play, though apparently impromptu. Sir Robert Peel is in my estimation one of the ablest men who ever had the direction of English affairs. He has great talents, great parliamentary tack. He understands the English character well. He found the protestant prejudices of his own Tory Party evidently against him on this Maynooth question, and like an able general, he raised this false alarm, in order to try the vigilance of his Troops in case of a real emergency—and, he succeeded. Both Catholicism and Protestantism, Oxford and Maynooth were all forgotten for the nonce, in the real hatred which the English nation feel towards our Government and its free institutions, in the jealousy of our increasing power, wealth, intelligence, energy, enterprise and empire. "They bite however at a file."[7] In spite of all the obstacles which they may attempt to place in our way, in spite of all their machinations publick and private, our course is onward, and while they dispute our passage north, they may as well be looking out for our limits on the Pacific *south* of the 42°. There are some good ports in the "Bay of St Francisco," as well as in the "Straits of Fuca," and what my Dear Sir can prevent the "Westward Ho" of the hardy pioneers of the West. We who have passed our lives almost among these people know, that if our own Government cannot stay the emigration of this rifle bearing population, these emigrationally "Sons of the Forest," no foreign government can arrest their settlement from Monterey to Nootka Sound, *if they so w*ill it—much less England whoose threats they despise, whoose oppositions they court. English diplomacy, ten years roll round, may find new questions of "annexation" for the exercise of their skill, their fraud or their bribery.

Peel seems to me to treat John Bull as the Spaniards treat his namesake in the arena, only that he acts double, he plays "Bandelero" and "Picadore," at the same time he flaunts the red rag of Oregon in his face one day, and sticks darts covered with fire work's on his hide in the form of an "Income Tax" on another. The poor animal groans and bellows but must bear it. Who is ultimately to play the "Matadore" with him? He who rules the destinies of nations, as well as men can only tell. It will be a pitiable spectacle come when it may, but come it will sooner or later. The elements are even now at work which will ultimately shear Great Britian of her gigantick power, possessions, influence and wealth. She will then stand a monument, a landmark, to other nations, of the folly and madness which governed her Councils, of the Bigots which formed her Church, and of that lust of dominion, which instead of adding to her own strength and prosperity at home, sought conquests abroad on Continents, which God and nature never intended she should possess or possessing retain.

As to the "Oregon question" you may depend on it here, as well as throughout the whole West, with all parties. I might almost say with all men there is but one opinion, and that is strict accordance with the sentiments contained in your Inaugural address, our right, our perfect absolute right to that Territory. There may be with some, a disposition by way of compromise to settle our boundary by the forty-ninth paralell of Latitude. Where it ought to have been settled, in the negociation between Mr Webster and Lord Ashburton,[8] and where in my opinion it would have been settled but for the Anglican feeling of Webster, as most clearly manifested in the arrangement of our north eastern boundary. (The excuse of Lord Ashburton that he had no power, I consider all gammon.) But below that point (the 42°) they will not cede an inch of soil, a pebble, a grain of sand. They deem their right perfect, absolute, indefeasible. They are willing to do all that honorable and honest men would do in a question of private right, not affecting their honor. They look upon War as a great a national calamity. They would avoid it by any sacrifice that they could honorably make, but rather than yield one iota of what they deem their own, their own by discovery, by purchase, by settlement, by possession, by all those solemn and legal forms and muniments which give nations as well as individuals *title*, they would say to their Countrymen in the language of Camillus:

> "Arma aptare, atque ferro non auro,
> Rempublicam recuperare."[9]

Excuse the long epistle. Present my best regards to Mrs Polk, and accept for yourself the best wishes of ....

JOHN LAW

ALS. DLC–JKP. Addressed to Washington City.

1. Eli P. Farmer, not further identified, ran unsuccessfully against John W. Davis for a seat in the U.S. House.

2. For the August 1845 elections, see James Whitcomb to Polk, March 2, 1845.

3. Knox County, Indiana.

4. Judge of Indiana's Ninth Judicial Circuit from 1836 until 1843, Samuel C. Sample served one term as a Whig in the U.S. House, 1843–45.

5. An attorney and Democrat, Charles W. Cathcart represented La Porte County in the Indiana Senate from 1837 to 1840, served as a presidential elector in 1844, and won election to two terms in the U.S. House, 1845–49. Upon the death of James Whitcomb in 1852, Cathcart accepted an interim appointment to the U.S. Senate and served for one year.

6. See Jacob L. Martin to Polk, April 16, 1845.

7. Quotation not identified further.

8. See Jacob L. Martin to Polk, May 17, 1845, and Andrew Jackson to Polk, May 2, 1845.

9. Variant of Livy's phrase, "arma aptare ferroque non auro reciperare patriam iubet," which translates "make ready their weapons, and win their country back with iron instead of gold." *History of Rome*, Book 5, section 49, lines 3–4. Law's reference is to Marcus Furius Camillus, a 4th century B.C. dictator who led the defense of Rome against Gallic armies.

## TO WILLIAM S. PICKETT

My Dear Sir,                                    Washington 26th June 1845

Your letter of the 29th ultimo, covering a Statement of my account with your House came duly to hand. Your bill for the balance due your House is $2058.01 was paid by me on presentation on the 9th Instant. My crop of this year will be forwarded to your House.

*J. Knox Walker Esq.* has shown me your letter of the 26th ultimo, addressed to him, on another subject.[1] The situation which you desire at Marsailles is an important one. The present incumbent is a Virginian and was appointed last year.[2] Great interest is taken in his behalf, by leading gentlemen of that state, who earnestly entreat that he may not be removed. At one time my impression was that his removal would be proper. Subsequent information however satisfies me that if I were to remove him, it would give great dissatisfaction and produce excitement among many of my own political friends. The present incumbent is represented to be a gentleman of high character and standing and to agree with me in politics. If I were to remove such a man and appoint one who was related to me by marriage,[3] I would be subject to the charge, of looking more to the interest of my relations than to the public. This would be well calculated to do serious injury to my administration, and is I am sure what you would not desire. Early after I entered upon the duties of my office, I was not in possession of the information which has subsequently come to my knowledge in reference, to the situation which you desire at Marsailles; and which would now greatly embarrass me, if I were to make the change desired by your friends.

I have thought to be proper to speak to you thus frankly, that you may not be disappointed in failing to have your wishes gratified.

My position is a very responsible one and my first and great duty is to the country.

JAMES K. POLK

L. DLC–JKP. Addressed to New Orleans; marked *"Copy"* and *"Private."*
1. On May 26, 1845, Pickett wrote Joseph Knox Walker about Polk's intentions to appoint Pickett to the naval agency at Marseilles. ALS. DLC–JKP.
2. A Richmond merchant, Nathaniel Denby served as temporary navy agent at Marseilles in 1844.
3. Pickett married Mary Eliza Walker, Polk's niece.

## FROM JOSEPH H. TALBOT[1]

Dear Sir.                                    New York 26th June 1845

I shall leave this place early in the morning for Boston and from there come by the lakes home. I was received by those to whom you gave me letters in Philadelphia and this place,[2] with great cordiality, and through them I have made numerous acquaintances, which may be of profit to me hereafter.

On the 24th I was assigned a post of honor, in the funeral procession to the memory of deceased friend Genl Jackson. It was the most imposing spectacle I ever witnessed and I witnessed many old gray headed men in tears. It is astonishing what a hold Genl J. had upon the feelings of his countrymen. He is gone, and I fear it will be long before we have such another man. So far as I can learn your appointment of Mr Lawrence as collector at this port, will give general satisfaction to *all the business men*, and *none* can make *objections* to it, but it is evident, that the *Simon Pure*, V. Buren men, and the leaders of *clubs* are not pleased, for the reason that their *personal* expectation may not be realized. Mr Lawrence is now experiencing similar troubles, that have awaited you for some time past, but he is a firm and virtuous man, and will do all things right. That is, his intentions are pure, and will if possible surround himself with subordinates of integrity, and I feel assured, that you will never have cause to blush for that appointment. I have been much with him and studied him well, because I knew the solicitude you felt upon this subject, and feel well satisfied that in this matter you desire well of your country. I spent last evening with Mr Coddington, in company with Mr Van Buren and many other gentlemen, and although all present were Democrats, the subject of politics was not broached in my presents or hearing. There appears to be a perfect calm, which upon the whole is well enough, but it is not to be disguised that under this smoothe exterior there lurks some trouble which you may quell by a mild conciliating course, taking care not to give any of the *cliques* an ascendency in your administration, and thereby preserve the unity of the great Democratic family, upon which, I honestly believe depends the perpetuity of our political institutions. The suggestions I make you will treat as confidential, and if they should profit you in the smallest degree, I shall be greatly surprised. Remember me to your good lady, and for yourself accept my warmest wishes for a successful administration, health and happiness ....

JOS. H. TALBOT

ALS. DLC–JKP. Addressed to Washington City.
1. Talbot, a Madison County lawyer, succeeded his brother Eli as clerk of the Chancery Court of Williamson County in 1832, served several years as clerk of the Tennessee Supreme Court, and in 1838 became the first U.S. district attorney for the newly formed West Tennessee court. The following year he was succeeded by Henry W. McCorry, who served until 1849.
2. Letters not found.

FROM ALEXANDER J. ATOCHA[1]

Washington [June 27, 1845][2]

After briefly discussing his business interests in Mexico, Atocha gives an account of the background to his arrest and expulsion from the country in early 1845. He notes the republic's large foreign debt and stresses that every new administration has been forced to borrow from the merchants of the capital; almost all of the wealthy men among resident foreigners are creditors of the republic. Atocha himself made loans to the administrations of Bustamante[3] and Santa Anna. He claims that at present the debt that is owed to him amounts to about $190,000. Concerned about the unstable political situation, Atocha tried in 1844 to realize his securities and to withdraw his loans from the government. Well acquainted with Santa Anna, he visited Santa Anna and successfully prevailed on him to refund a portion of the debt. Stressing the "purely commercial character" of his relationship with Santa Anna, he denies any involvement in the domestic politics of Mexico and adds that he never advised Santa Anna about military or political matters. Unfortunately, in November 1844, with the outbreak of the revolution led by Paredes, Atocha's worst fears were realized.[4] He describes his arrest and expulsion from Mexico and demands redress and indemnity for his unjust explusion and consequent loss of property and income. Atocha argues that his securities fluctuate in value and that such securities are useful only to those who reside in the capital and are able to manage them carefully. He hints that the Mexican government's awareness of this fact, together with baseless suspicions about his relationship to Santa Anna, led to his expulsion.

NS. DNA–RG 76. Addressed locally.

1. A native of Spain, Atocha moved to New Orleans in the 1830's and became a naturalized U.S. citizen. In 1839 he took up residence in Mexico City and engaged in unspecified business endeavours. During Polk's administration, Atocha acted as an informal agent of Antonio López de Santa Anna to the U.S. government.

2. Date identified by Polk's AEI on the cover, which states that he referred this letter to the secretary of state on June 27, 1845.

3. Anastasio Bustamante. A Spanish general, Bustamante joined the independence forces during the revolution; he served first as vice-president, 1828–29, then as president, 1830–32 and 1837–41.

4. A Santa-Annista general, Mariano Paredes y Arillaga led the coup that ousted Santa Anna in 1844. Paredes' announcement of rebellion on October 31, 1844, together with congressional refusal to supply new troops and money, drove Santa Anna from the capital; rebel forces captured him near Jalapa on January 15, 1845. Santa Anna volunteered to go into exile and left Mexico on June 3, 1845. Leading a second coup in December 1845, Paredes served as president from January to July 1846.

## FROM J. GEORGE HARRIS

My Dear Sir                                         Nashville June 28, 1845

Yrs. of the 20th June inst.[1] was received by me this day at 11 o'clock a.m. I immediately mounted my horse and started for the Hermitage. At the first gate I learned that And. Jackson[2] had passed on to the city. I returned, found him, retired privately with him to a room at the Nashville Inn and under an injunction of secrecy disclosed to him the object of the interview, showing him your letter. I elicited from him the following facts, taking notes of his declarations, and reading them to him after they were taken, all which he fully approved as being strictly in accordance with the best of his recollections.

On Thursday the 5th of June, the General wrote a letter to his old friend & companion in arms Gen. Plauché of New Orleans[3] on Friday, the 6th he said to his son: "I want to write a letter to my friend Polk—it will probably be the last letter I shall write." His son replied: "Father, you seem to be too feeble to undertake it to-day: will you not postpone it until to-morrow." The General responded: "No, my son, never put off until to-morrow that which may be done to-day." And so saying he requested his son to hand him pen ink and paper,[4] when he commenced writing, as follows: "My Dear Friend: Although I feel very much debilitated, and am suffering great pain I cannot refrain from addressing to you, my friend, the last letter which I shall probably write, imparting to you important information which I have from reliable sources and warning you against some of the evils that threaten your administration. I am informed that the late Secretary of the Treasury, did, while in office receive benefits to the amount of about $90,000 from the New York Deposite Banks, for his own private purse, in consequence of favors shown them by him in the management of the public monies—and, my dear friend, I feel it to be my duty to impart this information to you that you may be enabled to guard the country from a continuance of the dishonorable practice." Mr. Jackson says this is the substance, and (as he believes) much of it the language used by the General in that connexion. He then devoted a portion of the letter to the subject of certain scrip for which holders were by a law of Congress entitled to public lands, but which he had abiding fears would so managed as to be recognised as *cash claims* against the Government. He warned the President against a train of evil consequences which must inevitably result from the slighest possible departure from the intention of the law. He alluded to our foreign relations—especially to our relations with Great Britain praying the President to be just and fear not using his favorite phrase "ask nothing but that which is right, and submit to nothing that is wrong."[5] He closed his letter with the re-assurance of his unabated friendship, wishing the administration perfect success. Mr. Jackson says the letter from the beginning to end breathed the strongest and most cordial friendship, containing frequent repetition of "my friend," "my dear friend" and other endearing terms. Repeating also that the great object of his letter was to implore you to set your face against any mismanagement of the public monies either in the making of deposits [or] of the management of our Indian Affairs.

After he had written about a page and a half of this letter (the whole of which covered about 2 1/2 pages of common letter-paper) he paused and called for some nourishment with which he revived and completed it. He then called in his son and said: "Here my son, read this letter, I want you to be a witness to the fact that I have warned the government against the disasters with which it is threatened—and have done my duty." His son then asked if he should reserve a copy of it—the General replied that if he would examine it attentively, a copy would be unnecessary.

Thus you perceive that Mr. Jackson is good authority with reference to the contents; and therefore have I been particular in detailing all he says concerning them.

Mr. Jackson thinks the letter (which he folded & sealed for the General *imself*) was sent to the Post Office at Nashville by the Genl's servant

Tom (the marketman)[6] on Saturday morning (7th inst.). He says, however, it may be possible that a visitor (he cannot imagine who) that left the Hermitage on Friday evening might have taken it to the office. That it was franked and sent to the Post Office by Gen. Jackson, by the hand of his old and faithful servant Tom or some curious visitor, Mr. Jackson is certain.

I have found it necessary, and I believe it is not imprudent, to disclose in a private manner to Mr. Cheatham (the P.M.) the fact of the non-arrival of the letter at Washington. He has in a careful way conversed with his principal clerks, and says "Mr. Wilson[7] answers in reply to the question whether any letter from Genl Jackson passed thro the office a few days before his death, that some 3 or 4 days before the General's death *four* letters (he thinks) from the Hermitage with the General's frank upon them were received at the office and mailed one of which was to the President entirely directed and franked in the General's own hand writing. He recollects from a remark made to his fellow clerk that the General would continue to write up to the day of his death. Mr. W. is the youngest clerk in the office. Col Sands (the principal clerk who wraps the packages)[8] recollects the bundle from the Hermitage and says it consisted of *three* letters, one from the wife of A. J. Donelson[9] to her husband franked by the Genl, one to Munson White & Co. or Gen. Plauché, he recollects not which, New Orleans under his frank,[10] and one directed and franked by his own hand to the President. Andrew Jackson informs me that two other letters were sent to the office at the same time, and in the same bundle, with that directed to the President. Col. S. also says it was only two days before the Genl's death. So it would seem to be probable that the letter was really mailed at Nashville, I have, however, several other points of inquiry which I shall cautiously make for the purpose of ascertaining with certainty whether the letter was or was not intercepted between the General's own hand and the Post Office.

If it was not thus intercepted, it would seem that the fault must be in the City P.O. of Washington; for, the Wash. City package of letters is made up at Nashville accompanied by a way-bill giving the No. of letters and is supposed to remain unopened until it arrives at its place of destination. If on the arr. of the package at Washn it did not contain as many letters as the way bill called for, their office should have been informed of the fact. I have inquired, and find that no such information has been received at the Nashville Po: Office. If then the letter *was* mailed here, the Wash Office is at fault either in one way or another.

I have appointed to meet Mr. Jackson again on Monday; when we shall undertake further and more minute inquiry.

The truth is that I have been apprehensive while making inquiries that some person who might have been near the General in his last hours, and who is as far from wishing a continuance of friendly relations between yourself & the dying veteran might have meddled in this matter either directly or indirectly. If so, he cannot escape the searching inquiry which Mr. Jackson and myself have taken steps to undertake in a proper manner.

Your letter was thrice welcome. I had almost dispensed of the honor of your frank, but I know that high and important duties consumed your time.

Gen Houston made a speech to between 2000 & 3000 people, nearer the latter than the former, at the Race Course today, commencing at 12 o'clock. He spoke for one hour and a half, eloquently & powerfully upon the past, present, & future condition of Texas, declared himself favorable to Annexation, and was cheered with enthusiasm from period to period.[11]

J. GEO. HARRIS

[P.S.] I have not made public the non-arrival of the Gen. last letter to you, thinking you would prefer to have it done at *Washington*.[12]

ALS. DLC–JKP. Addressed to Washington City. Polk's AE on the cover reads as follows: "J. George Harris—containing a statement of *Andrew Jackson Jr.*, of the contents of *Genl. Jackson's* letter to me, which letter never came to hand. Recd. 6th July 1845."

1. Letter not found. See Polk to A. O. P. Nicholson, June 28, 1845.
2. Andrew Jackson, Jr.
3. A New Orleans merchant and cotton broker, Jean Baptiste Plauché commanded a battalion of city militia under Andrew Jackson's command during the Battle of New Orleans. He won election as lieutenant governor of Louisiana in 1850.
4. For the text of Jackson's last letter, see Jackson to Polk, June 6, 1845.
5. This paraphrase of a passage from Jackson's second inaugural address does not appear in Jackson's letter of June 6, 1845. For the original passage, see Polk to Jackson, April 27, 1845.
6. Not identified further.
7. John G. Wilson, not identified further.
8. P. M. Sands, not identified further.
9. Elizabeth Martin Randolph Donelson.
10. Maunsel White and Jean Baptiste Plauché. An Irish-born sugar planter and cotton broker, White came to New Orleans in 1801. He led a volunteer company at the Battle of New Orleans; marketed Jackson's cotton crops until 1845; and represented Plaquemines Parish in the Louisiana Senate from 1846 until 1850.
11. See J. George Harris to Polk, June 17, 1845.
12. Harris wrote his postscript in the left margin of the final page of the letter.

## TO A. O. P. NICHOLSON

My dear Sir.                                    Washington City 28th June 1845

On yesterday the citizens of this city and District paid the last solemn tribute of respect to the memory of our venerable and lamented friend Genl Jackson. All parties united in the ceremonies. The public offices were closed & hung in mourning. All business in the city was suspended. Almost every door in Pennsylvania avenue through which the procession passed was closed & hung in mourning. Mr. Bancroft's eulogy delivered from the Eastern steps of the capitol to a very large assembly was solemn & eloquent, doing justice to the character of the venerable dead and great credit to his own head & heart. I forbear to give you a further account of it. You will see it in the Washington Union tho no written description can do justice to the occasion. [1]

From a letter received from *J. Geo. Harris Esq* some days ago [2] and also from a statement published in the Nashville Union immediately after Genl Jacksons death, and again in the same paper of the 21st inst, [3] I learn that the last letter which he ever wrote with his own hand was written to me on the 6th or 7th inst. [4] I have anxiously expected to receive that letter, but it has not come to hand. It was no doubt left on his table after he had written it and it may be that in the midst of the confusion incident to the mourning and dying scene, it may not have been sent to the Post Office and may yet be among his papers. If this be not so I am at a loss to account for its failure to reach me. Who handled & took possession of his papers after his death? I should prize the letter as above all price as being the last ever written by the greatest man of the age in which he lived, a man whose confidence and friendship I was so happy as to have enjoyed from my youth to the latest hour of his life. On the 26th of May he addressed in his own handwriting a most affectionate and kind letter to me breathing in every paragraph the purest patriotism, as well as his personal & political friendship for myself. This last letter of the 6th or 7th inst. you describe in the Nashville Union of the 21st upon the authority of his adopted Son, who had doubtless seen and read it to have been of this same character. [5] If on search it cannot be found I again ask you to ascertain who handled and had possession of his papers immediately after his death. If Andrew Jackson Jr or any of the family had laid their hands upon it after his death, it would beyond all doubt have been forwarded to me. As it has not been received, it must either have been put away unobserved with his other papers left on his table at his death or have fallen into other hands than the family, who have not forwarded it. Cheatham may be able to tell whether any such letter was mailed at his office. I have written this morning to *Andrew Jackson* Jr. on the subject.[6] Will you do me this special favour as soon as you receive this letter to the Hermitage, see *Mr Jackson* and have a thorough search made for it. If the letter cannot be found procure from *Andrew Jackson* Jr a statement of its contents as near as he can remember them and also all the conversation which the General had at the time of writing it and all he knows about what was done with it after it was written. I wish no noise or parade made about the inquiry which I wish you to make. You can do it quietly and in your own way. My great object is to get possession of the letter, and if I cannot do that to ascertain its contents and the probable causes which have prevented it from reaching me.

JAMES K. POLK

L, draft. DLC–JKP. Addressed to Nashville; marked *"Private"* and *"Copy."*
1. Polk refers to the Washington *Union* of June 28, 1845. The *Union*, noting that the day's ceremony began with the firing of minute guns and the tolling of bells throughout Washington City, suggested that a procession of thousands had arrived in the city for the occasion. In addition to describing the affair, the *Union* also published the text of George Bancroft's eulogy of Jackson.
2. Polk probably refers to J. George Harris to Polk, June 11, 1845.
3. Polk refers to the *Nashville Union* issues of June 12 and 21, 1845. The *Union*, noting that Jackson had penned his last letter to Polk on June 6, speculated that the letter dealt with foreign affairs and expressed confidence in Polk.
4. See Andrew Jackson to Polk, June 6, 1845.
5. Andrew Jackson, Jr.
6. Polk's letter has not been found.

FROM J. GEORGE HARRIS

My Dear Sir,                              Nashville June 30, 1845
Mr. Jackson[1] has not visited the city to-day. He promised to meet me here and I have accordingly been in waiting for him. If he does not come down to morrow morning I shall go to see him in the evening. Meantime I have inquired how many *free letters* were sent in the Washington packages of the 5th, 6th, 7th & 8th June from the Nashville Post Office. The record is as follows:

| Mail | Thurs. | morn | 5th | June | 21 | fr. | let. |
|------|--------|------|-----|------|----|----|------|
| " | Friday | " | 6th | " | 5 | " | " |
| " | Saturday | " | 7th | " | 25 | " | " |
| " | Sunday | " | 8th | " | 7 | " | " |

Gen. J's letter to the President[2] (according to Col. Sand's recollection, ɔrinc. clk P.O.) was with two others bearing his frank dropped into the common receiving box for letters upon the outside on Friday evening, and by Col. Sand's own hand forwarded in the mail which departed on the morning of Saturday the 7th. The way-bill on the Washington package of that mail called for 25 free letters, and the P.M. of your *City P.O.* found it to contain that no. unless the package arrived broken and without a bill. If he *did not*, it was his duty to inform the Nash. Office. No such information is received.

From all the evidence *now* before us, it would seem that the letter was duly mailed at Nashville on the morning of the 7th, and should have reached your hand about the 14th by due course of mail. And if so, it would also under all the circumstances, that it must have lodged in the city P.O. of Washington. I presume that the way-bill which accompanied the Wash. letters from Nash. on the morning of the 7th is preserved at your city P.O. where it will show for itself.

When in my letter of yesterday I alluded to the possibility that some person who was near the Genl in his last hours might have been interested in intercepting the letter either one way or another between the Hermitage & Po. office I was far from supposing that it was any member of *the family* of course. No one of them could possibly be capable of such a thing. But you know there were persons (casual visitors) leaving the Hermitage almost every evening, with some of whom the Genl often entrusted his letters for the P.O. It was to these that I referred. The explanation perhaps is scarcely necessary.

J. Geo. Harris

ALS. DLC–JKP. Addressed to Washington City.
1. Andrew Jackson, Jr.
2. See Andrew Jackson to Polk, June 6, 1845.

## TO JOHN HORN ET AL.[1]

Gentlemen:                           Washington City 30th June 1845

My public duties at the seat of Government must prevent me from accepting your invitation to unite with my Fellow Citizens of Philadelphia in "celebrating the ensuing anniversary of American Independence."[2] That anniversary will be attended with more than ordinary interest throughout our lands. It will be celebrated by a nation in mourning because of the death of her first citizen, who shed his youthful blood to achieve and spent his whole life to maintain her Independence. You have truly said in your letter that on the approaching 4th of July "the Cypress must be blended with the Laurel and the brightness of our glorious anniversary be clouded by the lamented death of the great and the good Jackson." While a whole people mourn his loss, they will rejoice with patriotic gratitude to the men of the Revolution and to that over ruling Providence by which they were guided and directed in securing and transmitting to their posterity the rich inheritance of our free institutions.

*Andrew Jackson* was among the last of the survivors of the eventful period of our Revolution, and having "filled the measure of his country's glory,"[3] now sleeps with his fathers. The voluntary expression of a nation's gratitude for his great service, in war and in peace, is now doing justice to his memory. It will be the test of the faithful historian to transmit his great and patriotic deeds to posterity, that they may be imitated by future generations of his admiring countrymen, and by the friends of freedom throughout the world. Thanking you for your invitation, I have the honour to transmit to you herewith a sentiment, to be presented, in my name, as requested in your letter.

JAMES K. POLK

*Sentiment*

The Memory of Andrew Jackson: Illustrious in war, his policy was peace: devoted to the interests of his own country, he was just to all Foreign Nations; In our Foreign policy, his country approves and adopts his maxim, to "*ask nothing that is not right, and submit to nothing that is wrong.*"[4]

ALS, draft. DLC–JKP. Addressed to Philadelphia and marked "*Copy.*"

1. Polk's letter is addressed to Horn, D. H. Tucker, J. A. Phillips, Robert F. Christy, and Charles H. Kirk.

2. On June 23, 1845, Horn et al. invited Polk to attend a public dinner in Philadelphia to celebrate the Fourth of July. LS. DLC–JKP.

3. Quotation not identified further.

4. Polk paraphrases a passage from Jackson's second inaugural address. See Polk to Jackson, April 27, 1845.

## FROM ANDREW JACKSON, JR.

Dear Sir                    Hermitage June 30th 1845

Your kind favor of date the 5th inst (marked private)[1] came to hand a few days after the decease of my poor Dear Father. If living, I have no doubt he would have cheerfully coincided in the view you have expressed in regard to our Foreign relations &c. It was my intention to have written you immediately after his decease, but my heart was sir too full, and our friend Geo. G Harris[2] and others promised me to write you forthwith. I have also written a few lines on the closing hours of my dear Father which you will see published in the Nashville Union.[3] The last letter written to any one, by him was to you on the 6th inst (Friday). Early the next morning I carefully put it into the hands of our boy Tom to have it placed in the Post Office at Nashville, which he told me he did. I have just seen our friend Harris & he states to me confidentially that the letter had not been rec'd by you as yet. It is strange, for the boy says he put it into the Nashville Office on Saturday the 5th inst at about 10 Oclock.[4]

I read the letter[5] by Fathers request, and folded & backed it to you. It was a kind and affectionate letter, intended to put you upon your guard against some former practices in the Treasury Department in relation to the Deposits of the funds of the Govrmnt. in some of the Banks in New York & to the Eastward, and also about the vile fraud (as he calls it) of the Treaty with the Indians in Mississippi, of the script that was intended to be forced upon the government by Congress. You will recollect all about it. The Indians you know first had reservations—then floats was issued &c. Thereupon a great many fraudulent claims came up all intended to be forced upon the government. This he also guarded you against.

He finally closed his letter to you having confidence in your administration, that you would do your duty, in our foreign relations, with a blessing.

Nothing else was touched up. I thus give you a short sketch of all the substance of it.

I have just rec'd a letter from our friend Genl Armstrong, addressed to Father the evening before he sailed from New York, and I deem it prudent to quote to you a few lines of his letter, as follows: "*No* one here intertains fear that we shall now have *War*, but in case we do my place is at home. I trust you have mentioned my wish to Presdnt Polk to enter the Army. I must come home, & what into line some place. *In case of no war*, I wish you to write him on the subject of the Bankers for the United States. Genl Harrison removed the fund out the hands of the Messrs Rothchilds to that of Barring & Brothers.[6] If I could in England have the credit and standing with my Government *so far as to influence* the return of these funds to the Rothchilds, it would give me some weight, not that they want the Deposits, but the withdrawal of them has hurt their pride and I understand the House show great feeling on the subject & to be known as instrumental in restoreing the funds would greatly benefit me. I requested Mr Vaulx[7] to show you my final settlement with the government."

I herewith enclose you two letters,[8] one from our old friend Gen! Davis,[9] the other from a lady,[10] perhaps you know &c.

My household with myself thank you for the kindness to my Brother Thomas & Mr. Taggart,[11] and Sir, you would confer a great favor by speaking to Mr. Secretary Bancroft, of Master John Adams midshipmans warrant,[12] whenever it can be done. It has been promised a long time by all the secretaries whenever it could be done or a vacancy occurs.

All pretty well now, and join me in kind regards to yourself & Mrs. Polk.

A. JACKSON JUNR.

P.S. I have in more details given the substance of my Fathers last letter to you to Geo. G Harris. He promised to write you forthwith.[13] We will endeavor to find out more about it in the Nashville Post Office. It is a strange affair to me, and hope ere this it has come to hand.

P.S. Private. I hope sir after the August Elections that you *will turn out of office* our Marshall Mr. Shepherd,[14] for reasons I can give you whenever it is desired. A.J. Jr.

ALS. DLC–JKP. Addressed to Washington City. Polk's AE on the cover states that he received this letter on July 10, 1845.

1. Polk's letter has not been found.
2. J. George Harris.
3. Jackson's reference is to an article, "The Last Days of Gen. Jackson," published in the *Nashville Union* of June 21, 1845.
4. Jackson probably meant to write June 7, not June 5.
5. See Andrew Jackson to Polk, June 6, 1845.
6. Taking advantage of Baring Brothers and Co.'s close association with Nicholas Biddle during the struggle between Andrew Jackson and the Second Bank of the United States, Rothchilds replaced Barings in 1834 as the official bankers of the United States in Europe. In 1843 the government's official account went back to Barings.
7. Possibly James Vaulx, not identified further.
8. Enclosures not found.
9. John M. Davis held commissions in the army, 1807–15 and 1816–21, and fought at the Battle of New Orleans. An ardent Jacksonian, he later served as U.S. marshal for the western district of Pennsylvania during the 1830's.
10. Not identified.
11. Thomas J. Donelson and James B. Taggart.
12. Jackson's reference not identified further.
13. See J. George Harris to Polk, June 28, 1845.
14. A former editor of the Jackson *District Telegraph and State Sentinel*, 1837–38, Benjamin H. Sheppard served as U.S. marshal for the Middle District of Tennessee from 1842 until 1846.

# CALENDAR

N.B. Items entered in *italic* type have been published or briefed in the Correspondence Series.

## 1845

| | |
|---|---|
| [1845] | From Mark Alexander. ALS. DLC–JKP. Advises Polk on internal improvements, tariff revision, the Zollverein treaty, and British interference in Liberia. |
| Jan 1845 | From John Chaney et al. LS. DLC–JKP. Urge on behalf of the Ohio Democracy that Samuel Medary be named Post Master General. |
| Jan 1845 | From Henry N. Cushman et al. NS. DLC–JKP. Recommend on behalf of the citizens of Franklin County and the Commonwealth of Massachussetts the appointment of Marcus Morton to Polk's cabinet. |
| Jan 1845 | From Isaac Davis et al. LS. DLS–JKP. Recommend Marcus Morton for a place in Polk's cabinet. |
| *[1 Jan 1845]* | *From George Bancroft.* |
| *[1 Jan 1845]* | *From Aaron V. Brown.* |
| 1 Jan | From Ethan A. Brown. ALS. DLC–JKP. Requests information regarding Polk's travel plans; explains that he and his friends would like to pay their respects when Polk reaches Louisville, Ky. |
| 1 Jan | From William Hendricks. ALS. DLC–JKP. Invites Polk to visit Madison, Ind., en route to Cincinati from Louisville. |
| *1 Jan* | *From Memucan Hunt.* |
| 1 Jan | From Achilles D. Johnson. ALS. DLC–JKP. Congratulates Polk on his election to the presidency. |
| 1 Jan | From James Maher. ALS. DLC–JKP. Proposes plan for widening Pennsylvania Avenue and planting 360 trees on the sides of same. |

| | |
|---|---|
| [2 Jan 1845] | From Nathan Gaither. ALS. DLC–JKP. Recommends Elijah Hise of Russellville, Ky., to be attorney general in Polk's cabinet. |
| [2 Jan 1845] | From Nathan Gaither. ALS. DLC–JKP. Introduces Thomas Strange of Warren County, Kentucky. |
| *2 Jan* | *From Cave Johnson.* |
| 2 Jan | From Richard M. Smith. ALS. DLC–JKP. Encloses "some half dozen marches & quicksteps composed & dedicated" to Polk by John F. Goneke of Athens, Ga., Polk's former friend and neighbor. (Enclosures not found.) |
| 2 Jan | From George Work. ALS. DLC–JKP. Announces the death of Williamson Smith of Mississippi; asks Polk's assistance in settling Smith's claim against the United States. |
| 3 Jan | From Daniel L. Brodie. ALS. DLC–JKP. Solicits an appointment to a government post in the Wisconsin Territory. |
| 3 Jan | From John DeMott. ALS. DLC–JKP. Encloses Lewis H. Sanford's legal opinion for Polk's perusal. (Enclosure not found.) |
| [3 Jan 1845] | From Charles Fenderich. ALS. DLC–JKP. Requests Polk's opinion as to the "lithograph likeness" that will be published in the near future. |
| *3 Jan* | *From Theophilus Fisk.* |
| 3 Jan | From Thomas Martin. ALS. DLC–JKP. States that although he has no desire to sell his recently acquired pair of carriage horses, he will let Polk purchase them at cost, which was $300 cash. |
| 3 Jan | From James C. Moses. ALS. DLC–JKP. Acknowledges receipt of payment for prior subscriptions to the *Knoxville Register*. |
| *3 Jan* | *From Samuel P. Walker.* |
| *4 Jan* | *From Alfred Balch.* |
| 4 Jan | From Edward A. Hannegan. ALS. DLC–JKP. Forwards a letter from the Indiana electors. (Enclosure not found.) |
| *4 Jan* | *From J. George Harris.* |
| *4 Jan* | *To Martin Van Buren.* |
| 4 Jan | From Hampton C. Williams. ALS. DLC–JKP. States that his devotion to the Democratic party and his Tennessee birth should qualify him to be heard on questions relating to the interests of the District of Columbia. |
| *4 Jan* | *To Silas Wright, Jr.* |
| *5 Jan* | *From Aaron V. Brown.* |
| *5 Jan* | *From Aaron V. Brown.* |
| 5 Jan | From Edward C. Delavan. ALS. DLC–JKP. Urges Polk to sign a declaration pledging total abstinence from alcoholic drinks. |
| *5 Jan* | *From Cave Johnson.* |
| *5 Jan* | *From Aaron V. Brown.* |

6 *Jan*          *From Aaron V. Brown.*
6 Jan           From John Chaney. ALS. DLC–JKP. Advises Polk that many leading Democrats in Ohio do not support LeGrand Byington's application to be appointed U.S. district attorney for the state.
6 Jan           From Nicholas Fain. ALS. DLC–JKP. Requests that Polk visit him in Springvale, Tenn., en route to Washington City.
6 Jan           From Ezekiel P. McNeal. ALS. DLC–JKP. Discusses payments of taxes due on Madison County lands owned by the estate of Polk's brother, Samuel W. Polk.
6 Jan           From James D. Wasson. ALS. DLC–JKP. Forwards Edward C. Delavan's request for Polk's signature to a temperance pledge.
7 Jan           From Charles T. and Lyvinnialla Falkenthal. LS. DLC–JKP. Ask permission to name their infant son after Polk.
7 Jan           From Samuel Nisbet. ALS. DLC–JKP. Solicits Polk's opinion on the idea of Congress appropriating surplus revenues to the American Colonization Society.
7 Jan           From John Pollock. ALS. DLC–JKP. Writes from Spring Mount, County Waterford, and requests information on any of Polk's relations bearing the Christian name Hugh or Charles who might have emigrated from the southern part of Ireland about sixty years ago.
7 Jan           From William Stale. ALS. DLC–JKP. Asks if Polk is a member of the Temperance Society and if so, invites him to attend a grand celebration of the Society to be held in Waynesville, Ohio, on February 26th.
7 Jan           From James Walker. ALS. DLC–JKP. Solicits appointments for his two sons-in-law, William S. Pickett and Isaac N. Barnet.
8 Jan           From Alexander Keech. ALS. DLC–JKP. Suggests several names for cabinet appointments.
8 Jan           From William George Read et al. LS. DLC–JKP. Tender the hospitalities of the City of Baltimore.
[8 Jan 1845]    From John G. Scrogin et al. LS. DLC–JKP. Invite Polk to visit Paris, Ky., on his way to Washington City.
8 Jan           From Frederick P. Stanton. ALS. DLC–JKP. Recommends George W. Murphy of Memphis, Tenn., to be appointed bearer of dispatches to China; notes that Murphy has rendered great service among their foreign population in "balancing the great increase of Whig votes in the County."
9 *Jan*          *From Robert Armstrong.*
9 Jan           From David R. Atchison. ALS. DLC–JKP. States that the Democracy of Missouri would approve the appointment of Robert J. Walker to the post of Treasury secretary.
9 *Jan*          *From Aaron V. Brown.*
9 Jan           From Edward A. Hannegan. ALS. DLC–JKP. Thinks tha

his constituency in Indiana would be pleased to see Robert J. Walker appointed secretary of the Treasury.

9 Jan     From Preston King. ALS. DLC–JKP. Transmits letter of Edmund Varney, a member of the New York Senate.

*9 Jan*     *From Samuel P. Walker.*

*10 Jan*     *From George M. Dallas.*

*10 Jan*     *From Andrew Jackson.*

*10 Jan*     *From Isaac McCoy.*

10 Jan     From Abraham Rencher. ALS. DLC–JKP. Congratulates Polk on his election and expresses general satisfaction with his position as U.S. chargé d'affaires at Lisbon, Portugal.

*11 Jan*     *From Cave Johnson.*

11 Jan     From John M. Patton. ALS. DLC–JKP. Transmits a letter of recommendation in behalf of John Y. Mason for a place in Polk's cabinet; states that all of the signatories are members of the Virginia legislature.

11 Jan     From Fernando Wood. ALS. DLC–JKP. States that Democrats in the New York legislature would prefer Churchill C. Cambreleng for a place in Polk's cabinet over any other.

12 Jan     From Robert Armstrong. ALS. DLC–JKP. Relates that Polk is scheduled to leave Nashville for Washington City by boat on February 1st; adds that if there is the danger of ice, he will arrange a comfortable stage for Polk and his family.

12 Jan     From Cornelius W. Lawrence. LS. DLC–JKP. Introduces William E. Lawrence, who will be visiting Washington soon and wishes to pay his respects.

12 Jan     From Jacob Thompson et al. LS. DLC–JKP. Recommend Robert J. Walker for a place in the cabinet as secretary of the Treasury; note that Mississippi has never had an appointment to such a post in the general government.

13 Jan     From Junius L. Clemmons. ALS. DLC–JKP. Maintains that Democrats in Davidson County, N.C., would prefer that Polk retain John Tyler's whole cabinet "with the understanding that they shall resign one at a time and at early periods."

13 Jan     From Henry Ewing. ALS. DLC–JKP. Introduces Evans Rogers, "an eminent merchant" of Philadelphia and "a tried Democrat of the old school."

13 Jan     From Richard French et al. LS. DLC–JKP. Recommend the appointment of William O. Butler of Kentucky to be secretary of war.

13 Jan     From Samuel H. Huntington. ALS. DLC–JKP. Solicits Polk's autograph.

*13 Jan*     *From Cave Johnson.*

*13 Jan*     *From Samuel H. Laughlin.*

13 Jan     From Ambrose H. Sevier. ALS. DLC–JKP. Urges the appointment of Robert J. Walker to be Treasury secretary.

14 Jan       From Joseph B. Boyd. ALS. DLC–JKP. Requests autograph of "the tenth President of the Republic."

14 Jan       From Henry Finck. L. DLC–AJD. Solicits appointment as U.S. consul at Ludwigsburg in the Kingdom of Württemberg.

14 Jan       From J. G. M. Ramsey. ALS. DLC–JKP. Suggests that Polk appoint persons who have made "solid attainments both in science & literature" because "the great *republic of letters* has been signally neglected especially under some of our Administrations."

14 Jan       From George D. Strong. ALS. DLC–JKP. Predicts that Polk will be called upon to serve a second term; notes that the "fence politicians" in New York are coming to the support of Texas annexation.

14 Jan       From Israel K. Tefft. ALS. DLC–JKP. Informs Polk that he has been named an honorary member of the Georgia Historical Society.

15 Jan       From Timothy Hoskins. ALS. DLC–JKP. Suggests that Henry Hubbard be named to a position in Polk's cabinet.

15 Jan       From John Rowan, Jr., et al. LS. DLC–JKP. Invite Polk to visit Bardstown, Ky., on his forthcoming journey to Washington City.

15 Jan       From Daniel B. Tallmadge. ALS. DLC–JKP. States that Robert J. Walker would make an excellent Treasury secretary, for he is well acquainted with both northern and southern views on the tariff.

16 Jan       From Shepard Cary. ALS. DLC–JKP. Urges Maine's claims for having a cabinet appointment and recommends Nathan Weston for the office of attorney general.

*16 Jan*       *From Amos Nourse.*

*17 Jan*       *From Aaron V. Brown.*

17 Jan       From Francis B. Fogg. ALS. DLC–JKP. Requests that Polk reply to a suit filed in favor of Sarah Hawkins Polk for recovery of her interest in a tract of land in Tennessee's Western District.

17 Jan       From Nathaniel Gammon. ALS. DLC–JKP. Solicits a clerkship in one of the departments of the general government.

17 Jan       From Thomas Martin. ALS. DLC–JKP. Regrets that he must decline Polk's invitation to accompany him on his forthcoming trip to Washington City.

17 Jan       From H. C. Meriam. ALS. DLC–JKP. States that the "agricultural press of this Country now includes about sixty different papers" and recommends that Polk write a short essay on agricultural interests for publication in those newspapers, which are non-partisan and eager to publish the views of eminent public men.

*17 Jan*       *From John M. Niles.*

| | |
|---|---|
| 17 Jan | From James G. Read et al. LS. DLC–JKP. Invite Polk to visit Jeffersonville, Ind. |
| 17 Jan | From Daniel Sturgeon. ALS. DLC–JKP. Recommends Robert J. Walker to be secretary of the Treasury. |
| *17 Jan* | *From Cornelius P. Van Ness.* |
| 18 Jan | From Francis P. Blair. ALS. DLC–JKP. Argues that appointing William H. Roane to the postmastership of Richmond, Va., in place of Claiborne W. Gooch would be regarded as an act of retributive justice by the Virginia Democracy. |
| 18 Jan | From L. Y. Craig. ALS. DLC–JKP. Relates that the pair of bay horses in Lexington are available for Polk's purchase and can be delivered to him in Louisville upon his arrival there. |
| 18 Jan | From James L. English. ALS. DLC–JKP. Urges Polk to moderate the "violent party spirit" that has been excited during the past twenty years and that has been so destructive to public morals and honest government. |
| 18 Jan | From Ransom H. Gillet. ALS. DLC–JKP. States that although his friends in New York have urged him to apply for the position of postmaster general, he would prefer an appointment connected with his profession, such as solicitor of the Treasury. |
| 18 Jan | From E. S. Haines. ALS. DLC–JKP. Introduces the bearer, Thomas D. Jones; states that Jones is a "young, self taught artist" of Cincinnati who wishes to model a bust of Polk. |
| *18 Jan* | *From Cave Johnson.* |
| *18 Jan* | *To John Schnierle.* |
| 18 Jan | From William A. Spark. ALS. DLC–JKP. Recommends the appointment of John Y. Mason to a place in Polk's cabinet. |
| 18 Jan | From M. B. Townsend. LS. DLC–JKP. Urges the appointment to Polk's cabinet of either Nathan Weston or John Fairfield. |
| *18 Jan* | *From Martin Van Buren.* |
| 19 Jan | From William B. Barry. ALS. DLC–JKP. Introduces Thomas D. Jones, a young Cincinnati artist wishing to take a bust of the "Peoples President." |
| 20 Jan | From Robert Armstrong. ALS. DLC–JKP. Introduces Beverly L. Clarke and George D. Blakey of Kentucky, who wish to urge the appointment of their friend, Elijah Hise, to federal office. |
| 20 Jan | From John Chaney et al. NS. DLC–JKP. Urge Polk to appoint Robert J. Walker to a seat in the cabinet. |
| 20 Jan | From Adeline Deaderick. ALS. DLC–JKP. Recalls hearing Polk speak of the favor her father, Ephraim McDowell, had done him; notes that she and Polk are related; and requests that her husband, James W. Deaderick, be appointed to the superintendency of Indian affairs at St. Louis, Mo. |

| | |
|---|---|
| *20 Jan* | *From Alexander Duncan.* |
| 20 Jan | From John S. Geyer. ALS. DLC–JKP. Urges Polk to support legislation granting indemnity for the French spoliations on American commerce prior to 1800. |
| *20 Jan* | *From Duff Green.* |
| 20 Jan | From John H. Harney. ALS. DLC–JKP. Recommends Elijah Hise of Kentucky to be U.S. attorney general. |
| 20 Jan | From Thomas J. Kelly. ALS. DLC–JKP. Relates that Young Stephenson, captain of the steamboat *Champion* and "one of the very few Democratic Steam Boat Captains to be found on our rivers," has offered to take Polk and his party from Smithland to Cincinnati. |
| 20 Jan | From John L. O'Sullivan. ALS. DLC–JKP. Requests that Polk resubmit the name of William H. Polk to be chargé at Naples; suggests that his name should not be given further consideration for that appointment. |
| *20 Jan* | *To Thomas Sherlock et al.* |
| [20 Jan 1845] | From John S. Skinner. ALS. DLC–JKP. Encloses a report of the Committee on Foreign Relations to the Senate of the Republic of Texas; explains that it places "in some new lights, the mutual advantages of immediate annexation." |
| 20 Jan | From Joseph A. Wright. ALS. DLC–JKP. Encloses a letter from Samuel Milroy of Indiana recommending Robert J. Walker to be appointed Treasury secretary. |
| 21 Jan | From Charles Mason et al. NS. Ia–HA. Recommend James Clarke of Burlington, Iowa Territory, to be U.S. marshal. |
| 21 Jan | From Roderick Murchison. ALS. DLC–JKP. Invites Polk to visit Jefferson, N.C., should he travel to Washington City via Raleigh. |
| 21 Jan | From F. N. Nicholas. ALS. DLC–JKP. Recommends appointment of Joel Pennybacker of Shenandoah County, Va., to a post in the general government. |
| [21 Jan 1845] | From S. H. Parker. ALS. DLC–JKP. Urges appointment of Joel Pennybacker to a post in the general government. |
| 21 Jan | From Robert A. Thompson. ALS. DLC–JKP. States that Joel Pennybacker served in the Virginia legislature with distinction and would render faithful service in the general government if appointed to office. |
| *21 Jan* | *From Silas Wright, Jr.* |
| 22 Jan | From Silas M. Caldwell. ALS. DLC–JKP. Requests assistance in settling some debts his son, James M. Caldwell, has incurred in Columbia; states that he has returned Polk's slave, Gilbert, to the farm at an expense of eighteen dollars. |
| *22 Jan* | *From Cave Johnson.* |
| 23 Jan | From James Russell. ALS. DLC–JKP. Recommends Marcus Morton for a place in Polk's cabinet. |
| 23 Jan | From James Wilkins. ALS. DLC–JKP. Asks if Polk wishes to |

|  |  |
|---|---|
| | retain his services as steward at the White House; encloses a recommendation from John Tyler. |
| [24 Jan 1845] | From L. R. Fish. LS. DLC–JKP. Requests that Polk accept a hat to be worn at his inaugural; states that he wishes to show Orlando Fish, also of New York City, that he can make "as good a Hat as he can and for as good a purpose, he having made one for Hon Mr Clay." |
| 24 Jan | From Thomas Ford. ALS. DLC–JKP. Introduces Edmund Roberts of Illinois, "a firm and consistent member of the democratic party." |
| 24 Jan | From Daniel Kenney. ALS. DLC–JKP. States that he does not wish to stand for reelection to the Tennessee House; requests that Polk consider him for any position Polk might judge suitable. |
| 24 Jan | From John B. Macy. ALS. DLC–JKP. Encloses recommendation from John Chaney and the Democratic members of the Ohio legislature urging Robert J. Walker's appointment to a place in the cabinet. |
| 24 Jan | From J. D. Test et al. LS. DLC–JKP. Invite Polk to honorary membership in the Athenian Society of Indiana University. |
| 24 Jan | From George B. Walker et al. LS. DLC–JKP. Urge Polk to spend a few hours in Evansville, Ind., on his trip to Washington City for the inaugural. |
| 24 Jan | From Taylor Webster et al. LS. DLC–JKP. Request that Polk visit Hamilton, Ohio, on his journey to Washington. |
| *[25 Jan 1845]* | *From Aaron V. Brown.* |
| *25 Jan* | *From Jacob L. Martin.* |
| 25 Jan | From Gayton P. Osgood. ALS. DLC–JKP. Maintains that Massachusetts Democrats support Marcus Morton despite his refusal to dismiss Whig office holders when he became governor in 1843. |
| 26 Jan | From Richard E. Byrd. ALS. DLC–JKP. Denounces Washington G. Singleton, also of Winchester, Va., for circulating a letter slanderous of his private as well as his political character. |
| 26 Jan | From Alexander Newman et al. LS. DLC–JKP. Recommend John Y. Mason for a place in Polk's cabinet. |
| 26 Jan | From John Norvell. ALS. DLC–JKP. Introduces Mathew Johnson, a former member of the Ohio legislature and "one of your warmest democratic friends." |
| 27 Jan | From Aaron Vanderpoel. ALS. DLC–JKP. Urges Polk to ignore slanders said to be circulating about the character of Churchill C. Cambreleng; holds that Cambreleng knows more about "men & things" than any other man in New York City who may be under consideration for a place in Polk's cabinet. |
| *28 Jan* | *From William C. Campbell.* |

| | |
|---|---|
| 28 Jan | From William R. King. ALS. DLC–JKP. Introduces his friend, Rufus Prince of New York City. |
| 28 Jan | From James K. Paulding. ALS. DLC–JKP. Warns Polk against appointing Fitzgerald Tasistro to a position in the new administration. |
| 28 Jan | From Thomas J. Read et al. LS. DLC–JKP. Inform Polk of arrangements worked out between the Louisville and Cincinnati committees appointed to escort the president-elect from the one city to the other. |
| *29 Jan* | *From Aaron V. Brown.* |
| 29 Jan | From John Davis. ALS. DLC–JKP. Congratulates Polk on his election to the presidency. |
| 29 Jan | From A. J. Fanning. ALS. DLC–JKP. Informs Polk of his election to honorary membership in the Apollonian Literary Society of Franklin College, located near Nashville, Tennessee. |
| 29 Jan | From Tolbert Fanning. ALS. DLC–JKP. Encloses a circular describing the agricultural education offered at his recently established Franklin College, which has sixty students and a full faculty. |
| 29 Jan | From Memucan Hunt Howard. ALS. DLC–JKP. Recommends Wilson Defendorf, an active member of New York City's Empire Club, to receive an appointment in the customs house or to some situation in Washington City. |
| 29 Jan | From Andrew Jackson. ALS. DLC–JKP. Recommends continuance and advancement of William Darby, formerly of New Orleans and currently a subordinate clerk in one of the government offices in Washington City. |
| 29 Jan | From John K. Kane. ALS. DLC–JKP. Expresses the high regard in which Romulus M. Saunders of North Carolina is held by the Democrats of Pennsylvania. |
| *30 Jan* | *To George Bancroft.* |
| *30 Jan* | *To Martin Van Buren.* |
| 31 Jan | From Anonymous. L, signed "John Price." DLC–JKP. Promotes the use of a patent fertility tonic available from his residence in New Orleans. |
| 31 Jan | From Anonymous. L, signed "John Price." DLC–JKP. Suggests that great fortunes may be made speculating in Texas debt. |
| [31 Jan 1845] | From Alfred Balch. ALS. DLC–JKP. Regrets that he cannot accompany Polk to Washington City; explains that unexpected litigation will require that he remain in Nashville for court proceedings on March 3, 1845. |
| 31 Jan | From Benjamin V. French. ALS. DLC–JKP. Prefers Marcus Morton over any other applicant for office from Massachusetts. |
| 31 Jan | From William Murray. ALS. DLC–JKP. Congratulates Polk |

|  | on his election. |
|---|---|
| [Feb 1845] | From John A. Bolles et al. LS. DLC–JKP. Recommend Marcus Morton for a place in the cabinet; note the unanimity of Massachusetts' 55,000 Democrats in urging Morton's appointment. |
| [Feb 1845] | From Joseph Boulanger. ALS. DLC–JKP. Applies for the position of White House steward. |
| [Feb 1845] | From Matthew Buchanan. ALS. DLC–JKP. Urges retention of Abraham B. Morton as register of public lands at Clinton, Mo.; worries that Thomas H. Benton will attempt to have Morton removed. |
| [Feb 1845] | From James Craig et al. LS. DLC–JKP. Recommend John B. Brown for appointment as receiver of public monies at Johnson Court House, Ark. |
| [Feb 1845] | From Andrew J. Donelson. L, fragment. DLC–JKP. Advises Polk on the future appointment of William G. Childress to office. |
| [Feb 1845] | From William A. Hayes et al. NS. DLC–LW. Request that Bradbury C. Bartlett be named naval agent for the naval yard at Portsmouth, N.H. |
| [Feb 1845] | From Reuben H. Hine et al. NS. DLC–JKP. Urge William L. Marcy's appointment as Treasury secretary. |
| [Feb 1845] | From Selah R. Hobbie. N. DLC–JKP. Solicits a personal interview to discuss arrangements for printing and distributing Polk's inaugural address in a timely way. |
| [Feb 1845] | From Charles D. Hoyt. ALS. DLC–JKP. Offers to sell the finest pair of family coach horses in the state of New York. |
| [Feb 1845] | From Littleberry H. Mosby. ALS. DLC–JKP. Desires to be retained as postmaster of Louisville, Ky. |
| [Feb 1845] | From A. H. Palmer. ALS. DNA–RG 26. States that Ezra Wilson is one of the oldest citizens of Defiance, Ohio, and would be the best choice for keeper of the light house in Cleveland harbor. |
| [Feb 1845] | From Asa Redington, Jr. ALS. DLC–JKP. Recommends Nathan Weston of Maine to be appointed U.S. attorney general. |
| *1 Feb* | *From Andrew J. Donelson.* |
| 1 Feb | From Andrew Jackson, Jr. ALS. DLC–JKP. Introduces James Taggart and wife of Washington City; mentions that Mrs. (Jane) Taggart is a sister of his wife (Sarah York Jackson). |
| 1 Feb | From John C. Mason et al. LS. DLC–JKP. Joins the undersigned Democratic members of the Kentucky legislature in urging Polk to visit Frankfort on his forthcoming journey to Washington City. |
| 1 Feb | From Ralph R. Wormeley. ALS. DLC–JKP. Hopes that in his inaugural address Polk will urge his countrymen to pay |

their foreign debts and so retrieve the honor of the debtor states and the Union as well.

3 Feb    From Andrew Jackson. ALS. DLC–JKP. Introduces Andrew J. Smith and supports his bid to be named U.S. consul at Havana; recalls that young Smith's father, David, fought in the battle of New Orleans.

[3 Feb 1845]    *From Cave Johnson.*

3 Feb    *From Dutee J. Pearce.*

3 Feb    From William S. Pickett. LS. DLC–JKP. Encloses an account of the sale of 101 bales of cotton; credits to Polk's account the sum of $2,127.44; and promises a further accounting when he has sold the remaining 28 bales.

3 Feb    From Thomas J. Read. ALS. DLC–JKP. Urges retention and promotion of George Gilless, a clerk in the Fourth Auditor's office of the Treasury Department.

3 Feb    From Richard M. Young. ALS. DLC–JKP. Introduces Peter Sweat of Peoria, Ill.

4 Feb    From Edward Burke. ALS. DLC–JKP. Tenders his services for refurnishing the presidential mansion, which he is led to believe is "in a dilapidated condition"; explains that he assisted a similar undertaking when Martin Van Buren went into office and retained the house plans used in that work.

4 Feb    *From John Catron.*

4 Feb    From Edwin Croswell. ALS. DLC–JKP. Recommends Gansevoort Melville to be U.S. marshal for the Southern District of New York; maintains that Melville possesses the ability and enjoys the support required for the position.

4 Feb    From Solomon Hillen, Jr. L, copy. MdHi. Presents the name of William Frick to be appointed collector of the customs at Baltimore; explains that Frick, an appointee of Martin Van Buren, lost that post solely for political reasons when the Whigs came to power in 1841.

4 Feb    From John K. Kane. ALS. DLC–JKP. Commends "to executive favor" Edward Worrell of Wilmington, Del.

[4 Feb 1845]    From William T. Leacock. ALS. DLC–JKP. Regrets that he cannot pay his respects when Polk visits Louisville, Ky.; explains that illness prevents his going out.

4 Feb    *From Nathaniel C. Read.*

5 Feb    From Preserved Fish and Cornelius W. Lawrence. NS. DLC–JKP. Support retention of John L. Graham as New York City postmaster; prefer Jonathan I. Coddington for that post should it become vacant.

5 Feb    From Andrew Jackson. ALS. DLC–JKP. Introduces Arthur P. Hayne, a brother of the late Robert Y. Hayne.

5 Feb    From Walter H. Overton. ALS. DLC–JKP. Introduces his neighbor, "Judge Brewer," of Alexandria, La.

5 Feb    From William S. Pickett. LS. DLC–JKP. Fears that a further

|         | improvement in cotton prices cannot be established on the basis of recent orders from Europe; states that he will hold the balance of Polk's shipment in hopes that delay will bring a higher price. |
|---------|---|
| *5 Feb* | *From John F. Ryland.* |
| 6 Feb   | From Robert H. Ball et al. LS. DLC–JKP. Invite Polk to visit the citizens of Covington, Ky. |
| 6 Feb   | From Andrew Billings et al. NS. DLC–JKP. Joins the undersigned Democratic members of the New York legislature in urging the appointment of William L. Marcy to the position of Treasury secretary in the new administration. |
| *6 Feb* | *From John P. Campbell.* |
| 6 Feb   | From Thomas Irwin. ALS. DLC–JKP. States that Democrats in Pittsburgh and western Pennsylvania hold Robert J. Walker in high regard and urge his appointment to Polk's cabinet. |
| 6 Feb   | From J. G. M. Ramsey. ALS. DLC–JKP. Recommends Hugh G. Crozier of Coffeeville, Miss., to be named U.S. marshal for northern Mississippi. |
| 6 Feb   | From D. A. Sarredas. N. DLC–JKP. Invites Polk and his suite to attend the National Theatre of Cincinnati. |
| 6 Feb   | From George C. Welker. ALS. DLC–JKP. Encloses resolution of the National Johnson Club's meeting at Philadelphia on November 20, 1844; asks that Polk offer Richard M. Johnson the post of secretary of war. |
| 7 Feb   | From William F. Coplan et al. LS. DLC–JKP. Invite Polk to visit and remain over night in Brownsville, Penn. |
| *7 Feb* | *From Andrew Jackson.* |
| 7 Feb   | From Andrew Jackson. ALS. DNA–RG 56. Introduces Frederick Derrive; wishes Polk well in carrying out "your own well digested views in forming your cabinet." |
| *7 Feb* | *From Miner K. Kellogg.* |
| 7 Feb   | From Nicholas Martin, Jr. ALS. MdHi. Notes that William Frick, with whom he served in the Maryland Senate, traversed the whole state in Polk's behalf during the presidential canvass; prefers to see Frick returned to his old office of collector of the port of Baltimore. |
| *7 Feb* | *From Gorham Parks.* |
| 7 Feb   | From John A. Rogers. ALS. DLC–JKP. Offers general advice on Polk's selection of advisers and office holders. |
| 7 Feb   | From William A. Spark. ALS. DLC–JKP. Encloses letter signed by the Democratic members of the Virginia legislature (Alexander Newman et al. to Polk, January 26, 1845). |
| 8 Feb   | From N. D. Coleman. ALS. DLC–JKP. Regrets that the press of business in Vicksburg, Miss., prevented his meeting Polk at Louisville and going with him to Washington City. |
| *8 Feb* | *From Andrew Jackson.* |

8 Feb         From Edward P. Scott. ALS. DLC–JKP. Desires that John
              Y. Mason be retained in Polk's cabinet.
*9 Feb*       *To Cave Johnson.*
9 Feb         From T. L. Smith. ALS. DLC–JKP. Suggests that Polk ap-
              point to his cabinet all the popular and influential men con-
              sidered for the presidential nomination at the last conven-
              tion.
*10 Feb*      *From George Bancroft.*
10 Feb        From John F. H. Claiborne.    ALS. DLC–JKP. Accuses
              William M. Gwin of having defrauded his creditors; urges
              Polk not to appoint Gwin to public office.
*10 Feb*      *From Levin H. Coe.*
10 Feb        From William Frick et al. LS. DLC–JKP. Communicate on
              behalf of a meeting of Baltimore Democrats their offer to
              accompany Polk from the Relay House to the City.
10 Feb        From Francis R. Shunk. ALS. DLC–JKP. Commends Henry
              Simpson of Philadelphia to Polk's notice for an appoint-
              ment in the customs house.
*10 Feb*      *From Martin Van Buren.*
10 Feb        From Philo White. ALS. DLC–JKP. Relates that he has set-
              tled in Racine, Wisconsin Territory, although his heart re-
              mains in North Carolina.
10 Feb        From Richard M. Young. ALS. DLC–JKP. Introduces Calvin
              A. Warren of Quincy, Illinois.
11 Feb        From John D. Dilworth et al. LS. DLC–JKP. Communicate
              a resolution adopted by the Democratic party of New Castle
              County, Delaware, who urge the appointment of James A.
              Bayard as attorney general of the United States.
11 Feb        From Samuel Fessenden. LS. DLC–JKP. Requests at the di-
              rection of a mass meeting of citizens of Portland, Me., that
              Polk conduct all activities of the new administration "with-
              out the presentation" of intoxicating drinks.
*11 Feb*      *From William D. Moseley.*
*11 Feb*      *From Martin Van Buren.*
12 Feb        From N. S. Benton. ALS. DLC–JKP. Recommends William
              L. Marcy of New York to be secretary of the Treasury.
12 Feb        From John B. Butler. ALS. DLC–JKP. Regrets that the re-
              ception committee from Pittsburgh, Penn., did not meet
              Polk at Wheeling; explains that they did not have proper
              information respecting the progress of Polk's journey.
12 Feb        From Edward A. Hannegan et al. NS. DLC–JKP. Joins the
              undersigned members of Congress from Indiana in recom-
              mending the appointment of Robert J. Walker as Treasury
              secretary.
12 Feb        From Robert H. Morris. ALS. DLC–JKP. Introduces a Mr.
              Bramson "for the purpose of exhibiting the extraordinary
              musical tallent of a young daughter of his."

| | |
|---|---|
| 12 Feb | From James C. O'Reilly. ALS. DLC–JKP. Introduces Abraham Sulger of New York, son of Jacob Sulger, Jr., of Philadelphia. |
| *12 Feb* | *From David Petrikin.* |
| 12 Feb | From Francis E. Rives. ALS. DLC–JKP. States that John Y. Mason would be the most popular choice of Virginians should Polk name one of their statesmen to his cabinet. |
| 12 Feb | From Ottis Scott. L. MdHi. Concurs with William Frick's many friends who urge his appointment as collector of customs at Baltimore. |
| 12 Feb | From Ether Shepley. ALS. DLC–JKP. Introduces Amos Nourse of Maine. |
| 12 Feb | From Daniel Smith. ALS. DLC–JKP. Forwards letter addressed to Polk at Uniontown, Penn. |
| *[12 Feb 1845]* | *From Laura Wilson Polk Tate.* |
| 13 Feb | From Calvin T. Chamberlain et al. NS. DLC–JKP. Joins the undersigned members of the New York Senate in urging the appointment of William L. Marcy to the cabinet as Treasury secretary. |
| 13 Feb | From John Chaney et al. LS. DLC–LW. Joins other Democratic members of the Ohio legislature in recommending William Medill to a post in Polk's administration. |
| 13 Feb | From Mrs. Connor. N. DLC–JKP. Offers her house on Missouri Avenue in Washington City for rent by Polk or his friends. |
| 13 Feb | From Ralph I. Ingersoll. ALS. DLC–JKP. Introduces his brother, Charles A. Ingersoll of New Haven, Conn. |
| 13 Feb | From Thomas J. W. Pray et al. LS. DLC–JKP. Urge at the behest of the New Hampshire State Temperance Convention that Polk not follow the practices of his predecessors in serving intoxicating wines and liquors in the President's House. |
| 13 Feb | From T. Booth Roberts et al. LS. DLC–JKP. Communicate a resolution on Texas annexation as adopted at a mass meeting of Democratic citizens at Wilmington, Del.; note that this endorsement was accidentally omitted from the proceedings of the meeting as published in the Wilmington *Delaware Gazette*. |
| 13 Feb | From John R. Waterman. ALS. DNA–RG 59. Offers to provide information about prospective appointees from his native state of Rhode Island; notes that he previously served several years in the state legislature and in the customs house at Providence. |
| 14 Feb | From John K. Kane. ALS. DLC–JKP. Introduces Francis Wharton of Philadelphia, "one of the most cherished members of our young Pennsylvania Democracy." |
| 14 Feb | From P. M. Marvel. ALS. DLC–JKP. Communicates a |

|          |                                                                                                                                                                                                                                          |
|----------|------------------------------------------------------------------------------------------------------------------------------------------------------------------------------------------------------------------------------------------|
|          | memorial from the Democratic members of the Massachusetts legislature.                                                                                                                                                                   |
| 14 Feb   | From Archibald C. Niven. ALS. DLC–JKP. Recommends William L. Marcy to be named Treasury secretary.                                                                                                                                        |
| *14 Feb* | *From Stephen C. Pavatt.*                                                                                                                                                                                                                 |
| 14 Feb   | From Enoch Tucker & Son. AN. DLC–JKP. Request an appointment to take Polk's measurements for an inaugural coat; explain that they had received an order for the work from a New York merchant last September but that they wished to check their earlier measurements before doing the work. |
| *15 Feb* | *From Andrew J. Donelson.*                                                                                                                                                                                                                |
| *15 Feb* | *From Andrew Jackson.*                                                                                                                                                                                                                    |
| *15 Feb* | *From Albert G. Jewett.*                                                                                                                                                                                                                  |
| 15 Feb   | From Richard K. Meade. ALS. DLC–JKP. Claims that he knows the sentiments of his fellow Virginians and that they would prefer the appointment of John Y. Mason to Polk's cabinet.                                                          |
| 15 Feb   | From Frank Nokes. ALS. DLC–JKP. Recalls that he served previously as Polk's hackman and asks that he be named driver of Polk's private carriage.                                                                                          |
| *15 Feb* | *From John L. O'Sullivan.*                                                                                                                                                                                                                |
| 15 Feb   | From James Page. ALS. DLC–JKP. Introduces George Follin and Ambrose W. Thompson of Philadelphia.                                                                                                                                          |
| *15 Feb* | *From William Wilson Polk.*                                                                                                                                                                                                               |
| 15 Feb   | From Charles Stewart. ALS. DLC–JKP. Urges retention of John Y. Mason as secretary of the navy; notes that within the previous four years the department has had six different secretaries.                                                |
| *15 Feb* | *From Martin Van Buren.*                                                                                                                                                                                                                  |
| 15 Feb   | From Campbell P. White. ALS. DLC–JKP. Introduces his son, John C. White, who with his sisters will visit Washington for the inauguration.                                                                                                 |
| 15 Feb   | From John T. H. Worthington. L. MdHi. Recommends the appointment of William Frick to be customs collector at Baltimore.                                                                                                                   |
| 16 Feb   | From Hugh J. Anderson. LS. DLC–JKP. Transmits a resolution adopted at the January 29 meeting of the Maine Temperance Union; urges Polk's support for "this truly philanthropic enterprise" (exclusion of intoxicating drinks from use at the inaugural festivities and at the executive mansion during his term of office). |
| 17 Feb   | From Anonymous. L, signed "A Son of New York Sed Amicus Patriae." DLC–JKP. Suggests that Lewis H. Sanford would be a suitable choice for the head of the Treasury Department. |
| *17 Feb* | *To James Buchanan.*                                                                                                                                                                                                                      |

| | |
|---|---|
| 17 Feb | From George Ford. ALS. Polk Memorial Association, Columbia. Solicits position as Polk's body servant; states that he serves as "an assistant to the messenger in the Bureau of Construction of the Navy Department." |
| *17 Feb* | *From William M. Gouge.* |
| 17 Feb | From Rufus McIntire. ALS. DLC–JKP. Details factional splits in Maine and relates same to forthcoming patronage appointments. |
| *17 Feb* | *From Thomas Ritchie.* |
| 17 Feb | From William H. H. Taylor. ALS. DLC–JKP. Explains that his clerks in the Cincinnati post office failed to give him correct information about Polk's arrival date there; regrets that he did not return from South Bend, Ind., in time to welcome Polk to the city. |
| 17 Feb | From Ambrose W. Thompson and George Follin. LS. DLC–JKP. Regret that they have to leave Washington City without first calling to pay their respects. |
| 17 Feb | From R. Wood. ALS. DLC–JKP. Requests Polk's autograph as a reward for campaign labors in West Haverford, Penn. |
| *18 Feb* | *From William C. Bouck.* |
| *18 Feb* | *From James Buchanan.* |
| 18 Feb | From Mary Burden. ALS. DLC–JKP. Implores Polk's charity to help her fend off creditors in St. Louis. |
| *18 Feb* | *From Edwin Croswell.* |
| *18 Feb* | *From Amos Lane.* |
| 18 Feb | From Thomas J. Read. ALS. DLC–JKP. Introduces Lucien B. Howe of Millersburg, Ill. |
| 18 Feb | From Aaron Vanderpoel. ALS. DLC–JKP. Commends to Polk's favorable notice Joshua Dodge, who was for several years employed by the general government "to secure the introduction of our tobacco in Germany & other portions of Europe, without the onerous duties with which it is charged." |
| 18 Feb | From John C. Wright. ALS. DLC–JKP. Adds his recommendation to others from members of the New York legislature in favor of William L. Marcy's appointment to a seat in Polk's cabinet. |
| 19 Feb | From John Baten. ALS. T–JKP. Solicits position as White House gardener; offers to send references from fellow citizens of Norristown, Penn. |
| 19 Feb | From Robert Keyworth. AN. DLC–JKP. Presents Polk a gold pen and requests its use when Polk signs his first official document. |
| 19 Feb | From Thomas C. Legate. ALS. DLC–JKP. Recommends Robert Thompson to be postmaster of Galena, Ill. |
| 19 Feb | From Felix G. McConnell. LS. DLC–JKP. Introduces John Willingman, applicant for the post of White House steward. |

| | |
|---|---|
| [19 Feb 1845] | From John and Julia Gardiner Tyler. N. DLC–JKP. Invite the Polks to dine at the White House. |
| 19 Feb | To Robert J. Walker. LS, draft. DLC–JKP. Offers Walker the post of attorney general; cancels signature and specific reference to the attorney generalship. |
| 20 Feb | From Ezekiel Brown. ALS. DLC–JKP. Quotes passage from a letter from Robert A. Linn of Sussex County, N.J., recommending Daniel Haines to be appointed U.S. minister to China. |
| 20 Feb | From John Galbraith. ALS. DLC–JKP. Introduces Murray Whallon, a lawyer from Erie, Penn. |
| 20 Feb | From Ralph I. Ingersoll. ALS. DLC–JKP. Introduces Norris Willcot of New Haven, Conn. |
| 20 Feb | From Henry Pirtle. ALS. DLC–JKP. Urges retention of Littleberry H. Mosby as postmaster of Louisville, Ky.; states that Mosby is "a quiet gentleman who has not meddled in the political strife in the slightest manner." |
| 20 Feb | From John A. Rogers. ALS. DLC–JKP. Recommends the employment of John Willingman as White House steward. |
| 20 Feb | From Jeremiah Russell et al. NS. DLC–JKP. Joins ten other Democratic members of Congress from New York in recommending William L. Marcy for a place in Polk's cabinet. |
| 20 Feb | From John Scott. ALS. DLC–JKP. Recalls how his Masonic affiliation and support of Indian removal resulted in his being set aside by the voters in his bid for reelection to Congress in 1831. |
| 20 Feb | From Aaron Vanderpoel. ALS. DLC–JKP. Introduces his nephew, Isaac Vanderpoel, who comes to Washington City to witness the inauguration, not to seek a job. |
| 20 Feb | From Amos E. Wood. ALS. DLC–JKP. Suggests that Polk ignore the patronage claims of the former office holders from Ohio and appoint first rate applicants who have never held office before; asserts that rotation in office is "necessary for the well being of our principles and party." |
| 21 Feb | From John Chaney. ALS. DLC–LW. Recalls the public record of William Medill as a member and Speaker of the Ohio House; advises that Medill's appointment "to some suitable and respectable situation" would be well received by Ohio Democrats. |
| 21 Feb | From John A. Gareschi. ALS. DLC–JKP. Informs Polk that he has been elected an honorary member of the Calocagathian Society of St. Mary's College in Baltimore. |
| *21 Feb* | *From Joseph Hall.* |
| *21 Feb* | *From John P. Heiss.* |
| *21 Feb* | *From Peter T. Homer.* |
| 21 Feb | From William G. McNeill. ALS. DLC–JKP. Urges the appointment of William Coventry H. Waddell of New York to |

|          | the post of Treasury secretary. |
|----------|----------------------------------|
| 21 Feb | From William E. Paxton. ALS. DLC–JKP. Informs Polk of his election to honorary membership in the Ciceronian Society of Georgetown College in Kentucky. |
| 21 Feb | From Arnold Plumer. ALS. DLC–JKP. Renews his previous suggestion that James Buchanan be named secretary of state; asserts that "ninety nine out of a hundred in Penna. would be gratified with his appointment." |
| 21 Feb | From George W. Samson et al. NS. DLC–JKP. Invite Polk to attend a concert of sacred music to be given at the E Street Baptist Church on Monday evening next. |
| 21 Feb | From Martin Van Buren. ALS. DLC–JKP. Introduces Theodore Fisk of New York City. |
| 22 Feb | From George M. Dallas. ALS. DLC–JKP. Encloses papers relating to the refurbishing of the White House (enclosures not found); recommends the Philadelphia firm of Bailey & Kitchen, "perhaps the best providers in their line of business in the United States." |
| 22 Feb | From Thomas Delong. ALS. DLC–JKP. Claims that he spent $400 campaigning for Polk in Oswego Co., N.Y., and asks reimbursement for his expenses. |
| *22 Feb* | *From John W. Edmonds.* |
| 22 Feb | From Moor N. Falls. ALS. DLC–JKP. Relates that he has just returned to Baltimore from Philadelphia where he examined and tried a pair of bay horses priced at $500 plus shipping; requests instructions. |
| 22 Feb | From John Hamm. ALS. DLC–JKP. Introduces Joseph H. Larwell, a member of the Ohio Senate from Wooster. |
| 22 Feb | From Arthur P. Hayne. ALS. DLC–JKP. Encloses letter of introduction (Andrew Jackson to Polk, February 5, 1845); recounts story of the last visit between Jackson and his brother, Robert Y. Hayne. |
| *22 Feb* | *From Andrew Jackson.* |
| 22 Feb | From John Jameson et al. LS. DLC–JKP. Recommend John W. Keenan of Missouri as messenger for the presidential mansion. |
| 22 Feb | From William Kerr. ALS. DLC–JKP. Requests that Polk hand to the next secretary of the navy the enclosed statement on lightning conductors. |
| 22 Feb | From Samuel Medary. ALS. DLC–JKP. Introduces Joseph H. Larwell and Rudolphus Dickinson of Ohio; thinks that both are known to Polk personally. |
| 22 Feb | From Rembrandt Peale. ALS. DLC–JKP. Commends Polk for his recent statement that he wished to be president of all the people and not of a party. |
| 22 Feb | From Selah B. Strong. ALS. DLC–JKP. Requests that if William L. Marcy is not chosen for a place in the cabinet, |

Polk would appoint Selah R. Hobbie to the postmaster generalship.

| | |
|---|---|
| *22 Feb* | *To Martin Van Buren.* |
| *23 Feb* | *From James Hamilton, Jr.* |
| 23 Feb | From Ambrose H. Sevier. ALS. DLC–JKP. Asks that no Arkansas patronage be awarded until he and Polk have had an opportunity to discuss the appointments. |
| 24 Feb | From William G. Angel. ALS. DLC–JKP. Recalls their friendship in Congress and congratulates Polk on his election. |
| 24 Feb | From Richard B. Carmichael. ALS. DLC–JKP. Commends Polk for his Nashville speech. |
| *[24 Feb 1845]* | *From John Catron.* |
| 24 Feb | From William Ford. ALS. DLC–JKP. Recommends the appointment of his friend, Benjamin F. Butler, to a place in the cabinet. |
| 24 Feb | From William Grason. L. DLC–JKP. Asks that Polk appoint William Frick collector of the port at Baltimore, a position held by Frick until his removal by John Tyler in 1841. |
| *24 Feb* | *From Russell Jarvis.* |
| 24 Feb | From Louis Leclerc. LS. DLC–JKP. Recalls getting up the French Meeting in New York City last October 30; wishes to be invited to Polk's inauguration. |
| 24 Feb | From John Y. Mason. ALS. DLC–JKP. Introduces Nicholas Gee, "a first rate dining room servant, and a most accomplished coachman." |
| 24 Feb | From Robert H. Miller. ALS. DLC–JKP. States that although he has signed applications for office from members of the Ohio congressional delegation, he urges that none be given appointments, for they have had "sufficient favors already." |
| 24 Feb | From James H. Piper. ALS. DLC–JKP. Says that the Virginia legislature will adjourn soon, that he will go home and then to Washington City, and that he awaits further indications of Polk's pleasure as to his future duties. |
| 24 Feb | From Jeremiah Russell. ALS. DLC–JKP. Recommends retention of Charles A. Wickliffe as postmaster general. |
| 24 Feb | From Francis R. Shunk. ALS. DLC–JKP. Notes that all of the aspirants for the postmastership at Pittsburgh are his friends; thinks that Chambers McKibbin's appointment to that post will be acceptable. |
| *24 Feb* | *From Joel B. Sutherland.* |
| 24 Feb | From George M. Weston. ALS. DLC–JKP. Maintains that if his father, Nathan Weston, is not named to the cabinet, Maine Democrats would prefer the appointment of Levi Woodbury of New Hampshire. |
| 24 Feb | From Silas Wright, Jr. ALS. DLC–JKP. Introduces Charles |

|            | Linsley, a Democrat and lawyer from Middlebury, Vt. |
| 24 Feb | From Silas Wright, Jr. ALS. DLC–JKP. Urges the appointment of Ver Planck Van Antwerp as head of the General Land Office. |
| *25 Feb* | *To Benjamin F. Butler.* |
| 25 Feb | From John I. DeGraff. ALS. DLC–JKP. Suggests that the Texas question has become popular and that if there is to be an annexation, then it should be accomplished without delay. |
| 25 Feb | From Jesse D. Elliott. LS. DLC–JKP. Introduces Sidney Jones of Philadelphia; notes that Jones, a manufacturer of oiled cloth for window curtains "upon which are represented various historical scenes," has worked hard to establish an efficient militia in Philadelphia and presently commands a "splendid corps of dragoons." |
| 25 Feb | From Henry D. Gilpin. ALS. DLC–JKP. Recommends the appointment of Henry Simpson of Philadelphia to any position of trust in the government. |
| *[25 Feb 1845]* | *From Gouverneur Kemble.* |
| 25 Feb | From Cornelius W. Lawrence. LS. DLC–JKP. Introduces Charles Augustus Davis of New York City; adds that Davis is "not politically with us but is a true American and personally one of our best and most reliable friends." |
| 25 Feb | From Edward J. Mallett. ALS. DLC–JKP. Introduces Levi C. Eaton, a member of the Rhode Island Senate and a faithful Democrat. |
| 25 Feb | From R. A. Mumford. LS. DLC–JKP. Wishes to serve as Polk's financial agent with the Bank of the Metropolis. |
| 25 Feb | From James S. Owens. L. MdHi. Requests that William Frick be restored to his post as collector of customs at Baltimore. |
| 25 Feb | From Joshua Poythress. ALS. DLC–JKP. Forwards a box of sea shells as a present to Sarah C. Polk. |
| 25 Feb | From Philip F. Thomas. L. MdHi. Urges William Frick's appointment as collector of customs at Baltimore. |
| *25 Feb* | *To Martin Van Buren.* |
| 26 Feb | From John Avery. ALS. DNA–RG 92. Solicits position in Philadelphia as an inspector of clothing for the army; encloses certificate of endorsement by numerous citizens of Nashville, Tenn. |
| 26 Feb | From Levin H. Coe. LS. DLC–JKP. Introduces Calvin W. Cherry, a merchant from Haywood County, Tenn. |
| 26 Feb | From William Ellis. ALS. DLC–JKP. Transmits an address presented on the occasion of the bicentennial of Dedham, Mass. |
| *[26 Feb 1845]* | *From William H. Haywood, Jr.* |
| *[26 Feb 1845]* | *From William H. Haywood, Jr.* |

| | |
|---|---|
| 26 Feb | From William U. Jacob et al. LS. DLC–JKP. Inform Polk of his election to honorary membership in the Franklin Debating Society of Eastville, Va. |
| *26 Feb* | *From Cave Johnson.* |
| 26 Feb | From Gayton P. Osgood. ALS. DLC–JKP. Introduces his friend, Charles Howard of Springfield, Mass.; notes that Howard formerly served on the state's Executive Council during the governorship of Marcus Morton. |
| 26 Feb | From John Pettit et al. LS. DLC–JKP. Urges the appointment of James Shields of Illinois as commissioner of the General Land Office should that post not be continued in the hands of a fellow citizen of Indiana. |
| 26 Feb | From John Tyler. ALS. DLC–JKP. States that James Maher "the public gardiner has superintended the public grounds about the Presidents House for the last four years" and that "for taste, neatness and diligence" he stands unsurpassed. |
| *[26 Feb 1845]* | *From John Tyler.* |
| 27 Feb | From A. R. Brown. LS. DLC–JKP. Requests that no appointment for postmaster of Lowell, Mass., be made until the Democrats of the city have expressed their preferences in the question. |
| *27 Feb* | *From Benjamin F. Butler.* |
| *27 Feb* | *From Benjamin F. Butler.* |
| 27 Feb | From Benjamin F. Butler. ALS. DLC–JKP. Introduces his personal and political friend, Samuel J. Tilden of New York City. |
| *27 Feb* | *To John C. Calhoun.* |
| 27 Feb | From Albert Constable. L, copy. MdHi. Notes that the Democracy of Baltimore elected William Frick to the Maryland Senate following his removal in 1840 as customs collector; urges Polk to restore Frick to his former post. |
| *27 Feb* | *From Martin Van Buren.* |
| *27 Feb* | *From Martin Van Buren.* |
| *27 Feb* | *From Levi Woodbury et al.* |
| 28 Feb | From Edward Burke. ALS. DLC–JKP. Informs Polk that he has brought from New York's principal houses the "largest assortment of Curtain Materials Furniture Coverings Carpetings & paper hangings in the Union," which will be of interest in furnishing the White House. |
| 28 Feb | From John Burnham. ALS. DLC–JKP. Asserts that in Maine both Whigs and Democrats favor the annexation of Texas, although the Whigs are constrained by their leadership to hold back their public support. |
| *[28 Feb 1845]* | *From John C. Calhoun.* |
| 28 Feb | From A. Campbell. ALS. DLC–JKP. Introduces Pollard McCormick, a manufacturer from Allegheny City, Penn. |
| 28 Feb | From John B. Cochran et al. LS. DLC–JKP. Invite Polk to |

|  | membership in the Union Philosophical Society of Transylvania University in Lexington, Ky. |
|---|---|
| 28 Feb | From David Craighead. ALS. DLC–JKP. Urges Polk to appoint Solomon W. Downs in place of Balie Peyton as U.S. district attorney for Louisiana. |
| 28 Feb | From John G. Gibbs. ALS. DLC–JKP. States that John T. Smith of Philadelphia will deliver a hat that was made "with great care" for Polk to wear at his inaugural. |
| *28 Feb* | *From William H. Haywood, Jr.* |
| 28 Feb | From Foster Hooper. ALS. DLC–JKP. Relates that Phineas W. Leland lost his job as customs collector at Fall River, Mass., because he voted Democratic in 1840; urges Polk to restore Leland to his former position. |
| *28 Feb* | *From Andrew Jackson.* |
| 28 Feb | From Daniel Schneider et al. LS. DLC–JKP. Ask that Polk accept for his inaugural dinner the gift of a sirloin of beef from Berks County, Penn., where "nearly nine thousand of those hardy yeomanry are proud to be your political friends and sincere well wishers." |
| 28 Feb | From Frederick Stanton and George Snodgrass. LS. DLC–JKP. Advise Polk of his election to honorary membership in the Belles Lettres Society of Oakland College in Mississippi. |
| 28 Feb | From John Thomas. ALS. DLC–JKP. Rejoices at Polk's election and tells of his electioneering efforts in York, Ohio, and in neighboring states. |
| 28 Feb | From Silas Wright, Jr. L. DLC–JKP. Urges the appointment of Joel Turrill to a suitable office; recalls that Turrill chaired the select committee appointed in the U.S. House to consider the question of abolishing slavery in the District of Columbia; and thinks that Turrill "was mainly and prominently instrumental in making that report what it was." |
| [March 1845] | From Anonymous. L, signed "an old federalist." DLC–JKP. Objects to the appointment of Elijah F. Purdy as surveyor for the the port of New York City; claims that Purdy hires such men as Isaiah Rynders "to do club law on his fellow-citizens." |
| [March 1845] | From Archibald Atkinson et al. NS. DLC–JKP. Recommend Joel Pennybacker of Virginia to a place in the general government. |
| [March 1845] | From James G. Bryce. NS. DLC–JKP. Encloses letter from John Slidell to Thomas Barrett regarding the collectorship at New Orleans, La. |
| March 1845] | From John C. Calhoun. ALS. DLC–JKP. Introduces Robert S. Chew, a State Department clerk selected to assist Polk's private secretary with the duties of his office. |
| March 1845] | From Walter T. Colquitt et al. LS. DLC–JKP. Recommend John Lewis for appointment as Librarian of Congress. |

[March 1845]      From Ezra S. Dodd et al. NS. DNA–RG 26. Recommend
                  Ezra Wilson for appointment as a lighthouse keeper; name
                  five places on Lake Erie and Lake Michigan that might be
                  suitable posts.
[March 1845]      From John Thomson Mason. ALS. DLC–JKP. Recommends
                  H. R. Smeltzer of Maryland "for the place of post office
                  agent for the U. States."
[March 1845]      From John Thomson Mason. ALS. DLC–JKP. Introduces
                  Peter McGee, who comes highly recommended by fellow cit-
                  izens of Frederick, Md., for the post of U.S. gardener.
[March 1845]      From Lorain T. Pease. ALS. DLC–JKP. States that he has
                  known Gideon Welles of Hartford, Conn., for many years
                  and thinks that he would make an excellent choice for the
                  post of second assistant postmaster general.
[March 1845]      From Catherine W. Polk. ALS. DLC–JKP. Solicits prefer-
                  ment for her brother, Josiah F. Polk; explains that their
                  business has failed, "owing to the increased number of Ho-
                  tels" in Washington City.
[March 1845]      From Smith Pyne. ALS. DLC–JKP. Offers Polk a pew at St.
                  John's Episcopal Church in Washington City.
[March 1845]      From Robert Reeves. ALS. DLC–JKP. Recalls that in his
                  interview with Polk at the National Hotel he was told to
                  renew his case after the inauguration; observes that he has
                  come to do that which duty forces upon him.
[March 1845]      From Henry Stevens. ALS. DLC–JKP. Reminds Polk of
                  their earlier conversation about "the light boat."
[March 1845]      From Jacob B. Wildman et al. LS. DNA–RG 45. Recom-
                  mend Jesse D. Elliott for appointment to one of the bureaus
                  of the Navy Department.
[March 1845]      From John Williamson et al. NS. DLC–JKP. Solicit advance-
                  ment for William N. Bronaugh, formerly a captain in the
                  army and presently a resident of Arkansas.
1 March           From William Allen. ALS. DLC–JKP. Requests an interview
                  for the next morning at 8:30 a.m.
*1 March*         *From Benjamin F. Butler.*
1 March           From Julius Dessoir. NS. DLC–JKP. Asks for the contract
                  to provide new furniture for the White House; appends tes-
                  timonial signed by numerous customers familiar with his
                  work as a cabinet maker.
*1 March*         *From John P. Helfenstein.*
1 March           From Dixon H. Lewis and Walter T. Colquitt. LS. DLC-
                  JKP. Prefer Romulus M. Saunders of North Carolina for the
                  postmaster generalship.
*1 March*         *To William L. Marcy.*
*[1 March 1845]*  *From John L. O'Sullivan and Samuel J. Tilden.*
*1 March*         *From Martin Van Buren.*
*1 March*         *To Martin Van Buren.*

| | |
|---|---|
| 1 March | From A. Young. ALS. DLC–JKP. Protests failure of the state and national governments to protect his fellow Mormons residing in Nauvoo, Ill. |
| *2 March* | *From John L. O'Sullivan.* |
| *[2 March 1845]* | *From Smith T. Van Buren.* |
| *2 March* | *From James Whitcomb.* |
| 3 March | To George Bancroft. LS. MHi. Invites Bancroft to serve as secretary of the navy. |
| 3 March | From James Buchanan. ALS. DLC–JKP. Introduces Reah Frazer of Lancaster, Penn.; notes that Frazer "acted a conspicuous part in the Baltimore Convention" and is "every thing he ought to be both personally & politically." |
| 3 March | From James H. Carson. ALS. DLC–JKP. Attests to the merits of Joel Pennybacker of Shenandoah County, Va.; adds that Pennybacker, a lawyer, formerly served in the Virginia Senate. |
| 3 March | From Asbury Dickins. ALS. DLC–JKP. Sends three volumes of the *Senate Executive Journal* and a copy of the *Senate Journal* for the session ending March 4, 1841. |
| 3 March | From Edward Everett. LS. DLC–JKP. Wishes to be informed as soon as possible whether or not he is to be recalled. |
| 3 March | From Henry Ewing. ALS. DLC–JKP. Regrets that he cannot attend Polk's inauguration but sends his sincere congratulations of the day. |
| 3 March | From George F. Fort et al. LS. DLC–JKP. Recommend John R. Thomson for a place in Polk's cabinet. |
| 3 March | From Augustine M. Gay. ALS. DLC–JKP. Writes from Phillips Academy in Andover, Mass., soliciting Polk's autograph. |
| *3 March* | *From Gouverneur Kemble.* |
| [3 March 1845] | From James Laurenson. ALS. DLC–JKP. States that he is a correspondent for both the Baltimore *Sun* and the Philadelphia *Ledger*; wishes to know which printing office will issue copies of Polk's Inaugural Address; and explains that he has been engaged to send a large number of same eastward by tomorrow's express. |
| 3 March | From John Law et al. LS. DLC–JKP. Urge the appointment of William O. Butler of Kentucky as secretary of war; assert that Butler's preferment would give great satisfaction not only to the citizens of Indiana but to the whole West as well. |
| *March* | *From William L. Marcy.* |
| *March* | *From John Y. Mason.* |
| *March* | *From John Y. Mason.* |
| *March* | *From John Y. Mason.* |
| March | From John Nelson. ALS. DLC–JKP. Encloses copy of his letter of this date to John Tyler by which document he resigns |

|              | his post as attorney general of the United States. |
|--------------|-----------------------------------------------------|
| *3 March*    | *From Henry E. Riell.* |
| 3 March      | From Henry D. Smith. ALS. DLC–JKP. Requests that Polk make no appointments in Connecticut until after the state elections in April next. |
| *[3 March 1845]* | *From Samuel J. Tilden and John L. O'Sullivan.* |
| *3 March*    | *To Martin Van Buren.* |
| *3 March*    | *From Smith T. Van Buren.* |
| *3 March*    | *From Silas Wright, Jr.* |
| 4 March      | From Anonymous. L, fragment. MdHi. Recommends William Frick to be reinstated as collector of customs at Baltimore. |
| *4 March*    | *From George Bancroft.* |
| 4 March      | From Clement B. Barrett. ALS. DLC–JKP. Recalls Polk's assistance at the town of Knoxville in August 1841 when he and his family were on their way north. |
| 4 March      | From Thomas H. Benton et al. LS. DLC–JKP. Recommend that Robert B. Mitchell be appointed subagent at Council Bluff in place of H. E. Elliott. |
| *4 March*    | *From George M. Bibb.* |
| 4 March      | From Theodorick Bland. L. MdHi. Urges the appointment of William Frick "to fill some respectable office" in the new administration. |
| 4 March      | From John G. Flugel. ALS. DLC–JKP. Congratulates Polk upon his inauguration and indicates a desire to remain as U.S. consul at Leipzig, Germany. |
| 4 March      | From George William Gordon. ALS. DLC–JKP. Congratulates Polk on his election; writes from his post as U.S. consul at Rio de Janeiro, Brazil. |
| *4 March*    | *From Daniel Graham.* |
| 4 March      | From J. Huddleson. ALS. DLC–JKP. States that he attended the President's inauguration and will return to Allegany County, Md., with copies of the best inaugural address yet given. |
| 4 March      | From Howard Kennedy. ALS. DLC–JKP. Recalls their conversation at Cumberland and regrets to say that the pair of horses under discussion will not answer Polk's needs; suggested to "a drover on his way to Washington with a span of horses" the possibility of the President's interest in looking at them. |
| 4 March      | From Trasimon Landry. ALS. DLC–JKP. Expresses pleasure in having cast one of Louisiana's electoral votes for Polk. |
| 4 March      | From Lucius Lyon et al. LS. DLC–JKP. Recommend as the sitting delegation to Congress from Michigan John Norvell for a major presidential appointment such as minister to a foreign court or comptroller of the Treasury. |

| | |
|---|---|
| 4 March | To William L. Marcy. LS. DLC–WLM. Offers Marcy post of secretary of war in the new administration. |
| 4 March | From Jesse Miller. ALS. DLC–JKP. Introduces Daniel Dobbins and urges Polk to restore him to his former place as an officer in the revenue cutter service on Lake Erie. |
| 4 March | From Josiah G. Peabody. ALS. DLC–JKP. Encloses communication from Democrats of Lowell, Mass., and requests that no appointment to the postmastership there be made without their approval; encloses letter to Polk from A. R. Brown. |
| [4 March 1845] | From Benjamin C. Presstman. L. MdHi. Recommends William Frick to be named collector of customs at Baltimore. |
| *4 March* | *From J. G. M. Ramsey.* |
| 4 March | From Francis R. Shunk. LS. DLC–JKP. Supports the claims of Daniel Dobbins for an appointment to office. |
| 4 March | From John Spalding. ALS. DLC–JKP. Extends sincere best wishes on the occasion of Polk's inauguration. |
| 4 March | From Enoch B. Talcott. ALS. DLC–JKP. Assures Polk that the citizens of Oswego County, N.Y., would approve the appointment of Joel Turrill to any place of confidence in the President's patronage. |
| 4 March | From J. B. Williston. ALS. DLC–JKP. Urges Polk not to retain the federal appointees in New York City. |
| *4 March* | *From Henderson K. Yoakum.* |
| 5 March | From Archibald H. Arrington. ALS. DLC–JKP. Prefers Thomas I. Pasteur of New Bern, N.C., over others suggested for the post of customs collector at Ocracoke, N.C. |
| 5 March | From Thomas H. Blake. N. DLC–JKP. Encloses a note "from Ex-President Tyler whilst at the ball last night"; Polk's AE reads, "John Tyler, Jr. Resignation as Sec. for signing Land Patents." |
| 5 March | From William C. Bouck. ALS. DLC–JKP. Introduces Archibald C. Niven, whom Bouck appointed adjutant general of New York in 1843 and who will serve in the next Congress. |
| 5 March | From Eber R. Butler. ALS. DLC–JKP. Solicits Polk's autograph. |
| 5 March | From Robert B. Campbell. ALS. DLC–JKP. Relates that he will depart Havana for New York tomorrow; has taken the liberty of sending Sarah Polk "two boxes of West India preserves." |
| March | From George A. Carnes. ALS. DLC–JKP. Requests Polk's autograph. |
| March | From Asa Dimock. ALS. DLC–JKP. Introduces Thomas C. McDowell of Cambria County, Penn. |
| March | From Andrew J. Donelson. ALS. DLC–JKP. Urges the appointment of William B. Preston of Sumner County, Tenn., |

to some subordinate office requiring "activity and energy and fidelity."

5 March        From Charles D. Ferris. ALS. DLC–JKP. Reviews contributions of William L. G. Smith in the late presidential campaign and urges his appointment as postmaster of Buffalo, N.Y.

5 March        From David Gilbert. ALS. PHi. Considers Henry Simpson fully qualified to serve as surveyor for the Port of Philadelphia.

5 March        From John P. Heiss. ALS. DLC–JKP. States that accompanying this letter are two splendid capons, the gift of Adams & Holt Company of Philadelphia.

5 March        From William S. Hubbell. LS. DLC–JKP. Encloses a letter from a mutual friend, William G. Angel.

*5 March        From Ralph I. Ingersoll.*

5 March        From Daniel Judson. ALS. DLC–JKP. Warns that the people have turned away from religious principles and will be punished for their evil ways.

5 March        From John A. McAllister. ALS. DLC–JKP. Requests Polk's autograph.

*5 March        From William L. Marcy.*

5 March        From J. W. Murphy. LS. DLC–JKP. Sends Polk a copy of his inaugural address printed on satin.

5 March        From Emery D. Potter. ALS. DNA–RG 26. Encloses a petition from Ohio citizens urging the appointment of Ezra Wilson as lighthouse keeper.

*5 March        From Sylvester S. Southworth.*

5 March        From William Taylor. ALS. DLC–JKP. Recommends Joel Pennybacker of Rockingham County, Va., for appointment to a situation in the government.

5 March        From Isaac Toucey. ALS. DLC–JKP. Recommends Gideon Welles be appointed assistant postmaster general; also urges consideration for Lorain T. Pease as receiver at the Green Bay land office and for William P. Eaton as a candidate for any responsible position.

5 March        From John Webb and Jonathan Smith. LS. DLC–JKP. Urge that Gabriel C. Smith be given some office of profit by which relief might be provided friends and relatives of the late Williamson Smith of Mississippi; explain that Smith's death leaves them burdened with his debts.

5 March        From Philo White. ALS. DLC–JKP. Introduces Augustine G. Danby, postmaster at Utica, N.Y.

*6 March        To John C. Calhoun.*

6 March        From M. C. Dougherty. ALS. DLC–JKP. Opposes the appointment of Albert Banta to be U.S. marshal for Indiana; notes that Banta's term as sheriff of Elkhart County expired in August 1844.

| | |
|---|---|
| 6 March | From John H. Eaton and William B. Lewis. LS. DLC–JKP. Introduce Sebastian Luchisi, who seeks employment in the White House; recall that Luchisi previously served Andrew Jackson and Martin Van Buren during their presidencies. |
| 6 March | From William Frick. ALS. MdHi. Asks to be restored to his former post as collector of customs at Baltimore. |
| 6 March | From Charles G. Greene. ALS. DNA–RG 45. Recommends Joseph Hall to be appointed surveyor in the customs house at Boston. |
| 6 March | From Curtis Guild, Jr. ALS. DLC–JKP. Requests Polk's autograph. |
| *6 March* | *From Andrew Jackson.* |
| 6 March | From Edward Jenkins. ALS. DLC–JKP. Complains that John Tyler appointed persons from out of state to positions in New York City; states that many of those outsiders had Whig connections; and warns that the old Democrats will not accept retention of the Tyler appointees. |
| 6 March | From Moses G. Leonard. L. DLC–FP. Certifies that John S. Harris of Rhode Island is a person of "good moral character and business capacities." |
| 6 March | From Moses G. Leonard et al. NS. DLC–JKP. Recommend Samuel Waterbury to be awarded the contract to furnish the President's House; assert that he owns a reputable cabinet shop in New York City, that he is a useful Democrat, and that he is a man of true integrity. |
| *6 March* | *From Edward J. Mallett.* |
| 6 March | From Joseph Stibbs. ALS. DLC–JKP. Requests permission to breed his mare with the Arabian stallions "presented to the President of the United States by the Immaum of Muscat"; explains that he hopes to improve his Ohio breed if Polk grants this privilege. |
| 7 March | From George M. Bibb. LS. DLC–JKP. Advises Polk of the death of Alexander W. Jones, register of the land office at Edwardsville, Ill. |
| *7 March* | *From Aaron V. Brown.* |
| *7 March 1845]* | *From Aaron V. Brown.* |
| *7 March* | *From Leonard P. Cheatham.* |
| 7 March | From Edward T. R. Coyne. ALS. DLC–JKP. Congratulates Polk on his inaugural address. |
| 7 March | From Dan A. Daniels. L. DLC–FP. Withdraws his endorsement of Walter R. Danforth and recommends John S. Harris for the post of customs collector at Providence, R.I. |
| 7 March | From Alfred Dobbins. ALS. DLC–JKP. Recalls that he rents his farm in Wayne County, Tenn., from Polk's brother-in-law, James Walker; promises that he will pray daily for Polk's success as president. |
| *7 March* | *To Andrew J. Donelson.* |

| | |
|---|---|
| 7 March | From Andrew Jackson. L. DNA–RG 60. Introduces William T. Thompson, who fought under Daniel T. Patterson in the defense of New Orleans in 1814–15. |
| 7 March | From Knock & Childs. LS. DLC–JKP. Solicit Polk's patronage of their tailor shop in New York. |
| 7 March | From William H. Merrick. N. DLC–JKP. Requests an "interview for a few minutes." |
| 7 March | From William D. Moseley. ALS. DLC–JKP. Discusses patronage questions relating to Florida Territory; notes that his Democrat friends want to run him for governor upon Florida's admission to the Union. |
| 7 March | From Samuel Nelson and John Savage. LS. DLC–JKP. Suggest that John L. Graham should be retained as postmaster of New York City; note that by unfortunate investments he has lost all of his property and that he needs to serve out his term for financial reasons. |
| 7 March | From J. C. Nisbet. ALS. DLC–JKP. States that there is a young lady in Cedarville, Ohio, who wishes to name her daughter for Mrs. Polk and requests that Polk send him "a paper that has Mrs. Polk's name in it." |
| 7 March | From N. S. Richardson. ALS. DLC–JKP. Requests Polk's autograph. |
| 7 March | From John Shiels. ALS. DLC–JKP. Applies for Polk's assistance in obtaining a pension for his naval service. |
| 7 March | From David Stewart. L. MdHi. Adds his voice in support of William Frick to be named customs collector at Baltimore. |
| [8 March 1845] | From Anonymous. L. DLC–JKP. Discusses New York politics and party divisions. |
| 8 March | From Olney Ballou. L. DLC–FP. Recommends John S. Harris to be collector of customs at Providence, R.I. |
| *8 March* | *From Augustus Beardslee.* |
| 8 March | From Francis P. Blair and Selah R. Hobbie. NS. DLC–JKP. Enclose numerous certificates urging an appointment for Charles P. Sengstack to some office in the government. |
| 8 March | From Henry D. Gilpin. ALS. DLC–JKP. Introduces Thomas M. Pettit, a friend and presiding judge of the district court in Philadelphia, Penn. |
| 8 March | From Nathaniel C. Hart, Jr. ALS. DLC–JKP. Congratulates Polk on his inauguration. |
| 8 March | From Thomas M. Hope. ALS. DLC–JKP. Thanks Polk for receiving him so cordially earlier in the day and encloses a letter received from Justin Butterfield, late U.S. district attorney for Illinois. |
| 8 March | From Thomas Lawrence. ALS. DLC–JKP. Complains of treatment by the pension office; states that he came to Washington City from New York to make his appeal to Polk in person. |

| | |
|---|---|
| 8 March | From John Y. Mason. ALS. DLC–JKP. Advises that the person recommended by Charles A. Wickliffe to be a marine lieutenant is named John C. Cash, not Thomas Cash. |
| 8 March | From Henry A. Oakley. ALS. DLC–JKP. Requests Polk's autograph. |
| 8 March | From Jesse Roberts. LS. DLC–JKP. Encloses thirty dollars and a copy of specifications for his "self filling pumper"; requests that Polk procure a patent for his invention. |
| 8 March | From Leathy R. Smith. ALS. DLC–JKP. Recalls the close friendship between Polk and her late husband, Williamson Smith; urges Polk's assistance in obtaining some preferment for her brother-in-law, Gabriel C. Smith, who promises to assign the proceeds of the office to her support and that of her numerous children. |
| 8 March | From Frederick Stoever. ALS. DLC–JKP. Sends congratulations of the Democracy of the city and county of Philadelphia; renews his recommendation of Henry Horn to be collector of customs and Andrew Miller to be postmaster. |
| 9 March | From James Walker. ALS. DLC–JKP. Requests that Polk direct J. Knox Walker to inspect the application papers of William S. Pickett and see that all of the recommendations are in place. |
| 9 March | From Levin H. Coe. ALS. DLC–JKP. Urges the removal of Marcus B. Winchester as postmaster of Memphis, Tenn. |
| 9 March | From Ezekiel P. McNeal. ALS. DLC–JKP. Acknowledges receipt of Polk's check on the Union Bank of Tennessee office at Jackson, Tenn.; discusses other financial matters relating to Polk's lands in Hardeman County. |
| 9 March | From William W. and Maria Grundy Masterson. LS. DLC–JKP. Request an appointment to some office lucrative enough to warrant giving up the postmastership of Green Hill, Tenn. |
| 9 March | From Arnold Plumer. ALS. DLC–JKP. Thinks that Samuel Hays' continuance in the U.S. House for over two months following his confirmation as U.S. marshal for western Pennsylvania is evidence of his declination of the appointment; refers Polk to James Buchanan for information about his former service as U.S. marshal from 1839 to 1841. |
| 0 March | From Anonymous. L, initialed "V. V." DLC–JKP. Denounces the "blackguard Empire Club" and opposes Elijah F. Purdy's bid for the New York customs collectorship. |
| 0 March | From Anonymous. N. DLC–JKP. Requests as the mayor of Georgetown an interview with Polk. |
| *0 March* | *From James G. Bryce.* |
| 0 March | From John C. Calhoun. ANS. DLC–JKP. Suggests several candidates for Polk's patronage. |
| 0 March | From Caleb Cannalt. ALS. DLC–JKP. Urges Polk to appoint |

|  |  |
|---|---|
|  | a judge for the western district of Pennsylvania. |
| 10 March | From Southy Grinalds. ALS. DLC–JKP. Requests that Polk renew his appointment as consul to Santa Martha, New Granada. |
| 10 March | From Jeromus Johnson. ALS. DLC–JKP. Approves of Polk's inaugural address and his selections for the cabinet. |
| 10 March | From Thomas Lawrence. ALS. DLC–JKP. Complains of the conduct of James L. Edwards, commissioner of pensions; requests a meeting with Polk. |
| 10 March | From Sackfield Maclin. ALS. DLC–JKP. Regrets leaving Washington City without having seen Polk; explains that his traveling companion, Archibald Yell, chose to leave earlier than expected; recommends Samuel Mitchell for office in Arkansas; and expresses the opinion that Chester Ashley is an *"expediency man* and not to be trusted." |
| 10 March | From D. B. Stockholm. ALS. DLC–JKP. Notes that Polk's inaugural address meets with the approval of all parties in Ithaca, N.Y.; discusses the military and commercial importance of the Oregon Territory. |
| 10 March | From William Taylor. ALS. DLC–JKP. Encloses a letter from citizens of Rockingham County, Va., asking Polk to retain Daniel Bryan as postmaster of Alexandria, D.C. |
| 10 March | From Levi Woodbury. ALS. DLC–JKP. Encloses a list of recommendations for federal appointments in Rhode Island; notes that Edmund Burke and Olney Ballou prepared the list. |
| 10 March | From Archibald Yell. ALS. DLC–JKP. Introduces his friend John Hogan of New York; observes that Hogan "fully comprehends all the machinery of N. York politics." |
| 11 March | From William Allen. ALS. DLC–JKP. Encloses a letter from Thomas H. Blake, who says that there is a mistake about the closing of the land office at Marion, Ohio. |
| 11 March | From Edmund Anderson. ALS. DLC–JKP. Solicits the position of postmaster at Richmond, Va. |
| *11 March* | *From Julius W. Blackwell.* |
| 11 March | From Sidney Breese. ALS. DLC–JKP. Encloses recommendation from members of the Indiana congressional delegation for James Shields to be appointed commissioner of the General Land Office. (Enclosure not found.) |
| 11 March | From Theodore C. Callicot. ALS. DLC–JKP. Solicits the autographs of Polk and his wife. |
| 11 March | From Ellen Knox Chapman. ALS. DLC–JKP. Offers Polk a part interest in the proceeds of a property settlement in Ireland in exchange for his legal assistance in prosecuting the case. |
| 11 March | From Daniel S. Dickinson. ALS. DLC–JKP. States that the bearer of this letter, John Hogan of Utica, N.Y., has enjoyed |

|  | a long and successful legal career and would perform ably in any position to which he might be appointed. |
| 11 March | From Joseph Hall. ALS. DNA–RG 45. Solicits post of surveyor for the district of Boston and Charleston, Mass. |
| *11 March* | *From Elijah Hayward et al.* |
| 11 March | From George W. Hopkins. ALS. DLC–JKP. Desires to be considered for appointment as consul to Liverpool despite his candidacy for reelection to the U.S. House. |
| 11 March | From William Horner. ALS. DLC–JKP. Promises to send Polk literature distributed by the New York Board of Missions, for which organization he serves as an agent in the Allen Township of Pennsylvania; requests payment for his services in exposing corruption in the post office at Easton, Penn. |
| 11 March | From Joseph C. Johnson. ALS. DLC–JKP. Desires to obtain Polk's autograph. |
| *11 March* | *From William Kennon, Sr.* |
| 11 March | From Walter F. Leake. ALS. DLC–JKP. Notes that George McDuffie and Daniel E. Huger are pressing for the retention of Robert B. Campbell at Havana, Cuba; withdraws his application for that consular post; and requests appointment as U.S. minister to Brazil should Henry A. Wise be recalled. |
| 11 March | From Dixon H. Lewis. ALS. DLC–JKP. Endorses Clement C. Clay's solicitation for office; encloses letter from Clay. (Enclosure not found.) |
| 11 March | From William C. McCanslen. ALS. Polk Memorial Association, Columbia. Solicits an appointment; claims to have been an active Democrat since 1822. |
| 11 March | From John C. Mallory. ALS. DLC–JKP. Introduces Edward Harden, collector of customs at Savannah, Ga. |
| 11 March | From William P. Maulsby. ALS. DLC–JKP. Urges the retention of Thomas L. Smith, register of the Treasury. |
| 11 March | From Thomas Ritchie. ALS. DLC–JKP. Declines on behalf of his son, William F. Ritchie, the appointment of postmaster at Richmond, Va.; explains that William has not yet returned to Richmond. |
| 11 March | From Nathan Selbert. ALS. DLC–JKP. Solicits Polk's autograph. |
| 11 March 1845] | From John Cotton Smith, Jr. ALS. DLC–JKP. Requests that the customs collectorship at Bridgeport, Conn., not be filled prior to the state elections scheduled for April 7th; explains that he is running for Congress and would oppose the appointment of Samuel Simons, who held that post under previous Democratic administrations. |
| 11 March 1845] | From Jesse Speight. ALS. DLC–JKP. States that although he will not oppose the appointment of Thomas I. Pasteur to the collectorship at Ocrakoke, N.C., he rejects the notion |

that Pasteur is the equal of Sylvester Brown, the incumbent.

11 March    From Joseph Towaler. ALS. DLC–JKP. Notes the misconduct of Wilson G. Lamb, an inspector at the port of Camden, N.C.

11 March    From William Wilkins. ALS. DLC–JKP. Recommends Isaac F. Quinby for a military appointment.

*12 March*   *From Alfred Balch.*

12 March    From Clement B. Barrett. ALS. DLC–JKP. Requests loan of $200 with which he might pay expenses of a trip from Hollowell, Me., to his native Virginia.

12 March    From Duncan Campbell. ALS. DLC–JKP. States that friends in Scotland have sent him a newspaper article reporting that Polk's ancestors resided in Dunbar prior to their immigration to America; relates that he came to Saint Marks, Florida Territory, in 1839 and was naturalized immediately upon his arrival.

12 March    From Auguste D'Avezac. ALS. DLC–JKP. Reponds to Polk's request that he indicate his preferences for a diplomatic appointment; places St. Petersburg at the head of his list.

12 March    From John H. Eaton. ALS. DLC–JKP. Requests that Polk retain Thomas L. Smith as register of the Treasury; notes that Smith has many influential friends and relations "who take a lively interest in his welfare."

12 March    From O. Fish. LS. DLC–JKP. Offers Polk the gift of a new black beaver hat.

*12 March*   *From Phineas Janney.*

*12 March*   *From Gouverneur Kemble.*

12 March    From Andrew A. Kincannon. ALS. DLC–JKP. Recommends James H. Tate, a neighbor and leading Democrat in Lowndes County, Miss., for the consular post at Rio de Janeiro, Brazil.

*12 March*   *From Jesse Miller.*

12 March    From Gayton P. Osgood. ALS. DLC–JKP. Asks Polk to retain Lemuel Williams as collector of customs at Boston, Mass.

12 March    From John M. Seely. NS. DLC–JKP. Encloses certificates supporting the appointment of Charles P. Sengstack as commissioner of public buildings.

12 March    From Albert G. Southall. ALS. DNA–RG 45. Requests that he be retained as agent for the preservation of live oak and other timbers on the public lands; notes that John Tyler became his guardian at infancy.

12 March    From Charles S. Wallach. ALS. DLC–JKP. Solicits the position of chargé d'affaires to Venezuela; claims that the presidential campaign bankrupted him and ruined his law practice.

[12 March 1845]   From J. W. Wetherell. ALS. DLC–JKP. Recommends E

|  | ward B. Hubley of Pennsylvania to be commissioner of Indian affairs. |
| 12 March | From Henry Wheaton. AN. DLC–JKP. Asks Polk to retain John G. Flugel as U.S. consul to Leipzig. |
| 13 March | From Anonymous. L, signed "An old Democrat." DLC–JKP. Expresses dissatisfaction with the appointment of William L. Marcy to the cabinet; argues that Churchill C. Cambreleng or Azariah C. Flagg would have proven more acceptable to the Democratic citizens of New York. |
| 13 March | From Anonymous. L, signed "D. W. Stone." DLC–JKP. Recommends William H. Haywood, Jr., for a federal office. |
| 13 March | From George M. Dallas. ALS. PHi. Encloses testimonials supporting the application of Horn R. Kneass for the office of attorney for the eastern district of Pennsylvania. (Enclosure not found.) |
| 13 March | From George Dennett. ALS. DLC–JKP. Denounces a "clique consisting of thirteen persons" attempting to manage the patronage in Portsmouth, N.H.; encloses an article from the *New Hampshire Gazette*. (Enclosure not found.) |
| 13 March | From John A. Dix. ALS. DLC–JKP. Urges Polk to retain Thomas L. Smith as register of the Treasury. |
| *13 March* | *From Augustus C. Dodge.* |
| *13 March* | *From Richard M. Johnson.* |
| *13 March* | *From Thomas Lloyd.* |
| *[13 March 1845]* | *From Jesse Miller.* |
| 13 March | From Bennet Redman. ALS. DLC–JKP. Offers Polk a house and lot in Paris, Ill., that he won betting on the election; wants Polk to come and visit him. |
| 13 March | From Ezekiel Starr et al. NS. DLC–JKP. Request appointment of a third member to the Cherokee Commission in order to resolve outstanding claims made under the Cherokee Treaty of 1835–36. |
| 13 March | From Aaron Ward. ALS. DLC–JKP. Introduces G. Sherwood of Westchester County, N.Y.; praises Polk's inaugural address. |
| 13 March | From U. P. Winder. ALS. DLC–JKP. Requests that Polk retain Albert G. Southall in his post as agent for the conservation of live oak trees; commends Polk's inaugural address. |
| 14 March | From Anonymous. L. DLC–JKP. Warns Polk that Charles A. Wickliffe is untrustworthy. |
| *14 March* | *To Benjamin F. Butler.* |
| 14 March | From John Catron. ALS. DLC–JKP. Asks Polk to secure an appointment for Ramsey L. Mayson; encloses letter from Eliza Mayson to Ephraim H. Foster. |
| 14 March | From Mary Clinton. ALS. DLC–JKP. Solicits an office for her brother, Thomas G. Clinton; communicates this letter and that of her brother through Sarah C. Polk. |

| | |
|---|---|
| 14 March | From Thomas G. Clinton. ALS, draft. DLC–JKP. Requests appointment to any position that might give him opportunity to pursue scientific subjects investigated these past two years. |
| 14 March | From William Fargo. L. DLC–JKP. Notes that he lost $300 betting on the presidential election and is stranded in Illinois; asks Polk to send him money so he can return to his New York home. |
| 14 March | From C. S. Fowler. ALS. DLC–JKP. Offers his services as a supplier of china and glassware for the president's mansion. |
| 14 March | From Hillory Galaway. ALS. DLC–JKP. Solicits the position of driver of Polk's carriage; names several prominent citizens as references. |
| 14 March | From Henry D. Gilpin. ALS. DLC–JKP. Introduces his brother, Thomas W. Gilpin. |
| *14 March* | *From Jefferson K. Heckman.* |
| *14 March* | *From John P. Heiss.* |
| *14 March* | *From Jesse Miller.* |
| 14 March | From S. K. Nurse. ALS. DLC–JKP. Requests Polk's aid in securing an appointment as assistant surgeon in the navy. |
| 14 March | From James H. Otey. ALS. DLC–JKP. Introduces William W. Horton, a young student at Yale College and a family friend from Huntsville, Ala. |
| 14 March | From William F. Ritchie. ALS. DLC–JKP. Declines appointment as postmaster at Richmond, Va. |
| 14 March | From Gabriel C. Smith. ALS. DLC–JKP. Solicits a federal office to pay his family's debts. |
| 14 March | From Henry A. Wise. ALS. DLC–JKP. Gives details of the court-martial of Alexander Gibson, formerly a lieutenant in the navy; supports Gibson's request for a restoration of lost rank; recommends George Slacum for the consulship at Ric de Janeiro. |
| *15 March* | *From Robert Armstrong.* |
| 15 March | From Patrick G. Buchan et al. LS. DLC–JKP. Introduc John Smyles, a Rochester physician and party operativ fully informed about politics in western New York. |
| 15 March | From Robert Butler. ALS. DLC–JKP. Congratulates Pol on his inaugural address; asks if Sarah Polk, the new "na tions mother," recalls when she lived with the Butlers i Nashville; on behalf of his family, now residing in Lak Jackson, Florida Territory, wishes the Polks health an happiness on this the anniversary of Andrew Jackson birth. |
| 15 March | From John P. Campbell. ALS. DLC–JKP. Expresses feelin₡ of "a deep and abiding interest" in Polk's administratic and requests a private interview. |
| 15 March | From Henry Hill. ALS. DLC–JKP. Informs Polk th |

Roswell Woodworth, a revolutionary war pensioner from New Lebanon, N.Y., has donated $100 for Polk's honorary membership of the American Board of Commissioners for Foreign Missions; encloses the certificate of membership.

March   *From Henry Horn.*

March   From Daniel Judson. ALS. DLC–JKP. Rebukes Polk for discrepancies between the rhetoric of his inaugural address and the expansion of slavery in the new territories.

March   From Dutee J. Pearce. LS. DLC–JKP. Recommends Asa Gray for the post of surveyor at the port of Tiverton, R.I.; regrets Polk's nomination of John S. Harris as customs collector at Providence; and asserts that Harris did not fully support Thomas Dorr in his efforts to bring democracy to Rhode Island.

March   From Samuel A. Rhover. ALS. DLC–JKP. Solicits $10 with which to pay his tuition at Indiana University.

March   From Thomas J. Smith. ALS. DLC–JKP. Informs Polk of his election as an honorary member of the American Literary Institute at Bethany College, Va.

March   From Thomas L. Smith. ALS. DLC–JKP. Requests continuance in his appointment as register of the Treasury; details the complex duties of his office.

March   From Albert H. Tracy. ALS. DLC–JKP. Offers his views on patronage and urges Polk to avoid a policy of partisan proscription.

March   From Luther Kidder. ALS. DLC–JKP. Informs Polk that Edward B. Hubley, a delegate from Pennsylvania to the Baltimore Convention, would accept an appointment as commissioner of Indian affairs.

March   From Thomas Lawrence. ALS. DLC–JKP. Asks Polk to commute the death sentence of a New York prisoner.

March   From Gervasio N. Pires. ALS. DLC–JKP. Congratulates Polk on his victory in the presidential election.

March   *From Thomas Ritchie.*

March   From Anonymous. L, signed "A friend to Virtue." DLC–JKP. Alleges that Robert H. Morris, former mayor of New York City, is a man of corrupt morals and deserves no favors from Polk.

March   From A. Boyles. ALS. DLC–JKP. Complains that the loyal rank and file Democrats of New Jersey have received little reward for their service to the party, while "demi-democrats" monopolize patronage in the state; expresses hope that Polk will correct this imbalance.

March   From Thomas Brinkerhoff. ALS. DLC–JKP. Praises Polk's inaugural address; solicits a position in the federal government.

March   *To James Buchanan.*

| | |
|---|---|
| 17 March | From Arnold Buffum. LS. DLC–JKP. Requests verification of Tennessee land titles signed by Polk during his gubernatorial term. |
| 17 March | From J. A. Collins. ALS. DLC–JKP. Congratulates Polk on his inauguration. |
| 17 March | From Joshua Dodge. ALS. DLC–JKP. Seeks appointment as chargé d'affaires to Buenos Aires. |
| 17 March | From George Evans. ALS. DLC–JKP. Informs Polk that Isaac C. Bates' funeral will be held in the U.S. Senate chamber on March 18 at noon. |
| 17 March | From Edward A. Hannegan and David R. Atchison. LS. DLC–JKP. Recommend that Polk appoint Daniel Kelso as a "sub agent" to the Potawatomi Indians. |
| 17 March | From John Hogan. ALS. DLC–JKP. Reports that Silas Wright and Addison Gardiner will support Polk's administration; notes that all factions within New York's Democratic party approve of Polk's inaugural address. |
| *17 March* | *To Andrew Jackson.* |
| *17 March* | *From Daniel T. Jenks.* |
| 17 March | From William L. Marcy. ALS, copy. DLC–WLM. Urges Polk to show William C. Bouck "some mark of confidence" as soon as may be convenient. |
| *17 March* | *From Henry Osborn.* |
| 17 March | From William S. Pickett. LS. DLC–JKP. Informs Polk of the sale of twenty-eight bales of cotton; reports the state of Polk's account current. |
| *17 March* | *From John C. Rives.* |
| 17 March | From Francis R. Shunk. LS. DLC–JKP. Thanks Polk for the greeting conveyed through Samuel Hays of Venango County; expresses regret that the U.S. senatorial election by the Pennsylvania legislature "has terminated adversely to our wishes." |
| [17 March 1845] | From Lewis Stirn. ALS. DLC–JKP. Offers to sell Polk a piano for "the National Palis." |
| 17 March | From Dan Storrs. ALS. DLC–JKP. Requests the loan of a few dollars. |
| 17 March | From Nathaniel Terry. ALS. DLC–JKP. Solicits an appointment for William W. Horton of Madison County, Alabama. |
| 17 March | From A. M. M. Upshaw. ALS. DLC–JKP. Introduces E. J. Dove, a local artist who wishes to take a miniature likeness of Polk. |
| *17 March* | *From Cornelius P. Van Ness.* |
| *17 March* | *From Reuben M. Whitney.* |
| 17 March | From Fernando Wood. ALS. DLC–JKP. Assures Polk of his continued support despite Polk's failure to honor his request. |
| 18 March | From Benjamin F. Butler. ALS. DLC–JKP. Accepts the ap |

|  | pointment of U.S. attorney for the Southern District of New York. |
|---|---|
| 18 March | From John F. H. Claiborne. ALS. DLC–JKP. Argues against the removal of Thomas Barrett, collector of customs for the port of New Orleans. |
| *18 March* | *From Andrew J. Donelson.* |
| 18 March | From Charles G. Harwell. ALS. NNC. Recommends Henry Curken of Barnstable, Mass., for a position in the federal government. |
| 18 March | From Ralph I. Ingersoll. ALS. DLC–JKP. Introduces Henry Eld, Jr., a naval lieutenant familiar with the Oregon Country. |
| 18 March | From Richard Nelson. ALS. DLC–JKP. Approves of Polk's inaugural address and offers best wishes for the success of his administration. |
| 18 March | From Francis O. J. Smith. ALS. DLC–JKP. Objects to the conflicting and capricious judgments of Treasury auditors in settling the accounts of public contractors; recommends an appeal process to the attorney general in remedying such cases. |
| 18 March | From John A. Williams. ALS. DLC–JKP. Asks Polk to meet with members of the Mechanical Association of Washington City. |
| 19 March | From Ellen Eliza Alden. ALS. DLC–JKP. Solicits a loan of $200 from Polk. |
| 19 March | From William N. Bronaugh. ALS. DLC–JKP. Seeks employment as a courier of dispatches to Texas. |
| 19 March | From John W. Campbell. ALS. DLC–JKP. Reports that he has collected a debt of $250.50 from Turley Hopper and has credited the funds to Polk's account in the Jackson branch of the Union Bank of Tennessee. |
| 19 March | From Daniel S. Dickinson. ALS. DLC–JKP. Informs Polk that the nomination of John H. Prentiss as U.S. marshal for the Northern District of New York has been rejected by the Senate. |
| 19 March | From John A. Dix. ALS. DLC–JKP. Returns a file of recommendations for alternate candidates for U.S. marshal of the Northern District of New York, in case John H. Prentiss' nomination is rejected by the Senate. |
| *19 March* | *From Andrew J. Donelson.* |
| 19 March | From Ransom H. Gillet. ALS. DLC–JKP. Thanks Polk for offering him a place in the Treasury Department; prefers the post of solicitor to that of any other bureau. |
| 19 March | From Edward J. Mallett. ALS. DLC–JKP. Recommends that Levi C. Eaton succeed him as postmaster of Providence, R.I. |
| 19 March | From John M. Niles. ALS. DLC–JKP. Urges the appointment of Joshua Dodge to a consular position in either Eu- |

|              | rope or South America.                                                                                                                                                                                                                                            |
|--------------|--------------------------------------------------------------------------------------------------------------------------------------------------------------------------------------------------------------------------------------------------------------------|
| 19 March     | From John Norvell. ALS. DLC–JKP. Solicits a position in Michigan as U.S. district attorney or superintendent of Indian affairs.                                                                                                                                    |
| 19 March     | From Martha Polk and Eliza Gray. LS. Polk Memorial Association, Columbia. Request that Polk assist Martha Polk find a position in the theater; claim that Martha Polk is a relative whose guardians have withheld from her the knowledge of her true parentage and have denied her the benefits of her parents' estate. |
| *19 March*   | *From James Reid.*                                                                                                                                                                                                                                                 |
| 19 March     | From John G. Ricard. ALS. DLC–JKP. Solicits a position as cook in the White House.                                                                                                                                                                                 |
| 19 March     | From John S. Settings.  ALS. DLC–JKP. Recommends Charles P. Sengstack for appointment as commissioner of public buildings.                                                                                                                                          |
| 19 March     | From Francis R. Shunk. ALS. DLC–JKP. Introduces Walter H. Lowrie of Pittsburgh.                                                                                                                                                                                    |
| 19 March     | From Joel B. Sutherland. ALS. DLC–JKP. Encloses a newspaper excerpt of a speech by Horace Greeley indicating that Henry Clay will be the Whig candidate for president in 1848.                                                                                       |
| 19 March     | From W. Williams. ALS. DLC–JKP. Requests an opportunity for his Ebon Minstrels to perform at the White House; notes that their vocal and instrumental music is of "a mirthful inspiring character."                                                                  |
| 19 March     | From John Woodruff. ALS. DLC–JKP. Wishes to add Polk's autograph to his collection.                                                                                                                                                                                |
| 20 March     | From William Anderson. ALS. DLC–JKP. Calls for the removal of Polk's political opponents from office, but counsels against taking such action prior to Tennessee's August elections.                                                                                |
| 20 March     | From Chester Ashley. ALS. DLC–JKP. Warns Polk of divisions within the Arkansas Democracy; supplies a list of persons suitable for public office in Arkansas; and urges Polk to reject Elias Rector's application to be U.S. marshal.                                 |
| 20 March     | To George Bancroft. ALS. MHi. Asks Bancroft to call as soon as may be convenient.                                                                                                                                                                                  |
| 20 March     | From John P. Campbell. ALS. DLC–JKP. Introduces P. J. Sullivan of Missouri and recommends his appointment to a government clerkship.                                                                                                                                 |
| *20 March*   | *From John F. H. Claiborne.*                                                                                                                                                                                                                                       |
| 20 March     | From John F. H. Claiborne.  ALS. DLC–JKP. Encloses his application to be appointed superintendent of live oak forests.                                                                                                                                              |
| *20 March*   | *From Henry Horn.*                                                                                                                                                                                                                                                 |
| 20 March     | From Henry A. and Hiester H. Muhlenberg. LS. DLC–JK                                                                                                                                                                                                                |

Recommend Edward B. Hubley, a personal friend of their late father, to be named commissioner of Indian affairs or naval officer at Philadelphia.

| | |
|---|---|
| *20 March* | *From Shadrach Penn, Jr.* |
| 20 March | From William V. Pettit. ALS. DLC–JKP. Introduces William F. Coplan, a member of the Pennsylvania legislature from Fayette County. |
| *20 March* | *From Henry E. Riell.* |
| 20 March | From Francis R. Shunk. ALS. DLC–JKP. Introduces William B. Foster, Jr., one of Pennsylvania's canal commissioners. |
| *20 March* | *From Henry Simpson.* |
| *20 March* | *From Daniel Sturgeon.* |
| *20 March* | *From James H. Thompson.* |
| 20 March | From E. J. Whittle. ALS. DLC–JKP. Solicits an appointment for her brother, Powhatan Whittle, to the United States Military Academy. |
| 21 March | From John B. Dawson. ALS. DLC–JKP. Recommends his son, R. G. Dawson, for appointment as U.S. marshal for the Eastern District of Louisiana. |
| 21 March | From David Higgins. ALS. DLC–JKP. Seeks appointment as a clerk in the Treasury Department. |
| 21 March | From James S. McFarlane. ALS. DLC–JKP. Details his objections to the Tyler appointees in New Orleans, La. |
| 21 March | From Daniel Saffarrans. ALS. DLC–JKP. Introduces Moses A. Nixon of New York City. |
| 21 March | From John F. Schermerhorn. ALS. DLC–JKP. Introduces Moses A. Nixon. |
| 21 March | From John S. Skinner. ALS. DLC–JKP. Asks to be retained as third assistant postmaster general. |
| 21 March | From Joseph L. Williams. ALS. DLC–JKP. Requests an interview with Polk; wishes to deliver a Cherokee petition "setting forth the horrible oppression & outrage" of John and Lewis Ross. |
| *22 March* | *From John S. Barbour.* |
| *22 March* | *From Peter V. Daniel.* |
| 22 March | From Jacob G. Davies et al. LS. DLC–JKP. Recommend Charles P. Sengstack to be commissioner of public buildings in the District of Columbia; note that the undersigned Democratic members of both branches of Baltimore's City Council feel that Sengstack's labors in the late election deserve the warmest thanks of Democrats throughout the Union. |
| 22 March | From Charles J. Ingersoll. ALS. DLC–JKP. Introduces Thomas J. Hester of Philadelphia. |
| 22 March | From Daniel T. Jenks. ALS. DLC–JKP. Encloses an article from the *Richmond Enquirer* in which Thomas Ritchie |

urges a union of Polk and Tyler supporters; argues that Tyler's friends secured Polk's victory in Pennsylvania. (Enclosure not found.)

22 March     From Amos Kendall. ALS. DLC–JKP. Requests the replacement of Charles H. Winder as a clerk in the State Department by Louis F. Whitney.

22 March     From John Kettlewell et al. LS. DLC–JKP. Recommend Charles P. Sengstack to be commissioner of public buildings in the District of Columbia; complain that the present commissioner gives but little employment to Democratic mechanics; observe that the undersigned mechanics of Baltimore know Sengstack to be one from whom "they would be certain of receiving even-handed justice."

22 March     From Thomas Lloyd. ALS. DLC–JKP. Objects to his removal as surveyor of the port of Baltimore; wishes to be allowed to resign instead.

22 March     From John B. Magruder et al. LS. DLC–JKP. Recommend Charles P. Sengstack for appointment as commissioner of public buildings in the District of Columbia; state that the Democrats of Bladensburg appreciate his service in the late election; and note that he is "a practical mechanick and working man of business knowledge and habits."

22 March     From Richard C. Murray et al. LS. DLC–JKP. Urge the appointment of Charles P. Sengstack as commissioner of public buildings in the District of Columbia; state that his abilities are highly regarded by the working men of Baltimore.

22 March     From John H. Prentiss. ALS. DLC–JKP. Thanks Polk for his nomination as U.S. marshal of the Northern District of New York, despite his rejection by the Senate.

*22 March*     *From Joel B. Sutherland.*

22 March     From Edward D. Tippett. ALS. DLC–JKP. Requests that Polk and the cabinet examine his design for a new steam engine. (Enclosure not found.)

22 March     From Daniel B. Turner. ALS. DLC–JKP. Introduces Robert T. Scott, a member of the Alabama legislature for Jackson County; notes that Scott serves as Alabama's agent for state claims against the federal government for expenses arising from the Creek hostilities of 1836 and 1837.

22 March     From Aaron Vanderpoel. ALS. DLC–JKP. Recommends Anthony J. Bleecker for U.S. marshal of the Southern District of New York.

22 March     From Campbell P. White et al. LS. DLC–JKP. Solicit the retention of Thomas L. Smith as register of the Treasury.

23 March     From Thomas H. Blake. ALS. PHi. Requests Polk to sign seven patents for lands reserved under the Creek Treaty of 1832.

23 March     From William Clare. ALS. DLC–JKP. Prefers appointment

|  | to a position in the customs house at New York or at Mobile. |
| --- | --- |
| *23 March* | *From Charles J. Ingersoll.* |
| [23 March 1845] | From John L. Lamson and Edward W. Smith. LS. DLC–JKP. Inform Polk of his election to honorary membership in the Hermean Society of the Caldwell Institute of Greensborough, N.C. |
| 23 March | From Ezekiel P. McNeal. ALS. DLC–JKP. Introduces Joseph Jones of Philadelphia. |
| 23 March | From D. Smith. ALS. DLC–JKP. Asks for Polk's autograph. |
| *23 March* | *From Archibald Yell.* |
| 24 March | From Edwin R. Ferris. ALS. DLC–JKP. Wishes to add Polk's autograph to his collection. |
| 24 March | From H. P. Haun. ANS. DLC–JKP. Asks that Polk lay before Cave Johnson the letter from Richard M. Johnson; explains that the letter in question is the one that he handed Polk during their conference a few days ago. |
| [24 March 1845] | From Andrew Jackson. ALS. DLC–JKP. Encloses Auguste D'Avezac's letter of March 15, 1845; encourages Polk to appoint D'Avezac to some suitable position in the government; and adds that he is too weak to correspond with D'Avezac on the subject. |
| 24 March | From Alexander Jones. ALS. DLC–JKP. Encloses a copy of the new British tariff schedule and a printed statement on the cotton market. (Enclosures not found.) |
| 24 March | From Rufus McIntire. ALS. DLC–JKP. Maintains that the gathering of numerous letters of recommendation may represent nothing more than the "mere personal scramble" for office; in most cases the public has formed no collective opinion on either appointments or removals. |
| 24 March | From William S. Pickett. LS. DLC–JKP. Encloses a statement of Polk's account with M. D. Cooper & Co. of New Orleans. |
| 24 March | From Roger B. Taney. ALS. DLC–JKP. Recommends his son-in-law, James Mason Campbell, for the office of U.S. district attorney in Maryland. |
| 25 March | From Ozias Balcom. ALS. DLC–JKP. Reports that many New York Democrats bet on Polk's election; solicits a loan of $200. |
| *25 March* | *From George C. Beckwith.* |
| 25 March | From Charles Callaghan. ALS. DLC–JKP. Reports that he served under Andrew Jackson in 1814; offers views on Texas annexation. |
| 25 March | From James Carroll. ALS. DLC–JKP. Recommends James M. Buchanan to be postmaster of Baltimore, Md. |
| 25 March | From William Chadbourne. ALS. DLC–JKP. Requests Polk's autograph. |
| 25 March | From David Darnell. ALS. DLC–JKP. Recalls their youthful |

|  |  |
|---|---|
|  | acquaintance and solicits an appointment as messenger. |
| 25 March | From John Goldbury. ALS. DLC–JKP. Asks for Polk's autograph. |
| *25 March* | *From Henry Horn.* |
| 25 March | From Edmund Laffan. ALS. Polk Memorial Association, Columbia. Sends receipt for two boxes shipped to Sarah Polk. |
| *25 March* | *From Ezekiel Starr et al.* |
| 25 March | From Ver Planck Van Antwerp. N. DLC–JKP. Requests an interview with Polk for purposes of discussing his prospects for a federal appointment. |
| 25 March | From Charles H. Winder. ALS. DLC–JKP. Solicits Polk's autograph. |
| 26 March | From Azariah C. Flagg and Silas Wright, Jr. LS. DLC–JKP. Recommend Dennis B. Gaffney for some federal appointment in a milder climate than that of New York. |
| 26 March | From Charles G. Greene. ALS. DLC–JKP. Expresses concern that all of the better patronage jobs are going to the friends of Martin Van Buren and not to those in Massachusetts who opposed his nomination; recommends that Polk appoint Benjamin F. Hallet to the U.S. district attorneyship, Henry Crocker to the naval agency, and Robert Rantoul, Jr., to a suitable post in the government's service. |
| *26 March* | *To Andrew Jackson.* |
| 26 March | From John C. LeGrand. ALS. DLC–JKP. Expands upon earlier discussion with Polk concerning applicants for Baltimore port appraiser; warns against appointing Alexander Young; recommends Robert M. Welch; encloses a letter recommending Welch from a "few gentlemen." (Enclosure not found.) |
| 26 March | From James W. McClung. ALS. DLC–JKP. Introduces Robert T. Scott of Bellefonte, Ala. |
| 26 March | From Robert M. McLane. ALS. DLC–JKP. Presents his friend and fellow Democrat, Joseph J. Turner of Baltimore, Md. |
| 26 March | From John V. L. McMahon. ALS. DLC–JKP. Supports retention of James W. McCulloh as comptroller of the Treasury. |
| 26 March | From R. E. Merrill. ALS. DLC–JKP. Wishes to obtain Polk's autograph. |
| *26 March* | *From Jesse Miller.* |
| *26 March* | *From Archibald Yell.* |
| [27 March 1845] | From William E. Cramer. ALS. DLC–JKP. Recommends Chesselden Ellis for the position of solicitor of the Treasury. |
| *27 March* | *From George M. Dallas.* |
| 27 March | From Herschel V. Johnson. ALS. DLC–JKP. Recommends his brother-in-law, James Purnell Polk of Somerset County, Maryland. |

| | |
|---|---|
| 27 March | From Peter W. Kenaday. LS. DLC–JKP. Claims to have lost his job as a riverboat captain for having supported Polk in the late election; solicits a customs house appointment in New Orleans for himself and a position as mail agent for his son, Alexander McConnell Kenaday. |
| 27 March | From Henry Liebenau. ALS. DLC–JKP. Recommends nomination of John I. Morgan as collector of customs at New York City. |
| [27 March 1845] | From Thomas Lloyd. ALS. DLC–JKP. Complains that his removal as surveyor for the port of Baltimore has damaged his reputation; believes that a letter from Polk will restore his honor. |
| 27 March | From William G. McNeill. AN. DLC–JKP. Solicits a personal interview. |
| 27 March | From Frances Robinson. ALS. DLC–JKP. Returns her husband's letter of dismissal; recalls Polk's assurances that no such action should be taken without prior notification. |
| 27 March | From James F. Simmons. ALS. DLC–JKP. Reminds Polk to delay the appointment of the collector at Providence, R.I., if Thomas F. Carpenter declines to serve. |
| 27 March | From James Walker. ALS. DLC–JKP. Explains that he remains in Washington City awaiting William S. Pickett's consular appointment; hopes that Polk will not deny Pickett's claim of patronage. |
| 27 March | From William R. Watson. ALS. DLC–JKP. Solicits reappointment as the collector at Providence, R.I., since Thomas F. Carpenter has declined it. |
| 28 March | From William J. Alexander. ALS. DLC–JKP. Requests consideration for a federal appointment. |
| *28 March* | *To Andrew J. Donelson.* |
| 28 March | From Joseph Hall. ALS. DNA–RG 45. Asks for the return of a letter recommending him for appointment as surveyor of the port of Boston; seeks to have his present position protected, as recent appointees in the Boston Customs House are hostile to him. |
| 28 March | From Robert Keyworth. ALS. DLC–JKP. Solicits contract for that portion of White House refurbishing that involves cleaning, repairing, or replacing the chandeliers, lamps, candelabra, silver pieces, and plated ware. |
| 28 March | From A. P. Longley. ALS. DLC–JKP. Requests money with which to continue his education at East Tennessee University. |
| 28 March | From William G. McNeill. ALS. DLC–JKP. Seeks an interview prior to his urgent return home to attend a gravely ill child. |
| 28 March | From John Y. Mason. ALS. DLC–JKP. Requests Polk's signature on several naval and marine corps commissions ap- |

|              | proved by the Senate. |
|--------------|------------------------|
| 28 March | From Marcus Morton. ALS. DLC–JKP. Acknowledges receipt of his appointment to the customs collectorship at Boston; states that his selection was "unexpected as well as undesired and unsolicited"; requests permission to delay his decision in order to consult with leaders of the party and "to consider how far the Official influence may be expected to harmonize and cooperate." |
| 28 March | From Henry Simpson. ALS. DLC–JKP. Encloses copies of his addresses and circulars written for the Hickory Club of Philadelphia; believes that they demonstrate his commitment to Polk's election and thus support his application for office. (Enclosure not found.) |
| 28 March | From Sylvester S. Southworth. ALS. DLC–JKP. Reports that Eliab Kingman, a correspondent of the *New York Journal of Commerce*, started a rumor of his appointment as "Consul to Japan"; notes that Kingman acted "for the purpose of 'humbugging' some of his contemporary letter writers." |
| 28 March | From Nathaniel Terry. ALS. DLC–JKP. Introduces Robert T. Scott of Jackson County, Ala. |
| 28 March | From James H. Thomas. ALS. DLC–JKP. Apprises Polk of political affairs in Tennessee; names several Democratic nominees for the upcoming state election. |
| 28 March | From Joseph G. Totten. NS. DLC–JKP. Inquires if Polk might wish the use of facilities at Old Point Comfort as a family retreat; notes that John Tyler visited there on two occasions during his presidency. |
| 29 March | From John S. Barbour. ALS. DLC–JKP. Recommends Henry Hill, Jr., of Albemarle County, Va., to be appointed warden of the penitentiary at Washington City. |
| 29 March | From John Bruce. ALS. DLC–JKP. Asks Polk to postpone appointing a new postmaster at Winchester, Va., until after the state elections. |
| 29 March | From Thomas F. Carpenter. ALS. DLC–JKP. Urges the appointment of Hezekiah Willard as customs collector at Providence, R.I.; supports the application of Burrington Anthony to be named U.S. marshal for the District of Rhode Island. |
| 29 March | From George M. Dallas. ALS. DLC–JKP. Introduces David McCallister of Delaware. |
| 29 March | From Paul Dillingham, Jr. ALS. DLC–JKP. Introduces David A. Smalley, a lawyer and Democrat from Burlington, Vt. |
| 29 March | From Jesse Miller. ALS. DLC–JKP. Restates his views on federal appointments in Philadelphia and Pittsburgh. |
| 29 March | From Josiah F. Polk. ALS. Polk Memorial Association. |

|            | Columbia. Solicits a promotion in office if changes are made in the second auditor's division of the Treasury Department. |
|------------|---|
| 29 March   | From Elijah F. Purdy. ALS. DLC–JKP. Encloses a synopsis of testimonials on file in the Treasury Department recommending him for appointment as customs collector at New York City. |
| 29 March   | From William R. Rucker. ALS. DLC–JKP. Threatens to withhold support from Aaron V. Brown's gubernatorial campaign if John W. Rucker, his brother, is not appointed U.S. marshal for the Southern District of Mississippi; asserts that Thomas Fletcher, son of Thomas H. Fletcher, is a Whig and should not be given the marshalship. |
| 29 March   | From Joel Turrill. ALS. DLC–JKP. Encloses private letters recommending him for a federal office; wishes to be considered for a consular appointment at Le Havre or Rio de Janeiro. |
| 29 March   | From Timothy Weller. ALS. DLC–JKP. Encourages the removal of Thomas L. Smith as register of the Treasury. |
| 30 March   | From John F. H. Claiborne. ALS. DLC–JKP. Encloses a tribute to Sarah C. Polk by William M. Smyth of the Jackson *Southern Reformer*. (Enclosure not found.) |
| *30 March* | *From Arnold S. Harris.* |
| 30 March   | From Benjamin Patton. ALS. DLC–JKP. Recommends Robert C. Grier for appointment to the U.S. Supreme Court; gives an extensive personal and political testimonial of Grier's qualifications. |
| *30 March* | *From Nathaniel P. Tallmadge.* |
| 31 March   | From Noyes Billings. ALS. DLC–JKP. Recommends Stanley G. Trott as postmaster at New London, Conn. |
| *31 March* | *From Benjamin F. Butler.* |
| 31 March   | From George A. Carnes. ALS. DLC–JKP. Renews his earlier request for Polk's autograph. |
| 31 March   | From John F. H. Claiborne. ALS. DLC–JKP. Submits the name of Solomon W. Downs as an applicant for the office of U.S. attorney for Louisiana; argues that Downs' appointment would remove him from the competition for the gubernatorial nomination and so unite the Louisiana Democracy behind Isaac Johnson. |
| 31 March   | From John F. H. Claiborne. ALS. DLC–JKP. Supports the application of Warren Stone to be named surgeon at the Marine Hospital in New Orleans; maintains that Stone, a surgeon at Charity Hospital, "is one of the boldest & most successful operators in the world & of great practice." |
| 31 March   | From John F. H. Claiborne. ALS. DLC–JKP. Makes one more appeal for the appointment of Mandeville Marigny as U.S. marshal of Louisiana. |

| | |
|---|---|
| 31 March | From Owen Connelly. ALS. DLC–JKP. Provides Polk with names of those individuals responsible for the recent gift of a horse. |
| *31 March* | *From Samuel H. Laughlin.* |
| 31 March | From Thomas Lloyd. ALS. DLC–JKP. Requests an answer to his letter of March 27, 1845. |
| 31 March | From William L. Marcy. ALS. DLC–JKP. Encloses reports of the commissioner of Indian affairs and paymaster general of the army; informs Polk of expiring commissions for several Indian agents and paymasters. (Enclosures not found.) |
| 31 March | From William H. Marriott. ALS. DLC–JKP. Offers opinions on patronage at the Baltimore Customs House. |
| 31 March | From Job Pierson. ALS. DLC–JKP. Recommends Gerrit Y. Lansing as chargé d'affaires to the Netherlands. |
| 31 March | From Josiah F. Polk. ALS. DLC–JKP. Requests a two-minute audience. |
| 31 March | From J. G. M. Ramsey. ALS. DLC–JKP. Recommends Henry A. Talman for a position in the New York Customs House; encloses a letter from H. W. Conner of Charleston, S.C., who asks Ramsey to assist with Talman's appointment; recalls that he has quoted from Conner's letters in past communications; and cautions against giving any patronage to William M. French or Hugh L. McClung, even if backed by Alexander O. Anderson. |
| 31 March | From William H. Roane. ALS. DLC–JKP. Urges Polk not to remove Nathaniel B. Denby as U.S. consul at Marseilles, France. |
| 31 March | From C. U. Schlater. ALS. DLC–JKP. Solicits Polk's autograph. |
| 31 March | From Thomas Parkin Scott. ALS. DLC–JKP. Recommends Michael McBlair, John J. Graves, and Joseph White as candidates for the appointment of naval officer for the port of Baltimore. |
| 31 March | From James A. Sedden. ALS. DLC–JKP. Requests that Polk retain Nathaniel B. Denby as U.S. consul at Marseilles, France. |
| 31 March | From Henry Simpson. ALS. DLC–JKP. Introduces William Ross, a merchant in Philadelphia County, Penn.; notes that Ross supposes that he and Polk may be related. |
| 31 March | From John Slidell. ALS. DLC–JKP. Responds to Polk's request for written advice on federal appointments in Louisiana; provides explanations for his recommendations on each position. |
| 31 March | From John B. Sterigere. ALS. DLC–JKP. Solicits appointment as collector of the customs at Philadelphia. |
| 31 March | From Jeremiah Y. Tifft. ALS. DLC–JKP. Wishes to add Polk's autograph to his collection. |

| | |
|---|---|
| 31 March | From Robert S. Wharton. ALS. DLC–JKP. Requests an interview; explains that directions for his reinstatement as a clerk in the Treasury Department have not been received by Robert J. Walker, who says that he will appoint another to the clerkship if no contrary instructions from Polk are in hand by the close of the day. |
| 31 March | From Levi Woodbury. ALS. DLC–JKP. Attests to the loyalty of Isaac O. Barnes, his brother-in-law; urges Polk to retain Barnes as U.S. marshal for the District of Massachusetts. |
| [April 1845] | From John W. Dana. ALS. DLC–JKP. Recommends Joseph Howard to be named U.S. attorney for the District of Maine; warns that the Maine Democracy opposes the appointment of Augustine Haines to that position. |
| [April 1845] | From Joshua Herrick. ALS. DLC–JKP. Requests that Jabez True be appointed U.S. marshal in Maine. |
| [April 1845] | From Lorain T. Pease. L. DLC–JKP. Appeals the dismissal of Bartholomew McGowan from the navy on grounds that his accuser, William C. Bolton, is of unsound mind; notes that the navy failed to give McGowan a hearing and did not give him the customary opportunity to resign. |
| [April 1845] | From Benjamin C. Presstman. ALS. DLC–JKP. Introduces William George Krebs and recommends his appointment to the postmastership of Baltimore, Md. |
| [April 1845] | From John H. Wheeler. NS. DLC–JKP. Requests acknowledgment of having received his shipment of Andrew Jackson's picture by Thomas Sully, Jr. |
| 1 April | From Jesse D. Elliott. ALS. DLC–JKP. Asks Polk to direct the navy to purchase its "Sails, Hammocks, and Bags" from Philadelphia canvas manufacturers. |
| *1 April* | *From John Fairfield.* |
| 1 April | From Daniel Freeman. ALS. DLC–JKP. Announces that he has named his son after Polk. |
| 1 April | From Thomas McElhiney. ALS. DLC–JKP. Promises to send Polk two copies of a book he has just published. |
| 1 April | From G. C. F. Morhard. ALS. DLC–JKP. Details project for constructing a railroad line to the Oregon country. |
| 1 April | From William Parmenter. ALS. DLC–JKP. Expresses appreciation for his appointment as naval officer for the port of Boston, Mass. |
| 1 April | From Joel B. Sutherland. ALS. DLC–JKP. Offers assurances that he supported Polk's nomination for the presidency; encloses a letter from Andrew Jackson supporting his claims. |
| April | From Hampton C. Williams. ALS. DLC–JKP. Recommends James Hoban as district attorney for Washington City; notes that Hoban is the unanimous choice of Washington citizens. |

| | |
|---|---|
| 2 April | From William J. Alexander. ALS. DLC–JKP. Introduces Robert Gibbon of Charlotte, N.C. |
| 2 April | From Samuel Beardsley. ALS. DLC–JKP. Introduces Jay Hatheway of Rome, N.Y. |
| 2 April | From Sidney Breese. ALS. DLC–JKP. Supports the application of Isaac Cook for the postmastership of Chicago, Ill.; observes that Cook is a "moral man and of strict integrity." |
| 2 April | From John Claiborne. ALS. DLC–JKP. Reiterates his desire to secure an appointment as attorney for the District of Louisiana; encloses a letter from John Slidell. |
| 2 April | From John F. H. Claiborne. ALS. DLC–JKP. Recommends William M. Smyth of Jackson, Miss., to be U.S. consul at Rio de Janeiro; notes that Smyth is the editor of the *Southern Reformer*. |
| 2 April | From Samuel Cushman. ALS. DLC–JKP. Expresses gratitude for his appointment as navy agent at Portsmouth, N.H. |
| 2 April | From John Jay. LS. DLC–JKP. Informs Polk of his election to honorary membership in the New-York Historical Society. |
| 2 April | From Preston King. ALS. DLC–JKP. Urges the appointment of Michael Hoffman of New York to an office in the federal government. |
| 2 April | From Eliakim Littell. ALS. DLC–JKP. Calls Polk's attention to a proposed constitutional change as "set forth in the Living Age," a copy of which is sent this day under separate cover. |
| *2 April* | *To Thomas Ritchie.* |
| 2 April | From John Slidell. L. DLC–JKP. Introduces Samuel Haight, appointed by Andrew Jackson to be consul at Tampico and then by Martin Van Buren to be consul at Antwerp; explains that John Tyler removed Haight without cause; and urges his reinstatement. |
| 2 April | To Robert J. Walker. ALS. NNPM. Introduces a "Mr. Thomas of Ohio" and urges his favorable consideration. |
| 3 April | From H. J. Anderson. ALS. DLC–JKP. Approves of Polk's inaugural address and cabinet selections; discusses Tennessee political affairs. |
| 3 April | From Joel H. Dyer. ALS. DLC–JKP. Declares that he is "poor and pennyless"; solicits a federal office to support his family. |
| 3 April | From John Fairfield. ALS. DLC–JKP. Recommends Ezra B. French for appointment as customs collector at Waldeborough, Maine; names several prominent citizens of Maine as qualified applicants for federal office. |
| 3 April | From Samuel Raub, Jr., and Thomas Wallace. LS. DLC–JKP. Urge the removal of William Noland as commissioner of public buildings in Washington City. |

| | |
|---|---|
| 3 April | From Henry Simpson. ALS. DLC–JKP. Expresses hope that Polk will make removals and appointments in the customs house, mint, and post office in Philadelphia; encloses an article from the Harrisburg *Democratic Union* on the subject of Pennsylvania's recent election of a U.S. senator. |
| 3 April | From John S. Stiles. ALS. DLC–JKP. Urges consideration of his application as naval officer for the port of Baltimore, Md. |
| 3 April | From William R. Watson. ALS. DLC–JKP. Praises James F. Simmons for his contributions to Charles Jackson's successful gubernatorial race; notes that the opposition attacked all who supported Thomas W. Dorr's release. |
| 4 April | From George W. Boyd. ALS. DLC–JKP. Regrets that "this dying thirst for office" has resulted in the removal of John McClintock as naval officer of Portsmouth, N.H. |
| 4 April | From Benjamin F. Butler. ALS. DLC–JKP. Solicits a position in the general government for Dennis B. Gaffney of Albany, N.Y. |
| 4 April | From John Cole. ALS. DLC–JKP. Seeks an interview. |
| 4 April | From Howell Hinds. ALS. DLC–JKP. Recommends P. O. Hughes as U.S. marshal for Mississippi. |
| *4 April* | *From Alexander Jones.* |
| 4 April | From Joseph W. Manson. ALS. DLC–JKP. Introduces Josiah B. French of Lowell, Mass. |
| 4 April | From Silas Reed. ALS. DLC–JKP. Wishes to be retained as surveyor of public lands in Illinois and Missouri. |
| 5 April | From James W. Armstrong. ALS. DLC–JKP. Solicits the appointment of postmaster at Macon, Ga. |
| 5 April | From Charles G. Atherton. ALS. DLC–JKP. Introduces Thomas P. Goodhue of Lowell, Mass. |
| 5 April | From James Buchanan. ALS. DLC–JKP. Suggests retention of Thomas Findley until his commission as Baltimore's postmaster expires in July; notes that Jane Findley Shunk, the wife of Francis R. Shunk, is Findley's niece. |
| 5 April | From John Fairfield. ALS. DLC–JKP. Introduces Eliphalet Case, former editor of the Portland *Eastern Argus*; warns that Case has aroused suspicions of Maine Democrats by his refusal to identify the persons financing the purchase of the *Argus*. |
| *5 April* | *From Thomas Hague.* |
| [5 April 1845] | From Adam Huntsman. ALS. DLC–JKP. Worries that a newly established newspaper at Trenton, Tenn., might take the public printing contract from the Western District's most influential newspaper, the Jackson *Republican*; notes that no Democratic newspaper has succeeded in the District's northern counties. |
| 5 April | From Robert W. Powell. ALS. DLC–JKP. Believes "every- |

|  | thing promises well for the Democracy" in Tennessee's state elections; supports John P. Chester's application for a special agency in the Post Office Department. |
| 5 April | From H. H. Wright. ALS. DLC–JKP. Requests a pardon for her husband, William S. Wright, who is held at the Washington penitentiary. |
| 5 April | From David Levy Yulee. ALS. DLC–JKP. Recommends Walker Anderson to be navy agent at Pensacola, Fla.; suggests delaying appointments until after the forthcoming state elections. |
| [6 April 1845] | From Robert Armstrong. ALS. DLC–JKP. Urges the appointment of Philip Poultney as naval officer for the port of Baltimore. |
| 6 April | From John B. Dawson and Dixon H. Lewis. LS. DLC–JKP. Introduce James Maher, public gardener during John Tyler's administration. |
| *6 April* | *From J. George Harris.* |
| 6 April | From Townsend Peyton. ALS. DLC–JKP. Solicits Polk's autograph. |
| *7 April* | *From Robert Armstrong.* |
| 7 April | From John B. Bouton. ALS. DLC–JKP. Asks for Polk's autograph. |
| 7 April | From Sidney Breese. ALS. DLC–JKP. Remarks that Polk's administration has the confidence of the nation; predicts that the administration "will be the most benign and most successful of any other that has preceeded it." |
| *7 April* | *From Edmund Burke.* |
| *7 April* | *From Benjamin Cowell.* |
| *7 April* | *From L. W. Gosnell.* |
| 7 April | From Edward A. Hannegan. ALS. DLC–JKP. Renews his recommendation that William J. Brown be appointed register of the U.S. Treasury. |
| *7 April* | *From J. George Harris.* |
| *7 April* | *From Henry Horn.* |
| 7 April | From Charles J. Ingersoll. ALS. DLC–JKP. Notes that he is now the only Democrat elected to Congress from eastern Pennsylvania; anticipates that Polk will consult him in making appointments in those congressional districts. |
| *7 April* | *From Andrew Jackson.* |
| 7 April | From Samuel Medary. ALS. DLC–JKP. Introduces William Neil of Columbus, Ohio. |
| *7 April* | *From Jesse Miller.* |
| 7 April | From Levi Reynolds, Jr. ALS. DLC–JKP. Maintains that Pennsylvania Democrats favor retention of Calvin Blythe as collector of customs at Philadelphia. |
| 7 April | From Henry W. Rogers. ALS. DLC–JKP. Suggests that Polk confer with John A. Dix, Ransom H. Gillet, Albert G. Jew- |

|  |  |
|---|---|
| | ett, John B. Skinner, and Augustine G. Danby concerning appointments in Buffalo, N.Y. |
| 7 April | From Charles Ruckoldt and D. T. Johnson. LS. DLC–JKP. Request that Polk await communication from the General Democratic Committee of New Haven, Conn., prior to appointing a postmaster and a surveyor for their city. |
| 7 April | From Stephen P. Slocum and Samuel J. Carr. LS. DLC–JKP. Quote text of resolutions adopted at a March 21st meeting of Whigs held in Newport, R.I.; quote text of resolutions adopted at a March 31st meeting of Newport Democrats; and congratulate Polk for having "incurred the high displeasure of the Algerines, of this place ...." |
| 8 April | From John Anderson. ALS. DLC–JKP. Introduces J. W. Robinson, one of Maine's principal merchant shipowners and a delegate to the late Baltimore convention. |
| 8 April | From Hartwell H. Brown. ALS. DLC–JKP. Asks if reports are true that Polk has appointed him to a position in the Memphis navy yard; recommends his near neighbor, James Coman of Limestone County, Ala., for the office of U.S. marshal. |
| *8 April* | *From Benjamin F. Butler.* |
| *8 April* | *To Franklin H. Elmore.* |
| 8 April | From Augustus Garrett. ALS. DLC–JKP. Recommends that Polk delay making any Chicago appointments without consulting "the interest and wishes of the Citizens of the City of Chicago." |
| 8 April | From Charles C. Haddock. ALS. DLC–JKP. Requests the reasons for his removal as postmaster at Buffalo, N.Y. |
| *8 April* | *From George S. Houston.* |
| *8 April* | *From Charles S. Jones.* |
| 8 April | From William L. Marcy. LS. DLC–JKP. Reports that eight officers and agents of the War Department have failed to render accounts for the last quarter of 1844. |
| 8 April | From William L. Roy. ALS. DLC–JKP. Encloses a copy of his Hebrew dictionary; expresses concern about the New York City Charter election. |
| 8 April | From Sylvester S. Southworth. ALS. DLC–JKP. Regrets to report that preliminary Connecticut election returns indicate the loss of three Democratic seats in the U.S. House; expresses concern about the New York Charter election scheduled for today; solicits a pursership in the navy, but only after an appointment as a bearer of dispatches to a European legation. |
| 8 April | From Ebenezer S. Thomas. ALS. DLC–JKP. Informs Polk about his efforts on Polk's behalf during the 1844 presidential campaign. |
| *9 April* | *From Robert Armstrong.* |

| | |
|---|---|
| 9 April | From Joseph E. Buzby. ALS. DLC–JKP. Solicits Polk's autograph. |
| *9 April* | *From John F. H. Claiborne.* |
| 9 April | From George W. Clinton. ALS. DLC–JKP. Expresses disappointment at not being named U.S. attorney for the Northern District of New York; reports that the people of Buffalo have reacted unfavorably to Philip Dorsheimer's appointment as postmaster of their town. |
| 9 April | From David L. Gregg. ALS. DLC–JKP. Recommends the immediate appointment of Thomas Dyer as receiver at Chicago; notes that he has not received his commission as U.S. attorney for Illinois. |
| *9 April* | *From J. George Harris.* |
| 9 April | From Robert R. Haskins. ALS. DLC–JKP. Congratulates the Polks on their Sabbatarian views. |
| 9 April | From Leonard Jarvis. ALS. DLC–JKP. Discusses possible nominees for the collectorship at Belfast, Maine; asks Polk to delay that appointment until after the state's elections in September. |
| 9 April | From Andrew Johnson. ALS. DLC–JKP. Recommends the appointment of John P. Chester as a special agent for the Post Office Department. |
| *9 April* | *From Alexander Jones.* |
| 9 April | From Samuel H. Laughlin. ALS. DLC–JKP. Encloses a list of Land Office employees with notes on their character and qualifications; provides news of efforts to secure an appointment to West Point for his son, Samuel Houston Laughlin. (Enclosure not found.) |
| 9 April | From William M. Lowry. ALS. DLC–JKP. Offers news of Tennessee's gubernatorial and congressional campaigns; solicits an appointment as a special agent for the Post Office Department. |
| 9 April | From Albert Smith. ALS. DLC–JKP. Expresses surprise at the appointment of Levi J. Horn as U.S. consul to Rio de Janeiro; informs Polk of Horn's "entire unfitness for the place." |
| 9 April | From Frederick P. Stanton. ALS. DLC–JKP. States that S. F. Moseley of Memphis will move to Texas and desires appointment as U.S. district attorney there. |
| 10 April | From Robert J. Chester. ALS. DLC–JKP. Advises that John H. Day and Francis McClennahan have purchased the Jackson *Republican*; worries that the government printing contract might be assigned to a newspaper in Trenton, Tenn. |
| *10 April* | *From James Hamilton, Jr.* |
| *10 April* | *From John N. Mars.* |
| 10 April | From Gideon C. Matlock. ALS. DLC–JKP. States that Pierce M. Butler, agent to the Cherokees, is a Whig; notes |

that the Cherokees are dissatisfied with Butler and desire his removal.

10 April    From Franklin Pierce. ALS. DLC–JKP. Approves of Edmund Burke for the post of commissioner of patents; expresses thanks for his appointment as U.S. attorney for the District of New Hampshire.

10 April    From Joel B. Sutherland. ALS. DLC–JKP. Encloses articles clipped from the Philadelphia *American Sentinel* and the Philadelphia *Spirit of the Times*; observes that the *American Sentinel* article was written with a view of bringing the Native Democrats back to the party.

10 April    From Thomas Willy. ALS. DLC–JKP. Warns that Philadelphia's Whigs, chagrined by Polk's success, will seek revenge against the Democrats and employ false rumors to divide them.

11 April    To George Bancroft. LS. NN. Repeats instructions stated in his letter of this date to James Buchanan and other members of the cabinet.

*11 April*    *To James Buchanan.*

11 April    From John F. H. Claiborne. ALS. DLC–JKP. Thanks Polk for the appointment of agent for the preservation of live oak timbers in Louisiana, Mississippi, and Alabama; urges the appointment of his cousin, John Claiborne, to some federal office.

11 April    From A. H. Everett. ALS. DLC–JKP. Encloses copies of his articles, written for the Washington *Globe*, discussing relations between the United States and Mexico. (Enclosures not found.)

*11 April*    *From Henry Horn.*

*11 April*    *From Andrew Jackson.*

11 April    To William L. Marcy. LS. DNA–RG 99. Repeats instructions stated in his letter of this date to James Buchanan and other members of the cabinet.

*11 April*    *From John Y. Mason.*

11 April    To Robert J. Walker. LS. Private Collection of Paul H. Bergeron. Repeats instructions stated in his letter of this date to James Buchanan and other members of the cabinet.

12 April    From Daniel B. Brinsmade. ALS. DLC–JKP. Solicits aid for the family of Elias Boudinot, a leader of the Treaty party of the Cherokee nation; reminds Polk of Boudinot's assassination in 1839 by members of the rival National party.

2 April    From L. J. Cist. ALS. DLC–JKP. Solicits Polk's autograph.

2 April    From John Fairfield. ALS. DLC–JKP. Encloses R. D. Rice's letter of April 7, 1845; notes that Rice is the editor of the Augusta *Age*; and comments that this letter will verify his assessment of public opinion in Maine. ALS. DLC–JKP.

*2 April*    *From Herschel V. Johnson.*

| | |
|---|---|
| 14 April | From John G. Palfrey. ALS. DLC–JKP. Encloses the Declaration of the Commonwealth of Massachusetts of March 24, 1845; requests that Polk communicate it to Congress. |
| 14 April | From Thomas L. Ragsdale. ALS. DLC–JKP. Criticizes John Y. Mason for supporting George W. Crump's appointment as chief clerk in the Pension Office; encloses his correspondence with Mason of April 12 and 14, 1845. ALsS. DLC–JKP. |
| 14 April | From James M. Smith. ALS. DLC–JKP. Complains about the appointment of Philip Dorsheimer, a bankrupt, as postmaster at Buffalo, N.Y. |
| 14 April | From Isaac Toucey. ALS. DLC–JKP. Introduces Gideon Welles, who will advise Polk on the Connecticut Democracy. |
| 14 April | From John Wentworth. ALS. DLC–JKP. Desires the immediate appointment of Thomas Dyer as receiver of public monies at Chicago. |
| 15 April | From George Bancroft. LS. DLC–JKP. Declines recommending the reinstatement of Josiah Colston, formerly a purser in the navy whose sureties are being sued for his defalcation. |
| *15 April* | *From Franklin H. Elmore.* |
| 15 April | From French S. Evans. ALS. DLC–JKP. Invites Polk and his family to attend the dedication of the Methodist Episcopal Church on Massachusetts Avenue on April 20. |
| 15 April | From David E. Harbaugh et al. NS. DLC–JKP. Endorse the appointment of John Norvell as U.S. district attorney for Michigan. |
| 15 April | From Charles Lewis. ALS. DLC–JKP. States that he killed an individual "attemting to disgrace you in the political world"; claims that he has given up his "wild ways" and taken residence with his wife, Mary, in Havana, Cuba; and requests that he be given a government appointment. |
| *15 April* | *From Austin Miller.* |
| 15 April | From Marcus Morton. ALS. DLC–JKP. Introduces Josiah B. French, a Democrat of much "purity and Patriotism." |
| *15 April* | *From John Norvell.* |
| 15 April | From George W. Owens. ALS. DLC–JKP. Introduces Edward Harden; urges Harden's retention as collector at Savannah, Ga. |
| 15 April | From John W. Rucker. ALS. DLC–JKP. Solicits appointment as U.S. consul at Havana, Cuba; states that Sarah Polk, "a little power behind the Throne," has known him all his life. |
| 15 April | From Sylvester S. Southworth. ALS. DLC–JKP. Applauds reports that Polk has removed Cornelius P. Van Ness from the collectorship of New York City; reaffirms his support for Jonathan P. Clement's restoration to his post as an inspector of customs. |

| | |
|---|---|
| 15 April | From Joel B. Sutherland. ALS. DLC–JKP. Anticipates that the Whigs will run Henry Clay in 1848; relates that Democrats in the interior of Pennsylvania are not united behind the appointments made by Francis R. Shunk and John K. Kane. |
| 15 April | From James H. Thomas. ALS. DLC–JKP. Recommends that Tennessee postmasters be left in place until after the August elections. |
| [15 April 1845] | From Jeremiah Towle. ALS. DLC–JKP. Wishes to be retained as naval officer for the port of New York; argues that he has been misrepresented by persons seeking appointment to the office. |
| *15 April* | *From Cornelius P. Van Ness.* |
| *15 April* | *From James Walker.* |
| 15 April | From Richard Wayne. ALS. DLC–JKP. Protests the removal of Edward Harden as customs collector at Savannah, Ga. |
| 16 April | From Benjamin Andrews. ALS. DLC–JKP. Complains of his removal as postmaster at Cleveland, Ohio. |
| *16 April* | *To Edmund Burke.* |
| 16 April | From Benjamin F. Butler. ALS. DLC–JKP. Introduces Tobias L. Hogeboom, "the patriarch" of New York's Democracy for the last half century. |
| *16 April* | *From Levin H. Coe.* |
| 16 April | From John W. Edmonds. ALS. DLC–JKP. Assures Polk that Tobias L. Hogeboom of Columbia County, N.Y., is a staunch Democrat. |
| *16 April* | *From Alexander Jones.* |
| 16 April | From Benjamin Kurtz et al. LS. Private collection of James S. Corbitt. Enclose a bound volume of proceedings for the National Lord's Day Convention, held in Baltimore in November 1844; offer praise of the Baltimore Sabbath Association for Polk's "respect for and attachment to the Sabbath." |
| *16 April* | *From Jacob L. Martin.* |
| 16 April | From S. B. Mirner et al. LS. DLC–JKP. Approve of John Norvell's appointment as U.S. district attorney for Michigan. |
| 16 April | From Pleasant Nelson. ALS. DLC–JKP. Recommends that Jeremiah Cherry be appointed postmaster at Columbia, Tenn. |
| 16 April | From Nathan Ranney. ALS. DLC–JKP. Solicits appointment as postmaster at St. Louis, Mo.; believes the country and the Democratic party owe him the office. |
| 16 April | From Henry R. Schoolcraft. ALS, copy. DLC–FP. Seeks appointment as commissioner to the Sandwich Islands. |
| 16 April | From Sylvester S. Southworth. ALS. DLC–JKP. States that Cornelius P. Van Ness threatened him with removal from |

his office in the New York Customs House for supporting Polk's election.

16 April    From Cornelius P. Van Ness. ALS. DLC–JKP. Requests copies of any charges made against him; claims that he can refute such charges and notes that rumors of his failure to support the Democratic ticket "can only have originated in malice."

17 April    From George Bancroft. LS. DLC–JKP. Submits naval commissions of George W. Latham and Nathan C. Fletcher for Polk's signature.

17 April    From John S. Barbour. ALS. DLC–JKP. Argues for the removal of John B. Dade, warden of the penitentiary at Washington City; supports application of Henry Hill, Jr., who seeks appointment to Dade's office.

17 April    From Ker Boyce. ALS. DLC–JKP. Suggests that Franklin H. Elmore could not accept an appointment as U.S. minister to Great Britain "without great sacrifice of his own interests and those of others dependant upon his presence."

17 April    From Sidney Breese. ALS. DLC–JKP. Encloses a letter from J. P. Cooper, who complains of James L. Edwards, pension commissioner.

17 April    From James G. Bryce. ALS. DLC–JKP. States that he would be "highly gratified" to accept a diplomatic post under Polk's administration; notes that he could serve with the mission to Mexico or as chargé d'affaires to Vienna.

17 April    From John C. Bucher. ALS. DLC–JKP. Urges appointment of Henry Horn as customs collector for Philadelphia; describes Horn as a consistent and orthodox Democrat.

17 April    From Ben F. Clark. ALS. DLC–JKP. Introduces S. B. Lowry of Louisville, Kentucky.

17 April    From Jonathan P. Clement. ALS. DLC–JKP. Claims that Cornelius P. Van Ness removed him from office because of reports that he supported Clay in the late presidential campaign; offers assurances of his devotion to the Democratic party and seeks reappointment as an inspector in the New York Customs House.

17 April    From James Conner. ALS. DLC–JKP. Asks Polk to appoint Alexander J. Bergen as U.S. consul to Havana, Cuba.

17 April    From Stephen A. Douglas. ALS. DLC–JKP. Recommends Ver Planck Van Antwerp for a position in the federal government.

7 April    From R. W. Dunlap. ALS. DLC–JKP. Argues against the appointment of non-residents to federal offices in Philadelphia; urges retention of Calvin Blythe as collector of customs.

7 April    From Jesse D. Elliott. ALS. DLC–JKP. Solicits command of naval forces in the Gulf of Mexico; notes that John Tyler

promised him the "humble privilege of the first blows" against Mexico.

17 April    From William Faulkner. ALS. DLC–JKP. Urges retention of John H. Townsend as postmaster at Norwich, Conn.; recommends Enoch C. Chapman for the office if Townsend's removal proves necessary.

17 April    From Robert Howe Gould. ALS. DLC–JKP. Desires appointment as secretary to one of the United States' European legations; cites his experience of twelve months as acting secretary to the American legation in London.

17 April    From Charles G. Greene. ALS. DLC–JKP. Introduces S. C. Foster of Maine.

17 April    From Thomas M. Hope. ALS. DLC–JKP. Expresses surprise at having been removed as U.S. marshal for the District of Illinois; affirms his continued support for Polk's administration.

17 April    From John M. McCalla. ALS. DLC–JKP. Encloses a letter from Henry Johnson; notes that Johnson, a brother of Richard M. Johnson, supported Polk actively in the general election.

17 April    From John C. McLemore. ALS. DLC–JKP. States that friends urge him to solicit appointment to a federal office, the salary of which would support his destitute family; notes that he would be satisfied with the office of agent for mineral lands in Illinois and Wisconsin.

17 April    From John M. Niles. ALS. DLC–JKP. Introduces Gideon Welles of Connecticut.

17 April    From Doyle O'Hanlon. ALS. DLC–JKP. Asks Polk to retain James Owen as naval officer at Wilmington, N.C., despite his affiliation with the Whig party; argues that Owen is old and depends on the office to support his daughters.

17 April    From Samuel K. Platte. ALS. DLC–JKP. Complains of his removal from office; encloses a copy of his letter to William L. Marcy.

17 April    From Levi D. Slamm. ALS. DLC–JKP. Encloses a copy of testimonials from recently elected members of the New York City government; requests Polk's attention to the claims of the individual for whom they have written. (Enclosure not found.)

17 April    From Henry H. Sylvester. ALS. DLC–JKP. Encloses his correspondence with Henry Hubbard; comments that he has urged Hubbard to forego any appointment that would require him from leaving his wife, who is in poor health.

17 April    From Harvey M. Watterson. ALS. DLC–JKP. Informs Polk about Democratic political activities in middle Tennessee, including his unanimous nomination as a candidate for the state senate.

| | |
|---|---|
| 17 April | From William Wright. ALS. DLC–JKP. Wishes to have the Tylerite appraisers at the port of Boston removed. |
| 18 April | From A. W. Auner. ALS. DLC–JKP. Solicits Polk's autograph. |
| *18 April* | *From John P. Campbell.* |
| 18 April | From John Fairfield and Thomas Robinson. LS. DLC–JKP. Urge Polk to appoint a new collector of the customs at Bath, Maine, from the list of candidates previously submitted. |
| 18 April | From James M. Howry and William C. Dunlap. LS. DLC–JKP. Recommend Kemp S. Holland for a position in the general government. |
| 18 April | From Edward J. Mallett. ALS. DLC–JKP. Reports that he is satisfied with the appointments of postmaster and collector at Providence, R.I. |
| 18 April | From John Y. Mason. ALS. DLC–JKP. Waives all objections to the appointment of his son, John Y. Mason, Jr., to the post of purser in the navy; thanks Polk for his support in this matter. |
| *18 April* | *From Robert H. Morris.* |
| 18 April | From Edward B. Robinson. ALS. DLC–JKP. Solicits an appointment as a purser in the navy, or some other position in the general government. |
| 18 April | From Truman Tyler et al. LS. DLC–JKP. Recommend Charles P. Sengstack for appointment as commissioner of public buildings. |
| *18 April* | *From Asa Whitney.* |
| 19 April | From John Fairfield. ALS. DLC–JKP. Requests that Polk appoint U.S. District Attorney Gorham Parks to a new post when he is replaced by Augustine Haines; concurs with George Bancroft that William B. Hartwell should be appointed purser in the navy; requests that Polk return to him a letter by R. D. Rice; and informs Polk that Thomas H. Blake acted without sanction when he offered advise on cabinet appointments. |
| 19 April | From Edward Harden. ALS. DLC–JKP. Solicits retention of his post as customs collector at Savannah, Ga.; encloses letters of support. (Enclosures not found.) |
| 19 April | From Micajah Hawks. ALS. DLC–JKP. Thanks Polk for his appointment as surveyor and inspector for Eastport, Me.; presents six reasons for retaining Bion Bradbury as customs collector at Passamaquoddy, Me. |
| 19 April | From Henry Horn. ALS. DLC–JKP. Introduces James Magee, whose high standing among Philadelphia Democrats and disinterest in acquiring office will allow him to judge dispassionately the claims of various office seekers. |
| 19 April | From Samuel H. Laughlin. ALS. DLC–JKP. Encloses a letter from Henderson K. Yoakum; mentions that he has ad- |

vised William R. Rucker of local objections to his appointment to the post of U.S. marshal for South Mississippi; solicits a position in Washington for his son, Samuel Houston Laughlin. (Enclosure not found.)

19 April — From John M. Niles. ALS. DLC–JKP. Introduces Noyes Billings of New London, Conn.

19 April — From Francis R. Shunk. ALS. DLC–JKP. Explains that he is unable to grant a state appointment to Augustus L. Roumfort of Philadelphia County, Penn.; requests that Polk find a position for Roumfort in the general government.

19 April — From Joel B. Sutherland. ALS. DLC–JKP. Encloses two of Francis I. Grund's letters published in Philadelphia newspapers; notes that Grund is U.S. consul at Antwerp. (Enclosures not found.)

20 April — From Virginia L. Beverley. ALS. DLC–JKP. Asks that Polk reappoint her brother, McKenzie Beverley, to his post in the Treasury Department.

20 April — From Auguste D'Avezac. ALS. Private Collection of Paul H. Bergeron. Urges Polk to appoint P. J. Sullivan to a post in the State Department.

20 April — From Josiah B. French. ALS. DLC–JKP. Introduces Thomas P. Goodhue and recommends his appointment as postmaster of Lowell, Mass.

20 April — From John B. Macy. ALS. DLC–JKP. Discusses the possible nomination of David T. Disney to a federal office; suggests that Disney's friends desire his appointment to a foreign mission.

*20 April* — *From Dutee J. Pearce.*

20 April — From Shadrach Penn, Jr. ALS. DLC–JKP. States that he is pleased with the selection of Thomas Ritchie as editor of the "Administration organ"; announces the cessation of the pro-Benton St. Louis *Missourian*.

20 April — From George H. Richards. ALS. DLC–JKP. Asks Polk if he is acquainted with a young man by the name of Lewis Polk.

20 April — From Albert G. Southall. ALS. DLC–JKP. States that his removal as agent for the preservation of live oak timbers, although painful, has not affected his support for Polk or the Democratic party.

21 April — From John S. Bagg. ALS. DLC–JKP. Offers thanks for his appointment as postmaster at Detroit, Mich.; states that he has assumed the duties from his predecessor, Thomas Rowland.

21 April — From George Bancroft. LS. DLC–JKP. Submits several naval commissions for Polk's signature.

21 April — From Seth Barton. ALS. DLC–JKP. Encloses copies of the New Orleans *Picayune* and the *Jeffersonian Republican* relating news of affairs in Texas. (Enclosures not found.)

| | |
|---|---|
| 21 April | From Joseph B. Boyd. ALS. DLC–JKP. Solicits a letter from Polk for his collection of autographs of the "distinguished public men of our country"; notes that he has obtained autographs from all of Polk's presidential predecessors. |
| 21 April | From Granville S. Crockett. ALS. DLC–JKP. Declares that he would thankfully accept an appointment as U.S. consul at Tangiers. |
| 21 April | From Ransom H. Gillet. ALS. DLC–JKP. Encloses a letter from Seneca Indians in New York discussing their land claims and treaty obligations. |
| 21 April | From Ransom H. Gillet. ALS. DLC–JKP. Encloses Azariah Walton's letter, which discusses the appointment of Peleg Burchard, presently collector of customs at Cape Vincent, N.Y.; insists that local Democrats desire Burchard's retention. |
| 21 April | From Ransom H. Gillet. ALS. DLC–JKP. Encloses a letter from Levi Blossom advocating the removal of Nathaniel P. Tallmadge as territorial governor of Wisconsin. |
| 21 April | From John L. Graham. ALS. DLC–JKP. Sends copies of his correspondence with George D. Strong; encloses copies of letters from prominent New York citizens supporting his retention as postmaster at New York City. |
| [21 April 1845] | From Samuel Haight. ALS. DLC–JKP. Wishes to be reappointed U.S. consul to Antwerp; submits copies of letters conceding the injustice of his removal by John Tyler. |
| 21 April | From Thomas K. Handy. ALS. DLC–JKP. Apologizes for using Polk's name to secure an appointment in the New Orleans Customs House; explains that William H. Polk had assured him the President's favor; and requests a letter supporting his appointment to the post. |
| 21 April | From Henry Haw. ALS. DLC–JKP. Warns that John H. C. Mudd, an applicant for office, made "the most violent whig speeches" during the late presidential contest; refers Polk to John T. Hoddert, a witness to Mudd's actions. |
| 21 April | From William McClure. ALS. DLC–JKP. Solicits appointment as collector of customs at Pittsburgh, Penn. |
| 21 April | *From Abijah Mann, Jr.* |
| 21 April | *From John Y. Mason.* |
| 21 April | *From David Petrikin.* |
| 21 April | *To Francis W. Pickens.* |
| 21 April | From Augustus L. Roumfort. ALS. DLC–JKP. Assumes that his application for the consulship at Le Havre is a "forlorn hope"; calls attention to letters outlining his political history; and refers Polk to John Y. Mason, Roumfort's acquaintance of many years. |
| 1 April | From James S. Sandford et al. LS. DLC–JKP. Transmit resolutions of the Democratic Republican Committee of New |

York City's fifteenth ward protesting the removal of Cornelius P. Van Ness as collector of customs; solicit Van Ness' retention and praise him as a man "of great ability and the highest character."

21 April   From Lyman Sherwood. ALS. DLC–JKP. Notes that the appointment of Michael Hoffman as naval officer of New York City would please the local Democracy.

21 April   From John Stickney. ALS. DLC–JKP. Wonders why Polk has not removed James C. Sloo as register at Shawneetown, Ill.

21 April   From Aaron Vanderpoel. ALS. DLC–JKP. Explains that his general recommendation of Levi D. Slamm for federal office does not override his specific recommendation of Anthony J. Bleecker for U.S. marshal of New York.

22 April   From Hugh J. Anderson. ALS. DLC–JKP. Introduces James White, a resident of Belfast, Me., and currently treasurer of the state.

22 April   From Joseph F. Ballister. ALS. DLC–JKP. Seeks to add Polk's autograph to his collection.

22 April   From Edmund Burke. ALS. DLC–JKP. Accepts the position of commissioner of patents.

22 April   From William Ennis. ALS. DLC–JKP. States that his subordinates in the customs house at Newport, R.I., wish his continuance as collector at that port; explains that the recommendation of William Littlefield by several influential Democrats had been prompted by a false rumor that Edwin Wilbur would be appointed to the collectorship; observes that those recommendations have been withdrawn.

22 April   From Richard French. ALS. KyLoF. Recommends the promotion of William R. Lovitt to the rank of major in the army.

22 April   From Joseph Hall. ALS. DLC–JKP. Introduces Abner Greenleaf, editor of the Portsmouth *New Hampshire Gazette.*

22 April   From William H. Stiles. ALS. DLC–JKP. Details recommendations for federal appointments in Georgia.

*22 April*   *From Jeremiah Towle.*

22 April   From Levi Tyler. LS. DLC–JKP. Encloses letters recommending his brother, John W. Tyler, for appointment as postmaster at Louisville, Ky. (Enclosures not found.)

23 April   From J. Brooks. ALS. DLC–JKP. Observes that the painting and redecoration of the president's mansion will commence on June 1 and presumes that Polk will vacate the White House; offers the use of his home, "the most pleasant summer residence in the vicinity of Washington."

23 April   From Edmund Burke. ALS. DLC–JKP. Announces that he will assume the duties of commissioner of patents on May 5; requests a short leave of absence in June or July to move hi

|  | family to Washington City. |
| 23 April | From William E. Creutzfeldt. NS. DLC–JKP. Solicits employment as gardener of public grounds in Washington City. |
| 23 April | From William Morton. ALS. DLC–JKP. Recalls his service to Polk during his tenure as Speaker of the U.S. House and reminds Polk of the promise that he would "not forget it in times to come"; wishes to be retained as a clerk in the office of the first auditor of the Treasury. |
| 23 April | From Dyre Tillinghast. ALS. DLC–JKP. Attests to the sound character of Abram Hogeboom of Niagara Co., N.Y., but admits that he can express no preference among Democrats in his district. |
| 23 April | From Edward D. Tippett. ALS. DLC–JKP. Claims that his invention in steam power is "worth millions to the government"; seeks an appropriation of $150 to finish the project. |
| 23 April | From Edward D. Tippett. ALS. DLC–JKP. Declares that he has been unemployed for six months; begs for immediate attention to his claim as an enlisted soldier in the army. |
| *24 April* | *From William Allen.* |
| [24 April 1845] | From C. L. Andrews. ALS. DLC–JKP. Wishes to obtain Polk's autograph. |
| 24 April | From J. Barnard. ALS. DLC–JKP. Reports that John P. Heiss, publisher of the *Nashville Union*, has offered him an interest in the paper with James G. Shepard; observes that many Whigs believe that Aaron V. Brown will triumph in Tennessee's gubernatorial contest. |
| 24 April | From Edward Bradley. ALS. DLC–JKP. Reports that William A. Richmond, recently appointed superintendent of Indian affairs in Michigan, was a defaulter to the Treasury in 1840 when he was the receiver of public monies in Michigan. |
| 24 April | From Charles Fletcher. ALS. DLC–JKP. Encloses a plan to establish a network of post offices linking the Iowa Territory to the Oregon country. |
| 24 April | From Edward Harden. ALS. DLC–JKP. Assures Polk of his continuing support, despite his removal as collector of customs at Savannah, Ga. |
| 24 April | From Hopkins Holsey. ALS. DLC–JKP. Introduces Albon Chase, editor of the *Southern Banner* at Athens, Ga. |
| 24 April | From Henry Horn. ALS. DLC–JKP. Refutes his opponents' argument that he is too wealthy to be appointed customs collector at Philadelphia. |
| 24 April | From Isaac S. Ketcham. ALS. DLC–JKP. Solicits appointment as subagent to the Wyandot Indians. |
| 24 April | From William S. Pickett. LS. DLC–JKP. Encloses an invoice for supplies for the Mississippi plantation; wishes to know whether Polk's private accounts are to be sent to Washing- |

ton City for inspection.

24 April     From William S. Pomeroy. ALS. DLC–JKP. Believes his
             qualifications for appointment as the collector of customs
             at Fairfield, Conn., surpass those of his rivals, Samuel Si-
             mons and Stephen Lownsberry.

24 April     From David R. Porter. ALS. DLC–JKP. Recommends Ben-
             jamin Parke of Harrisburg, Penn., for an auditorship in the
             Treasury Department.

24 April     From Levi Reynolds, Jr. ALS. DLC–JKP. Questions James
             Buchanan's opposition to him and fears that his friendship
             with Calvin Blythe might result in Blythe's removal as col-
             lector at Philadelphia.

*[24 April 1845]*     *From Robert B. Reynolds.*

25 April     From H. M. Brooks. ALS. DLC–JKP. Requests Polk's auto-
             graph.

25 April     From Isaac Estill. ALS. DLC–JKP. Understands that Hop-
             kins L. Turney has recommended him for a government job;
             wishes to know what his prospects may be.

25 April     From M. J. Grove. LS. DLC–JKP. Informs Polk of his elec-
             tion as an honorary member of the Franklin Literary Soci-
             ety of Fredericksburg, Penn.

25 April     From David Higgins. ALS. DLC–JKP. Solicits appointment
             as chief clerk of the Patent Office; mentions that Robert J.
             Walker has assured him of a position when an appropriate
             vacancy occurs.

25 April     From F. Randolph Hulbert. ALS. DLC–JKP. States that
             many merchants in New York City are dissatisfied with
             Polk's appointments to foreign consular posts; reminds
             Polk that in the late election City merchants raised $18,000
             when all other campaign funds had been spent; urges the
             appointment of Alexander J. Bergen to the consular post at
             Havana, Cuba.

25 April     From George W. Jones. ALS. DLC–JKP. Notes that Henry
             Dodge has informed him of his restoration to the post of
             surveyor general for Wisconsin and Iowa; explains the delay
             in transmitting his account as pension agent.

25 April     From Jesse Miller. ALS. PHi. Urges Polk to appoint James
             M. Ramsey to the post of navy purser.

*25 April*     *From Francis R. Shunk.*

25 April     From John Ward. ALS. DLC–JKP. Says that William
             Thompson, a justice of peace for Washington City, charged
             at a local Clay club meeting that Ezekiel Polk had been
             Tory and should have been killed.

26 April     From Anonymous. L. DLC–JKP. Asks that Polk appoint
             Robert Tyler and Thomas A. Cooper to office.

*26 April*     *From Alfred Balch.*

26 April     From Seth Barton. ALS. DLC–JKP. Encloses a letter from

Solomon W. Downs; urges prompt issuance of Down's commission as U.S. attorney for New Orleans, thereby allowing time for proper preparation of the "Maison Rouge Case" (*U.S.* v. *King and Cope*). (Enclosure not found.)

[26 April 1845]   From F. Hanson Bell et al. NS. DLC–JKP. Request that Polk remit the fines and court costs of James Harvey's conviction for interfering with the mails; explain that as members of the jury they had no choice in the case but that the interference on the constable's part followed from imperfect knowledge of federal law.

*26 April*   *From Lewis Cass.*

26 April   From Leonard P. Cheatham. ALS. DLC–JKP. Opposes any association by Thomas Page with the *Nashville Union*.

26 April   From Owen Connelly. ALS. DLC–JKP. Lists a large number of persons from the Washington area that Polk should either remove from office or deny application for office; claims that Democrats in Washington have been persecuted by Whigs, who dominate the federal departments.

26 April   From R. W. Dunlap. ALS. DLC–JKP. States that James Buchanan's partisans in Philadelphia are reporting the imminent removals of Calvin Blythe and Joel B. Sutherland in favor of George F. Lehman and Henry Welsh.

26 April   From James Dunlop. ALS. DLC–JKP. Recommends the appointment of Isaac Clark, Thomas Carbery, and Hamilton Lufborough to posts in the federal penitentiary.

26 April   From Lewis Eaton. ALS. DLC–JKP. Endorses Lorenzo A. Besançon of New Orleans for a federal office.

26 April   From James Hamilton, Jr. ALS. DLC–JKP. Details his travel plans from New York City; requests an interview on Wednesday morning regarding Texas affairs.

26 April   From J. Harrison Hodges. ALS. DLC–JKP. Wishes to add Polk's autograph to his collection.

*26 April*   *From Daniel T. Jenks.*

26 April   From Austin Miller. ALS. DLC–JKP. Recommends William Arrott for a surveyorship in the Philadelphia Customs House.

26 April   From Lewis Sanders, Jr. ALS. DLC–JKP. Warns Polk about John D. Elliott, the collector at Natchez, Miss.

*7 April*   *To Andrew Jackson.*

7 April   From George G. Leiper. ALS. DLC–JKP. Introduces Levi Reynolds, Jr., of Pennsylvania.

8 April   From George Bancroft. LS. DLC–JKP. Submits several naval commissions for Polk's signature.

8 April   From Matthias J. Bovee. ALS. DLC–JKP. Alleges that local Whigs will "resort to slander & falsehood" to defeat his application as register of the land office at Milwaukee; observes that the removal of Nathaniel P. Tallmadge and ap-

pointment of Henry Dodge as governor of the Wisconsin territory "gives universal satisfaction."

28 April    *From Daniel S. Dickinson.*

28 April    *From Henry Horn.*

28 April    From Edward B. Hubley. ALS. DLC–JKP. States that his friends have written letters recommending him for appointment as commissioner of Indian affairs; complains that Thomas Hartley Crawford, the present commissioner, has replied to these "private letters" with the claim that "the office is not vacant."

28 April    From S. Johnston. ALS. DLC–JKP. Warns Polk to avoid appointing J. D. Stevenson of New York City to any office; declares that Stevenson defaulted as a tax collector and assisted in Whig pipe laying.

28 April    *From John K. Kane.*

28 April    *From Francis W. Pickens.*

28 April    From John S. Skinner. ALS. DLC–JKP. Believes that a letter on his behalf, written by Dixon H. Lewis, was responsible for his appointment as third assistant postmaster general; states that he values Lewis' correspondence "as containing the sentiments of one whose friendship I highly prize"; and asks Polk to return the letter.

28 April    From Joseph Thompson. ALS. DLC–JKP. Expresses surprise over his removal as customs collector at Fairfield, Conn.; and asks permission to serve until the expiration of his commission.

28 April    *From Henry Welsh.*

28 April    *From Henderson K. Yoakum.*

29 April    *From George M. Dallas.*

29 April    From Alexander Hamilton. ALS. DLC–JKP. Notes that he has reviewed the news from Mexico and concludes that the Mexican government plans to capture American ships in the Pacific; suggests that Polk dispatch "some fast sailing vessels" to warn merchants of the danger.

29 April    From Isaac S. Ketcham. ALS. DLC–JKP. Requests a meeting with Polk for himself and Thomas Hartley Crawford.

29 April    From Joseph J. McDowell. ALS. DLC–JKP. Introduces John W. Price of Hillsboro, Ohio.

30 April    From Anonymous. L. DLC–JKP. Warns Polk about the continued presence of Whigs in the federal offices of Washington City.

30 April    *From Aaron V. Brown.*

30 April    From Andrew Jackson. ALS. DLC–JKP. Encloses a letter from Thomas F. Marshall requesting the appointment of Charles W. Field to West Point; maintains that this appointment would defeat Whig slanders in Kentucky.

30 April    From Cave Johnson. LS. DLC–JKP. States that Bernard

Peyton has requested the return of several letters by Thomas Jefferson respecting Peyton's appointment as postmaster at Richmond; adds that the Jefferson letters are not on file in the office of the postmaster general.

30 April — From Thomas J. Kelly. ALS. DLC–JKP. Relates that Polk's family in Columbia, Tenn., are well and that he hears of "very little sickness here for the last week or two."

30 April — From Samuel H. Laughlin. ALS. DLC–JKP. Solicits the appointment of Hampton C. Williams as chief clerk in the patent office.

30 April — From William G. McNeill. ALS. DLC–JKP. Denies charges of excessive expenditures in his post as chief engineer of the Brooklyn naval yard; requests that his removal order be reconsidered.

30 April — From Benjamin Patton. ALS. DLC–JKP. Urges retention of J. Albert Helfenstein, his brother-in-law, as receiver of public monies at Milwaukee, Wis.

1 May — From Casper C. Childs. ALS. DLC–JKP. Apologizes for the seemingly critical tone of Alexander J. Bergen's article published in the New York *Plebeian* of April 29; encloses clipping of Bergen's piece demanding New York's share of the consular patronage.

1 May — From Jonathan P. Clement. ALS. DLC–JKP. Asks that he be reinstated as an inspector at the New York Customs House; denies that he ever supported Whig candidates.

1 May — From J. L. S. Cramer. ALS. DLC–JKP. Advocates creation of a steam-powered navy to protect American commerce in the event of war; hopes that the government will make arrangements with the Baltimore & Ohio railroad for the shipment of adequate supplies of Cumberland coal, "the very best for steam ships."

*1 May* — *From Henry Horn.*

1 May — From Ezekiel P. McNeal. ALS. DLC–JKP. Acknowledges receipt of Polk's check for $211.50; discusses rental arrangements for Polk's properties.

1 May — From James Magee. ALS. DLC–JKP. Declares that he is too ill and fatigued to travel from Philadelphia to Washington City by the following morning; states that he will call on Polk in the evening if able to make the journey.

1 May — From H. G. Parks. ALS. DLC–JKP. States that veterans of a Missouri regiment of mounted volunteers have submitted claims for the loss of 200 horses; alleges that Peter Hagner, third auditor of the Treasury, has delayed settlement of some claims for six to eight months; and asks that the claims be "acted on at once."

1 May — From Leonidas Polk. ALS. DLC–JKP. States that his friend Nathaniel S. Wheaton, an Episcopal clergyman and former

president of Trinity College at Hartford, Conn., plans to travel to Europe for the benefit of his health; solicits letters of introduction for Wheaton's visit with the American ministers at Paris and London.

1 May   From David Scott. ALS. DLC–JKP. Solicits information on the heirs of the late Rees Price of Chester County, Penn.; claims that Polk descends on his maternal side through Price's daughter, Mary Price (Mrs. John) Alexander of North Carolina.

1 May   From Aaron Vanderpoel. ALS. DLC–JKP. Introduces James K. McLanahan of Pennsylvania; declares that McLanahan would be qualified for any office to which he might be appointed.

2 May   From Anonymous. L. DLC–JKP. Provides details of the May 1 public meeting of Philadelphia Democrats, convened to sustain Polk's Oregon policy; claims that the occasion, at which Buchanan and Dallas supporters battled for control of the platform, represented the "first movement of Buchananism in Philadelphia."

2 May   From George Bancroft. ALS. DNA–RG 45. Details case against Alexander Gibson, a navy lieutenant dismissed from service and subsequently restored; finds that Gibson has received lenient treatment; and denies that he has a just claim to seven years of lost rank.

2 May   From Auguste D'Avezac. ALS. DLC–JKP. Encloses a letter from John Bruce relating to the conduct of the post office at Winchester, Va.; expresses his gratitude to Polk for his appointment as minister to the Hague. (Enclosure not found.)

*2 May*   *From Andrew Jackson.*

2 May   From James McCarty. ALS. DLC–JKP. Maintains that office seekers disrupted the Democratic meeting of the previous day at Philadelphia's Independence Square; urges Polk to retain the incumbents and ignore the "hungry office seekers and President makers."

2 May   From Thomas McCully. ALS. DLC–JKP. Encloses a copy of the proceedings of the meeting over which he presided the previous day in Philadelphia. (Enclosure not found.)

2 May   From Edward Merton. ALS. DLC–JKP. Deplores the disgraceful behaviour exhibited at the Democratic meeting in Philadelphia on the previous day; holds that James Buchanan and George M. Dallas "appear to be the cause of the excitement, each aiming at the Sucession."

2 May   From William Murry. ALS. DLC–JKP. Informs Polk that he has changed addresses in New York City.

2 May   From William Quarles. ALS. DLC–JKP. States that John B. Dawson is too ill to write; praises Dawson's efforts in Louisiana politics.

| | |
|---|---|
| 2 May | From Frederick Stoever. ALS. DLC–JKP. Encloses a newspaper account of the proceedings and resolutions of the Democratic meeting over which he presided the previous day in Philadelphia. |
| 2 May | From John Tomlin. ALS. DLC–JKP. Wishes to exchange the postmastership of Jackson, Tenn., for a clerkship in Washington City. |
| *2 May* | *From Nicholas P. Trist.* |
| 3 May | From William J. Alexander. ALS. DLC–JKP. Introduces John W. Gibbon, assayer of the mint in Charlotte, N.C. |
| *[3 May 1845]* | *From James Buchanan.* |
| 3 May | From John S. Elliot. ALS. DLC–JKP. Wishes to add Polk's autograph to his collection. |
| *3 May* | *From Ransom H. Gillet.* |
| 3 May | From Francis Hayre. ALS. DLC–JKP. Complains that although his information against William Morton resulted in that clerk's removal, Robert J. Walker appointed another to the vacant post. |
| 3 May | From William L. Marcy. LS. DLC–JKP. Transmits monthly reports of the War Department bureaus and copies of his instructions to the receiving and disbursing officers. |
| 3 May | From Marcus Morton. ALS. DLC–JKP. Introduces Abner Loring Cushing of Boston. |
| 3 May | From Thomas L. Ragsdale. ALS. DLC–JKP. Informs Polk that John K. Cook would settle in Florida in order to secure appointment as live oak agent there; adds that if Cook cannot be appointed, then he would solicit the appointment. |
| 3 May | From Bradford Sumner. ALS. DLC–JKP. Introduces Abner Loring Cushing of Boston. |
| 3 May | From Gideon G. Westcott. ALS. DLC–JKP. Condemns the activities of "a *secret* and *private caucas*" for using the Philadelphia meeting of May 1 to promote their chances of patronage; names James Page, John Horn, John K. Kane, William D. Kelly, and Ellis B. Schnabel as "self-constituted regulators of the Democratic Party and the people." |
| 3 May | From Campbell P. White. ALS. DLC–JKP. Encloses a memoir from Thomas Herring regarding the single-term principle. |
| 3 May | From Hampton C. Williams. ALS. DLC–JKP. Encloses a list of offices suitable for his appointment; prefers the chief clerkship in the Patent Office. (Enclosure not found.) |
| *May* | *From John F. H. Claiborne.* |
| May | From Owen Connelly. ALS. DLC–JKP. Discusses the Whigs in the Navy Department; complains of his proscription by John B. Jones of the Washington *Madisonian*. |
| May | From Augustus C. Dodge. LS. DLC–JKP. Requests that no appointments be made in the Iowa Territory until he writes |

|          | again. |
|----------|--------|
| 4 May    | From Charles G. Greene. ALS. DLC–JKP. Wishes Polk would replace Cranston Howe with Samuel A. Allen as an assistant appraiser in the Boston Customs House. |
| 4 May    | From John Tomlin. ALS. DLC–JKP. Solicits a federal position, since no other West Tennessean has applied for federal patronage. |
| 5 May    | From Alexander J. Bergen. ALS. DLC–JKP. Seeks appointment as consul to Havana or Havre. |
| 5 May    | From Joshua P. Bird. ALS. DLC–JKP. Wishes to add Polk's autograph to his collection. |
| 5 May    | From James G. Bryce. ALS. DLC–JKP. Recommends Henry T. Williams for appointment as surveyor-general of Louisiana. |
| 5 May    | From James Buchanan. ALS. DLC–JKP. Requests that Polk ask Henry Horn not to remove Sandy Harris, Benjamin F. Crispin, and Bernard Maguire from their positions in the Philadelphia Customs House. |
| *5 May*  | *To Benjamin F. Butler.* |
| *5 May*  | *From George M. Dallas.* |
| 5 May    | From T. Legaré Fenn. ALS. DLC–JKP. Introduces himself as a student from Phillips Academy, Andover, Mass.; states that he is from Charleston, S.C., and is a cousin to the late Hugh S. Legaré; requests the favor of Polk's autograph. |
| *5 May*  | *From Royal R. Hinman.* |
| 5 May    | From George W. Jones. ALS. DLC–JKP. Presents his friend, S. F. Rodolf of Iowa County, Wisconsin Territory; notes that Rodolf is connected by marriage to Henry Dodge. |
| 5 May    | From Samuel D. McCullough. ALS. DLC–JKP. Informs Polk of his election to honorary membership in the Society of Adelphi in Lexington, Ky.; wishes to obtain Polk's autograph for the Society's collection. |
| 5 May    | From M. L. McLain. ALS. DLC–JKP. Writes on behalf of James I. Randolph, a nephew of William Henry Harrison and former clerk in the General Land Office, who seeks reappointment in order to support his large family. |
| 5 May    | From William G. McNeill. ALS. DLC–JKP. Notes that he has submitted letters which detail his conduct as chief engineer at the Brooklyn dry docks; hopes that they provide sufficient evidence to refute "the alleged charge of prodigal or extravagant, expenditure of the Public money." |
| *5 May*  | *From Jesse Miller.* |
| 5 May    | From Robert H. Morris. LS. DLC–JKP. Expresses appreciation for his appointment as postmaster at New York City |
| 5 May    | From Charles G. Smith. ALS. DLC–JKP. Solicits Polk's autograph. |
| 5 May    | From James W. Stone. ALS. DLC–JKP. Recommend |

|  |  |
|---|---|
|  | Thomas P. Moore for federal office; states that Moore's appointment would please the citizens of Mercer County, Ky. |
| 5 May | From John M. Thayer. ALS. DLC–JKP. Relates background information on two of Daniel Webster's appointees to consular posts; states that John H. Payne in Tunis took an active part in the 1840 presidential campaign as a song writer and singer; notes that John F. Mullowny in Morocco, also a Whig partisan, had "but slight qualifications for the office." |
| *5 May* | *From Archibald Yell.* |
| 6 May | From Anonymous. L. DLC–JKP. Encloses a poem "from a little American girl." |
| *6 May* | *From Benjamin F. Butler.* |
| *6 May* | *To Andrew J. Donelson.* |
| 6 May | From F. W. Golladay. ALS. DLC–JKP. Desires appointment to a clerkship in the government. |
| *6 May* | *From James Hamilton, Jr.* |
| 6 May | From William G. McNeill. ALS. DLC–JKP. Affirms his allegiance to Polk and the Democratic party despite the decision to remove him as chief engineer at the Brooklyn dry dock. |
| 6 May | From Ely Moore. ALS. DLC–JKP. Expresses thanks for his appointment as U.S. marshal for the Southern District of New York. |
| *6 May* | *To Robert J. Walker.* |
| *6 May* | *From Charles A. Wickliffe.* |
| 6 May | From John York. ALS. DLC–JKP. Asks for a loan of $60 to pay his debts. |
| *7 May* | *From Benjamin F. Butler.* |
| 7 May | From W. L. Crandal. ALS. DLC–JKP. Requests that the nomination of a postmaster at Syracuse, N.Y., be delayed; alleges that A. S. Smith, an applicant for the office, "made political bargains to secure the appointment" and "acted in *bad faith* towards others." |
| 7 May | From John L. Graham. ALS. DLC–JKP. Encloses latest news received by the English steamer *Hibernia*; notes that despite the "great injury" occasioned by his removal as postmaster at New York City he tenders best wishes for Polk's administration. (Enclosure not found.) |
| 7 May | From Benjamin Hartley. ALS. DLC–JKP. Solicits assistance in his effort to secure appointment as an inspector of customs at Philadelphia. |
| 7 May | From George F. Lehman. ALS. DLC–JKP. Expresses gratitude for his appointment as postmaster at Philadelphia. |
| May | From Gansevoort Melville. ALS. DLC–JKP. States that disappointment over his failure to secure a federal office has not diminished his desire that Polk's administration "may be honorable and triumphant." |
| May | From Henry M. Phillips. ALS. DLC–JKP. Regrets that |

he did not receive an appointment as district attorney for Philadelphia; discusses proceedings of Philadelphia's Oregon meeting of May 1.

7 May        From Archibald Roane. ALS. DLC–JKP. Wishes to be reinstated as inspector of customs at New York City; claims to be a grandson of Archibald Roane, second governor of Tennessee.

7 May        From Abraham Sulger. ALS. DLC–JKP. Encloses a letter of introduction from James C. O'Reilly, a physician in Mulberry Grove, Tenn.; solicits appointment as inspector of customs at Philadelphia.

8 May        To George Bancroft. ALS. MHi. Requests all papers relating to the appointment of surgeon for the marine hospital at New Orleans.

8 May        From David Craighead. ALS. DLC–JKP. Approves of Polk's inaugural address and selection of cabinet officers; offers opinions on Oregon, tariffs, and patronage.

*8 May*      *From Robert H. Hammond.*

8 May        From James E. Harvey. ALS. DLC–JKP. Reports that the State Department has ignored his requests for information relating to the status of the U.S. consulate at Florence; expects that Polk will prompt the department to fulfill its duty.

8 May        From Selah R. Hobbie. ALS. DLC–JKP. Encloses a letter from F. B. W. Stockton; offers assurances that Stockton is a Democrat and deserves retention as an agent of the Bureau of Topographical Engineers.

8 May        From Merit Jordan. ALS. DLC–JKP. Encloses a letter of introduction from John O. Bradford. (Enclosure not found.)

*8 May*      *From Ebenezer Knowlton.*

*8 May*      *From William B. Lewis.*

8 May        From Ellis B. Schnabel. ALS. DLC–JKP. Seeks appointment as weighmaster at the customs house in Philadelphia.

8 May        From Benjamin G. Shields. ALS. DLC–JKP. Recommends James E. Saunders, editor of the Mobile *Commercial Register*, for the collectorship at Mobile, Ala.

8 May        From Henry Simpson. ALS. DLC–JKP. Claims that "*incompetency*" necessitates the removal of all appraisers at the Philadelphia Customs House; solicits appointment as either treasurer of the Philadelphia Mint or "*principal*" appraiser of customs.

8 May        From William M. Smyth. ALS. DLC–JKP. Asks Polk to delay proceedings against Thomas Barrett, collector of customs at New Orleans, who is charged "with 'holding' and 'exercising' the functions of a Foreign Consul."

[8 May 1845] To Robert J. Walker. ALS. DLC–JKP. Encloses a letter from George W. Jones discussing his accounts as pension agent for Wisconsin; asks Walker to report on the settlement of

|  | Jones' accounts. |
| [8 May 1845] | From Samuel C. White. ALS. DLC–JKP. States that he has failed to secure an interview with the Treasury secretary and cannot remain in Washington City; fears "influence" will be used against his application for office; asks that Polk personally read his application papers. |
| 9 May | From George Bancroft. LS. DLC–JKP. Submits naval commissions for Polk's signature. |
| [9 May 1845] | From John P. Campbell and Leonard H. Sims. LS. DLC–JKP. Submit recommendations for appointments in Missouri. |
| 9 May | From Lewis Cass. ALS. DLC–JKP. Recommends the appointment of Charles G. Hammond as collector of customs at Detroit; believes that Hammond's selection will strengthen the Democratic party in Michigan. Encloses a letter from William Hale of the Michigan Senate. (Enclosure not found.) |
| 9 May | From George W. Thompson. ALS. DLC–JKP. Solicits appointment as postmaster at Wheeling, Va; argues that his community favors his nomination and states that he has long labored for Polk and the Democratic cause. |
| *9 May* | *From Henry Welsh.* |
| 10 May | From Benjamin F. Butler. ALS. DLC–JKP. Discusses duties of appraisers and assistant appraisers of customs; tenders recommendations for removals and appointments of appraisers in the New York City Customs House. |
| 10 May | From James Conner. ALS. DLC–JKP. Encloses resolutions of the Grand Council of the Tammany Society; discusses the status of Cornelius P. Van Ness as collector at New York City; and claims that citizens are "alarmed at the delay" in Van Ness' removal. (Enclosure not found.) |
| 10 May | From John S. Du Solle. ALS. DLC–JKP. Believes that his decision to avoid party factionalism and "remain *independently Democratic*" will prompt the removal of his brother-in-law, Robert Ford, from his office in the Philadelphia Customs House; asks Polk to secure the retention of Ford as an inspector of customs. |
| 0 May | From William F. Havemeyer and John L. O'Sullivan. LS. DLC–JKP. Introduce James McCullough of New York City; state that during the presidential campaign McCullough supported Polk and Dallas. |
| 0 May | From Adam Huntsman et al. LS. DLC–JKP. Recommend Thomas Ewell of Jackson, Tenn., for a federal office. |
| 0 May | From Joshua A. Lowell. ALS. DLC–JKP. Recommends Sullivan S. Rawson to replace Bion Bradbury as collector at Passamaquoddy, Me. |
| 0 May | *From Rufus McIntire.* |

| 10 May | *From David Petrikin.* |
| 10 May | From Thomas M. Pettit. ALS. DLC–JKP. Expresses appreciation for his appointment to the post of U.S. attorney for the Eastern District of Pennsylvania. |
| 10 May | From Thomas L. Ragsdale. ALS. DLC–JKP. Encloses copy of a note that he has sent to William L. Marcy, who refuses to reinstate him to his former position in the War Department. |
| 10 May | *From Brigham Young et al.* |
| 11 May | *From Andrew J. Donelson.* |
| 11 May | *From Andrew J. Donelson.* |
| 11 May | From William D. Moseley. ALS. DLC–JKP. Predicts that his opponent, Richard K. Call, will triumph in the Florida gubernatorial contest; assures Polk that David Levy Yulee, candidate for the U.S. Senate, is a "good Democrat of sterling integrity." |
| 12 May | From Pierce B. Anderson et al. LS. DLC–JKP. Report that Oscar H. Lide from McMinn County, Tenn., desires a clerkship in the federal government. |
| 12 May | From Jacob G. Davies. ALS. DLC–JKP. Introduces J. Smith Hollins of Baltimore. |
| 12 May | From James E. Harvey. ALS. DLC–JKP. Complains about the response of James Buchanan to his inquiries on behalf of Edward Gamage, U.S. consul at Florence. |
| 12 May | *To Andrew Jackson.* |
| 12 May | *From John Law.* |
| 12 May | From Dutee J. Pearce. ALS. DLC–JKP. Congratulates Polk on recent appointments in New York and Pennsylvania and discusses the distribution of offices at the customs houses in Newport and Bristol, R.I. |
| 12 May | From John J. Thompson, Jr. ALS. DLC–JKP. Reports that he has just returned from Texas; believes that "annexation is paramount to all other objects"; states that the Texas Congress will convene on June 16 to accept unanimously the United States' joint resolutions. |
| 12 May | From Silas Wright, Jr. ALS. DLC–JKP. Introduces Thomas Brownell, a lieutenant in the navy. |
| 13 May | From Anonymous. L, signed "A Friend." DLC–JKP. Declares that the recent "intolerably bad" appointments in New York City have "almost destroyed" public confidence in the Democratic party; denounces William L. Marcy and urges the removal of Cornelius P. Van Ness. |
| 13 May | From Felix Bosworth. ALS. DLC–JKP. Urges the appointment of Jeremiah Y. Dashiell as superintendent of the U.S. mint at New Orleans. |
| 13 May | From Edward Brooks. ALS. DLC–JKP. Complains about his sudden removal as collector for the port of Detroit, Mich. |

|            | claims that Lewis Cass had assured him that he could re-main until his commission expired. |
|------------|---------------------------------------------------------------------------|
| *13 May*   | *From Henry Horn.*                                                         |
| *13 May*   | *To Henry Horn.*                                                          |
| 13 May     | From Alexander Jones. ALS. DLC–JKP. Claims that his role in securing the support of "the Democratic portion of the Native American party in New York" enabled Polk to win the 1844 election; seeks appointment as a despatch agent for the State Department. |
| 13 May     | From Archibald C. Niven. ALS. DLC–JKP. Observes that the "greater portion" of New York Democrats do not favor the removal of Cornelius P. Van Ness. |
| 13 May     | From Alexander S. Rowles. ALS. DLC–JKP. Requests information concerning a Morgan County, Tenn., land grant that was made to Charles W. Parks in 1841. |
| 13 May     | From Henry Simpson. ALS. DLC–JKP. Solicits the position of appraiser for the port of Philadelphia. |
| 14 May     | From George Bancroft. LS. DLC–JKP. Submits naval commissions for Polk's signature. |
| 14 May     | From Benjamin H. Brewster. ALS. DLC–JKP. Urges the retention of Michael Cochran, postmaster at Pottsville, Penn.; notes that he has "great influence with the mining population" of the region. |
| *14 May*   | *From Andrew J. Donelson.*                                                |
| *14 May*   | *From Andrew J. Donelson.*                                                |
| 14 May     | From James B. Hunt. ALS. DLC–JKP. Introduces Orville B. Dibble, one of Michigan's delegates to the Baltimore Convention; recommends Dibble for government employment. |
| 14 May     | From John M. Lea. ALS. DLC–JKP. Acknowledges the request of "your nephew, Mr. Walker" to delay until June 5 payment of a note due from Polk to the estate of William McNeill. |
| 14 May 1845] | From George Sykes. ALS. DLC–JKP. Introduces John W. Allen of New Jersey; recommends Allen to replace James A. Nichols as collector at Perth Amboy. |
| 5 May      | From George Bancroft. L. DNA–RG 45. Informs Polk that the appointment of L. B. Cully was cancelled because Congress refused to appropriate funds for the salary of a "Naval Constructor" at Memphis. |
| 5 May      | From Lyman Gilbert. ALS. DLC–JKP. Offers information on "a defaulter" who has been recently appointed to an important office in New York City. |
| *5 May*    | *From Duff Green.*                                                        |
| *5 May*    | *From Charles S. Jones.*                                                  |
| 5 May      | From William B. Lewis. ALS. DLC–JKP. States that although he is anxious to leave Washington City, he is unwilling to depart until Polk answers his inquiries about his |

15 May · removal from office.
15 May · *From William R. McDougal.*
15 May · From Seaton W. Norris. ALS. DLC–JKP. States that William W. Wick, Democratic candidate for Congress, requests a delay in the appointment of a postmaster at Indianapolis until after Indiana's August elections.
15 May · From John Norvell. ALS. DLC–JKP. Introduces Lansing B. Mizner of Michigan.
15 May · From Thomas Simpson and Thomas Boulter. L. DLC–JKP. Declare that they wish to emigrate to Oregon; ask Polk to write them with "all particulars" about when another vessel will be sent to that territory.
15 May · From Peter von Schmidt. ALS. DLC–JKP. Reports that he referred a proposal for the defense of harbors to George Bancroft, who declined to investigate it.
16 May · From Anonymous. L. DLC–JKP. Offers advice on patronage in Mobile, Ala., "this citadel of Whiggery."
[16 May 1845] · From Robert Armstrong. LS. DNA–RG 94. Discusses the case of Benjamin S. Roberts, who was forced to resign from the army in 1839; declares that "*Justice*" requires that he be reinstated and restored to his former rank; includes an addendum in which Andrew Jackson writes in support of Roberts' case.
16 May · From Eli C. Davis. ALS. DLC–JKP. Recalls his part in the Battle of Horseshoe Bend; appeals to Polk for a position in the federal government.
16 May · From Joseph B. Gilman. L. DLC–JKP. Reports that he has tendered his resignation as postmaster at Fall Branch, Tenn.; recommends Anson Gwinn as his successor.
16 May · From Hugh Gilmour. ALS. DLC–JKP. Calls Polk's attention to the case of William T. Gillespie, whose mother requests his discharge from the army; encloses copies of Gilmour's correspondence with William L. Marcy and Roger Jones.
16 May · From John T. Hudson. ALS. DLC–JKP. Claims that he was the first member of the New York delegation at Baltimore to propose Polk's nomination; complains about the rejection of his application for the office of collector at Buffalo.
16 May · From William G. McNeill. ALS. DLC–JKP. Requests an interview to discuss his prospects for restoration as chief engineer at the Brooklyn dry docks.
16 May · *From William D. Moseley.*
16 May · From William P. Rowles. ALS. DLC–JKP. Writes that Polk' bold stand on Oregon is popular in Middle and West Tennessee; adds that "millions of freemen" are determined "t extend the area of freedom & open it to the occupancy of the greatest number of persons."
16 May · From Nathaniel Terry. ALS. DLC–JKP. Advises Polk tha

|  | public sentiment in Mobile, Ala., favors the nomination of Theophilus L. Toulmin as collector of customs. |
| *17 May* | *From John F. H. Claiborne.* |
| *[17 May 1845]* | *From William E. Cramer.* |
| 17 May | From George Croghan. ALS. DLC–JKP. Encloses a letter that he received from John Tyler. (Enclosure not found.) |
| *17 May* | *From Augustus C. Dodge.* |
| 17 May | From Franklin H. Elmore. ALS. DLC–JKP. Introduces Robert W. Gibbes of Columbia, S.C. |
| 17 May | From Benjamin B. French. ALS. DLC–JKP. Seeks renewal of his commission as a magistrate for the district of Washington City. |
| 17 May | From Ralph Graves. ALS. DLC–JKP. States that he has lived in Texas for seven years but looks forward to the "hour that will place me and my Dear family under the protection of the U.S. of A"; recommends A. Walker for office. |
| 17 May | From Amos Kendall. ALS. DLC–JKP. Claims that Francis I. Grund, U.S. consul at Antwerp, is "politically faithless" and "morally depraved"; urges Polk to remove him from office. |
| 17 May | From Daniel P. Leadbetter. ALS. DLC–JKP. Introduces William S. Taneyhill of Holmes County, Ohio. |
| 17 May | From John M. McCalla. ALS. DLC–JKP. Anticipates that his leave of absence will last three weeks; recommends that James Eakin, chief clerk, take charge of the bureau during this period. |
| *17 May* | *From Jacob L. Martin.* |
| 17 May | From Robert J. Walker. ALS. DLC–JKP. Encloses correspondence from James Shields and William L. Marcy with documents relating to public lands set aside for the Seminoles in Florida. (Enclosures not found.) |
| [18 May 1845] | From John B. Dawson. LS. DLC–JKP. Discusses patronage in Louisiana. |
| 18 May | From James R. Knox. ALS. DLC–JKP. Writes as a professor of religion and as a relation; urges Polk to publish an address calling for a general fast to protect the nation from harm. |
| 18 May | From John Y. Mason. ANS. DLC–JKP. Discusses the president's authority to grant reprieves and pardons. |
| 19 May | From Anonymous. L, signed "A Friend." DLC–JKP. Warns that recent appointments, particularly that of Ely Moore, have created a "feeling of indignation" among New York City Democrats; claims that Moore and Van Ness are "the directors general" of "Calhoun's movements in New York for the Succession." |
| 9 May | From A. H. Bodman. ALS. DLC–JKP. Solicits Polk's autograph. |
| 9 May | From John Chambers. ALS. DLC–JKP. Describes the bitter |

territorial dispute between Iowa and Missouri; expresses his concerns about the outbreak of "a civil war."

19 May From Charles G. Eastman. ALS. DLC–JKP. Introduces John C. Haswell, former editor of the Bennington *Vermont Gazette*.

19 May From Reah Frazer. ALS. Private collection of George E. Webb, Jr. Recommends A. Boyd Hamilton for appointment as a purser in the navy.

19 May From John F. Gillespy. ALS. DLC–JKP. Discusses matters relating to claims of the Cherokee Indians.

*19 May* *From William H. Haywood, Jr.*

19 May From Daniel T. Jenks. ALS. DLC–JKP. Warns that the removal of Joel B. Sutherland "would produce a very great dissatisfaction" among pro-Texas Democrats; recommends Sutherland for the position of treasurer of the U.S. mint at Philadelphia.

19 May From David Lewis. ALS. DLC–JKP. States that his farm will be sold to pay his debts; requests a loan.

*19 May* *From William B. Lewis.*

19 May From William L. Marcy. LS. DLC–JKP. Notes that Richard Delafield has invited Polk to visit West Point.

*19 May* *From J. G. M. Ramsey.*

*19 May* *From Joel B. Sutherland.*

*19 May* *To Levi Woodbury.*

20 May From Peter Bescançon, Jr. ALS. DLC–JKP. Informs Polk that passengers on a schooner from Veracruz have brought news of Mexico's declaration of war; adds that he does "not give full credence to the reports."

*20 May* *From John Catron.*

20 May From George C. Dromgoole. ALS. DLC–JKP. Urges the appointment of David H. Branch of Petersburg, Va., to a consular post.

20 May From Joseph Grimes et al. LS. DLC–JKP. Recommend James Sheely for appointment as surveyor at the port of Alexandria, D.C.

*[20 May 1845]* *From Michael Hoffman.*

20 May From William Horner. ALS. DLC–JKP. Claims that he is entitled to a seat in the U.S. House to represent Pennsylvania's Tenth Congressional District; states that opponents employed "*bribery, fraud and deception*" to defeat his candidacy as the "*patriot volenteer candidate.*"

20 May From Charles V. Morris. ALS. DNA–RG 45. Provides details of his service in the navy; asks Polk to place his name "at the foot of the present list of Lieutenants."

20 May From Aaron Vanderpoel. ALS. DLC–JKP. Introduces James Lee, a New York City merchant.

*[20 May 1845]* From Robert Wilson et al. NS. DLC–JKP. Petition Polk as

Missouri citizens; recommend the appointment of Ebenezer H. Wood as register of lands at Fairfield, Iowa Territory.

21 May     From Anonymous. L, signed "An Old Democrat." DLC–JKP. Reports that "sober-minded" Democrats in Louisiana are disappointed that Seth Barton acts as "the door of admission" to Polk's administration.

21 May     From John Fairfield. ALS. DLC–JKP. Introduces Anson G. Chandler of Maine.

21 May     From Richard M. Gaines. ALS. DLC–JKP. Introduces John Chamberlain, a professor of mathematics at Oakland College in Mississippi.

21 May     From Peter Hagner. ALS. DLC–JKP. Returns H. G. Parks' letter about the claims of the Missouri veterans; reports that his office will send Parks a response in a day or two.

21 May     From Thomas H. Hopkins. ALS. DLC–JKP. Regrets that his wife solicited an office on his behalf; states that he would accept an appointment to satisfy his "pecuniary embarrassments."

21 May     From William H. Irwin et al. LS. DLC–JKP. Recommend appointment of James Sheely as surveyor for the port of Alexandria, D.C.

[21 May 1845]     From Jacob Keck. ALS. DLC–JKP. Informs Polk that Benjamin E. Carpenter, appointed appraiser for the port of Philadelphia, is not qualified to fulfill the duties of the post.

21 May     From John Norvell. ALS. DLC–JKP. Introduces Orville B. Dibble of Detroit, Mich.

21 May     From John C. Park. ALS. DLC–JKP. Addresses Polk concerning the case of James M. Duggan, imprisoned for a violation of the revenue laws.

21 May     From Reuel Williams. ALS. DLC–JKP. States that Anson G. Chandler, the bearer of this letter, can provide Polk with a true account of the difficulties among Maine Democrats.

21 May     From Silas Wright, Jr. ALS. DLC–JKP. Writes on behalf of Alexander J. Bergen, an applicant for the U.S. consulship at Havana; claims that he is not familiar with Bergen's qualifications for the post and therefore cannot recommend him over other candidates.

22 May     From H. Andrews. ALS. DLC–JKP. Requests Polk's autograph.

22 May     From Jacob Bindernagel. ALS. DLC–JKP. States that a few disaffected German Democrats have denounced Cornelius P. Van Ness and have urged the appointment of Jonathan I. Coddington to the collectorship at New York City; argues that their views do not accurately reflect the sentiments of a majority of German Democrats.

22 May     From Thomas B. Eastland. ALS. DLC–JKP. Declares that the appointment of William F. Wagner as U.S. marshal for

Louisiana will prove "satisfactory to all *true* Democrats."

| | |
|---|---|
| *22 May* | *From Duff Green.* |
| *22 May* | *To Andrew Jackson.* |

22 May     From Daniel T. Mouier. ALS. DLC–JKP. Writes on behalf of the merchant community to urge the removal of Cornelius P. Van Ness; claims that he has neglected his duties and has hired men from "the prize fight rings" to replace respectable officers.

22 May     From Wyndham Robertson, Jr. ALS. DLC–JKP. Complains that his anticipated appointment to a clerkship has been tendered to another individual.

22 May     From James W. Schaumburg. ALS. DLC–JKP. Encloses a printed statement that deals with his case for reappointment in the army. (Enclosure not found.)

22 May     From Levi D. Slamm. ALS. DLC–JKP. Reports that he has discussed his application for the office of naval storekeeper with George Bancroft; believes that a word from Polk would influence Bancroft's decision.

22 May     From Samuel R. Smith. ALS. DLC–JKP. States that he possesses letters from Andrew Jackson, John Tyler, and William H. Harrison; notes that he has not received a reply from Polk.

22 May     From John J. Thompson, Jr. ALS. DLC–JKP. Warns Polk that some of the recent appointments in Louisiana have stirred up "dissatisfaction" among Democrats; announces that he will depart for Texas in a few days.

22 May     From Hezekiah Williams. ALS. DLC–JKP. Introduces Anson G. Chandler.

*22 May*     *From Levi Woodbury.*

23 May     From Noyes Billings. ALS. DLC–JKP. Discusses the qualifications of the applicants for the postmastership at New London, Conn.; recommends Stanley G. Trott.

*23 May*     *From Aaron V. Brown.*

23 May     From L. D. Dewey. ALS. DLC–JKP. Solicits a pardon for William Hoff, imprisoned at Hudson, N.Y., for mail robbery.

23 May     From John F. Gillespy. ALS. DLC–JKP. Informs Polk that the Cherokee commissioners are hard at work on their report.

*23 May*     *To Michael Hoffman.*

23 May     From John Lester. ALS. DLC–JKP. Requests reappointment as appraiser for the port of Baltimore.

23 May     From William O. Slade. ALS. DLC–JKP. Claims that William J. Bronaugh, a clerk in the Post Office Department, will not settle debts owed to the estate of H. C. Slade, his late brother; hopes that Polk will give the matter "an impartial consideration."

23 May     From Ver Planck Van Antwerp. ALS. DLC–JKP. Complains

that Missouri has been slighted in the dispensation of federal patronage; demands that a decision "may be made *at once*" on his application for office.

23 May    From Silas Wright, Jr. ALS. DLC–JKP. Introduces Charles Jewett of Berrien County, Mich.

24 May    From Anonymous. L, signed "Democrat." DLC–JKP. Informs Polk that the Irish American citizens of New York, "who it is admitted carried the election in this state," are disappointed over their exclusion from federal office.

24 May    From Anonymous. L. DLC–JKP. Criticizes the appointment of Lorin Spencer as recorder of land titles for Missouri.

24 May    From Franklin B. Carpenter. ALS. DLC–JKP. States that a woman in Otsego County, N.Y., intends to name her daughter after Polk's wife and wishes to know her Christian name.

24 May    From Madison Caruthers. ALS. DLC–JKP. Claims that those who oppose his appointment to the collectorship at New Orleans have spread false rumors about his "political character"; reaffirms his support for the Democratic party and its principles.

24 May    From Henry Ewing. ALS. DLC–JKP. Encloses for Polk's acceptance John M. Lea's draft in the amount of $1,103.60; states that Polk may arrange payment as suits his convenience.

24 May    From John P. Helfenstein. ALS. DLC–JKP. Discusses politics and patronage in Wisconsin Territory.

24 May    From Henry Horn. ALS. DLC–JKP. Argues that public sentiment supports the dismissal of William B. Whitecar from his office in the Philadelphia Customs House; recommends Reuben Hanse to replace Whitecar as assistant appraiser.

24 May    From Elisha A. Maynard. ALS. DLC–JKP. Comments on Polk's nominations for collector and postmaster at Buffalo, N.Y.; notes that he favored the appointment of John J. Hudson over Henry W. Rogers for the collectorship.

*24 May*    *From Shadrach Penn, Jr.*

24 May    From James Rain. L. DLC–JKP. Declares that he is glad Polk defeated Henry Clay.

24 May    From A. G. Sloo. ALS. DLC–JKP. Encloses a copy of a memorial discussing the establishment of a "steam mail packet line along the Atlantic coast." (Enclosure not found.)

[24 May 1845]    From John A. Stemmler. ALS. DLC–JKP. Encloses resolutions passed by the German Democratic Republican Association of New York City. (Enclosure not found.)

26 May    From Charles E. Babcock. ALS. DLC–JKP. Warns Polk that the removal of Royal R. Hinman from the collectorship at New Haven, Conn., has angered "the Tyler party" in Con-

necticut.

26 May          *To Andrew J. Donelson.*
26 May          From William F. Giles. ALS. DLC–JKP. Introduces Thomas
                L. Murphy of Baltimore.
26 May          *From Andrew Jackson.*
26 May          *From Charles S. Jones.*
26 May          From W. D. Lansing. ALS. DLC–JKP. Asks for Polk's auto-
                graph.
26 May          From John A. Mairs. ALS. DLC–JKP. Apprises Polk of af-
                fairs on his Mississippi plantation.
26 May          *From Benjamin Patton.*
26 May          From John O. Rees. ALS. DLC–JKP. States that his support
                for Polk and the Democracy has prevented his employment
                as a shipmaster; requests a naval appointment.
26 May          From John A. Stemmler.   ALS. DLC–JKP. Introduces
                George C. De Kay of New Jersey; notes that he published
                "The Young Hickory, a Jersey Flagstaff" following the Balti-
                more Convention; claims that De Kay has influence among
                German Democrats.
26 May          *From Levi Woodbury.*
27 May          From Seth Barton. ALS. DLC–JKP. Encloses a letter from
                Solomon W. Downs discussing changes in the land office at
                Ouachita, La. (Enclosure not found.)
27 May          From John W. Davis. ALS. DLC–JKP. Reports that he has
                been nominated as the Democratic candidate for the U.S.
                House in Indiana's Sixth Congressional District; believes
                that he "shall have no difficulty if the Whigs do not procure
                some Democrat to run."
27 May          From Solomon W. Downs.  ALS. DLC–JKP. Recommends
                Samuel Locke, a hardware merchant, for the collectorship
                at New Orleans.
27 May          From Henry Ewing. ALS. DLC–JKP. Acknowledges receipt
                of Polk's draft in the amount of $1,100.66.
27 May          From Daniel Graham.   ALS. DLC–JKP. Discusses Ten-
                nessee's state and congressional elections.
27 May          From James Lee.  ALS. DLC–JKP. Recommends the ap-
                pointment of Jonathan I. Coddington to the collectorship
                at New York City.
27 May          From Richard D. Letter et al. LS. DLC–JKP. Condemn ef-
                forts of a faction within Tammany Society to convince Polk
                to remove Cornelius P. Van Ness as collector of customs at
                New York City; declare that the undersigned members of
                the Society support his retention.
27 May          To Dolly Madison. N. MoHi. Extends an invitation for her
                to join "half a dozen friends" on a visit to Mount Vernon.
27 May          From James M. Porter. ALS. DLC–JKP. Observes that the
                advanced age and poor health of Peter Hagner, third audi-

tor of the Treasury, warrant a search for a successor; recommends William Hackett, of Pennsylvania.

27 May From Anthony Ten Eyck. ALS. DLC–JKP. Supports John Martin's application for federal office.

27 May From Joel Turrill. ALS. DLC–JKP. Wishes to replace Reuben G. Beasley as U.S. consul at Havre.

27 May From William Williams. ALS. DLC–JKP. Discusses patronage at Boston, Gloucester, Marblehead, and Newburyport, Mass.

28 May From Aaron V. Brown. ALS. DLC–JKP. Asks Polk to secure an appointment for Jesse B. Clements.

28 May From James Buchanan. PL in Moore, ed., *The Works of James Buchanan*, VI, pp. 162–63. Transmits papers and letters relating to the Mexican government's payment of claims under the Convention of 1843.

28 May From Madison Caruthers. ALS. DLC–JKP. Denies reports that he has "spoken disrespectfully" of Polk; encloses a letter from George Eustis.

28 May From Joseph Cowdin. ALS. DLC–JKP. Claims that the petition and letters supporting his application for office have been misplaced.

28 May From Adam Diller. ALS. DLC–JKP. Directs Polk's attention to the Philadelphia *Home Journal and Citizen Soldier*, "not strictly speaking a party paper," but an advocate of "Republican institutions" and "a well organized and well disciplined militia"; solicits for the paper a printing contract to advertise public land sales.

28 May From Anthony Duyro et al. N. DLC–JKP. Deny newspaper reports that German Democrats favor the removal of Cornelius P. Van Ness; send Polk an account of one of their recent meetings.

28 May From George Eustis. ALS. DLC–JKP. Writes on behalf of Madison Caruthers to relate details of a conversation in which Caruthers expressed "his great respect & warm attachment" for Polk.

28 May From James Guthrie. ALS. DLC–JKP. Introduces William R. Jouett, a captain in the army.

28 May From Edward Harden. ALS. DLC–JKP. Encloses letters supporting his claim that "twenty greedy office hunters & their immediate relations" prompted his removal from the collectorship at Savannah, Ga. (Enclosures not found.)

28 May From Edward Harte. NS. DLC–JKP. Alleges that John J. Mumford, now employed in the New York Customs House, owes him $36 for work as a correspondent and editor at the *New York Standard*; claims that after the *Standard* became a Tyler newspaper, he was discharged.

28 May From George W. Jones. ALS. DLC–JKP. Thanks Polk for his

appointment as surveyor of public lands for Wisconsin and Iowa territories.

28 May     From William M. Lowry. ALS. DLC–JKP. Predicts that Aaron V. Brown will win the Tennessee gubernatorial contest; notes that Brookins Campbell has withdrawn from the race in the First Congressional District.

28 May     From Edward Lucas. ALS. DLC–JKP. Introduces Benjamin Moor, master armorer at Harpers Ferry.

28 May     From George R. Parburt. ALS. DLC–JKP. Seeks appointment as postmaster at Canandaigua, N.Y.

28 May     From William T. Thompson. ALS. DLC–JKP. Claims that during his absence from New Orleans, his enemies have tried to damage his reputation; requests that Polk send him a copy of the charges made against him.

29 May     From Edmund Burke. ALS. DLC–JKP. Encloses Levi Woodbury's letter explaining his reasons for declining appointment as U.S. minister to Great Britain.

29 May     From John I. DeGraff. ALS. DLC–JKP. Warns Polk that Matthias J. Bovee, an applicant for the office of register of lands at Milwaukee, is "wanting" in financial integrity.

29 May     From John T. Johnson. ALS. DLC–JKP. Seeks employment as steward at the White House.

29 May     From William S. Pickett. LS. DLC–JKP. Encloses a statement of Polk's account.

29 May     From Fernando Wood. ALS. DLC–JKP. Urges Polk to retain Cornelius P. Van Ness in the collectorship at New York City; suggests that Van Ness' removal "would disturb important commercial interests."

[30 May 1845]     From P. S. Loughborough. ALS. DLC–JKP. Introduces William R. Jouett.

31 May     From Hugh J. Anderson. ALS. DLC–JKP. Supports retention of Nathaniel M. Lowney as collector of customs at Belfast, Me.; does not believe rumors about Treasury Department charges against Lowney.

31 May     From Anonymous. L, signed "Radical of the 8th Cong. District." DLC–JKP. Encloses material commenting on the political character of William W. Woodworth of N.Y. (Enclosure not found.)

31 May     From George W. Crabb. ALS. DLC–JKP. States that poor health forces him to seek appointment to federal office in either Florida or Texas.

31 May     From Morven M. Jones. ALS. DLC–JKP. Solicits Polk's autograph.

[31 May 1845]     From William R. McDougal. ALS. DLC–JKP. Requests an interview with Polk; notes that he has "given up the idea" of securing a government office.

*31 May*     *To Louis McLane.*

| | |
|---|---|
| 31 May | From David Myerle. ALS. DLC–JKP. Refers Polk to James K. Paulding's letter in the Washington *Union* about Myerle's contract for water-rotted hemp; mentions the sad plight of the "unfortunate Indians" living in Missouri. |
| 31 May | From Shadrach Penn, Jr. ALS. DLC–JKP. Maintains that David T. Disney "is one of the ablest statesmen in Ohio" and "a good French scholar." |
| 31 May | From Shadrach Penn, Jr. ALS. DLC–JKP. Encloses a letter from Thomas Harney concerning the reinstatement of his cousin, William A. Harney, as a cadet at West Point. |
| 31 May | From David Petrikin. L. DLC–JKP. Recommends Andrew Beaumont for federal office. |
| 31 May | From Joel R. Poinsett. ALS. DLC–JKP. Supports the application of Henry L. Pinckney for the collectorship at Charleston, S.C.; informs Polk that the Democratic party "is divided on the subject of making changes in the federal offices held in this state." |
| 31 May | From John Willbank. ALS. DLC–JKP. Recommends George W. Williams of Philadelphia, Penn., for a federal office. |
| June 1845 | From John P. Beekman et al. LS. DLC–JKP. Urge retention of the Mechanics and Farmers' Bank of Albany, N.Y., as an agency for the disbursement of pensions; claim that the bank's stockholders and directors have always supported the Democratic party. |
| June 1845 | From John H. Gardner et al. CS. DLC–JKP. Recommend the continuance of the Mechanics and Farmers' Bank as the agency for disbursing pensions in Albany, N.Y. |
| [June 1845] | From D. H. Stover. ALS. DLC–JKP. Solicits an office for her son-in-law, Isaac K. Hanson, who was dismissed from his clerkship in the Treasury Department. |
| 1 June | From Daniel S. Donelson. ALS. DLC–JKP. Desires employment as sutler to troops on the Rio Grande; mentions that Andrew J. Donelson, his brother, urged him to apply for the post. |
| 1 June | To William L. Marcy. ALS. CtY. Requests a meeting with Marcy. |
| 2 June | From Anonymous. L, signed "R.F.R." DLC–JKP. Urges Polk to station troops on the Columbia River and Rocky Mountain passes to "vindicate" the nation's rights and protect settlers emigrating to the Oregon country. |
| 2 June | From John Brough. ALS. DLC–JKP. Withdraws as an applicant for office; complains about William Medill. |
| 2 June | From Robert Campbell, Jr. ALS. DLC–JKP. Sends news of Polk's plantation in Mississippi; remarks that "Old Father Polk" died recently; adds that he "retained his mind to the last & as a Polk made no profession." |
| 2 June | From George Guier. LS. DLC–JKP. States that George W. |

|  |  |
|---|---|
| | Williams of Philadelphia is "an active and efficient Democrat and original Jackson man." |
| 2 June | From Jane Harris. ALS. DLC–JKP. Writes from Nashville, Tenn., that her husband has regularly beaten her and has threatened "to make negro men sleep in my room"; adds that he has abandoned her for "a mullato woman"; seeks Polk's aid in a suit against her husband, a wealthy Whig and Mason. |
| *2 June* | *From Michael Hoffman.* |
| 2 June | From Henry Horn. ALS. DLC–JKP. Informs Polk that questions have arisen about the collector's authority to remove subordinates without the concurrence of the Treasury Department; notes that he has received a communication from Robert J. Walker on this matter. |
| 2 June | From William Medill. ALS. DLC–JKP. Reports on the attendance of postal officials for the month of May. |
| *2 June* | *From Ely Moore.* |
| *2 June* | *To A. O. P. Nicholson.* |
| 2 June | From Shadrach Penn, Jr. ALS. DLC–JKP. Wishes to secure for the St. Louis *Missouri Reporter* the printing contracts for public land sales in Missouri, Illinois, Iowa, and Wisconsin. |
| 2 June | From Georgeanna H. Sherburne. ALS. DLC–JKP. Solicits an appointment for her father, John H. Sherburne, who was removed as an inspector at the port of Philadelphia. |
| 3 June | To Edward Everett. ALS. MHi. Introduces Robert Armstrong. |
| 3 June | From Alexander Ewins. ALS. DLC–JKP. Seeks restoration as a measurer at the Boston Customs House. |
| 3 June | From Arthur P. Hayne. ALS. DLC–JKP. Encloses a "sketch of my life." (Enclosure not found.) |
| 3 June | From Joshua Herrick. ALS. DLC–JKP. Discusses his application for federal office. |
| 3 June | From Albion and Thomas S. Hurdle. LS. DLC–JKP. Request that Polk retain William Noland as commissioner of public buildings. |
| 3 June | From S. C. Kell. ALS. DLC–JKP. Writes on behalf of a society in England that was formed to diffuse "information on Commercial & Economical subjects"; forwards an issue of *The Economist*. |
| *3 June* | *To Cornelius W. Lawrence.* |
| 3 June | From William L. Marcy. ALS. DLC–JKP. Introduces Joshua A. Spencer of New York. |
| 3 June | From William H. Merrick. ALS. DLC–JKP. Introduces Henry Prince, Jr. |
| 3 June | From William Moore. ALS. DLC–JKP. Assures Polk of the "unanimity of sentiment on the subject of Annexation" i |

Texas; offers his services in some confidential office.

3 June      From John D. Perkins. ALS. DLC–JKP. Reviews the factional divisions within the New York Democracy in 1844; complains that the Van Buren faction has received most of the federal patronage.

3 June      From James H. Thomas. ALS. DLC–JKP. Discusses several legal cases; reports that Tennessee Democrats are confident of victory in August.

3 June      From Ver Planck Van Antwerp. ALS. DLC–JKP. Apologizes for the "exceptionable and offensive" tone of an earlier letter.

3 June      From Charles A. Warland. ALS. DLC–JKP. Wishes to add Polk's autograph to his collection.

*3 June*      *From Charles A. Wickliffe.*

4 June      From George Bancroft. LS. DLC–JKP. Informs Polk of the status of War Department activities regarding the Cherokee commission and the Choctaw Indians.

[4 June 1845]      From Lawson Gifford. ALS. DLC–JKP. Reports news of the state election campaign in East Tennessee; solicits for the Jonesboro *Tennessee Sentinel* the publication of public land sales.

4 June      From William H. Haywood, Jr. ALS. DLC–JKP. Introduces David W. Stone of Raleigh, N.C.

[4 June 1845]      From Cave Johnson. ANS. DLC–JKP. Encloses a list of postmasters whose commissions will expire during the current recess of the Senate.

4 June      From John L. H. McCracken. ALS. DLC–JKP. Seeks retention of Cornelius P. Van Ness as collector of the port of New York.

4 June      From Robert Tansill. ALS. DLC–JKP. Writes to protest his 1843 court-martial conviction; requests that Polk reverse the sentence.

4 June      From J. C. Thompson. ALS. DLC–JKP. Urges Polk to retain Cornelius P. Van Ness as collector of the port of New York.

4 June      From Frederick E. Westbrook. ANS. DLC–JKP. Encloses resolutions of a meeting of New York City Democrats calling for the removal of Cornelius P. Van Ness.

*4 June*      *From Charles A. Wickliffe.*

4 June      From Abraham D. Wilson. ALS. DLC–JKP. Opposes the removal of Cornelius P. Van Ness as the collector of the port of New York.

June      From George Bancroft. LS. DLC–JKP. Confirms the commission of Joseph Sinclear as subagent to the Miami Indians.

June      From George Bancroft. LS. DLC–JKP. Proposes dismissal of Frederick P. Baldwin as a midshipman in the navy.

5 June 1845]      From Noyes Billings. ALS. DLC–JKP. Recommends Stanley

G. Trott as postmaster of New London, Conn.

5 June      From John Blair. ALS. DLC–JKP. Reports on Democratic politics in East Tennessee; asks that Lawson Gifford receive the printing contracts for public land advertisements.

5 June      From John Claiborne. ALS. DLC–JKP. Explains his unwillingness to accept appointment as live oak agent; encloses copies of letters from John F. H. Claiborne on the matter.

5 June      From Jonathan I. Coddington, Jr. ALS. DLC–JKP. Recommends the appointment of his father, Jonathan I. Coddington, as the collector of the port of New York.

5 June      From James Conner. LS. DLC–JKP. Urges Polk on behalf of the Tammany Society to remove Cornelius P. Van Ness as collector of the port of New York.

5 June      From Charles J. Ingersoll. ALS. DLC–JKP. States that he has received Polk's letter introducing Robert Armstrong; mentions plans to publish an "historical sketch of the war of 1812."

5 June      From Cave Johnson. ALS. DLC–JKP. Reports on the attendance of postal officials for the month of May.

5 June      From John Kettlewell. ALS. DLC–JKP. Introduces John Neff of Alleghany County, Md.

*[5 June 1845]*      *From William L. Marcy.*

5 June      From Wyndham Robertson, Jr. ALS. DLC–JKP. Thanks Polk for his appointment to a clerkship in the Post Office Department; desires a promotion as soon as possible.

5 June      From A. Vanzant. ALS. DLC–JKP. Asks Polk to find and certify an application for power of attorney that was sent to John Tyler.

5 June      From Robert J. Walker. ALS. DLC–JKP. Encloses a report by James N. Barker, comptroller of the Treasury, regarding a contested appraisal of imported goods. (Enclosure not found.)

*6 June*      *From David T. Baldwin.*

6 June      From George Bancroft. LS. DLC–JKP. Encloses for Polk's signature a warrant for George Williams as a boatswain in the navy. (Enclosure not found.)

*6 June*      *To Sam Houston.*

*6 June*      *From Andrew Jackson.*

*6 June*      *From William H. Polk.*

6 June      From James Robertson. ALS. DLC–JKP. Recommends William C. Bouck for the collectorship of the port of New York.

6 June      From Frederick Stahl et al. LS. DLC–JKP. Request a modification of U.S. Lead Mines' instructions on the leasing of land in Wisconsin Territory.

*7 June*      *From David T. Baldwin.*

7 June      From George Bancroft. LS. DLC–JKP. Encloses minutes of

|  | a meeting with John T. Mason regarding the Cherokee Commission. |
|---|---|
| 7 June | From George Bancroft. LS. DLC–JKP. Encloses a communication from John T. Mason. (Enclosure not found.) |
| 7 June | From George Bancroft. LS. DLC–JKP. Encloses a report from Thomas Hartley Crawford, commissioner of Indian affairs, on the request of David Myerle. |
| 7 June | From George Bancroft. LS. DLC–JKP. Reports that Thomas Hartley Crawford has sent Polk a paper regarding the Treaty of Dancing Rabbit Creek. |
| 7 June | From Cornelius S. Bogardus. ALS. DLC–JKP. States that he has informed Cornelius P. Van Ness of his interview with Polk on Wednesday last; mentions that if not for the opposition of "numerous friends in New York," Van Ness would have resigned; encloses an extract of a Van Ness letter. |
| 7 June | From Thomas Claiborne, Jr. ALS. DLC–JKP. Requests that Polk renew his offer of a clerkship. |
| 7 June | From George Croghan. ALS. DLC–JKP. States that he has received a copy of the court of inquiry proceedings on allegations of misconduct; wishes to express his views of the matter to Polk and the court. |
| 7 June | From Joseph P. Hoge. ALS. DLC–JKP. Encloses a memorial from Illinois citizens on the granting of leases to mineral lands. |
| *7 June* | *From Cornelius W. Lawrence.* |
| 7 June | From Matthew C. Perry. ALS. DLC–JKP. Recommends Alexander S. MacKenzie for a "mission or agency" to the government of Paraguay. |
| *8 June* | *From Sam Houston.* |
| 8 June | From Sam Houston. LS. DLC–JKP. Introduces Joseph C. Eldridge; reports that Eldridge can provide information regarding public opinion on the issue of Texas annexation. |
| [8 June 1845] | From Cave Johnson. ALS. DLC–JKP. Sends Polk the latest information on Democratic victories in the Florida elections. |
| 8 June | From Amos Kendall. ALS. DLC–JKP. Expresses concern over the delay in the appointment of his son to federal office; warns Polk that George Bancroft's decision to cancel arrangements with Messrs. Benson, of New York City, has stirred up discontent among "the western friends of Oregon." |
| 8 June | From Mary A. Lewis. ALS. DLC–JKP. Writes on behalf of her husband, Charles Lewis, who accidentally killed Isaac Goodall in June, 1844; notes that they have moved to Havana, Cuba; requests a position in a "safe place any where in the Indian nation." |
| 9 June | From Robert Armstrong. ALS. DLC–JKP. Recommends |

John J. Mumford, a New York Democrat, for a federal position.

9 June     From Robert Armstrong. ALS. DLC–JKP. Introduces E. Prescott of Louisiana.

*9 June*     *From Alfred Balch.*

9 June     From Ransom H. Gillet. ALS. DLC–JKP. Believes that Cornelius W. Lawrence will accept the collectorship at New York; adds that the appointment is "satisfactory" to the New York Democracy.

*[9 June 1845]*     *From J. George Harris.*

9 June     From James Henry Horn et al. N. DLC–JKP. Invite Polk to attend a public dinner in Philadelphia on July 4th.

9 June     From Hillary Langtry. ALS. DLC–JKP. Encloses his resignation as postmaster of Columbia, Tenn.; mentions upcoming elections in Tennessee; notes that in Columbia "many are joining the Methodist church under the great excitement which has continued for about three weeks." (Enclosure not found.)

*9 June*     *From William H. Polk.*

9 June     From Campbell P. White. ALS. DLC–JKP. Introduces Thomas Herring of New York City.

9 June     From David Levy Yulee. ALS. DLC–JKP. Informs Polk that after the recent elections, Florida enters the union with "a thoroughly Democratic organization"; suggests that Polk postpone, for a few weeks, federal appointments in the state.

10 June     From David Babe. ALS. DLC–JKP. Expresses thanks for his reprieve from a death sentence.

10 June     From Robert B. Campbell. ALS. DLC–JKP. Introduces Edward H. Barton, a New Orleans physician and for the past two years a resident of Havana, Cuba.

*10 June*     *From Ransom H. Gillet.*

*10 June*     *From J. George Harris.*

*10 June*     *From Cornelius P. Van Ness.*

10 June     From John P. Van Ness. PL, broadside. DLC–JKP. Demands retention of Cornelius P. Van Ness as collector at New York City; states that the people of New York will not "tolerate the ignoble slander" of his removal.

10 June     From George C. Washington and John T. Mason. LS. DLC–JKP. Discuss the question of the tenure of office of the Cherokee commissioners.

10 June     From Campbell P. White. ALS. DLC–JKP. Introduces Thomas Herring of New York City.

11 June     From David T. Disney. ALS. DLC–JKP. States that he could not accept the position of postmaster at Cincinnati; adds that his friends have urged his appointment to a foreign mission.

| | |
|---|---|
| *11 June* | *From J. George Harris.* |
| 11 June | From Francesco Orsini. ALS. DLC–JKP. Asks to meet with Polk "not to beg for office but for some private business." |
| 12 June | From James R. Bruce. ALS. DLC–JKP. Wishes to receive a letter from Polk. |
| 12 June | From Franklin H. Elmore. ALS. DLC–JKP. Introduces Marcellus Duval of Arkansas; notes that Duval is the "assistant & confidential clerk" of Pierce M. Butler. |
| [12 June 1845] | From Franklin Gage. ALS. DLC–JKP. Requests "a few moments conversation" with Polk; reports that he was asked by American citizens residing in Cuba to apprise Polk of "certain facts relative to their interests on that island." |
| *12 June* | *From J. George Harris.* |
| 12 June | From Gouverneur Kemble. ALS. DLC–JKP. Protests the possible appointment of Levi D. Slamm as naval storekeeper at Brooklyn, N.Y. |
| *12 June* | *From Louis McLane.* |
| 12 June | From Marcus Morton. ALS. NN. Advises Polk about the collector's appointment at Newburyport, Mass. |
| 12 June | From Robert Barnwell Rhett. ALS. DLC–JKP. Solicits a favorable appointment in the army for his nephew, Thomas Rhett. |
| 12 June | From James H. Thomas. ALS. DLC–JKP. Discusses Polk's financial affairs in Tennessee. |
| *12 June* | *To Robert J. Walker.* |
| *12 June* | *From Robert J. Walker.* |
| 12 June | From William L. Yancey. ALS. MB. Solicits an appointment as a purser in the navy for E. A. Semple. |
| *13 June* | *From George Bancroft.* |
| 13 June | From Benjamin H. Brewster. ALS. DLC–JKP. Recommends Thomas S. Bryant for appointment as a quartermaster in the army. |
| *13 June* | *To Edward Everett.* |
| 13 June | From David Hayden. ALS. DLC–JKP. Encloses a copy of the New Orleans *Picayune*, a Whig newspaper; notes that its enthusiasm for Texas annexation demonstrates the widespread support for the administration's course. (Enclosure not found.) |
| 13 June | To Cave Johnson. ALS. DLC–WM. Requests an abstract of the applications and recommendations for the deputy postmasters whose commissions expire in June. |
| 13 June | From Robert Lucas. ALS. DLC–JKP. Solicits reappointment as governor of Iowa Territory. |
| 13 June | From John L. O'Sullivan. ALS. DLC–JKP. Introduces Charles A. Secor of New York City. |
| 14 June | From Anonymous. L, signed "John Smith." DLC–JKP. Denounces Polk as "a lying scoundrel" for reneging on a |

Polk to consider him for a federal office.

16 June — From Hamilton Lufborough. ALS. DNA–RG 42. Recommends Richard Shekell for wardenship of the federal penitentiary in Washington City.

16 June — From Hiester H. Muhlenberg. ALS. DNA–RG 156. Asks Polk to appoint a commission to evaluate the suitability of Reading, Penn., as a site for a national foundry.

16 June — From William Potter. ALS. DLC–JKP. Appeals to Polk on behalf of Delight S. Boudinot, widow of Elias Boudinot.

16 June — From Henry Simpson. ALS. DLC–JKP. Solicits an appointment in the federal government.

17 June — From Simon Cameron. ALS. DNA–RG 156. Encloses a memorial requesting an evaluation of Reading, Penn., as the site for a national foundry. (Enclosure not found.)

*17 June* — *From J. George Harris.*

17 June — From Joab Hill. ALS. DLC–JKP. Recommends Samuel Toree of Missouri as Indian agent either to the Sauk and Fox or to the Cherokee.

17 June — From Jesse Miller and John Laporte. LS. DLC–JKP. Recommend Chambers McKibbin to replace James Peacock as deputy postmaster at Harrisburg, Penn.

17 June — From James E. Saunders. ALS. DLC–JKP. Introduces David Salomon of Mobile, Ala.

17 June — From Francis R. Shunk. ALS. DLC–JKP. Prefers the appointment of Chambers McKibbin or Thomas Phillips over J. B. Guthrie for the postmastership at Pittsburgh, Penn.; claims that Guthrie "was one of a few democrats in Pittsburgh" who opposed his nomination in Pennsylvania's gubernatorial contest.

17 June — From Harvey M. Watterson. ALS. DLC–JKP. Believes that he will win election to the Tennessee Senate; predicts that Aaron V. Brown will triumph in the gubernatorial election.

18 June — From John F. Gillespy. ALS. DLC–JKP. Criticizes the report of the Cherokee commissioners; denies the charge of "malignity" toward the commissioners.

18 June — From Henry D. Gilpin. ALS. DLC–JKP. Introduces "Captain Loper" of Philadelphia.

18 June — From Emanuel B. Hart and William V. Brady. CS. DLC–JKP. Write on behalf of the Common Council of New York City to invite Polk to attend "a public testimonial of affection and reverence" for Andrew Jackson.

8 June — From Robert Patterson. ALS. DLC–JKP. States that he has ordered a militia parade in honor of Andrew Jackson; invites Polk to attend the June 26th commemoration in Philadelphia.

8 June — From James Robertson. ALS. DLC–JKP. Claims that he played a vital role in Polk's nomination and victory in New

York; attacks Polk's choices for the cabinet and federal appointments.

18 June        From Samuel Wescott et al. LS. DLC–JKP. Urge the appointment of Watts Sherman as pension agent at Albany, N.Y.

18 June        From Alfred M. Young. ALS. DLC–JKP. States that he is "mortified" over Polk's choice for U.S. marshal in Louisiana; notes that his own "claim to that office" was "paramount to those of the present incumbent."

19 June        From William J. Brown. ALS. DLC–JKP. Encloses a note from Philip E. Engle verifying the correct form of his name. (Enclosure not found.)

*19 June*        *From John Catron.*

19 June        From Thomas Claiborne, Jr. ALS. DLC–JKP. Thanks Polk for his appointment to a clerkship.

19 June        From Charles J. Ingersoll. ALS. DLC–JKP. Tells Polk that he has not seen Joseph H. Talbot of Tennessee; mentions that he is hard at work on a "historical sketch."

19 June        From Cave Johnson. ALS. Polk Memorial Association, Columbia. Informs Polk that L. H. Woldridge has been appointed postmaster at Franklin, Tenn.

[19 June 1845]   From Cave Johnson. ALS. DLC–JKP. Requests a meeting with Polk to discuss the appointment of a postmaster at Cincinnati.

*19 June*        *From William McLain.*

19 June        From David Myerle. ALS. DLC–JKP. Seeks a brief interview with Polk to discuss the government ropewalk at Memphis, Tenn.

19 June        From Shadrach Penn, Jr. ALS. DLC–JKP. Encloses articles from the St. Louis *Missouri Reporter*; states that he will work "to effect a union of the two branches of the party" in Missouri.

20 June        From George Bancroft. LS. DLC–JKP. Encloses a report on the "subject of leasing or otherwise disposing of the mineral lands of the Upper Mississippi." (Enclosure not found.)

20 June        From Hiram N. Bishop et al. LS. DLC–JKP. Inform Polk of his election as an honorary member in the Philomathesian Society of Kenyon College in Gambier, Ohio.

20 June        From W. D. Collins. ALS. DLC–JKP. Discusses the persecution of Christian Indians in the Creek nation; solicits Polk's aid in securing the religious liberty of the Creeks.

20 June        From Thomas H. Harvey. ALS. DLC–JKP. Submits details of James B. Bowlin's efforts to secure his removal as superintendent of Indian affairs at St. Louis.

20 June        From Henry Horn. ALS. DLC–JKP. Reports that he has met Joseph H. Talbot; hopes that the Philadelphia ceremony in honor of Andrew Jackson "shall be divested of party character."

acter."

| | |
|---|---|
| 20 June | From John B. Macy. ALS. DLC–JKP. Regrets that David T. Disney is unwilling to accept the postmastership at Cincinnati. |
| 20 June | From Benjamin Rawls. ALS. DLC–JKP. Expresses sorrow over the death of Andrew Jackson; quotes an article in the *Charleston Courier* criticizing Jackson's conduct as president; notes that it was written by a "dyed in the wool *Federalist.*" |
| 20 June | From John T. Smith. ALS. DLC–JKP. Supports the application of George W. Williams for the office of commissioner of public buildings in Washington City. |
| 20 June | From Mary W. Thompson. ALS. DLC–JKP. Encloses a copy of a sermon delivered on the occasion of the death of her husband, Alexander R. Thompson; notes that her departed husband greatly admired Andrew Jackson. |
| 20 June | From John H. Wheeler. ALS. DLC–JKP. Seeks appointment to federal office. |
| 21 June | From J. Ellis Bonham et al. LS. DLC–JKP. Invite Polk to attend a July 4th celebration in Cumberland County, Penn. |
| *21 June* | *From J. George Harris.* |
| 21 June | From David Hayden. ALS. DLC–JKP. Encloses for Sarah Polk a "beautiful and touching line, on the death of the lamented Genl. Jackson"; notes that it was written by George W. Reeder, an inspector in the New Orleans Customs House. (Enclosure not found.) |
| *21 June* | *From Daniel T. Jenks.* |
| 21 June | From David Koones. ALS. DLC–JKP. Complains that his removal from a clerkship in the Post Office Department has placed him "in a very unhappy situation." |
| *21 June* | *From Marshall Tate Polk, Jr.* |
| 22 June | From John F. H. Claiborne. ALS. DLC–JKP. Introduces H. Warren, a "respectable merchant & influential democrat"; solicits a transfer of government commissary business at New Orleans from Samuel J. Peters to Warren. |
| 22 June | From John F. McWhirter. ALS. DLC–JKP. Notes that he lived in Columbia, Tenn., until 1833; recommends the removal of Benjamin Holladay as postmaster at Weston, Mo. |
| 23 June | From John Horn et al. LS. DLC–JKP. Invite Polk to attend a public dinner on Independence Day in Philadelphia. |
| 23 June | From John Peirce. ALS. DLC–JKP. Presses his application for the office of assistant appraiser in the New York Customs House. |
| 23 June | From James Whitcomb. ALS. DLC–JKP. Claims that the appointment of Henry W. Ellsworth as chargé d'affaires to Sweden is "not a fortunate one"; discusses applicants for U.S. marshal and the postmastership at Indianapolis. |

| | |
|---|---|
| 23 June | From William Willison. ALS. DLC–JKP. Inquires about the laws that regulate the sale of government lands. |
| 23 June | From John P. Wingerd et al. LS. DNA–RG 42. Recommend Richard Shekell for appointment as warden of the federal penitentiary in Washington City. |
| [24 June 1845] | From Benjamin Lloyd James. ANS. DLC–JKP. Requests that "no persons be appointed to be postmasters in and for any office of the U.S. who cannot write plainly their own name and that of the town county and state in which they reside." |
| 24 June | From Brantz Mayer. ALS. DLC–JKP. Encloses a copy of his edited version of the journal of Charles Carroll, commissioner from Congress to Canada in 1776. (Enclosure not found.) |
| 24 June | From Caleb Pierce. ALS. DLC–JKP. Seeks reinstatement as an inspector in the Philadelphia Customs House. |
| 24 June | From William H. Robertson. ALS. DLC–JKP. Praises his predecessor as consul at Bremen, Ambrose D. Mann, for his able defense with his pen of U.S. interests; reports that German and Swiss immigration to the United States is increasing. |
| 24 June | From George Selden. ALS. DLC–JKP. Complains that the cannon salute to mark the death of Andrew Jackson disturbed the observance of the Sabbath in Erie, Penn. |
| 24 June | From James Whitcomb. ALS. DLC–JKP. Explains his objections to the appointment of Alexander F. Morrison as postmaster at Indianapolis; urges Polk to make no appointment to that post until the state elections have been held on August 1st. |
| 25 June | From Edward B. Hubley. ALS. DLC–JKP. Introduces Samuel Ludvigh, editor of a German newspaper in New York. |
| *25 June* | *From Memucan Hunt.* |
| 25 June | From Joseph Wood et al. LS. DLC–JKP. Invite Polk to an Independence Day celebration with the Democratic citizens of Philadelphia. |
| 26 June | From Seth Barton. ALS. DLC–JKP. Requests a leave of absence from his duties as solicitor of the Treasury. |
| 26 June | To James Buchanan. LS. DNA–RG 59. Encloses an executive order closing all public offices on June 27, in memory of Andrew Jackson. |
| 26 June | From William G. Childress. ALS. DLC–JKP. Discusses Oregon and Texas annexation; gives his opinions on the state election campaign in Tennessee. |
| 26 June | From Wheeler H. Clarke et al. NS. DLC–JKP. Request that the Mechanics and Farmers' Bank continue as the pension agency in Albany, N.Y. |

| | |
|---|---|
| 26 June | From R. R. Collier. ALS. DLC–JKP. Wishes to know why his charges against the appointment of William N. Friend as postmaster at Petersburg, Va., were disregarded. |
| 26 June | From Joseph Cowdin. ALS. DLC–JKP. Awaits word on his possible appointment as consul at Glasgow or Belfast. |
| 26 June | From Franklin H. Elmore. ALS. DLC–JKP. Introduces Arthur P. Hayne of Charleston, S.C. |
| [26 June 1845] | From Daniel T. Jenks. ALS. DLC–JKP. Warns Polk of "a most unfortunate state of cliqueism" in the Pennsylvania Democracy. |
| 26 June | To Cave Johnson. PL in St. George L. Sioussat, ed., "Letters of James K. Polk to Cave Johnson, 1833–1848," *THM* I (September, 1915), p. 255. Informs Johnson that the commission for the postmaster at Columbus, Ohio, has not been received. |
| 26 June | From Philip Barton Key. ALS. DLC–JKP. Solicits appointment as U.S. attorney for the District of Columbia; encloses information on the political views of another candidate. (Enclosures not found.) |
| *26 June* | *From John Law.* |
| *26 June* | *To William S. Pickett.* |
| 26 June | From James W. Schaumburg. ALS. DLC–JKP. Encloses extracts from the "official legal opinions" of Roger B. Taney and William Wirt relating to his case for reappointment in the army. |
| *26 June* | *From Joseph H. Talbot.* |
| 26 June | From Robert J. Walker. ALS. DLC–JKP. Introduces William Parker of New Orleans. |
| 26 June | From Robert J. Walker. ALS. DLC–JKP. Introduces David D. Porter, son of David R. Porter; suggests that the younger Porter "is no less worthy brave & democratic than was his lamented father." |
| 26 June | From William C. Zantzinger. ALS. DLC–JKP. Urges Polk to examine the case of his father, William P. Zantzinger. |
| *[27 June 1845]* | *From Alexander J. Atocha.* |
| 27 June | From Roger S. Baldwin. CS. DLC–JKP. Encloses resolutions of the General Assembly of Connecticut regarding the "purchase and proper distribution of the Reports of the Decisions of the Supreme Court." |
| 27 June | From James Gordon Bennett. ALS. DLC–JKP. Introduces Charles Ausringer of the Kingdom of Bavaria. |
| 27 June | From Jacob G. Davies. ALS. DLC–JKP. Invites Polk to attend a funeral procession in Baltimore in honor of Andrew Jackson. |
| 27 June | From Abraham P. Eyre et al. L. DLC–JKP. Write on behalf of the Democracy of Pennsylvania's Fourth Congressional District to invite Polk to a July 4th celebration. |

| | |
|---|---|
| 27 June | From John Hayes et al. LS. DLC–JKP. Urge the appointment of Charles P. Sengstack as commissioner of public buildings in Washington City. |
| 27 June | From George H. Jones. ALS. DLC–JKP. Informs Polk that Ransom H. Gillet will call to discuss the question of Jones' promotion to chief clerk. |
| 27 June | From Charles L. Moses. ALS. DLC–JKP. Solicits an interview to urge his application for a midshipman's commission. |
| 27 June | From William H. Watson et al. C. DLC–JKP. Invite Polk to Baltimore to attend a "public demonstration of respect and sorrow" for Andrew Jackson on July 1st. |
| 28 June | From Edward Brooke et al. LS. DLC–JKP. Write on behalf of the temperance societies of Washington City to invite Polk to an Independence Day celebration; note that the occasion will be held, with Polk's "kind permission, within the grounds of the presidential mansion." |
| *28 June* | *From J. George Harris.* |
| 28 June | From John Long et al. LS. DLC–JKP. State that the undersigned Democratic citizens of Albany, N.Y., favor the appointment of Watts Sherman as pension agent; advise Polk that Thomas W. Olcott, the incumbent agent, "abandoned his political principles and his party" in 1840 and thus deserves removal. |
| [28 June 1845] | From Wendell Long et al. LS. DLC–JKP. Recommend Watts Sherman as pension agent at Albany, N.Y. |
| *28 June* | *To A. O. P. Nicholson.* |
| 28 June | From Charles P. Sengstack. ALS. DLC–JKP. Notes with concern Polk's "considerable debility and exhaustation" at the time of his last interview; explains the circumstances behind his application for commissioner of public buildings. |
| [28 June 1845] | From Francis J. Shafer et al. LS. DLC–JKP. Support the application of Watts Sherman for appointment as pension agent at Albany, N.Y. |
| 28 June | From Egbert Somendike et al. LS. DLC–JKP. Invite Polk on behalf of the Democratic citizens of Pennsylvania's Third Congressional District to a July 4th celebration. |
| [28 June 1845] | From George C. Washington. N. DLC–JKP. Invites Polk "to partake of some refreshments" following the funeral ceremony in honor of Andrew Jackson. |
| 28 June | From Nathan B. Whitfield. ALS. DLC–JKP. Introduces himself as "an old college mate at Chapel Hill"; wishes to see Polk. |
| [28 June 1845] | From Jesse D. Williams et al. LS. DLC–JKP. Recommend the appointment of Watts Sherman for the office of pension agent at Albany, N.Y.; urge the removal of Thomas W. Olcott. |

| | |
|---|---|
| [28 June 1845] | From W. W. Wright et al. LS. DLC–JKP. Support Watts Sherman as a "suitable candidate" for the office of pension agent at Albany, N.Y. |
| 29 June | From David Hubbard. ALS. DLC–JKP. Recommends William L. Hunter for appointment as an agent to one of the Indian tribes of Arkansas; claims that Hunter is related to the Polk family. |
| 30 June | From David R. Atchison. ALS. DLC–JKP. Introduces William Gilpin of Missouri. |
| *30 June* | *From J. George Harris.* |
| 30 June | From John C. Haswell. ALS. DLC–JKP. Requests Polk's intervention to reverse his removal as a clerk in the office of the register of the Treasury. |
| *30 June* | *To John Horn et al.* |
| 30 June | From J. Huddleson. ALS. DLC–JKP. Promises to write Polk soon concerning the postmastership at Cumberland, Md. |
| *30 June* | *From Andrew Jackson, Jr.* |
| 30 June | From Eugene McDonnell. ALS. DLC–JKP. Complains that Robert J. Walker refuses to approve his appointment to a clerkship in the Treasury Department; claims that his exposure of "the robbers of the public Treasury" to a congressional committee is the true reason for Walker's refusal; adds that his exposure of corruption extended to "Mr. Tyler and others." |
| 30 June | From John Minge. ALS. DLC–JKP. Denies that he gambled on the presidential election; warns Polk about George H. Jones, a man who is "utterly destitute of character." |
| 30 June 1845] | From Charles L. Moses. ALS. DLC–JKP. Asks for Polk's assistance in procuring an appointment as midshipman. |
| 30 June | From Henry Simpson. ALS. DLC–JKP. Regrets that James Buchanan's influence has denied him appointment to public office; complains of the incompetence of the principal appraisers at the Philadelphia Customs House. |
| 30 June | From John C. Smith. N. DLC–JKP. Requests permission for the teachers and students of the Fourth Presbyterian Church school "*to pass before the President in his door* and salute him" on July 4th. |
| 30 June | From George W. Williams. ALS. DLC–JKP. Solicits appointment as commissioner of public buildings in Washington City. |

# INDEX

*577*

# Date Due

UML 735